Also by Thomas Dyja

Nonfiction

The Third Coast: When Chicago Built the American Dream

Walter White: The Dilemma of Black Identity in America

Only Connect: The Way to Save Our Schools with Rudy Crew

Fiction

Play for a Kingdom

Meet John Trow

The Moon in Our Hands

Praise for **New York, New York, New York**

"[A] tour de force, a work of astonishing breadth and depth that encompasses seminal changes in New York's government and economy, along with deep dives into hip-hop, the AIDS crisis, the visual arts, housing, architecture, and finance. . . . [Dyja has] in this outstanding work, done all that a historian can do to light the way forward, by so vividly illuminating the past."

—Kevin Baker, *New York Times*

"Superb reflections on a city resurgent . . . Dyja goes far beyond politics and Wall Street: he is equally interested in and intelligent about everything from Aids to Hip Hop, Keith Haring and Anna Wintour, Spike Lee, Jay-Z and Elaine Kaufman . . . This is an especially important book for the majority of New Yorkers too young to remember the remarkable trajectory the city has experienced."

—Charles Kaiser, *The Guardian*

"[A] psychedelic express subway ride, from pre-1970s fiscal crisis to post-pandemic."

—Sam Roberts, *New York Times*

"This engaging book has the potential to become a classic text."

—*Library Journal*

"[A] cogent narrative studded with pithy insights and vivid profiles . . . Dyja's exhaustive knowledge of the era, dazzling prose, and all-embracing sympathy—and scorn when it's merited—make for a stimulating study of New York's never-ending upheaval."

—*Publishers Weekly* (starred review)

"[A] mammoth undertaking—a whirlwind history of the city from the late 1970s to the present . . . fast-moving, punchy prose . . . He's a master of using perfectly chosen adjectives to sketch a character."

—*New Statesman*

"Morally and politically charged, an urgent, readable story of Gotham's fortunes."

—*Kirkus Reviews*

"[Dyja] boldly anatomizes New York in a phenomenally intricate and revelatory web of provocative juxtapositions . . . A dynamic, passionately knowledgeable, surprising, and gutsy chronicle of a world-shaping city and humanity itself in all its paradoxical wonder."

—*Booklist* (starred review)

"An exhaustively researched, eye-opening look at the great city's tumultuous, transformative recent history and what comes next."

—*People*

"[A] book as marvelous and maddening as the city itself . . . Dyja's energetic storytelling, eclectic interests, and supple prose make *New York, New York, New York* a tour de force, and his intellectual integrity overcomes the passionate political convictions that help to make his chronicle so pungent."

—Daniel Akst, *Reason*

"Dyja's prose sparkles and sings, revealing endlessly fascinating details while never bogging down or losing an overall sense of forward momentum. This is brilliant work on a broad canvas."

—*Passport Magazine*

"Dyja's stellar achievement with this indispensable book has been to write of the last four decades of New York in the very way that the city likes to think of itself—as propulsive, alluring, energetic, infuriating, scrappy, lyrical, nostalgic, omniscient, staggering, memorable, magical. The result is a history like no other for a city like no other."

—Simon Winchester, *New York Times* bestselling author of *The Professor and the Madman* and *The Men Who United the States*

New York, New York, New York

Four Decades of Success, Excess, and Transformation

Thomas Dyja

Simon & Schuster Paperbacks
New York   London   Toronto   Sydney   New Delhi

Simon & Schuster Paperbacks
An Imprint of Simon & Schuster, Inc.
1230 Avenue of the Americas
New York, NY 10020

First Simon & Schuster trade paperback edition March 2022

SIMON & SCHUSTER PAPERBACKS and colophon are
registered trademarks of Simon & Schuster, Inc.

For information about special discounts for bulk purchases, please contact
Simon & Schuster Special Sales at 1-866-506-1949 or business@simonandschuster.com.

The Simon & Schuster Speakers Bureau can bring authors to your live event.
For more information or to book an event, contact the Simon & Schuster Speakers Bureau
at 1-866-248-3049 or visit our website at www.simonspeakers.com.

Interior design by Kyle Kabel

Manufactured in the United States of America

1   3   5   7   9   10   8   6   4   2

Library of Congress Cataloging-in-Publication Data
Names: Dyja, Tom, author.
Title: New York, New York, New York : four decades of success, excess, and
transformation / by Thomas Dyja.
Description: First Simon & Schuster hardcover edition. |
New York : Simon & Schuster, 2021. | Includes index.
Identifiers: LCCN 2020032025 (print) | LCCN 2020032026 (ebook) |
ISBN 9781982149789 (hardcover) | ISBN 9781982149796 (paperback) |
ISBN 9781982149802 (ebook)
Subjects: LCSH: New York (N.Y.)—History—20th century. |
New York (N.Y.)—Politics and government—1951- | New York (N.Y.)—
Social conditions.
Classification: LCC F128.55 .D93 2021 (print) | LCC F128.55 (ebook) |
DDC 974.7—dc23
LC record available at https://lccn.loc.gov/2020032025

ISBN 978-1-9821-4978-9
ISBN 978-1-9821-4979-6 (pbk)
ISBN 978-1-9821-4980-2 (ebook)

To Suzanne,
Who Brought Me Back

Contents

x | Contents

III. Reformation

IV. Reimagination

When asked to name his three favorite American cities,
Holly Whyte said,
　　　　　　"New York.
　　　　　　New York.
　　　　　　New York."

Introduction

S now again this morning—four inches, said the AccuWeather
Forecast—after a foot and half last week. Snow across the hundred
acres of broken boards, mounds of brick, bent pipe, and garbage around
Charlotte Street and Boston Road. Snow edged the sills of burnt-out
apartment buildings, dusted shards of glass and mattresses left behind.
There'd been some 63,000 fires in the South Bronx in the last two years;
little point in plowing.

Today, Valentine's Day 1978, was officially "I Love New York" Day.

Jimmy Carter had visited these desolate blocks last October, made
thin promises as photographers focused on a landscape hopeless as
the moon. We'd given up on the moon by then, along with just about
everything else. Saigon had fallen; Nixon had resigned. Three decades
of economic expansion had ended with a thud. Factories were closing.
A dollar bought half of what it did ten years before; the speed limit,
to save gas, was now a poky 55. So as America's big, bright, exceptional
promise of eternal growth blew apart, Carter had offered up Charlotte
Street as a ruin so apparently complete that the rest of the failing nation
could say that at least they weren't *there*.

At Southern Boulevard, 18 feet in the air, the #5 train emerged
from behind a hollowed building, bubbly orange, green, red, and blue
words—"Daze," "Blade," "Futura"—painted on its sides. Inside, it
stunk of pot and piss; dense black scribbles over the windows and

walls. Every stop along the way to Brooklyn, bundled riders winced at the graffiti, at the smell, at the parade of annoyance and threat that was daily life in New York circa 1978: track fires and dog shit, bad reception and cockroaches, that high-heeled lady upstairs with no rugs and the mugger around the next corner. "Hello from the gutters of N.Y.C.," wrote serial killer Son of Sam to the *Post*, "which are filled with dog manure, vomit, stale wine, urine and blood." In their camel hair coats, Frye boots, and shiny Yankees jackets, New Yorkers stepped over and through it all this "I Love New York" Day, shoved past mounds of uncollected garbage bags. Some 6.8 million people lived in New York City in 1978, down a million from ten years before; middle-class Blacks and Puerto Ricans had joined the White flight. Pocked with cracks and empty corners, old New York was coming apart in chunks. A dump truck fell through the West Side Highway. Famed exorcist Malachi Martin knew for a fact that demons hunted lost souls on the benches of Bryant Park. Few New Yorkers bothered with self-control. "People see it as bad," one young man told the *Times*, "and they feel they can't do anything about it. So they do their little bit to make it worse." Public space was yours to use as you pleased—go ahead and toss your hot dog wrapper on the sidewalk, piss between parked cars. Keepers at the Children's Zoo had stood by watching as a man molested one of their geese.

Then the change began. Over the next thirty-five years, three different New Yorks evolved in lurches; three very similar cities with much of the same DNA, but each bigger, faster, and sleeker than the one before, each one more merciless and beautiful. The Koch era was the Renaissance; after brutal Retrenchment came dazzling, greedy years that spiraled back down amid crack, AIDS, and a social gout of too much too fast. The next four years of David Dinkins left the city's liberal traditions battered but laid the foundation for the safe streets and dotcom excess of Rudy Giuliani's Reformation in the '90s. After the planes hit on 9/11 and a brief state of grace, the shaky city handed itself over to technocratic, philanthropic billionaire Michael Bloomberg who wove City Hall into his personal empire, reimagining New York to look very much like him: visionary and strategic, driven by data and good taste, rich beyond measure, and fatally detached from those it left behind.

By New Year's Eve 2013, when Bloomberg delivered his good-bye atop a desk in City Hall, New York had experienced the most dramatic peacetime transformation of a city since Haussmann rebuilt Paris, greener and safer than it had ever been, from Bryant Park's lawn and the blocks of tidy homes across the South Bronx to the million-dollar brownstones in Bed-Stuy. Rumpelmayer's and Billy's Topless were gone, along with CBGB, subway graffiti, and that dog shit on the sidewalk. Good luck finding a place to smoke. The murder rate had dropped to a then all-time low of 333. Entire neighborhoods had been culturally, racially, economically, and physically remade; bedraggled Williamsburg was hip, Sunset Park burst with Fuzhou Chinese. Altogether some 3.6 million immigrants had come through since 1978, and 1.5 million—the entire population of Philadelphia—stayed. City Hall was solvent.

But the city of our memories, that thrilling cesspool where anything could happen, site of secret rituals officiated by Santera priests, home of dowagers on Beekman Place, refuge from everything straight and common—*that* city seemed to have slipped under a sea of gold. The rich were no longer rich; they were imperial. Chain stores devoured mom and pops. Camp had been domesticated; rage, sex, and high art defanged, rents out of reach, the NYPD an army. Hip Hop was mainstream, but the Twin Towers were nowhere to be found. Depending on your mood, your age, your bank account, New York was now horrifying, or wonderful, and even that changed day-to-day, moment-to-moment.

That was the fall of 2013, when I started this book, angry at the closing of Big Nick's, a pretty lousy burger place and longtime symbol of the free-for-all character of the Upper West Side I'd moved to back in 1980. The election of progressive Bill de Blasio had surely signaled the end of an era; it was time, I thought, to sort through the facts of those years and get to the bottom of this slimy feeling I had that while so much had gone right in New York, way too much had gone wrong. Everyone had their opinions about what had happened: Some saw only villains and victims, used terms like Neoliberalism, Quality of Life, Broken Windows, and Gentrification with little sense of their original meanings, context, or applications; others told rose-colored stories about Giuliani's cops cleaning up Dodge and Bloomberg's enlightened reign, ignoring the profound damage done to the city and its people. Either way, four complex decades were reduced to a morality play. I wanted to get down to the actual ideas, policies, and technologies behind it all. What was the process? Who were the people?

As I researched and wrote over the next seven years, some things about the city and the world changed in remarkable ways—Donald Trump, for example, whom I'd originally seen as a bit of side comedy occasionally bursting in the door with a wacky catchphrase, became president of the United States. In other ways, the city stayed tragically the same.

Then, in a matter of days Covid-19 thrust New York back to the dark, empty streets of our memories, but this time no one was allowed to wander them. A city fueled by the energy of density, the pressure, the motion, the countless daily face-to-face interactions was suddenly frozen, and we sat helplessly listening to the sirens that never stopped. Some 17,000 New Yorkers died over three months, six times as many as died on 9/11. Hundreds of thousands lost their jobs. And then a White woman in the Central Park Ramble threatened to call the police on an African American birdwatcher, George Floyd was murdered by cops in Minneapolis, and the streets of New York burst into violent protest along with other American cities.

We no longer have the luxury of dogma, assumptions, and unexamined opinions about New York, not from any side of the many divides that separate us in this city. A fourth evolution of New York is clearly imminent; economics, public health, and social justice demand it. And that makes it crucial to learn the practical lessons of its earlier transformations. Covid has revealed cities, as nothing ever has, to be organisms built of countless intricate networks that exist to facilitate human exchange; their general health, maintenance, and momentum, their need to stay afloat through whatever hits them, transcends politics and sometimes, sadly, individual need. For us to learn anything from how New York became at once kinder and meaner, richer and poorer, more like America and less like what it had always been, we need a fine-grained look at how New Yorkers, public and private, created new methods of urban living that together saved the city, then in too many places overwhelmed it. We must confront the bitter fact that the things that brought New York back—connection, proximity, density—are exactly what sent Covid-19 burning through its streets, that too much that was objectively "good" depended on casting off, pushing aside, building upon, chewing up, and spitting out New Yorkers simply trying to make their own lives. And we must understand that the greatest challenge we will face is one that New York failed badly in its last three evolutions: the cure can't be worse than the disease.

Seven main themes weave through this book and point to the future: how City Hall made an ungovernable city governable; how the one Great Conversation of New York culture broke apart; how AIDS transformed Gay New York and the city as a whole; how the built landscape and public space were fundamental to new growth and community while also creating inequality and new forms of control; how millions of immigrants stabilized and globalized the city even as its People of Color confronted diminished power, dislocation, and brutality; the impact of technology on nearly every aspect of life in New York; and finally, the rise of Brooklyn as an expansion of the city's consciousness of itself.

All these themes hang on the deeper structures of how people connect in cities. New York's passage through Renaissance, Reformation, and Reimagination was really a shift from mass society to networks. Until the '70s, political scientists described New York as a game played by all its interests with City Hall as the referee. But as Information took over from Industry, the collective world of unions, borough machines, the archdiocese, and even the Mob gradually gave way to one of individuals who define themselves primarily by the networks they belong to. The gameboard became what I imagine as a galaxy of 8½ million lives connected to each other in ways beyond counting: those with the most connections—and therefore the most access to favors, advice, job tips, and string pulling—shone the brightest, and the reconnection and reorganization of New Yorkers sent new tastes, ideas, resources, and behaviors coursing through every borough, unleashing financial, human, and social capital. Like a giant brain, the more connections, the more synapses firing, the higher functioning New York became. Those without wide connections, or with none at all, were left behind.

But social capital isn't an unqualified good; a street gang can produce just as much as a congregation, and the same kinds of connections that catalyzed the response to AIDS and spread Hip Hop also produced toxic levels of social capital in Wall Street, Nouvelle Society, and post-gentrification PTAs, until, by the end of the Bloomberg years, New York was one vast web of business, government, philanthropy, and culture that exemplified the best and worst of a networked world. "[T]he larger the web gets," writes historian William McNeill, "the more wealth, power, and inequality its participating populations exhibit." And the more vulnerable it is to any sort of contagion, including a very nonmetaphorical virus.

The energy released by all this breaking and building of new connections, the movement between Order and Disorder, is the catalyst of urban life, the human fission that fuels a city. Though much visible effort goes into preserving Order, cities, especially democratic capitalist ones, thrive on the energies and possibilities of toggling back and forth, so how New York manages and manipulates Order and Disorder explains much of what happens during these years. Deregulation of markets, for example, creates profits by creating Disorder to speculate on; the Mob made money by enforcing Order on the Disorder of places like the Garment District and Fulton Fish Market. Hip Hop came to life out of Disorder and then became an Orderly thing, while Koch's Housing Initiative helped create Order in neighborhoods. The most familiar example—enforcing Order in the streets and parks—touches the troubling knot at the core of the city's transformation: Using Order to facilitate exchange between people wasn't the same as using it to enforce oppressive, if familiar, norms about sex, race, and class. And a city without Disorder, or at least *public* Disorder, is barely a city at all.

That brings us to *Who*. Over these thirty-five years, the greatest changes were the work of New Yorkers obsessed in their own individual ways with fixing, changing, building, saving, serving the city more than their political party, social ties, or corporate affiliation. Even when it was a fig leaf for their own agendas, you still find possibility, identity, history, justice, and a sense of Home—a search for actual results, not just votes or dollars. Elizabeth Barlow Rogers was obsessed with Central Park, just as Marcy Benstock was obsessed with stopping Westway, Larry Kramer was obsessed with fighting AIDS, Jack Maple was obsessed with crime, and Reverend Johnny Ray Youngblood was obsessed with affordable housing. Everyday New Yorkers rebuilt communities by rebuilding their connections to government and to each other. What happened in these years didn't just happen *to* New York; its people had agency. Not all the time and not nearly enough, but when people connected in practical, humane ways, when they participated in urban life, sometimes—many times—they found sweet spots that balanced the networks of power and money, that made us love the place even as we hated what it was becoming. Instead of standing by and watching Jane Jacobs's street ballet, they jumped in and danced. New Yorkers rediscovered trust which, deserved or not, offered hope even as they despaired at what was lost. The greatest lesson of these thirty-five years is that keeping a city fertile demands the active, daily participation of its citizens.

I've chosen words like *transformation* and *evolution* quite consciously, because neither *failure* nor *triumph* fully describes these years. Along with the potential for contagion, what left New York vulnerable at their end was that too many good ideas, practical strategies, and necessary temporary measures became permanent, inflexible policies applied to a place in constant flux. The gentle urbanism that taught New Yorkers how to responsibly share public space was turned into a means of controlling them; proactive policing made heroes out of the NYPD, until it became in many places an occupying army. The Jane Jacobs–style gentrification that revived the taste for urban living turned life in New York into a consumer good. The list, as we'll see, goes on, into the Arts and Media, Wall Street, and our neighborhoods. No one knew when to say "When." Or wanted to even when they did. At the same time, some basic services that everyone relies on were taken for granted or outright ignored; increasing cultural diversity did not add up to enough practical change. The result was a city flush with cash and full of poor people, diverse but deeply segregated, hopeful yet worryingly hollow underneath the shiny surface. A city wide open to a virus that would not only exploit poverty and density, but also the very thing that makes New York great—its vast web of human contact.

As it tries to balance its wild heart with the realities of public health, its need for public safety with our inalienable civil rights, the New York ahead will confront the same issues it confronted between Koch and Bloomberg. The fight over public space will illuminate new kinds of inequality and privilege based on age and health along with wealth, class, and race. In the name of health and security, new methods of control will be deployed against New Yorkers and their behaviors. Technology will play a key role, from the virtual workplace to vaccines to methods of surveillance and monitoring that will extend beyond the annoyance of the security desks that appeared with the *fatwa* against Salman Rushdie. An immense amount of reason and soft logic will be needed to keep digital solutions from sharpening themselves into the tools of authoritarianism and a random sniffle from being accorded the same fear and distrust as a terrorist act.

More than ever, balancing public and private, inside and out, me and we, will be central tensions of New York, and if we intend to hand a peaceful, prosperous, and generative city to our children, then we must all play active roles in its next evolution and consciously participate in civil life beyond work, shopping, and leisure. We will have to rethink our networks; our own personal networks—who's in them and what are they connected to—but also carefully and inclusively rebuild collective powers to confront the ones that have torn us apart, ones that can guarantee everyone access to basic resources like health care, housing, and justice. Everyone must be able to walk the streets of New York without worrying about being assaulted by a gang member or a cop. We will have to be constantly aware of race, gender, and class in ways and places that are new and often uncomfortable, but always with the understanding that we remain connected by the potential to be fully human, a potential we're offered the unique opportunity to realize every day by how we live in our city.

On February 14, 1978, New Yorkers peered out at a snowstorm and a very uncertain future for their city. We know where it ended up, for better and worse. The years in between are not just a period to get past. Many great and valuable things took place during them along with many terrible ones, and they are all teachers. The next New York will be built on the lessons we learn—or fail to learn—from the previous three.

I. Renaissance

Chapter One

"I Love New York" Day

S tanding alone, bald, and surprisingly tall, Ed Koch watched the snow fall through the windows of Tavern on the Green while the guests filed in for Hugh Carey's "I Love New York" Day lunch. Only six weeks into his term and the City had already spent twice the year's budget for snow plowing.

He'd been born in the Bronx, around the corner from Charlotte Street, back when garmentos were escaping from the Lower East Side. The kids who grew up in Crotona fought at Anzio and Guadalcanal, then came home for a few years of City College before making their own escape to the suburbs. As the shops along Jennings Street closed, torahs given to new congregations, Robert Moses gouged the Cross Bronx Expressway through the borough's gut, pushing more Whites out to Co-op City. Black and Puerto Rican families moved into their apartments, so the landlords let the broken windows stay broken. Then the drugs hit, along with the fires started by owners to collect insurance, by bored kids and worried fathers who knew that fire victims got preference for the projects, until history was consumed and it all became just "the South Bronx." Services were pulled back until all that was left were the sirens of Engine 82 and Ladder 31, up to 150 times a day. Koch wasn't from a place as much as a time passed.

These days New Yorkers were rustling through closets in search of their own lost times: Depression-era *Annie* filled the Alvin Theatre; the

3

Manhattan Transfer and *film noir* retrospectives; Bette Midler in her peep-toed pumps; anything that reached back to the mythic New York that had died in 1975 when the City had nearly gone bust. London and Chicago had great fires, San Francisco an earthquake; the disaster that forced New York into its future was the Fiscal Crisis. To understand how the City pulled itself up, it's important to know what knocked it down.

Five-borough New York was still young when Governor Al Smith and Mayor Fiorello La Guardia stitched them together into a "workers' paradise" with its own free university, hospitals, low transit fares, and lots of public housing that balanced the mansions along Fifth Avenue. The third maker of modern New York was Robert Moses, whose power came from his ability to please those in both the public housing and the mansions. Tall and severe, part of New York's "Our Crowd" of German Jews, he built the radiating system of highways, parks, and beaches for the State then, as City Parks Commissioner, a frenzy of bridges, parks, roads, and pools that put the Depression-era unemployed to work on a regional plan crafted by blue bloods largely to keep *them* at arm's length. New Yorkers adored Moses for providing both bread and circuses, but he became besotted with his own considerable genius. After a disastrous run for governor in 1934 exposed his distaste for the *hoi polloi*, Moses used the tolls from the Triborough Bridge to subsidize a network of public authorities answering only to him. A series of weak mayors then handed him control of the City's planning and construction, and in the name of urban renewal, he destroyed healthy neighborhoods, scattered their social capital, deepened segregation, ignored mass transit, and undercut manufacturing by favoring highways over railroads.

In 1953, the City's balance of power wobbled when reformer Robert Wagner won City Hall with the votes of the Blacks and Puerto Ricans moving into the buildings, jobs, and benefits left behind by Whites headed to the suburbs. Wagner made all civil servants subject to the unions, which let him sidestep the borough machines and political clubhouses and deal directly with a big chunk of the City's working-class vote. When Medicaid passed in the early '60s, the State forced the City to foot a large percentage and worse, because now the poor could use private hospitals, its aging public hospital system became one huge, unnecessary but politically untouchable expense. So to keep paying for the Workers' Paradise, Wagner went down two slippery slopes: he increased borrowing and imposed new taxes that sped up the exodus of Whites and corporations. His successor, handsome young John Lindsay, took over in 1965 as a breath of fresh air focused on social justice and modernizing the City's sclerotic systems. The new mayor's idealism and city plan were a rebuke of Moses, whose reign finally ended when the MTA took over his seat of power, the Triborough Bridge Authority. Lindsay used Great Society programs like Model Cities to reconnect the people to their city after decades of Moses's control, creating community boards and pumping Federal money into long-ignored neighborhoods. Then it all fell apart.

In October 1969, with the Amazin' Mets dousing the mayor with champagne after their surprise World Series win, New York's economy began an 84-month swoon. Nixon chopped away at the Great Society, and the optimism of Lindsay's first term curdled. Generational and economic change met sloppy, weak governance; Model Cities proved to be corrupt and chaotic, and the capital budget was raided to pay expenses, a breach of responsible accounting that made long-term maintenance and planning impossible. "Nobody was willing to say no," said one official, and it was true whether you wore a three-piece suit, a dashiki, or a hard hat. *Especially* if you wore a hard hat. Even as New York's public union members led the charge to the suburbs, the unions, not City Hall, seemed in charge; a corrupt NYPD watched the murder rate more than quadruple between 1961 and 1972, while striking sanitation workers let garbage pile in the streets. School decentralization led to a battle in Brownsville that tore apart the alliance between Blacks and Jews. People Power devolved into entropy, and the urban legend of Kitty Genovese, screaming for help while her neighbors listened, became the truth of the city: No one will help you, so why should you care about anyone else? New Yorkers hadn't reconnected with governance; they'd split further apart. Experts deemed the city ungovernable.

Larger, global forces added fuel to the crisis. With Daniel Bell announcing *The Coming of Post-Industrial Society*, Japan and Germany emerged as industrial competitors, London overtook New York as the premiere financial market, and the US lost its first war. And then the

Oil Crisis. In theory, bad economic times should pull prices down, but the glut of global petrodollars kept pushing inflation *up* while high unemployment held wages down, giving birth to Stagflation. Lindsay raised taxes to make up for sliding revenues, but it wasn't enough, and here's where the nosedive began. State funds and property taxes come to the City twice a year, so to maintain cash flow it has to regularly borrow hundreds of millions of dollars. The banks had always played along because it was easy money, and as the debt rose, the City floated short-term bonds of various sizes and flavors that were really just increasingly dodgy ways of getting money to pay interest on existing debt. By the end of Lindsay's second term, the City was living week to week, and the budget had no basis in reality. "The only agenda," says one former staffer, "was to keep the city afloat." By the time a rumpled five foot two accountant out of the Brooklyn machine named Abe Beame took over City Hall in 1974, Wall Street was on to New York's problems. Robert Caro's damning biography of Moses, *The Power Broker*, revealed the corruption beneath New York's imperial rise, while on the Bowery, a bar called CBGB became the center of what Legs McNeil also called his new magazine: *Punk*. "Punk wasn't about decay," said McNeil. "Punk was about annihilation . . . Nothing worked, so let's get right to Armageddon."

The State's own problems brought things to a head. Governor Nelson Rockefeller had, with the help of his brother David, Chairman of Chase Manhattan Bank, created hundreds of public authorities with exotic bond issues that had the effect of letting the State print its own money. When the Urban Development Corporation (UDC), builder of large-scale affordable housing, defaulted in March 1975, the banks announced they wouldn't buy any more City bonds. This wasn't New York's first fiscal crisis, and everyone believed the City would ultimately pay its bills, so the real reason was economic philosophy. Though the banks had it in their power to restructure the debt, most of the business elite felt the Workers' Paradise and other big cities had been kept alive since the New Deal with political pork that just subsidized bad (read: Democratic) management. Here was an opportunity to take control of what they considered the most inept, bloated, bleeding-heart government of them all: New York City. So on April 14, 1975, New York found itself unable to redeem a $600 million bond issue, and the credit market shut its doors.

Beame's City Hall was indeed inept. When Governor Carey asked just how many people the City employed, Deputy Mayor James Cavanaugh had pulled out an envelope with some numbers jotted on the back. "Many things which would in other cities or in a corporation be on computers," admitted one insider, "were handled by people writing out in pen." While City workers labored around the clock to patch failing systems, Beame named an economic panel with no economists. Impeaching the feckless mayor was considered before Carey assembled an advisory board of bankers, businessmen, and officeholders called the Municipal Assistance Corporation, or MAC. Led by Lazard Frères's elegant, pursed-lipped Felix Rohatyn, it had emergency authority to issue bonds, though it could find no takers. One State senator who'd caught a ride back from Albany on the State jet said the diminutive Beame at this point looked "so distraught and so unhappy . . . you wanted to pick him up and put him on your lap." In September 1975, Carey effectively suspended democracy in New York City by creating a new and much more powerful Emergency Financial Control Board (EFCB) to take in all City revenue and direct all major expenditures. Beame was forced to restaff his City Hall with business-savvy officials and some actual businessmen.

With City Hall no longer in charge of how to spend its own tax dollars, Rohatyn assembled traditional competitors like labor, banking, business, and real estate interests to plan its next moves, putting New York City under the control of a network of powerful interests political scientists call a "crisis regime." Bankruptcy, it was decided, would devastate everyone, so the union pension funds bought bonds while the banks gave extensions on interest payments and bought bonds, too, now at much higher rates than before. Real estate developers prepaid their taxes. The lights stayed on, the ballot box remained, but the Workers' Paradise was over. In October, this united front pled the city's case to a Washington tired of paying urban subsidies, but the resulting *Daily News* headline "FORD TO CITY: DROP DEAD" shifted sympathies. David Rockefeller personally lobbied the White House, and on Thanksgiving Eve, as Macy's blew up its balloons, President Ford announced a deal for Federal aid through 1978.

Over the next two years, the City laid off some 61,000 employees. When State courts ruled the deal illegal, panicking banks demanded that the EFCB become a permanent unelected body overseeing the City's government. New York—and America—faced a Rubicon moment. To his credit, Rohatyn refused, saying, "It would mean the end of democracy." Instead, the EFCB would remain in charge until City Hall could deliver three balanced budgets in a row without Federal help. Two years had passed since then, and the state of emergency remained. Albany and Washington still provided 40% of the City's operating revenue and a plan had to be in place by summer for new Congressional funding or New York would be right back where it was in 1975, this time with all deferrals deferred and extensions extended. And for all the snow piling up outside Tavern on the Green, June wasn't far away.

*　　*　　*

Inside Tavern on the Green, Diana Ross and Yul Brynner chatted with Governor Carey. Americans hated nearly everything about New York City except for Broadway, so the State had launched a campaign around a logo dashed off by its designer Milton Glaser in the backseat of a cab. Though just three letters and a red heart, "I Love New York" had drawn a record 16.7 million visitors in 1977 despite the Blackout, Son of Sam, and Charlotte Street, so the $400,000 tourism budget had been multiplied by ten for things like this party to debut a slightly elegiac disco jingle touting Broadway. For symbolic reasons, if not culinary (*Times* restaurant critic Mimi Sheraton considered its food "below minimum standards of acceptability"), there was no better place for it than Tavern on the Green, revived by new owner Warner LeRoy with heavy applications of Tiffany glass and chintz. "I just love it here," Andy Warhol had said at the reopening. "I want to come back someday and get a chicken sandwich on potato bread. It's only $2.50." Today he was here with Paulette Goddard on his arm for free veal, prawns, and avocado.

Outside, the busy city observed Valentine's Day. "It was *really* a celebration," Warhol wrote in his diary, "a big holiday." New York, so close to death, was freshly beloved by New Yorkers. "It's in danger of dying," said Paul Mazursky, "so there's something tender about it." Though *Annie* took place during the Depression, "Tomorrow" was very much a song about today, and if you were still here, some crazy part of you loved the place no matter what, the intimacy and decay, the smell of cabbage crashing into *bacalao*, opera and salsa battling in the air shaft. Woody Allen was scouting locations for *Manhattan*. Isaac Bashevis Singer ordered the soup of the day again at the Famous Dairy Restaurant on 72nd, and Edward Gorey donned his big fur coat to see Suzanne Farrell dance Balanchine. White-gloved waiters polished samovars at the Russian Tea Room, while in a warm, quiet corner at *The New Yorker*, Mr. Shawn applied his pencil. *Metropolitan Life* by Fran Lebowitz just hit the shelves at Scribner's. Chevy Chase was about to replace Raymond Burr as host of that week's *Saturday Night Live*, and at 8:00 p.m. Robert LuPone would again shout "Step, kick, kick, leap, touch!" to start tonight's performance of *A Chorus Line*. Banjo-hitting shortstop Bucky Dent had stirred things up today in spring training, begging Yankees manager Billy Martin to let him bat in clutch moments.

On the Upper East Side, the old-money types lurched toward sequins. Just yesterday Halston had opened his new showroom at Olympic Towers (Scaasi said it would be bare shoulders for the spring, and dots dots *dots!*). Every night neurotic, romantic Liza Minnelli blew her lines in *The Act* with "brashness, pathos and desperate energy." International jet setters, unable to pass the boards of any of the dozen or so Park Avenue co-ops they'd deign to inhabit, consoled themselves by shake shake shaking their booties amid the nightly roller-skating, disco ball–spinning, coke-sniffing debauch at Studio 54. "It's like the last days of Rome," shouted writer Bob Colacello into the large powdered ear of Diana Vreeland. She responded, "I should hope so, Bob."

There were countless other New Yorks to love then, too, networks freely and frequently intersecting. Temples, parishes, and private schools; ethnic New York that made a nice *ragu* Sundays, played *Gaelic* in Riverdale, slurped borscht at the Kleine Konditorei. Fulton Street simmered with mobsters and fishermen while across town in the Meatpacking District, both sides of beef and gay men hung from hooks. A port city, New York had always been a gay city. In the '20s, when your public appearance defined gender, "fairies" had solicited "men" in Bryant Park and posed Elmo-style for photos with tourists in Times Square where, during World War II, thousands of American soldiers and seamen would discover new truths about themselves. Despite postwar rigidity over gender and sexuality, New York's "Sad Young Men" had developed an awareness of their identity and their rights that led to the Stonewall Riots. Since then, gay men had been exploring the boundaries of sex as a language, forming what Charles Kaiser called their own "completely democratic society," a network that connected men across lines of class and race. Some, like writer Larry Kramer, wondered if they'd gone too far. "[A]ll we do is live in our Ghetto and dance and drug and fuck," shouted the narrator of his novel *Faggots*. A coterie of adventurous, envious straights imitated gay life through glam-punk androgyny or by cavorting with other love-handled swingers on the wrestling mats at Plato's Retreat, but otherwise most New Yorkers considered homosexuality something to hate and fear. Koch's election was a watershed. As a congressman he'd supported gay rights, and the presence of Bess Myerson at his side during the campaign had fooled no one. While Gay New York claimed Koch as one of their own, he suspected that Cuomo's teenaged son Andrew had distributed the "Vote for Cuomo, not the homo" flyers in Queens. One of his first acts in office was to ban discrimination based on "affectional preference." New York's unique sass, its fast-talking, funny, cynical attitude part Jewish, part Black, part working class, came with a healthy dollop of camp. Susan Sontag's "ultimate Camp statement"—that something can be "good *because* it's awful"—helped make life in post-crisis New York endurable but also justified some of its rot.

From the start New York had also been a city of Color, its first two hundred years built with the labor of enslaved Africans whose numbers would in time be second only to Charleston's. Along with its historic Black population, it now had a significant Latino one, too, mostly Puerto Rican, and a growing Asian community. Crumbling Harlem continued its tenuous hold on Black consciousness, even as the Black middle class headed for the suburbs, the Rockefeller Drug Laws kicked in, and West Indians once again poured into Brooklyn. Racial peace was delicately held. "The city has to be tolerant," wrote E. B. White back in 1949, "otherwise it would explode in a radioactive cloud of hate and rancor and bigotry." This remained true. Up in the Bronx, a high school electronics nerd named Joseph Saddler had perfected a way to regulate the beat between two different records on two separate turntables, letting him stretch out that big, creamy moment that made you move—the "break"—for as long as he wanted. He called it the "clock theory" and now known as Grandmaster Flash, he was the city's hottest DJ.

Something was growing beneath the ashes of abandoned New York, something fed and watered on tension, anger, and creativity. Dancing through the fall of Rome required a kind of heroism; battling through circumstances you couldn't change was the very heart of camp. Did New Yorkers really want things any other way? "To be contented," said Mrs. Vreeland, "that's for the cows."

New York Governor Carey gritted his teeth at Ed Koch as he went to the microphone. Starting at only 2% in the polls, Congressman Koch had run as an outsider, bellowing "How'm I doin'?" into his megaphone at subway exits, running artless ads that stressed competence. His post-Blackout calls for the death penalty and the endorsement from Rupert Murdoch's conservative *New York Post* had drawn White ethnics and now, after beating Carey's man, Mario Cuomo, he'd become the city's biggest cheerleader, venting the anger of most New Yorkers and expressing their hope. "I realized," he reflected later, "that if I was to harness the energies of the people of the City of New York and give them back their pride, I would have to become bigger than life." They bought his rumpled bachelor persona, the $257-a-month rent-controlled apartment, and $3 bottles of wine. His lack of filter amused—those who crossed him were "Wackos!" or "Vile!"—and his distance from clubhouse politics looked for now more like principle than ego. New Yorkers believed Koch would turn things around. So did Ed Koch. "The world started when he became Mayor," said the corporate counsel. Hugh Carey didn't agree. That morning PR man Bobby Zarem had cajoled him into extending a last-minute invitation to Koch, and now the two joined Yul Brynner, Diana Ross, and Frank Langella in a rousing chorus of "I Love New York." Ed Koch just had to do what he was told.

I Won the Election, Not You.

The next morning, the mayor tucked his long frame into the backseat of a dented '74 Chrysler Newport with bad brakes—Beame had bought it during the Crisis to avoid being seen in the official limo. Koch had spent his first weeks learning the full extent of the City's decay; the 2,300 miles of potholed streets, the rusting bridges, doomsday budget, and the fact that no one knew exactly how many cars the City owned. Since then he'd ordered all vehicle requests be made public, which meant using the Chrysler for this visit to David Rockefeller. Both men believed that they ran New York City. Both felt the other was a fool.

Looking at his reflection, Ed Koch saw a self-made man. After his father, Louis, had lost his job, they'd moved to his uncle's house in Newark where, for eight years, nine high-volume people shared two bed-rooms while the Koch family begged for tips at a hatcheck concession. "To live on the largesse of people," said the mayor later, "is something I consider demeaning." Gangly Ed got a reputation for his brains and big mouth, happiest when alone with the person he most admired: himself. After CCNY and a short, violent tour of duty in 1944, he went to NYU Law and opened a one-man practice in Lower Manhattan, living with his parents and dodging questions as to why he was still single until 1956 when he moved to Bedford Street and took up the guitar. Greenwich Village was in transition then, the old Italians and Jews under siege, their rents rising because of bongo-drumming Beat poets and wannabes like Koch. That same year, followers of Adlai Stevenson organized the reform-minded Village Independent Democrats to challenge the regular Democrats' Tamawa Club. An Adlai man himself, Koch jumped into politics and rose to district leader by flipping back and forth between the two clubhouses, battling his own party as much as the Republicans. In 1965 he broke away to endorse Lindsay, who returned the favor by *not* endorsing him for City Council. Koch never forgave him and two years later won his old East Side congressional seat as "a liberal with sanity," which meant, like Adlai, a progressive aside from race.

Now, as *Mayor* Koch, he intended to do as he saw fit, starting with taking down the Lindsay kids' treehouse at Gracie Mansion. "I owed nothing to the political system," he said later, part lone wolf, part Man of La Mancha. "I had no commitments. I was absolutely my own man." That wasn't just directed at "the richies," as he called them; he was equally dismissive of Labor leaders like Jack Bigel, who'd offered their help as "partners." "You're not my partners," Koch had replied. "I won the election, not you." Which was true. But he could hardly do what he wanted; with the EFCB and MAC overseeing the budget, he effectively reported to *them*, not the people of New York. Since more decisions would be made in his office, he'd gained personal power at the expense of both the City Council and the Board of Estimate, but he had simple, sweeping, nonnegotiable directives from the Commission on City Finances: cut taxes, cut debt, cut spending, restore the capital budget, and improve management. If he hoped to get that new Congressional loan, he'd have to cut 20,000 more jobs, freeze salaries, restructure debt, and cut social spending, even with poverty in the City up more than 40% since 1969 and median family income down 18%. Cuts, though, weren't enough. The City needed revenue. New taxes were out of the question, leaving only one option, the last directive from the Commission: encourage development. "Growth" had always been the point of New York City, even during the Workers' Paradise. Growth meant more jobs, better jobs; it meant mobility and hope, and part of the mayor's job in the old Game of New York had been to direct it where he wanted it to go. Now the job was to lure businesses, people, and jobs back with whatever inducements the City could conjure and hope the resulting activity would throw off enough tax revenue to pay the bills.

Koch wasn't against much of this, in theory. He was in favor of trimming government, and he agreed that private sector accountability could make an enormous difference in terms of management. But he was no businessman. He'd appointed a genial millionaire retiree named Robert Milano as Deputy Mayor for Economic Development, though the *Times* sniped, "[i]f either he or the Mayor knows what encourages business expansion . . . they have given no sign of it." And he didn't seem to recognize, or want to admit, how much City Hall was now interlocked with business networks. Though he called the banks just another of the City's "pressure groups" and scoffed at their idea of New York being run as a business, or *by* its businesses, the mayor was now required to attend a monthly meeting with a Management Advisory Board of nine CEOs and bankers, while the Department of Operations had to produce a "Mayor's Management Report" twice a year to track performance data on all thirty-one City agencies, as well as embed on-loan executives to help develop more efficient public administration. One way or another, the Crisis Regime would have its say.

As the Newport headed toward Liberty Street, stout, needle-nosed David Rockefeller—to Bill Moyers "the most conspicuous representative of the Ruling Class"—waited at a 30-foot granite table lined with black leather chairs. His grandfather John, founder of Standard Oil, had passed down both a vast fortune and a sense of obligation to the family, first to his son John Jr., who'd built Rockefeller Center, and then his five grandsons. David was the youngest by three years; dumpy, dyslexic, a beetle collector, he'd run in the trails of his older brothers, especially Nelson ("I idolized Nelson"), through a childhood of summers on Seal Island and the Unicorn Tapestries just down the hall, until he was packed off to Harvard. A student of Hayek, an intern for La Guardia, he joined Chase National Bank in 1946, and as Ed Koch wrote wills and stumped for votes, he'd flown around the world learning the *realpolitik* of oil. New York was not so much the Rockefellers' home as their fiefdom. On top of being major landowners, the family had played roles in the creation of Rockefeller Center, Rockefeller University, the Museum of Modern Art, the UN Headquarters, Riverside Church, the Cloisters, the Asia Society, and Lincoln Center, and funded various civic initiatives, including low-income housing. Mayors would come and go, but there would always be Rockefellers exercising *noblesse oblige* in some proportion to their profits; now it was David's turn to exert their vast shadow power. He'd already played a major role in the bailout, lining up with Citibank CEO Walter Wriston to make the case to Wall Street, real estate, and the business community that joining forces as civic leaders rather than angry bondholders would push New York from an industrial economy to an information-based one.

And that was, to the Crisis Regime, the answer to the question as to where new Growth would come from. The movement from Industry to Information would prove to be the fundamental economic shift of the next four decades, and it was hardly some secret conspiracy even then.

Going forward, as Daniel Bell had explained, knowledge would replace labor, services would replace goods, and a new knowledge-based power class would emerge that would increase the role of women in the economy. Between 1950 and 1977 there'd been some fifty books explaining this transition, and all through those years, manufacturing in New York had been sliding as factories moved south and west and Moses built highways instead of railroads. Not only were trucks more expensive and dirtier, they clogged streets, presenting an opportunity to the five Mob families who stepped into time-sensitive arenas like waste hauling, ports, the Garment District, and the Fish Market, jacking up the cost of doing business. Congestion, red tape, taxes, and extortion mounted, and major industries left, pockets of small, interrelated factories began to die of old age; the Yellow Pages still had listings for bungmakers and spats salesmen. The gut punch, though, was the death of the port, long the city's largest employer of unskilled labor, now outdated and squeezed by the Mob. When the Port Authority diverted the new container shipping technology to New Jersey in the mid-'50s, away from the crumbling Hudson piers, the city's manufacturing sector largely split apart—the executives drifted up to Midtown and labor went overseas.

Rockefeller and Wriston, though, each saw their own, albeit related, set of opportunities. For Wriston, it was all about finance and the nature of money. The seismic event for information in New York was when Nixon went off the gold standard in 1971. Overnight, cash lost its intrinsic value; money was now just numbers on a screen, and collecting and moving that information wouldn't just be the future of banking, it was the future, period. Finance would *be* the economy and everything else would be the games to bet on. Lean, urbane Wriston, a native of Appleton, Wisconsin, insisted that New York's saving Growth would come by pampering the finance, insurance, and real estate corporations—the FIRE sector—as they wove a global network, buying, selling, lending, and borrowing across borders, their boards and interests interlocked. "Capital," he liked to say, "will go where it is wanted and stay where it is well treated." If Washington would only unleash the financial sector, its relentless innovation would turn New York into the world's money factory while the city itself put the needs of FIRE above everything else. The philosophy that had driven the banks to shut the credit market in 1974 would now rule the city. Schools, housing, libraries, all of the investments in human capital that its taxpayers had made for decades, were to be deemed "redistribution of wealth" (an idea that somehow coincided with those investments being made for People of Color). Growth would be measured in purely financial terms; all that mattered now for cities was, wrote Paul Peterson, "the maintenance and enhancement of their economic productivity."

In return, Wriston planned to get rid of the old vaulted temples to Mammon and put more of that money information in the hands of everyday folks, while he turned Citibank into a "financial supermarket" that would help them figure out what to do with it, especially with cozy old passbook savings accounts melting away under 10% inflation. A week before "I Love New York" Day those plans took a giant leap forward when eighteen inches of snow fell, completely shutting down New York: If you didn't have cash, you were out of luck—no bread, no milk, no subway tokens, and only 38% of Americans had credit cards then. But Citibank had just installed automatic teller machines in all of its 271 branches; Citibankers carried on as usual and New Yorkers finally saw the point of ATMs—you could get your money whenever you wanted it, *no matter what*! Over the next three years, Citibank's deposits in New York would double and ATMs became standard, providing an early lesson for many Americans about trusting computers. More important, ATMs helped demystify money, and soon credit cards would be increasingly easier to get as the once shameful idea of carrying debt would gradually become a sign of financial savvy.

David Rockefeller, on the other hand, a native New Yorker, understood that the city's ultimate resource was its real estate, so he saw the move from Industry to Information in those terms. In many ways the Rockefellers were supersized versions of the leading families in postwar American cities like Pittsburgh and Baltimore who'd redeveloped their business centers to lure back fleeing Whites, but New York had two "downtowns"—thriving Midtown and the flagging Financial District where the Rockefellers had much of their holdings. As the action moved north, those who owned the land beneath the closed warehouses and factories Downtown cared about commercial and residential possibilities, or even eminent domain, more than saving industry, so stretches of

Manhattan from the gritty section below Houston to the South Street Seaport and Times Square went to rot while their owners waited to see what would happen next. That didn't work for the Rockefellers, so in 1955 David decided what that "next" would be. First, he convinced the Chase board to build their new headquarters on Liberty Street.

Koch's Newport stopped in front of One Chase Manhattan Plaza, a bracing 60-story Modernist slap that declared Chase king of New York finance, even when that wasn't entirely true. Advised by Moses and inspired by his old boss La Guardia, Rockefeller had then founded the Downtown Lower Manhattan Association, a kind of mini Crisis Regime for the Financial District that developed plans with the Port Authority for a World Trade Center that would clear out the tiny electronics district. Meanwhile, David and developer William Zeckendorf orchestrated a game of musical chairs wherein Zeckendorf convinced various banks to relocate throughout the Financial District, making the Information Age appear nigh. Thus frothed, the Regional Plan Association (RPA) produced a new regional plan and the City revamped its zoning rules to favor office buildings. Even David's brother Nelson called a surprise press conference to announce plans for a 100-acre mixed-use, mixed-income development on the landfill excavated for the World Trade Center, to be called Battery Park City. (David hadn't known about it until he read it in the *Times*—"I must say I was annoyed.") Moses joined in with his Lower Manhattan Expressway meant to connect the West Side Highway and the Manhattan Bridge across "Hell's Hundred Acres." Two years later, the Planning Commission offered its own revised city plan that included a replacement for the West Side Highway, a convention center, redevelopment in Downtown Brooklyn and the West Side, and the renovation of Times Square. "In the long run," one draft of the plan admitted, "New York does not want to retain the low skill, low wage segment of its industrial mix."

But then very little happened. "Expressways are never wiped out at a single stroke," Jane Jacobs said later. "They're nibbled to death by ducks. So let's all be ducks and nibble this thing to death." Which activists did; the expressway died, opening the way for SoHo. The 10 million square feet of the World Trade Center sucked up all the demand for office space. Battery Park City foundered, and now its acres of landfill, called "The

Beach" by locals, sat empty along the Hudson where an underground sex and art scene thrived on the abandoned piers. The path ahead wasn't obvious because even the Crisis Regime wasn't entirely—mostly, but not entirely—in sync. Citibank had overtaken Chase, and Rockefeller remained desperate for Downtown development in a way that Wriston with his new angled skyscraper in Midtown didn't have to be.

So who would run New York? Ed Koch headed up the stairs and past Isamu Noguchi's sunken Zen garden. Ed Koch was not a Zen guy. He loved the chaos of New York, the yelling out the window, the fuhgeddaboudits. He only cared about what his New York *did*. Amid the low murmur of flowing capital, he was whisked up to the 17th floor, led through corridors of creamy carpets and ficus trees. Back at City Hall, file cabinets overflowed and toilets didn't flush. He'd found La Guardia's desk in a hallway.

The boardroom doors opened.

The room stood. This was Rockefeller's Business Labor Working Group, a network of business and union leaders founded during the Crisis and now interested in learning just how much it could flex on the new mayor. Guided toward the seat between Rockefeller and labor leader Harry Van Arsdale, Koch made note of people who'd never given him a check or the time of day. Bob Milano and Planning Commissioner Robert Wagner Jr. were there for the City. The mayor sat. And only then did everyone sit back down. Rockefeller hovered, inquiring as to how Koch liked his coffee, then, guest served, wasted no time. Every new plan was stuck, he said. Losses mounting, he intended to tear down Radio City Music Hall and put up a hotel. He left it to the assembled executives and union leaders to make the case for the convention center, the proposed underground highway along the Hudson called Westway, and the stalled Battery Park City. While Koch and Wagner listened politely, an overwhelmed Bob Milano babbled his admiration for Rockefeller and his plans.

The mayor left making no promises, though he soon fired Bob Milano. "[H]e broke into tears," reported the mayor, not much for crybabies, or discretion. For the next few weeks he mulled what he'd heard. At a point when he was pulling every string to get more funding from Congress, he wasn't thrilled about greasing the way for a

Rockefeller, though all the jobs promised by Westway sounded good. As to Battery Park, Wagner pointed out that the deal as it was put the City on the hook for overages; money it didn't have. Shy, with pleading, scholar's eyes and a stiff smile, Robert "Bobby" Wagner, the late mayor's son, was politically dead but had Koch's ear. Relieved of the duty to chase his own family legacy, he wandered City Hall as head of the Planning Commission, wise and a little in the clouds as he guided the mayor toward understanding how essential the built environment was to Growth; on one hand, real estate development would be the quickest way to create it, but long-term the City needed more housing and more taxpaying homeowners. And both relied on infrastructure spending, which the Crisis had all but stopped.

By the end of March the snow melted, and Rockefeller had dashed off a testy follow-up bemoaning the City's inaction. Amid the stink of thawing garbage, vast puddles spread; on April 13, Reggie Jackson hit a three-run home run that drove fans to whip giveaway Reggie candy bars onto the field. President Carter finally delivered the national urban policy he'd been promising since his walk along Charlotte Street, one that all but sent a message directly to Koch. Ending the Great Society idea that repairing cities was the responsibility of the Federal government, Carter proposed instead "a working alliance of all levels of government, with the private sector of our economy and with our citizens." The days of simply pouring money into cities were over; city governments, businesses, and citizens would have to work together to rebuild. Carter would help New York, but Koch would also have to play ball with the likes of Rockefeller. A week later, the City struck a deal that kept Radio City Music Hall open and lowered its exposure on Battery Park City in return for endorsing the Federal mortgage supports needed to finally start building the project. The wobbly strolls along the line between public and private had just begun.

It was a tense summer. The Yankees stunk and Senator William Proxmire did all he could to dynamite the new aid bill in Congress. By July, California passed Proposition 13, weepy Billy Martin resigned as Yankees manager, and the City had managed to skate into the new fiscal year without more borrowing. Congress reluctantly authorized the aid, and after signing off on a $4.5 billion workable, if still dismal, four-year financial plan, the EFCB dropped the *Emergency* from its name—though it would continue oversight for the next thirty years. New York had officially survived the Fiscal Crisis.

At which point the Yankees woke up. They finished the season tied with the Red Sox for the AL East and with two on and two out in the seventh inning of the one-game playoff at Fenway Park, interim manager Bob Lemon believed the way New Yorkers were starting to believe. He sent Bucky Dent to the plate. From his ungainly crouch, Dent hit a 1–1 fastball over the Green Monster to launch the Yankees into the playoffs and an eventual World Series win. Ed Koch led a ticker tape parade down Broadway, shouting "We're number one!" on the steps of City Hall. When the Yankees win the World Series, New York feels right again, even when it's not.

In the days ahead, sitting behind La Guardia's little desk propped up on blocks, or tossing his balled-up socks onto the Gracie Mansion floor, Koch couldn't shake the memory of that boardroom. They'd all stood up. Rockefeller had leapt up to bring him coffee. *Him*, Ed Koch, who'd once begged for tips!

Chapter Two

Something It Hadn't Been

B eing in charge of a zoo is a pretty big deal if you're the father of a three-year-old, so in January 1978, the week he'd taken the job as Parks Commissioner, Gordon Davis had brought his daughter, Elizabeth, to the Central Park Zoo. First stop was the Monkey House, where the gorillas Kongo and Lulu were lying motionless on the floor, staring at the ceiling as their daughter, Patty Cake, picked paint off the bars. Next, the neurotic lions pacing cages the size of an Upper East Side bedroom and the tigers sleeping amid a bitter, desperate stink. The eland couldn't stand. One lonely sea lion floated in the sea lion pool—the Federal government had barred the zoo from getting another. In the Children's Zoo, Whaley the cracked fiberglass whale grinned maniacally as if numbed to the pain of these 125 wild animals crammed into a single acre, uncared for, unprotected, occasionally tortured by visitors and park employees.

"Daddy," said Elizabeth, "never bring me here again."

The possibility that he'd made a big mistake had struck Gordon Davis as soon as he'd walked into Parks Department headquarters. The encrusted windows, holes in the walls, and junk shop furniture; everything about the old crenellated Arsenal at 64th and Fifth summed up the collapse of City government. Over the last decade, public agencies, foundations, and advocacy groups had all done extensive damage reports on the city's infrastructure, so even though precomputerized New York had no complete inventory of its capital plant, *what* had to happen was known. Estimates put the city's capital requirements for the next decade up to $40 billion, but money aside, the enormity of it all had sucked the will out of most everyone, especially at Parks, the city's very last priority at a time when the Transport Workers Union deemed conditions in the subways "bad enough to cause a major disaster at any time." The Arsenal represented the other side of Retrenchment that wasn't about pleasing banks and Congress, the part about improving City management. Koch had to make the city function.

The impulse here is to add "again," but making New York "work" had not always, and maybe not ever, been a goal for those who welcomed disorder as the way to overtime or a palmed twenty. City government had never been run for maximum efficiency; the point of patronage was jobs, with results a distant second. Management was the province of reformers and the public agencies, foundations, and advocacy groups who'd erected a virtuous scaffolding around City politics, assuring things actually got done while City Hall focused on giving special interests their taste. Everyone else got pinched, especially the middle class and small businessmen who paid for their independence by having to slash through thickets of red tape, following absurd union rules and paying inflated prices. Koch liked to tell about the time an old woman tugged his sleeve and said, "Mr. Koch, Mr. Koch, make the city what it once was." To which he said, "Lady, it was never that good." "Everybody who was any good working for Koch in that first term," says Davis, "understood that they were part of a puzzle trying to restore the city to something it hadn't been." All New Yorkers deserved orderly governance and delivery of services, but that would require profound changes both in how City government operated and how New Yorkers thought of their city.

The crisis had made them more conscious of the place than they'd been in a long time, and that included business leaders, many of whom had grown up here; most good government groups like the Citizens Budget Commission were resolutely nonpartisan. Mayor Lindsay had created the Urban Fellows Program to create young administrators, but given that his attempts to introduce modern management theories also included the RAND-inspired Productivity Program that advised letting the South Bronx burn, many were reasonably suspicious of all this talk about efficiency and budgets when it led to cuts that hurt mostly People of Color. In fact, the person most responsible for laying the foundation for a functioning New York City wasn't a Republican but a Growth Democrat. As part of the bailout, Lindsay's former City Planning Chair, John Zuccotti, son of a captain at the El Morocco nightclub, was brought in as essentially a shadow mayor to Beame. Along with developing a reporting system that culminated in an annual Mayor's Management Report, he created a Management Improvement Program to blast through decades of bureaucratic sludge and instill some seemingly obvious business principles at City Hall, altogether changing the mayor's job into something closer to CEO. Zuccotti left a clear charge for Koch: Build a nonpartisan managerial tier and develop clear strategies and structures that will let them manage for results. Every administration over the next thirty-five years would define itself by how it pursued that goal, and every administration would claim it came up with the idea.

Koch was on board. "Removal of incompetents," he declared, "is not anti-labor. It is anti-those-who-do-not-want-to-labor." According to Davis, Koch "set a tone that the glass is half-full, not half-empty. And you better work your ass off to at least be accountable." Instead of one deputy mayor, Koch hired seven with Policy and Management's David Brown the first among equals and tried to make civil service merit-based instead of subject to union rules, to help create that tier of managers. But the mayor needed his own attitude adjustment. While he'd shown an admirable openness to ideas, he liked to set people against one another and relied more on press conferences and threats to get things done than on systems. The early returns hadn't been promising. The August 1978 Mayor's Report included the first results from Project Scorecard, a study of street cleanliness created by the Fund for the City of New York, and they were dismal; the city was a stinking mess. False alarms and venereal disease were up. That summer, the pier at Bethune Street collapsed into the Hudson.

Commonplace Civilization

All the talk of productivity and work rules spoke to what so many felt had disappeared in New York: personal accountability and trust. New Yorkers needed to see the city and their fellow citizens as something more than adversaries, and that's why Parks mattered so much. In 1978, the Parks Department oversaw 24,000 acres in 572 parks that included Frederick Law Olmsted's jewels—Central Park, Riverside Park, and Prospect Park in Brooklyn—plus Bryant Park, 3 zoos, 4 stadiums, 14 golf courses, 6 beaches, 104 swimming pools, and some 2.6 million trees. One-sixth of New York was parkland, a higher percentage than any other American city, but in terms of acres per person, it was next to last, and those acres were dangerous and worn. New Yorkers desperately needed spaces to throw balls, stroll or, as more people were doing, jog. Parks weren't passive. "A park is a work of art," wrote Olmsted, "designed to produce certain effects upon the minds of men," the only places in cities where you'll find "with an evident glee in the prospect of coming together, all classes largely represented, with a common purpose." Parks were fundamental to a democracy; they were shared land devoted, as Adam Gopnik writes, to "commonplace civilization"; public space controlled by common trust and expectations. The inability of New Yorkers to share and care for their parks expressed the loss of trust; changing public spaces and the attitudes toward them was the third process involving the built environment that would eventually transform the city.

The problems started at the Arsenal, long a dumping ground for political favors. Lindsay's first commissioner, Thomas Hoving, once called the Clown Prince of Fun City, offered up the parks as entertainment without thinking much about their care, and his patrician successor August Heckscher had placated the unwashed masses by surrendering public control; vandalism was just another way to use the park. Then five commissioners in five years and deep budget cuts had devastated what morale remained; a comptroller's audit found a "systematic pattern of loafing" among Parks employees. Not surprisingly, a dozen candidates turned the job down before it fell to Gordon Davis, thirty-six years old, a fair-skinned African American from an august Chicago family. As reporter Orde Coombs wrote, Davis "honed a superior wit, he refused to tolerate fools, and he took great comfort in his intelligence." Six foot five and half, Davis had played basketball at Williams College, then got his law degree at Harvard. He'd worked in Lindsay's budget department, then as his liaison with Model Cities and speechwriter during his brief presidential run. In private practice now, with a seat on the City Planning

Commission, Davis thought the Parks job was impossible, too; plus, he'd voted against Koch. But he took the job, and over the next five years, he'd make Parks a laboratory for the procedures and partnerships that would eventually transform the city's public administration and begin the use of public space as a way to reeducate New Yorkers about the rights and responsibilities of urban life.

Before he could attack any of the big problems, though, Davis had two months of coordinating salt and shovels and finding his way around the Arsenal. Olmsted himself had hated the place; he'd circled it with large trees in hopes of hiding it and complained about the same kinds of shenanigans that now had Davis secretly hoping to be fired. Then one crisp morning in April 1978, he paid a surprise visit to Inwood Hill Park, where grinning park workers lounged in the springtime sun as garbage cans overflowed and papers swirled overhead. The commissioner was not amused. "We have cutbacks in the department," shrugged their supervisor, "and we have a fiscal crisis."

This was Davis's moment of satori. Using the Fiscal Crisis as an excuse, New Yorkers simply accepted the miserable state of their parks as another one of the many indignities to be soldiered through like so many piles of dog shit. There was no real chance of changing crime, dirt, or subway delays. Didn't all the experts say New York was ungovernable? Yet simply accepting that the city's social capital had rotted away also meant accepting the pain that inflicted on other living beings, whether they were guinea pigs having their eyes put out in the zoo or hungry children in the South Bronx. For the City's services to improve, New Yorkers would have to improve, too. So Davis started to set limits. He took the advice of a Parks Council report and began to say no. He canceled the annual Taste of the Big Apple festival in Central Park and, much to the shock of the March of Dimes, kept their deposit when they didn't clean up after their walkathon. Permits and management would be taken seriously now. He restructured the department and negotiated broader job definitions for some union employees. He engendered a sense of good faith effort and accountability at the Arsenal. He got the windows cleaned.

And he admitted what he didn't know. New York's unusual breadth of services had created a belief that City Hall could—and should—manage its own holdings as a public trust, but in too many cases too much money had been paid out for terrible public management of things like zoos and golf courses. On the other hand, much of the city's successful cultural infrastructure was, like the bridges and subways, the product of public-private partnerships, beginning in 1869 with the American Museum of Natural History, followed by the Metropolitan Museum of Art, the New York Botanical Gardens, and the Bronx Zoo. By now, the Department of Cultural Affairs included 15 private institutions known as the Cultural Institutions Group (CIG) that either received City money or stood on City land. Even the New York Public Library wasn't really a "public" creation; Carnegie money had merged with the private Astor and Lenox libraries. Though the City now paid for the branch system, the research libraries were still privately funded. With all this in mind, Davis tested the idea of outside vendors running some Parks operations in hopes of turning money-losing propositions into small gains.

That left the issue of poor public behavior in parks, a textbook example of the "Tragedy of the Commons" wherein a public good is destroyed because every individual takes advantage of it with no thought of the greater good. But why couldn't "public" mean shared space with generally agreed upon limits on behavior and use? This debate applied to all public spaces in New York including, in the summer of 1978, the sidewalks. After the Yankees' soap opera, the city's other obsession was dog crap. The '70s had brought dogs to New York in greater numbers than ever before and all those dogs, large and small, produced approximately 125 tons of waste *a day* that the Department of Sanitation had neither the interest nor the funds to clean up, making stepping in dog shit a trope of New York life. The battle lines were drawn: one side felt sidewalks were theirs to use as they pleased, while the other felt shared public space should be clean. Dog owners fought every City Council pick-up bill, with the ASPCA claiming that New Yorkers would set their dogs loose or kill them before they'd pick up their poop. Said the leader of the Dog Owners' Guild—without shame—"Like the Jews of Nazi Germany, we citizens, including the old and infirm, are being humiliated by being forced to pick up excrement from the gutter." In June 1977, State Assemblyman Edward Lehner and State Senator Franz Leichter (whose mother had been a German intellectual actually murdered by the Nazis) had finally pushed through a bill in Albany that required people in cities with more than 400,000 residents—only New York City and Buffalo—to pick up after their dogs, and on August 1, 1978, State Health Law 1310 went into effect, compelling dog owners on the Upper East Side and in Brooklyn Heights who huffed and puffed about graffiti to admit their own civic responsibilities. A year later, the city would ban public drinking.

Around this time, Davis went out to the Rockaways to stare at the spotless sands of Jacob Riis Park, built by Moses in the mid-1930s and a national park since 1972. Studies showed that people tend to operate in public space according to certain latent rules, motivated of course by individual choice but also dictated to some degree by the setting. Sadly, in New York's big parks, none of those rules seemed to matter. Bryant Park was, says Davis, "a shithole." The police would make a show of force, pull out as soon as crime went down, and then crime would go right back up. As he pondered, a little envious, a Park Ranger walked by in her Smokey the Bear hat. People snapped to in her presence and walked their trash over to the cans. Here was Davis's second big thought: he needed "somebody with a uniform who conveys a message that there's a certain positive way to use public spaces." And so were born the Urban Park Rangers, whose job was "to set a tone," to persuade New Yorkers in major parks to treat them, and by extension one another, with the respect they'd convinced themselves was undeserved, not their responsibility, maybe even uncool. "[P]arks, open spaces, when they work best, change people's behavior . . ." says Davis. "They're there because they *want* to behave differently."

So now all the ideas percolating about public space, urban management, and public-private partnerships met, as so many New Yorkers do, in Central Park. Rusted, broken playgrounds, dry water fountains, cracked benches, and clogged sewers flooding the transverses all testified to its overuse and abuse. Graffiti was scrawled everywhere. "Somehow," wrote artist Robert Smithson, "I can accept graffiti on subway trains, but not on boulders." Like Times Square and Bryant Park, Central Park was a male domain—one survey counted 83% of those at Bethesda Fountain as men; 71% in the Sheep Meadow. Courts had nearly closed the zoo, the park's top attraction, and talks with the New York Zoological

Society to take it over had stalled. Relearning *how* to love at least this one part of New York in a guileless way, not in spite of its flaws and not *because* of them, but for what it could be, might help New Yorkers relearn how to behave in the city at large.

The perfect choice for this job worked in the Arsenal basement. As the park had hit bottom in the '70s, nonprofits like the Central Park Community Fund, supported by the unlikely pair of Richard Gilder and George Soros, had formed and within the Parks Association was a steel magnolia from San Antonio named Elizabeth Barlow. Raising two kids on East 89th Street had made the park's everyday value evident, but her master's in city planning from Yale taught her that its vistas, ponds, and thatches of trees were one huge work of experiential art shaped out of nature. Barlow traveled in the best circles, was genteel, tough, and, most important, she was obsessed. Davis named her Central Park Administrator, with the plan that she would imitate the other CIGs, recruit a board, and raise money for the massive task of not so much restoring the park as nurturing it into a new life.

That would take a very long time, though, and Davis wanted something everyone could see. Since last January, he'd walked countless times past dry Bethesda Fountain. Told that repairing its broken pipes would cost hundreds of thousands of dollars, Davis in early April 1979 sent over plumbers and an electrician, and a week later water started to trickle. Reaching its full glory would take more time and more money. But a fountain was working again in the middle of Central Park, a fountain that had been shut off four years earlier simply because no one had felt like dealing with it. The Angel of Bethesda had been healed. At the zoo, new vets were hired and humane procedures put in place while Davis negotiated a deal with the Zoological Society that transferred management of all three City zoos to people who actually knew how to run them, while a Kevin Roche redesign of Central Park would be paid for by Lila Acheson Wallace.

Around that time, Davis and Barlow brought Governor Carey to see the new Dairy Building, restored with money from the Central Park Community Fund. As they passed the dust bowl that was once the Sheep Meadow, Carey offered State money to reseed the grass, which Davis jumped on as the way to launch the entire restoration. "We're going to hang by this," he said, "or we're going to fly by this." James Taylor gave a concert in July 1979 to raise the rest, and then a five-foot fence went up all around the 15 acres of new sod. In a small victory for commonplace civilization, no one pulled it down.

Back to the City

Lunchtime on a warm November afternoon. Office workers ate dirty water hot dogs and grabbed sun where they could. At Sixth and 41st, a lanky man in his sixties strode up the steps to Bryant Park, wove through the dealers, and established a recon post near a dry fountain. Holly Whyte had the demeanor of a cheerful country gentleman, but on Guadalcanal he'd been a Marine intelligence officer and now he took stock of these desperate acres hidden behind shrubbery and an iron fence, the smell of piss and pot smoke rising through the plane trees. Bryant Park had been left for dead. A brave few finished lunch with furtive eyes, but most just sprawled across the benches or huddled, selling and smoking, sizing up buyers and prey. In the '30s, Robert Moses had imposed a formal French design on Bryant Park to keep out vagrants and the "fairies," but instead of an oasis, he'd created a secret garden whose worst uses chased away everything else. Since then, the park had slipped ever deeper under the assumption that ruin was the reality of city life.

Whyte pulled out a stopwatch to tally five minutes of arrivals. Through a week of lunchtime visits, the numbers had stayed about the same—500 or so when it should be 9,000 on a day like this, less than a quarter women. On the other side of the fence on Sixth Avenue, New Yorkers smiled and talked and flirted. "What a city does best," he wrote, "is bring people together, face to face, for the exchange of ideas and goods and services. This New York does superbly. This is its export industry, its reason for being." Cities exist to let people make networks. To Whyte, fixing Bryant Park—and New York—meant letting New Yorkers do what they knew how to do and inviting in more people to do it.

Koch's inaugural address had explicitly called for "urban pioneers" to join in the work of saving New York, but a movement had begun on its own in the '50s as millions had been going the other way, a push-back against suburbia and White flight that used language of return, reclamation, and embrace of the past to define a new way of urban living that would eventually redraw the social and economic map of New York. One early and essential voice in this Back to the City movement belonged to this gentle ex-Marine counting junkies. As a young officer, William "Holly" Whyte was fascinated by maps, in particular the close observation required to make them. "My strength," he wrote later, "has been the simple ability to see things other people have missed." After the war, he covered America's surge for *Fortune*; his 1956 bestseller *The Organization Man* explored corporations and suburbs as a form of collectivism and sold some two million copies, freeing Whyte from worrying about a day job. In 1958, just as the Rockefeller Foundation was funding the first department of Urban Design at MIT, he edited a collection titled *The Exploding Metropolis* that asked whether the city would ever "reassert itself as a good place to live." Instead of Moses-style urban renewal, he wanted choice: "Little plans, lots of them, are just what are needed—high rise and low, small blocks and superblocks, and let the free market tell its story." Laurance Rockefeller, headiest of the brothers, pulled Whyte under the family umbrella and so from a small office on the fifty-fifth floor of 30 Rock amid the Rockefeller Brothers Fund, he consulted for both public and private interests, exercising a subtle but strong influence on the life of New York and cities around the world by applying his observational skills from Guadalcanal. Where did people walk? Where did they stop and talk? How did people actually *use* spaces? His data would help shape the City's response to Midtown overdevelopment, a zoning revision in 1961 that encouraged developers to trade public space for height in hopes of creating more light and street life.

The next chapter in the counternarrative was a book by one of the authors in *The Exploding Metropolis*—Jane Jacobs. As a lead writer at *Architectural Forum*, then America's preeminent building magazine, she'd seen too many visionary plans destroy tired yet vibrant neighborhoods. Holly Whyte heard her call out the planning establishment at a Harvard conference on urban design and asked her to contribute a piece to *Fortune*, "Downtown Is for People," that persuaded the Rockefeller Foundation to underwrite a book. It took owlish Jacobs two and a quarter years to write *The Death and Life of American Cities*, turning her famous bobbed hair white in the process, but when it appeared in

1961, it forever changed how people viewed life in cities. Jacobs added poetry to Whyte's data, described the street ballet of the West Village with passion and romance, and offered a theory of the city as a kind of self-sufficient organic system, imperfect and alive, constantly changing and innovating and best left alone to grow as it would without government-abetted development. Her solution was similar to Whyte's—short blocks, high density, mixed use, and old buildings with new construction, a vision that not only resisted change but called for the return of a way of life that had existed in places like Crotona, one that valued communities full of networks and social capital.

Jacobs also changed how people approached power in New York. While Holly Whyte and his cracker-barrel common sense made connections with power, she'd been fighting planners since Moses tried to open Washington Square to cars, and just when *Death and Life* came out, she led a very visible battle against the designation of her part of the West Village as a slum. The Right liked her opposition to big government and her support of market solutions; the Left saw her as a grassroots activist who appreciated "authentic" urban life, but like Saul Alinsky and James Rouse, Jacobs defied categories; she spoke only for the city, embracing the messy complexities of urban life and economy with the same joy as she embraced her messy home. She didn't blindly support manufacturing or labor, and her campaign in the West Village had the ultimate effect of letting luxury housing push out low-income housing. Yet public opinion solidly backed Jacobs, who made the battle about preserving the idiosyncrasies of Greenwich Village rather than the diverse needs of New Yorkers. The "slum" designation was removed, showing that not only could you fight City Hall—you could win.

Jacobs's book and her victory in the West Village established a popular template for what a city was now "supposed" to be. And yet the world of 555 Hudson Street was just one very magical way a city could function; not all cities are Greenwich Village, nor do they have to be to succeed, and not all urban renewal and planning was bad. Though huge developments like Penn Station South and Stuyvesant Town were anathema to Jacobs, they helped stanch White flight in Manhattan and their residents loved them. On the Lower East Side, the Cooper Square Committee had won another, and arguably more successful, grassroots fight against urban renewal in 1961 when the City chose to adopt its community plan instead of bulldozing eleven blocks. The first of its kind in New York, it expressly preserved low-income housing as opposed to Jacobs's market-oriented "deslumification."

But *Death and Life* had created a taste—maybe a rarified one—for a very specific kind of urban experience, one that could only be found in certain parts of New York, one that drew not just from the living streets, but from the aesthetics of the city's past. "New ideas must use old buildings," she said, and this was, beyond all her practical prescriptions, maybe her most influential concept, a restatement of Walter Benjamin's belief that Modernity's search for the next thing always leads to the past: "Modern" cities shouldn't bulldoze the past; they should engage it. Along with Robert Venturi's *Complexity and Contradiction in Architecture*, she proclaimed the end of Moses's Modernist frog march of progress. The way forward now in cities would blend past, present, and future, the point no particular style of architecture but the act of curating Time.

And then Pennsylvania Station was demolished.

If a building can be a martyr, Penn Station gave its life for New York's preservation movement, which now became another thread in Back to the City. Though the State Bard Act allowed New York to declare landmarks on purely aesthetic grounds, the City didn't use it. But as more and more New Yorkers read *Death and Life*, as buildings fell and Carnegie Hall barely escaped the wrecking ball, Mayor Wagner grudgingly formed a toothless Landmarks Preservation Commission, albeit too late to save Penn Station. The long grief of its three-year demolition helped force passage of the City's landmarks law in April 1965, energized later that year by Lindsay's election. Marathon hearings ultimately declared 321 sites and 13 districts landmarks, including the Astor Library, which became the Public Theater, and Brooklyn Heights, the city's first historic district and core of the next stage in the return—the Brownstone Movement.

As the first concerted movement of middle-class Whites back to New York, the importance of Brownstoning transcends just historic preservation. After the war, as Truman Capote wrote, Brooklyn Heights was full of "brave pioneers bringing brooms and buckets of paint: urban, ambitious young couples, by and large mid-rung in their

Doctor–Lawyer–Wall Street–Whatever careers, eager to restore to the Heights its shattered qualities of circumspect, comfortable charm," followed in the early '60s by "brownstoners" inspired by neighborhood restoration efforts in Savannah and Charleston. Everett Ortner, an editor at *Popular Science*, and his wife, Evelyn, paid $32,500 for their Park Slope brownstone in 1963 and began to host wine and cheese parties that became the Brownstone Revival Committee. In 1974, supported by the Municipal Art Society, the City's Economic Development Council, and the National Trust for Historic Preservation, the committee hosted the first Back to the City conference at the Waldorf with the goal of "encouraging middle-class people to return from the suburbs to inner-city neighborhoods." The Ortners were not alone in their efforts. "This summer," reported the *Times*, "a link with the revival committee was established in London, where the movement is known as 'gentrification.'"

And so "gentrification" spread through Brooklyn. As Bronx neighborhoods were melting into an amorphous, ominous South Bronx, the huge stretch once known only as South Brooklyn was being carved into invented places such as Cobble Hill, Boerum Hill, and Carroll Gardens. These neighborhoods weren't really being gentrified, though, because they'd never existed; most residents had identified with the borough as a whole and their own block, but little in between. Gay men in the Village and lesbians in Park Slope created safe spaces for themselves and also furthered the Jacobs ideal of neighborhoods scraped and varnished by White, educated, and usually well-to-do homeowners who superimposed their own social, cultural, and economic networks onto formerly working-class areas. Yes, the change was supposed to come from within, but people who renovated entire buildings with their own hands reasonably considered themselves "within." Bringing in "urban pioneers" who owned their own homes did help real estate prices and tax revenues, but they immediately began to redefine what a "community" was and who really belonged to it.

Mayor Lindsay had encouraged this new urban identity and community participation in part because he *had* to—charter reform in 1963 had created Community Planning Boards that gave neighborhoods a voice, if not a vote, in local development. Lindsay was particularly interested in Brooklyn, especially its downtown. With the Heights landmarked and Cobble Hill and Park Slope next, Brownstone Brooklyn gave hope—a racist hope—to the owners of the large department stores along Fulton Street who feared the increasing number of Black and Brown customers even though profits remained strong. To stave off this so-called blight, the 1969 City plan put a special emphasis on Brooklyn, including the transformation of Fulton Street into a mall. The first malls had required stores to pay a surcharge, but in the middle of the Fiscal Crisis, Fulton Mall business owners were in no mood to throw more money at City Hall, so in 1975 the State empowered an Improvement Association to collect "contributions" from storeowners. Two years later, four more Business Improvement Districts were chartered in Manhattan and Queens. In the years ahead, BIDs would be one of the many tools, both promising and risky, that would change the face of the city.

Brooklyn brownstones weren't the only place attracting new residents. Since at least the 1850s, artists and writers, free thinkers and rebels had searched for cheap raw space Downtown in industrial areas like Coenties Slip, Water Street, and the cozy West Village, so when a Korean artist named Nam June Paik, part of the avant-garde Fluxus group, moved into an empty loft south of Houston in 1965, it was just the next frontier. The battle over the Lower Manhattan Expressway had created uncertainty here; amid its few remaining sweatshops were hundreds of lofts left empty by owners waiting for their eminent domain check, so in 1967 a Lithuanian named George Maciunas—one of the founders of Fluxus—started converting these empty loft buildings into artists' co-ops as a kind of aesthetic intervention. The next year Donald Judd bought 101 Spring Street and Paula Cooper left the galleries along 57th Street for 5,000 square feet on the third floor of 96 Prince Street, next to a workingman's bar named Fanelli's. OK Harris Gallery was next, and when the City officially dropped the expressway, the rush was on. Gordon Matta-Clark opened a restaurant at Prince and Wooster; collaborative galleries popped up, Leo Castelli went into 420 West Broadway, and SoHo was born, landmarked as the Cast Iron District in 1973, then explicitly as an artists' district with the 1974 Loft Law.

New York now had a new official Art district. But it soon became something more. During the week, it was still trucks and dark, mysterious streets; on Saturdays it was "a souk," wrote Calvin Tomkins, "a pageant," with the serious galleries open, air kisses kissed, fellow artists greeted and snubbed. What was new was Sundays. On Sundays the galleries were closed, but the Bridge and Tunnel crowd came in from Westchester and Long Island to shmy; Upper East Siders trickled down for leisurely walks across cobblestoned streets, among the cast-iron façades covered in posters, in and out of boutiques stocked with one-of-a-kind items, every man a *flaneur*. They people-watched at cafés and imagined life with exposed brick walls. Manhattanites began to consider and even mourn the passing Industrial Age, even as their increasing presence in SoHo sped the passage of old warehouses and small factories into new lofts and stores. No other place so completely expressed Jacobs's idea of the past as a necessary ingredient for the modern. As in Brooklyn, Time was being stopped here, or at least slowed down a bit—but progress wasn't; in fact, it was racing ahead because shopping and ownership were at the heart of SoHo, more than the Village ever was. With every ATM and credit card making consumerism just that much easier, buying something in a cool, artistic place like SoHo elevated shopping to a creative act. If the hallmark of the Upper East Side was to do things the way they'd always been done, here every choice expressed identity. Movies like *An Unmarried Woman* and *Manhattan* further established the meaning of SoHo. Jill Clayburgh found a new life in Alan Bates's loft; Woody Allen and Mariel Hemingway whined and opined as they shopped at Dean & DeLuca. Wandering around SoHo became one of the things New Yorkers *did* on Sundays, along with lolling in bed with all five pounds of the *Times*, going to H&H for bagels, and standing in line to buy tickets to the new Truffaut, then standing in another line for a seat. "SoHo was not only a new neighborhood," wrote the *Voice*, "but a metaphor for the new good life." SoHo was a "lifestyle."

And if visiting on Sunday was great, *living* in SoHo had to be even better. The once bizarre idea of living in a factory now had an intangible value, an amenity that made up for the absence of things people traditionally looked for in a home, like schools nearby, grocery stores, or maybe even a tree. Landowners who'd been playing the long game now saw their payday and shoved out manufacturers along with many of the artists who'd reclaimed the raw spaces. SoHo didn't need artists to exist now; it just needed their style. "Because our artists' eyes could see what was not there . . . ," wrote Ingrid Bengis, "we created a psychology which, without our knowing it, was going to remove us from the very world we had built." The City estimated in 1978 that 10,000 illegal conversions had been done in the last five years; by the time it stepped in to help SoHo manufacturing, it was too late. New York now sold Time as much as space; Lifestyle as much as practical use. Living in New York became for many a consumer good, a collection of Lifestyle expectations that would redefine communities and connect residents more than any prior ethnic, racial, or economic history; a ticket to the Jacobs cavalcade of urban life that required only appreciation and money. Real estate's value would be based not just on square footage but on a bundle on ineffable qualities that generations would chase across the city, creating new capital by restoring "authenticity" to old properties, warping society and economics, overriding ethnicity and tradition.

Up in 30 Rock, Holly Whyte may have helped point the way to Lifestyle, but he remained devoted to the return of commonplace civilization. "New Yorkers fervently deplore the city," he wrote. "It is their favorite form of self-praise. Only the heroic, they imply, could cope." New York, to Whyte, needed to produce more than just money; it needed to produce social capital. Even as New York careened, he celebrated its street life—"Characters are flourishing," he wrote. "It is the work of a great city to be tolerant of them, and New York is." Unfortunately, the 1961 zoning had been a conspicuous bust, Sixth Avenue a windswept mile of monoliths and vacant plazas. But two pocket parks to the east, Paley and Greenacre, had worked. To learn why, Whyte and his staff set up hidden cameras to film New Yorkers sitting, eating, walking, and schmoozing (his favorite word). Patterns emerged: People went where there were other people. They went where there was food and comfortable places to sit, especially if there were chairs you could move so you could own your surroundings. "Moveable chairs is a big idea," says Fred Kent of Project for Public Spaces, the consulting firm Whyte seeded. People liked sun, water, and openings that invited impulsive visits. Based on that research, the Planning Commission in 1975 amended zoning to require higher standards of public space from developers and a review process over public-private space. As Dutch architect Rem Koolhaas argued just then in *Delirious New York*, New York had invented the "culture of congestion." What it needed now were crowds.

But before the crowds came buyers. As early as 1975, the co-op market had begun to take off. There was "safety in concrete" for savvy New Yorkers, wrote *New York*. "Investors are buying real estate, despite its relatively low return, because it's now the prime hedge against inflation," soon to hit almost 15%. The action helped fire optimism. Cranes were going up in Manhattan, Bloomie's Bags were blooming, and Gordon Davis was eyeing the Bethesda Fountain. Private sector employment had risen for the first time in nine years, and *New York* noted signs of "a revival now going on in *parts* of New York." But they didn't include battered neighborhoods in outer boroughs. Although homeownership was central to Koch's vision for Growth, the city needed more than just the Lifestyle market in Manhattan to fully revive. Unfortunately almost all new construction was high-end; building codes made even cheap housing expensive to build, rent control limited profits, and Washington had switched from constructing public housing to subsidizing the private side with the Section 8 program, which provided low-income renters with vouchers instead of actual apartments. Early on, the mayor had pushed Housing Preservation and Development to explore building small homes on City-owned land and pushed to clear the inventory of abandoned or foreclosed rentals, known as *in rem*. Once rehabbed, the City sold them to tenant groups, community organizations, and qualified private management companies—10,243 units in 1979 and double that the next year. Tax breaks were another crucial tool for creating more affordable housing. The State's 421a plan encouraged middle-income building in the outer boroughs, and the City's J-51 gave owners breaks for renovating multi-unit residential properties or converting commercial or industrial spaces into residential ones. But their abuse turned Koch's move toward the stability of homeownership into something disruptive; in theory a way to help people "un-slum" neighborhoods, J-51s unintentionally spurred arson in the South Bronx and spread gentrification. A month after "I Love New York" Day, the *Times* reported that conversions from manufacturing, office, and hotel space into residences were "providing housing for a population of well-educated and relatively affluent young people strongly motivated to remain in Manhattan."

Meanwhile, the exploding market for condos and co-ops punished the middle class that had stayed in Manhattan. Faced with high oil costs and diminishing margins, many of the big real estate families were cashing out by converting their rental buildings into co-ops, historically in New York either large union-sponsored complexes, publicly backed Mitchell-Lama developments, or exclusive Upper East Side buildings that excluded anyone shareholders didn't want to live with. But now approved conversion plans tripled from 79 in 1977 to 249 in 1979 and many longtime New Yorkers had a very difficult choice forced on them. Offer plans appeared under doors and buildings turned into battlefields with landlords, renters, and prospective buyers pitted against one another, all still sharing the elevator as everyone decided whether they could afford to stay. All this new product should have meant dropping prices, but average co-op prices tripled and interest rates shot past 10% when usury laws were changed late in 1978 (a win for Wriston). Thousands of those "well-educated and relatively affluent young people" moved their Cuisinarts and pints of Häagen-Dazs into the apartments of those who couldn't, the leading edge of a coming social, physical, and financial Lifestyle upheaval. "I wouldn't think of building a new apartment building for the middle-income family," said Harry Helmsley. Asked what middle-income Americans should do, he replied, "There's always trailers down South and used houses, though not in the best areas. This is what a lot of people are going to have to get used to."

So Bad It's Good

Of all the things Abe Beame can be blamed for, Donald J. Trump is by far the worst. By 1978, tax abatements were fueling commercial real estate, too, particularly the ones from the Industrial and Commercial Incentive Board created during the Beame years. The first person to line up hat in hand had been this smirking thirty-two-year-old bad boy developer from Queens who held the options on the West Side properties owned by bankrupt Penn Central Railroad as well as the one on the musty Commodore Hotel next to Grand Central Terminal.

Donald's father, Fred, a fan of Norman Vincent Peale, had built an empire of tract housing in Queens and Brooklyn, but rich as they were, the Trumps gave off a pungent blend of shadiness and gauche; financial shenanigans ultimately got them banned from all FHA and State projects, and in 1973 they settled a huge racial discrimination suit with the Federal government. By then loutish Donald had emerged as Fred's favorite among his five children; after two years at Fordham and a transfer to Penn, he let his father pay the tab for his postgraduate studies at Oleg Cassini's Eurotrash hideaway Le Club, where Fred's friend, amoral lawyer Roy Cohn, taught him where to put his napkin, how to work the ropes, and mostly how to bluff and bully. As he always would, Fred underwrote his son's caviar dreams of owning the Manhattan skyline, in this case arranging a line of credit to help him buy the musty Commodore for $10 million, rehab it into a Hyatt, then sell it back to the UDC for $1 for which he would get a 99-year lease and pay $250,000 a year in lieu of taxes for forty years.

To a city bailing hard to stay afloat, this had seemed like a terrible deal, but desperate Penn Central had turned the screws, saying it would close the hotel otherwise, and Donald, already known for making grand and dubious claims, said what was good for him was good for New York. Fred had written some significant checks to the Brooklyn machine, so Mayor Beame pled his case. He and Carey had both attended Donald's wedding to a shiny Czech model named Ivana, plus there were some valid arguments to be made: the area around Grand Central was sliding, the Chrysler Building had been foreclosed on, the Terminal was in disrepair, and no one else was jumping in to help, so Trump got his tax break and launched his career in Manhattan real estate.

Grimy details aside, the deal woke up the crucial intersection of 42nd and Lex. MassMutual now sank $40 million into the Chrysler Building, Mobil bought theirs, and in June 1978, the Supreme Court guaranteed that the path of New York City's future would be through its past with a 6-to-3 ruling blocking construction over the landmarked Grand Central Terminal, thus establishing the protected status of hundreds of structures and their air rights. The hope was a revival movement west across 42nd Street, the belt of the island. At Fifth Avenue the New York Public Library had become a haven for petty criminals and vagrants, its bathrooms unusable, its books regularly stolen or crumbling in the stacks. Only Brooke Astor's recent $5 million donation kept the lights on. In 1978, retired Time Inc. head and creator of *People* Andrew Heiskell joined the board and resolved to jolt the NYPL out of its torpor. Many of its problems were intimately bound up with Bryant Park—as Davis recognized, eliminating crime and undesirables in one place just sent them to the other—and various halfhearted attempts had been made to reclaim the park until Heiskell saw a $1.5 million gift from the Rockefeller Brothers Fund as the chance to take one more shot. A founder of the Urban Coalition in the '60s, he pulled Gordon Davis into a network made up of his point person Marshall Rose, the NYPL, the Rockefeller Brothers Fund, and the 42nd Street Development Corp. For inspiration, they looked to Davis's Central Park Zoo deal and the State's recent BID legislation; a new BID formed by the businesses around Bryant Park would lease it from the City and manage it using revenue from a restaurant to be built inside. The RBF hired Holly Whyte and the Project for Public Spaces to do a study, which was why he'd been out there with his stopwatch. "The situation is bad, yes, but so bad it's good," wrote Whyte, bullish as ever, "and from this level even modest actions can have a dramatic effect on these spaces and peoples' perception of them."

To manage it all, the new Bryant Park Restoration Corporation hired Dan Biederman, a twenty-six-year-old fresh from Harvard Business School, already chairman of Community Board 5 and a consultant working on the City's rudimentary computer systems. Firm-jawed, straight-spoken Biederman didn't smoke or drink, and in the few moments he wasn't working liked to climb rocks; he would've made an excellent Mormon save for the fact that he was Jewish. A quiet loner from Scarsdale, he'd grown up marveling at the stoops out the window as his mother drove him in to visit his grandparents on Fifth Avenue. One Passover night when he was around ten he fell in love for good. Seder finished, his father and uncle took a stroll, and while the elders talked business, Biederman and his cousin walked ahead in the spring air, taking everything in until they looked up and saw the Empire State Building looming above. At 29th Street they finally turned around and walked back up to 76th. "I was sold," he says. But the treeless gray reality shocked someone who'd formed his image of New York from the backseat of a car. Deciding he wanted to make his living somehow changing all that, he joined the Community Board, and there he met Holly Whyte, who'd brought him to the BPRC.

Where Davis envisioned Bryant Park as a public version of Gramercy Park, Biederman looked at the parks of Paris and Boston's Faneuil Hall, Rockefeller Center, and Disney World, going so far as to consider outsourcing the management of Bryant Park to the last two. If Holly Whyte saw a city that could be fixed, Biederman saw one that needed new management and, like Elizabeth Barlow, he was obsessed. With no secretary and the Library still hesitant, he forged ahead raising money for maintenance and graffiti removal. It would be thirteen years before Biederman would see his dream realized.

Across Sixth Avenue began the world of Times Square and 42nd Street, another microclimate like the Library and Bryant Park where class and culture converged. Under the flashing Spectacolor sign atop Times Tower, theatergoers dodged into the Booth to see *The Elephant Man*, Puerto Rican families stretched their dollars at double features of third-run flicks, and men gave blowjobs in the Capri. "[L]ife is at its most rewarding, productive, and pleasant," wrote Samuel Delany, sounding much like Olmsted, "when large numbers of people understand, appreciate, and seek out interclass contact and communication conducted in a mode of good will." Delany was writing about gay life in Times Square, but the idea of democratic space was the same. Little Michael Eisner had scooted down from Park Avenue for the arcades and double features just like Robert Diggs and Dennis Coles had cut school in Staten Island for Bruce Lee flicks a few blocks from where Sarah Bernhardt had once played Phaedra and the sixteen-year-old Robert Mapplethorpe had stared at his first gay porn. Kids from the Bronx haunted Downstairs Records in the subway station. Artist Charlie Ahearn went to see *Mad Monkey Kung Fu* and *7 Grand Masters* on 42nd, his feet stuck to the floor, "rats chasing popcorn back and forth, kids yelling at the screen." This was where the city's wild things were. And it was also a place you avoided if you weren't looking for something wild. Recently, a syndicate led by Fred Papert and banker John Gutfreund had drawn up plans for The City at 42nd Street, a combination of Lincoln

Center and Disneyland with Ziegfeld's New Amsterdam Theatre at its core. Every big player in town was on board.

By 1979, thirty buildings were under construction, most still on the East Side, including the AT&T Building, which alone got some $20 million worth of tax abatements, and the 51-story Palace Hotel rising up behind the Villard Houses. In total, some 129 projects had gotten abatements for an estimated $54 million; no one had ever been turned down. Koch wanted to pump the brakes. If commercial real estate was surging, why keep subsidizing it when schools were being cut? At which point Donald Trump pushed his way back to the trough. In March 1979, he announced he would demolish Bonwit Teller's beloved Art Deco department store at 56th and Fifth and using the air rights he'd bought from neighboring Tiffany's, build a 60-story tower featuring 320 luxury condos. Given Trump's claim that the atrium stores would fetch "the highest prices ever paid for Fifth Avenue real estate—literally twice as high as anyone has ever gotten," it seemed absurd that he should get yet another tax break, but as should have been clear from his bulky suits and wide-cuffed trousers, Trump had no fear of looking absurd. He applied for a nearly $40 million abatement. "There was no question that I was entitled," he wrote later. "We were out to make Trump a brand and begin an empire . . . ," said his vice-president. "We were about getting more per square foot than the guy next door." Who until a few years ago happened to be the late Aristotle Onassis, owner of Olympic Tower, one of the few condo buildings in New York then, with some three-quarters of its owners foreign or corporate. After a dinner party at Adnan Khashoggi's apartment, Trump had decided that he, too, wanted to give rich foreigners a place to park their cash. While co-ops in the city had a sorry history of discrimination, Trump's condos would open the doors not so much to other New Yorkers, but to foreign capital and a network of global socialites with little or no interest in homegrown New York.

The City was starting to work just a bit better and everyone, it seemed, was coming back. The question was whether they'd be able to live together.

Chapter Three

New York Equalize You

On June 15, 1978, two White cops in Crown Heights pulled over a Black man named Samuel Miller for driving with a suspended license.

At least that was their story. Some said it was a shakedown of the man with him, his brother, broad-shouldered Arthur from Barbados who owned a construction company on Nostrand and ran his local block association. There were no smartphones then so what exactly happened next remains unknown, but one witness claimed to see Arthur shake his head no to a police demand. Things turned violent. Reinforcements arrived, one officer reportedly pointed his gun at the growing crowd and shouted, "You niggers stay back!" as the beating commenced. When it was over, fifteen cops stood over Miller's dead body. Police captain Jack A. Clark objected to the report that he'd been "choked to death" because "you get the impression of somebody with two hands around the neck." No, the police medical examiner concluded that it had been done with "a rod-like object, such as a forearm or stick," which apparently deserved greater respect.

"This city," wrote Koch the next month in his newsletter to City employees, ". . . is in the midst of a renaissance." But this "renaissance" was by no means general. Underneath the reawakening pride was a greasy sense that "*their* turn was over," that it was time to return the city to safe, sane—White—control. There were six other instances that summer of

White gangs or police attacking Blacks; Koch named a commission. He was bluntly pragmatic about Retrenchment. "When you reduce expenses," he explained, "it impacts upon poor people because our budget is primarily devoted to poor people." A bootstrapper himself, he made no secret of how he felt about welfare: "The good-government groups and social workers destroyed the city for twenty years." Much of his distrust for the liberal Establishment came from race. During his run for district leader in 1964, J. Raymond Jones, the first and only Black leader of Tammany Hall, had backed his opponent, and the national Democrats had more than once quashed his attempts to inject a proto–All Lives Matter strain into the Civil Rights movement. Koch backed down, but never forgot. As he made peace with the White-dominated machines in the Bronx, Brooklyn, and Queens, the mayor investigated welfare payments and trimmed job training. Haskell Ward, his new head of community development, was Black, but he had no connections to the city's Black networks. "The blacks Koch has can't find their way to Bed-Stuy," said Congressman Charles Rangel. For the first time in twenty-five years there was no Person of Color on the Board of Estimate, whatever traditional roles they'd had in City government erased. Squeezed by growing immigration, the breakdown of old political networks, a changing economy and soon, waves of drugs, crime, and disease, New York's African Americans would be forced over the next thirty-five years into new cultural and social strategies that would in turn change the world.

What made the situation particularly bitter was that Black votes had put Koch in office. Rangel and the rest of Harlem's Gang of Four—protégés of J. Raymond Jones that included Percy Sutton, Basil Paterson, and then City Clerk David Dinkins—had endorsed him instead of Cuomo after Sutton had finished fifth in the mayoral primary. Koch, who'd once claimed "Blacks don't vote," promised to stop talking about "poverty pimps," leave the poverty programs alone, and hire more minorities. "If you can't get who you want," the pugnacious Rangel said of his fellow congressman, "at least get who you know." The new mayor made the bait and switch clear with his first executive order, dated January 1, 1978, bringing all the City antipoverty programs under his control. While you could argue that Lindsay's subsidies had worked—"New York City didn't burn," says Gordon Davis, because "the people who would have led riots were all on the payroll"—even the reliably liberal journalist Jack Newfield had come to the conclusion that "the poverty programs are enriching a few political hustlers and not improving the quality of life for the poor people of this city." Virtually everyone conceded that Model Cities had been corrupt and without direction. But poverty programs weren't just about serving the poor. As blue-collar employment in Harlem dropped from 1950 to 1970, white-collar employment rose, mostly into jobs left behind by departing Whites, many in Great Society programs. Brooklyn State Senator Major Owens called those jobs "our foot in the door," and Black politicians wanted to control them for exactly the same reasons White politicians had. Though cutting waste and fighting corruption made objective sense—and the next generation of community organizations *would* ultimately transform the South Bronx and Brooklyn—these stable middle-class jobs had been as important for the community as much as the scholarships and training they administered. Koch considered all this another example of New Yorkers incentivized to preserve disorder while the workers saw themselves more like the Fire Department—a permanent force charged with fighting a permanent problem.

Whites generally ate it up when Koch took on People of Color, but he was just as dismissive when they challenged him. In February 1978, he attended a meeting of the Queens Citizens Organization, a group of fifteen or so parishes and congregations around Flushing Meadows seeded by Saul Alinsky's Industrial Areas Foundation. As Jane Jacobs once wrote, "If you are a nobody, and you don't know anybody who isn't a nobody, the only way you can make yourself heard in a large city is through certain well-defined channels." IAF community organizing offered a way for everyday people of all races to create new local networks that would let them be heard, and they were heard that day in Queens when the moderator warned the mayor to stick to the agenda. Koch declared, "I'm not here under subpoena" and stomped out to cascades of boos. Afterward, a Lutheran minister in Brownsville asked Alinsky's successor Ed Chambers for a meeting. Chambers didn't sing "Kumbaya." Don't fall behind one charismatic person, he told them; get bigger and more diverse. Sign on 150 leaders and 30 churches, raise $250,000 of their own money. The goal of organizing was "the power to demand recognition and reciprocity and respect," said one IAF leader. It took, said Chambers, "a special cold, rational kind of anger." Community organizing would ultimately prove a crucial force in the evolution of New York.

The other kind of anger—hot and emotional—was easy to find, especially after Arthur Miller's senseless death. Two weeks into his term, the mayor was heckled in Harlem during a service honoring Dr. Martin Luther King Jr. and tensions escalated into spring, with the *Amsterdam News* running a daily "KOCH MUST GO!" headline. On Eastern Parkway, there'd already been sparks between the Hasidim and the West Indians; a protest nearly became a street fight against a Policemen's Benevolent Association march a block away. That December in Boro Park, a mob of Hasids stormed the 66th Precinct; 62 police officers were injured, but remarkably, no arrests were made. A few weeks later, buried in a back page of the *Times*, came news that a grand jury returned no indictments in Miller's death; it had been just "a tragic, unforeseeable accident." Brooklyn, said one resident, was "a volcano that's sleeping."

The Seven-Mile World

Meanwhile in the Bronx, every bombed train, every kid in white shell toe Adidas pointed to a secret world being born in plain sight. Jeff Chang calls it "the Seven-Mile World"—seven square miles that cooked up new kinds of music, dance, and visual art that together gave cultural, political, and ultimately economic voice to people who'd lost theirs. It would become the mainstream of not just Pan-African culture, but "young urban American culture" as a whole, and just like Wriston's new economy, Hip Hop had everything to do with globalization, technology, democratization, and freedom.

It started with kids just having fun. In August 1973, Clive Campbell, aka Kool Herc, had hosted a back-to-school dance party with his sister in the rec room of their building at 1520 Sedgwick Avenue. A tall, broad-shouldered former graffiti writer, he put two James Brown records on two different turntables and by flipping back and forth, lifting and resetting the needle, he sent the party up into a new level of groove by making the percussion break go on and on. Campbell had moved with his family from Jamaica; in 1965 the UK shut down immigration from the Caribbean just as Congress reopened it, drawing West Indians to the US, in particular to New York, a city that had been, according to historian Robert Farris Thompson, "founded as a way station to the West Indies"; for two hundred years, most of its enslaved had been "seasoned" there first before being brought north. Later, in the 1950s, Afro-Cuban rhythms had met jazz to create mambo, then there was rock and roll–inflected boogaloo, followed by salsa. And now Afro-Caribbean culture was about to create another hybrid. Herc took his massive speakers outside to imitate Jamaican dancehall parties; heavy beats throbbing out to an entire park or school gym, and soon clubs where he remixed the Funk and Soul songs Disco had pushed off the radio, danced to by kids who couldn't get into the hi-class, leather-shoes-only clubs—and increasingly didn't want to.

Those were the musical underpinnings, but Hip Hop had other deeper roots. Along with all the socio-economic failures of the '60s, gangs and heroin had torn up the Bronx. Taking cues from the Hells Angels and the martial arts movies in Times Square, gangs like the Savage Skulls and the Black Spades in their fur-edged, sleeveless denim jackets had divvied up the borough. Graffiti marked the boundaries, but after a while the kids with that talent started to pull away, creating a secret society of all races, from all neighborhoods, that transcended turf. Their names on a train—Blade, Daze, Futura—represented an act: Working nonstop on boards laid over the third rail at the Mosholu Yard, scaling up the sketches they'd made in their blackbooks, throwing color at the dreary ghetto palette. Making themselves seen.

Meanwhile, the gang members who'd survived (and their girlfriends) were tired of the violence and the long sentences mandated by the Rockefeller Drug Laws, so Herc's parties put the fun up front, with MC Coke La Rock doing call and response. To the east, at the Bronx River Community Center, warlord Afrika Bambaataa began morphing the Black Spades into the Zulu Nation, charging his parties with the message that they should be "warriors for their community" while he blended African and Cuban numbers in with Go-Go, Sly Stone, Kraftwerk, and the occasional Bugs Bunny cut. Down in Morrisania, Grandmaster Flash launched the clock theory while his MCs the Furious Three fired up dancers with improvised rhymes. One of them, Keith "Cowboy" Wiggins, christened what they were doing "Hip Hop."

The gangs now melted into crews. Violence still hung in the air—"Apache" wasn't just a song by the Incredible Bongo Band; it was also a gang-hazing gauntlet—but the taste for competition was being sublimated into stylized conflicts between DJs, MCs, and b-boys, whose capoeira-like dancing was "a fight with steps instead of fists." "[H]ip hop wasn't a nice place," says Charlie Ahearn, "It was cutthroat." "[H]ip hop gatherings had an edge," wrote Nelson George, "a balance between pain and the celebration of music and movement." Teenagers in sheepskins, Kangol hats, and Pumas filled the clubs and parks, everything clean and sharp; a statement against the shabby denim shells worn by the gangs. Still, all the angel dust made security necessary. For his "peace guards," Kool Herc relied in part on Five Percenters, a Harlem-born splinter off the Nation of Islam that became a jailhouse faith in the '70s. Its uplifting, imaginative—and misogynist—cosmology considered every Black man a God and shooting dice a path to mystical wisdom. Five Percenters made proselytizing a high duty, and "building" their secret knowledge for others stressed verbal dexterity and creativity; it was, according to one rapper, "a religion about talking." Their ideas, along with the arms-crossed, legs-stiff posture they liked to strike, filtered into Hip Hop and its lexicon: using "Word" as an affirmation, for one, came from the Five Percent Nation. Along with Bambaataa, the Five Percenters bridged '70s gangs and Hip Hop.

As the city fell apart and Punk took off Downtown, cassettes from the Bronx spread through the boroughs, from the Queensbridge Houses out to Russell Simmons and Carlton Ridenhour in the far reaches of Queens; in Harlem to DJ Hollywood and Eddie Cheeba. When the Blackout hit in 1977, spray paint and stereo equipment went out the windows first. Identity is above all else the product of shared experience, so Hip Hop let the boroughs develop new identities with their own styles and stars, all connected by subways bombed by artists like Lee Quiñones, Dondi, and Zephyr. The Seven-Mile World expanded into a citywide youth network made from scavenged pieces of the blown-up American dream, customized with wit, bravado, and energy. "A shift was occurring," wrote George, "and you either were drawn to it or feared it." By 1978, Disco was for Studio 54 and Xenon; Punk and New Wave were south of 14th, and Hip Hop competed with the horns and timbales of Latin Fania for Sound of the Streets.

Most of those streets, though, were empty. Since 1970 the South Bronx had lost 43,000 apartments, 16% of its housing, and 14% of its population. Community groups like the South East Bronx Community Organization and the Mid Bronx Desperados had been fighting to stabilize sections of the borough since the late '60s, but Charlotte Street remained windswept and piled with plywood and bricks. Koch had put it in the hands of handsome Deputy Mayor Herman Badillo, the first Puerto Rican congressman and first Puerto Rican borough president. Everything Badillo did seemed like an audition for higher office, and he'd already raised eyebrows by bringing in former UDC head Ed Logue to work on a massive plan that so far couldn't decide whether it was primarily commercial or residential. A more enlightened version of Moses, Logue had built a significant amount of middle- and low-income housing, but he'd also created the concrete desolation of Boston's Government Center and the UDC had gone bankrupt under him, so the South Bronx offered redemption.

Unfortunately, Badillo failed to count his votes before presenting the plan to the Board of Estimate in February 1979. Since the 1898 consolidation, the mayor, the comptroller, the Council president, and the five borough presidents had convened every other week in its chapel-like meeting room in City Hall to approve contracts and land use proposals, but the Board's deeper purpose was to maintain the City's balance of power through its intricate voting math that made alliances necessary. Though the Crisis Regime had mooted some of its power, it exercised what it had here, rejecting the plan 7–4. Badillo resigned, leaving it to Logue to find a new way to save the South Bronx and his reputation.

And the kids kept on riding into the void on bits of funk and soca, searching for something for themselves. Austrian artist Stefan Eins saw what was happening. He moved his "white wine, white walls, white people" SoHo gallery Fashion Moda to a storefront on Third Avenue near the Hub to let Downtown artists meet the people of the South Bronx. Like Afrika Bambaataa's mixes, he threw good things together and let them cook.

When no one else would speak for it, "the Bronx," wrote Robert Farris Thompson, "started to talk back."

Soon We Pay Mortgages

One of the four princes of a dying kingdom, gravel-voiced Charles Rangel had earned his sharp suits and handshakes at Sylvia's. He'd come home to Harlem after the Korean War with a Bronze Star, a Purple Heart, and sergeant's stripes, but they didn't mean anything to White New York, and the day a box of lace fell off his truck in the Garment District and a menacing cop said, "You better clean that up, boy," he knew he had to finish high school. He got his law degree from St. John's while working as the night manager of the Hotel Theresa, joined the Carver Club, and in 1971, beat Adam Clayton Powell Jr. for Harlem's congressional seat by 150 votes.

But like Ed Koch, Rangel was a product of a time more than a place, because Harlem now wasn't Harlem then, and the racial demographics he'd built his career on were changing. The Workers' Paradise had existed during a period of exclusion, but since the Hart-Celler Act in 1965 had upped national quotas for immigration, an estimated 80,000 legal immigrants a year, along with as many as half a million illegals, had already come to New York, complicating and globalizing ethnicity, class, and culture in New York; discussing the city solely in terms of White and Black missed that tidal change. The number of Chinese had tripled since 1960 and would grow faster. Negotiations over Hong Kong sent worried money into underpriced real estate in Manhattan's Chinatown, pushing its boundaries well beyond a few colorful blocks south of Canal. Those with capital started restaurants, which employed almost exclusively men, while women went to the garment industry; New York's biggest local, Local 23-35 of the ILGWU (International Ladies' Garment Workers' Union), was two thirds Chinese. Dominicans, the next largest group of immigrants, moved into Washington Heights, where they worked in light manufacturing, auto repair, grocery stores, and building services. The first Korean groceries opened. The Refugee Act of 1980 would bring a new and incredibly diverse surge: political refugees from Ethiopia, South and Central America, and the

Soviet Union. As early as June of 1981, Brighton Beach was known as Little Odessa, with a quarter of its businesses owned by Soviet Jews. City Planning now had a Department of Immigrant Affairs. "Soon we be like American people," said one émigré. "Soon we pay mortgages."

Few of those new seeds were landing in Harlem, though. Eventually "most of the people with disposable income chose to leave Harlem for greener pastures," said Lloyd Williams, president of the Greater Harlem Chamber of Commerce, taking their money with them to Long Island or Brooklyn, weakening the networks that had once held the neighborhood together. Manhattan was becoming proportionally Whiter not because of Whites moving in but because of Blacks leaving Harlem—60% of its population left between 1950 and 1980. A community is the sum of potential connections around institutional networks, so less density and failing institutions meant a more fragile community with fewer ties to the rest of the city. Those who stayed in Harlem remembered its Jane Jacobs past of watchful eyes and kids playing in the streets, all the same things Whites fetishized about their own old neighborhoods, but trying to hold on amid a 40% poverty rate and an infant mortality rate twice the rest of the city's didn't draw the attention of SoHo lofts. Brownstoning here wasn't about Lifestyle; it meant keeping buildings from going *in rem* or helping squatters rehab abandoned shells. Rangel and the rest of the Gang of Four offered few answers. Much of their patronage now came through the HUDC, a UDC subsidiary charged in the early '70s with devising an old-school urban renewal plan for Harlem and used by the Gang of Four to direct jobs and money to their chosen banks and developers. The problem was that there wasn't any new private development and the HUDC's big plan, an International Trade Center on Lenox, showed no signs of ever being built.

With Harlem fading and despite the collapse of neighborhoods like Brownsville and East New York in Brooklyn, the surge of West Indian immigrants was shifting Black power to that borough. The city's original Black residents, later generations of Afro-Caribbeans had long played a central role in Harlem politics, but those who arrived post-1965 headed directly to Bed-Stuy, Crown Heights, and Flatbush, where they usually considered themselves an ethnicity separate from native-born African

Americans, cutting their own deals with Brooklyn's White regulars. Even within the Caribbean community there were divisions: Older émigrés tended to look for cultural leadership from Trinidad, whose steel drums and calypso echoed along Eastern Parkway during the annual Labor Day Parade, while the new generation leaned toward the reggae and leftism of Jamaica. Still, Caribbean identity mattered more than race or your particular island home: "They haven't to know who is who," sang Mighty Sparrow in a calypso tribute to Brooklyn, "New York equalize you." Aside from politics, West Indians affected the city's present economy in ways that weren't always noticed since demographers usually considered them "Black" rather than a separate ethnicity. A substantial number of civil service jobs, for example, were held by West Indians, especially women in hospitals and nursing, "a giant sponge soaking up surplus, unskilled labor," while men found work in nonunion trades like the construction generated by growing homeownership. As immigrants do, the West Indians developed informal networks to share information about jobs—networks that African Americans tended to consider unfair—and developed more weak ties outside of their communities. They also liked to own their homes, great news for City Hall. While all this added diversity to New York's Black community, though, it also let Koch triangulate against African Americans. Floating Shirley Chisholm for Schools Chancellor, for instance, pleased the West Indian community *and* the Brooklyn machine, but not so much Harlem. The *Village Voice* worried "that when Koch is through as mayor, he will have created a bitter ethnic rift that will divide this city."

The most lasting divide, though, would be between African Americans and Koch. A charm offensive in 1979 sputtered with a *New Yorker* profile in which he said all Whites were racists and all Blacks anti-Semitic; wearing an afro wig to that year's Inner Circle dinner did not help. Anger crested when he announced the closing of Sydenham Hospital, a handsome nine-story building fronting the corner of Manhattan Avenue and 124th Street, famed for being the first hospital in the country with an integrated staff, now a last resort. Management was inept; Medicare had made it obsolete; the emergency room was up a flight of stairs. Though Koch's alternative offered the possibility of better care for many of the estimated 1.25 million New Yorkers considered "medically indigent," doing it by fiat erased history and felt like a gratuitous demonstration of just how much power Harlem had lost. Councilman Fred Samuel called it "a declaration of war against the poor," and Haskell Ward resigned. "What was happening in my community," said Rangel, "was far more important than anything they could come up on the balance sheet." Like SoHo and the Village, Harlem wanted to stop Time, too, but that would require money it didn't have. On September 16, demonstrators broke in and began a sit-in that exploded into an ugly conflict with police; thirty were injured. The occupiers were ultimately removed and Sydenham was closed. Koch would later call it "a mistake," but whatever relationship he may ever have had with Black New York was dead. Communities were made of more than just houses.

Chapter Four

Every Night a Different Channel

Bathed in blue light, Ann Magnuson, a New Wave version of the young Shirley MacLaine, took the stage at Irving Plaza in early November 1978 to introduce a "newer than new, wower than wow" take on vaudeville. Flyers flapping off East Village lampposts had asked for

EMOTIONAL CRIPPLES
4 EGYPTIAN SLAVES
ROBOT/MONSTERS
GLAMOUR GIRLS
CRETINS
NAZIS
1 PIANO PLAYER

Many had answered the call. One of the Egyptian slaves introduced a man who played harmonica to his dog, followed by more campy to corny musical numbers that added up to kids having a very silly, very stoned, good time. Then with stiff, robot steps a wide-eyed, geisha-faced figure in a clear plastic cape took the spotlight. As Saint-Saëns's delicate *Samson et Dalila* began to play, an Austrian pastry chef named Klaus Nomi launched into "Mon Coeur s'ouvre à ta voix" in a crystal countertenor that suddenly invested the evening with genius and wonder. Another new spirit was born Downtown, another set of voices eager to chime in on the Great Conversation. But it was the beginning of the end of the cozy, private world of New York's cultural elite.

A few weeks earlier, Sid Vicious had stabbed Nancy Spungen, bringing Punk's brief, furious era of purity to an end. With Television split up, Diana Vreeland watching Stiv Bators at CBGB, and the Ramones crowned "Doyens of Punk Rock" by the experts at the *Times*, the moment called New York Punk was over. Which didn't mean that Punk was dead—it just became shorthand for "fuck you" to anything mainstream, just one more element in the glorious mess that was Downtown in the late '70s. South of 14th Street the grid melted away and getting lost was the point, your geography earned by living in tiny, roach-infested apartments amid old worlds still clinging to the same blocks their grandparents had fought over. From Alphabet City west to the piers on the Hudson, Downtown offered risks and freedoms not available Uptown—cheap rent, cheap drugs, and an understanding that this was stage and sanctuary for all those who needed to get away from somewhere else and become who they really were; an abandoned city at the service of your imagination. "To be hip," wrote Glenn O'Brien, "is to belong to . . . an elective tribe located within a larger community, outsiders inside. It is detached from the main thing and proud of its detachment." And Downtown was *very* proud of its detachment. "[W]hen people told you that they never went above Fourteenth Street," wrote Carlo McCormick, "it was not simply a truth but a matter of pride."

Being an outsider, though, isn't the same as being an outcast. No one comes to New York to be alone; they come to find their people and through the '70s, thousands of art school graduates who'd heard Andy Warhol say that art was just a job had headed Downtown; a far cry from thirty years before when Duchamp, asked how many people he thought really liked avant-garde art, had replied, "Oh, maybe ten in New York and one or two in New Jersey." They found one another at places like the Kitchen, Artists Space, and the Mercer Arts Center, St. Mark's Poetry Project, and the Judson Dance Theater, William Burroughs's "bunker" at 222 Bowery. Art collectives and bands were formed; Disco music was born in the lofts of SoHo when Black and Latino gay men excluded from the White gay scene threw their own parties. And as Minimalism froze on the walls of Midtown galleries, the next generation of visual artists, three waves of one tide, would combine the criticism of Derrida and Kristeva that exposed modes of power in Western Culture with shards of the Beats, Pop Art, Marxism, and Symbolist poetry, assembling new forms heavy on what the French called *bricolage* ("do it yourself"). The first, the so-called Pictures Generation, focused on the image itself. "[U]nderneath each picture," wrote critic Douglas Crimp, "there is always another picture," so who was making or using it and how was the point, who would see it and why: the faux film stills of Cindy Sherman, for example, and Richard Prince manipulating ads. Though part of the Downtown art world, they still positioned themselves within the conventional world of galleries, museums, and collectors.

The second group broke away from those ideas of artistic "progress" and galleries—often because they didn't have one—and formed collectives such as Colab, short for Collaborative Artists, made up of forty or so artists, including Tom Otterness, Kiki Smith, and Jenny Holzer. Colab claimed to approach art as "a radical communications medium," putting up content-driven shows relating to subjects ranging from *Doctors and Dentists* and *Income and Wealth* to *Batman*. Its other interest was new media—film, public access television, and early computers. Jane Dickson, for example, had a weekend gig programming Times Square's Spectacolor sign, the first computer light board, while her boyfriend Charlie Ahearn and his brother John shot Super 8 movies on the subways and in the projects under the Brooklyn Bridge. A Chicago native with wavy hair and a deep practical streak, Dickson's taste for Hogarth and Ivan Albright spoke to her "desire to confront scary things." Colab, she says, was like "stone soup. We'll each pitch in what connections we have and they will make a greater whole for everyone." Walter Robinson took a more gimlet view: Colab "provided a kind of social context for all these basket cases to actually function in the art world."

Meanwhile, odd graffiti appeared on Lower East Side walls; phrases like SAMO © SAVES IDIOTS and SAMO © AS A NEW WAVE ARTFORM; an omen of the third wave. Martin Wong and Kenny Scharf had moved Downtown in 1978, as well as a lean, baby-faced twenty-year-old School of Visual Arts student in nerd glasses named

Keith Haring, a former Jesus freak and Deadhead who'd moved from Kutztown, Pennsylvania, when he realized that he was gay. After a couple days at the Y on 23rd Street, and some nights spent cruising Christopher Street, Haring moved into an apartment on Bleecker and kept an earnest journal—"The public has a right to art . . .The medium is not the message. The message is the message." At SVA he made friends with Scharf and John McLaughlin (soon to be known as John Sex), working constantly, looking constantly. He especially liked the graffiti on the trains for its fluidity and "the hard-edged black line that tied the drawings together!" Influenced by semiotics and a meeting with William S. Burroughs and his friend, artist Brion Gysin, he spent a year morphing thirteen letters into a pictogram code, but it still wasn't what he was looking for.

Downtown, Haring fell in with a network of fellow suburban refugees raised on sugared cereals and midnight movies. After a few performances, *New Wave Vaudeville* moved to the basement of Holy Cross Polish National Church at 57 St. Mark's Place where Ann Magnuson programmed evenings like Monster Movie Club and Elvis Memorial Night. Club 57 became a members-only clubhouse full of mushrooms, acid, bingo nights, and sex; a Saturday morning cartoon version of Dada wobbling happily between satire and homage. "[E]very night was a different channel," said Magnuson. If the *Wizard of Oz* singalong wasn't for you, there was the Mudd Club in TriBeCa for "coolness and being hip and shadowy and mysterious," and by the time Madonna and Eric Fischl landed, they joined a circle of some 500 insiders floating around, through, and next to one another below 14th. Scharf introduced Haring to an eighteen-year-old runaway named Jean-Michel Basquiat who'd been exposed as SAMO—he and his friend Al Diaz said "SAMO" meant "Same old shit." Photographer Tseng Kwong Chi arrived from Paris; the *East Village Eye* and *SoHo Weekly News* were the papers of record, Glenn O'Brien hosted *TV Party* on public access and introduced Debbie Harry and Chris Stein to a precocious graffiti artist in Ray-Bans named Fred Brathwaite, aka Fab Five Freddy, godson of Max Roach.

Over it all reigned the spirit of Andy Warhol, ambiguous essence of everything cool in New York. "He was the father," said Scharf, "and we were the children." A daunting waif in his white wig and bland affect, artist, filmmaker, socialite, collector of cookie jars, and devoted son, Warhol's arrival at an event turned it into an Event, his interest an immediate stamp of approval. He'd first come to New York in 1949 after a sickly childhood spent in bed with his coloring books, a rare bloom amid smoky Pittsburgh, and then a stint at Carnegie Tech where he met the all-encompassing aesthetic of Moholy-Nagy along with the unromantic Bauhaus emphasis on production. Full of high art aspirations, he found himself a hot commodity in New York as a graphic designer and window dresser until a show of his shoe drawings finally landed him among Lichtenstein, Oldenburg, and the aborning world of Pop, where Art melted into consumerism and media. Warhol donned a silver wig and turned into a character Truman Capote called "a Sphinx with no secret." The New York art world was not impressed: "[H]e was about the most colossal creep I had ever seen in my life," said one socialite. But after his famous *Campbell's Soup Cans*, Warhol created his own social laboratories disguised as clubs—first the Dom and then the Factory—where he performed human experiments on a cast of characters he turned into "superstars," using and abusing them as he twisted Moholy's vision of Art as a human universal into Art as a throwaway. Diana Vreeland brought him Uptown, and as his easel painting fell away, he applied his creative efforts to appearances at parties, shopping, and his most elevated art form: making money. Warhol's cold affect never made it clear how he felt about that, which was very much the point. "Warhol both glamorized and satirized his subject," said Lita Hornick. "[He] was always a double agent." These days Warhol was spending much time with the likes of Imelda Marcos and Calvin Klein in Studio 54, but he was always hunting for the next thing, so Ross Bleckner brought him to the Mudd Club.

The set for all this art, drugs, and sex was made possible by rock-bottom real estate prices in a section of New York left intentionally to ruin by landlords waiting for the next opportunity, its oddball ideas still charged with an innocent exuberance. As Calvin Trillin marched with his four-year-old between drag queens in the new Halloween parade, he noted that "the original bohemians were mainly people who came from small, peaceful towns, and they settled in the Village partly because . . .

it had the sort of informality and neighborliness they were used to at home. In other words, it reminded them of the Midwest."

Blockbusters

Anyone could make a reservation at Elaine's. The question was, where would you sit? Most who made the hike up to Yorkville, land of ex-Bund members and *kaffe mit schlag*, waited at the crowded little bar on the left as the empty tables not meant for them filled up with George Plimpton, William Styron, and Larry King. Sometime into your second drink, Elaine in her caftan and glasses would cut through the waves of the waiting like a stout Coast Guard tug to rescue some *Saturday Night Live* types and drop them safe and dry along the Line—ten red-checker-clothed tables down the right wall that surged and smoked with middle-aged male literati and their dates. At this point, some at the bar would leave, a little sour-green, while those who stayed would eventually be led past this thick-cut slab of New York's cultural Establishment, the heart of what deconstructionism was deconstructing, past the booth in back reserved for Woody Allen, and deposited in Siberia or even worse, the Paul Desmond Room, where you couldn't even crane your neck to watch Lauren Bacall nibble cashews. The food was expensive and mediocre, the service not worth discussing, but how often did you get to see Woody Allen eat chicken française?

If Downtown was about outsiders transforming themselves into insiders, then Elaine's was the epitome of insiders showing just how inside they all were. There were other places to parade and preen: the Oak Bar at the Plaza had a stodgy, J.Press charm, and the Algonquin had Round Table nostalgia. Society ladies preferred Mortimer's on Lex where they poked at chicken paillard or La Caravelle for translated French; the new Mr. Chow's on 57th was for power Chinese; the Four Seasons and 21 for just raw power. Studio 54's nexus of style, fame, and entertainment presaged the future. Warhol and Capote went to them all, but Elaine's table-hopping, squeeze-in-another-chair, *you*-wait-at-the-bar calls were the final judgments in 1978. New York then was still the City of the Word, home of three daily papers and the *Wall Street Journal* plus dozens more in other languages; *Time, Vogue, Esquire, Sports*

Illustrated, *The New Yorker*, and just about every other magazine, book publishing house, and TV network you could name; a dense network of public intellectuals who all knew each other and who all had to eat. Mercurial Elaine Kaufman had opened the restaurant in 1963 and as the first writers had trickled in, she'd kept tabs, cashed checks she took her time to deposit, probably had a few crushes, too, but most of all, she genuinely loved being around writers. Elaine's became what Jules Feiffer called "a men's club for the literary lonely," with its owner always eager to introduce two people she thought would get along, making herself the hub of the city's literary network, connecting big names like David Halberstam and Gay Talese in his very tight three-piece suits to the midlist novelists and magazine editors who'd nervously groom each other when Norman Mailer pounded his chest. Politicos dropped by, too, actors and the women who wanted to meet them; occasionally a peculiar transit cop in spats and a bowler. And Woody, who just then was making a luscious and perverse black-and-white valentine to this whole scene, starring himself as a man very much like himself having an affair with a stunning seventeen-year-old Dalton senior. (He wasn't alone in his tastes: twelve-year-old Brooke Shields played a child whore in *Pretty Baby* that year, complete with nude scenes.) Writers weren't quite rock stars or quarterbacks, but they were revered and envied as necessary to what made New York superior to all other cities. New York was home to the gatekeepers of Western civilization, and Elaine Kaufman was their guard dog.

But money, technology, and the nature of media itself were starting to change all of that. The fall of 1978 had been unusually restful in the tweedy parts of town; a four-month newspaper strike along with balmy temperatures had, according to *The New Yorker*, "conspired to produce a uniquely relaxed and pleasurable atmosphere in our city." Once the presses rolled, new doorstops from old names like Wouk and Michener sat atop the *Times* Best Sellers list, but the summer's big hit had been *Scruples*, a trashy first novel by Judith Krantz. Everything about it—the huge advance, the splashy release, the miniseries in the making—felt more like Hollywood than New York. Of course, ur-literary agent Swifty Lazar in his thick black glasses had always been around, Mr. Magoo with movie connections, and the odd Jackie Susann or Harold Robbins would pop up as a final guest on *The Tonight Show*. But for all its sloppy habits—the hard drinking and the fights and affairs that came with it—publishing remained a gentleman's game, many of the eighty-six or so houses such as Doubleday, Viking, and Scribner's privately held, run by men like Thomas Guinzburg and Roger Strauss, who'd nurtured countless seasons of American letters. It was a calling, entered for prestige, not wealth, full of unspoken rules, a guild-like apprenticeship, and ways of doing business that relied heavily on accepted wisdom. The Xerox machine allowed more than one copy of a manuscript to be printed now, but most agents still sent them to editors one at a time in search of the right fit that would provide their clients with that steady stream of income to pay for the kids' tuition at Ethical Culture and the place in Sag Harbor.

Computers were partly to blame for the massive deals being made by Krantz's lawyer, Mort Janklow. A premature frenzy over their potential in the '70s had led big media corporations to buy up independent publishers who, when on their own, had usually relied on bank financing for the (very) rare big author advance. Now someone like Dick Snyder, head of Simon & Schuster, only had to have his spending authorized by higher-ups. Though no longer personally on the hook, he now had to deliver profit margins far beyond what it used to cost to repay the loans. Enter the blockbusters; big commercial fiction that didn't advance the Great Conversation but sold like crazy in that other new development democratizing information—chain bookstores. "Up to now, only a certain class read books," said Snyder, "and the book distribution mechanism was for that class. Now, all of a sudden—boom!" The computers at the new B. Dalton at 666 Fifth tracked sales in real time, making guesstimating obsolete. Like City Hall, another dusty institution that made multimillion-dollar decisions based on hunches, publishers began to confront data. And that threatened to end civilization as it was known along the line at Elaine's.

Blockbusters and conglomerates weren't just for publishing. On the chilly morning of December 20, 1978, lines formed early at the Metropolitan Museum of Art. After two years of traveling America and Steve Martin singing "King Tut," *The Treasures of Tutankhamun* had arrived in New York. Over the next five months thousands of New Yorkers would, according to Hilton Kramer, "lie, bribe and risk mental and physical health" to see 55 minor items, each spotlit, from the cursed tomb of the boy king. "Art Museum" went on every city's wish list along with "Festival Marketplace." If blockbuster publishing was creating new readers, blockbuster art shows were spreading mainstream interest in the Fine Arts, with the same caveat: Would money bully aside quality in the name of giving the public what it wanted? More than aesthetics were at stake. During the Cold War and the Great Society era, governments, foundations, and corporations had all poured billions into the Arts as a means of spreading "the American Way," a hard machinery of financial support that had helped produce everything from the Batman Show to King Tut, and a public art movement had emerged led by Creative Time and the Public Art Fund placing high-quality art in public spaces. Fifth Avenue between 82nd and 105th became "Museum Mile." In 1974, a report by the Mayor's Committee on Cultural Policy identified the Arts as a vital industry in New York City, its 1,500 cultural institutions generating some $100 million in tax revenues. According to the National Endowment for the Arts, 18,182 graphic designers lived in the city, 15,374 painters and sculptors, 7,877 musicians and composers, and 4,382 authors (though with twice as many men in all these areas as women), along with tens of thousands who made their living raising curtains, stretching canvasses, and reading slush piles. Mostly, though, the Arts were used to attract business. The head of Exxon's Public Affairs called the Arts "a social lubricant. And if business is to continue in big cities, it needs a lubricated environment." Between 1970 and 1978, corporate giving was up 150%—Mobil was, according to *New York*, the "corporate equivalent of the Medicis."

And then the era of the Fiscal Crisis and Proposition 13 sent the Arts to the chopping block just when cultural institutions geared up to meet the growing demand. As the Met's new director Phillippe de Montebello intended to make it "the world's premier encyclopedic museum by the year 2000" and MoMA bought up West 53rd Street, the Arts were forced to chase even after more money in corporate boardrooms, putting more executives on their boards who focused on the bottom line, and selling badges of good taste in the form of O'Keeffe posters and Monet tote bags. Big shows like the Met's retrospective of photographer Richard

Avedon—"a convergence," wrote Roberta Smith, "of social, intellectual and media clout"—now aspired to instant zeitgeist, part appreciation, part advertising campaign, with fashion raised up to a level of Fine Art for reasons that had as much to do with underwriting as they did with costume as an art form.

The key player in this nexus was legendary *Harper's Bazaar* and *Vogue* editor Diana Vreeland, brought into the Met in 1971 to consult at the Costume Institute by then-director Thomas Hoving. "A little bad taste is like a nice splash of paprika . . . ," she once said, lighting another Lucky. "No taste is what I'm against." Her exotic, almost Asian, looks and air of a naughty countess happy to slum with the help had elevated her snobbery to a kind of genius, even if High Fashion still provoked anti-elitist invective from the sorts who admired Bella Abzug's hats. "People with something important to do do not care about living stylishly . . ." wrote the *Voice*. "If you have nothing in your head, you put purple on it." To which Vreeland would likely have said, *Indeed!*

In Washington Square Park, Jean-Michel Basquiat sold hand-painted postcards for ten dollars.

Chapter Five

To Lake Ladoga, and Beyond

U p in Central Park, spirits had been high through the spring rains. Protected by the fence, green shoots had appeared across the Sheep Meadow . . . until the entire 15 acres turned brown. Hardened New Yorkers chuckled. Of course, the grass died—this was fucking *New York*. If you want grass, move to Larchmont. Gordon Davis, resolute, put down more sod and crossed his fingers. It had been a long winter. Koch got praise from the *Times* for his "moxie" and had a 3-to-1 approval rating, but the best that could be said about New York was that he had it drifting in a better direction. Though the Bronx had stopped burning, over the last five years spending had dropped 34% for fire, 30% for sanitation, 26% for education, and 18% for transit. "Out there around '83," claimed Budget Director James Brigham, "there's a future." Until then, New Yorkers would have to fend for themselves. On any given night there were only 2,500 or so cops on the streets; in TriBeCa, muggers stabbed a young Scottish fashion designer in the heart. A week later, a subway train derailed at Columbus Circle injuring 21 passengers.

Deputy Mayor David Brown resigned in December 1978, warning about chaos inside City Hall that rivaled the Yankees clubhouse. Koch proved too impulsive, distracted, and political to put his weight behind Zuccotti's management initiative. No one analyzed the monthly commissioners' reports or compared month-to-month performance. Meetings wandered, the daily message drifted, and union pressure in

Albany killed civil service reform. All the City's labor contracts were keyed to the MTA's deal with transit workers, so it had no control over the numbers, no leverage for productivity. With American Airlines and Olivetti packing to leave the city, Koch still focused more on balancing the budget than pleasing corporate honchos.

Not all the City's problems could be blamed on him or the pains of Retrenchment. Quietly and comprehensively, computers had been altering how the world worked since 1948 when mathematician Claude Shannon laid down the foundation of Information Theory in Bell Labs at West Street and Washington. Only two miles away, City Hall had never bothered to keep up; instead, its swelling volume of data—reports, budgets, payrolls, vendors, contracts—ultimately crushed its manual systems, causing what James Beniger calls a Control Crisis. The City had lost control in the '70s not just because of debt, but because it couldn't effectively manage its information; its budget was, said one expert, "completely unauditable," which was the other reason the banks kept the City out of the credit market. Before New York could borrow again, it had to catch up. Corporate America had its own tech problems, though, and for the big banks, the issue was the same as the City's: The sheer magnitude of data they produced outstripped their ability to handle it. At Wriston's own Citibank, the back offices were so awash they'd nearly lost UPS as a client when they couldn't produce a monthly statement. Chase had it even worse; Rockefeller confessed that its poor performance in the mid-'70s was the result of "an almost total collapse of our operations management systems." After ignoring warnings from the head of IBM, Rockefeller blamed the City's inefficiency on the Great Society while his own bank fumbled with a back-office system one executive called "garbage in, garbage out, and a backlog of garbage." For a short time, Chase had had to fall back on manual record keeping.

The City initially responded to Tech as a real estate opportunity, offering tax incentives to retain back-office data processing, but this didn't help City Hall function better or get the budget under control. In 1975, Operations had hired American Management Systems (where Dan Biederman was working) to develop accounting and budgeting platforms, spending tens of millions of dollars on huge, water-cooled mainframes in Chelsea, but things hadn't improved much when Koch took over. "We had no idea what was going on," said Deputy Mayor Peter Solomon. Only the consultants really understood how the system worked. Still, by April 1979, some 55 departments were replacing battered file cabinets with computers: databases of child welfare cases, fuel use, purchasing, payroll, benefits, and schedules; byte by byte, the ungovernable city started to find order in a few corners, for entirely nonpartisan reasons.

More computers were proving a better idea than more deputy mayors; everyone simply shopped for the DM they wanted to deal with. "There are now three big growth industries in New York," said Wagner, "Fast-food joints, massage parlors, and deputy mayors." To finally get control of City Hall, Koch needed a captain, and he found him the day in August 1979 when the Yankees' own foul-mouthed, ball-busting captain Thurman Munson crashed his Cessna into the runway of the Akron airport. Prickly and unkempt with a walrus moustache and gut, Munson was loved by New York, and the team wouldn't be the same for a good 15 years. That sad afternoon, Koch reorganized City Hall, shedding four deputy mayors and making Bob Wagner Deputy Mayor for Policy. For Deputy Mayor of Operations, the captain of City Hall, he chose a thin, thirty-six-year-old Brooklyn native with a porn-star moustache and a taste for opera named Nat Leventhal, who'd gotten results out of a famously torpid HPD. "I cracked the whip," he said of his monthly grillings of deputies. "No one was frankly telling them it made any difference." Picking up where Zuccotti left off, Leventhal would over the next few years drag City Hall management closer to the modern age.

His first target was Sanitation. New York had a toxic relationship with its sanitation workers, many of whom rode the trucks only because they'd flunked Police or Fire exams. If a garbageman ever woke up ready to do a good job, he faced decrepit work conditions and New Yorkers who blamed him for filthy streets while they dropped trash where they stood. So Leventhal went positive. His Productivity Council and Labor-Management committees forced Sanitation head Norman Steisel to make nice. New trucks were ordered. Koch visited repair depots and transfer stations; Jets tickets and days off were handed out for high performance, and productivity and Project Scorecard numbers crept up, allowing Steisel and Leventhal to begin negotiations over trimming three-man truck crews down to two. Fixing Sanitation didn't mean cuts; it involved giving workers self-worth, responsibility, and the right tools. In City Hall, Leventhal added analysis of mistakes and problems to the Mayor's Management Report, lending it heft and accountability, and got Operations a voice on the budget. With Koch offering political cover for any tough choices, he began to move the needle. "[W]e . . . put the day-to-day management of the government on a reasonably businesslike basis," said Leventhal. City government could do more than react, problems *could* be solved. All this added momentum to what Davis was doing at Parks, and a network of administrators finally began taking shape who would over the next four decades move between public and private with a continuity of goals and methods that would drive the evolution of New York in terms of management and the built environment, people like Amanda Burden, Alair Townsend, Harvey Robins, and Felice Michetti. To them, public-private cooperation of the sort Carter had called for was an opportunity for practical innovation and common sense. From the Arsenal to the Mayor's Advisory Group, private money, power, and ideas were being woven into the practice of governance. In January, S&P announced that if the City could produce two balanced budgets with no gimmicks, it could test the bond market.

But it wasn't enough for David Rockefeller and the Crisis Regime. Even as Koch went back on his campaign promise and joined the push for Westway, as the State funded a new convention center and took over the flailing Battery Park City, Rockefeller complained that "Special interest groups had learned the techniques of stopping almost anything." New York needed a return to "catalytic bigness." Dictates hadn't worked with Koch, though, so Rockefeller went back to offering him coffee and Danish. Control came from generosity, and as philanthropy emerged as the "third sector" in the public-private urban nexus, he decided that giving back to New York would once again be the way to steer its direction. Since the rise of the large foundations of the Fords and the Carnegies, and others like the Kaplan Fund and the Twentieth Century Fund largely in New York, seeding independent research and advising governments ostensibly for the common good, by now "what is public and what is private," wrote Daniel Bell, "and what is profit and what is not-for-profit, is no longer an easy distinction." In order to be "an equal partner with government," business, said Rockefeller, would have to "assume greater responsibility in the urban area." And so, in December 1979, he and Walter Wriston announced the founding of a civic-minded Chamber of Commerce they called the New York City Partnership. Its goal would be to serve New York . . . by improving conditions for business.

The Market Would Provide Meaning

Around town, cleaning crews scrubbed the façades of St. Patrick's, Rockefeller Center, the Helmsley Building, Grand Central Terminal, and some of the Broadway theaters. Graffiti disappeared in Bryant Park. Compared to bankrupt Cleveland, New York wasn't looking so bad, and the upside of inflation was that it let the City pay down some debt. As Koch began to impose some order in City Hall, New York regained control of its destiny, if not its old identity. The next New York that had been brewing underground peeked out.

In the Bronx, art was everywhere in 1979, even though budget cuts and inflation had decimated the standard of living for many—a $258 grant in 1975 was now effectively worth $129. But on Walton Avenue, John Ahearn and Rigoberto Torres made casts of their neighbors, communal works of art that created trust and pride as little girls, gang members, and smiling grandmothers coolly endured twenty minutes encased in plaster to be immortalized in the South Bronx Hall of Fame shown that fall at Fashion Moda. More tightly wound than his brother Charlie, John had come to the East Village after Cornell but "Everybody seemed way too happy" so he ended up moving to the South Bronx. "I felt comfortable," he says, "and I trusted what I was doing." On the trains, graffiti writers went all out, capped by an entire car painted with Campbell's Soup cans. When Kool Herc got stabbed, Grandmaster Flash took over the scene and Grand Wizard Theodore invented scratching; DJs could toy with the music now, shock it with the electronic. "Rapper's Delight" by Hip Hop's version of the Monkees, the Sugarhill Gang, was a 14-minute imitation of what full-time pizza maker and part-time bouncer Hank Shocklee had heard in clubs, but the song proved to be Rap's breakout hit with both White and Black kids and suddenly the game changed.

Hip Hop captured another aspect of this next New York—it would be electronic. Answering machines had just hit the market and home computers were Radio Shack novelties, but the future was out there. Back on the week of "I Love New York" Day, the cover of *Time* had featured "The Computer Society," which announced that tomorrow belonged to "the microchip, a ladybug-sized bit of electronic scrimshaw that may change our lives as profoundly as the industrial revolution." While most were wary, NYU's new Interactive Telecommunications Program ran right into the question of what was next. Founded by Red Burns and George Stoney, the ITP would play with computers and telephone lines to send words and images, envisioning "small-scale community networks which can reinforce community consciousness." Up on 53rd, Citicorp Center offered a vision of what the new white-collar FIRE economy and its public-private partnerships would look like. With a Conran's housewares store and gourmet food court, perfect for a curious city where hundreds were trying an odd Japanese dish called *sushi* (though, warned *New York*, "doctors are against it"), this "first vertical shopping mall" was open to all, but private money paid to empty the garbage and keep junkies from nodding off under the ficus. Caviling about it being a suburban-style mall just sounded dreary. After decades of Modernism promising unitards on the Moon, then the fumbling malaise of the '70s, the future on display featured cleaner air and natural fabrics. The City miraculously ended FY79 in the black. It was time to try that *sushi*.

To which a middle-aged couple keened in a *Times* op-ed, "It is not our city anymore, our city is gone . . . What do we do? Where do we go?"

New York, they were certain, had lost its soul. Their city of Roseland and Miss Subways, the assumptions, tastes, and power of their generation were being challenged, the promise shot through with panic, and with good reason—crime was rising, a record 1,814 murders in the year to come, and the economy remained clenched in Stagflation. Bestsellers like *The Crash of '79* urged readers to hoard gold and canned goods. With 16 tax brackets topping out at 70% for married filers earning $760,691 in 2020 dollars, inflation shoved people into increasingly higher brackets though their real wages stayed flat; millions flowed into flimsy tax shelters meant to fail. In October, in hopes of bringing inflation under control, Fed Chairman Paul Volcker let interest rates float, sending the economy on a three-year thrill ride and launching New York toward its Renaissance by turning bonds, long the most boring thing on Wall Street, into something volatile. Gold went through the roof, chaos reigned on bond floors as prices yo-yoed.

But chaos doesn't have to mean apocalypse. Disorder in the bond market meant winners and losers, and the winners began stocking up on real estate, art, and collectables, largely because they promised to beat inflation. As the Iranian hostage crisis overwhelmed the Carter White House in November, the auction season "produced a bonanza," reported the *Times*. Not just for reliable Impressionists and Expressionists but also for things like Art Deco clocks, carved goose decoys, and Lalique vases, just because the buyers thought they could sell them for more later. Citibank and Sotheby's formed an art advisory division, and syndicates borrowed money to buy paintings. The eternal exchange between wealth and art was once again very clear. "Say you were going to buy a $200,000 painting," wrote Warhol. "I think you should take that money, tie it up and hang it on the wall." Said Joseph Kosuth, "The market would provide meaning." Leading the way would be a medium-sized jungle cat in Gucci pumps named Mary Boone, a twenty-six-year-old who'd opened a gallery at 420 Broadway in February with a show for barrel-chested Brooklyn native Julian Schnabel, his ego as big as the canvases he covered in broad strokes of paint and broken plates glued in vibrant, almost childlike mosaic. After years of silence and still points, here was sweaty, voluptuous painting again that electrified the art world with passions on both sides, a controversy that was terrific for art, and for Boone.

But not everything was about money yet. Klaus Nomi had captured the sweet, bizarre heart of the moment Downtown, and on December 15, 1979, David Bowie did three numbers on *Saturday Night Live* backed by Joey Arias and Klaus. A gay opera singer from Weimar, he'd come to New York in hopes of someday joining Callas on stage but that hadn't happened so he'd peeled vegetables in restaurants, delivered packages, and kept practicing until *this*. At home on St. Mark's Place, he baked pies and sang falsetto into the courtyard.

This is Lake Ladoga!

Anomie still lingered in the subways, though. "New Yorkers seem to have made a pact," wrote James Lardner, "to enter a state approximating suspended animation, and to stay there until they get where they are going." When they did, they were often late; 30% of doors didn't work, 80% of cars were covered in graffiti. When the gang epic *The Warriors* had come out, the ads had read, "These are the Armies of the Night . . . They could run New York City." Most riders thought they already did, but in fact they were statistically safer there than on the streets. Fear of crime was as harmful to New York as crime itself, so City officials couldn't make up their minds about the Guardian Angels, the teenaged vigilantes in berets assembled by the night manager of the Fordham Road McDonald's, Curtis Sliwa, and the Shaolin Protectors—Jeff and Jerry Monroe, black belt brothers in the African American kung-fu subculture with its lore of honorable men fighting corrupt authorities with only their fists. Did they make people feel safer or more scared?

Cheap public transportation had been New York's original antidote to "a city of the very rich and very poor." Immediately swamped, the first trains fell into an impossible cycle—heavy use raised the cost to private operators while politics forced them to keep fares low. By 1953 the New York City Transit Authority had assumed responsibility for all the lines, and in 1968 the MTA swallowed up the NYCTA to become North America's largest railroad system, responsible for the subway system, the buses, bridges, tunnels, three commuter lines, and the New York Coliseum. But the current sorry state of the subways choked the free movement of people to work, to shop, to go to school, and fewer riders meant fewer fares, accelerating the system's downward spiral. For decades, no mayor or governor had treated transit as a priority, and even if a mayor wanted to, the MTA was out of their hands because it was a public authority under State control, led now by Harold Fisher, Hugh Carey ally and treasurer of the Brooklyn machine. Fat, crooked, and uninterested, Fisher proved that government unchecked ends up the same way. Experts were out of ideas; *Setting Municipal Policy*, an influential annual study, offered three obvious options: "Muddling Through," "Paying Whatever Is Necessary," and "Reducing Transportation Expenditures."

By September 1979, even Carey had seen enough and replaced Fisher with forty-six-year-old former UDC head Richard Ravitch, who had the burly sense of purpose found in fighting mammals of the Upper Midwest. Raised on the Upper West Side, he'd attended Columbia, then Yale Law, and after a stint in Washington, had come home to take over the family construction business. Principled and civic-minded, he'd saved the UDC from bankruptcy, resigned from MAC because it cared more about Wall Street than New York, and thrown Donald Trump out of his office when he'd lobbied for the Commodore tax break. Everyone told Ravitch not to take the MTA job, and like Gordon Davis, that's why he did. Though Carey and Koch both refused to raise fares and taxes, by spring 1980 Ravitch had wheedled more money out of the State and a minor fare hike, just in time for negotiations on the Transit workers' new contract, which Koch now used as a referendum on Retrenchment, and himself. Bent on balancing the budget, he urged a hard line while a last-minute deal worked out between Ravitch and union head John Lawe fell through. At 12:01 a.m., April 1, 33,000 MTA employees went out on an illegal strike. What came next—according to Koch, at least—changed "the course of history for the city of New York."

Early that warm morning, at an emergency meeting with police commissioner Bob McGuire, the mayor looked out a window at One Police Plaza expecting to see empty streets; instead, he saw thousands of New Yorkers crossing the Brooklyn Bridge. "This is going to save us," thought Koch, picturing New York now as besieged Leningrad. "This is Lake Ladoga!" Running out with the press in tow, he greeted the walkers and bikers as if "a dybbuk had overtaken" him, waving his hands and shouting, "Walk over the bridge! We're not going to let these bastards bring us to our knees!" Instead of booing, they cheered, so for eleven days, every morning and evening commute Koch riled up New Yorkers at the bridges. Women took to wearing sneakers over their stockings and carrying heels in their purses while the mayor, who'd never learned how to ride a bike, faked his way through photo ops. Despite a rainy

April 10, when a quarter of a million cars turned Midtown into one monstrous traffic jam—the birth of the term *gridlock*—New Yorkers didn't simply accept their fate and stay home as they had under Lindsay. The strike was settled on the eleventh. "We changed the mood of the people of the city of New York . . . ," Koch said later, "I was standing up for them." But *he* hadn't changed the course of history. The white-collar office workers had done it—instead of identifying with the strikers, they'd backed the people who signed their checks. The transit strike announced the end of New York as a union town.

A month later, on May 9, Retrenchment officially ended when Koch presented a three-inch thick "technically balanced budget" for FY81 that included $1 billion in capital spending. The City could begin to sketch out a future. On June 18—New York Construction Day—ground was broken on the first buildings in Battery Park City and the new convention center on the West Side, another deal built on Trump's Penn Central options.

The Capital of Street Culture

With the grip of the Crisis Regime now loosened, Koch now shot down The City at 42nd!, that pie-in-the-sky plan to weave everything from 41st to 43rd, from Seventh to Eighth, into one big performing arts theme park. Taking a swipe at its air of ersatz Disney, he declared that he'd prefer something "seltzer instead of orange juice," though the real reason was that he suspected there was more money out there for the City. "Glitzy," had been the verdict of Herb Sturz, head of City Planning, the man behind the mayor's decision. A fan of John Dewey and Dylan Thomas, Sturz cared more about liberal action than purity, and his pragmatism inspired and informed much of what was to come in New York, particularly in Times Square. Founder of the influential Vera Institute of Justice, his entire experience in planning consisted of having read Mumford and Jacobs, but he envisioned using the built environment to share the wealth through Growth. After fighting for the Great Society, he now embraced private involvement in public projects. "You can do an enormous amount," he said of government, "but to effect real change, why would you expect government to do it alone?" So Sturz committed City Planning to encouraging the catalytic bigness Rockefeller wanted, focusing on their benefits to the city rather than any potential harm.

The priority from the start was Times Square. Sturz brought in Holly Whyte to do a study of 42nd Street and after weeks of filming from an abandoned hotel he concluded, "This is the national cesspool." In his sunny way he recommended that "the best way to handle the problem of undesirables is to make a place attractive to everyone else." As in Bryant Park, the answer was to change the use and create density. Sturz never envisioned a sex-free Times Square; to him, the undesirables were specifically those responsible for child prostitution and sexual violence, and to clean them up he brought in Lindsay veteran and former Legal Services lawyer Carl Weisbrod to take over the Office of Midtown Enforcement while plans were drafted for new economic development that would invite in "everyone else." In July 1980, a memo of understanding committed the City to jointly developing Times Square and 42nd Street with the State, kicking off an almost two-decade-long saga.

Meanwhile, Howard Johnson's kept frying clams, and the peep shows rolled on; no one could imagine New York without that madness in the middle, and with Joey Arias dancing at Fiorucci on 59th and Diana Vreeland slumming at the Mudd Club, Uptown and Downtown were now just states of mind. In the face of this, John Ahearn and Tom Otterness wanted to stage Colab's next show in "a central location that would be open to people from all parts of New York." That could only mean Times Square; "the capital," says Charlie, "of street culture." After scouting a derelict four-story former massage parlor at 41st and Seventh, they met with the Durst Organization, who they talked into two months' rent free. Grants from the NEA and others came through and *The Times Square Show* was on. On June 1, the doors opened on the consciously "activated space" and never closed for the next month. As MoMA gave itself over to Picasso and the Met opened its new André Meyer Galleries full of Impressionists, here graffiti crews, artists, scenesters, and local vagrants hung out at this "raw, raucous, trashy" playhouse shocked to life with some 150 funny, biting, sexy, political works—from the staircase David Hammons sprinkled with broken malt liquor bottles to the first public paintings of Basquiat, Haring, and Scharf. What mattered most about *The Times Square Show*, though, was that it united all the city's artistic undergrounds—Stefan Eins and Joe Lewis brought people down from the Hub to meet the B-movie Club 57 aesthetic; Charlie Ahearn met Fab Five Freddy, who'd done the Soup Can train and worked with the reclusive graffiti legend Lee Quiñones. The next day, Lee and Fab painted a gigantic FAB 5 on the side of the building, a statement to the art world that "you've got to make some room here for these people." Small worlds joined forces "to attack," wrote the *East Village Eye*, "the wasteland of our mass culture by producing stuff that is alive."

Something young and street smart had been added to the SoHo art explosion. To Diego Cortez, graffiti was "the soul of the underground scene" and the '60s-era debate over it returned with the photos of Martha Cooper, the debut of Henry Chalfant's panoramic photos of bombed trains at the OK Harris Gallery, and a show at the New Museum that December. The *Voice* explicitly connected graffiti to Dubuffet's *art brut*, but millions of subway riders remained unconvinced, and unnerved. While the likes of Dondi and Lee offered wit and beauty along with their criminality and protest, too much was simply a visual mugging and unfortunately graffiti writers resisted the distinction. If every train rolling by actually had, as Claes Oldenburg once claimed, brought "a bouquet from Latin America," public opinion might have been on the writers' side, but a big piece running on the #6 seemed more honest: "New York City," it read. "Where else could I get away with this shit?" Koch wanted wolves prowling the train yards, but Ravitch wisely focused on cleaning.

Meanwhile, Jane Dickson rented a studio on 43rd Street, where she and Charlie moved into another space on the sixth floor, pretending they were a film company to put off inspectors until they realized no one cared. "[T]he landlord couldn't care less because he knew [redevelopment] was going to happen," she says. "It was dark and desolate between the neon things." Nearby the tiny bar Tin Pan Alley gave haven to transvestite boosters, strippers, hookers, artists, cops, and combinations of the above amid art by Cookie Mueller and Nan Goldin. Kiki Smith worked the grill. Charlie and Fab decided to make a movie about Hip Hop that they titled *Wild Style*, while Jane documented the final days of Times Square with canvases of red and yellow neon blaring through the velvety 2:00 a.m. black; Peepland stripped down to its lurid studs; old New York dying while the next thing grew.

Everything Falls Into Place

The green shoots had finally taken. By fall 1980 a luscious expanse of front-yard quality green stretched across the Sheep Meadow. "Only five years ago," wrote Carter Wiseman, "few New Yorkers would have stood still for fenced-off public lawns. Something has happened. If you walk by the Sheep Meadow these days, you see people doing, it would seem, nothing more than watching the grass grow. They seem almost worshipful; strange expressions of puzzled delight come over their faces as they let the cool green grass slide between their toes." The sudden appearance of this lawn "had a psychological impact," says Gordon Davis. "I could feel it. It was a statement. You *can* do something remarkable."

It was now possible to imagine a New York that wasn't dark, dangerous, and depressed. The new Central Park Conservancy let Elizabeth Barlow solicit contributions and by October, it had raised $6.5 million to restore Cherry Hill and the Conservatory Pond. A planning team began examining its 843 acres "as if it were a patient on an operating table," cataloguing each of its 24,000 trees in a database in preparation for a decade of work. The Parks Department embarked on 39 projects in all boroughs, from seawalls to ballfields. Work on a new extension began at the Brooklyn Museum, and Andrew Heiskell hired an outgoing Armenian with a gray goatee named Vartan Gregorian, former provost at Penn, as the new president of the NYPL. The two instructed their beleaguered staff that from now on "we will say only what's good about the Library" and the endowment began to refill. Technology helped fuel the optimism. "A computer or calculator does the job quicker, more efficiently," wrote *The New Yorker*, "and then it sits there saying, 'What's next?' And people have to formulate new questions. It makes demands, forces one to stretch one's imagination." City Hall had created the first computer security unit, built a database of City property, and most important, now had the country's "most sophisticated computerized accounting system" that the *Times* called "the most significant reform arising from the fiscal crisis." In February 1981, the credit market opened again to New York City.

Just then Gordon Davis was mulling whether to allow Bulgarian artist Christo and his wife Jeanne-Claude to erect some 15,000 arches over 25 miles of Central Park paths, with a saffron banner hanging down from each. New York is "a walking city," said the artist, and *The Gates* would be "something very simple about walking." In a 100-plus page report that served as his manifesto for Central Park, Davis turned down their request, feeling that at this fragile moment, with New Yorkers just learning how to let the grass tickle their toes, the park was spectacle enough. The fact was, Davis was still treading water when it came to the rest of the system; only 26% of parks citywide were rated "Good" and old attitudes died hard. *Times* reporters skeptical of his approach also saw fit to write off a park visitor dropping trash under their noses with a glib "What am I going to do with it?" as nothing more than a "mirror to some of the troubles of the city in general."

But that attitude of willful powerlessness was being challenged, the relationship between a community and the government being redefined, especially in Brooklyn where the churches working with the IAF had formed East Brooklyn Congregations (EBC) and hired streetwise Chicago organizer Mike Gecan to help them reach the next level. A warrior for practical power, Gecan quickly formed a partnership with Reverend Johnny Ray Youngblood, the pastor of St. Paul's Community Baptist Church in East New York, and the two ignited a movement when they brought a delegation to meet Brooklyn Borough President Howard Golden. Armed with questions, all Golden offered them were garbage cans so they returned to St. Paul's on fire. Building on two of IAF's prime rules—Never do for others what they can do for themselves, and Anger is a useful basis for organizing—East Brooklyn Congregations became a local action force, tackling details of park repairs, street signs, and rip-off grocers, rebuilding community from the ground up instead of buying a Lifestyle, another kind of hopeful green shoot.

In December, as he waited for the F train at Sixth and 41st, Keith Haring noticed a rich void of black matter paper pasted over an expired ad. "Suddenly, everything fell into place," he explained later. He ran upstairs to buy some white chalk, then returned to the station where he made his first subway drawings, the dancing men, barking dogs, radiant babies, and flying saucers that he was soon drawing every day on his way to work during the absolute nadir of the MTA, when packed platforms had officials afraid of riders being pushed onto tracks. But when you looked out the window of the car, there was that baby again, that man with an Egyptian dog head, and the barking dog, signs of human life amid the underworld; messages in a bottle from Haring, who just wanted to say hello.

Big development, though, captured the headlines. James Rouse, developer of Boston's Quincy Market, was bringing his "festival marketplace" approach to South Street Seaport while in Midtown, two flashy hotels debuted: Trump's Hyatt and Harry Helmsley's Palace. For decades, the crafty Helmsley had kept his old basset hound face out of the news until Leona Mindy Roberts (née Rosenthal), a notoriously aggressive pioneer in co-op conversions, put him in her sights and Harry tossed aside his wife of thirty-four years along with whatever good taste and sense he'd ever had. While he'd admirably restored Gilded Age opulence to the old Villard Houses, the tower behind it was, to *New York Times* architecture critic Ada Louise Huxtable, "a curtain wall of unforgiveable, consummate mediocrity." She favored the mirrored bronze and steel of Trump's Hyatt—"It is urbane and elegant New York." If only Trump had been, too. After promising to donate the reliefs on Bonwit's façade to the Met, he decided they were "Just junk." So he ordered them destroyed and lied about it when he was caught.

On the same day Dorothy Day died on the Lower East Side, *Man of La Mancha* fan Ed Koch traded in his Rocinante and leased a new Lincoln Continental. The Renaissance had begun.

Chapter Six

The Age of the Individual

Brooke Astor had quite the quandary. Tap tapping a pencil on her desk in the Money Room, she mulled the list. The Kissingers, of course. The Wristons and Rohatyns. But some would *have* to go; sixty was such a small number in a city made of so *many* fascinating people and they all seemed to want to meet the Reagans. That George Will, so persistent, had goaded her into a dinner for the President and the First Lady—it was her *duty*. So why was it called the Money Room? Well, it was, she'd declared when she'd created this duplex at 778 Park, the room "where I am going to give Vincent's money away!" And she had with great brio—$130 million so far. Sister Parish's decorating expressed her brand of grandeur: timeless yet relaxed; privilege gracefully deployed amid animal figurines, ten coats of lacquered red paint, and some Canalettos.

So who else? Tap. The point was to introduce Mr. Reagan to a group of people he might not meet at his usual sort of party, which was, when you thought about it, a rather *broad* group, so yes to Victor Gotbaum and the head of the 100 Black Men. Bill Paley and David Rockefeller because one must. That nice Tom Brokaw. The De La Rentas, who were just so *interesting*; both Oscar and Françoise worked hard and Mrs. Astor liked that. Not everyone did but that was such an *old* way of thinking; married off at sixteen to a gambler and, it turned out, a wife-beater, Brooke had learned to most admire those diamonds set amid some higher purpose. The editors from all the newspapers went on the list. But no politics at *all*! She was devoted to Ed Koch, but there *were* limits. It was settled, then. Five courses for sixty, the evening of December 9, to welcome President Reagan and the First Lady, who looked so *good* in red Adolfo.

With Carter gone, American aristocracy emerged from hiding in puffed sleeves and pinstripes, sent their cutaways to be cleaned at Jeeves of Belgravia, placed exotic Maia bouquets in the foyer niche. Guests at the Fall Antiques Show Benefit tucked into a spread laid out by forty-year-old Westport stockbroker Martha Stewart, now trying her hand at catering. This collective awakening converged with Margaret Thatcher and what one British wag called "the horrible renaissance of the upper-class twit" and another on the opposite side of the globe. In September the People's Republic of China had announced reforms to encourage business—Mao, like Bella Abzug, had gone out of fashion—and New York society was celebrating with a blitz: Bloomingdale's had transformed itself into an Orientalist fantasia of PRC goods, while a massive trade show at the Coliseum displayed 20,000 items from ivory dragon boats to industrial chemicals that, according to *Mother Jones,* projected an "enthusiasm for the consumption ethic." A few days later, "the 650 people you know best," wrote Warhol, floated into the opening gala for *The Manchu Dragon: Costumes of China,* some 150 imperial robes presented by Diana Vreeland at the Met's Costume Institute. While Mrs. Vreeland wasn't single-handedly sewing government, consumerism, and art together, she certainly lent her needle, offering guidance for the era at hand: "Everything is money and power and how to use them both," she said. "We mustn't be afraid of snobbery and luxury." The delightful fireworks display over the park illuminated what turned out to be John Lennon's last hours, and when the ambulance drove off with his body that unseasonably warm December night, the dinginess and drear of the '70s seemed scrubbed away throughout the Upper East Side, hair shirts folded and donated to the MSK Thrift Shop. The next evening, after Mrs. Astor had rung the silver bell and the spaghetti ai funghi was enjoyed, the president-elect raised his glass and admitted he'd heard "wonderful things about New York."

From 57th to 96th between Fifth and Lex, with colonies on Sutton Place, Beekman Place, and Gracie Square along the East River, social New York was its own Seven-Mile World. Money could be found anywhere in the city, but this was the land of "the 400," the mother of all networks, and so much that was simply *known*; the countless discrete indicators expressing generations of membership as surely as any gang jacket or graffiti, with the most important word there being *discrete*. Vast wealth never disappeared during the postwar years; it simply learned to disport itself quietly—*Vivre caché pour bien vivre*, as the French say: live hidden to live well. But now the president said it was time to glitter and gleam again. New York's Old Moneyed Establishment were coming through the Retrenchment inconvenienced at worst and with Reagan promising tax relief and deregulation, the rich and powerful began to make more visible use of their riches and power. Their networks were about to change, though, along with attitudes toward wealth. This would form the basis of Renaissance New York, just now fastening the clasp on its pearls and preparing to make its entrance.

The Point Is the Gleam

Because he distrusted the poor even more than he disliked the rich, Koch now helped well-to-do New Yorkers embrace their luxuries. "The old climate was that profit was evil," he said. "I have created the impression, 'We love you if you are rich.'" Despite endorsing Carter, he'd spoken so warmly of Reagan through the election season that Norman Podhoretz claimed him as a brother neocon, but Koch saw the strategies of Retrenchment as a way to *use* the rich, pushing responsibility onto them for the arts and the parks. And Reaganism had nothing to do with old rock-ribbed calls for good government in the face of party machines. A think tank called the International Centre for Economic Policy Studies had opened on the Upper East Side in 1978, and a month after the inauguration, its program director George Gilder published *Wealth and Poverty*, expanding on Ayn Rand's proudly antisocial philosophy with Orwellian inversions of logic wherein the poor were greedy, racism didn't exist, and true goodness belonged only to those who did whatever the hell they wanted, hereinafter referred to as "entrepreneurs." Loudly praised by the president himself, *Wealth and Poverty* replaced the Social Gospel preached at Rockefeller's Riverside Church with a rationalization for greed, justifying policies that actively hurt the poor as punishment for their willful depravity. After a gushing review from Roger Starr, the man behind planned shrinkage, *Wealth and Poverty* flew out of the Madison Avenue Bookshop at 69th Street, literary provider of choice for High Society, and began a run on the *Times* Best Sellers list. Until the Invisible Hand fixed New York by cutting their taxes, those with the power to change things would try not to get shit on their John Lobb shoes. "A millionaire should not give to charity," said Harry Helmsley. "The only thing you can ask from a millionaire is the opportunity for them to give you a chance to work."

They didn't have to wait long. On August 13, 1981, Reagan signed tax cuts into effect: Over the next three years, the top bracket would go down from 70% to 50%, meaning a couple with a gross income of $20,000 would be paying $764 less, which was certainly nice, but if that same couple had a gross income of $250,000, they'd get some $35,000 more to play with. Deductions were increased for retirement accounts and capital gains tax cut to help spread the enthusiasm for bonds into moribund stocks where the long bear market had driven prices down at the same time as inflation had driven assets high; the result was a wave of leveraged buyouts, mergers and acquisitions, and the sudden existence of twenty-something millionaires.

"The point," said Diana Vreeland, "is the gleam . . . the positiveness, the *turn-out.*" D.V. exchanged the Roman excess of Studio 54 for Versailles as a court formed in New York connected to the Reagans by their California friends Betsy Bloomingdale and her husband, department store heir Alfred. Fashionistas like Nan Kempner and attendants of means such as walker *cum* real estate heir Jerome Zipkin got to work building a bigger and brassier circle behind the façade of the Social Register the way Helmsley had erected his tower behind the staid Villard Houses. In the Hamptons now "there was a certain mood . . . ," wrote Marie Brenner. "Anyone who really tosses money around gets sneered at, but it's a sneer that is tinged with respect." But the bargain for public acceptance of wealth once kept under satin wraps would be that now anyone could buy in. Another big seller at the Madison Avenue

Bookshop, *The Preppy Handbook*, was ostensibly a comic guide to the secret codes and questionable style choices of Old Money, yet while Muffy and Biff guffawed, a generation carefully watching from outside learned about Fair Isle sweaters, popping collars, and all the other markers that allowed easy entrance into the New York Yacht Club. "In a true democracy everyone can be upper class and live in Connecticut," read the introduction. "It's only fair." Seeds of a new class were buried in the comedy of that line. Of course the old Marxists on the Upper West Side, the Line at Elaine's, and anyone else who'd come to New York to continue the Great Conversation greeted all this garish excess with bemusement. How could anyone take seriously the likes of the much-feted Debutante of the Year Cornelia Guest who chirped, "I don't want to learn anymore. I think men have to go to college, but women don't." Yet that idea of individual achievement being rewarded with a spot in something that looked like the upper class thrummed on the same frequency that had sent Koch's marchers across Lake Ladoga. Though a Topsiders ad asked, "Can you imagine strolling through Southampton faking it?," the reality was that "faking it" was now at the heart of Society. "Fake it," after all, had long been Vreeland's motto.

And Reagan was making it the American Lifestyle.

It Seemed Like We Had Won

As champagne flowed at La Grenouille, the rest of New York begged for water. City Hall had declared a drought emergency; no open hydrants, no washing streets or sidewalks and worst, a PSA featuring Koch surrounded by a clutch of kids all chanting, "If it's yellow, let it mellow; if it's brown, flush it down." Amid a city record 637,451 felonies in 1981, Manhattan snapped awake. The Empire State Building was named a landmark, and Philip Johnson stuck a Chippendale top on his new AT&T Building. *New York*'s new fashion editor, Anna Wintour, late of *Harper's Bazaar* and ladies softcore *Viva*, offered help to the uncertain in this incoherent New Wave era of neon and lace, tutus and jumpsuits. Out went the Conran's industrial shelving and in came bibelots and paintings of spaniels. The brave sampled exotic international fare such as guacamole, kung pao chicken, and pad thai. Chlamydia had arrived, some 200,000 cases in 1979, so doctors advised women to carry condoms. They were also well advised to avoid "Ugly George" Urban walking Midtown streets in his bulging silver lamé shorts, cajoling a surprising number of women into flashing their breasts for his public access show. For $1,000 you could watch a handful of old movies on your own Betamax, this year's Sony-made necessity along with the soon ubiquitous Walkmen playing Hall and Oates and the Police, and pay for it all with a Visa or MasterCard—consumer debt was easily had after the Supreme Court's ruling that state usury laws didn't apply to credit cards from national banks.

TriBeCa was now the hottest place to be, with Printed Matter, Franklin Furnace, and the Clocktower at its artistic core and its social center a casually white-apron brasserie on West Broadway perfect for this new decade trading Nik Niks for button-downs. Anna Wintour thought Odeon was *too* downtown, but guided by Keith and Brian McNally, ex-pat English veterans of Mr. Chow's, it became "a plutocracy all its own," hangout for media players like Lorne Michaels and Jonathan Demme and then the Schnabel–Eric Fischl–David Salle circle of artists after their big joint show that spring. To Fischl, it felt like they were "riding inside the curl of the perfect wave." "Given the choice," conceded Calvin Tomkins, "most artists would probably prefer to live at a time when art is in demand, even if for the wrong reasons." Said one, "It's no longer chic to be poor. I want goods, products, services."

Though the attitude in the East Village wasn't quite so blatantly craven, Rap and Reaganism hit America hand in hand. Just before the election, Kurtis Blow's "The Breaks" became the first Hip Hop song to sell 500,000 copies, and a week before the inauguration, Debbie Harry and Blondie released "Rapture," the first pop song to include a rap (albeit one delivered by a White woman). A month later, she hosted *Saturday Night Live* with her musical guests "the Funky Four Plus One More," the first Rap music on national television. That same afternoon, there'd been another significant debut; two breakouts amid the unfiltered, anarchic *New York/New Wave* show at PS 1 in Long Island City: the lush black-and-white erotic photos of Robert Mapplethorpe and the wall given over to Jean-Michel Basquiat. Calculated yet vulnerable, his genius deformed by the pull of fame, his brief life would tell the future of the East Village.

By now everyone Downtown knew him, long and gracefully loping in his old coat, a tuft of short dreads flowing back from his head. Just twenty years old, his placid face sweet and bebop cool; innocent and ambitious. He'd grown up in Brownstone Brooklyn, son of a striving Haitian accountant and sometimes abusive Puerto Rican mother who often took him to the Brooklyn Museum. As their marriage dissolved, Jean-Michel drifted, an angry middle-class runaway who liked Hitchcock, *Guernica*, and dropping acid in Washington Square until the SAMO graffiti brought him into the Downtown scene. After *The Times Square Show*, he'd written in one of his notebooks: "IT'S TIME TO GO AND COME BACK A DRIFTER," so out he went in search of his art. Where Haring found an inner order in New York, Basquiat picked through its rubble: faces and teepees, police cars, airplanes and crowns, sometimes swimming in rich colors, other times stark on white paper, or painted à la folk art on whatever he could find. According to his father, the morning after *New York/New Wave* opened, Basquiat went to the house on Pacific Street in a suit and tie and announced, "Papa, I have made it."

If the East Village scene had an official start, it was that summer, at the opening of Patti Astor's Fun Gallery. As MoMA packed up *Guernica* for its return to post-Franco Spain, she regularly hosted what Walter Robinson would call "minifestivals of the slum arts" and "a crisscross of island-mediated African influences now illuminated New York . . . ," wrote art historian Robert Farris Thompson, "multiple streams of sub-Saharan and Western culture began to converge at every minute of every day." Afrika Bambaataa came to Haring's black light art show, b-boys and graffiti writers partied with punks at Negril, and Klaus Nomi released a silly and startling cover of "Lightnin' Strikes." Martin Wong's paintings found the tenderness and textures of Alphabet City, more galleries opened: Nature Morte, Civilian Warfare, Gracie Mansion. Jane Dickson put Haring and Holzer on the Spectacolor sign in Times Square. You couldn't hide from the new beat: a *20/20* segment explained that the music throbbing out of boomboxes, and the *Village Voice* ran a front-page piece about the Puerto Rican kids reviving breakdancing on the Upper West Side. Bambaataa and his Soul Sonic Force cut a trippy blend of singsong rap and electronica titled "Planet Rock" while Sugar

Hill released another influential if synthetic hit "The Message" with Melle Mel and the Furious Five pulling Rap away from "yes yes y'all" to "Don't push me." NYU student Rick Rubin cleared the furniture out of his dorm room to start a record label he called Def Jam. Haring spent his weekends at Paradise Garage on King Street, dancing to the trancelike funk and diva grooves of DJ Larry Levan; "gay life," wrote Ingrid Sichy, "at its most pagan and communal." Global music arrived— King Sunny Ade at the Roxy and Haitian show bands in Queens. Cool itself, one of New York's greatest exports, was finally being defined by the members of the Afro-Atlantic diaspora who'd inspired it; the qualities of cool swallowed whole by American culture—the remove, the composure, the balance, the command—identified finally as African. "Many Westerners . . . ," he continued, "have been using the ecstasy and the brilliance of the arts of cool people, even performing these traditions, without considering their philosophic power. The tradition is known as an idiom of the streets but rarely comprehended for what, in fact, it is: a symbolically generous aesthetic organization of reality." Cool was changing from being about *against* to being about *for*; urban blasé understood as courage in the face of horrors. "It seemed like we had won," says Charlie Ahearn. "The apartheid culture that I'd been so against disappeared."

Meanwhile, dealer Annina Nosei had installed Basquiat in the basement of her gallery where she now brought collectors to watch him light joints, crank Billie Holiday, and turn out paintings part Charlie Parker, part MC, lush and playful but with jagged edges and concrete poetry that explored America, history, and the streets, and how he fit into each of them. Thompson saw it as a "search for wholeness," but the spectacle of Basquiat seemed as much on display as his art. He played along with this plantation arrangement, though, and a year after he'd been scribbling on his own refrigerator door, he made his SoHo debut alongside Haring, Barbara Kruger, and Jenny Holzer. His paintings now fetched as much as $10,000 so he pumped them out as fast as he could, cash hanging out of the pockets of the Armani suits he now painted in, mocking—and living—the big-dick, big-time artist mythos of Schnabel. In the new year, Nosei moved him into a loft. Still only twenty-two, drowning under drugs and his dreams coming true, Basquiat brought his girlfriend Suzanne Mallouk in for ballast but instead they just sunk, papering the windows while he entertained paranoid fantasies about the CIA and obsessed over how much race may have factored into his fame. "He very much wanted to be colorless," said Mallouk. Money was the only measure he could truly count on. Mallouk left and Basquiat, freebasing now, had his frame stretcher drive him aimlessly through the streets.

It Begins

Just two nights before Reagan had signed the tax bill in August 1981, some 80 men had packed into a book-lined apartment overlooking the Washington Square Arch, a clean, open space, white and charcoal gray. Unlike Mrs. Astor, Larry Kramer hadn't carefully trimmed the guest list; he'd invited every gay man he and his friend Paul Popham knew. No one wanted to be there. Kramer's novel *Faggots* had satirized these men, from the high-fashion, influential Disco A-list to the Stonewall activists, mocked them for being shallow and obsessed with sex, and since then he'd been *persona non grata* in much of Gay New York.

But something strange and horrible was happening.

It had come on quickly that spring, after the first few deaths in the fall. Young men straggling nervous and puzzled into St. Luke's, NYU, and Beth Israel, their lymph glands swollen, bodies covered in spots ranging from large dark lesions to pink and hard to see. At first doctors couldn't make a diagnosis because what they saw was so unlikely—Kaposi's sarcoma was usually found in old Jewish or Italian men, or in Equatorial Africa. But by April a number of doctors including NYU dermatologist Dr. Alvin Friedman-Kien had seen dozens of cases and the men were developing other cancers, too, were contracting meningitis, going blind; their immune systems had seemingly collapsed, allowing infections like pneumonia to ravage them swiftly and brutally from within. Death came with delirium, pain, and diarrhea; a terrifying wasting away that made dignity almost impossible. Was it poppers? All the patients had used them. They all had a history of sexually transmitted diseases, too, but who didn't? Straight or gay, if you fucked around, you eventually caught *something*—Chlamydia was just the latest to join syphilis, gonorrhea, shigellosis, amebiasis, heps A, B, and C, and the dreaded herpes, all of which were on the rise in New York City; certain GI infections were up 7,000% in the last five years. Still, no one could say *for sure* sex was involved. Through the spring, as David Stockman slashed the Federal budget and more men stumbled into emergency rooms or were carried in the arms of their lovers, doctors in New York, San Francisco, and Atlanta compared notes. In June, the CDC published the first report followed a month later by a *Times* piece titled "Rare Cancer Seen in 41 Homosexuals."

Soon after it came out, Larry Kramer went for a checkup from Friedman-Kien, who'd been quoted in the article. While there, he'd run into a friend who worked at the Joffrey Ballet. They chatted, waiting for their results, until finally his friend said he had Kaposi's. Kramer, a writer, had no words. Some kind of horror lay ahead for this man, maybe for him, too; a withering, wracking path that didn't even have a name, then an early end. He'd never been an activist—"Larry was anti-movement before he got involved in the movement," says journalist Andy Humm—and many other gay men were considering how to respond. But Kramer couldn't wait. He'd sounded the alarm.

Dr. Friedman-Kien explained to the room what they knew so far and asked for money to help start research. "It was completely sobering and scary," says Humm. "You could have heard a pin drop." What should they do in the meantime? Stop having sex, said the doctor. This didn't go over well. After fighting so long for their sexual freedom they weren't about to suddenly go celibate because of some new bug. "Gay liberation then," says playwright William Hoffman, "was about fucking anyone you wanted to at any time of the day or night and the rest is bourgeois nonsense." It didn't help matters that Kramer's relationship with his own homosexuality was complex; while a Yale undergrad, he'd tried to commit suicide when he'd realized he was gay. Stout and intense, his deep dramatic passions could fog his better judgment. After a stint in the William Morris mailroom, he'd found success in the movie business but less so in the clubs, the bathhouses, and the Pines on Fire Island, where he never found the community Samuel Delany had in the gay theaters of Times Square. When he finally fell in love, the man he loved didn't want to commit. "[N]o relationship," said Kramer later, "could withstand the baggage that we were putting on it by having so much sex with so many different people." So he wrote *Faggots*, which chased his lover away and now he was alone. There were no paintings on his walls; he'd rather watch the shadows move, the moonlight filtering through the trees.

That night raised $6,635. But Kramer wanted to create a new kind of gay network. His first article about the epidemic in *The Native* touched off accusations that he was overreacting. He pled for more news coverage, begged Herb Rickman, Koch's liaison to Gay New York, for money, help, education—while health commissioner Dr. David Sencer advised Koch that no funding was necessary. Given that even some of the gay community needed to be convinced there was a problem, the administration's lack of action in the early stages was not altogether unsurprising, but Koch's silence was bitter. When asked whether he was gay, he answered, "Fuck off. There have to be some private matters left."

One of Us

So began the Age of the Individual in New York, led by a man who considered himself one above all else. Going into the election that fall, Koch had political capital to burn. "I always like to tweak people if I can," said the mayor. "Especially if I don't like them. This is something vicious in me." "Vicious or not," nodded *New York*, "the city loves the mayor's act. He's one of us." And who exactly "we" were at the end of the Retrenchment was coming into focus. Most of "us" were not gay and maybe too excited about this year's Met Gala—The Eighteenth Century Woman—or the new Big Apple Circus at Lincoln Center to notice the babies born in the Bronx with symptoms oddly similar to those of the sick gay men; or the street people, mostly needle users, appearing in hospitals with what just looked like the same diseases of filth, poverty, and despair that had forever killed the poor. "We" would all get around to doing something about *those* things once everything else was fixed.

Nor were "we" one of those unfortunates living on the street, once upon a time called hobos but now known as "the homeless." No one knew the exact scope of the problem; a much-discussed 1981 study guessed that there were some 36,000. City psychiatric wards were overrun, beds lined hallways, certain streets, plazas, and intersections given over to poor, often mentally unstable, often drug- and/or alcohol-addicted men and women. The seeds went back to the '50s. Until then the City had considered SROs the lowest—albeit necessary—rung on the ladder, but the social push toward the nuclear family led it to gradually drive out housing varieties aimed at singles, encouraging the conversion of SROs to market apartments just as the number of at-risk singles exploded; 127,000 units in 1970 had fallen to 20,000 in 1981. At the same time, professional consensus shifted to outpatient treatment, allowing the State to empty its mental hospitals. Patients' rights cases and new drug therapies all but ended involuntary commitment and conservatives were only too happy to slash those budget lines. Between 1968 and 1978, State psychiatric hospitals had gone from 78,000 patients to 26,000, dumping those discharged into the remaining Upper West Side SROs, and admitting only the most severe new cases. Recent budget cuts hadn't helped, but the system had already been gutted. "We are not a shelter," said Sarah Connell of the State Office of Mental Health.

The City, on the other hand, was legally bound to provide clean and safe shelter for *every* homeless person due to Robert Hayes, a twenty-five-year-old lawyer whose suit on behalf of six homeless men living near his Chelsea apartment had led to a consent decree in August 1981 requiring New York to make that unprecedented and ultimately impossible promise. No one would ever be satisfied; Hayes and his Coalition for the Homeless fought on for higher quality shelters when the City couldn't even provide enough that was poor. City Hall viewed homelessness as a health issue fueled by State cuts and, as with the terrifying ailment striking gay men, there was no easy solution; there weren't even difficult ones. Two new urban crises were striking at once—in one, people suffered because of their network; in the other, because they had none. Yet it was easier to keep looking up because no one wanted to fall back into the hole.

Especially because the hole still yawned open. Unemployment was nearing 10% while the limited, intense Growth of the "Wall Street, Madison Avenue, and Broadway recovery" threatened to burn out before it could spread. "[T]he average middle-class tenant has already been forced from most of Manhattan," wrote *New York*, and rising commercial rates were thwarting the City's attempts to keep back-office operations; GM, Union Carbide, Texaco, and Celanese were considering moving altogether. The prices were, in part, a product of the tax abatements already baked in, which meant the abatements originally handed out to encourage risk in a lagging real estate market were now given to discount the high prices they'd help create. Koch called for a review of all of them and denied Trump's application for Trump Tower, dubbing him "Piggy, piggy, piggy." Trump sued.

The nation dipped into what was then its worst recession since the 1930s with manufacturing strangled, often by its own hand as consumers paid higher prices for a "Made in America" label that meant something less than the best; Japanese domination seemed inevitable, and the Vapors' pogo-friendly breakup song "Turning Japanese" became a fatalist anthem. If New York appeared to be holding its own it was because it had a head start in the shift to FIRE, and Retrenchment already had it dealing with the kind of damage Reagan's budget cuts would now inflict nationally. Even with the return of White white-collar workers, though, population continued to slip, driving tax revenue down some $2 billion over the next two years, and FIRE was already proving fickle: the City's 1982 surplus was projected to become an $854 million deficit in 1983.

Balanced budget or not, the Crisis Regime remained unconvinced about the unpredictable Koch. David Rockefeller asked him to bring in former Salomon Brothers partner Ken Lipper as an economic advisor, and it was Rockefeller who'd put on a hard hat at 4:30 a.m. to tour fetid subway tunnels and the next day deliver the Republicans votes in Albany for the MTA rescue plan Ravitch had cobbled together while Koch fixated on graffiti. In March 1982, after reading an *Atlantic* article titled "Broken Windows" that pointed to evidence that "disorder and crime are usually inextricably linked," he'd asked the NYPD to enforce Quality of Life laws "to protect the rights of New Yorkers to safely enjoy the streets of their city." Then he convinced the State legislature to delay the real estate capital gains tax at the heart of the rescue deal, letting developers keep millions the MTA could have used to fix broken windows. By picking through the new tax law, Ravitch found a way to save $600 million on subway cars, then orchestrated a bidding war that saved millions more. When years ahead the trains finally ran on time, it was because Ravitch had figured out how to pay for it. Of course, $1 billion in Federal aid had been available all along if the City had traded in Westway.

And still Ed Koch ended his first term as "the most popular mayor in memory," according to *New York*. "The rebuilding of mayoral power and the easing of the City's fiscal problems . . . ," wrote Charles Brecher and Raymond Horton, "have occurred more rapidly than more observers would have predicted early in 1978." Though he ran on both the Democrat and Republicans lines in 1981, Koch never called himself a "fusion" candidate. Koch was Koch. When 75% of New Yorkers voted for him, they voted for someone who'd enacted startling, painful cuts to the budget, was hated by People of Color (though 60% of Blacks voted for him), and who clashed with the unions. And Reagan's Federal cuts now let him blame the pain on Washington rather than City Hall and the Crisis Regime; the mayor who'd once said, "We love you if you are rich" now called Reaganomics "regressive politics" and launched a misguided, ego-driven run for governor against his old nemesis Mario Cuomo.

The threads were winding together—new building and public space; energized culture and big money; fresh thinking in City Hall. New York was changing into something more creative than ever, but greedier and more violent, even deadly. On April 8, 1982, two thousand men danced at Paradise Garage, under six-foot-wide rolls of paper Keith Haring had covered with black-and-white drawings in Japanese ink. A second meeting at Kramer's apartment had led to the founding of the Gay Men's Health Crisis and this was its coming-out party, the city's favorite dance club miraculously full of gay men writing checks and holding hands as the New York City Gay Men's Chorus sang "He Ain't Heavy, He's My Brother." The illness now went by many names: GRID, for Gay-Related Immunity Deficiency, or ACIDS, Acquired Community Immune Deficiency Syndrome. Some called it Saint's Disease after a particularly unfettered club that most of the victims had visited. By March 1982, 285 cases had been reported, half in New York, yet Koch refused to meet with the GMHC. By May, there were 351; some 40%

percent had died. "I'm worried that I could get it by drinking out of the same glass," wrote Warhol, "or just being around these kids who go to the Baths." *New York* reassured its mainstream readers, calling it "The Gay Plague." Doctors, though, had settled on Acquired Immune Deficiency Syndrome.

AIDS.

Chapter Seven

Be a Card-Carrying Capitalist

While the Salomon Brothers' Executive Committee twiddled their thumbs back in the conference room, Henry Kaufman listened to his secretary read the memo back. Round-headed and jowly, with pointed ears and a unique checkerboard pattern of wrinkles on his forehead, Dr. Kaufman was Salomon's chief economist, his deadpan pronouncements considered delphic by Wall Street. Brought to America at the age of ten to escape the Nazis, his nickname Dr. Doom came from his demeanor as much as his negativity about the economy: At his desk at 7:30 every morning. Gone at 6. He'd spent his recent European vacation considering 10% unemployment, the stock market wallowing under 800, GE trading at 1⅛. For years he'd predicted higher rates and always been right, but with numbers like that, rates *had* to start coming down.

On this morning, August 17, 1982, Dr. Doom officially became a bull.

Kaufman told Helen to release the memo, then went back into the conference room where John Gutfreund, Salomon's CEO, gave him a dirty look. The Jewish outlier on WASPy Wall Street, Salomon Brothers saw itself as a kind of warrior brotherhood, a swaggering meritocracy steeped in ethics where, until its recent merger with Phibro, displays of wealth had traditionally been discouraged. Outside, the news spread of Kaufman's change of heart. Within the hour bonds were up and the opening bell rang in a rally. By ten, stocks and bonds were charging and Gutfreund gleefully canceled the meeting. Dow up 9.32 at 10:30 a.m., on massive volume. Another surge at 1:00 p.m. When the bell rang at 4:00, the Dow finished at 831.24, up 38.81, its biggest day ever.

The world would never be the same. New York's drought had ended: Reservoirs were filling up again Upstate and the Bull Market had arrived. With the goals of the Crisis Regime and the city's young professionals fully merging, the Renaissance flowered. Over the coming thirty years, three booms and busts would each ask serious questions about the power of the FIRE sector, but none would challenge the belief born during the next five that its needs and desires were always in the best interests of New York, turning the pursuit of broad, healthy Growth into the production of ever-greater Wealth.

The conversion was not immediate. Anyone under thirty knew the stock market as the place where retirees put their money, and older generations had scars from earlier crashes, but after eighteen months of the White House promising ponies, America was losing patience; it wanted to be rich again, it wanted to be #1 again, it wanted to *have*. Nine days after the coming of the Bull, *Forbes* published its first list of the 400 richest Americans, with shipping magnate Daniel Ludwig #1, J. P. Getty's son Gordon #2, and David Rockefeller in a twelve-way tie for #3. Thirteen had the rarified, Scrooge McDuck title of "billionaire." The same day, the market traded 137.3 million shares, its fourth 100+ session in a row. By March 1983, "nearly all the doubters have been routed," claimed *New York*. And then the Great Miracle that converted the remaining bears. On May 19 William Simon's company Wesray took Gibson Greeting Cards public. They'd bought it for $80 million, $79 million of which they'd borrowed against its inflated assets; eighteen months later Gibson ended its first day of trading worth $290 million and Simon's personal stake of $330,000 had sprouted like magic beans into $66 million, a return of 20,000%. It was *that* easy, as spectacular and unreal as Reagan's Star Wars defense plan to shoot down Soviet missiles from spaceships. So would begin this cartoon age of garish society and paper profits, of calling ketchup a vegetable.

Unfortunately, the Bull that gilded Renaissance New York did little for most Americans. Eighties Wall Street was about institutional money released by deregulation, mergers and acquisitions, and, most of all, the debt that made it all possible. As John Kenneth Galbraith points out, financial euphoria always starts with new ways to borrow money; this time it was triggered by the Savings & Loan crisis. Volcker's rocketing interest rates had forced S&Ls to offer double digits to new depositors while only getting back single digits on the old thirty-year mortgages on their books. S&Ls were going under, and getting a mortgage was nearly impossible, so in March 1980, with the banking system *and* the housing market on the brink, Carter had signed a law to allow them to issue credit cards, invest in commercial real estate, and offer checking accounts in order to stay in business. Reagan then took it a step further with a change that encouraged S&Ls to sell their mortgages in search of higher returns, freeing up a $1 trillion that needed to be invested in *something*. Which takes us back to Salomon Brothers, where in 1978 one Lew Ranieri had repackaged an old investment product the government had clamped down on during the Depression: A group of home mortgages all backed by government insurance would be bundled together, then sliced into bonds, thus converting the debt some people owed on their homes into an asset for others. Ranieri had been a bit ahead of the curve then—the same high interest rates that killed the S&Ls also made his bonds unattractive—but now deregulation let Salomon buy up the S&Ls' mortgages at a deep discount, bundle them into bonds, and sell them back to the S&Ls who believed they'd diversified into the bond market when in fact they'd just bought ground meat made out of their own steaks. In June 1983, Salomon Brothers and Freddie Mac together issued the first collateralized mortgage obligation bonds (CMOs), which bundled up debt and cut it into tranches based on the amount of risk: you could choose between ground chuck and ground sirloin. It would be years before technology would allow doing this on a huge scale, but the immediate impact was that all kinds of debt, not just mortgages, were bundled, cut into bonds, and sold: credit card debt, car loans, you name it. Between 1983 and 1988, some $60 billion of CMOs were sold; GM's financing arm became more profitable than its cars. America began to make debt instead of things.

The other signature debt product of the '80s was the Junk Bond. Large corporations guarantee a steady flow of operating capital by issuing low-risk bonds, but in the late '70s, Michael Milken at Drexel Burnham had shown that the high-risk, high-yield bonds issued by smaller companies delivered consistently higher returns. These "junk bonds," he claimed, performed a patriotic duty—aggressive ownership could use them to buy underperforming American companies and whip them into globally competitive shape, not through Japanese *Book of Five Rings* managerial brilliance but through the productivity gains (read: layoffs and asset stripping) that they'd have to achieve to service the massive debt they'd undertaken to buy the company in the first place. A network of corporate raiders formed around Milken, buying and selling companies based only on balance sheets. All of this together jolted American business awake, hijacked its purpose, and turned the nation's industrial base into a board game played for tiaras and mansions. By 1983, almost every major bank had an M&A department; financial machinations got priority over research as rowdy traders and Ivy League bankers fought over the new landscape of wealth. Of course, all this was terrific for New York. As the Bull got higher it also got wider, and sustaining that volume mattered to the city more than setting records because it was everything that surrounded the act of buying and selling that stoked its economy. Or Manhattan's. Or at least the parts of Manhattan where a thin layer of New Yorkers were getting absurdly rich.

Loading Software

If money was information, information was money. Since traders in the '50s playing with the racing wire, through Quotron and the Ultronic Stockmaster to Reuters' '70s video terminal that displayed live bids and offers, Wall Street had always wanted as much market information as it could get, as quickly as it could get it. Quotron and ADP were the current leaders in computer services, but one Monday in June 1983, a short man with a nasal voice crammed into a taxi cradling the computer system he believed would change all of that. For six months, Michael Bloomberg and his staff had been working around the clock on this prototype, due today to their one client, Merrill Lynch, but it still wasn't booting. They had to deliver *something*, though, so as the techs kept working, he headed downtown toward another humiliation.

The Bloombergs had been the only Jews in Medford, Massachusetts, and Michael had grown up idolizing Johnny Tremain "sticking it to old George III." As a Johns Hopkins frat boy, he got mostly Cs, but he also had the ingenuity and balls to usually get what he wanted, like the time he offered the guy at the front of the line at the movies twenty bucks to buy him tickets. The combination also got him into Harvard Business School and in 1966 a job at Salomon Brothers, where he came early, left late, and got to know both managing partner Billy Salomon and John Gutfreund, who liked him but didn't love him—"bright, aggressive, fast-talking," was Gutfreund's description. He wasn't the only one with doubts. "He thought he knew more than the people he was working for," said one partner, in particular his boss, who in 1975 exiled Bloomberg to Information Services, Salomon's graphics department off on a vacant floor. Though he took his lumps, Bloomberg still didn't make the cut when Salomon merged with Phibro; Gutfreund personally handed him his pink slip and $10 million severance. Out on the street at thirty-nine, he bought his wife a sable coat and then spent $4 million starting his own company. While there he'd learned the importance of data and that technology needed to be usable to matter, so Innovative Market Services would produce a computer with a desktop terminal and customized keyboard that would give users data on bonds and also let them develop personalized analytics. And today was the moment of truth. He plugged in the components of the first Market Master machine and as it hummed slightly, he shifted into nervous patter with the curious Merrill traders. Then, he later recalled, "I noticed out of the corner of my eye a flashing message on our screen saying 'Loading Software.'" The bug had been fixed.

Bloomberg's timing was perfect. As 100 million+ share days became common—five years before, 20 million was the norm—everyone was using computers to keep up with the volume being created by other computers. But bond traders didn't love Bloomberg; they made their money off other peoples' bad guesses and the Market Master helped turn guesses into educated predictions. Back in the '70s a Brooklyn-born broker named Bernie Madoff, whose bearing and strong Florentine prow belied the fact that his father had invented the punching bag stand, had also tried to democratize Wall Street, developing what he called "a screen-based trading mechanism" for the Over the Counter market, the start of Nasdaq. Bloomberg sold Merrill Lynch a 30% stake in his company and over the next two years he crawled on his hands and knees through offices, literally laying the foundation of the future: a network producing a constant stream of addictive, customizable data, all of which he owned. As Malcolm Forbes once told his grandson Steve, "You make more money selling information than you do following it."

As Finance sped the passage of Renaissance New York into the Information Capital of the World, the loss of manufacturing seemed increasingly evolutionary. City Hall tracked potholes, welfare benefits, and deadbeat dads with computers; Planning could now produce a map in an hour that once took thirty-five. But even as the phone lines of NYTel, the state's largest employer, hummed with data, information was taking at least as much as it gave. Satellite dishes and desktop computers allowed companies to send back-office work not to New Jersey but to Barbados at $1.50 an hour instead of $9. India was next. It wasn't just factories being pushed out; the information economy didn't need low-level paper pushers. "If nothing is done," wrote *New York*, "Manhattan will continue its metamorphosis into a 1980s version of Shanghai in 1937; an international settlement and paradise for the wealthy."

A Pursuit, a Game, a Sport

"No city had ever been so well arranged to meet the world . . . So much was happening . . . ," wrote Diana Vreeland. "Highlife, lowlife, life, life—grandeur and poetry—and a real sense of fun. Life was vital and meant to be lived . . . Society was a pursuit, a game, a sport. Fashion was competition." D.V. wasn't writing about New York, though; she was writing about Paris during La Belle Époque, that exquisite era before World War I when high society danced across continents from Newport to Deauville to St. Petersburg, with the City of Light as its hub. Of course, she did intend the comparison: La Belle Époque was the theme of the Costume Institute's 1982 gala, when the likes of Prince and Princess Edouard de Lobkowicz, the Bloomingdales, the Erteguns, *la* Zipkin, and just *all* the great designers—Perry Ellis, Versace, and Halston to start—in all some 750 members of New York's grande elite of wealth, blood, and style entered the Met's Great Hall, transformed by Vreeland (and $500,000 from Pierre Cardin) into a Parisian street scene and from there on to an exact replica of Maxim's built solely for this dinner. "Don't forget that the belle époque was the culmination of everything having to do with the grandeur of high society, so of course the show is lavish," said Vreeland, a sudden stickler for historical accuracy. "It was a time when women had a lavish belief in their own ecstatic beauty . . ."

Oh, such breathtaking stuff! And it was all happening so quickly, like a ravishing. That the subways were filthy and the streets dangerous only added to the thrill of the limousines, the Scaasi gowns, and the gold-rimmed crystal shimmering in the candlelight; with the contrast came so much of the joy. After Mrs. Astor had given her ruling in the pages of *W* magazine—"People with money and taste are always welcome," she said—and faded Grizabella's envious mewling in *Cats* struck a little too close to home, Old Society with their dry little William Poll sandwiches at last succumbed to what John Fairchild would call Nouvelle Society. "You don't need the oratorical skills of Harold Acton for the power elite to marvel," said *New York*, "your net worth will do nicely." After all, while they worshiped the Windsors and swooned when Charles and Di tied the knot, one of the highest spots in their pantheon went to history's greatest gold digger, Wallis Simpson. Dealmakers and swashbucklers, craven as they were, now got their due for elevating dull banking into an architecture of money. Salomon's merger with Phibro had sprayed a little perfume on its culture, perfume that could have come out of the refrigerator John Gutfreund's wife Susan had in her boudoir for the expressed purpose of chilling her scent. A formidable blonde eighteen years younger than John, she threw elaborate dinners for fifty at their hypermodern duplex in River House. Rail-thin fashion designer Carolyn Roehm wed Henry Kravis, whose KKR controlled companies from Beatrice Foods to Motel 6 for only as long as it took to "reorganize" them and sell the bones. At the very top were the Steinbergs. "I'll own the world," boasted the portly Saul, head of Reliance Group Holdings and part of Milken's network. He'd built up Reliance in the '70s until an ill-advised attempt at taking over Chemical Bank left him, according to one contemporary, "an untouchable." Gayfryd rehabilitated him. Upon arrival, she bought the twenty-one-foot George III dining table, the harp, the Old Masters that lined the walls of their 34-room triplex, all of which he paid for by threatening companies with takeover unless they bought out his position. Even some of the *nouvelle* found them *un peu gauche*.

All this money pulsed through the city like a sugar rush, or maybe long fat rails of coke, all sexy, jumpy, and arrogant, full of stories. Diana Vreeland had captured the moment exquisitely by featuring La Belle Époque and its demimonde, its Odettes and Swanns who transcended class and history by negotiating complex arrangements of sex and power poignantly mirroring those of New York's parvenues. Like the young artists in the East Village, this new "elite" was largely a brigade of middle-class strivers come to New York to become someone else: Ivan Boesky's father owned a deli in Detroit; Carolyn Roehm had been born Jane Smith in Missouri; Susan Gutfreund had been an airline hostess; Gayfryd Steinberg's father was a clerk. Ralph Lauren, born Ralph Lifshitz on the Grand Concourse, transformed the old Rhinelander mansion at 72nd and Madison into what John Taylor called "a sort of elaborate stage set on which the professional classes could act out the seemingly bottomless well of aristocratic aspirations . . ." Vreeland understood "the Working Rich" as she herself had always worked, as an editor at *Harper's Bazaar* and then *Vogue*, where she'd set the terms of fashion and elegance until she was fired without ceremony in 1971 for her almost gleeful disdain of budgets but also the sense that her passion for excess had fallen out of step; Hoving had brought her into the Costume Institute as an act of mercy. Her position as New York's style doyenne was indeed a job, but one that she, like Warhol keeping tab of every cab fare and dinner at Le Cirque ("the new Republican restaurant," he called it), lived completely. No great beauty, something her mother had repeatedly told her and everyone within earshot when she was a child, Vreeland made style into something forgiving, an exercise of the mind and soul that the new rich could use to seal away their past.

But while the *nouvelle* caught up on Proust, what they *really* craved was public confirmation that their ascent was deserved. Ultimately the biggest difference between the new and the old was something sociologist Jerome Karabel observed: In a meritocracy, the winners, believing they've earned their success, "may be more self-righteous about their elite status than is a more traditional ruling group." The *nouvelle* felt unconnected to any of the responsibilities that traditionally went with aristocracy; *noblesse* without the *oblige*. "Sometimes," wrote Fairchild, "no, often—they forget that the rest of the world is living another way." But they never really forgot; making inequality visible was the whole point, a constant reminder of how far they'd come.

To scale the true aeries of High Society, though, they'd have to learn how to give it away. Philanthropy is the glue that binds High Society. Taxes, it is felt, pay for the poor, while philanthropy supports the pillars of their way of life, the museums, the operas, and hospitals while weaving together Society, Business, and Government through intersecting boards, reciprocal donations and galas. On one level this was easy enough. For the second wife of an everyday millionaire to be photographed in a Saint Laurent gown, she had to be invited to galas, and to be invited she had to donate. The cause was not always deeply held; fundraisers for the NYPL complained that "when they go to people for money, they are sometimes told to go back to Brooke Astor and ask her for more." True power philanthropy, though, involved more than buying tickets. At the upper reaches of society you were invited to literally buy your place: the New York Public Library, the Metropolitan Opera, the Zoological Society, MoMA, or one of the other cultural institutions would offer you a seat on the board in exchange for a suitably hefty donation and access to *your* power network, which would in turn connect you to the networks of your fellow board members and their own respectability, influence, and soft power. Those in a hurry selected smaller targets; the Steinbergs, for instance, made PEN their cause, to the annoyance of some of its literary membership. But the best things were not rushed. The board of all boards was the Metropolitan Museum of Art, and even Henry Kravis who'd knocked at the door by donating $10 million, still had to sit quietly and wait for it to open.

We Decided We Liked the Place

Finance wasn't solely responsible for the excess. That first *Forbes* list included thirteen New York developers, many of whom now made themselves more visible as the broad real estate market rose and the changing built environment made big fortunes even bigger. Development had always required strong, ongoing relationships with everyone from construction unions to community boards, but now families such as the Tishmans, the Speyers, and the Roses turned more conspicuously philanthropic and social. Helmsley and Trump, for their part, just turned more social. Harry and Leona displayed almost touching pretentions; ubiquitous ads positioning her as "the Queen of the Palace" had her poking around hotels rooms in a tiara to assure guests of the highest quality towels and cocktail shrimp. "She has done," wrote Bernice Kanner, "for her hotels what Frank Perdue has done for his chickens." While her goofy persona offered the common man a taste of the new grandeur, when the tiara came off, she said, "We don't pay taxes. Only the little people pay taxes."

Donald Trump hadn't even belonged on the first *Forbes* list. With a net worth only around $5 million—much of that financed with debt secured by his father—he tried to convince the reporter that he was the richest developer in New York City, worth nearly a billion dollars. "This was a model Trump would use for the rest of his career," wrote the reporter later, "telling a lie so cosmic that people believed that *some* kernel of it had to be real." *Forbes* credited him with $100 million, a public overestimate he then parleyed into credibility and entree into Nouvelle Society for their gold leaf, petty dictator tastes. "In fifty years," claimed Ivana, "Donald and I will be considered old money like the Vanderbilts." Trump Tower opened in November 1983, after the State Supreme Court awarded him his tax break for housing the Saudi royal family and Baby Doc Duvalier. Inside its handsome Der Scutt exterior was a five-story pink marble and bronze mall resembling the world's largest powder room, its three-speed "waterwall" plashing encouragement amid the wares of Asprey and Buccellati. Though *The New Yorker* joked about doormen in "operetta uniforms," its measured first-person plural bought in: "We decided we liked the place. Liked the patina, the crowds. Liked riding the elevators."

Few topped Trump when it came to taking public money, and few so avidly handed New York over to foreign investors. "New York was conquered by outside people like myself," said Greek architect Constantine Kondylis, who would design dozens of unremarkable "luxury" buildings in Manhattan, including Trump Plaza. "The city became more international, more cosmopolitan." Indeed, New York City was playing a smaller role in the American economy, but a larger role in the world one; its companies now tended to operate globally as the number of foreign banks in the city went from 84 in 1976 to 191 in 1985. But all the foreign attention wasn't necessarily beneficial. Every visitor from Monte Carlo dining at Mrs. Astor's table validated the emphasis on attracting tourists and a global business elite over New York's long-term health. The infusion of foreign money in real estate, for one, boosted prices to levels that drove pension funds out of their traditional investments in middle-income housing, into Salomon's lucrative bonds.

The City tried to keep ahead. As rising Midtown rents shuttered small and beloved old retailers, City Planning rezoned Chelsea and the Flatiron District to encourage manufacturing, but that only brought "commercially driven gentrification" south. Viking Press moved to the old Stern's department store at 40 West 23rd Street with computer terminals and open loftlike spaces that, said *New York*, "could be the model for the Flatiron district's future." Other publishers like Farrar, Strauss and Giroux, Abrams, and Scribner's followed, lunching amid casual Boomer elegance at Danny Meyer's Union Square Cafe. In Times Square, Jane Dickson dodged drug dealers to keep painting strip joints and muggings even as she and Charlie had their first kid, but reality now outweighed the romance. "It was ugly, and it was desperate," recalls Charlie. "If anyone went there in the '80s and thought it was cool, they just didn't know better." Despite some legendary productions between 1984 and 1987—*Sunday in the Park with George, Fences, Glengarry Glen Ross*, to start—half the legitimate theaters on Broadway were dark. But the City and the State had news about Times Square.

After Koch had chosen seltzer over orange juice, the State had taken the lead in its redevelopment—it had broader powers of eminent domain and could get around much of the City's regulatory process—but with Sturz directing behind the scenes. The 42nd Street Development project they came up with would put the risk on the developers to buy the land in return for, yes, some abatements, but mostly the right to build massive office buildings that would let them recoup their money fast. In June 1981, the City had issued 150 pages of guidelines for four million square feet of office space, a hotel, and a merchandise mart, while Koch charged the new Theater Advisory Council with figuring out what to do with forty-four theaters within a special district intended to transform the area into a preserve of middle-class entertainment. The public wouldn't be out of pocket—but Times Square wouldn't really be theirs anymore; it would be handed to the FIRE sector, which only became apparent two years later, when Philip Johnson and his partner John Burgee presented their almost amusingly awful plan in December 1983: four massive, insipid towers that would stuff sexy, dirty, beyond the pale Times Square, meeting place of classes, races, genders, Eugene O'Neill, *shaolin*, and Tin Pan Alley into a faddish postmodern suit whose lapels already felt a little too wide. "We're giving Times Square an identity it doesn't have now," said Burgee about the most identifiable 13 acres in all of New York. Jaws dropped. Holly Whyte said "undue despair" was not called for—*yet*—and the two went back to their drafting tables.

Forty-seven lawsuits were filed, bundling two groups of unlikely allies. Adult bookstore and peep show owners lined up with landlords who didn't want their property taken, while the second group, led by the Municipal Art Society and fueled by the dismal Marriott Marquis rising on 45th Street, challenged the quality of the plans. Architect Hugh Hardy, originally a set designer, feared another Pennsylvania Station tragedy; his subcommittee, run with Nicholas Quennell, defined Times Square as a "Bowl of Light" and organized a one-night blackout of the area to demonstrate the potential impact of Johnson's plan. Still, in November 1984 every major player in the State and City argued to the Board of Estimate that it was the City's chance to do something big again. To general dismay, the Board voted yes and 99-year leases were signed. Abatements and zoning laws were amended, bonuses offered, to direct the future of Manhattan into higher, denser buildings west of Sixth Avenue.

The Bull stomped forward. The Renaissance gleamed. An ad for Citicorp/Diners Club proudly suggested "Be a Card-Carrying Capitalist." That fall, the other oxford dropped after *Wealth and Poverty*, with permanent effect on New York, and America. George Gilder chose a new president for his think tank, the very nonacademic former encyclopedia salesman William Hammett, who repackaged it into the

Manhattan Institute for Policy Research and published *Losing Ground* by Charles Murray, a disaffected liberal academic who claimed that welfare recipients were making the same kind of cost-benefit analysis as any businessman, choosing what paid the highest return in the short term even if it damaged their long-term prospects. The fault, he believed, was on liberals for not incentivizing poor, young, black men to leave their damaged communities and their self-defeating sensibilities. Hammering an intellectual veneer on Gilder's greed, it changed future debate over public spending from how do we help our fellow Americans to an argument about why we shouldn't.

The Bull got fatter. From 1984 to 1987, LBOs and other buybacks took more than $250 billion worth of stock out of the market, driving demand up further for what remained. Between July 1982 and July 1986, the Dow had doubled. *Harper's* editor Lewis Lapham called money "the sickness of the town." In January 1986, Drexel Burnham was making a deal for 47 floors at 7 World Trade Center. One-third of Yale's Class of 1986 applied for analyst jobs at First Boston. "That," said one old hand, "is the sign of a top." Ivan Boesky defined the era with a speech he delivered to Berkeley's business school that spring: "Greed is all right . . . ," he said. "I think greed is healthy. You can be greedy and still feel good about yourself." *Wall Street* director Oliver Stone would boil it down even further for Gordon Gecko: "Greed is good."

Chapter Eight

They Begin to Blossom

The day before Dr. Doom heralded the Bull, *New York* ran an article titled "Downward Mobility," with dry-as–melba toast sketches depicting moments of quiet desperation among the city's thirty-something professional class. As one couple cleaned up their cramped apartment after a dinner party and another decided to use the husband's raise on an exterminator, the piece warned that "the baby boom generation may never achieve the relative economic success of the generation immediately preceding it or following it." Indeed, the dollars of those who'd dropped acid at Woodstock and fought at Khe Sanh were worth a third of the ones they'd grown up with, and after My Lai, Watergate, and Iran, they were disillusioned and scared they'd never have the classic six they were meant to have; scared they'd spend their lives running in place. In one drawing, a doctor with the start of a paunch tells his friend, "When I said I didn't care about 'things,' it was the '6os, when 'things' were still in reach."

And then Henry Kaufman had changed his mind.

Not only did the Bull make its glorious return in 1982, but *The Big Chill* began filming, Martha Stewart published *Entertaining*, and in February, gap-toothed, white-bread David Letterman debuted *Late Night* on NBC, announcing the coming-of-age of the television generation. Those young White, white-collar workers now had a name: the Yuppies, short for Young Urban Professionals. And suddenly they could have all

111

the expectations they wanted because the Bull provided this disillusioned generation with a purpose again and a means to finally climb over Dad. It was time to either jump up or fall. There was money to be had now, money you deserved because the President said so and because you'd gone to a good school. Or because you didn't: the New Deal laws that had kept banking safe and dull had also kept strivers out, but breaking those laws down opened the sector to hungrier, smarter people from the other side of the tracks. In July 1982, New York for the first time employed more people in the FIRE sectors than in manufacturing, a "growing breed of middle-echelon white-collar worker" that *New York* felt was "the only really good thing" the city's economy had going. While the dirt and crime let these twenty- and thirty-somethings consider themselves Urban Pioneers, they were a different breed than that first wave of Back to the City types. Sinatra's new and inescapable cover of "New York, New York" called to the world's bootstrappers and social climbers to make it there so they could make it anywhere.

Yet while each Yuppie came individually wrapped in the confidence that they were an exceptional member of the meritocracy, they expressed their individuality by doing what all the other Yuppies were doing at the moment, connected to each other by one of the unpleasant truths of social network theory: "Like goes to like." Daniel Bell called this a "status society," and it applied to Yuppies as much as it did to the Nouvelle Society; in a meritocracy, your class is something active, made of your networks and your primacy in them. *Where* you worked mattered more than what you did; where you went to school mattered more than what you learned, because those places created ties. The density of young, largely White professionals pouring into New York meant all kinds of new weak ties connecting friends to friends of friends; a twenty-six-year-old lawyer on the Upper East Side could have literally thousands more connections than someone their age in the Bronx, and through those connections came useful information: job tips, stock tips, heads up on an apartment, a cute guy your sorority sister could fix you up with; altogether a mountain of social capital that made them an immense force. The problem was, they only liked to share with each other. As Charles Kadushin points out, social networks are "essentially unfair" because of one of their other basic rules: he who has a lot gets more. Fed by fear as much as greed, Yuppies grafted the upper-class tastes and entitlements they'd internalized onto the Back to the City movement, creating the vast generational Lifestyle network that would drive Renaissance New York.

If David Letterman's cheerful cynicism and good suits embodied Yuppiedom, the yuppiest of all neighborhoods was the Upper West Side, the next stop of the renewal impulse after SoHo and Brownstone Brooklyn. Unlike the wealthy, White, and respectable Upper East Side, the Upper West Side began the decade down in all three categories. Born a bourgeois district of brownstones and sprawling apartments between two Olmsted parks, it had aged into a gracious dump full of elderly Jews, gays, counterculture liberals, angry Puerto Ricans displaced by Lincoln Center, and junkies in the once-glorious Belleclaire Hotel; Riverside Park was off-limits after dark, and residents mapped their itineraries to avoid dangerous blocks. But it was also a vibrant dump, the "authentic" alternative to the tight-ass, Republican East Side across the park, home of Debbie Harry and John and Yoko. "It was very hippie," said Bil Rock, a graffiti artist who grew up there. "Not sandals and Grateful Dead, but more like sneak cokeheads and Sly and the Family Stone." Much of the city's Black intelligentsia lived there, too, people like Maya Angelou, Harry Belafonte, and Miles Davis, with Mikell's at 97th and Columbus their musical and literary locus, jazz and funk mingling with sightings of James Baldwin. And there was sex. The Soldiers and Sailors Monument at 89th and Riverside had been a gay pick-up spot since at least the '30s and of course there was Plato's Retreat in the Ansonia. But when a club called Ruelle's opened in 1979 on Columbus Avenue, a Whiter, more fashion-forward sort began visiting, small boutiques sprouted, and by 1982, there was a new street to saunter SoHo-style, featuring shops like Charivari, the first "curated fashion store" with its Japanese and Belgian designers. Few tears were shed for the old businesses being shoved out—"Most of what has had to go was filthy and full of junk," said one local.

Food played a larger role in defining Lifestyle here than Dean & DeLuca or Raoul's had in SoHo. When City Hall streamlined the process for sidewalk cafés in 1981—"one more tool," said one local, "in giving the sidewalks back to the people"—their number almost tripled, especially along Columbus. Twenty-four-hour Korean groceries served up fresh fruit and vegetables along with pools of bright light on dark streets. Specialty grocer Fairway and its neighbor on Broadway, Citarella seafood shop, began to expand, and the Silver Palate built on the identities of nearby Jewish deli stalwarts like Zabar's, Murray's, and Barney Greengrass. Dining out was rougher until Keith McNally ventured up from Odeon to open Café Luxembourg: "What a joy," kvelled Gael Greene, "to have something wonderful to eat besides Chinese food north of Columbus Circle." Throughout the city, "[a]ffluence begat gourmets who wanted tomatoes and mozzarella, not meat and potatoes." Yuppies explored daring new cheeses like Havarti and chèvre, sipped oaky Chardonnay and sliced their own bread; it was snobbery, but it was also a generation raised on TV dinners, uninterested in the high social haute cuisine of Lutèce and La Côte Basque, discovering real food for themselves. Fine dining now was, reported Patricia Morrisroe, "a necessary social ritual . . . More and more people feel entitled to what was once the preserve of the wealthy, and in accommodating these people, restauranteurs have democratized dining." As diners learned more, quality mattered more; by 1984, more than half restaurants passed their health inspection the first time around. The 1986 arrival of Le Bernardin from Paris was arguably New York's comestible coming-of-age.

Tastes of all kinds are spread through networks, so Yuppies were susceptible to many raging epidemics—mid-century furniture, cocaine, and the natural fiber preppy looks of the Popular Club Plan catalogue that morphed into J.Crew. They went to Shea Stadium to watch the Mets, a team as loud, abrasive, and impressed with itself as a cab full of junior analysts, and hung out at Rouse's South Street Seaport, which proved to be no Quincy Market. Most important, Yuppies began to make the digital part of their daily lives. Compact discs arrived—"these cute little devils will make the LP obsolete," warned one writer. With the New York Public Library still offering a free research phone line, PCs cracked the consumer market in 1983. A mostly male audience browsed the latest software at J&R to run on their 48K of memory. An idea that NYU's ITP had been playing with for years quietly emerged as the first bulletin board systems. "Not since the advent of the telephone," wrote New York, "have people experienced such a totally new method of relating to one another." The transforming moment, though, took place during the third quarter of Super Bowl XVIII the night of January 22, 1984, in a commercial clearly inspired by Orwell: As ragged gray figures shuffle past a massive screen of Big Brother, a busty blonde in a bright white tank top runs in and flings a sledgehammer at the screen, smashing it to pieces. "On January 24th," said a voice, "Apple Computer will introduce Macintosh. And you'll see why 1984 won't be like *1984*." In those sixty seconds, Steve Jobs and director Ridley Scott flipped the meaning of computers; buying an Apple with its "mouse" and "icons" and "windows" was a way to fight The Man. Even Warhol himself started shilling for Commodore—"I'm gonna tell everyone to get one," he said at a press event. Personal computing made money only that much more unreal. Computer banking began in 1983 with Chemical Bank's Pronto system. Gone was Manny Hanny's vault on Fifth Avenue, long a sign of stability and strength; Wriston's dream of the financial supermarket came true as Yuppies streamed into Citibank bearing the regularly bad advice of Louis Rukeyser's *Wall Street Week in Review*.

Yuppies also changed sex and parenting in New York. The city's historically high number of singles young and old was one reason real estate was so expensive, but the free love era now ended. Yuppies were not obsessed with sex. Money had gone from an aphrodisiac to the point itself. Herpes and that gay plague also had both sexes thinking twice before hopping in the sack; personal ads thrived in the *Village Voice* and *New York*, but instead of declaring fetishes, they now featured words like *commitment* and *marriage*. Biological clocks ticked loudly over the pick-up lines. "[W]ith yuppies and AIDS," said Alexander Liberman, "I think New York is the unsexiest place on earth." Children in Manhattan had long been something of a curiosity, but Yuppies approached parenting with their characteristic fever for acquisition and competition. The result would be generations of what Richard Sennett would call "Intense Families" driven by their own internal needs more than the needs of any given community. *New York* devoted an entire issue to the dressing and feeding of children, which restaurants would put up with them, and how to find good help. It also reported on a new phenomenon: "formal 'play dates' that often involve time-consuming transport and lack the spontaneity of backyard play." Those blessed with the unique burden of a "gifted child" were advised to "accept the child's special talents and not worry that they are being elitist." White children were a *truly* blessed event—between 1970 and 1980, their numbers had dropped 45% in New York. Many who once considered the public school system akin to sanitation were now reassured that "[t]here is an upper tier of public schools that do an excellent job of educating children"—of course, the *White* before *children* was simply understood. But that wasn't good enough, not really, and so the great race began to get Jason or Jennifer into the right nursery school. Once again, the cash-waving meritocracy pried open a preserve of the wealthy, creating a new business for tutors as "the pressure to get into a brand-name college . . . reached a critical point." One particularly horrifying Nickelodeon ad featured precocious moppets making shock statements like "Our father is a lawyer, our mother is a judge" and "We have two cars, three cats, and my mother earns more than her father ever did. No wonder I'm a Yuppie Puppie!" In one of the few kindnesses of the age, that phrase did not stick.

The foundation of all this on the Upper West Side was homeownership. For twenty years the City had been encouraging with little success a combination of brownstone revival on side streets and urban renewal on the avenues, but now a combination of practical factors beyond taste had launched this stampede into its rambling old apartments. First, mortgage rates dropped from 16% to 10.5% from 1981 to 1983. Second, a new four-tier property tax system was put in place that encouraged people to buy brownstones and apartments, while walloping small businesses with commercial rent taxes. Over the next twenty years, the effective property tax for homeowners would drop more than 65% even as it ate away at local businesses. Third, there was supply. J-51 tax breaks had fostered a wave of apartment conversions, but also Federal tax changes incentivized the big real estate families to convert more of their middle-class rentals into co-ops, which then leased the street-level retail to third-party landlords. Add to that three major new developments at 68th, 79th, and 96th, and a series of large, publicly funded low- and middle-income sites north of 86th. Finally, obviously, the Bull was throwing off the money to pay for it all.

This suddenly regenerating Upper West Side—according to *New York,* "without doubt one of the most striking examples of urban revitalization in recent memory"—vindicated Jane Jacobs at least as much as anything about the West Village; rather than government plans, a few smaller, directed changes had let the market do the work. If SoHo was an act of repurposing the city's industrial history, the Upper West Side offered a return to upper-middle-class domesticity with a diversity not found on the East Side; a Lifestyle that let you eat your cake and consider it a *mitzvah*. But the problems that arose over the next fifteen years spoke directly to some drawbacks in Jacobs's thinking. The new building and conversions meant displacement; brownstones went from multi-unit apartments into single-family homes, SROs went co-op, and some early J-51 buildings aged out of their abatements, allowing the landlords to jack up rents. A culture clash became palpable in schools and playgrounds, in the buildings filling up with professionals; at the Columbia on 96th, for example, fully a third of new buyers were lawyers. "[T]here's a real schism between the pre-conversion and post-conversion people," said a resident of a nearby building. "A new breed is taking over, and there's a lot of hostility. People are separated by age and economic class." But they were also separated by culture. Rather than restoring networks or adding new connections, Lifestyle usually superimposed new networks onto the old neighborhood. Fresh Yuppie arrivals wanted things the way *they* wanted them, so positive involvement in parks and public schools often became battles for control in a neighborhood that already had a powerful tradition of activism. Attempts to create commonplace civilization turned into hostile takeovers as Yuppies unilaterally "saved" spaces and forced longtime residents into siege mentalities with the message, as one writer described it, "Fuck you, Jack. I *won* this contest already." On the other hand, sincere attempts by newcomers to enter existing networks were often rebuffed, with locals pulling into their own tighter, self-defeating ones. Sometimes the conflicts were internal; buying your co-op turned you from an aggrieved tenant into a taxpaying owner who suddenly had a financial interest in the surrounding area. Old hippies reading their buildings' new bylaws understood time was not on their side.

A force of change and an invading army, Yuppies weren't just on the Upper West Side. Chelsea was attracting interest; 61% of its residents were single in 1987 and the revamped Barney's was opening on

18th. City Hall accepted Manhattan's high real estate prices as a way to spread growth into the other boroughs. "[I]t's not a penal sentence to live in Flatbush," said Louis Winnick. But those who did move didn't always do so because of the rent—Lifestyle was out there, too. "The whole notion of having to live in Manhattan is getting very outdated," opined one theater producer, as artists scoped out loft spaces in Brooklyn and Queens. Citywide, close to 100,000 rental units were converted from 1981 to 1986, changing the texture of many neighborhoods: 37% of owners had higher median incomes than the people they replaced, usually about twice as much, and until 1983 most co-op conversions involved evictions.

Old Crisis Regime dreams of catalytic bigness met Yuppie aspirations in a new piece of the city's built environment: Battery Park City, which the State had taken over and put in the hands of UDC head Richard Kahan. His first task was a full redesign, and that job went to another member of the new generation of administrators, Amanda Burden. Unlike Nat Leventhal, whose father had sold trousers, her stepfather was CBS CEO William Paley and her mother the premier socialite Babe Paley, and though *Vogue* had featured the willowy debutante at twenty-one, lounging with her husband Carter Burden in their Dakota apartment, she'd grown up steeped in the workings of the city courtesy of her civic-minded stepfather. In 1972, divorced with two children, she went back to college in hopes of joining Jane Goodall in Gombe until she ran into her friend Fred Kent, who introduced her to Holly Whyte. "Holly lifted a scrim off the city," says Burden, "from how we were used to looking at the city and opened our eyes to what makes cities work." After a stint at the Project for Public Spaces, she went to the UDC where she became vice president for design review and public space for Battery Park City. Burden wanted it to be "an extension of the city" imbued with Whyte's precepts, so architects Cooper and Eckstut studied the UWS, Gramercy Park, and Fifth Avenue as they developed guidelines that each developer would interpret in their own ways, compressing the organic process of a diverse urban landscape. Olympia & York won the bidding and starting with the Esplanade in 1983, "the largest and most expensive real estate venture ever undertaken in New York City" rose with a stately sort of idiosyncrasy. While most applauded the triumph of Jacobs-style development, it was largely forgotten that Nelson Rockefeller's democratic ideal of an explicitly mixed-income community had been transformed into a luxury enclave. Upper West Side by the Sea would ultimately house some 2,200 units full of young financiers drawn by its proximity to Wall Street more than its brilliant underpinnings. Art on the Beach held its last event in 1985, a Sun Ra concert and a David Hammons construction called *Delta Spirit* and over time West Street became a kind of moat.

For all their narcissism and consumerism, though, Yuppies represented a version of hope. They believed New York had a future, and for every asshat with slicked-back hair snorting baby powder at velvet-walled Nell's there were two midlevel executives who sincerely wanted to raise their kids here because of its diversity, stimulation, and exchange, who were throwing their lot in with New York and showing their faith by demanding more from it. Yuppies saw things they could fix and put themselves to the task. There were more trees and fewer broken windows. And some *were* having second thoughts about the constant pursuit of success and status. "This is a treadmill," said one young analyst, "and once you jump off, even for a second, you are *gone*." The number of psychologists in the city had doubled since Koch took office and Wellbutrin was now readily available. Channel 4 ran a special report in 1986 about "a whole new class of poor in New York. The Middle Class. People with decent jobs. Respectable salaries. And less to show for it than ever before." But ultimately, Yuppies' greatest interests were their own well-being, their hero now Jerry Rubin, who'd gone from Yippie provocateur to Yuppie banker. "The most dramatic shift in the city's psychology . . . ," said Felix Rohatyn, "has been the recognition of the absolute need for business to be here to support the city." With its values entirely internalized, the Crisis Regime stood down and watched the Bull roar ahead. Yet this upbeat, better-groomed city of *The Cosby Show* and *Kate & Allie* remained unsafe and disgusting; trash incineration was phased out, so the roach population exploded. Manufacturing continued to drop. It proved dangerous to place hope in the hands of Yuppies. As they chose between a Yamamoto jacket and one of Donna Karan's Seven Easy Pieces, or tucked into one of those tall salads at Gotham Bar and Grill, that whisper reminding them of their connection to the rest of the city became fainter; what started in fear became a race with no finish and for too many, no shame.

Playwright Wallace Shawn wrote the following about his Yuppie friends in the published edition of his 1985 play *Aunt Dan and Lemon*:

> [T]hey begin to blossom, to flower, because they are no longer hiding . . . there are those who live gracelessly in a state of discomfort, because they allow themselves to be whipped on an hourly basis by morality's lash, and then there's another group of cheerful, self-confident people who've put morality aside for now, and they're looking happy.

And Counting . . .

Meanwhile, gay men died on gurneys in hospital hallways, waiting for a quiet pick-up by Redden's on 14th Street, the only funeral home that would take their bodies. Though 400 cases had been reported in the New York area since June 1981, the September 1982 Management Report made no mention of AIDS, while the city's one defenestration fatality got its own paragraph. Larry Kramer's March 14, 1983, *New York Native* piece titled "1,112 and Counting" called out everyone he considered complicit in this unfolding tragedy: hospitals like Sloan Kettering that admitted one Kaposi's patient a week; Koch, of course; and the press, like *Times* editor Abe Rosenthal who didn't allow the word "gay" in his paper. He blasted GMHC for providing services he thought the City should be giving, but most of all he lit into other gay men for caring more about sex than death. Koch finally agreed to meet with gay representatives, including two from GMHC, but not Kramer. He left the group.

Without question "1,112 and Counting" spread the sense of responsibility among gay men, but a *Newsweek* cover story a month later stirred a cyclone of panicked fearmongering among Straight New Yorkers who'd just discovered some empathy after watching loveable Harvey Fierstein growl his way through *Torch Song Trilogy*. Though the CDC knew by this point how AIDS was spread, the AMA falsely claimed simple contact was enough, and when a Mineola, New York, grandmother died after a blood transfusion, nurses began to hold their breath around patients, refused to draw their blood, or just ran at the sight of them. Models wouldn't touch brushes used by gay men. Inmates rioted at Rikers Island. New Yorkers avoided swimming pools, the subway, the Village in general; coworkers, neighbors, dear friends were now suspected carriers of a deadly, incurable disease caused by their sexual predilections. "Any homosexual or Haitian has become an object of dread," wrote *New York*. Violence against gays multiplied, but the police kept no statistics. The City Council shot down the discrimination bill again. As hysteria blossomed alongside those beautiful lives Shawn described, the Health Department set up "a system of active surveillance" of AIDS and the City opened an Office of Gay and Lesbian Health Concerns, but its one program, funded through the Salvation Army, signed up all of seven men over fifteen months. By the end of 1983, New York's entire contribution to AIDS services and education totaled $24,500. Commissioner Sencer said the worst was over.

Gay men were left to confront AIDS on their own. Above all else, this was a crisis of connection; the virus exploited sexual networks. Men who'd focused their lives on physical contact were now literally untouchable and gay life had become, wrote Andrew Holleran, "a vast empty space from which everyone has withdrawn." Some died within weeks of their diagnoses; others, years. AIDS didn't cause things to happen as much as it allowed them to, so a host of horrors descended on the sick: blindness, gums consumed by tumors, dysentery, pancreatic failure, stroke, it went on. Gay men weren't just forced out of the closet—many were literally thrown out into the street, bitchiness and camp wilting at the sight of young men under heavy coats creeping along Christopher Street with their canes, their names soon to be struck from address books, their apartments bleached down for the next renter. Some families tended their dying sons and brothers, but too many didn't, leaving the gay community to cook, clean, visit, and care for those rejected. Death proved homosexuality to be not a choice but an essential identity, and activism took on a new importance as gays reconsidered the terms of their community, their networks, and the straight world. Sex didn't end. "[S]topping promiscuity," writes Holleran, "was like stopping Niagara Falls." Many advocated closing the bathhouses, though Douglas Crimp argued that public sex wasn't necessarily dangerous sex and that bathhouses were exactly where education would be most effective; network theory certainly supported that idea. In June 1983, a pamphlet called *How to Have Sex in an Epidemic: One Approach* advocated condoms—which gay men usually disdained—for "safe sex." Condom use took off, and STD rates plummeted.

Yet still the red tide rose. Intravenous drug users had astronomical rates of infection—87% at one clinic. One-third of the beds at St. Vincent's held people with AIDS, and their faces were faces most of New York didn't want to see: gay men, homeless drug users, Black women and children; marginal people seen in the rearview mirror of a city rushing toward gold. In the spring of 1985, two plays forced New York to look. The first, *As Is*, was by William Hoffman, an influential member of the city's gay theater community who never saw himself as political—"I considered myself a very independent soul." The play, a wrenching story of a gay couple in mid-breakup discovering that one of them has AIDS, is an exquisite chamber piece compared to the blaring sirens of Larry Kramer's play that opened a month later. What it lacked in artistry, *The Normal Heart*, a bitter roman à clef, made up in agitprop and the gay community was not united in its support for a play that made Kramer the Cassandra hero of the entire epidemic. But just before the opening, Koch announced "a comprehensive expansion of city services" for AIDS patients. The death of Rock Hudson that summer and the controversy over young Ryan White, thrown out of his Indiana school after his diagnosis, made America confront AIDS, though sympathy wasn't the result; Gallup polls showed that 57% of Americans felt homosexuality should be illegal, up 14 points since the late '70s.

If AIDS had arrived back then, Straight New York may have reacted differently, but the Reagan years sanitized the reasonable goal of a cleaner, brighter commonplace civilization. "AIDS rewrote the sexual revolution out of existence," says scholar Marvin Taylor. Over the next decade, the deaths of more than 50% of Manhattan's gay Baby Boomers, most within three years of their diagnosis, would be a strong if unspoken reason why New Yorkers stood by while some of their most beloved places and outrageous ways of life were bleached out of existence. The reasonable "Cleaning up" of New York became something coded and pointed as the administration used public health concerns to make moral choices. The new health code law passed in October 1985, for example, made any kind of penetrative public sex illegal, so the piers were cleared, bars like the Mine Shaft and Plato's Retreat closed along with bathhouses like the St. Marks', driving sex clubs and parties underground; deadly privacy was, it seemed, preferable to safe public sex. Technology also played a role in decreasing public sex. VCRs made porn easy to find and secret trips to Times Square unnecessary. Meanwhile, Straight New York colonized the physical and intellectual voids left behind as the deaths of longtime leaseholders throughout the West Village and Upper West Side let landlords raise the rents on their vacant apartments. Roommates were put out and areas long identified with Gay New York would become simply quaint, full of exactly the delicious urban experiences Yuppies wanted; Time captured and sold, just like at Battery Park City. Singles inhabited 53% of Manhattan housing units, and a third of all the ones in the city, but now old men became harder to find: Three times as many women than men over sixty-five now lived in New York.

Ed Koch, meanwhile, remained a maddening puzzle. After the Archdiocese won its suit to overturn his antidiscrimination Executive Order 50, he went to Rome for the installation of his close friend John Cardinal O'Connor, who'd just sued him. Inside City Hall, heroic things were done by people such as the administrator at HRA who'd secretly created a system to help AIDS patients manage the health bureaucracy. When he finally confessed what he'd done, Koch embraced him and said, "Why didn't you come to me a year ago?" It was impossible to tell whether lives or votes mattered more.

Art for the People?

The idea of Art and the Arts for just a rarified cognoscenti continued to erode. But tensions grew as to who exactly they *were* for and Richard Serra's *Tilted Arc*, a 120-foot long, 12-foot-high gently curving arc of CORTEN steel on the Javits Federal Building plaza went right to their heart, its success as an art work offset by its failure as an addition to a very busy section of the city. Serra insisted the work was right where he wanted it to be: "Art is not democratic," he said. "It is not for the people." Even if they'd paid for it. Meanwhile, there was Charles Osgood of CBS *Sunday Morning* following Keith Haring through the crowd at the Shafrazi Gallery and his first one-man show, full of masturbating Mickey Mouses, dancing Smurfs, and a customized Venus on the Half Shell. The reporter dubbed Haring's work "Art for the people, all for the price of a subway token." City Hall pledged much more than that now for public art—after the death of Doris Freedman, the City Council passed her Percent for Art bill and the MTA started its own Arts & Design program.

Yet time, taste, and technology wore at things that had seemed eternal. George Balanchine died in April 1983, ending more than forty years at the New York City Ballet during which he produced arguably the most crystalline, most exquisitely New York expressions of Modernism after the Seagram Building. "It is all but unthinkable . . . ," mourned Arlene Croce, "Those ballets were, and remain, central to what art in the twentieth century is all about." Refined, luxurious, sensual yet deeply cerebral, Suzanne Farrell spinning *en pointe* truly seemed to be the still point amid the mayhem outside. A last call of sorts rang for movies, too, as the Thalia's monthly calendar went uncircled now that you could rent videos of *Breathless* and *The Battle of Algiers* and watch them at home. The deepest change, though, was the sudden larding of money lust throughout the culture. With factories closing, Americans didn't turn to Marx; they tuned to *Dynasty* and *Family Ties* starring the charmingly avaricious Michael J. Fox, or *Lifestyles of the Rich and Famous* with Robin Leach. Crowed Leach in his Brighton carney's accent, "We've taken the rich out of the closet."

Media conglomerates, once slow basking fish happy to share the pond with smaller cousins, now gobbled up independent book publishers, newspaper chains, and magazines. The fastest-growing power brokers—Rupert Murdoch and the Newhouse brothers—passed Malcolm Forbes on his own list by helping Americans vicariously live the good life. Murdoch liked money, but as he'd shown with his influential endorsement of Koch back in 1977, he was playing for more. Having steered the *Times* in London and the *New York Post* firmly to the right, he now purchased John Kluge's television stations as the first step to his own network and the foundation of a new conservative political order. The homegrown Newhouse brothers, on the other hand, particularly Si, consolidated and reinvigorated a wide swath of New York Media en route to becoming the ultimate arbiters of society and culture. In 1979 they'd inherited Advance Publications, grown by their father from the *Staten Island Advance* into a media conglomerate that owned Condé Nast and its magazines, such as *Glamour, Mademoiselle, GQ,* and *Vogue*; the next year they bought Random House, which included Knopf and Pantheon, then *The New Yorker* in 1983. The brothers topped it off with a reboot of the style bible of the '20s and '30s, *Vanity Fair*, shocked awake by import Tina Brown, recent editor of British throwaway *Tatler* whose "Life Is a Party" philosophy captured the "New Snobbism" of the Thatcher era. Only thirty, her ambition, mother wit, and well-timed romances had brought her precocious literary success and now she was ready for Act Two: "New York was the big time," she wrote in her diary, ". . . and that's where I, a girl of the arena, wanted to be." Her (much older) husband was Harry Evans, legendary editor of *The Sunday Times*, since devoured by Murdoch. Together they would have an immense impact on New York Media. Buxom and sensibly bobbed, Tina wielded her deft, cinematic editorial chops—and Si's deep pockets—to produce what she called "sophisticated boom boom"; "We give intellectuals movie star treatment," she wrote, "and movie stars an intellectual sheen." When she put Joan Collins on the October cover with the cut line "She Rhymes with Rich," sails billowed and *Vanity Fair* began cutting through the waves. Yet countless dinner parties next to Jerry Zipkin took their toll. While Brown had punctured toffs in her *Tatler* days and confessed to her diary concerns about Reagan's "gift of instinctive collusion between imagery and national mood," her magazine polished the veneer of his White House more than it ever tried to punch through; with Vreeland fading, Brown had, intentionally or not, taken over her mission to merge culture and power.

At *The New Yorker,* meanwhile, firebreaks were dug around its hallowed editor William Shawn. Iconic as the magazine was, its epic articles of great import had too often become more obligation than pleasure, yet supporters such as writer George W. S. Trow spoke of the magazine as if it were a plummy New England boy's school and Shawn its Mr. Chips. "*The New Yorker,*" said Trow, "is a place where an honorable man is teaching other men who are trying to be honorable," and its own moral mission, the polished sensibility and erudition, were under siege from sophisticated boom boom. Which didn't explain why there couldn't be photographs.

In books, Mort Janklow's outsized deals set the new standard, while more than a few writers grumbled with Serra that great art doesn't come out of giving the people what they want. Nor did it necessarily return great profits; despite all the blockbusters, hardcover sales were down 16% in 1982. Yet profit margins increasingly determined culture. Where boozy sex gossip had once been the hot topic at book parties, now it was auctions and foreign rights. And money *did* have its consolations. "It was suddenly glamorous," says Joni Evans, "unbelievably glamorous, to be in the book publishing industry." It also now had a cool kids' table, chaired by Gary Fisketjon at Vintage and his friend Morgan Entrekin at Simon & Schuster. Club hopping young book editors on Page Six added to publishing's sudden glamour, its ur-text Jay McInerney's *Bright Lights, Big City*, his 1984 Renaissance New York update of Fitzgerald's Lost Generation featuring Odeon and the Twin Towers on the cover.

Money Is the Opposite of Magic

So wrote Haring in his diary. "The worlds of art and money are constantly intermingling. To survive this mixture the magic in art has to be applied in new ways. Magic must always triumph." The next few years in the East Village saw a great flash and then, as often happens at the end of magic, things disappeared.

The scene blew up in 1983. The Rock Steady Crew showed up in *Flashdance* and the Whitney Biennial officially defined the cutting edge as Haring, Basquiat, Holzer, Schnabel, Fischl, Salle, Sherman, and Barbara Kruger. Galleries multiplied, "Holiday" played everywhere, sung by the husky-voiced twenty-four-year-old waitress and club dancer Madonna, whose look of perpetual postcoital disarray captured the mood. That fall was, says Charlie Ahearn, the "apotheosis," producing two works that established the moment's music and art as global phenomena. *Wild Style*, the Rosetta Stone of Hip Hop, starred Lee Quiñones as a graffiti writer trying to break into the art world, his journey an immersion in the people, places, and music of the era. After Ahearn debuted it in Japan, Times Square crowds went crazy at the scenes of Lee bombing cars, the basketball court throwdown between the Cold Crush Brothers and the Fantastic Romantic Freaks; the parents of little Dante Smith and Nasir Jones both took their boys. At the same time, Henry Chalfant had been filming *Style Wars*, his own documentary on graffiti writers, and his collection of subway car photos, *Subway Art*, was the first and best book of its kind.

But the East Village grew beyond Planet Rock. Back in the fall, when his show at the Fun Gallery had briefly brought him "back to his roots," Jean-Michel Basquiat had lunch at The Factory. He was obsessed with Warhol, who claimed to have once bought sweatshirts from him. "He was just one of those kids who drove me crazy . . . ," Andy told his diary, feigning indifference at first but then swooping in, pulling Haring as well into his trickster world alongside Basquiat, who moved into a loft Warhol owned on Great Jones Street. Despite his social cache, Warhol's reputation as a working artist had slid to where he was painting portraits of the LeFraks so, vampire and father figure, he sucked youth and energy out of Basquiat in return for press and occasional pep talks. Bouncing behind club diva Dianne Brill from Limelight to Area to 8BC, the Downtown 500 contracted, its icons Madonna and Keith Haring seemingly less concerned with subverting the Establishment than getting their own place at the table. Club 57 closed; instead, Haring now threw parties in his Broome Street apartment for "the downtown cultural elite" as he called it, "my 'in' scene." As Madonna racked up gold records, Haring huffed that "the art world in general kind of looks askance at what I'm doing" while executing commissions in Europe and Japan and giggling at Mr. Chow; he'd stopped drawing in the subways. Basquiat got great reviews for his first show with Mary Boone, and Haring threw the party of the summer—a huge birthday bash for himself at the Paradise Garage. Klaus Nomi was not there. While in the hospital for fatigue, he'd learned he had Kaposi's sarcoma. After a final visit back to Essen to say good-bye to his Aunt

Dodo, he went on to Munich for a chilling performance of Purcell's aria "What Power Art Thou" while wearing a frilled collar to hide his lesions. Once back in New York, his friends avoided touching him and as he slid closer to death they avoided him altogether. He died in early August 1983, alone. Though few knew it yet, "[t]he party was over," said Kenny Scharf, "and now it was about surviving." AIDS was only one of the coming horrors.

All three—Basquiat, Haring, and Madonna—were producing exceptional work, navigating the complex perils of success, but the original impulse that involved and empowered People of Color was giving way to selling versions of their style to White kids, and the plucky ingenuity of people like Gracie Mansion and Patti Astor was veering into big money. By the end of 1984 there were some seventy galleries in the East Village and artists cranked out paintings—"You give them a group show called *Shit in a Road,*" said one, "and they'd paint pictures for it." Critics called out their illusions of purity: Craig Owens called it "a kind of Junior Achievement for young culture-industrialists." Reagan's drastic cuts to arts programs certainly forced artists to now sell as much and as hard as they could, but as Yuppies scouted apartments on Avenue A, most locals were loath to admit they were packaging their magic for sale, scooting behind Warhol's fig leaf of subversion while shipping what Calvin Tomkins described as "Art that is bright in color, upbeat, humorous" straight to "banks, insurance companies, and brokerage firms." Chase bought 1,305 pieces in 1984 alone. The result was what Elizabeth Currid would call "the Warhol Economy," a new economic sector in New York that regarded youth culture as a constant wildcat strike of fashion, music, and art, with Media as the prospectors. In that spirit, graffiti got its shot at the big time when old-guard dealer Sidney Janis opened *Post-Graffiti* at his gallery on 57th, but something happened on the way down from the South Bronx; canvases by Daze, Crash, and Lady Pink felt strained and reviews were patronizing at best. In September 1983, police killed graffiti writer Michael Stewart. Not only were the writers *not* being welcomed into the academy, the cops could still kill them if they felt like it. "The MTA *thought* we were vandals," said Lee, "and the galleries *wanted* us to be vandals."

Then the next plague landed. By 1983, crack had saturated New York. The flattened refrigerator boxes disappeared and talented young men and women melted into the night. Grandmaster Flash spent the better part of the next two years in crack houses; Kool Herc took to the pipe, too. "Hip Hop as a culture . . . was dying," says Charlie Ahearn, its future and its legacy in the balance while the East Village scene drifted toward its own overripe climax. In February 1985, the cover of the *New York Times Magazine* featured Basquiat as a voodoo exotic, shoeless in a sumptuous Armani suit. The measured piece paid respect to him as a painter but took note of the mounds of heroin and cocaine which looked more like indulgence than saintly indifference. A narcissist and an addict, Basquiat sneered at the Establishment as it paid his bill at the Ritz. His next show at Mary Boone bombed. Too much, too fast, too expensive to hold on to, the East Village came apart, too. Faced with a new rent bill ten times what she'd been paying, Patti Astor closed the Fun Gallery and the exodus began. "They'll all be forced out," said real estate investor Tom Pollak, newly arrived from Aspen. "They'll be pushed east to the river and given life preservers." Artists and musicians died of AIDS, smoked too much crack, drifted off to Berlin or the cheap desolation of Brooklyn. Magic had not triumphed. Or at least not in the way Haring had imagined. "[T]he East Village will continue to exist," wrote Carlo McCormick, "as the simulacrum of itself." Through the Holiday on St. Mark's would still pour drinks, Veselka would still serve late-night pierogis, noise rock would still be played at CBGB, new bohemians would find the price of romance baked into their rent.

The Warhol-Basquiat show in September 1985 was a bust. Shafrazi had billed it as a boxing match and *Times* rendered its verdict as "Warhol TKO in 16 Rounds," calling Basquiat his "mascot." "Oh God," wrote Warhol. The friendship ended. Haring's second Party of Life, for 5,000 at Palladium—Schrager and Rubell's sequel to Studio 54—stopped traffic on 14th and featured, he said, "endless celebrities." There was backlash. "[B]y 1985 and 1986," said a friend, "we all felt we lost Keith to fame." Though he claimed his Pop Shop on Lafayette was an "art experiment," one writer contended that it marked his "speedy regress from the locomotive to the caboose of cool." But what is "cool"? "To be cool," wrote Robert Farris Thompson, "means to be composed in a sharing sense, to remember the way one ought to be. To be cool means a return to laughter, people, and responsibility." Faced with his almost inevitable fate, Haring did workshops with children across the country and murals for hospitals, including the big *Crack is Wack* at 128th Street. Whatever craven philosophies Warhol had whispered in his ear, Haring believed that wealth and fame came with a duty. Money, he wrote, "can actually be very effective for 'good' if it is used properly and not taken seriously." His work became overtly political. The Martin Wong show at Semaphore East—full-size, textured renderings of Lower East Side storefronts—brought the gates down on the East Village. Downtown plunged into plague years of sacrifice and weekly funerals for friends. But the controversy over MoMA's *Primitivism* show and its vision of Tribal Arts as Picasso's trusty Man Friday proved the Establishment no longer told the only story.

In SoHo and TriBeCa, Suzi Gablik's observation that art had "become dangerously overinstitutionalized" didn't particularly bother the artists who'd never hidden the transactional nature of their job. They got paid while commodities traders with pinky rings got stamped "Cool." But Paula Cooper had noticed "that artists and collectors started wearing the same clothes, eating the same food, drinking the same wine." Fischl saw the Willy Loman in it all. "I've become much more sympathetic to the mentality of the middle class and to their fright," he said. But many simply had no problem with Yuppies because they were Yuppies, too; Jeff Koons, for instance, *was* a commodities broker. Born in York, Pennsylvania, the genial Koons had no urge to rebel against the suburbs; he'd had a happy, comfortable childhood, encouraged from his earliest days to pursue his art by his father. Pieces like the silver replica of his father's travel bar spoke to the façade and spectacle of middle-class America, relishing their cheerful absurdity without obviously condemning them. Influenced by Dalí's showmanship and the bold, colorful irreverence of the Chicago Imagists, he was never taken with the romance of the starving artist, working on Wall Street while preparing his first major work—pristine Hoover vacuums encased in Plexiglas, shown at the New Museum the same summer as *The Times Square Show*. When Mary Boone passed him over in favor of Basquiat, he regrouped with his parents in Florida and then came back to the city as a trader at Smith Barney, no longer dependent on galleries to make his art. His 1986 *Statuary* series was highlighted by *Rabbit*, a replica of an inflatable rabbit cast in stainless steel, which produced an almost inexplicable wonder many viewers found disturbing.

As the Tilted Arc case wound through the courts, the City erected its first Percent for Art piece at 120th and Sylvan Place, next to some senior housing, a hopeful if tentative treelike sculpture called *Growth*.

Chapter Nine

The Devil and Ed Koch

Alone, and in the spotlight—this was Ed Koch's dream.

The mayor watched himself get out of bed, 1010 WINS burbling on as he dressed, consciously, happily, profoundly alone; so alone, said Bess Myerson, "he never even walks a dog." The spotlight followed him as he did what needed to be done, said what needed to be said to politicians, businessman, and minorities; Hero, Villain, Victim, whoever Koch had to be to get what he wanted but always the star and all eyes were on him now as he grabbed a big inflatable apple and burst into song.

Up on the stage of the Village Gate this May night in 1985, actor Lenny Wolpe captured the self-involved essence of Ed Koch, the image he wanted to show even if the facts didn't all add up. Back in January of 1984, the mayor had settled scores with a self-serving autobiography that fluffed his ego after Mario Cuomo's punishing win for governor; *Mayor* had gone straight to the top of the *Times* Best Sellers list while he'd marched up and down Fifth Avenue signing books, which was a lot more fun than being governor anyway. Now, a year later, Charles Strouse, composer of *Annie*, had turned it into a musical; something, Koch hoped, like "Berlin cabaret." Though *Mayor* wasn't exactly *Threepenny Opera*, it conveyed some of the salty, exhausted reality of daily life in Renaissance New York for most New Yorkers: the racial strife, need, and new money rubbed in their noses along with his *chutzpah*.

(And yes, of course, there *was* a song with that title in the show.) Yet *all* New York's a stage at that moment, and all the men and women with swollen portfolios and six-figure publicists merely players. While Leona and Donald, Cardinal O'Connor and David Rockefeller all challenged for the spotlight in *Mayor*, no one seriously challenged him for City Hall; by the time Lenny Wolpe leapt into song this opening night, "he is at the height of his power," read the show's stage direction, "he knows it, and so do those around him."

Deep into Koch's second term, the Fiscal Crisis seemed a thing of the past, even if he hadn't accomplished much of what the Crisis Regime had charged him with aside from balancing the budget—five in a row now. The mayor of course gave credit for all that was good to his own City Hall: "[I]t has been a long time," wrote Koch in his 1985 management report, "since anyone has seen this City's government pioneering in so many fields. Perhaps it has never been seen." That was an exaggeration. But these years of sudden surplus had shifted City Hall away from its Retrenchment commitment to productivity and management; the Mob went unchecked, Koch stopped bothering with civil service reform, and no one was incentivized to come up with metrics on the quality of services. Labor raises were too small to make the unions happy and too big for anyone in the Crisis Regime still watching City Hall instead of their own balance sheets.

The only other department still focused on productivity was the MTA, since handed over to former Boston transit chief Robert Kiley and David Gunn, a railroad veteran obsessed with rolling stock since he was a kid. The DOT forecast that daily traffic would soon match the strike levels that had inspired the word *gridlock*, so a $925 million surplus payment released by MAC went into new track, signals, and maintenance, while new union rules let the MTA create the management tier it desperately needed. Station rehabilitations began, the Arts for Transit program installed its first works, and 1,375 cars now had air conditioning. Meanwhile, Gunn tackled perceptions. With George Kelling's "Broken Windows" article in the air, he agreed that order, or at least the appearance of order, had to be established, and that meant methodically strangling graffiti. The 1984 Clean Car Program stuck to one simple goal: "Once a train was entered into the program and cleaned," said Gunn, "it would never again be used while graffiti was on it." Writers could bomb cars that hadn't been cleaned, but if they hit a clean one, it got an immedite chemical wash. Security and lighting were beefed up at the yards and Kelling himself was hired as a consultant.

Instead of pushing for more such fine work, though, Koch went back to what was familiar: borrowing and hiring. Bond sales of $75 million in 1981 hit $1 billion in 1985, allowing the City to project a ten-year, $26.8 billion capital plan while starting work on new police stations, laboratories, libraries, and office buildings. Funds were earmarked for 900 small parks and there were now 31 CIGs; BAM's Next Wave Festival was a rousing hit. Work on the long-planned third water tunnel had begun, and the DOT resurfaced as many streets in the first half of FY85 as it had the entire year before. The City had restored most of the jobs cut during Retrenchment, but they were concentrated on teachers, cops, and corrections officers—77% of the increase on 13% of the budget lines. All this added up to a general sense of recovery. So Koch had reasons to sing. But his hand-waving, name-calling sass had lost its charm. Mario Cuomo's win in the governor's race had been an embarrassment, the press had turned against him, and Sunday night Chinese wasn't enough to patch up rifts with people like the Gotbaums and Ravitchs. Even with City staffing at pre-Retrenchment levels and the proportion of women and minorities at new highs, Koch remained anathema to liberals and Blacks. Whenever faced with a choice, he'd gone with the conservative option, and six years after riding a bus to his inauguration, he'd thrown a Haring-like combination sixtieth birthday party/fundraiser for 1,500, tickets $2,500 a pop. Meanwhile, wages stayed flat. "The key to economic success in New York is not a good job," wrote Brecher and Horton, "it is two jobs." Accidentally on purpose, he turned his head away from the corrupt borough machines of Stanley Friedman in the Bronx, Donald Manes in Queens, and Brooklyn's Meade Esposito. If Wall Street or real estate slipped, New York's credit rating would slip, too, and the cycle would start all over.

In the spring of 1985, four major plans for the city's built environment all came to a crossroads: a five-borough affordable housing initiative, Westway, Columbus Circle, and Times Square, along with critical moments for parks and public space. Each would have a profound impact on the city going forward and speak to the changing nature of power and possibility. They'd also show who Ed Koch had become. Back in February 1984, Koch brought Barbara Walters up to the Bronx for a *20/20* segment. Standing outside 1660 Crotona Park East, he'd proudly said, "I was born in this building." To which someone stuck their head out a window and informed the mayor that he'd been born next door, at 1663. Koch had forgotten, literally, where he was from.

Lights on Charlotte Street

Efforts to revive homeownership in New York predated Koch. After Nixon froze Federal funds for housing projects, Lindsay had designated six neighborhood preservation areas while the Ford Foundation's Bedford Stuyvesant Restoration Corporation and the Community Preservation Corporation worked with community groups like SEBCO and the Desperados in the Bronx, Los Sures and St. Nick's in Brooklyn, and dozens more to provide private capital for housing, achieving at best tenuous success. In Harlem, everyone called for more outside investment, but the fact that it would likely come from Whites stirred a backlash; City auctions of brownstones brought protests even when the winners were local working-class Blacks. Further north, Alinsky-style organizing hadn't been able to stop the transformation of Washington Heights into a drug market. For all this frustration, though, the land, money, and people *did* all exist; the City, for example, held large parcels of empty land that could be used for housing, including almost 65% of Harlem. The trick was bringing them all together.

The most visible and unusual effort to do that was made by Ed Logue. Despite experts insisting that high-density building was the only sensible option for the South Bronx, the Mid-Bronx Desperadoes community group led by Genevieve Brooks told him that they wanted the same opportunity that White ethnics had had in the past and that gentrifiers had now: to own homes and increase their value by improving the surrounding area. In 1981 he'd presented his South Bronx plan—25,000 residential units and five million square feet of industrial and commercial space. "We're trying to be pragmatic and sensible," he said. But the first phase of that "pragmatic and sensible" solution was the last thing anyone ever expected in the Seven-Mile World: suburban-style ranch houses. Ninety of them at $60,000 apiece, spread over the 15 acres of Charlotte Gardens. Buyers like David and Irma Rivera, owners of a shoe store on the Grand Concourse, and textile foreman Julio Cruz would choose their own siding and carpeting. Basic as the homes looked, they were hard to build and expensive. The Mob kept concrete prices high, contractors were slow, the approval process glacial. Even just the cost of carting away rubble was exorbitant, so instead, as rappers and writers had been heading down to Negril, a six-ton weight was pulverizing the bones of the old South Bronx. And buildings alone were not enough to create a community. The Local Initiatives Support Corporation, backed by the Ford Foundation, directed money toward community organizing, and Logue convinced the Port Authority to turn eight blocks near the Cross-Bronx Expressway into Bathgate Industrial Park. Urban Park Rangers were stationed in Crotona Park, the pond cleared of abandoned cars and restocked with fish. In March 1984, Mayor Koch dedicated Charlotte Gardens. "The people who have bought them," he said, "will defend them with their lives." By May, kids were fishing for trout. Gentrification may have been killing the East Village, but Logue's version brought the Renaissance to the Bronx.

On the private side, David Rockefeller had backed up his faith in homeownership by starting the Community Preservation Corporation in the '70s, and in January 1982 he announced the NYCP's Housing Partnership with a five-year goal of 30,000 homes. After a one-time grant, market-rate two- and three-story buildings would let owners earn their mortgage payments from rent. The City gave land and infrastructure, while the Partnership took care of the rest with seed money from the Rockefeller Brothers Fund and Brooke Astor. Out in Brooklyn, the EBC went from demanding street signs to leveraging its discovered power against the problem of housing. Reverend Youngblood called it the Nehemiah Plan, after the prophet who'd rebuild the walls of Jerusalem: "Let us rise up and build," he'd said. Ed Chambers pointed them toward the crusty former *Daily News* columnist and builder I. D. Robbins, who for ten years had been promoting row houses as the way to rebuild cities, and together they established the rules of Nehemiah Housing: Only single-family, owner-occupied homes, attached to hold down costs and built in volume "to foster a renewed sense of neighbor-hood." Instead of public grants, they wanted low-interest mortgages, a ten-year tax deferral, and a $10,000 interest-free loan on each unit. Enlisting the help of Bishop Mugavero, they scraped together a building fund, and though Koch hated both the IAF and Robbins, Mugavero sold him. The first bulldozer got to work in November. "Grass roots are fragile roots," said Youngblood at the ground breaking. "*Our* roots are deep roots." Charlotte Gardens was full by mid-1984, and the first of some 2,300 EBC homes in East Brooklyn opened later that year; the Housing Partnership began construction the next. Meanwhile, City programs had put more than 140,000 units into the low- and mid-dle-income market. Government, business, and average New Yorkers were together showing the way forward on housing.

In the years to come, Cuomo and Koch would each describe their conversion to the cause in their own egotistical ways. The governor had supposedly told his new head of the Battery Park City Authority Meyer Frucher that he wanted him to "give the project a soul." (Which hap-pened, allegedly, after visiting Soviet officials had expressed surprise that the City had underwritten luxury housing.) Frucher suggested issuing housing bonds against the cash Battery Park was already throwing off, and when minority groups told him they wanted the money directed to their communities, not on site, Cuomo had a win-win: Affordable housing and happy rich White people. "[C]lassic Robin Hood," said an aide. Koch's tale was of course about *him*. "I got so mad at the *New York Times* for demanding that we give the homeless housing that I said, at one point—I mean facetiously—'We'll show them. I'm going to spend every fucking dollar on housing now on the homeless. I didn't really mean it. But out of that frustration came our housing program." In May 1985, they announced a $1.2 billion joint program to build and rehab 75,000 low- and middle-income apartments over the next five years, followed in April 1986 by Koch's own sweeping plan to throw everything the City had at housing: zoning bonuses, tax breaks, bond-ing authorities, and mortgage help, plus new taxes on hotels and co-op sales and, for the first time, money from the City's own capital budget; in total, $4.2 billion over the next ten years with the goal of 250,000 low- and middle-income units. But instead of one big program, the

City started six smaller ones to tap into a variety of groups and learn what worked best. No Federal funds were used, except what Rockefeller wheedled out of his friend Samuel Pierce at HUD. Under Paul Crotty, the new Office of Housing Coordination interlocked a host of foundations like James Rouse's Enterprise Foundation with groups public and private, communities, corporations, churches, risk takers, visionaries, and, of course, Mrs. Astor for heroic acts of city making. In the years ahead, homeownership went up among all races in all boroughs. The Koch housing initiative was possibly the single greatest contribution to the transformation of New York, the groundwork for many of the better-known improvements still to come.

A Manhood Question

In June 1985, *Mayor* into the second month of its run, all the way on the other side of the spectrum, the biggest and most contentious development project in the city's history to date hung in the balance. For the third and final time in the courtroom of Judge Thomas Griesa, Southern District New York, Westway was on trial and it was all coming down to the testimony of an amateur scientist named William Dovel, whose stare expressed not so much hostility as a lack of interest in anything not related to his subject of expertise, fish; in particular, the striped bass. Despite the immense stakes—a billion dollars, six lanes of traffic, and landfill a thousand feet into the Hudson—fifteen years of courtroom battles had placed Westway somewhere between earthquakes and asteroid strikes as an active concern of most; fifteen years of bureaucracies grinding against each other in the form of permit hearings, fish surveys, and air-quality measurements during which the purpose of Westway changed. Nelson Rockefeller had sold it as the necessary replacement for the West Side Highway; when the City had heaved into the Fiscal Crisis, the Crisis Regime touted it as a billion-dollar cure-all. And now in Renaissance New York? Well, now it was, according to Herb Sturz, "a manhood question." "[T]he bigger a person's biceps," wrote *The New Yorker*, "the surer his support." But "manhood" just meant "power." "[T]he real purpose of Westway," said one activist, "has been to create hundreds of acres of real estate in the Hudson River"—110, to be exact.

When Westway advocates pointed to the park, they usually ignored the wall of luxury towers sketched in behind it, a seeming afterthought.

Most New Yorkers opposed Westway for two reasons: first, it would have a dire impact on the city's environment, and second, the billion dollars from the Federal government could be traded in at any time for mass transit money. Environmentalists lead by the Clean Air Campaign felt the same way about the Hudson as Holly Whyte felt about the city's streets—they believed. The CAC's head was Marcy Benstock, a mild-seeming activist in bangs who could whip herself into a righteous tornado over the course of a sentence. A self-described "dreamy English major" from Harvard with a master's in economics from The New School, she'd written and edited books for Ralph Nader and run the City's air-pollution compliance campaign on the Upper West Side. Confident that the Hudson remained a vital, living thing despite the sewage, PCPs, and oil leaks, she became the hub of a citywide network of community groups.

Once the Army Corps had given its approval—called a Section 404 permit—claims that Westway would create the vague and impressive number of between "13,400 and 124,600 permanent new jobs" suddenly sounded more compelling to Koch, who cut a deal with then governor Carey in July 1981. Reagan presented them with a large ceremonial check for $85 million, but the Clean Air Campaign challenged the permit, leading to two trials during which it became clear that someone had toyed with the environmental impact study. With an injunction in force, the Army Corps hired Dovel to conduct a study of striped bass habitats in the Hudson piers. Much happened while Dovel counted. Retrenchment ended, the Bull market arrived, and most directly, the deadline for the mass transit trade-in was moved up to September 30, 1985; if Westway wasn't signed by then, the money would go to the MTA. As the clock began to tick, the enterprise began to lose steam in Cuomo's office and the *New York Times*, but the Powers That Be remained bent on Westway.

Dovel, meanwhile, kept counting. His initial research indicated that the Hudson inter-pier areas were indeed important nurseries for young striped bass, and his first draft of the new environmental impact study said Westway would have a "significant adverse impact." But somehow, even though the data didn't change, "significant" became "minor" in the final study. Desired results in hand, the Army Corps reissued its Section 404 and by March of 1985, Westway looked like it would beat the deadline—until someone noticed the differences between the draft EIS and the final. Judge Griesa, a flinty Nixon appointee, called for a *third* trial in late June that now hinged on Dovel's testimony. "Westway," Dovel firmly testified, "like other similar habitats in the vicinity, is not critical to the survival of striped bass." And then he melted on the cross, admitting that he'd been paid by a Westway lobbyist and venturing thin explanations as to why the final report was altered. Unamused, Judge Griesa issued a permanent injunction against the permit. In September, the Second Circuit reversed it but upheld the rejection of the permit. Though the Army Corps and the rest of the Westway team were technically free to take another run, Congress voted against emergency funding.

The Clean Air Campaign had run out the clock. Westway was dead.

There'd be no wall of towers blocking the sunset over the Hudson. At least not yet. One of the most transformational events in modern New York history was a case of something *not* being built, just as the end of the Lower Manhattan Expressway ten years before had set the stage for SoHo. Instead, the MTA would get the billion dollars, the West Side would get a permanent grade-level highway, and the City would now focus on the potential of its waterfront, what one Zeckendorf executive called "the last frontier." A year after the ruling, thirty-two projects were planned for the city's shoreline.

They're Only Numbers

At the climax of *Mayor*, the prickly specter of Fiorello La Guardia warned Koch that people matter more than numbers. Unfortunately, government was now driven by them, like the $1.4 billion in tax revenues that a redeveloped Times Square might produce over the next twenty years. "If you had asked me fifteen years ago what I would work on through the 1980s," said Ruth Messinger, "I wouldn't have mentioned a sophisticated understanding of taxes, revenues, the hard number side of economic equity." As the Bull charged on, Growth in New York was merely in line with most other big American cities during these years. To Ken Lipper, now Deputy Mayor of Budget, Taxes, and Economic Development, and Herb Sturz, priming Growth meant more building, so the City shifted its fundamental purpose of mediating between the needs of the People and the developers toward simply making life easier for the developers. Sturz, who'd expanded the concept of "planning" to include worthy but far-ranging efforts such as trying to sell Rikers to the State and developing an office of immigrant affairs, put City Planning largely at the disposal of the Public Development Corporation and City Hall. Small business made up 87% of city businesses, but they provided only a third of its jobs, so for all the rhetoric, the City felt it needed to keep offering them tax abatements, tax deferrals, and zoning incentives. Checks on developers were loosened, more pro-development appointees named to the Planning Commission. and aspects of the 1982 zoning changes undermined. When Harry Macklowe illegally tore down SROs and Bruce Eichner built CitySpire on 57th Street 14 feet too high, both developers simply considered their fines the price of doing business. "[T]he city," wrote Carter Wiseman, "has largely abdicated its leadership role in shaping the future of these spaces, consigning it instead to the perceived needs of private interests." Ruth Messinger accused City Hall of turning over "the job of urban planning to the development community."

At the same time, City Hall began to take full advantage of its real estate holdings; Koch, "continuing to function as referee . . . ," said the *Times*, now "stepped in as quarterback." Shearson American Express bought a vacant lot on Greenwich Street for $23.9 million, and Ports and Terminals issued RFQs for four sites that would return $375 million. The development rights to the Coliseum, the MTA's white elephant at Columbus Circle, came in a deal with the State for a $75 million contribution to the Convention Center. An RFP went out in February 1985 with one paragraph of guidelines that put no limit on height, or anything else for that matter; only a requirement to apply for a 20% density bonus in return for renovating the Columbus Circle subway station. The top consideration would be the amount; the last—"Overall benefit to the city." All that mattered was the number. The bidders made their presentations the week *Mayor* opened, and on July 11 the

MTA announced that Boston Properties would pay $455.1 million for the rights to build two enormous angular Moshe Safdie towers with Lipper's old firm Salomon Brothers committed as major tenants. The price tag made their hulking density necessary and threatened to cast shadows over the south edge of Central Park. For the MTA it was a shocking windfall. "Critics of the Coliseum sale claim that our primary motivation was the amount of money it would generate," said Robert Kiley. "They are absolutely right." New York, like all cities, is the product of battles between competing goods.

Picking Up Papers

The renegotiation of public and private space continued throughout New York; who could use it and how, but mostly who would pay for it. In 1983, Gordon Davis stepped down from Parks, but on his way out, he signed the Bryant Park deal: based explicitly on the one he'd made for the Central Park Zoo, the City would lease it to the Bryant Park Restoration Corporation and then they'd split the cost of maintenance. The deal, Laurie Olin's final plans, and the restaurant to be built by Warner LeRoy all still had to pass the City's Uniform Land Use Review Procedure (ULURP), Landmarks, and just about every other committee you could name. Now one of the city's established philanthropies, the Central Park Conservancy had Exxon, Chase, and Bankers Trust as sponsors and Central Park was again, to Orde Coombs, "the single most democratic space in the city." Twelve proposals for BIDs were waiting for Board of Estimate approval when Biederman, frustrated as Bryant Park slogged through approvals, took a second job at the request of the mayor as head of the Grand Central Partnership, created to keep Exxon from leaving. Dozens of zoning deals allowed developers to trade private services in public spaces in exchange for extra height or density. Would all these public-private partnerships maintain truly public spaces and add to the common good? Or was the City selling off control to a chain of extra-legal governments?

The new Parks commissioner Henry Stern thought it was the latter and hit the brakes. "[A] tree-loving pixie and master politician," said the *Times*, with "what his detractors say is a mean streak in private," wiry Stern had the quirky yin air of a mid-'70s PBS host and a deep knowledge of New York. Suspicious of the Bryant Park deal, he tried to block the restaurant and reduced the grant to the BPRC from 35 years to 15, but circumstances did even more; City Planning considered digging a parking garage under the park, which inspired the library to expand its underground stacks until, in March 1986, an exhausted LeRoy finally pulled out.

Morale at the Arsenal deteriorated under Stern, who snacked on peas from the can and insisted that all his staff have walkie-talkie nicknames. Despite his populist stance and fifteen times the capital funds available to Parks than Davis had in 1978, the small parks still suffered. But Stern's work in Union Square did demonstrate an alternative to Davis's outsourcing. Over the years, Union Square had sunk to the same desperation as Bryant Park. Charles Luce, the CEO of Con Edison, pulled together the 14th Street–Union Square BID without taking a lease on Union Square Park; instead, it worked with community groups and Parks to develop it as a "special district" zoned to "encourage residential and mixed use development." Various stakeholders paid for everything from subway station improvements to a horticulturist and a police crackdown along 14th Street. When the north end plaza opened in 1985, the greenmarket expanded. Uniformed sweepers came through the park twice a day, though, explained one official, "it is not a yuppie park." While the major stakeholders drove the agenda, Union Square achieved much of what Bryant Park was trying to do without giving up City and community control. There was one crucial difference, though: no one lived around Bryant Park, whereas Union Square's residential neighbors, especially the ones in the new Zeckendorf Towers, had a stake in its survival.

Public involvement also changed the direction of Times Square. With the first new and uninspired buildings to the north of Times Square topping out, New Yorkers began to feel wary, if not betrayed. "Reluctantly," wrote Brendan Gill, who'd just a few years before had applauded Gordon Davis, "we must confront the fact that the city we have cherished is being taken from us even as we are encouraged to believe that it is being marvelously transformed for our sakes." The Municipal Art Society sounded the alarm. Hardy and Quennell presented a 12-minute computer-generated film (groundbreaking at the time) to City Planning that depicted what exactly Times Square would look like if the plan were approved, and it moved the needle. Times Square had to change—that was agreed—but its essence needed to be preserved. Johnson and Burgee were sent back to the drawing board a third time, Prudential signed on to underwrite the purchase of properties along 42nd Street, and City Planning and MAS spent two years on new design and zoning regulations. Approved by the Board of Estimate in 1987, they required minimum sizes for commercial signs and a new standard of light intensity to guarantee "bright, festive, gaudy lights and signs." Most New Yorkers considered it a win. Whatever happened, at least Times Square wouldn't look like Wall Street.

Slowly and inefficiently, the system *was* working in various crucial ways. Trump's much touted redo of Wollman Rink, his one civic act and supposed proof of government ineptitude, was paid for with City money and granted every possible waiver. Elsewhere, people flexed their power; independent advocacy groups such as the Parks Council and the Straphangers Campaign stepped up to perform roles that City Hall, the City Council, and the Board of Estimate had abdicated in the name of Growth. The court cases and the agonizing process that aggravated every Type-A developer who just wanted to cut the damn red tape existed precisely to be agonizing, detailed, and rigorous so that the City wouldn't solve one problem by causing new ones. Individual New Yorkers like Mike Gecan, Marcy Benstock, Reverend Youngblood, Gene Russianoff, Dan Biederman, Genevieve Brooks, Larry Kramer, just to start, were claiming power. As the AIDS crisis intensified, Kramer gave a speech that connected them all to Gordon Davis's sense of urban responsibility, Rockefeller's coffee, and the creation of urban networks:

> Power is little pieces of paper on the floor. No one picks them up. Ten people walk by and no one picks up the piece of paper on the floor. The eleventh person walks by and is tired of looking at it, and so he bends down and picks it up. The next day he does the same thing. And soon he's in charge of picking up the paper. Now—think of those pieces of paper as standing for responsibility. This man or

woman who is picking up the pieces of paper is, by being responsible, acquiring more and more power . . . All power is the willingness to accept responsibility.

It was possible for everyday people to have power in post-Crisis New York, but they had to join networks that consolidated it. While the chorus in *Mayor* passively bitched about rent and alternate side of the street parking, real-life New Yorkers joined groups like Sutton Area Community Council, Civitas, and the Natural Resources Defense Council who banded together to stop a 42-story condo from going up near the Queensborough Bridge. STAND—Stand Together Against Neighborhood Decay—forced a settlement from Bruce Ratner's Metrotech complex in Brooklyn.

In September 1985, *Mayor* hit a rough patch. All the principals offered to defer royalties except Koch, who demanded his weekly $375. Koch spent $6.3 million to beat Carol Bellamy, running as a Liberal, 74% to 10%; said State Senator Franz Leichter, "[T]he line between a bribe and a contribution is almost invisible." In one of the debates, Bellamy said, "Since you lost to Mario Cuomo, you've become a fraud and a phony." But those houses on Charlotte Street were real, and they wouldn't have been there without Koch. "Being Mayor," he'd later write, "forces you to adopt many personalities . . .—for your own sake and the sake of the city."

Mayor closed five days after his third inauguration.

Chapter Ten

From Queens Come Kings!

"Welcome, Massa, to the Ole Plantation." So read a sign greeting Ed Koch to Harlem in April 1983. Both Chicago and LA had elected Black mayors and yet Koch still complained about the struggles of a White mayor governing Blacks. "Anyone else who would say and do what Ed Koch says and does," said Rangel, "people would refer them to a psychiatrist." Racial violence rose with the skyscrapers: a White mob beat Black transit worker Willie Turks to death in Gravesend and in June 1983, "wolf packs" wandered Manhattan after the make-up date for a rain-shortened Diana Ross concert in Central Park. ("[O]h you should have seen it," wrote Warhol, "Jerry Zipkin in the soaking rain.") Reverend Calvin O. Butts, youth minister of the Abyssinian Baptist Church, convinced Rep. John Conyers to hold a Congressional hearing on police brutality, but Koch refused to stand for the playing of "Lift Ev'ry Voice and Sing" and after twenty out-of-control minutes, Conyers shut it down. At summer's end, eleven police officers beat Michael Stewart into a fatal coma.

Economically, Renaissance New York was splitting apart. Real incomes rose in 1983 for the first time in fourteen years, but poverty was growing faster here than in the rest of the country, concentrating in places like Mott Haven in the Bronx, where more than 61% lived below the poverty line. Household incomes were going up only because more households now had two earners. More women were entering the workforce—good news—but available jobs and capital were concentrating among a smaller cohort. Not good news. Only 14% of New Yorkers lived in two-parent families considered middle-class or higher; within the highest income group of that 14%, 70% had both parents working. At the same time, female-headed single-parent households also shot up—most straight into poverty—along with single individuals on the margins. Segregation deepened at the workplace, and the burger-flipping jobs that used to be entry points for teenagers went to desperate adults. The common "mismatch theory" held that Blacks weren't profiting from the Renaissance because they didn't have the skills for the kinds of jobs it offered, but education levels for Blacks and Whites rose at about the same level through the '80s, and in construction, the fastest growing unskilled sector in the city's economy, Blacks actually *lost* 11,000 jobs. Skills weren't the issue. The most reliable source of employment for Blacks was the public sector; more than 30% of Blacks with some college were employed by the government, and overall, wrote Roger Waldinger, "all of the industries in which native blacks were over-represented were characterized by large, bureaucratic organizations in which affirmative action measures can be charted." Cuts had wiped away an entire structure of family supports and early-warning networks, and those knocked off welfare often had to reapply a few months later. Attempts at workfare were a bust, with less than 40% of those on welfare considered employable.

Immigration continued to add to the inequities. The New York population considered "Other," meaning Asians and Latinos not from Puerto Rico, was up 105.8% since 1978, and incomes in that category were up 43% and 31%, respectively. West Indian and Nigerian immigrants often arrived with money and education; they took advantage of Koch's housing initiative and established microcommunities dense with their own professional and social networks. The rising housing prices putting pressure on some minority families also built home equity for others who'd entered the real estate cycle like the Latinos in Sunset Park who'd bought their homes from the Whites leaving when the piers died. Now they were selling them at a profit to Asians. Korean, Chinese, Indian, and Pakistani enclaves grew in Flushing and Jackson Heights; South and Central Americans moved into Elmhurst; Haitians and Senegalese went to Crown Heights, Flatbush, and even the Upper West Side. All their travels on the subway—especially on the #7 train—helped the MTA make good on its bonds.

Meanwhile, with New York's White power and money coalescing into new networks, only 2,733 African Americans in the Tri-state area earned more than $50,000 a year. Most qualified People of Color refused to work in Koch's City Hall, yet Black politicians hadn't formed a united front, unconnected to the new generation fired up by South Africa and Reagan, yet keeping an arm's length from the Nation of Islam's Louis Farrakhan whose antidrug efforts came larded with references to Judaism as a "dirty religion" and Hitler as "a great man." Jesse Jackson's empowering presidential run in 1984 hit the rocks when he referred to New York as "Hymietown." In Brooklyn, the Eastern Brooklyn Congregations registered some 10,000 new voters and doubled turnout in their areas, but the Black political establishment distrusted the EBC as much as Koch and Rockefeller did, and the feeling was often mutual. In 1984, "nosy and newsy" Andrew Cooper, former director of PR for Schaefer Brewery, started *The City Sun* as a Black-interest newspaper with coverage of Caribbean and African topics along with sports, culture, and local politics. Jailhouse convert Reverend Herbert Daughtry had taken over his father's Brooklyn ministry in 1959 and had since offered one of the few consistent independent voices of protest.

In Harlem, the Abyssinian Baptist Church, historic home of Adam Clayton Powell and New York's stolid Black middle class, was just trying to hold on; almost half of its 6,000 Sunday congregants now came in from the suburbs. Through the '60s and '70s, activists had touted community-driven, publicly funded solutions that became less realistic as Harlem got progressively weaker and poorer and public funds dried up. The Revolution would not be starting here, especially with the Gang of Four so invested in the status quo. But to Harvard professor William Julius Wilson, change wasn't really what was needed so much as for the past to return. His 1987 book *The Truly Disadvantaged* suggested that the exodus of the Black middle class was responsible for the dismantling of Harlem. Rebuilding the community meant rebuilding its dense networks of block and church, school and corner bar, and to do that, it needed its own Back to the City movement—the middle class, and middle-class Lifestyle, had to come home to Harlem. And that had to start with housing. The Gang of Four didn't like independent CDCs, so the Koch housing initiative had largely targeted Brooklyn and the Bronx, but now some fifty or so congregations formed the Harlem Congregations for Community Improvement, and at Abyssinian, Reverend Butts called out from the pulpit for a "housing ministry" to bring in public and private money. The State UDC joined in, albeit in a typically ineffectual way; in 1985, for example, it transferred 145 vacant brownstones at prices so high that the new owners couldn't afford renovations and the buildings remained empty. Still, it would ultimately play a significant role in rehabbing and building thousands of housing units in Harlem, and in March 1988 hosted the Building Harlem for Harlem Through Unity conference with Wilson as the keynote speaker. The gentrification of Harlem was started by people in Harlem.

It Takes a Suburb

But the people of Hollis, Roosevelt, and other outlying Black middle-class neighborhoods knew that a backyard didn't guarantee justice. Hardshell New Yorkers already liked to complain about "suburbanization." Ed Logue's ranch houses were suburban. The Pooper Scooper law and the Sheep Meadow were suburban. Anything trimmed, clean, orderly, and requiring a specific set of behaviors was suburban and therefore inauthentic. But cities and their suburbs are in dialogue, and as much as any rational urbanist program, New York was a product of fantasies about what a city is "supposed to be." If the male gaze and the White gaze influence their subjects, the suburban gaze alters the city and the suburban gaze wasn't necessarily White. Rap promoter and manager Russell Simmons had learned his very urban deal-making skills in the low-density wilds of Queens. Simmons was born in Jamaica, Queens, in 1957, and then his parents moved the family to nearby Hollis and its blocks of tidy homes owned by industrious Black families. "[B]lack people from Strong Island," wrote Greg Tate, "have all the funk of inner-city ignays, an African villager's sense of community, preppy educations, and the bicultural savvy of a "burb upbringing." Simmons's parents both went to Howard and made sure Russell attended integrated schools, but then heroin arrived, police stopped policing, and neighborhoods like St. Albans and Hollis managed to be at once prosperous *and* drug bazaars. Simmons lived the same way; partying as hard as he worked, landing his CCNY classmate Kurtis Walker, aka Kurtis Blow, the first major record deal for a rapper and an opening spot on the Commodores' tour.

"Hip hop was not just a fuck you to white society," said Bill Stephney, "it was a fuck you to the previous Black generation as well." And now Simmons was about to bring, as critic Frank Owen put it, "the anger, style, aggression and attitude of urban America to a worldwide audience." Like all networks, Hip Hop was sustained by stories, by celebrations of identity and, in the case of his brother Joey's group, Run-DMC, the look: Black jeans. White polished Adidas. Black leather jackets and hats. "They made costumes out of their regular, everyday outfits," said Simmons. "[I]t takes a bit of a suburbanite, as we were, coming from Queens—to see the power in ghetto culture." Just as the Ramones, another Queens band in black leather, had boiled down rock and roll, Run-DMC with their raw beats and relentless drum reduced Rap to its pounding essence and secured its future.

Another suburbanite redefining urban culture was that NYU student running a record label out of his dorm, Rick Rubin, a doted-on only child from Lido Beach whose parents had paid Def Jam's bills. "Authentic" then was about sound and spirit, and Rubin was a genius at finding them. Joining forces with Simmons, the two produced "I Need a Beat" by another kid from Queens, sixteen-year-old James Smith, aka LL Cool J, short for "Ladies Love Cool James." Rubin saw Run-DMC and LL Cool J as "young male fantasies of power . . . ," wrote Simmons, "inflated into larger-than-life, over the top cartoons." Def Jam signed a seven-figure deal with Columbia in 1985.

Carlton Ridenhour grew up in the suburbs, too, dreamed his astronaut dreams out in Roosevelt where his mother had founded the local theater group. "Long Island was Hip Hop crazy" in 1979 when he began studying graphic design at Adelphi. He joined the DJ crew of Hank Shocklee as "Chuckie D" and they soon got their own Saturday night radio show on WBAU, the Adelphi station. All this was happening out of sight of *Wild Style* and Planet Rock, away from the velvety Luther Vandross and Lionel Richie being pumped into the Black mainstream by Black music executives on "Rap-free" radio stations. Chuck rapped all day with his wiry, google-eyed, Jheri-curled friend William Drayton, known as DJ Flavor, as they made deliveries for the Ridenhour family furniture store, Drayton's insinuating trickster pose setting up Chuck's urgent flow. Bill Stephney, former WBAU station manager, now at Def Jam, believed Rap needed someone who could "bring a higher level of thinking to it," so in June 1986 he signed Chuck D, Flav, and the rest of their circle who became Public Enemy, "the Black Panthers of Rap." Yet the "Blacker" Rap got, the more White listeners came to it. As Chuck D was pulling together their first album *Yo! Bum Rush the Show!*, the Beastie Boys released *Licensed to Ill*, and Run-DMC and Aerosmith collaborated on "Walk This Way."

Suburbanites, White and Black, had merged the fuck you of punk and the fuck you of Black nationalism to make Hip Hop the primary expression of post-Boomer urban youth. And it didn't require a young Black man to leave his "known culture" to make it big. New York's post–Planet Rock Golden Age of Rap also featured the swirling jazz samples of Eric B. and Rakim, two Queens Five Percenters; Rakim's intense, almost spoken flow let you hear the internal rhymes and rhythms. By any definition, this was poetry. But it was still party music, and drugs had always been central to Hip Hop culture the same way they'd been central to rock and roll. Now Hip Hop was about to become the soundtrack for the kind of problem it had been meant to solve.

Crack It Up

Crunching and glistening in the light, the morning-after streets of Renaissance New York sparkled from broken glass vials and their colorful plastic tops scattered across sidewalks and gutters. Back in 1979, out in LA, Rick Ross, a good Reagan-era entrepreneur, had demystified and democratized rich man's cocaine by selling small amounts of it cooked, at low prices. Crack quickly rolled out, and over the next decade it would, with AIDS, devastate a generation of New Yorkers and deepen social and economic divides. "Crack is a businessman's drug," said Haring, and New York was a businessman's city, bent on immediate gratification, where stock analysts hung on quarterly reports and Yuppies indulged tightening cycles of desire with Sony devices, Le Creuset pots, and Mac computers that were obsolete after eighteen months. The frenzy to have *NOW* and to have *again* was the nature of all modern life. As the price of cocaine dropped from $50,000 a kilo in 1980 to $35,000 in 1984, on its way down to $12,000, crack presented itself as a chance to escape for a few minutes, to make a few bucks, or maybe a fortune which was, after all, our patriotic duty.

Despite the nationwide moral panic, kids all over America didn't become crackheads. But crack's effects were very real in the parts of New York City already reeling. "[W]hen it landed in your hood," wrote Jay-Z, "it was a total takeover. Sudden and complete . . . It was an irreversible new reality." The *Amsterdam News* announced in February 1986 "CRACK, SUPER DRUG, HITS NEW YORK STREETS." Addicts frightened of AIDS traded needles for pipes; paycheck-to-paycheck users slipped once and were lost. Kids weren't beaming up as much as Mom and Dad, uncles and aunts. "In this multigenerational chaos," wrote Nelson George, "few could raise their head above water or plan intelligently for the future." Rates of child abuse, child abandonment, and homelessness exploded. Left to their own devices, kids began to deal, and in many homes, authority flipped; parents looked the other way as their children paid the bills by selling crack to other parents, last Halloween's Ghostbuster waved a Glock. The economics of cheap cocaine meant that smaller operators could set up all over, free radicals smashing into each other, thriving in decayed urban landscapes and actively trying to create more. On any given day, some 150,000 New Yorkers were plying the drug trade. Neighborhoods fought back. In East New York, St. Paul's bought the strip of stores along Stanley Avenue to give church members safe places to shop. In Washington Heights, Coogan's Restaurant opened as a demilitarized zone, but doors and windows stayed locked, children kept inside. Every morning, communities swept up lighters, used condoms, needles, broken vials and pipes. They marched. They begged for police help. Already shaky social services required huge injections of money, but instead Washington launched the War on Drugs as Gilderized New Yorkers saw crack as a window onto the twisted minority soul. Why didn't they Just Say No? After peaking in 1981, crime had actually been dropping in Renaissance New York, murder had fallen to a fifteen-year low in 1985, but when a squirrely, harassed White commuter named Bernie Goetz shot four teenagers menacing him on the #2 train in December 1984, he found himself a vigilante hero, his feeling that "New York is out to get me" heard by many as an expression of their growing sense of futility: an estimated 1.7 million felonies committed in 1983 resulted in 22,000 convictions, meaning you had a 3% chance of ever getting punished for committing a felony, and a 2% chance of doing time. Yet even with that, the State's prisons were filling up.

One reason the police couldn't stop crack was that stopping crime wasn't in their job description. For a good hundred years or so, American criminology had approached crime as a result of root social problems and the technocratic "Just the facts ma'am" policing philosophy of the '60s and '70s involved mostly driving around in patrol cars and responding to 911 calls. Small crimes were ignored; a cop assigned to Needle Park on the Upper West Side was told to "Just keep the junkies moving. Don't let 'em stop." Top brass questioned whether the presence of cops really had any impact on crime at all. Said Commissioner Robert McGuire, "Nobody seems to know why crime goes up and down." Or what the relationship was between crime and cops or, for that matter, what the police actually did; pressure in a specific place could deliver temporary relief, but nothing permanent. An Us vs. Them sensibility had replaced Officer Friendly with what George Kelling called "stranger policing"; another example of the suburban gaze altering the city, given how many cops lived in suburbia. Meanwhile, One Police Plaza rebuffed any calls for structural reform. Fearing that too much interaction with the public led to brutality and corruption, now only detectives could make drug arrests. "No precinct commander ever lost his job because of a crime increase," wrote one reporter. "But a corruption scandal could bring down an administration."

A few months after the Conyers debacle, McGuire resigned and Koch brought in Ben Ward, whose biracial identity and deep store of Yiddish couldn't compensate for his drinking, philandering, and inability to interact smoothly with anyone, of any race; White cops especially held against him a false rumor that back in 1972 he'd pulled officers out of a Nation of Islam mosque after the fatal shooting of one of theirs. Sturz had pushed hard for Ward, a Vera Institute veteran, who believed like Koch in "community policing," which increased the visible presence of police but more importantly created partnerships with community groups. Ward's Operation Pressure Point cleared out public dealing and hit gambling and drug fronts on the Lower East Side; his Community Patrol Officer Program in the 72nd Precinct and the Total Patrol Concept both focused on Quality of Life, arresting for low-level street crimes and increasing interaction with communities until crack finally overwhelmed the police and the courts, and Sanitation took back the job of writing tickets for littering, dog poop, and the like. Ultimately, though, Ward's demons overshadowed his efforts. On Palm Sunday 1984, ten women and children were slaughtered as part of a 75th Precinct drug war; to that point, the worst mass killing in New York history. Off on a bender, Ward couldn't be found. African Americans supported his programs and the inroads he made in minority hiring, but dirty cops and a jump in "abuse of authority" by police officers mattered more, especially the case of Edmund Perry, a Stanford student shot by an officer who falsely claimed Perry and his brother tried to mug him. Drug-related murders jumped, with young-Black men the prime victims, though they were hardly the only ones; teenager Shavod Jones shot officer Steven McDonald in Central Park in 1986, paralyzing him for life.

Racial tensions crackled. In the spring, a gang of Whites stabbed nineteen-year-old Samuel Spencer to death in Coney Island. After a November 1986 shoot-out with cops, Larry Davis went on the lam for 17 days, helped by people wherever he went. "He did something brave," said LL Cool J. "Whether it was right or wrong doesn't matter to a lot of people." Gangly, curly-haired Howard Stern, whose family had moved out of Roosevelt right about the time the Ridenhours had moved in, became a hero to many young Whites with his softcore radio freak show where dwarves, Klan members, and pimply sorts who lived in Mom's basement egged on prostitutes to make out, turning the goofy "One of us" of the Ramones into a big White, working-class, libertarian middle finger extended to anyone who told him he was in bad taste, or that racism and sexism existed. The Establishment wasn't Dad's Rotary Club anymore; it was Yuppie do-gooders handing out checks to Black crackheads.

On the night of December 20, 1986, Michael Griffith pulled his sputtering Buick Regal over onto the shoulder of the Cross Bay Parkway. Griffith, twenty-three, from Trinidad via Bed-Stuy, along with his stepfather Cedric Sandiford and Timothy Grimes, decided to leave his young cousin with the car while the three Black men walked north three miles to Howard Beach for help. On the face of it, Howard Beach was everything Koch and Logue loved about neighborhoods—mowed lawns, split-levels, and block patrols. It was also the home turf of mobster John Gotti. Around 12:30 a.m., Griffith, Sandiford, and Grimes crossed paths with a few drunk White kids; insults were exchanged. At New Park Pizza at 157th and the Parkway, the men ate slices and asked for directions to the subway at which point a dozen White teenagers attacked them with a tree limb and a baseball bat. Separated, Griffith was chased on to the Shore Parkway where he was fatally hit by a passing blue Aspen. When Cedric Sandiford finally found his way to the police, he was questioned as if he were the criminal for entering Howard Beach.

"This incident," said Ed Koch, now a year into his third term, "can only be talked about as rivaling the kind of lynching party that took place in the Deep South." This sort of thing didn't happen in New York. Except for all the other times it had since 1626. The minstrel show was invented on the Bowery. "The Civil Rights movement never came to New York," wrote one activist, "there was never a real, true confrontation with the status quo in New York." That it hadn't come was due to the same fragmentation that produced the man who said that, Reverend Al Sharpton. Another Hollis native, larger than life in his velvet track suits, gold chains, and mane of processed hair, Sharpton's effect on racial politics in New York was like Run-DMC—loud, relentless, and straight from the streets of Queens. "I learned before I got out of the maternity ward," said Sharpton, "that you've got to holler like hell sometimes to get what you want." Once a precocious, loquacious young minister, he'd spent time at Adam Clayton Powell's knee, toured with Mahalia Jackson, met the widow of Marcus Garvey ("You're going to be like Garvey," she told Sharpton, "because you got a big head like Garvey"), and started the National Youth Movement under the guidance of Jesse Jackson and Bayard Rustin. After losing a 1978 run for State Senate as part of Shirley Chisholm's circle, he'd left activism to work with James Brown. But he'd also briefly advised the family of one of Goetz's victims, and as he met with Sandiford, battered and swollen from his beating, he saw a chance to expose New York's hypocrisy.

On Monday, December 22, the day three White teenagers were charged with second-degree murder, Sharpton led a caravan of cars to New Park Pizza. Most expected that they'd just circle the block, but instead Sharpton pulled over, bought a hundred dollars' worth of pizza, photographers clicking all the while, and got back in his car. Nothing else happened, but he'd put a protest on the front pages of the newspapers. While two outspoken Black lawyers, Alton Maddox and C. Vernon Mason advised Sandiford, Sharpton led another larger march that Sunday where a White child shouted "You ain't nothing but a nigger yourself" at Police Commissioner Ward. A local church booed Ed Koch. Afraid the White teens would get just a slap on the wrist, Maddox, Mason, and Sharpton advised Sandiford to not cooperate with the prosecution.

The city's Black leadership split between those who wanted to fix the system and those who wanted a whole new one. *The City Sun* gave Maddox and Mason a regular platform and West Indians, seeing one of their own killed, began to shift away from the Brooklyn Machine. As Sharpton called a New Year's Eve meeting between the mayor and twenty-three Black leaders "a coon show," Maddox called for a Black boycott of New York pizzerias, pissing off Governor Cuomo and many Italian Americans who were now more angry about the politicization of pizza than they'd ever been about the murder.

While New York simmered, a *Times* poll stated that "a third of New Yorkers say that many or almost all whites and blacks in the city dislike each other." Def Jam might have been selling the same music to White kids and Black kids, but they wanted to listen separately. John Ahearn still lived in the South Bronx, and the Percent for Art program commissioned him to make three bronze casts for the plaza in front of the new 44th Precinct a few blocks from where he lived. Planet Rock, though, was dead. By March, Dennis Rivera had closed his shoe store on the Grand Concourse. The owner of the building had quadrupled his rent because the South Bronx was coming back, so he was a peddler now, trying not to lose his miracle home on Charlotte Street. The trees in the yard had died. You could plant things in New York, but not everything survived. On the plus side, Goldman Sachs had named its first African American partner.

Chapter Eleven

Building the Bonfire

There was a stink in the air by 1986, a blend of David's Cookies, gamey homelessness, and the sweet, toasted plastic of burning crack, all topped with spice notes from Susan Gutfreund's Après L'Ondée. After the sudden thrill of survival, Renaissance New York had curdled into something overripe, cynical, and more dangerous than it had ever been during the Fiscal Crisis. "We're in a time," wrote Arthur Schlesinger Jr., "when private interest is the solution to all problems and the sense of public purpose has faded away." The gap between ostentatious wealth and desperate poverty had gone from an ethical challenge to the natural, yea proper, state of man. As TB, VD, AIDS, child abuse, and homelessness all rose, "Money," wrote Michael Bloomberg, "was emerging as the big story that needed telling at the end of the century."

Two new magazines started that year, both aimed at young, college-educated New Yorkers fascinated and repelled by the glamorous absurdity. *Manhattan, Inc.* provided juicy details about blockbuster deals, boardroom dickslapping, and luxury lifestyles while still pushing back against the avarice. *Spy* was a sneakier beast, aimed at Yuppies who knew better. Named by its founders Graydon Carter and Kurt Andersen after the magazine Cary Grant and Jimmy Stewart write for in *The Philadelphia Story*, it was beloved by the sort of person who was amused that it was named after the magazine in *The Philadelphia Story*. Under the motto "Smart, fun, funny, and fearless," *Spy* mocked New York power and fame

159

in all its pretentious excess, but from the inside, where its readers aspired to be; "snark" and media gossip were born here, its "satirical journalism" a mix of envy, disdain, and amusement written by and for people who'd gone to good schools and walked through velvet ropes, who understood the city's romance and brilliance as only those who come from somewhere else can, and pined, ironically, for more of those qualities now amid the manufactured glitz. Until then, it mercilessly mocked the likes of Liz Smith, fawning over her sequined masters, and "short-fingered vulgarian" Donald Trump. Satire was indeed called for when even Felix Rohatyn suggested there were too many charity galas. "In order to get the city's rich to give a lousy thousand dollars to the poor," he railed, ". . . you have to parade little black kids in front of them and give them party favors." *Plus ça change*, responded Annette Reed as she recalled failed attempts in the '70s to solicit donations without the presence of the Lester Lanin Orchestra. "They want to be seen," she said.

Tina Brown understood that visible inequity was a feature, not a bug. After another evening spent watching the B-list preen at a postdinner soiree, she wrote in her diary, "This is what I appreciate most about the city at night, the life force of New York aspiration, wanting, wanting to be seen." Those stomping their Manolos in affront at Rohatyn chose not to notice how their passion for gracious living had developed a reek, like the cigarette smoke in their furs. How, for instance, did every spin land on Ivan Boesky's number? No one wanted to ask or know, but SEC litigations climbed. The mayor hadn't wanted to know anything either, but the bizarre suicide of Queens Borough President Donald Manes, who stabbed himself in the heart, revealed an administration shot through with corruption, boroughs run as petty fiefdoms more corrupt than any Model Cities program, computerization used to gull taxpayers. Three out of the four bosses who'd endorsed Koch were crooks, as were five of the last ten party leaders and the last two county leaders in Queens and the Bronx. Koch had a mini-stroke from the shame, but New York was shameless. Every boldface name in Liz Smith looked to be in on the game, while the rest of the city grabbed what it could, all the way down to the 75th Precinct where a dozen or so dirty cops, the "Buddy Boys" in their "Killing Fields" t-shirts, went beyond shaking down dealers to providing protection for cartels.

The Mob provided vicarious thrills along with pervasive corruption. Killing his own boss while begging to be in the public eye, "John Gotti broke every old-world, old-school code of the American Mafia," wrote Jack Newfield. Whites fretting over Gangsta Rap cheered him on and lined up to see *Scarface* and *Wiseguys*, their nostalgia for *The Godfather*'s archaic honor system an ethnic version of the Lost Cause that Hip Hop happily assimilated out of a shared love of the hustle. In real life, the Five Families squeezed Renaissance New York hard. The Gambinos forced companies in the Garment District into permanent trucking "marriages"; the Luccheses took over cargo handling and unions at JFK—from 1977 to 1987, its share of American air freight fell from 41% to 33% in part because of them. The Genovese Family controlled Fulton Fish Market and had control of Javits Center from the groundbreaking. Conventions demand intricate timing, and once again the Mob taxed time and disorder: A trade show at Javits cost 2½ times what it did cost in Chicago, where only three workers were required to unload a forklift, not nine, and you didn't have to pay a licensed electrician $80 to plug in a lamp. Concrete cost up to 70% more in New York than other cities, so the City finally just built its own plant. But the problem wasn't just the Mob—it was acceptance of the Mob, who helped make building in Manhattan an estimated 20% higher than what it cost in the rest of the country, and affordable housing that much harder to build. And yet as Governor Cuomo's 1985 Organized Crime Task Force began to investigate the construction industry, the real estate business defended the Mob. To them, wrote Ray Rowan, "the monetary costs of corruption are more than offset by the money saved or earned through corruption." Immigrants offered nonunion labor of often better quality.

But there *was* one man in a white hat: New York's version of Eliot Ness, Rudolph Giuliani. Since being named US Attorney for the Southern District of New York in 1983, Giuliani had become "a kind of folk hero," said *New York*. Staring his Grand Inquisitor's stare, thin hair greased down, he'd brought RICO suits against all five Mob Families, cracked the Pizza Connection heroin case, and prosecuted dirty New York pols. Pudgy little Rudy, so the story went, had always stood up for what he believed; raised a Yankee fan, he'd risked his life by wearing pinstripes on the streets of Brooklyn. At Bishop Loughlin High, he'd led the JFK committee and considered the priesthood until the reality of celibacy sank in, at which point he'd headed up to Manhattan College with one eye still wandering to the collar. ("You should be guilty," he told an interviewer once. "It gives you an opportunity to improve your behavior.") After NYU Law School, Giuliani took his "Jesuitical view of the world" to the Southern District as a clerk and then the US Attorney's office, where he ran the narcotics department. "He told me he wanted to become the first Italian Catholic president of the United States," said an old girlfriend of a man who would make a career out of lambasting identity politics. His convictions tended to follow his ambitions; Rudy became an Independent under Ford to serve as Associate Deputy Attorney General, and then signed on as a full-fledged neocon when Reagan tapped him for the #3 spot in the Justice Department. Giuliani burst into his current US Attorney post with a gangbusters attitude, arguing that press coverage of him helped deter crime; in fact, crime kept rising, but the press loved him. His Catholic righteousness made him look above politics. Which was a very good thing when you wanted to enter politics.

Giuliani's next target was Wall Street. Mike Milken the Junk Bond King made $550 million in 1986, and while Ivan Boesky wasn't as big a fish, his streak of arbitrage wins looked suspicious. Giuliani made his first move days before Boesky's "Greed is good" speech at Berkeley, arresting Drexel managing director Dennis Levine for insider trades. Wall Street bankers "expressed dismay," said the *Times*, but they did not express surprise. Tugging Levine's string revealed a web, and Boesky, presented with the evidence, surrendered to Federal authorities that fall. But he didn't go down; instead, he flipped in exchange for one Federal felony charge and a $100 million fine. Giuliani had tossed him back; Ahab wanted the whale. In February 1987, Federal agents hauled two traders in handcuffs out of Goldman Sachs and Kidder, Peabody; another was arrested in the lobby of his apartment building. Giuliani expected them to crumble, but they fought the charges and eventually won. Still, the point had been made—the days of quietly settling things among gentlemen was over. Wall Street now officially hated Rudy Giuliani, and the feeling was mutual. Asked if he understood the resentment, the DA replied, "I'm probably considerably more intelligent, much more creative, much better able to run things than lots of people who do."

Wall Street had other reasons to be skittish—Mexico's debt problems and the hundreds of S&Ls going belly-up; by the end of 1986, the FSLIC (Federal Savings and Loan Insurance Corporation) was insolvent and $125 billion had been lost. Washington responded with firing up more risk—the long erosion of Glass-Steagall began here when commercial banks were allowed to earn revenue from investment banking. The old structure of one bank to one company had given way to interlocking networks of bankers and clients, allowing everyone maximum speed and flexibility to work with and against, inside and out, all in the interests of profit. Oracles of the Bull had predicted the Dow would hit 2000 the summer of '86 and then correct. The Dow did hit 2000. But it didn't correct. Instead, the glut of luxury apartments pulled co-ops and condos down 15.2%. Everyone sold CMOs now—so Salomon reacted with a strategy Michael Lewis called "Hit and run": waves of young traders churning fast and hard with little concern for anything but their next shot of Jägermeister. The monastic brotherhood was long gone, replaced by man-children fueled by what Lewis called the "eerie popular feeling that no job was worth taking outside investment banking." John Gutfreund himself led the way; at a dinner party that year he reportedly looked his table partner in the eye and said, "Well, you've got the name, but you don't have the money." It was a question as to how long he'd have his own: a slipping bond market forced Salomon to fend off a hostile takeover by Ron Perelman. Everyone was a speculator: in 1987, $1 billion were spent on baseball cards; $350 million were spent on tickets to actual baseball games. Everyone was a gambler: State lotteries spread, Las Vegas and Atlantic City became family destinations, and Indian gaming would soon be legal. Easy credit was now a way of life—the pleasures of the '80s had been charged to credit cards; $375 billion worth in 1987 alone—Robert Heilbroner predicted "a vast crisis" if the US continued to send industrial jobs to Mexico while it concentrated on "handicrafts."

For his part, Michael Bloomberg kept getting up at 5:00 a.m. every morning. He still had no secretary, still made his own plane reservations even as those first 22 Market Master terminals had become 2,500. He'd bought out Merrill Lynch and changed the company's name to Bloomberg LP. In May of 1987, the *Wall Street Journal* and AP began to use it as the official source for US government bond prices. Having a Bloomberg terminal became a necessity on Wall Street, their speed and breadth of information cultivated the sense that money made you smarter than everyone else, as every bit of news, information, and gossip, every timely joke and meme in this pre-meme world came through a grapevine that started with some guy who had one.

The Bull hit 2700, New York retired the last of its Federal debt, *Forbes* published a World Billionaire list, and the party kept going— loud, tense, and sloppy—even as the first sour light crept through the blinds.

The End of Cool

"Oh I'm not going to make it," Andy Warhol had told all the doctors, "I'm not coming out of the hospital." But all the doctors told him that in fact the surgery had gone very well, and on the evening of February 21, 1987, he stretched comfortably on his bed, watching television in the Baker Pavilion at New York Hospital, minus the gallbladder that had been causing him so much pain the last few months. He'd been on something of a New Age kick, making regular rounds between his chiropractor, nutritionist, and shiatsu masseuse, even wearing crystals, but still he'd nearly collapsed after a Fendi fashion show on Tuesday and begged off on the dinner afterward. Sonograms the next day revealed that the gallbladder, damaged by Valerie Solanas's bullet, was severely infected and close to gangrene. Scared as he was, on Friday Warhol had given his Blue Cross number by heart to the admissions office and checked in under the name Bob Robert. After surgery Saturday afternoon and an uneventful recovery, he'd been brought up here to the eighth floor and put in the care of a private nurse, Min Chou. Around 9:30 p.m. he'd called his housekeeper to check in on Archie and Amos, the miniature dachshunds.

Though still claiming to be starstruck by the likes of Sting, Warhol had complained recently about feeling bored, sounding a little puzzled by a culture now so aggressively jaded. He'd gotten his wish—the lines between art, celebrity, and wealth were being erased; fame had overwhelmed meaning—but in the last few years, he'd shown flashes of what could only be called conscience. "I wish someone great would come along in public life," he'd written in *America*, "and make it respectable to be poor again." (He had just sold a painting of a dollar sign to Pia Zadora.) After breaking off with Basquiat, he'd begun volunteering at the Church of the Heavenly Rest on holidays. "You see people with bad teeth and everything," he told his diary in 1985, but the next Christmas he wrote, "If there's this many hungry people there's really something wrong."

Nurse Chou took his blood pressure at 10:00 p.m., and as he slept, she reported to his doctor that the patient was doing fine. Chou didn't record many basic aspects of her care that night; the hospital may have given Warhol a drug he was allergic to; staff may have failed to monitor his status, but whatever the cause, Chou noticed that he was pale at 4:30 a.m. and by 5:45, he'd turned blue. When she finally told a staff nurse, the cardiac team was called, but rigor mortis had already set in. Andy Warhol was pronounced dead of a heart attack at 6:31 a.m.

With Roy Cohn dead from AIDS the year before and now Warhol, New York culture lurched into unknown territory. Si Newhouse finally pried *The New Yorker* away from William Shawn and placed it in the hands of former Knopf editor in chief Bob Gottlieb, who, so far to great relief, only added more cartoons. Max Frankel, the new editor of the *New York Times*, finally allowed the word "gay" to be used and even considered printing color photos. Obscure battles were fought over cable rights; future billions rode on the outcome, yet few New Yorkers paid attention. Elaine's lost some of its sheen—a middle-aged man of means had more choices now as to where he could overpay for pasta and bump into catalogue models. Laws were passed that told you where you could smoke. More than 2,000 mourners filled St. Patrick's Cathedral for Warhol's funeral on April 1—artists, writers, socialites, and celebrities, Factory survivors, and a recording of Lou Reed. Yoko Ono and John Richardson delivered eulogies. "It is hard to imagine what NY will be like without Andy," wrote Keith Haring in his diary. "How will anybody know where to go or what is 'cool'?" But was that really so bad? Warhol, wrote Tina Brown in her journal, "along with Roy Cohn, was one of the two most amoral men of our times . . . Warhol was the manipulative void, the dead star . . . a devouring maw that had to be fed with decadence." Their passings announced the end of an era but also a liberation.

This age of constant funerals also tested the value of cool. Too many had died, were dying—Keith Haring, Tseng Kwong Chi, and Robert Mapplethorpe had all been diagnosed by now; Perry Ellis, Charles Ludlam, Liberace, and Michael Bennett were gone. The *Times* called this moment "The End of the Beginning"; as new infections among gay men slowed, they now confronted the reality that some 30,000 of them were expected to die over the next few years. "Everywhere," wrote Ingrid Sischy, "there was this soft whisper of sadness." On national television at the Statue of Liberty rededication, Reagan's pal Bob Hope quipped, "I just heard the Statue of Liberty has AIDS, but she doesn't know whether she got it from the mouth of the Hudson or the Staten Island Fairy." You had to be angry now. You had to *do* something, but what? A quarter of all people with AIDS were New Yorkers. Tests were available, but in a city where doctors openly complained about caring for AIDS patients, most gays were opposed to testing. The process of approving new drugs was slow and in the meantime, as the AIDS Quilt was unfurled, Burroughs Wellcome gouged prices on the uncertain hope offered by AZT.

Larry Kramer, though, kept on picking up pieces of paper. In March 1987, Nora Ephron asked him to step in for her when she had to cancel a speech at the Gay and Lesbian Community Center. That night he delivered one of his usual tirades to an overflow crowd, but this time he brought factions together behind a new strategy, direct, angry, and demanding. One woman, the story goes, stood up and shouted, "Act up! Fight back! Fight AIDS!" Two nights later, AIDS Coalition to Unleash Power—ACT UP—was born to bully and shame the governmental and scientific communities into throwing everything they had at finding a cure for AIDS. On March 24, 600 protestors tied up traffic on Wall Street and hung the director of the FDA in effigy at Trinity Church. Strident, desperate, and very Out,

ACT UP was not interested in Paradise Garage, Gianni Versace, or Judy Garland. Its logo was a pink triangle recalling Nazi Germany with the words "Silence=Death." ACT UP was profoundly not cool. It would assume the vanguard of the fight against AIDS and herald the future of activism.

La Belle Époque was about to end.

II. Reconsideration

Chapter Twelve

The Age of Atonement

M ost analysts had spent the weekends on their computers, looking for the order in this increasingly disorderly market. The Dow had dropped 235 points the past week, and elfin oilman H. Ross Perot, #3 on the latest *Forbes* list, warned "there's a big one out there waiting to happen." Quantification had New York in its grip, from the Mayor's Management Reports to your daily mutual funds results, Rotisserie baseball team, or T-cell counts. Bill Gates was #29 now on *Forbes* and rising; David Rockefeller had slumped to #45. Wall Street, built on numbers, was in the thrall of young computer geniuses nicknamed quants, short for "quantitative analysts" who developed arcane and highly confidential programs called "statistical arbitrage," a modern alchemy that claimed to make money without risk using formulas so obscure as to become a sort of numerology. A visitor to a Santería diviner during this time noticed that the chain thrown to tell the future used the same binary code as a computer. "The entire universe is made of something's and nothings . . . ," said the *babalawo*. "All the knowledge that can be had lies between the one and the zero." But despite this more than passing connection to the mystical, quantitative analysis was based on the belief that everyone behaved rationally—a lot to assume from people whose prime motivation was money. Meanwhile, firms employed "computer assisted trading strategies," such as "portfolio insurance," that hedged stocks by shorting index funds: if your individual stocks went down, you'd make it up by betting the whole market was going down.

And it was going down as traders hit their desks that Monday morning, Asian and European markets plummeting on their screens. The opening bell rang and the slaughter began. Sell orders from portfolio insurance holders still hadn't caught up from Friday and so, anticipating bigger drops, nearly everyone sold more, with much of that "everyone" being computers programmed to sell when a stock hit a certain low. This rational cycle fed on itself for a few minutes until ten; then a large institution put up $100 million blocks of shares and the bottom fell out. Some trading floors went wild—traders screaming, climbing on desks, ordering steaks from Delmonico's in *Titanic*-like oblivion. Others sank into meditative silence. Wall Street was, said Paul Tudor Jones later, "gripped with complete fear." Some reported having out-of-body experiences. For the first time, traders watched their fortunes disappear live on computer screens. Crowds gathered in Times Square, in front of TVs at bars; thousands more flocked to the Stock Exchange to witness what looked like the start of another Great Depression. This was less a repeat of the past, though, than it was what Jim Chanos called, "the first global crisis of the modern financial world." Margin calls and fund redemptions mounted; the ticker ran on a two-hour delay. The final hour was the worst; the Dow fell 3.5 points a minute as computers proved their efficiency, letting sellers sell faster than they'd ever been able to sell before. Increasingly baroque, the algorithms had created the risks they were intended to expose. At the bell, the Dow had dropped 25%, 508 points, on a record volume of 604 million shares. But it wasn't over. The next day the entire financial system nearly buckled, the meager gains of an opening rally desperately consumed by lunchtime, and the New York Stock Exchange considered shutting down trading. Though the markets finally settled, at day's end the Dow stood clutching the ropes at 1738, down 1,000 points from its August high. In two months, a trillion dollars had evaporated.

The Bull lay motionless on the Street. A *Times* headline read, "The Plunge: A Stunning Blow to a Gilded, Impudent Age." "[T]he expansiveness and the money fever have spent themselves," wrote *New York*. ". . . the city is gripped by foreboding." La Belle Époque had ended in flames and now came judgment from on high, declared by Tom Wolfe whose *Bonfire of the Vanities* landed in bookstores amid hosannas. A self-proclaimed "status theorist" and Balzac admirer, Wolfe seemed to have snuck into every room, listened at every boudoir door for this second draft that vividly, viciously skewered "social X-rays" and the "Masters of the Universe" entitlement of his bond trading antihero Sherman McCoy, the Murdoch-corrupted press, and grandstanding Black activists. The age of atonement began. Business schools suddenly included classes on ethics and bankers performed public self-flagellation, while on the seventeenth floor of his new offices in the Lipstick Building, Bernie Madoff, desperate for cash, falsified his first trades. What action there was on Wall Street came from M&As orchestrated for quick profits; by 1988, 121 of the S&P 500 had been consumed. The real estate market melted.

Wealth in New York does trickle down, but not in a rational, even shower of largesse; it travels through networks of Who You Know—who's your hairdresser, your wallpaper guy, your dermatologist?—while leaving out those who aren't in networks. So City Hall projected a disastrous dive in tax revenue. The future of Renaissance New York had been predicated on the FIRE sector riding a smooth path to infinite Growth, but now, for example, Salomon Brothers pulled out of the Coliseum and suddenly that budget windfall disappeared. Amid warnings of dirty streets, fewer cops, and more potholes ahead, Koch's shift away from Retrenchment made it look to some critics as if nothing had really changed from the Fiscal Crisis, even with balanced budget laws and improved technology. The good times *had* papered over many old problems: the ten-year capital plan, for one, had only begun in earnest so the Williamsburg Bridge, in precarious shape, needed to be closed in April 1988. Battening the hatches, Koch froze hiring and rediscovered productivity and efficient management; he assembled the Cary Commission, 160 executives and City managers who came up with fifty money-saving actions. At least he was on the record for having tried.

And then a forgotten leftover from Retrenchment contaminated everything. On May 13, 1988, trucks jammed West Side streets as developers raced to pour foundations for eleven new office towers and four hotels to beat the deadline for the 1982 zoning bonus. With tax revenue about to drop, the City would now have to give breaks to developers for adding the equivalent of all the office space in Pittsburgh. Times Square was pushed to the brink; a stalled market meant no deals, which meant no recent comps, which meant as the Times Square Construction Authority began buying up properties, all the appraisals were based on the exorbitant boom values of a few years before. Suddenly the cost of buying all this land was higher than all the tax breaks could ever return over all ninety-nine years of the lease. The project was put on hold, but New Yorkers wanted something to happen in Times Square, plus 17 million tourists helped pay 400,000 salaries in 1987, so if something big didn't happen there now, that industry would take a huge hit. There was no going back.

Protect Me from What I Want

It was time to worship something other than the Bull. The goal of Claude Shannon's Information Theory in 1948 had been to eliminate "meaning" as much as possible in order to simplify the transmission of information, but art and humanity are all about "meaning"—the static in the transmission—and meaning suddenly enjoyed a new, if passing, vogue. After years of Bolivian marching powder and kamikazes, the word *recovery* now entered common parlance with an entire culture of "12-step" programs; New Yorkers talked (constantly) about getting sober, letting go, and letting God as part of a general purge and quasi-spiritual awakening that embraced Eastern practice along with New Age quackery and crystals. The hot summer convinced a growing number that "the greenhouse effect" was real, and the White House confirmed that the Reagans consulted an astrologer. The unsettling phrases Jenny Holzer carved into marble captured the unease: "PROTECT ME FROM WHAT I WANT," read one.

Boomers heading toward middle age still wanted, but they couldn't afford to want quite as much now, so they went back to conscience. The *avant-garde* continued drifting to Brooklyn's smaller scale and slower pace; BAM was already established as the home for Cage, Cunningham, Monk, and Morris. "If there's one thing Brooklyn's not, it's pretentious," said art dealer Ivan Karp. Even *Spy* deemed it "certifiably chic" in a not entirely tongue-in-cheek way. Aging Downtown survivors like David Byrne and Spalding Gray, Laurie Anderson and Philip Glass had transitioned from young rebels into bourgeois provocateurs, aiming polished yet still countercultural works at audiences that needed to get home in time for the babysitter. The moment's graphic look—spare, sophisticated collage with fussy, retro type or bold social and political statements—flowed from Tibor Kalman, a former SDS organizer at NYU who'd designed the Barnes & Noble scribe logo for his friend Len Riggio. His globalist, activist—and yet unashamedly materialist—aesthetic on everything from Benetton ads to the menu at Florent made consumer identity a form of political statement and helped Boomers balance their good intentions with their resolve to hold on to whatever they had, thus warming the bed for the Clinton years ahead.

Public spaces offered some hope. New plans for Bryant Park were approved, and in March 1988, Dan Biederman and the Bryant Park Corporation formally took over responsibility. Boards went up and in July backhoes dug up the entire lawn. A month later, the Central Park Zoo reopened, offering a taste of what New York could be. If this wasn't the zoo you remembered, it was the one that should always have been here, the kind of safe, celebratory space you went to other cities to find, its former condition shameful and inexplicable now except to those who fetishized past brutalities as nostalgia. Some complained the new admission fee was exclusionary, but it let the City stop doing a half-assed job so responsible professionals could properly run a humane facility. Elizabeth Barlow and the Conservancy had restored Belvedere Castle, Bethesda Terrace, and the Grand Army Plaza. Crime in Central Park had dropped 50%, so now its biggest problem was the private schools and other nearby stakeholders who'd used it wherever, whenever, and however they liked. Then the Conservancy began to require permits. As with pooper scoopers, the largely White users squealed until they figured out the system, at which point they acted as if they'd always been excellent stewards of the park and welcomed permits as a way to limit access.

Another public space New Yorkers could feel positive about was the subways. Though the entire rolling stock was graffiti-free, other improvements were hard to see for the homeless and panhandlers. The

MTA's original plan was to roust or arrest them all and spray down the platforms, a plan George Kelling told them was "immoral," so instead, they ran ads: "The Subway. We're coming back so you come back." But riders didn't come back. So with Kelling's input, and the precedent of the Urban Park Ranger program, Kiley and Gunn rolled out Operation Enforcement in October 1989; the Transit Police would either arrest you or throw you out of the subway for nuisance crimes like panhandling, urinating, or drinking alcoholic beverages. The initiative didn't last long; transit cops considered these arrests beneath them, and in the first in-depth legal encounter with what would be called "order-maintenance legislation," Judge Leonard Sand ruled that begging was protected speech. The public and the press came out largely on the MTA's side; riders wanted to feel safe. The meaning of "Quality of Life" took a step away from creating a shared life in the city toward enshrining Lifestyle over speech.

On the Lower East Side and the East Village, the response to most everything was "Die Yuppie Scum!" Basquiat was alive, but barely. Some claimed he had AIDS, which wasn't true but wouldn't have surprised anyone who saw him with sores on his face, teeth falling out, drunk or strung out. Severing most connections, he made weak attempts at cleaning up and had one last show in April 1988. "New York's changed," he told a friend. "I hate it here." Tompkins Square Park showed how messy Olmsted's vision of Democracy can be. Through the summer of 1988, tents went up that rendered it part homeless camp, part political squat, and unsafe, especially for the much-loathed stroller pushers who wanted bohemian cachet without bohemian poverty. The City imposed a curfew, and culture clash became literal when bottles were lobbed at the police. Two nights of teargas, helicopters, and searchlights ensued; cops in riot gear chanting "Kill, kill, kill" and brutalizing both protestors and residents with such indiscriminate vigor that they had the unlikely effect of temporarily unifying everyone who lived around the park. Already scarred by scandal, Koch looked cruel, the city slipping out of his control. A few days later, Basquiat was found dead in the Great Jones Street loft. "[I]t was not a surprise to anyone," said Haring. His father buried him in Green-Wood Cemetery, not far from where he was born. Back on Avenue A, Ann Magnuson stumbled awake in the middle of the night to feed her cat. When she tipped the box of Purina Cat Chow, out spilled thousands of cockroaches. In tears, she booked a flight to California.

Of course, not *everyone* would have to atone.

Diane von Furstenberg summed up the extent of breast-beating among *nouvelle society*: "A lot of us became fat and rich. And plunged right into the Establishment we condemned," she said. "Which is okay, I guess . . ." Black Monday hadn't stopped the galas; two weeks after, Christian Lacroix had debuted his new line at the World Financial Center for 610 guests at $500 a person. In November, Random House had published *The Art of the Deal* by Donald Trump, whose disdain for tradition and good taste had by now convinced striving classes that he was one of them. The people who resented him were the meritocracy who followed the rules; those on top and those on the bottom both knew Balzac had it right: "Behind every great fortune," he'd written, "there is a great crime." For Liz Smith, the love of money could still excuse anything. "It is refreshing," she wrote of "The Donald," "to find a rich person who isn't pretending to be broke or modest and unassuming, hopping and skipping on hot coals to avoid being called crass and vulgar when it comes to the most absorbing subject known to the average man and woman in 1988: money . . ." She finished, "Let's not kill Donald. Don't you want to see what happens when he grows up?" In the meantime, he borrowed $407.5 million to buy the Plaza, taking out full-page ads promising to make it "perhaps the greatest hotel in the world." He mulled public office. "I'm not running for president," he said, "But if I did . . . I'd win." The Helmsleys, on the other hand, were sacrificed for the sins of their class; Giuliani indicted them for tax evasion.

"We have dined out on the decadence," wrote Tina Brown, "and now must deconstruct the collapse." She said Donald Trump's book party in December 1987 was "the last party of the Reagan era." That may have been so, but it wasn't the last party. Social New York danced on with the kind of nervous energy that came from wondering if the next great crime to be discovered would be yours. The city, wrote Liz Smith, "is divided into people who have enough to shield the rest of the world out and those who don't." Just days after the Helmsleys' indictment came the $3 million Royal Wedding of Laura Steinberg and Jonathan Tisch.

"[I]t will have to be cleared by the SEC," quipped one minor Tisch. The cake alone cost $17,000, and Gayfryd had redecorated Central Synagogue with a few things from their home—"We tried very much to respect the integrity of the synagogue by using period pieces," she reassured reporters.

With Warhol dead, who decided what was cool? Artist Ashley Bickerton appropriated logos to create what Adam Gopnik called "embittered and vengeful parodies" while Jeff Koons's *Banality* series of porcelain sculptures, including most famously *Michael Jackson and Bubbles*, made kitsch comments on kitsch that produced an unsettling barbershop-mirror infinity. To the Style Industry cool now just meant being in constant production. Between 1979 and 1989, 2,500 new magazines came out. When Tina herself threw the "best party in Manhattan since Truman Capote's Black and White Ball" to celebrate the fifth anniversary of *Vanity Fair*'s reboot, she could make as good a claim as anyone that she had taken Warhol's role, too. Auctions had become standard practice in publishing, with agents pushing for faster and faster responses until Jeffrey Archer finally sent an entire manuscript by fax to Joni Evans, forcing the business to find yet another gear. *The Art of the Deal* wasn't an end; it announced that "the Deal" was now the information that counted most.

Waiting

A little over a month after Black Monday, fifteen-year-old Tawana Brawley had been found inside a plastic bag, beaten, her hair cut off, covered in feces with racial slurs written on her body. She'd claimed that a White man with a badge had abducted her and had, along with five other White men who appeared to be law officers, subjected her to four days of rape and sodomy before dumping her in the woods near her home in Wappingers Falls, a good hour north of the city in Dutchess County. Brawley's story was horrifying. So much so, in fact, with its grind house plot of a passel of Southern fried lawmen preying on a pretty Black teenager that it sounded almost too horrible to be true; the local police certainly weren't buying it. But Howard Beach *had* been true. Michael Stewart *had* been true. And four White men had just been arrested in nearby Peekskill for harassing a Black man. It *was* possible and Tawana did appear traumatized.

Brawley's story kicked off an acid year of protest, libel, and racial murder. Among all the strange poison in New York race relations, this would be the strangest. For counsel, the family chose Maddox, Mason, and Sharpton, who'd by now commandeered Black activism in New York. Maddox, beaten by police while an undergraduate at Howard, used his cases to raise consciousness more than achieve specific justice, but his guerilla courtroom tactics could backfire; though he'd represented Michael Stewart's family and successfully defended Cornell student Jonah Perry against charges that he'd tried to mug a cop, he'd also once gotten into a courtroom brawl and his brutal cross of a White model slashed by his Black client tarnished any claim he had to higher ground. In December, with the jury still out on Howard Beach, Sharpton and Maddox led protestors to pull the emergency cord on eight subway trains at 5:00 p.m., paralyzing the city with their first Day of Outrage; the next day, three White teens were found guilty of manslaughter in the death of Michael Griffith. In February, Officer Edward Byrne was shot while sitting in his patrol car, in revenge for the conviction of a drug kingpin. When a special prosecutor was named on the Brawley case, Maddox advised her to not cooperate: Negotiations ensued, spots on *Geraldo* and *Phil Donahue* where she spun her tale out into a gothic, statewide conspiracy implicating officials up to New York Attorney General Robert Abrams himself. Maddox and Sharpton wore thin; after a few months, 55% of Blacks had an unfavorable opinion of Sharpton, and when it was revealed that he'd once worn a wire for the FBI, the three became known to some Black leaders as "Fire, Liar and Wire."

On October 6, 1988, the State grand jury declined charges in the Tawana Brawley case. Through that year, wasted over what all the evidence said was a hoax, a record 1,867 homicides had been committed in New York City, half of them related to crack. The hottest ticket that fall was for the Lincoln Center production of *Waiting for Godot* starring Robin Williams and Steve Martin, though for many, especially kids, Godot was coming every day. Child abuse cases had nearly doubled and the seventeen City agencies dealing with the 89,331 involved still weren't connected, their data unreliable, tracking weak. And 26% of kids in New York between

12 and 17 were regular drug users. When it came to the homeless, New Yorkers had gone from sympathy to oblivion to now something close to hostility as politics outweighed common sense. Forty-year-old schizophrenic Joyce Brown, who also called herself Billie Boggs, lived on a sewer grate at 65th and Second where she swore and spat at passersby, ran into traffic, exposed and relieved herself as she saw fit. Forcibly hospitalized under administration procedures issued to deal with anyone in Brown's state, she claimed that she was being unfairly imprisoned. The New York Civil Liberties Union took her case and won, and though she lost on appeal, the hospital released her in February 1988. A cause célèbre, she spoke at Harvard, and in weeks was back swearing and spitting in Port Authority. Koch still denied homelessness was a housing problem even as tens of thousands of units moved out of range of the poor; in 1987, 63% of welfare families not in public housing had to pay more than their shelter allowance for rent. Families were warehoused in for-profit hotels like the Carter and the Martinique, while he declared an emergency that let the City place the homeless in armories and barrack-style shelters; the homeless hated them, and so did their neighbors. One of the few new ideas came from the governor's son, Andrew Cuomo. A dark sort of prodigy raised in smoke-filled rooms, he'd been a part-time AAA mechanic and political operative with no compunctions about getting up in someone's face in order to put muscle in his father's philosophy, and now he'd created a public-private form of transitional housing he called HELP. Otherwise, City services were visibly slipping.

For many, Godot wasn't even close. Black Monday had simply let off some steam; there'd been 49 billionaires on the *Forbes* 400 list when the market crashed and a year later there were 51. And then a bizarre new threat: in February 1989, the hated Ayatollah Khomeini of Iran issued a fatwa against novelist Salman Rushdie and Viking Press over Rushdie's novel *The Satanic Verses*. The Viking offices became an armed camp as guards took the unheard-of precaution of requiring identification to enter. Soon every office building was doing it. When he came, Godot would now have to sign in at security.

Chapter Thirteen

A Psychic Turning Point

Lou Reed was back. Tickets for his six-night run at the St. James Theatre the last week of March 1989 had sold out immediately to thousands desperate for a bit of the old Downtown. His new hit album *New York* had songs about AIDS and the Halloween parade, Jesse Jackson's anti-Semitism, welfare hotels, and young ghetto lovers: Manhattan was "sinking like a rock." As he took the stage, though, it was clear that more than just the city had changed. Standing in front of the chain-link backdrop wasn't the strung out, bisexual Lou of the Velvets; this Lou was middle-aged and married, wearing what could only be described as a mullet with sensible wire rims. He looked more like Letterman than Kerouac. Nothing about New York stays the same, even the things it considers timeless.

Regretful now, resentful, the city started a free-for-all mayoral election. Rudy Giuliani had resigned his post as US Attorney to run, but some of the shine was already off the man *Spy* called "The Toughest Weenie in America." Though an unforgiving moralist and gangbuster, he displayed a surprising affection for Mob ways, and stories dribbled out about him sneaking around in disguise to buy up copies of any publication where his name appeared. He'd made an enemy out of Republican Senator Al D'Amato by going after his friend Mike Milken and positioning himself as a Fusion candidate à la La Guardia; on the other hand, the Republicans hadn't seen the inside of City Hall for quite a while. D'Amato convinced the funereal cosmetics heir Ronald Lauder to run just to pressure him. On the Democratic side, Koch's own polling showed only an astonishing 17% wanted him back. Over the past four years, 184 members of his administration had been convicted of crimes, and the man who'd once tossed around the Big Apple now looked stunned and ineffectual. But, he would say later, "I was too proud to put my tail between my legs and get driven from office." "The city is war-weary," said one labor leader, "disgusted with itself, ready to turn a corner." In 1988, Jesse Jackson had won 64% of the city's vote in his primary win over Al Gore, a win orchestrated by Jackson's New York campaign head, Bill Lynch, who believed that a coalition of minorities and White liberals—and a united Brooklyn and Harlem—could put a Black candidate in City Hall, namely Manhattan Borough President David Dinkins.

But if New York was ready for a Black mayor, it wasn't clear that Dinkins wanted it to be him. One of the first Black Marines during World War II, the Trenton housekeeper's son had never been the most gifted, the most ambitious, the most *anything* out of the Harlem Gang of Four. Pushed by his parents to get his mathematics degree after the war, he pledged Alpha at Howard and married Joyce Burrows, whose father nurtured his new son-in-law through Brooklyn Law and into the George Washington Carver Democratic Club, where he met Sutton and Rangel and learned the delicate art of advancing Black interests amid the hypocrisy of Northern Democratic politics. Calm, kind, and measured in public, he played tennis every day, but in his office lacked the quick thinking, gut instinct, agility, and power he displayed on the court, prone to odd, unforced errors. When Abe Beame, for instance, named him Deputy Mayor, Dinkins had suddenly realized he hadn't filed a tax return for four years, banishing him to the underwhelming post of City Clerk for a decade, followed by two failed runs for Manhattan borough president against the underwhelming Andrew Stein. He finally won in 1985, but in office his strongly held convictions about justice and equality got lost as he dithered over the options, his well-intended if toothless initiatives on AIDS and homelessness obscured by business-as-usual deals with developers. The chalice was being thrust at him, though, and his graceful air of rectitude, the pragmatism that led him to support the Times Square plan many liberals had fought, and his soothing racial rhetoric made him the right man for these very tricky times. "He'll be a lousy candidate, he'll be a terrible mayor," said one Democratic player, "and I'll support him." Then a horrible crime lit race relations on fire.

Do the Right Thing

A brisk night in early spring. Around 9:00 p.m., a twenty-eight-year-old Salomon banker named Trisha Meili ran into Central Park at 84th for a quick stress-busting jog. A Yale graduate with a big toothy smile, she was a seasoned long-distance runner who felt she had the right to run where she wanted, when she wanted. She was one of "us." The first night of Passover, there was no school the next day so as Meili entered the park, a group of twenty-five or so teenaged boys, Black and Puerto Rican, also headed in at 110th Street, including Antron McCray, Kevin Richardson, Yusef Salaam, Raymond Santana, and Korey Wise. As the group rolled on, some stones were thrown at people, a bicycle rider assaulted, and each of the five made for the exits, but not before Santana, Richardson, and McCray were caught by police and brought to the Central Park Precinct for questioning. Sometime around 1:30 a.m., when it was assumed that they'd all get desk tickets, a woman was found along the 102nd Street path in only her bra, gagged, raped, and beaten, her skull fractured, an enormous amount of blood lost; taken to Metropolitan Hospital, doctors expected—even hoped, given her condition—that she would die. Over the next few hours the three boys were manipulated into confessing to her brutal assault, as well as implicating Wise and Salaam, arrested soon after.

"Wolf pack teen declares: 'IT WAS FUN,'" read one headline the next day, and "Wilding"—the word one of boys had used to describe the group mayhem. The confessions were generally accepted as true, even by many Blacks. "They had only one goal," wrote Pete Hamill, "to smash, hurt, rob, stomp, rape. The enemies were rich. The enemies were white." That these five kids went to school, ate regularly, had parents who cared about them only made it worse. What was their problem? "It has suddenly become permissible to vent frustration," wrote Joe Klein, "to ask questions and say things—often ugly things—that have been forbidden in polite discourse for many years." Why, asked Klein, have Blacks been "resistant to incubation"? Whose fault was it? Well, *theirs* was the answer that needn't be said. The Central Park Five, as they'd come to be known, served to vindicate to many Whites the policies creating an increasingly dual New York. *New York* called it "the metaphor of the deepening crisis so many feel is enveloping New York today . . . a psychic turning point for the city and its people." Superhero comics became adult fare just as frantic predictions of a generation of "superpredators" seemed to be coming true. "[T]he waves of vagrants and petty thieves who filled the streets," wrote Andrew Kirtzman, "would cause citizens for the first time to think of themselves as victims and the less fortunate as the victimizers." Ethnic Whites, especially moderate Democrats, were, according to *New York*, willing "to cede greater police and policelike powers to government." Donald Trump took out ads calling for the reinstatement of the death penalty, and Klein blamed "the unwillingness of black leaders to acknowledge the role of black crime in feeding white racism." The arresting cops celebrated in Elaine's while *The City Sun* ran Trisha Meili's name, citing Tawana Brawley's constant presence in the media as a precedent. Giuliani announced that he was running for mayor, and the Long, Hot Summer began.

While White New Yorkers puzzled over why minorities still hadn't gotten it together after *all* they'd done for them, Fab Five Freddy landed a new gig hosting *Yo! MTV Raps!* and presenting rappers as young Black men and women developing their talents, dreams, and identities; it became the hottest show on MTV. Young college-educated African Americans gravitated to the banged-up, stately neighborhood around Fort Greene Park, most notably a stick figure Morehouse grad from Bed-Stuy in chunky black glasses named Spike Lee whose stylish 1986 film *She's Gotta Have It*, shot in the neighborhood, announced a new generation of Black creativity that defied preconceptions; savvy about business, people like Lorna Simpson, Chris Rock, and Erykah Badu considered Blackness less in relation to Whiteness than as *their* identity on *their* terms. Trey Ellis summed it all up as something bigger than just Brooklyn in his essay "The New Black Aesthetic." The NBA was middle class and made up of "cultural mulatto[es], educated by a multi-racial mix of cultures, [who] can also navigate easily in the white world."

Lee's new film *Do the Right Thing* told the tragic events of the hottest day of the year on one block of Bed-Stuy, informed by the killings of Michael Stewart and Arthur Miller, gentrification, and the pizza parlors of Howard Beach. Sal refuses to put a picture of an African American on the wall of his pizza joint and later, when Radio Raheem refuses to turn off his boom box inside, cops strangle him with the same sort of chokehold used to kill Stewart; Lee's character Mookie, Sal's delivery guy but also his friend, throws a garbage can through the window, inciting the mob to burn it down. (Once again, beloved pizza under attack from Black aggression!) An expression of the anger boiling in New York, *Do the Right Thing* also showed the true bonds and genuine affections that made the hatred so bitterly sad. For the soundtrack, Lee went to Public Enemy, an on-target choice but fraught, as Chuck D had just forced out Professor Griff over a series of anti-Semitic quotes. Spluttering White critics took the song "Fight the Power" as an assault. After calling Lee "a classic art-school dilettante when it comes to politics," Joe Klein then, by the racial-transitive theory, accused David Dinkins of being "wishy washy" over the Central Park Five because he'd asked about the boys' lives without demanding their executions. When it opened two weeks later, the gauzy New York of *When Harry Met Sally* felt like a fairy tale.

Into August the races went, toward the September primary. Damp and vampiric, Giuliani was miserable on the stump, inexperienced and off-putting with the tentative humanity of a priest in street clothes. "Every time you take a veil off," said Koch, "you find some putrescence." Constantly lashing at critics, Giuliani looked too thin-skinned to run such an endlessly nettling city, so he ran to Roger Ailes for help. Despite Klein's patronizing assessment of Dinkins as "sort of like Babar, proud and slow and kind," the endorsements began to arrive for his metaphor of New York as "not a melting pot but a gorgeous mosaic" (Canada uses the same one). Rudy, meanwhile, took Ailes's advice to put emotion ahead of substance.

In Bensonhurst, another White enclave like Howard Beach, four Black teenagers went to look at a used 1982 Pontiac on sale for $900. Gina Feliciano, who'd recently broken up with Keith Mondello to date a Black kid, was having a party nearby. Mistaking the four car buyers for Gina's boyfriend, Mondello rounded up a gang to surround the teens, and Joey Fama put two bullets into the heart of sixteen-year-old Yusuf Hawkins, armed only with the Snickers bar he'd bought coming out of the subway.

"I'm tired of hearing 'sorry,'" said Hawkins's father.

Marches began in Bensonhurst, where residents claimed this whole Hawkins thing was just a terrible misunderstanding: Mondello and his pals hadn't meant to kill *him*; they meant to kill some *other* Black kids. "They are blowing this up into a racial thing," said one local. And then they waved watermelons and threw firecrackers at the Black marchers. Dinkins performed like enough of a statesman to win the primary. Giuliani easily beat Lauder.

And the bell rang for the main event.

Ron Lauder jumped to the Conservative line, so the primaries had only eliminated Koch, but that changed the entire calculus. Giuliani had assumed that he'd be running against him as a center-left, pro-choice, law-and-order, Fusion Republican who'd appeal to Koch-hating African Americans as well as Democrats open to voting for another Lindsay. With Dinkins his rival now, though, Rudy tacked right. But instead of running as a reformer against a corrupt Machine, he decided to run on race, and in a fit of political kitsch, named as his honorary campaign chairman moth-eaten Jackie Mason, who thanked him by calling Dinkins "a fancy *schvartze* with a moustache." Rudy flip-flopped on abortion, then called the whole issue "silly and irrelevant." Dinkins leaned back, Ali in Zaire, absorbing the punches as the Great White Hope slipped 23 points behind, "a snarling, unfocused neophyte" according to Andrew Kirtzman.

Through the summer, the economy had only gotten worse. Except for those bonus buildings, construction had stopped. Mitsubishi bought Rockefeller Center from David Rockefeller and with the world's ten largest banks all Japanese and some 600 Japanese restaurants in the city now, the red sign atop 30 Rock felt like a flag of conquest. Mike Milken's indictment for racketeering and fraud started a leak in the junk bond market then, on October 13, a 200-point "minicrash" in the Dow once and for all ended the Bull market. Michael Lewis's *Liar's Poker* revealed just how absurd Wall Street had become, junk bonds went back to being junk, and the recession everyone had been waiting for settled in.

The race for City Hall slid deeper into the mud. Giuliani used everything he had on Dinkins: links to Black nationalists, dodgy business dealings, mash notes Dinkins allegedly wrote to a lover. Giuliani, on the other hand, had gotten his Vietnam deferment by claiming his job was too important for him to "be sent overseas to get shot at," he'd annulled his first marriage after fourteen years when he found out his wife was his second cousin, and his father had done time for being a Mob enforcer. Dinkins's huge lead melted down. Something profound was shifting. In 1989, 69% of New York's voters were Democrats; 14% registered Republicans, and 15% independent, but in presidential elections, somewhere around 35% could be counted on to vote Republican. That meant a quarter of New Yorkers who called themselves Democrats were open to voting Republican, and though Dinkins entered Election Day with a safe lead, he won by less than 3 points. Lagging behind Jesse Jackson's 1988 numbers in some Black areas, Dinkins had still rolled up big wins in areas such as the Upper West Side and the Village. He may not have been the first choice of Black New York, but he was the Black mayor White, liberal New Yorkers wanted. For a few moments, the city congratulated itself; even Giuliani shouted down booing supporters.

Make Things Look Better Than They Really Are

The Koch era was over.

"Seizing the soul of the city, holding on to it, asserting it and marching up Fifth Avenue with thumbs up," said Daniel Moynihan, "it is a huge, intensely personal achievement." Diana Vreeland had died in the fall of 1989, after a few years out of public sight. "Make the best of things," was how one writer summed up her credo, "and make things look better than they really are," a philosophy that could easily describe New York under Koch.

On his last days in office, Koch got up at 5:00 a.m. and went to the gym, as usual. "I leave with joy," he told reporters as he cleaned out his desk, holding back tears. Your nutty uncle had become a cranky old man, and the death of Billy Martin on Christmas Day had made the passage of time so clear, the fact that New York had become something so much larger, faster, and hungrier than it had been on "I Love New York" Day. There'd been a Renaissance; unequal, precarious, and even bloody sometimes, as the one in Italy had been, but a rebirth nonetheless. New York was computerized, or at least well on the way, fueled by the constant production of wealth, serviced by a class of aspirational white-collar workers on one level and a low-end service class further down. The budget was balanced; Westway had been stopped; Battery Park City quietly blossomed, and who the hell knew what would happen in Times Square. Central Park would be a jewel again. The housing program had opened a door to the middle class, especially for immigrants who would over the next twenty years provide talent, energy, and creativity to the city's regeneration. But New York had also veered back in peril, vulnerable now to the fortunes of finance and real estate. Drugs, crime, and homelessness were shredding all five boroughs. The Big Bang of technology and reorganized civic administration had—in a few places, at least—cleared out a static bureaucracy with innovation and cooperation until the money rolled in and, said bond advisor James Lynch, "Everybody was fat, dumb and lazy in giving the store away." Charter reforms approved by voters that year made the City more democratic on paper; the Board of Estimate was eliminated, and each district now contained around 145,000 people, compared to 240,000 before. But as global capital consolidated, such "democratizing" reforms undermined collective powers like political machines and unions that had, among other things, served as way for those with little power to throw in with others. In theory, outlawing the Board of Estimate gave power to the people, but it also continued the herding of individual voters toward the personal and moral realm, safely away from the growing networks of public and private power that now went forward with less oversight. Those who weren't in strong networks would be less than full players.

It rained the night of December 31. At midnight, David Dinkins stood before his old friend and law partner Fritz Alexander and swore the oath as New York's 106th mayor while Koch hosted a final New Year's Eve party. He moved to a two-bedroom apartment on the sixteenth floor of Two Fifth Avenue with excellent views of the Empire

State Building. Among his new neighbors were Bella Abzug and Larry Kramer. "I spent the last nine years trying to get him out of office," said Kramer. "Now I've got him on my doorstep. I can't believe it."

A few months later, while Koch did his grocery shopping at Balducci's, a guy yelled, "You were a terrible mayor!" Koch yelled back, "Fuck you!" Everyone watching applauded.

At least that's how Koch told the story.

Chapter Fourteen

Dave, Do Something!

Deep behind the baseline, David Dinkins in spotless tennis whites bent his knees, loosely held the racket, and got ready.

The first serve came fast and hard, as soon as he entered office.

Income tax receipts had fallen another 30% since October; the gap was suddenly $800 million, and with its own $1.4 billion deficit, the State wouldn't be much help. Add mandates from the new charter and Dinkins had to find $1.8 billion to balance the budget. His entire platform zipped past in a blur. At his inauguration, Desmond Tutu at his side, he'd announced that New York would once again lift up the weak and powerless. Now not only would those senior aides and after-school programs, help for the homeless, and more lead paint tests not happen, but he'd have to make cuts.

Two weeks later, a dispute broke out between Haitian immigrant Ghislaine Felissaint and the Korean employees at the Family Red Apple market in Flatbush; either she'd been unfairly accused of shoplifting or tried to walk out after paying $2 for $3 worth of produce. Things got physical, peppers thrown, hands placed in anger. The police arrived amid flying rocks and bottles. Felissaint called C. Vernon Mason and Sonny Carson, who once said, "I don't hate just Jews. I hate all white people." The two established a picket in front of the Family Red Apple that soon spread down the street to another Korean market. The three tabloids happily fanned a small if symbolic argument between two minorities:

Koreans had woven the crime and harassment they'd experienced here into the racism they'd learned from decades of US military presence in their homeland, while Blacks felt colonized. Dinkins had been elected to exert a Tutu-esque moral suasion, but he was no Desmond Tutu. Delivering platitudes without visiting the store, the mayor appeared frozen and feckless. Whites shook their heads; Blacks felt he hadn't backed Felissaint enough.

30-Love.

On February 1, Mayor Dinkins presented his first budget. Parks would lose $12.3 million; pools would be closed, maintenance reduced to a minimum. The Clean Teams that manually cleaned streets would be phased out, the next class of police cadets delayed. Dinkins plugged the hole with short-term fixes like diverting the Battery Park City housing funds into the general budget. It might as well have been game, set, and match. The press offered acid flashbacks of the Fiscal Crisis—piles of garbage, mayhem in the streets—and decided that the problem of the '80s hadn't been Wall Street's ethos of greed—it was City Hall, the unions, and the spending Koch had restored. And Dinkins would have to pay. He would never fully recover, but his term would prove to be an inflection point in New York City history. Fifty years of assumptions about the world fell with the Berlin Wall; the Japanese bubble burst, and the threat of nuclear war ended just as Peak AIDS, Peak Crack, and Peak Crime converged on New York. In the next four years, crime would drop, Disney would come to Times Square, and both the Internet and Brooklyn would emerge as new frontiers, yet Dinkins's few significant wins would never cohere as a legacy, leaving him at best a well-intended relic of Great Society policies; at worst, a man not up to his job.

I Was Not Born with That Desire

Big names now crashed in colorful ways: Buster Douglas knocked out Iron Mike Tyson on February 11, the same day Liz Smith dropped the gossip bomb that Donald and Ivana were splitting up, launching a cottage industry of nonstop coverage including chorine Marla Maples's front-page confession to a friend that he was "the best sex I've ever had." Ed Koch said he was on Ivana's side, though he didn't even know what that side was. Baseball commissioner Fay Vincent banned George Steinbrenner from the Yankees.

The recession bit hard now. Between 1989 and 1992, New York would lose almost 14% of its jobs, its 13% unemployment double the national rate; more than one million New Yorkers would soon be on some form of welfare. Norman Steisel, now first Deputy Mayor, had to explain that New York was "in much better shape than it was in 1976." It remained active in the bond market, and the safeguards built in since the Fiscal Crisis meant the greatest threat now was for the Financial Control Board to take over management of the City's budget again. Work continued on the capital plan and the housing initiative, and Labor wasn't convinced there even *was* a budget problem, yet the debate focused on how the City "still" didn't work, as if nothing had changed since 1978. The administration featured some familiar names: Nat Leventhal ran the transition, Steisel dealt with the Crisis Regime. But to balance him politically, Dinkins named his progressive, aggressive campaign manager Bill Lynch second Deputy Mayor. Carrying himself like the humble editor of a small-town paper, Lynch had long worked to unite the city's Black leaders and create Black political power, but says Gordon Davis, he "didn't understand the city and how to run it." The main problem, though, was Dinkins. "I wish I could say," he wrote later, "that when I was young I thought, Gee, one day I'll be mayor of New York, but unlike some, I was not born with that desire." He did bring style and gravity to City Hall, rotating his four tuxedos through the galas, banquets, and ribbon cuttings he considered as important as anything on his desk; the *Post* took to calling him "Dapper Dave," his penchant for showering multiple times a day quickly noted by a press corps regularly forced to wait for his tardy arrival at events. His bearing, read by some as aloof, had been literally beaten into him as a boy—his mother once slapped him for addressing one of her friends by their first name—but manners to him were mostly an expression of self-respect. "I want to be heard as a man," he said, "not as a black man." This was not an entirely popular statement among some Black New Yorkers who, proud as they were to have a Black mayor, already found him *too* comfortable operating in the White world. Yet he kept the city cool when only Joey Fama was found guilty of the Bensonhurst murder. Marching alongside Nelson Mandela down the Canyon of Heroes was maybe his finest moment. The press, though, treated him with thinly veiled racism. In July, for example, sporting Mob Boss sunglasses after an eye injury, he talked about being tough on crime. The reporters present laughed in his face. "I'm a follower of Martin Luther King and I'm an admirer of Gandhi," he said, leaving in a huff, "but I'm also a marine, and I don't intend to be shoved around." His power represented a collective struggle that he was trusted not to debase, so he refused to entertain the largely White, largely hostile press corps at the annual Inner Circle dinner.

Yet Dinkins too often came off as an irritable retiree behind the wheel, deliberate one moment, rash the next. "There's no sense of strategy at City Hall," said Ray Horton of the Citizens Budget Commission, "no sense of how the pieces . . . fit together." Matters came desperately, tragically to a head that September. In for their annual visit to the US Open, the Watkins family of Provo, Utah, was on its way to Tavern on the Green when a gang attacked them on the E train platform at 53rd and Seventh. Brian Watkins, twenty-two, stepped in to protect his mother and was stabbed once in the chest. As he lay dying, the attackers went off to Roseland. So brutal and so random, the crime made New York City look like a madhouse again, to which the mayor said, "It really gets to be a function of how these things are reported," as if the press was the issue, not the murder. After the fallout from that, he tried again: "If, as has been observed, it is necessary for me to express myself in a different fashion so as to convey to the television and radio audience that which may not get conveyed otherwise, I will try to learn to do that because it's important that people know that I am angry and I am concerned." No one felt better. Confronted with the *Post* headline "DAVE, DO SOMETHING" and a withering cover story in *Time* titled "The Rotting of the Big Apple," Dinkins ordered up an expensive anti-crime initiative that he announced a day after settling on a generous raise for the city's teachers. A week later, as he was floating a hiring freeze and 15,000 layoffs, Dinkins ordered City workers to craft a new cherry headboard for his Gracie Mansion bed, at a cost of $11,500. When he finally went to the Family Red Apple to buy $10 worth of produce, not only did no one care, it came so late as to be insulting. "In the past," said Bobby Wagner, "New Yorkers were willing to tolerate a lot if they had the sense they were getting leadership."

Couch Potatoes

All this post-crash uncertainty had festered into an existential crisis, a reconsideration of New York itself just a few years after it had been "saved" by Koch. "The city has careened into a remarkable fit of despair," cried Joe Klein in *New York*, "a panic over crime, real estate values, the economy, racial animosity, and the future of urban life itself." Lifestyle was under siege. While Lew Rudin convened an emergency meeting of some thirty labor, finance, and businesspeople to light the Bat Signal, New Yorkers White and Black, rich and poor, crawled into their holes, locked the doors, and hunkered down, from Yuppie co-op owners unable to sell their apartments to poor families doubled up in public housing to kids from the Bronx and St. Albans, kept inside no matter if Mister Softee was right downstairs. Seniors were even more vulnerable. Cops hesitated to attend union meetings because they were afraid to go out at night. Polls showed virtually everyone was considering leaving the city, but you couldn't give a one-bedroom away. Intense families became even more intense as couples with small children, once hoping to trade up, got used to the crib in the living room. "There is a great deal of sullenness and hopelessness," said a psychic consultant in Queens. "You now see frightened people huddling in their own little space." AA meetings were bigger than the Tunnel now, and no more chasing fads like Mexican and Creole food. "Most everything's been done," reported one jaded restaurateur.

New Yorkers turned their self-imprisonment into a trend; they became "couch potatoes." Faith Popcorn called it "cocooning," a return to the womb after all that '80s id. With the murder rate about to crack 2,200 in 1990 and the Central Park Jogger on their minds, those afraid of going out after dark made a mad rush to the video store on the way home from work, wrestled neighbors for copies of *Joe Versus the Volcano* and *The Little Mermaid*, or tucked into Boomer-friendly television like *Moonlighting*, *Thirtysomething*, and *Hill Street Blues*. Stalled Yuppies binged on old movies and Ken Burns's twelve-hour documentary about the Civil War, surrounded themselves with mid-century hokiness that Kurt Andersen called "camp lite," coming into their majority by lying on the couch watching television just like Mom and Dad. The Knicks, a hard, perpetually pissed off basketball team, became a citywide passion; the banging manic intensity of Patrick Ewing, Charles Oakley, Anthony Mason, and John Starks expressed the world outside your apartment, something that you increasingly didn't have to experience now that an influx of Mexican immigrants let you order in more than just pizzas and Chinese. Fax machines, enjoying their brief Golden Age, sent legal documents and song requests. Outside of the Central Park Zoo and Nora Ephron movies, commonplace civilization seemed finished. "There is the loss of a sense of public order," said Fred Siegel as the Central Park Five convictions came down, "and no faith that it can be restored."

Taking Back the Subway

The desk cop snuck a look up from his newspaper as Chief William Bratton entered Transit Police headquarters that day. In a light *Bah-stun* accent, Bratton ordered him immediately reassigned. Later, walking near Grand Central, he came across one of his own who wouldn't cut it as a security guard. No resources, uninterested workers who considered themselves second-class: Bratton's first day on the job in April 1990 was a lot like Gordon Davis's back in 1978.

The son of a mailman, William Bratton had received a standard issue Irish-Catholic childhood in '50s Dorchester, Massachusetts, he studied hard, went to Mass, and wore his Sam Browne belt with pride. At the age of eleven, he came across a big yellow book in the library titled *Your Police* that made joining the force sound like the best thing a good boy could do if he didn't want to join the priesthood, so after a tour of duty as an MP in Vietnam, he joined the Boston Police and quickly rose, ambitious, progressive, to be the youngest number two in the force's history. The old guard chopped the legs out from under him then, so he jumped to chief of the Boston Transit Police and turned it around. Then he went to the Metropolitan Police and turned that around, too, drawing the attention of George Kelling and MTA head

Robert Kiley. With Operation Enforcement falling apart, they reached out and Bratton became the new head of the Transit Police.

Police and policing in New York were about to undergo historic change. Crime was about to drop and incarceration, after a steady rise into the '90s, would by the end of the decade plummet at a rate nearly as dramatic. Just how related all these facts are is a matter of debate, but what can be said for sure is that no single person or policy by themselves made any of them happen, whatever happened didn't happen all at once. The terms and ideas central to these years regarding crime and punishment—concepts like Community Policing, Broken Windows, Disorder, and Quality of Life—had been discussed and to some degree employed by One Police Plaza since the earliest days of Koch, and in other cities as well. For the next twenty years, they would be conflated, redefined, appropriated, and misappropriated; justice would be done, then abused. It's possible that the fever of crime would have broken no matter what.

But it all started underground. Thanks to Gunn and Kiley, New Yorkers in 1990 were traveling in a cleaner, more reliable subway system than they had for decades. Kiley had hired management consultant John Linder, who'd assigned managers to every station, putting their name and picture up on the wall to instill pride and ownership. But 20% of New Yorkers still thought graffiti was a serious problem; women claimed that between 40% and 50% of the crimes in New York City were committed in the subways when the real numbers were 3% of the felonies. Bratton needed to make the subways safer, but it was at least as important that he made people *believe* they were, and to do that, he'd have to make "probably the most demoralized police force in America" believe first. With Linder's help, Bratton prioritized fare evasion first, disorder second, and crime third, then issued the motto "Taking Back the Subway for the People of New York" to his force. He let himself be seen on the trains, leading officials through the tunnels. Monthly ejections went from 2,000 to 16,000.

One of the many people trying to decide whether Bratton was for real was head of the Central Robbery squad Jack Maple, a 5-foot-8 fireplug with a leprechaun's twinkling eyes and well out on his own island. Raised in Richmond Hill, he'd taken the civil service test at sixteen and gone to transit because he couldn't stand another day not being a cop. Along the way he'd unloaded UPS trucks and worked for a while at 21, where he "realized that even the powerful people pull down their zippers to piss." Brilliant, brave, and a pain in the ass, Maple clocked so much overtime, arrested so many perps that he was asked to tone it down. After four hundred collars and nearly getting shot in the face in Bryant Park, he made detective in 1980 at the age of twenty-seven, the youngest in department history, at which point, something snapped, but in a very unique way. While some cops became gangsters, Maple decided to play the city's other game. First, he went on a diet—30 cups of coffee a day. Nothing else. In five weeks, he went from 225 pounds to 160. He bought three suits, a homburg, some bow ties, and with Phil Rizzuto's buzz-saw voice in his head, went over to The Money Store, where he signed for a $25,000 loan. Every morning he left his wife and kids in Queens for a secret life as a Yuppie in Koch's Renaissance Manhattan, going to Broadway shows, drinking at Elaine's, buying an Alfa-Romeo. This lasted a year. The day he saw all the money was gone, he confessed to his wife and began, slowly, to pay it back. Their marriage was never the same, but he kept the homburg and the suits and now he set up undercover patrols in Times Square, his story immortalized by a profile in *New York*. He was still just a lieutenant in 1990 because the brass didn't know quite what to do with him.

Maple approached Bratton with ten pages of ideas and the two began to talk. One of his ideas changed everything. Maple suggested that they check *everyone* they arrested—fare jumpers, token suckers, smokers on the platform—for outstanding warrants. According to Bratton, they discovered "that many of the people we were arresting were exactly the ones who were causing other problems once inside . . . By focusing on fare evasion to control disorder, we were preventing a lot of the criminal elements from getting on the trains and platforms in the first place." This wasn't exactly Kelling and Wilson's Broken Windows theory, which among other things held that disordered places gave the appearance of a power void that allowed crime to breed. If that were strictly true, the perception of crime should have fallen once the subways began to improve. But Bratton and Maples weren't using Broken Windows to create order; they were using it as pretext to stop people they considered likely criminals. The difference is significant. In one, the theory is that with enough new paint and Keep Off the Grass signs you'd get rid of crime. In New York, the results on that were mixed: crime and crack had taken off on the Upper West Side even in the face of gentrification. Maple and Bratton were essentially co-opting Broken Windows (Maple claimed to never read the article) and well-intentioned attempts to restore a sense of the commons as tools for their crime fighting. They saw that people who did shitty things tended to do shitty things all along the spectrum of shitty things. The goal wasn't to get rid of disorder in the space; they used disorderly acts as a reasonable cause to snare serious criminals. The Transit Police was now actively trying to prevent crime. Maple employed charts and data in ways that other departments in the City had been doing for years, yet still long before the NYPD, such as plotting crimes on some 55 feet of maps. They opened files on everyone arrested in the subways and when they got out of jail, an officer would drop by to let them know that they were aware that they were out. Then Brian Watkins was murdered, "the catalyst," wrote Bratton, "for the turnaround of crime in New York City." Within days Governor Cuomo gave Bratton an extra $40 million to spend on uniforms, vehicles, and radios that actually worked underground. "The Transit Police," he said, "were becoming the Marine Corps."

Upstairs, though, New Yorkers were still hiding in their apartments. Throughout his twelve years in office, Koch had never been directly tied to the rise or fall of crime, and the NYPD had actively dissuaded anyone from thinking they could actually stop it, but now it was expected of Dinkins as if he, Black and liberal, had a personal responsibility for the mayhem. His commissioner, Lee Brown, had played football at Fresno State and after a stint as a cop in San Jose, had gotten his doctorate in criminology at Berkeley. Since 1982, he'd been commissioner in Houston, where he'd had some success with the kind of Community Policing Ward had tried on a limited level, and now the plan was to scale it up. Many in the force still doubted its efficacy, worried that arresting more criminals would make the streets more dangerous because there'd be fewer cops around; strange logic at first glance, but since the arresting officer had to stay with a suspect until arraignment, a process that could take thirty hours, it was a legitimate concern. Bratton supported Brown's vision of Community Policing. "Lee Brown's definition is a good one," he told an interviewer. "[P]olice form a partnership with members of the community to solve problems." No one saw Community Policing as the opposite of Kelling's Broken Windows as Setting or Bratton's Broken Windows as Pretext. All three belonged to the same movement and the new approach was working in places such as Sugar Hill, where Patrolman James Gilmore teamed up with the community to take down the Jheri Kurl Gang.

And then Brian Watkins was killed.

Dave had to do something. He asked Brown how many people he needed. "It was a remarkable request," wrote Brown's then number two Ray Kelly, who was given forty days to completely reorganize the NYPD. Kelly was to the NYPD what Bill Bratton had been to Boston; a product of the Upper West Side, he was Irish, too, and a Vietnam vet; groomed for leadership from the start, first in his class at the academy with a St. John's law degree earned between shifts, a master's in public administration from Harvard's Kennedy School of Government, and the nickname Popeye for his strong jaw, flat nose, and squint. A rivalry began smoldering between him and Bratton that would last for the better part of the next two decades. Kelly's advantage was that he was a lifer at the NYPD; he'd worked all five boroughs, including an undercover assignment to the Mineshaft where, he proudly reported, he "breezed right past the notoriously fickle bouncers." Kelly's 536-page report requested 5,000 new cops, tackling productivity the way most every other department had long ago, using metrics to maximize efficiency and implementing Community Policing throughout the city. Management was as much the point as money. In early October, Dinkins announced "Safe Streets, Safe City: Cops and Kids," the "Kids" part an extensive plan to use schools as community centers. It was expensive—$1.8 billion—and took months of arm-twisting before passage in February 1991.

In the meantime, homicide in New York had hit its peak: 2,245 in 1990. The State's Department of Substance Abuse announced that crack use had peaked, and the City's jail population also hit a peak at close to 22,000. Operation Pressure Point and ramped-up drug enforcement through the '80s had jacked the number of inmates on drug convictions from 834 in 1973 to 11,225 in 1992, and as young Black and Latino men sentenced under the draconian Rockefeller Drug Laws took up more and more prison beds, the State began to fund a range of advocacy and intervention programs to try to get that number down. Brooklyn DA Charles Hynes created a Drug Treatment Alternative to Prison program to push back against mandatory sentencing. Crime began to drop in Midtown—dramatically. "I've never seen such a sharp decrease in robbery anywhere in the city before," said Assistant Chief Thomas P. Walsh. With Business Investment Districts adding their own security, Bryant Park and 42nd Street basically closed, and the huge number of West Side and Times Square construction sites, there were fewer people around to be criminals or victims. A White man stabbed Sharpton in Bensonhurst, and the city stayed calm. In March, Rodney King's LA beating aired across the globe, and New York stayed calm.

Dinkins responded to these hopeful signs with the worst political miscalculation of his career. After signing off on big union contracts, he called the bluff of fiscal hardliners with a doomsday FY92 budget that threatened to lay off 10,000 teachers, cut caseworkers for AIDS, defund Parks, and shut off one out of every four streetlights. With critics calling it a "petty and unsophisticated" negotiating ploy, Felix Rohatyn once again suggested MAC take over, and Moody's downgraded the city. As the battle went into the spring, Dinkins deferred hiring the cops to August 1993, meaning the mayor as of 1994 would get credit for the 5,000 new police recruits he'd made possible. Crime continued dropping, but those who noticed considered it a fluke.

Virtual New York

Another symptom—or cause—of Couch Potatoes and social atomization was technology. As '80s Downtown cool had aged out, died off, moved away, and sold itself to the highest bidder, computers were making a new kind of cool full of its own secret languages, gear, and amazing things like those beautiful morphing heads at the end of Michael Jackson's "Black or White" video. "The world of electronically enhanced media is here," wrote Red Burns of NYU's Interactive Technology Program. "Technology ought to be the verb, not the noun." By 1990, Tim Berners-Lee had created the World Wide Web, Photoshop was released, and Windows 3.0 gave PCs the same easy, graphic interface as Macs. After weathering the screech, static, and *boing* of connection, New Yorkers were gingerly pulling onto the Information Superhighway, and though many headed straight to the sex chats, others grappled with the implications of being able to communicate in real time with everyone in the world, and the city of networks began its path toward becoming a networked city. A virtual New York began to exist. In 1990, ITP grad Stacy Horn hosted a "community of personalities" called ECHO, for East Coast Hang Out. "Like salons," explained *Fortune*, "these computer conversations are gatherings of people who like to communicate and argue, but they are not hampered by boundaries of geography or time." "Cyberspace," was developing its own etiquette, messages, and rituals—the *Times* helpfully defined a few terms such as *post, flame,* and *emoticon*—as some expressed themselves now entirely through words. "It is a revealing, not a transforming, medium," wrote Horn. "In cyberspace, we build worlds with the thing we say." This was very different from the physical New York that thrust everyone jostling, sweating, bumping, groping, swerving into each other. Your dirty talk in that adult chat room could be with an elderly woman in Dubuque, a chubby Black guy in Schenectady, or your mailman. As Times Square struggled in the development bardo, its anonymity—the glory hole, the hand job in the seats—was re-created in cyberspace without the fuss and fear, but also without the feel of warm, human flesh. Architect Richard Saul Wurman, soon to create the TED conference, warned about the sudden overload of data and "Information Anxiety."

As the chat rooms filled up, Prozac became the most widely pre-scribed antidepressant in the country. "You feel that it's worth making an effort," according to one user, "you don't feel hopeless anymore." Prozac further shifted the paradigm away from Freudian motivations toward measurables and action. "[O]ur modern technological society," wrote psychiatrist Peter Kramer, "demands the ability to face outward, expend high degrees of energy, take risks, and respond rapidly to multiple competing stimuli." Without the time and expense of the old leather couch, Prozac wrote a new map of the mind that didn't involve id, ego, and superego, and by eliminating the narrative and just dealing with actions, it dovetailed nicely with the Gilder-Murray mind-set that saw no reason to ask *why* people committed crimes. The negotiated middle, the synthesis, began to cede to Right and Wrong, Black and White, and what made Prozac truly express the age was that not everyone could afford it. Everyone was anxious in New York, but only those who'd done well had the luxury to, as the Nike ads said, just do it.

There was also war, the first since Vietnam. The Gulf War resolved little in the Middle East, but how it was covered pointed to coming media upheavals. After Iraqi dictator Saddam Hussein invaded Kuwait in 1990, George Bush launched Operation Desert Storm on the night of January 16, 1991. New York Couch Potatoes turned on CNN, then the only global 24-hour news network, to hear Peter Arnett and Bernard Shaw describe the first strike on Baghdad à la Edward R. Murrow while tracer fire burst on screen. Streets emptied. The whole world was watching CNN, even in Iraq, igniting a revolution in television. Back in the '70s the Big Three had commanded 92% of all TV viewers; by this point brand-new Fox and cable channels had chipped that down to 65%, and now the birth of a 24-hour cycle that presented news as a constant feed. The bombs were dropping while you watched! "To viewers," wrote one critic, "it was real life, not 'television.'" Along with Prozac and the aborning Internet, CNN provided the first drops of what would become the anesthetizing drip of constant information.

At Trump Tower, New York's vengeful id had spent the spring lying on his bed, talking nonstop on the phone about either his very public divorce proceedings or the opening of his Taj Mahal casino in Atlantic City. By June, Donald Trump was on the brink of defaulting on the $675 million in junk bonds he'd floated to pay for the whole thing; his Plaza employees were instructed to pick through the garbage for recyclables because every nickel counts. No one extended him credit, so he borrowed $30 million from his siblings—their shares of Fred Trump's estate—and sold half his interest in the casino. No one wanted his boat or failed airline. *Forbes* dropped him from the 1990 list of the world's richest people. "Oh, he'll be back," said *Spy*, "in all likelihood recast as a never-say-die survivor." But in the meantime, "Somebody pinch me."

What Went Wrong?

Though gangsta Rap and the Rodney King beating had made LA the new flashpoint of racial aggression, the peace in New York was only provisional, and it ended in Crown Heights that August.

The conflict was a long time coming. Back in the '40s, Lubavitch Hasidim had bought Rebbe Yosef Schneersohn a three-story gothic home at 770 Eastern Parkway that his son-in-law Menachem Schneerson took over after his death, along with leadership of the Lubavitchers. As the sect spread, thousands moved to Crown Heights at the same time as West Indians, producing friction between two immigrant populations elbowing for space that had nearly sparked into flame when police killed Arthur Miller in 1978. Since 1987, Crown Heights's population had risen some 25%, a dramatic increase matched nowhere else in the city, and violence between the two groups rose again.

Out of respect for the Rebbe (and the considerable block of votes he controlled), City officials afforded him a motorcade for his regular visits to his wife's grave, and on the night of Monday August 19, its three cars headed west on President Street. Yosef Lifsh, driving the back car, sped through an intersection to keep up. Some say the light was green; some say it was yellow; others red. Either way, a truck hit him and sent his station wagon onto the sidewalk and into two children, Gavin and Angela Cato, both seven. Lifsh was being angrily dragged out of the car when the police, EMS, and an ambulance arrived, so for his protection, the police removed him while the paramedics tried to free Gavin, pinned to an iron gate. Delivered to the hospital only twelve minutes after he was hit, the boy still died. Violent arguments began. Rumors spread. Within the hour, police were fielding calls about a riot in Crown Heights, but it didn't really ignite until a few hours later as growing crowds joined, then broke apart into separate gangs burning cars, throwing rocks, and finally one, with cries of "Kill the Jews!" attacked a twenty-nine-year-old graduate student named Yankel Rosenbaum. He died later that night. The police mostly stood back and around 4:00 a.m. the rioters dispersed. Brown and Deputy Mayor Milton Mollen assumed that the rain forecast for Tuesday would keep things from flaring up again, but it didn't rain. Instead, Sonny Carson whipped up another mob that looted, set fires, attacked any Whites they saw including cops, who appeared on TVs across the nation either idly standing by or waddling haplessly in pursuit. Wednesday was worse. As cameras rolled, kids screamed about Hitler and burned Israeli flags. Jimmy Breslin was pulled from his car and beaten. No strangers to street violence, the Hasidim fought back, but they were outnumbered. Even after his car was attacked, Brown allowed Dinkins to go to Crown Heights, where he was nearly mobbed and a sniper wounded eight police officers. A furious Dinkins read out Brown, and Kelly took over, quelling the riot within hours.

The damage was profound. "David Dinkins has failed his city," wrote Mike McAlary in the *Post*. Beyond the deaths of Cato, Rosenbaum, and an elderly Holocaust survivor who'd reportedly committed suicide, 38 civilians had been injured, along with 152 police. Sharpton, Daughtry, and others turned the boy's funeral into a platform for anti-Semitism; Rebbe Schneerson never extended his condolences to the Catos. Whites had just seen all their nightmares of superpredators come to life, complete with a Black mayor unable or unwilling to stop it. Dinkins's approval rating fell to 32%. The *Times* declared that "New Yorkers are losing heart." When a December Rap show at City College turned into a stampede, the duty captain refused to send in his men despite the reports of chaos inside. "They're not people," one cop said, "they're animals." Nine died of suffocation.

Hearts were hardening even as crime fell in nearly every category in every precinct, in every borough. The fever was breaking but not quickly enough, and after years of racial friction and roller-coaster change, that was beside the point. Like that plaintive couple ten years before, certain New Yorkers were sure that it wasn't their city anymore. And they wanted it back.

Chapter Fifteen

Mayor School

B ack in the fall of 1990, crime at its peak, Dinkins on his heels, the city found itself with some new allies. "New York looks quite healthy indeed," wrote Peter Salins in the premier issue of a magazine called *City Journal*. His article "Is New York Going Down the Tubes" argued that the city was actually in good shape. It had half the crime rate as Portland, Oregon, was the home of the arts and tastemakers, and rebounding FIRE industries would require the "agglomeration" of highly educated, highly skilled workers who wanted exactly what New York offered. "The question is not whether New York will survive," he declared, "but will New York thrive?" A breath of fresh, if sometimes wonky, air, the real surprise was that *City Journal* was published by the Manhattan Institute which, despite its history with Gilder and Murray, now drew disaffected liberals like Fred Siegel, Henry Stern, and Bobby Wagner to its roundtables. "[N]o one on the left-liberal side that has put out anything remotely as fine-grained as they have," said Jim Sleeper. "The city government is tired, bloated, and anachronistic," wrote Joe Klein. A new kind of Democrat was in the making in New York, a new kind of Crisis Regime emerging, and *City Journal* would lead a dialogue that would warp Retrenchment goals of good government and commonplace civilization into political tools, setting the stage for the city's next evolution.

By this point capitalism had won, if only by a nose, so even though its triumph was more a result of communism's faults than its own strength, the post-Crash articles about Wall Street excess had disappeared, and after three historic pastings suffered by Carter, Mondale, and Dukakis, the Left had stopped functioning in any meaningful way, sucked into the downdraft of the Soviet Union and leaving no critical counterweight to capitalism. Quantitative analysis and economics made everything about measurables now; Prozac Nation didn't care about narrative causes. Arkansas Governor Bill Clinton talked tough on crime and wrapped his love of the free market inside long-winded policy dives and a generational appeal to Boomers whose hippie dreams had been dipped in realism. *Reinventing Government* by Ted Gaebler and David Osborne was already a basic text for Democrats looking to bridge liberal goals with corporate management; they blamed outdated systems—not people. Government had to "turn bureaucratic institutions into entrepreneurial" ones by measuring performance, outsourcing, and bringing management and labor together.

All of which may sound familiar because it was. They and the Manhattan Institute were "discovering" policies that had been around since at least John Lindsay. Gaebler and Osborne illustrated some of their principles with examples from the Koch administration, things like the two-man garbage trucks, labor-management councils, and Project Scorecard. The chapter on "Community" led with Lee Brown's Community Policing program in Houston. Until Koch had decided that the Bull's sudden surpluses made productivity and lean staffs less imperative, New York had, in fact, been way ahead of the curve on "reinventing government"; Broken Windows, Quality of Life, and Community Policing, productivity and technology upgrades had all begun on his watch. But the constant drumbeat of emergencies under Dinkins and his very visible political choices allowed the narrative to grow that nothing had changed since 1975 even though Dinkins's City Hall *was* trying to implement programs you might find in *City Journal*. An advisory task force on management and productivity was in place, and in August 1991, Dinkins announced the Reform and Renaissance Program in hopes of reigniting Leventhal-style productivity, directed by Deputy Mayor of Operations Harvey Robins, who'd been leading an effort to "reinvent government" before *Reinventing Government* even came out. A '60s radical devoted to the dream of a smoothly run, equitable city, he'd been the one who'd set up the secret AIDS program under Koch. Robins beavered through the budget line by line, stripping out waste. Every morning he could be found at Ellen's coffee shop at Chambers and Broadway, "in the back all alone," reports one impressed City Hall regular. "No hangers-on, no entourage, just writing notes to himself about things he was going to do that day." Robins required monthly status reports from all departments as Leventhal had, while Steisel developed a cheaper approach to Medicaid that incentivized doctors to get people healthier instead of billing for endless visits. As to privatization, Koch had learned that it could have unexpected effects; when General Services, for example, had outsourced capital projects to private consultants, the best people left and the City paid through the nose for the services of its former employees. But the 1989 Charter Reform now mandated that Dinkins create structures for privatization along with a new Procurement Policy Board and Office of Contracts. Too often, though, politics still mattered too much, as when the mayor named Andrew Cuomo head of a new commission on homelessness, and then quickly announced his own plan, largely just more government-funded shelters.

Ultimately, Dinkins created an agency devoted to the homeless along Cuomo's public-private model, while the most dramatic example of effective, responsible public-private partnerships was still at work in neighborhoods far from the Manhattan Institute. Koch's Housing Initiative continued to help communities rebuild in the face of crack, AIDS, and crime while HPD head Felice Michetti pushed through the *in rem* inventory, growing again because of the real estate bust. Abraham Biderman, Koch's final housing commissioner, called it "one of the best examples of government accomplishing something." Here was a decentralized citywide network that didn't need lessons from *City Journal* about how to fix broken windows. But only as long as government had the will: Once diverted to help close the budget gap, the Battery Park City bond money never found its way back into affordable housing—"a breach of faith," said Sandy Frucher later.

For the old guard at the Manhattan Institute, though, all this concern with delivering services was nice, but it missed the real point. The affable Myron Magnet, for one, a former Columbia professor and Janis Joplin devotee festooned with Van Buren side chops, had gone neocon in the '70s after one of his neighbors was murdered by a regular at a nearby Morningside Heights soup kitchen; the pastor in charge told upset locals that they'd just have to curfew themselves. To which Magnet had said to himself, quite reasonably, "Fuck you." The real issue, he decided, wasn't hunger or need—it was morals, in particular, the lack of morals among Blacks and the liberals who'd corrupted them. Yes, the Institute had a whole list of the usual demands about rent control, taxes, and zoning for this Dinkins-era crisis, but in the end, just like *Losing Ground*, it wasn't about better serving "Them" when "They" were considered the heart of the problem. "What happened in the 1960s," said William Stern, former UDC head, "which Fred Siegel called moral deregulation and I would call a kind of disguised paganism." When did it begin? Well, according to Murray, by some amazing coincidence it began in 1964, the very same year that the Civil Rights Bill was signed. As Magnet explained in his book *The Dream and the Nightmare*, the courts stopped regulating antisocial behaviors (though many would point to *Brown vs. Board of Education* as the moment when they finally actually *did* begin to regulate them) and then welfare incentivized them. New Dems like Joe Klein could talk about the Information Age and how the paradigm was now "the decentralized flexible computer network," but "the moral foundations" had "shifted," and no matter what you tried to do for "Them," it wouldn't make a difference. The *City Journal* was now asking the same questions that the Fiscal Crisis had asked, but with a new assumption: the poor weren't *really* citizens. Renaming citizens "customers" provided a subtle way to divide the herd; while citizens have rights, customers must wear shirts and shoes and have money in their pockets to get service. And if the poor aren't really citizens, then social services are no longer a basic responsibility, and democracy's essential act becomes not speech, as Olmsted would have it, but purchase. Taxes are a way of buying services, and if you don't pay taxes, you're lucky to get services.

The Manhattan Institute was just one planet in a conservative universe forming in New York around Rupert Murdoch. Rush Limbaugh had moved to the city in 1988 to do his radio show; Roger Ailes was a political consultant in Hell's Kitchen, and young Harvard grad Eric Breindel, who'd lost his political future when he was busted for heroin possession, now made a career running down the poor, the drug addicted, gays, and single mothers in the pages of the *Post*. Their ideas seeped down and out among those who'd risen through the meritocracy. "All New Yorkers must accept their responsibility for making New York a better place," a City report had stated. "Government is accountable to its citizens, but citizens are also responsible for their city." This had been the core of Gordon Davis's work, and people like Benstock and Kramer practiced it in their own ways: picking up papers matters. But going forward, many New Yorkers in marginal areas who'd once prided themselves for their Jane Jacobs intentions now considered themselves under attack, any hopeful sense of fixing urban problems lost in a rising panic over Black hands on White bodies. Prozac had opened cracks in the clouds. Maybe they *didn't* deserve to live this way. Time to buy some Combat and be codependent no more. "They say it's because of their environment," one crime victim said, "but I think that's kind of a sucker story."

Policies to help New Yorkers rejoin the city in small, simple ways, that created social capital, that stressed civic responsibility and cooperation would now be used to enshrine Yuppie and White ethnic understandings of what "community" in New York was. The seemingly anodyne Communitarian ideas often found in *City Journal* that involved letting "average" New Yorkers determine standards assumed that "average" meant "White," a cauldron of majority mores passing as melting pot nostalgia. While crickets greeted William Julius Wilson's argument in *The Truly Disadvantaged* that deindustrialization, not single mothers, had gutted inner-city communities of social and financial capital, Nicholas Lemann questioned whether concepts of community and neighborhood even applied there anymore, and Alan Ehrenhalt in *City Journal* bemoaned the "triumph of individualism," "the decline of authority," and "the whole egalitarian ethic." What he really hated, though, was that "middle-class people are no longer entitled to separate themselves physically or even morally from those who are **unlike them**." Bold and itals mine; the word *White* left unspoken. It's hard to find a statement that less accurately described the delirious New York the Manhattan Institute supposedly harkened back to, whose vast social capital came out of the fact that it was statistically so much *more* integrated than New York in 1991 in terms of race *and* money. Ehrenhalt's vision of small, dense, separate communities didn't mention Howard Beach or Bensonhurst.

As *City Journal* demanded that "average" New Yorkers control their neighborhoods, People of Color kept on trying to do just that. By now, Reverend Calvin O. Butts had taken over Abyssinian Baptist Church. Born in the Wald Projects on the Lower East Side, a Morehouse grad, he'd firebombed a store in Atlanta after the assassination of Reverend Martin Luther King Jr. and in his early years at Abyssinian had refused to condemn Farrakhan, but stepping up to the pulpit had changed him. "I came from the Left," he told a reporter, but now he was "trying to work in the center," coming out for teen curfews and stepped-up enforcement against public drinking and condemning Gangsta Rap while still calling for the boycott of Korean grocers, slamming Clarence Thomas, and defending the Central Park Five. He endorsed Ross Perot in 1992, sat down with Rudy Giuliani, who "charmed" him, and though Dinkins was loath to send money beyond the reach of the Gang of Four, Butts was able to finally steer Housing Initiative funds into Harlem, resulting in some 6,000 units from 1989 to 1994. And since the 1975 charter reform, "average" New Yorkers had been trying to get more control of their neighborhoods through 197a growth and improvement plans drafted by their Community Boards. Once approved by the City Council, all City agencies were then supposed to take them into consideration. The rub was that each Board had to come up with the money for consultants and studies, and obviously the districts most in need of help had the hardest time raising the funds. But 197a did inspire building social capital, even if they went largely unheeded; after learning that the City planned to level Melrose in the South Bronx, the community came together around the group We Stay! Nos Quedamos! "The idea that prosperity meant our community residents had to be sacrificed was inconceivable," said founder Yolanda Garcia, another heroic obsessive. "Our community is dedicated to assist in the process of rebuilding itself." The group met 168 times over the course of a year to develop the 30 blocks of high-density, mixed-income Melrose Commons and within two years, it had City Council approval. On the stump, Democratic presidential candidate Jerry Brown talked about burned-out buildings in the South Bronx, but when he landed in town for the primary, he couldn't find one for a photo-op.

New immigrants were also creating new communities rich in social and financial capital outside both the mainstreams of both Yuppies and White ethnics. Between 1980 and 1990, nearly one million new people born in other countries had lived in New York for some time, shoring up what was left of manufacturing, providing a low-cost labor pool, buying homes just like earlier waves of European immigrants did, adding new services and retail outlets, spreading what Richard Sennett calls "Migrant knowledge." Some Manhattan Institute members like Louis Winnick welcomed them as the next cycle of American urbanism. Most Asian immigrants, for example, believed in the American Dream, and as long as not too many of their kids applied to the schools that White middle-class kids were applying to, they were seen as part of the globalism developing around America, the lone superpower. In the '60s, a handful of Korean medical students came to escape the military dictatorship. Unlike the Chinese, who preferred enclaves, many of them moved into White middle-class neighborhoods like Flushing, where they parleyed their education, Presbyterianism, and access to capital from family and ethnic networks into small businesses. The first Korean grocer in New York was Do Sup Kwack, who in 1973 bought a produce store in Brooklyn. Others soon followed, opening near subway stops in food deserts (in 1990 there was 1 food store for every 5,762 residents of the Upper East Side, but 1 for every 63,818 in Williamsburg), then spreading into Manhattan; an estimated 1,300 Korean groceries now added fresh flowers to daily life and what *New York* called "a welcome twist on city eating habits: the salad bar." The annual number of Koreans increased until the late '80s when some 175,000 arrived and the first wholesalers opened in Koreatown. In the ten years after President Bush signed the NAFTA treaty and the Immigration Act of 1990, the city's immigrant population would rise more than 40%; the 61,000 Mexicans would triple, Chinatown continued to spread, Russian Jews doubled their numbers, post-Solidarity Poles went to Greenpoint. But assimilation wasn't always the goal now; the assumptions as to what made you an American were changing. Rather than throwing all in with their adoptive home, many new immigrants flew back and forth to the West Indies, called their parents in Bangladesh, and sent emails to Odessa, considering themselves transnationals. The Department of Immigrant Affairs was now a mayoral office.

In January 1992, another planet formed in New York's conservative universe. A procession of experts Right and Left on homelessness, economics, and education began filing through the offices of law firm Anderson Kill on Thursday afternoons at 3:00 p.m. to sit with new partner Rudy Giuliani, who took notes. After his defeat, he'd been licking his wounds "almost entirely ignored by the city's governing and policy elite," wrote James Traub; now he called for "innovations like privatization, increased emphasis on productivity, an effective business-labor council to create a common purpose and goal" as if he'd come up with them. Among the people chief policy aide Richard Schwartz introduced him to was Dan Biederman, who mentioned *City Journal*, "out there pitching some of the same things" he was doing at Bryant Park and Grand Central. The spring 1992 issue Giuliani picked up was a look at "The Quality of Urban Life," featuring pieces by Kelling, Peter Salins, and Nathan Glazer about transit, education, and housing, though the one that caught his eye most was Siegel's piece on "Reclaiming Public Spaces." Invoking Jacobs and Whyte, it recounted the efforts of people like Davis and Biederman, the role of BIDs and other public-private structures not to help restore democracy and civilization but "civility" to the streets and parks of New York. Here was the core of a platform for Giuliani's next run at City Hall: a city for the deserving who did what they were told. Wagner and Siegel organized sessions at the Manhattan Institute for Giuliani to meet with the likes of Andrew Cuomo, educator Benno Schmidt, and George Kelling. White hat Rudy had returned, willing to listen and learn. Waving a copy of *City Journal* during a speech, he said, "I don't know if you can plagiarize policies, but if you can, here is where I plagiarize mine." (Of course, where *they'd* gotten them was another question.) "Imagine having a politician actually listen to your proposals!" wrote Magnet later, still tickled.

Dinkins vs. Giuliani II had begun.

Another City Altogether

The buds had just opened in Bryant Park. Dan Biederman mounted the small stage April 20, 1992, next to Mario Cuomo, Dinkins, and Parks Commissioner Betsy Gotbaum, and stared out at twelve years of work. Thousands of tulips, anemone, glory of the snow, and blue squill lined both sides of a lawn that could hold a thousand people; summer would bring phlox and day lilies, and asters in the fall. Wide entrances invited passersby. "All the hiding places have been eliminated," said Andrew Heiskell, about to retire. Almost baffling to New Yorkers were the public restrooms. They were clean. They were safe. They had attendants, friendly ones in uniforms, and flowers in a vase. "Will they be able to keep it this way?" asked one visitor, reluctant to fall in love because he knew, just *knew*, that the city would quickly devour this sweet baby chick of a park.

Bryant Park had undergone something more profound than a renovation. It "feels," reported Paul Goldberger, "like part of another city altogether." The mood was "easy, relaxed, chatty, like the square of a small town." Like the Sheep Meadow a decade before, here was a space that made trust happen, and the chairs had a lot to do with it. Holly Whyte had insisted on a thousand or so of the sort found in the Luxembourg Gardens and as a test, Biederman had put out 400 plastic chairs; to his amazement, none of them had been stolen. Further north, the Pulitzer Fountain splashed again in Grand Army Plaza, and the regilded Sherman Monument shone a little too brightly. Other major parks now had their own conservancies. In June, the NYPD announced a "phenomenal" drop in Midtown crime the first four months of the year, praising the Safe Streets, Safe City program and Community Policing. Biederman's Grand Central Partnership dramatically lit the Terminal. Light helped, wrote *The New Yorker*, "to ratify the future of New York." In the works were a comprehensive plan for the waterfront and 350 miles of bicycle and jogging paths. The Democratic Convention arrived in this eye in the hurricane. Dinkins had "hit his stride," said one observer, and a year after Crown Heights, New Yorkers crept home without incident to watch LA burn on CNN. Carl Weisbrod brokered a deal with the US Tennis Association for the US Open that would put more money straight onto New York's bottom line than any of the major sports franchises.

Then the winds picked up once again. Suffolk County police arrested Michael Dowd and three other cops from the 75th Precinct for dealing cocaine; the NYPD's Internal Affairs Division had investigated Dowd fourteen times and done nothing. Dinkins appointed Deputy Mayor Milton Mollen to head an investigation, and when Brown resigned, named Kelly interim commissioner. Police killed drug dealer Kiko Garcia in Washington Heights, touching off another brief riot while Dinkins, assuming yet another police murder, went to Garcia's family. Unfortunately, this time the shooting had been justified, so on the morning of September 16, 1992, ten thousand off-duty cops swarmed City Hall. Drunk by 11:00, they climbed onto buses and cars waving signs of the mayor with a huge afro and big lips, calling him a "washroom attendant" and of course the N-word. Three hundred on-duty officers watched as they rushed City Hall; watched as protestors racially slandered an African American city councilwoman; watched as cops blocked traffic on the Brooklyn Bridge. In rode Rudy Giuliani. Clambering up on a flatbed truck, he grabbed the mic and, after shouting "bullshit" out to the drunken cops, yelled, "The reason the morale of the police department is so low is one reason and one reason alone: David Dinkins!"

The Police Riot was as frightening and abhorrent as Crown Heights. Fully one-third of the NYPD, openly racist, drunk, belligerent, self-pitying, had told New Yorkers exactly how they felt about them, and Giuliani had their backs. But the panic over community self-definition wasn't just a panic over governance; it was a panic over losing cultural supremacy.

Chapter Sixteen

The End of the One-Tribe Nation

"THOUGHT POLICE" shrieked the cover of *Newsweek* on Christmas Eve, 1990. Inside, urgent team coverage from college campuses across the nation hyperventilated over "political correctness," a "powerful movement . . . seemingly at odds with what most Americans believed"— though the fact that *Newsweek* simply assumed "what most Americans believed" seemed to argue for its need. While cogently posing the actual dilemma of PC—it "represents the subordination of the right to free speech to the guarantee of equal protection under law"—the article implied that Maoist reeducation camps were nigh. On Broadway, wise elders defended the casting of Jonathan Pryce as a Vietnamese hustler in *Miss Saigon* against the howls of PC's inconvenient sidekick, multiculturalism, and its challenge to a singular Western, male-dominated culture. "Multiculturalism is a lie," keened Maggie Gallagher in *City Journal*. "Multiculturalism is anticulture." But that all-knowing *New Yorker* "we" no longer spoke for everyone.

Media swaggered through the city's latest crisis of faith. New faces squeezed into Elaine's, topped by walrus-mustachioed *Daily News* columnist Mike McAlary who with Jimmy Breslin and Pete Hamill now gave New Yorkers *three* hard-drinking voices of Every White Man to choose from in the tabloids. Woody Allen still came by, but quietly, since his creepy trade-in of Mia Farrow for her adopted daughter Soon-Yi. New York's official Brooklyn-born Jewish comedian was now Jerry Seinfeld, whose smirking persona cared about nothing in a very un-Existentialist way. After their 1992 merger, the Time Warner behemoth aimed at "synergy," a state of corporate nirvana wherein the same content was sold across all platforms—books, TV, music, movies. "Money was no object," says Joni Evans. J. Walter Thompson chairman James Patterson, for example, got $1 million for his first two novels and Madonna published a book of photos about sex called *Sex* which became, not surprisingly, the bestselling coffee table book of all time. At Pocket Books, editor Judith Regan published a series of bestsellers by Beavis and Butt-Head, Howard Stern, and Rush Limbaugh. "I don't sit around all day thinking whether this is good or bad for the culture," she said. "I don't have those thoughts in a day."

No, she did not. By then Martha Stewart had sold 2 million books, had a monthly magazine, Lifetime cable specials, a series of videotapes and CDs, and seminars. Barnes & Noble was opening superstores across the country, forcing publishers to ask whether a book that Barnes & Noble didn't want should be a book at all. With her "ratlike cunning"— Harry Evans's words!—Tina Brown had steered *Vanity Fair* into the black, but now found herself reportedly "fed up with the money culture." Thus began a high-stakes game of musical chairs in the summer of 1992. Robert Gottlieb was sent back to Knopf. Graydon Carter, who'd lampooned Powers That Be in *Spy* then covered them in the insidery *New York Observer* finally became one of them when he was given *Vanity Fair* and Brown, in what one literati described as "an act of cultural vandalism," took over at *The New Yorker*. Long-feared changes began, the likes of John McPhee and Elizabeth Drew no longer encouraged to wander out into the weeds in search of a pure, timeless knowledge that could now seem as specific a product of time, place, and class as a straw boater. Shawn's defender George W. S. Trow resigned, to which Brown responded, "I am distraught at your defection, but since you never actually write anything, I should say I am notionally distraught." All this swagger and deck chair rearranging, the garments rent over the swishy new Styles of the Times section, masked greater uncertainties. Synergy, for its logic, often came apart in the marketplace and the next generation wasn't buying into the narratives of progress and power the Boomers had nursed on; unmotivated and slightly ill-tempered

Gen Xers searching for nonexistent jobs lacked both the optimism and the delusions of their elders.

Looming behind it all were the Culture Wars, fought largely in the art world where by 1989 Japanese syndicates had stopped swooping in for Old Masters and Adam Gopnik sensed a "calmly embittered spirit." That fall, after an NEA-funded show in Richmond, Virginia, included Andres Serrano's photograph of a crucifix submerged in urine, and the Corcoran Gallery canceled a Robert Mapplethorpe show, Senator Jesse Helms pushed through a law stopping the NEA from funding anything considered "obscene." Meanwhile photographer Nan Goldin curated a show about Lower East Side artists dying from AIDS titled *Witnesses: Against Our Vanishing*, whose catalogue included an essay imagining Jesse Helms on fire and referring to Cardinal O'Connor as a "fat cannibal." Its author, gaunt, gap-toothed writer, filmmaker, musician and artist David Wojnarowicz, had been a teenage hustler in '70s Times Square, part of the art and sex scene on the West Side piers. In works such as his short film *A Fire in My Belly*, Wojnarowicz appropriated and assembled images of intense graphic power; often violent, often sexual. After his friend and mentor Peter Hujar died of AIDS in December 1987 and David himself was diagnosed a few months later, he'd begun spending more time on the fringes of ACT UP, whose weekly meeting at Cooper Union was now the social highlight of Gay New York. That year he'd made the photograph *Untitled (Buffalo)*, a close-up of a museum diorama; a buffalo tumbling off a cliff, writhing eternally, beautifully, in midair as it faces certain death.

When the NEA pulled its grant from *Witnesses*, and two days later, beloved actress and writer Cookie Mueller died of AIDS. Wojnarowicz launched into protest and artmaking. In December, he debuted a performance piece at The Kitchen called "In the Shadow of Forward Motion" intended to "shake the boundaries of the illusion of the ONE TRIBE NATION. To keep silent is to deny the fact that there are millions of separate tribes in this illusion called AMERICA." On the 10th, he joined some 5,000 ACT UP protestors outside St. Patrick's Cathedral. A few months earlier, activists had caused a near riot when they'd chained themselves to railings at the New York Stock Exchange and unfurled a banner condemning pharmaceutical company Burroughs Wellcome for price gouging on AZT. Burroughs Wellcome cut prices. "[F]or three of four years," said Larry Kramer later, "ACT UP was like molten lava." Queer rather than gay, its members increasingly identified outside traditional gender norms and binary sexual preference, its '70s clone look of tight jeans, white T-shirts, work boots, and leather jackets worn now as confrontation, and by women, too, who'd come aboard as much as a form of gender activism as health advocacy. Protestors chained themselves to pews, blew whistles, threw communion wafers on the floor; 111 were arrested. While Keith Haring died on February 16, Wojnarowicz continued creating some of his most powerful work, including *"Untitled (One Day This Kid . . .)* an image of himself as a buck-toothed, jug-eared boy in suspenders surrounded by text that starts "One day this kid will grow larger" then goes on to tell sentence by sentence the harrowing experience of growing into a gay life. As he sued a radical Christian group for misappropriating his work in fundraising materials, Wojnarowicz prepared an installation for the New Museum about "identity."

With the Culture Wars raging, MoMA staged *High and Low*, a comprehensive if old-school attempt to understand the relation between High Art and popular culture that now felt two steps behind in a world of computer screens, graffiti, and Wojnarowicz's anger; the walls of all museums were suddenly too small as "special interests" now demanded space and power. The new City Council, expanded by the 1989 Charter Reform, was its most diverse. Amid an often naïve and occasionally prurient public discussion of gender and sexuality, Straight New York stumbled toward the light wearing red ribbons to remind themselves that AIDS was still around. Gay couples appeared in magazine stories about Valentine's Day. Crowds wound around the block to see *The Crying Game* with its shock ending and the documentary *Paris Is Burning*, about the African American and Latino drag ballroom scene that inspired Madonna's "Vogue." Drag was no longer White middle-class camp but an expression of competition and family. K. D. Lang, Martina Navratilova, and the public dalliance between Sandra Bernhard and Madonna ushered in Lesbian Chic.

On July 22, 1992, eight days after 10,000 protestors walked in the AIDS March, David Wojnarowicz died. He had won his case, though. For damages, he received one dollar.

For Us; By Us

When Al Sharpton woke up after surgery in January 1991, the first thing he saw was the worried face of David Dinkins. Stabbed by a White man in Bensonhurst, Sharpton had the potential to set a match to the city so the mayor had sat vigil, waiting for him to wake up and defuse things. Dinkins's attitude toward his own community had lacked coherence and it returned the mixed feelings. "Black people were the first to come out of the bag criticizing Dinkins," wrote Chuck D, and that included Sharpton, who believed he'd "sold so many pieces of himself to so many different people that he will never again own himself." But the Reverend had long been running his own game and guided by Cornel West and Jesse Jackson, he realized as he struggled to walk again that "somehow, in my night journey through the New York City of the eighties, I had wandered away" from the message of Dr. King. When Sharpton reemerged and announced his intention "to formally throw my hair into the ring" for the 1992 Senate race, it was in a suit and tie, not a velour tracksuit.

On the face of it, he'd had a deathbed conversion, but really, he'd just rebranded. There'd always been more than one way to be Black, and every generation had created new ways to assert Black identity. That year, the General Service Administration announced that while excavating for a building on Duane Street, it had discovered bodies at the site of what turned out to be until the late 1700s the city's African burying ground. Over the objections of Mayor Dinkins, an archaeological dig began that stopped only after it had exhumed 419 skeletons, more than half under the age of twelve, almost all displaying signs of malnutrition and abuse. A decade of controversy would follow as to how the GSA had handled the site and what should happen next to the resting place of an estimated 20,000 people. But most important was the stunning reinsertion of brutal enslavement and Black presence into the whitewashed history of New York City. Back in the 1600s, burying grounds had been the first assertion of Black identity in America, and they would now be the starting point for correcting the false narratives of a colorblind New York and a North without slaves. Discovering the erasure inspired new identity.

The other issue with identity was very immediate—how to maintain control over the ideas, purposes, and possibilities beneath the Black cultural product that Whites had always appropriated. Though the Seven-Mile World now had ranch houses on it, the idea of an authentic Black cultural unity through Hip Hop had expanded its meaning beyond the "Peace, Unity, Love and Having Fun" of Planet Rock. "[L]ike its bebop predecessor," wrote Adilifu Nama, Hip Hop "was about creating community right where you were and adopting a standard of validation based exclusively on black peers, not on what outside critics had to say or what white societal norms dictated." In terms of the music itself, the heady, trippy Afrocentrism of Brooklyn's Native Tongues collective—groups like the Jungle Brothers, A Tribe Called Quest, and De La Soul—couldn't compete commercially with pap like MC Hammer and Vanilla Ice, or LA's powerful combination of chronic and "Fuck the Police." The R&B update New Jack Swing had also slowed down Hip Hop New York, but in 1990, Andre Harrell at Uptown Records had hired a new intern, a former Harlem altar boy raised in Mount Vernon named Sean Combs who, like Simmons, knew how to balance city and suburb. At Howard he'd posted mostly Cs, but "Puffy" threw legendary parties and was, according to Harrell, "the hardest-working intern ever." In between parties and promotions—the tragic CCNY charity show had been his—Combs produced *What's the 411?*, the first album of nineteen-year-old Mary J. Blige, a former telephone operator from Yonkers. Blige's diva voice didn't *sound* like Hip Hop, but she looked and lived it. Hip Hop wasn't about rapping or sampling; it was about what those first kids scratching and spinning on cardboard had always known—it was about being real.

Branding Hip Hop's Authenticity would establish it as a cultural position. With Rick Rubin gone and the Sony deal bleeding the company, 1990 was "the coldest year" for Russell Simmons and Def Jam. In the dumps, he spoke with a friend going through his own financial crisis, "the official bling-bling white man"—Donald Trump. What would get him through, Trump said, was his name. ("The hip-hop community is a branding community," Simmons later said. "They love Donald for having the knack for branding himself.") Simmons decided to make "the Def Jam brand seem larger than just that of a record company," so, a master of weak ties, he began connecting it in new ways to other cultural networks. HBO's *Def Comedy Jam* would make stars out of Martin Lawrence, Steve Harvey, and Bernie Mac. White people watched it, too, and so, said Simmons later, "It made Def Jam seem part of the larger culture." His most successful play was in fashion. Though Snoop's heavy-lidded, out-of-jail look was definitely authentic, Simmons needed clothes that let him express his age and status at serious tables while still feeling Hip Hop. Just like Yuppies, African Americans bought brand names like Tommy Hilfiger to mark identity but also as a transgressive act that changed their meaning, so, inspired by the FUBU brand, in turn inspired by W. E. B. Du Bois's call to African Americans to create products and services "For us; by us," Simmons started Phat Farm. Hip Hop could now be expressed in the form of Mary J. Blige or Dr. Dre, but also beltless pants or a $50 t-shirt. And despite what Murray and Lehman said about the need to leave the inner city, "hip-hoppers," wrote Nama, "do not equate social mobility with escape but embrace the ghetto as a site and source of social identity." Hip Hop's constant authenticizing had reclaimed the evanescence of cool, and created the basis of a racial business culture. More than any given form, what mattered was *who* was making it and *why*.

And now John Ahearn, good soul of the South Bronx, was about to learn just how much had changed since Planet Rock. With his old collaborator Rigoberto not involved in the bronze casts for the 44th Precinct, John's process was slightly different: before, he says, "the neighborhood work went first and then I made the artwork after that." But now, after the balance he'd seemed to have found between himself, his art, and his community, he says he was "wading into an area intentionally" with people who stood for more dangerous, though maybe in some ways even more authentic, aspects of the place: Raymond, a hardcase with his pit bull; Daleesha on her roller skates, and Corey cradling a basketball; three young locals standing "more as guardians than as saints." At least that was his intention, but a few weeks before the final pieces were to be installed at the 44th, two City workers complained to the Department of Cultural Affairs. Officials tried to explain Ahearn's art and the role he played in the neighborhood, but Arthur Symes, an architect and resident of Battery Park City, insisted, "He's not of the community because he's not Black—it's simply that." It was a statement further complicated by the fact that the part of the South Bronx in question was now predominantly Hispanic. The City backed Ahearn and on September 25, 1991, a crane placed the three bronze statues on their pedestals. "There was a disquiet to the day," remembered Ahearn. Some locals began to protest that these were the kind of people residents were afraid of; others felt Ahearn had no right to represent *any* People of Color, though the three had let themselves be cast. The works did have their supporters, but any discussion of aesthetics or content really just masked the basic fact that everything had changed in the years since John and Rigoberto had first opened up the card table on the sidewalk and bridging cultures was the goal. Symes would later compare these pieces to telling family secrets; John had indeed become a part of the community, but he belonged to many networks and he'd tipped his own delicate balance by being unclear about which small world he belonged in, and which he just had ties to. Multiculturalism could expand the world, but cultural interpreters were no longer wanted.

Five days after the bronzes went up, Ahearn paid to have them removed. As the One Tribe Nation cracked, the issue wasn't that art couldn't lead us to any common humanity. It was that fewer people wanted to go there.

O, Pioneers!

And so, as the old idea of making art as a way to relate to other cultures dimmed, the toxic leftovers of Industrial America beckoned from the far shore of the East River. Williamsburg had echoes of early SoHo; empty warehouses smelling of spices and potato starch, closed factories that once made chemicals, pottery, sugar, and beer. Downtown had always been a function of the imagination with the Empire State Building pointing the way out whereas this really was another place, its waterfront covered in scrub and toxic dirt, the flimsy three- and four-story buildings thrown together like riders on a rush-hour bus. McCarren Park had some trees. Northside was mostly Poles with some Ukrainians and Hasids. Southside was Puerto Rican and poor. Heroin was everywhere. Cabbies did not like to go to Williamsburg.

The first artists came in the '60s, people like Dan Flavin and Mark di Suvero, then some big group shows in the early '80s and the East Village exodus; Fred Tomaselli with his delicate constellations of colors and prescription pills, Amy Sillman and Roxy Paine. A spattering of small galleries and art collectives opened with the Ship's Mast on North Fifth Street passing for the Odeon with Guinness on tap and a free buffet. The subway stop at Bedford became a portal: you got off and went straight to your destination—quickly. Restaurants, bookstores, and bright lights were back in the Village. As the recession deepened and technology rolled ahead, some defining elements of a post-Warhol reconsideration cohered. First, the "scene" found itself in huge, inclusive warehouse parties inspired by the Rave scenes in Chicago and Europe. The organizers of Cat's Head I had expected 250 people, but 750 showed up for a carnival of music, performance, and multimedia. All were welcome. Second, it was Do It Yourself. With finished quality not always a prime consideration, some wondered whether what David Brody would call the "low-key, inclusive niceness" of Williamsburg could produce anything of import, but the art was made to be experienced and discussed more than bought. Finally, instead of rehashing the past through camp and cartoons, they were asking what was next. Williamsburg probably had more computers than paintbrushes; artists were creating plugged-in works that flashed, dripped, and spun in silly and serious ways; "electro-mechanical bricolage," said Brody, that explored the space where, wrote Jonathan Fineberg, "human parts are recycled and the mind is entered directly by the computer." More than the problems of the moment, Williamsburg looked ahead to a future that would value simulation at least as much as "reality," what artist Kit Blake called a "global metaculture" that would produce a "generic" art in constant relation to everything else but drawn from no specific culture. "Place is not important," wrote Blake. "Access is."

The scene snapped together when Annie Herron arrived. Small, with bobbed hair, green doe eyes, and still stinging from the end of the East Village, she dove into Williamsburg. "It is here, it is all here," she wrote." In 1991, she opened Test Site, a 5,000-square-foot gallery on North First Street and held the *Salon of the Mating Spiders* the next year. As a catalyzing moment, it probably comes closest to *The Times Square*

Show in terms of size and intent, if not talent; hundreds spilled out of a former auto repair shop carrying contraptions, paintings, and things to hang from the ceiling, milling happily in front, eating sandwiches and dancing, chatting with their neighbors, East Village in the air, but with less edge and fewer Black and Brown faces, "a street fair, New Music performance, picnic and art happening, all rolled into one" that some later compared to Woodstock. A few months later Williamsburg was discovered, or at least noticed, in a *New York* piece titled "The New Bohemia." Locals rolled their eyes, but while Condé Nast was playing musical chairs and Wojnarowicz was dying, an estimated two thousand artists were browsing used record stores and eating Thai, showing work at new spaces like Momenta Art. "We feel protected by the river and the recession," said club owner Jeff Gompertz. Others liked the "slow track compared to the hip hop pace of the East Village," which raises the unspoken point that there were virtually no People of Color around. For all the hypocrisies of that earlier scene and the bitter taste it left for some, Planet Rock had grown out of encounter between punks, graffiti writers, suburban émigrés, and rappers, whereas Williamsburg was largely a scene apart from the Hasids, Poles, and Dominicans next door.

The next summer, limos pulled up to the Old Dutch Mustard factory for Organism, which James Kalm called a "combination of Bacchanalia, anarchy, social club and creative space." The corner of Bedford and Metropolitan appeared on TV shows, and real estate prices shot up. Williamsburg artists could distance themselves from the East Village, but not the process it started. The Ship's Mast closed. "Everything's changing around here," said eighty-year-old Charles Garbacki. What Ward Shelley would call the Golden Age of Williamsburg had pretty much come and gone. But Williamsburg had just started. Another network now existed, as much Lifestyle as Community, that would expand the city's understanding of itself.

Decentering the Whole

Nineteen ninety-three was the year of discovering "identity"; of Toni Morrison winning the Nobel Prize; of slackers and grunge ("a direct rebuke to the very idea of trendiness," said one writer), and the Children of the Rainbow curriculum in the public schools. The Whitney Biennial featured a 600-pound cube of gnawed chocolate, a film of the Rodney King beating, and admission buttons spelling out the sentence "I can't imagine wanting to be white." Though Elisabeth Sussman says she "knew the territory of controversy," she and her co-curator Thelma Golden "didn't expect that we were going to get the reaction that we did." "I hate the show," was how *Times* art critic Michael Kimmelman put it. Roberta Smith called it "a pious, often arid show that frequently substitutes didactic moralizing for genuine visual communication." "Mope art," sniffed John Taylor. Twenty years later, Jerry Saltz called it "the moment in which today's art world was born." Western Civilization wasn't just under siege at the Biennial; the show questioned whether it even existed. "[I]dentities declare communities," wrote Sussman, "and produce a decentered whole"—an aesthetic restatement of Dinkins's "gorgeous mosaic" line. Golden questioned whether the center even mattered now that "decentralization and the embracing of the margins have become dominant." In other words, there was no such thing as a monoculture; culture was simply the sum of all its networks. Though the show explored theories of abjection and the body, race, and feminism, Sussman wanted something full of "art you *got*." So along with Matthew Barney's satyrs and Cindy Sherman's rubber genitalia, there was Ida Applebroog's fairy tale rendering of Hansel and Gretel titled *Jack F: Forced to Eat His Own Excrement*, and Charles Ray's *Firetruck* and his unnerving fiberglass rendering of a nuclear family, all the same size, all naked. No Schnabel heroics or East Village goofiness; these were expressions of "the socially marginalized subcultural groups within a predominantly white, male, heterosexual society."

The questions pushed forward here in 1993 would determine cultural discourse for the decades ahead: What is Art for? *Who* is it for? How do cultures interact when, as Coco Fusco wrote in the catalogue, appropriating imagery and experiences of other cultures could now be considered "symbolic violence." For years, critics had been complaining that professionals fueled the Art World more than art itself, but as off-putting as Roberta Smith may have found the Biennial, its works were in another essential way more embracing and universal than Degas because aesthetic "universals" could no longer be defined exclusively by ideals and assumptions set by European males. Smith, who considered "identity, difference, otherness" to be "fashionable buzzwords," felt the King tape made the show "less about the art of our times than about the times themselves," which one would think was a good thing, especially if you wanted art to be about something other than the Art World. Culture was no longer one broad mainstream with a naughty little counterculture running ahead, breaking plates, and creating new styles to sell. Multiculturalism ended the idea of "progress" in art. Instead of the quasi-capitalist hunt for the Next Big Thing, the avant-garde now led horizontal explorations of culture and self and while those once hidden, once silenced, began to claim their right to be seen and heard in public space, the largely White, largely male bastions panicked more than they ever did about AIDS, hunger, or stopping crack. *City Journal*'s discussions of public space and control were as much about controlling the multiculture as they were about throwing litter in a trash can. *New York* featured John Taylor on the "culture of victimization," and Christopher Byron's fears of the "rolling tide of undocumented immigrants for the city to absorb and support." With Morley Safer mocking contemporary art on *60 Minutes* and Rush Limbaugh railing against the city while eating burgers at 21 with Roger Ailes, debate over New York's public spaces became a proxy war over culture and politics.

Technology was the nonpartisan truth connecting this fracturing culture. By 1993, vinyl was dead. You could argue all night that your albums sounded richer and warmer, but after a few listens to *Kind of Blue* without the hisses and pops, you left Bleecker Bob's to the collectors. From chat rooms in cyberspace to *Jurassic Park*, encyclopedias on a single disc to the islands of *Myst*, all that mattered was your mood today, and that was the whole point: choice. As your faxes faded in the file cabinet, email was obviously the next step and the Internet, called by *Fortune* "a loosely confederated network of networks, public and private," would, along with increasing computing power, bring "a revolution of random access to information." Reagan's philosophy of the Individual was about to become the functional mode of modern life: all media, all retail, all politics was soon to be all about You. Just *You*. Your dreams, your opinions, your tastes, your budget, your hatreds, your lusts.

"I think what will happen," said the avatar of virtual reality, Jaron Lanier, "is that the rest of the country will start to inhabit virtual New York." But what would happen to New York in real life? The city looked west at the millionaires being minted in the Bay Area and Seattle and despaired that it had missed out on the future. Desperate real estate owners around the Flatiron District rewired old buildings, and a few infant tech companies made the move. By 1993 there were enough to christen the neighborhood Silicon Alley.

Chapter Seventeen

You Were on Your Own

Munching unbuttered popcorn, Michael Bloomberg watched a purple tang scoot around one of his company's many soothing fish tanks. And with its three luxurious floors on Park Avenue, no private offices, and free snacks sprinkled on those who swam hard wasn't Bloomberg LP really just one big fish tank, too? These days when he wasn't flying helicopters, Bloomberg pulled on Spandex shorts and Rollerbladed around Central Park. He was having a good time because as early as February 1991, Goldman Sachs had advised investors to move back into equities and they'd been right: on paper, the recession ended in March, and by April the Bull had come back to life, this time without pinstripes and a yellow tie. This was the "People's Market"; Main Street Boomers relentlessly reminded of their coming retirement and the high cost of college, their real estate underwater, were all pouring money into Wall Street even as it pulled away from broader economic realities. Few investors would admit—or understood—that they were just gambling, and many had no choice. The Economic Recovery Tax Act of 1981 loosened up rules on IRAs and a crafty benefits counselor in Pennsylvania launched the first 401(k) that November, allowing corporations to cut pension costs with retirement plans that limited their contributions while giving employees "control" over a nest egg they could take with them even if (when) they got laid off. The new Fed chairman, clarinetist and Ayn Rand devotee Alan Greenspan, blissfully inattentive to the irony of a free market Objectivist orchestrating the economy's fortunes, trimmed away at interest rates until by December 1991 they were at 3%, down from 20% in the early years of Koch. Savings accounts were no better than your mattress, and that yeasty inflation that made raises juicier and mortgages less a weight over time—that was gone, too—so instead of using low interest rates to buy more big things, which might have boosted the economy, everyday Boomers went in search of higher returns, taking on more risk while executives who knew better cashed in. Swamped fund managers bought everything, pumping portfolios higher as the overall economy got worse, and Congress played along again, voting down a bill to force companies to reveal the cost of executive stock options. Back in 1980, 6% of households had investments in mutual funds; by 1992, it was 27%. The Dow ended the year up 20%; Nasdaq a heart-thumping 56.8%.

Among the new wave of media analysts conjuring belief in this "New Economy," Michael Bloomberg's name became ubiquitous. For ten years, he'd collected data on virtually every stock, bond, and corporation you could think of, along with news, sports, weather, and even horoscopes, and in March 1991, just as the recovery had begun, Bloomberg Business News took on Reuters and Dow Jones as the prime source of business information. "There might be better traders than me," he told Forbes, "and there might be people who know more about computers. But there's nobody who knows more about both." By the end of 1993 Bloomberg had broken into the Forbes 400 (Warren Buffett was number one). Yet even if they couldn't avoid his name, few New Yorkers could pick him out of a lineup, and this seemed to extend to his wife Susan, who asked for a divorce because he was away so much.

One of the city's other human brands had also stirred back to life. Donald Trump had spent a year and a half restructuring all his debt, losing millions for investors in the process. "It's always good to do things nice and complicated," he told a reporter, "so that nobody can figure it out." With liens on his properties and a cap on his personal spending imposed by his creditors, he reemerged to push for a gargantuan development on the West Side and discovered that the banks refused to deal with him. His status as a serious New York real estate player was over. Instead, the Municipal Arts Society and community groups hammered together a Riverside South plan that he desperately claimed as his own while he explored new opportunities overseas. "His fame is now his currency," said one writer. A man, wrote Mark Singer, "with a suspicion that an interior life was an intolerable inconvenience," The Donald saw only blue skies over Manhattan: "When Trump is back," he boasted, "New York is back." Bernie Madoff's ass-covering maneuvers on Black Monday had blossomed into something much bigger and now, after a lax SEC probe, he leased more space in the Lipstick Building, where he computerized a Ponzi scheme alongside his legitimate trading business.

This was the financial backdrop to Dinkins's New York: New rims for an economy that couldn't get out of first gear, an every man for himself Recovery. Though Magellan Fund shares were up 24% in 1992, all the '80s gains in real median household income had been wiped out. Inequality kept spreading—the top 20% were up 16%, the bottom 20% were down 23%. "On August 6, 1979," wrote Luc Sante, "I hit the street clutching a $10 bill . . . I bought three slices of pizza, a can of Welch's Strawberry soda, a pack of Viceroys, six joints, two quarts of orange juice, two containers of yogurt and a pint of milk." Fourteen years later it would have cost $92.75—"or $22.75 for everything but the pot." As Bloomberg stared into his fish tanks and Mayor Dinkins kept herding cats, 1993 would be full of portents and plans that would drive the future of New York.

The First Attack

It was lunchtime at the World Trade Center, on a slushy February 1993 day. Mechanic David Peter took out his sandwich in one of the basements, as did Joseph Cacciatore; attorney Joseph Gibney folded a slice of pizza in his wheelchair on the thirty-seventh floor while Japanese executives opened menus at Windows on the World. Orders began zipping up the elevators—all food was cooked a hundred floors below. Another elevator full of kindergartners headed down. Though some 200,000 people spent some part of every day there, the World Trade Center had never found a place in New Yorkers' hearts. The Port Authority's ads had always come across as strangely pathetic and, as in the case of the latest one—"The World Trade Center Is a Point of View"—sometimes didn't even make much sense; if it mostly felt like a government complex it was because that's what it ultimately was.

The Empire State Building expressed the romance of height; the World Trade Center just expressed power.

As Peter, Cacciatore, and Gibney tucked into lunch, a twenty-minute fuse sizzled toward 1,500 pounds of explosives inside a yellow Ryder van parked on the B2 level of the parking garage.

At 12:17 p.m. it exploded.

Both towers swayed as a shock wave bounced back and forth in the protective concrete bathtub that kept New York Harbor out of the basement. Steel beams shot through walls, tons of concrete fell as fire and smoke shot up the stairwells and elevator shafts of Tower One. Metals burned inside a cavern 200 feet by 150 feet and four floors deep; broken sewers created a subterranean lake. The TV stations, the police and operations centers, all communications and exhaust systems were out of service. Thick black smoke choked the thousands streaming down the stairs in darkness. "You were on your own," said one survivor. Random people hauled Gibney down in his wheelchair. Hundreds were stuck in elevators, including the kindergartners from PS 95, who sang the theme from *Barney* over and over as they waited to be rescued. The Fire Department radios weren't strong enough. Survivors staggered to nearby hospitals or sat in the mounting snow. With Dinkins at a conference in Japan, Steisel and Kelly directed the response. A police helicopter plucked six from the roof, but heavy clouds made further air rescue impossible. At 11:25 p.m., the last people were pulled out of an elevator. Six had died, more than a thousand were injured. Diligence and some blind luck led to the quick capture of the culprits; a piece of the van was found with ID numbers that led straight to the rental company in Jersey City. But in the course of foiling another plot in June, it was discovered that the FBI had been trailing them for years and hadn't stopped them. Islamist terrorism, hinted at by Rushdie's *fatwa*, had arrived, and the World Trade Center entered New York's emotional memory.

Of Mice and Women

On a rainy Friday afternoon a month later, Robert A. M. Stern and Cora Cahan waited with hardhats at the New Amsterdam for Disney CEO Michael Eisner, his wife Jane, and their teenaged son. Shaking off their umbrellas, they all stepped into the gloom, playing their flashlights over the ornate peacocks and roses carved in the wood, the vast frieze over the stage and the holes in the ceiling. Built in 1903, the New Amsterdam was 42nd Street's grandest venue, home of Ziegfeld's *Follies* and host to every great name in stage until it was turned into a movie theater and left to slowly decay through decades of third-run gunfights. The Municipal Art Society had secured its landmark designation in 1979, but renovations cost too much, so the lights went out, the pigeons took over, and every night the ghost of Ziegfeld's lover Olive Thomas, once the most beautiful woman in New York, floated across the stage bearing the blue bottle of mercury pills she'd used to kill herself.

If time had stopped inside, any plans for Times Square and 42nd Street had slowed to a crawl. Carl Weisbrod, now running the project, had brought Rebecca Robertson over from City Planning to deal with the preserved theaters. Architect Robert A. M. Stern, a Disney board member, recommended a slightly retro, high/low approach and with that in mind, along with reports by Hugh Hardy on the Liberty and Victory theaters, she solicited proposals in October 1988. Meanwhile, John Burgee presented a third, Johnson-free take on the towers that complied with the "Bowl of Light" regulations but didn't fool Ada Louise Huxtable. "The emperor," she wrote, "got measured for a new set of clothes." Media giant Viacom had moved into the neighborhood, thinking that its culture brands like MTV and VH1 could profit from the edginess, but "disaster" was more the vibe now as the stink of another failed urban project mingled with the chestnuts and kebabs. Forty-Second Street was a void, its marquees blank and windows boarded. "The ground was covered in crack vials," says Jane Dickson. "It was gross and it was wild."

All this was about to change, though, because of four talented and very well connected women: Rebecca Robertson, Marian Heiskell, Cora Cahan, and Gretchen Dykstra. Like Elizabeth Barlow in Central Park, they would forever alter how the city saw itself and how the world saw the city by turning a risk-oriented, male-dominated area into a safe space for all ages, races, classes, and especially sexes. Robertson had taken over the entire 42DP in April 1990, when Carl Weisbrod left to run the City's office of Economic Development. A Toronto native, she'd worked in planning in Mexico and Venezuela, and Herb Sturz had recruited her for City Planning. When she'd taken over 42DP, real estate was crashing, Prudential was on the hook for $241 million, and the UDC had already taken control of 9 of the 13 planned sites on 42nd, so a new deal was struck: Instead of building new skyscrapers, the developer Park Towers and Prudential would simply renovate what they'd bought and sell when the market improved. Prudential would get a hefty tax break for keeping its money and jobs on the table, the City would buy the lots remaining on 42nd Street, and the Johnson-Burgee plans were officially dead. An interim plan—42nd Street Now!—was formed as a lifeboat until real estate headed back up.

The plan, though, wasn't really an interim plan. The city now had the "opportunity to go back to the mythology of what makes Times Square and 42nd Street interesting," says Robertson. But "we had to develop a plan that no one would think was a major plan . . . [I]f we do a plan that just looks like the interim, then we get what we want and nobody will notice it's about the whole thing." With the success of The Gap's new superstore on Broadway and the huge McDonald's on 42nd Street, they decided to include retail to increase foot traffic and technology was factored in. Now that you could watch kung fu films on your VCR and video games were coming into their own, entertainment wasn't enough. Instead, Robertson would sell what Hardy and Quennell had created with the "Bowl of Light" zoning: spectacle. To do that, she turned to Robert A. M. Stern, a former student of Robert Venturi whose path to Post-Modernism involved reinflating familiar vernacular styles, sometimes to the verge of popping. Robertson wanted "positive chaos and populism," "things that would change over time all the time," "a mixture of new and old, razzle-dazzle, amazing entertainment, and, crowds, crowds." Stern in turn brought in Tibor Kalman. He "got it," says Robertson. "He was nuts." Times Square, he said, "should be a zoo, like the rest of New York, but a well-maintained zoo instead of a depressed, unemployed, and crack-smoking kind of zoo." Which was literally what happened with the Central Park Zoo; a place crippled by nostalgia had been transformed into the best version of what it could be. "We had to cure the street," said Kalman later. He drove Stern to the brink but delivered the authentically crass, bright, loud, 30-foot-high Marky Mark in underpants sign sensibility Robertson wanted.

David Rockefeller
and Mayor Abe Beame
during the Fiscal Crisis
(*AP Photo*)

Mayor Ed Koch and Parks
Commissioner Gordon
Davis swear in the first
class of Urban Park Rangers.
(*NYC Parks Photo Archive*)

William "Holly" Whyte,
godfather of New York urbanism
(*Alex Gotfryd/CORBIS/
Corbis via Getty Images*)

Afrika Bambaataa, one of the founders of Hip Hop
(*David Corio/Michael Ochs Archives/Getty Images*)

Andy Warhol and Jean-Michel Basquiat at their joint show at the Tony Shafrazi Gallery
(*AP Photo/Richard Drew*)

Keith Haring at work in the subway
(*Laura Levine/Corbis via Getty Images*)

Publishing's power couple, Harry Evans and Tina Brown
(Ron Galella, Ltd./Ron Galella Collection via Getty Images)

Elaine Kaufman in front of her restaurant
(Fred R. Conrad/The New York Times/Redux)

Diana Vreeland and Pierre Cardin enter
the Met's La Belle Époque party.
(Ron Galella/Ron Galella Collection via Getty Images)

Nehemiah Homes in Brownsville
(*Gilbert Santana @soillgo*)

Irma and David Rivera
at their new house on
Charlotte Street in the Bronx
(*Arty Pomerantz/New York Post
Archives/@NYP Holdings, Inc.,
via Getty Images*)

Rap impresario
Russell Simmons
(*Ari Mintz/Newsday RM
via Getty Images*)

Michael Bloomberg and his partners in Innovative Marketing Services
(*Fred R Conrad/The New York Times/Redux*)

Playwright and AIDS
activist Larry Kramer
(*Catherine McGann/
Getty Images*)

Donald Trump and
his father, Fred
(*Dennis Caruso/NY Daily News
Archive via Getty Images*)

Mayor-elect David Dinkins
gives his victory speech.
(*AP Photo/Ron Frehm*)

Chuck D and Flava Flav
of Public Enemy
(*Al Pereira/Michael Ochs
Archives/Getty Images*)

Reverend Al Sharpton at
a rally for Tawana Brawley
(*Francis Specker/Alamy Stock Photo*)

Installation *Fire Truck*, 1992–93 by Charles Ray. *1993 Biennial Exhibition* (February 24–June 20, 1993). Whitney Museum of American Art, New York, NY.
(© *Charles Ray, Courtesy Matthew Marks Gallery; Photograph Jerry L. Thompson; Digital Image* © *Whitney Museum of American Art/Licensed by Scala/Art Resource, NY*)

Daniel Biederman
at play in Bryant Park
(*Bryan Thomas*)

Three of the women
who remade Times Square:
Cora Cahan,
Rebecca Robertson,
and Gretchen Dykstra
(*Chang W. Lee/
The New York Times/Redux*)

Mayor Rudy Giuliani and son, Andrew, at his inauguration
(*AP Photo/Mark Lennihan*)

Mayor Giuliani and Police Commissioner William Bratton
(*Gerald Herbert/NY Daily News Archive via Getty Images*)

Wade Boggs celebrating
the Yankees' 1996
World Series win
(*AP Photo/Ron Frehm*)

Stacy Horn, founder
of ECHO, New York's
first Internet "salon"
(*W. A. Funches Jr./New York Post
Archives/@NYP Holdings, Inc.,
via Getty Images*)

Curtain call at the Broadway premiere of *Rent*
(*AP Photo/Wally Santana*)

Pastor of the Abyssinian
Baptist Church Reverend
Calvin O. Butts
(*Anthony Barboza/Getty Images*)

Harlem's longtime
Congressman
Rep. Charles Rangel
(*Maureen Keating/CQ Roll Call
via AP Images*)

Nas, whose album *Illmatic*
took Hip Hop to a new level
(*Mika-Photography.com*)

Robert Hammond and
Joshua David at the High
Line groundbreaking
(*Scott Rudd/Patrick
McMullan via Getty Images*)

Harvey Weinstein
celebrates with
Madonna, Ben Affleck,
and Gwyneth Paltrow.
(*Patrick McMullan/
Patrick McMullan via
Getty Images*)

Condé Nast publisher
Si Newhouse with Anna
Wintour, editor of *Vogue*
(*Richard Corkery/NY Daily
News Archive via Getty Images*)

The Pit at Ground Zero, one month after 9/11
(*Allan Tannenbaum/Getty Images*)

Daniel Libeskind presents his concept for Memory Foundations, with Mayor Michael Bloomberg and Governor George Pataki.
(*Allan Tannenbaum/ Getty Images*)

Amanda Burden,
Bloomberg's director
of City Planning
(*Daniel Acker/Bloomberg
via Getty Images*)

Deputy Mayor Daniel Doctoroff in quest of the 2012 Olympics
(*Getty Images for NYC 2012*)

Police Commissioner Ray Kelly during the 2004 GOP convention
(*Darren McCollester/Getty Images*)

Groundbreaking at Atlantic Yards. From left, Bruce Ratner, Mayor Bloomberg, Governor David Paterson, Borough President Marty Markowitz, and Jay-Z.
(*WENN Rights Ltd/ Alamy Stock Photo*)

Christo and Jeanne-Claude at the opening of *The Gates* in Central Park
(*AP Photo/Richard Drew, File*)

John Thain, CEO of Merrill Lynch, shakes hands with Ken Lewis, CEO of Bank of America, its new owner.
(*Mario Tama/Getty Images*)

Occupy Wall Street
(*Uschi Gerschner/Alamy Stock Photo*)

Mayor Bloomberg in his bullpen at City Hall
(© *Larry Fink*)

Jeff Koons and *Play-Doh* at his Whitney Museum retrospective (*Timothy A. Clary/ AFP via Getty Images*)

Mayor Bill de Blasio welcomes the USNS *Comfort* to Covid-ravaged New York. (*AFP/Getty Images*)

Police and activists clash during the George Floyd protests. (*Anadolu Agency/Getty Images*)

In the meantime, crime was down on 42nd Street, but the heart of New York felt enervated. Jane Dickson and Charlie Ahearn had finally moved; the final straw the day their son disappeared for a few hours on the way home from school in Chelsea. Before they left for their new place in TriBeCa, Charlie made an elegiac short film called *Jane in Peepland* that juxtaposed her paintings of strip joints and street life with the violence and sleaze of the real thing, and as part of a Creative Time project to liven up the dead storefronts of 42nd Street, Jane turned a former peep show into a bridal shop, an apt metaphor for Times Square being made a lady. Tibor Kalman painted the word *EVERYBODY* on a huge yellow billboard, then stuck some chairs to the wall just high enough off the ground to make sitting on them an act of faith. "You had to trust that the chairs would hold," said Kalman. Once again, chairs taught how to trust.

The next two women had stepped into the job Robertson had left behind. Short, precise Marian Heiskell was the wife of Andrew Heiskell, the former Time Inc. executive who'd driven the renovation of Bryant Park and the NYPL, but it's more accurate to say that he was her husband; the eldest child of Iphigene and Arthur Sulzberger, she was New York royalty. Despite her considerable abilities, though, she hadn't taken over the family paper à la Katharine Graham at the *Washington Post*; the *Times* had gone to her younger brother Punch while she married its publisher Orvil Dryfoos, joining the board of Times Corp in 1963. Some of that may have been the era, but it may also have been because of her profound dyslexia, undiagnosed through a difficult youth; Marian never graduated from high school. "Impeccably stylish and quietly influential," hair gray since her twenties, Heiskell would become the first woman on the boards of Ford, Merck, and Con Ed, and the city's community gardens and farmers' markets were largely the result of her Council on the Environment of New York City. After Dryfoos died, she'd married Heiskell. Her executive director would be Cora Cahan, then head of the Feld Ballet, and after reviewing all the proposals, they chose, like Ed Logue in the South Bronx, to do the very last thing anyone expected: they would turn what had once been Minsky's Burlesque and 42nd Street's first X-rated movie house into a family theater. To tie it all together, Gretchen Dykstra constructed the massive Times Square BID, virtually everything from Sixth Avenue to Eighth, from 40th to

53rd, plus Restaurant Row on 46th. At the center of 5,000 businesses and 400 property owners, she'd provide sanitation, security, and the marketing that made sure the world saw them being delivered.

But all these plans needed a major player to provide the spark.

Michael Eisner knew Times Square well. When he was young, his parents had taken him to Broadway shows for his birthday, and on his own he'd come down for double-features or pinball. Once he'd even run away and spent a dismal night at the Hotel Dixie. Eisner grew up fascinated with built New York, bristling at the shadow cast by the new Pan Am Building, and "obsessed" as the 3,000 aluminum panels of 666 Fifth Avenue were bolted to their frames. Embedded in Our Crowd, his father, Lester, played golf with the Loebs and Lehmans and owned trade shows of the sort that ran at the Kingsbridge Armory until Moses built the Coliseum. When Moses didn't renew his contracts, Lester became Eastern Regional head of the Housing and Urban Renewal Authority, where he advised Jane Jacobs in her battle to save the West Village—"We owed a lot to Lester Eisner," she said later. Following his graduation from Denison University, Michael bought and renovated a building on East 82nd Street, then made his way up the ladder at ABC, a New Yorker until his pregnant wife was, on the same day, nearly shot and then almost hit by a falling brick. The Eisners had promptly moved to California and never looked back until their walk through the dank shell of the New Amsterdam.

Robert A. M. Stern had pitched him the idea the day before, even though associating Disney with New York seemed contrary to every middle-class, Middle American thing the company stood for. But much had changed about the company, and the city. After aging badly through *The Apple Dumpling Gang* '70s, Disney had found a multigenerational sweet spot by understanding that history's first teenagers had erased the cultural divide between child and adult; the managed video release of its backlist made Disney a partner in parenting, as if Mary Poppins had come back to be nanny for *your* kids. And it was a gold mine. Under Eisner, CEO since 1984, Disney Stores had rolled out and the parks were expanded and upgraded with architects like Stern, Michael Graves, and Arata Isozaki lending a sophistication that let grown-ups indulge. By the time *The Little Mermaid* came out in 1989, Disney was a juggernaut again. *Beauty and the Beast* opened the New York Film Festival and had, according to Frank Rich, the "best Broadway musical score of 1991." But Eisner worried that the company was growing complacent. Intent on now producing *Beauty and the Beast* as a Broadway show, he'd seen that if Disney owned its own theater, it wouldn't have to hand over a cut to the Shuberts or Nederlanders.

Not too long before, Marian Heiskell, an old friend of the Eisner family (he'd gone to dancing school with her daughter) had come to a charity dinner at his house and she'd also suggested buying the New Amsterdam. He'd nodded politely but now it made sense. Walt had tried to leap out of the land of make-believe with EPCOT and failed, but Eisner actually loved cities and had learned much about them scouting locations for new Magic Kingdoms and planning Celebration, Florida, a community loosely connected to the New Urbanism movement. Negotiations began. In the end, Disney would execute the entire design and renovation, and the City and State would pay—a lot. The final budget was $34 million. But suddenly there were signs of life in Times Square. On September 15, Kalman and Stern presented 342 pages of guidelines that channeled Whyte and Jane Jacobs as much as Stern's old professor Venturi. The slightly cartoony illustrations looked similar to the 42nd Street everyone remembered: huge neon signs, lots of shops and businesses, all just slightly larger and louder than life, like the 60-foot globe of changing images, the "noise tower," and tickers with sports scores. Grumblings about "Disneyfication" immediately began; ironic, since an avowed Socialist was behind it. Luc Sante felt it was all too calculated, but Disorder had to be managed now; if left to the marketplace, spontaneity in Times Square would be simply programmed into profits and Johnson's French mansard roofs. New Yorkers wanted order, but only so much.

The final piece of the Times Square revival evolved out of the early Midtown Enforcement efforts of Sturz and Weisbrod. In the fall of 1993, the Midtown Community Court opened on West 54th Street. Rather than gum up the courts with every prostitute and pot smoker collared in Times Square, it brought minor offenders directly before a judge who meted out quick justice stressing restitution rather than punishment, with social services involved when appropriate. Amanda Burden, now on the City Planning Board, designed the space and organized the public-private partnership between the City, local businesses, and social services agencies. In the years ahead, others would be opened in Red Hook and Harlem.

One thing this new 42nd Street would still have: sex. Said Gretchen Dykstra, "A few porn shops never hurt anyone." The City bought the few places left at the end of the block and sent everything else off to Eighth Avenue; by 1987, only 19 out of 430 retail businesses in the area were related to sex, but certainly not *gay* sex. In 1993, the most important Gay presence remaining in Times Square was Tony Kushner's *Angels in America* at the Walter Kerr Theatre. An epic meditation on AIDS and gay America, it arrived as the plague peaked and immediately took its place as the most critically acclaimed artistic statement on the epidemic. "A Gay Fantasia on National Themes," *Angels in America* was at least as much about the social sickness at large in the land as it was about AIDS.

Another important product of Times Square landed in November of 1993. Robert Diggs and his friend Gary Grice had long talked about creating a Staten Island crew based on the movies they watched on 42nd Street about the Wu-Tang, perennial cool bad guys to the Shao-lin's cowboys. A brotherhood of artists connected by an idea and a brand, the Wu Tang Clan expressed the ethos of trained and deadly outsiders. Diggs became RZA; Russell Tyrone Jones, Ol' Dirty Bastard; Gary Grice, GZA, and with six others constructed *Enter the Wu-Tang (36 Chambers)*, a motherfuckin' ruckus laid down over tight beats, jazz samples, and snippets of dubbed dialogue from Wu-Tang movies. The individual artists were encouraged to sign with other labels, building an immense and profitable network that embedded Wu-Tang throughout Hip Hop. The visions of Times Square held by not just forty-somethings like Kalman, Dykstra, and Robertson, but Kushner and the Wu-Tang Clan, too, expressed the turnover of the Dinkins years and the hopes and expectations percolating under the chaos.

Dinkins vs. Giuliani II

Senator Daniel Patrick Moynihan, august and liver-spotted, took the podium at the Sheraton in April to address the Association for a Better New York. A Jesuit-trained sociologist and voice of the conscienced middle, he'd never run from a fight and often sought them out; as UN ambassador he'd campaigned against anti-Zionist measures and written a notorious report warning that welfare was undermining the Black family. Though anathema to the Left, the Brahmin accent he'd somehow developed in East Harlem made him sound Kennedy-esque even when he suggested things like a period of "benign neglect" toward Black America. His speech today came from an article he'd published that winter in *The American Scholar* titled "Defining Deviancy Down." Mayor Dinkins was in attendance, sharply pressed and expecting a fellow Democrat to follow President Bill Clinton and endorse him for reelection. Instead, Moynihan took him to task for allowing an entire tier of crimes and social disorders to become the norm. He quoted Fred Siegel: "In the great wave of moral deregulation that began in the mid-1960s, the poor and the insane were freed from the fetters of middle-class mores." Of course, while the poor and the insane had been capering, fraud became rampant on Wall Street, 48 out of 50 states now marketed gambling as a necessary source of budget income, and other sorts of deviance—sexual abuse, alcohol abuse, pederasty, wife beating, and smoking—were being defined *up*. The real import of the speech wasn't its questionable logic, though. Validating John Taylor's belief that Giuliani was "a post-ideological technocrat, a neo-progressive in the Clinton mold," he all but instructed Democrats to vote Republican.

Indeed David Dinkins had exhausted many people's patience. "This is a stronger, safer New York than it was four years ago," he insisted and that was true in absolute numbers: Crime was down; the Dow was up. The parks were greener. The subways were cleaner, cooler, and on time. Crack and AIDS were ebbing. The pension gap was closing. But it still *felt* as if New York was up for grabs. Despite his 53% approval rating that winter, a *Times*-CBS poll showed that fully a third of Blacks wished someone other than Dinkins was running and 84% of Hispanics felt that race relations and quality of life had gone down during his four years. Amid terrorist bombings, cultural anxieties, and social fragmentation, New Yorkers wanted someone in charge who acknowledged and supported their right to work, build, raise families, create art, and make money safely.

Yet no one felt safe, even with the most qualified police commissioner in generations. Educated and unafraid of the people he was charged with protecting, Ray Kelly appeared on WLIB's *The Breakfast Club* to talk about relations between minorities and a police department only 11% Black and 14% Hispanic; on Sundays, he visited Black churches and made himself visible to cops and New York in general. Murders slipped again in 1993, now three years in a row, but, said Kelly, "I believe the most prudent posture is to simply let the facts speak for themselves." He politely declined feelers about heading up the FBI. But inside One Police Plaza, the bureaucracy forced Kelly to go slowly with change. "What you've got to do," said one of his top officers, "is lob a grenade on the thirteenth floor." When the Mollen Commission held its public hearings in the summer of 1993 and dirty cop Michael Dowd explained to the cameras how the Police Academy taught cadets to never give up a brother or sister cop, Kelly pushed back against its conclusion that the NYPD couldn't police itself.

Usually a report like this would damage a sitting mayor, but these were the same cops who'd held up nooses at City Hall. Giuliani's campaign director David Garth called the Mollen Commission "a very, very good way to get people's minds off the problems of the city," as if it weren't a problem that a large percentage of New Yorkers were only marginally more frightened of criminals than they were of the police. In July, the Governor's 600-page report on the Crown Heights riot absolved Dinkins of any personal responsibility while cataloguing a long, humiliating list of mistakes. And yet the race stayed a dead heat; New Yorkers still got the willies thinking about the alternative until a warmish ad featuring Rudy playing catch with his son Andrew humanized him just enough. The press turned on Dinkins, and New York, with articles discounting the drop in crime, describing streets crowded with prostitutes and drug dealers. Pete Hamill had had it up to here with the homeless. "During the years when sentiment triumphed over reason," wrote one of the town's more sentimental writers, "most New Yorkers believed that these men were harmless." But "New Yorkers don't want to hear much about the homeless anymore . . . They don't want to listen to any more sad songs." Homelessness wasn't the problem; the homeless were. Poverty wasn't a problem; the poor were.

In September, Giuliani took control of the race with his vision for "One Standard for One City." Coming from White Hat Rudy who'd gone after Wall Street, the Mob, and Leona Helmsley, that all sounded fine and egalitarian: New York was one city, and the one identity that mattered here was being a New Yorker. But who would decide what that standard was now that multiculturalism and identity politics were pleading their own special interests against the interests of the Irish, the Italians, the Catholics, the Jews, the Yankees (just then in the process of holding up the city for a new stadium). Well, Rudy, of course. And to Rudy, the Irish, Italians, Catholics, and Jews were no longer special interests; their cultural networks and needs were now all part of White Western Civilization, which needed no explanation or defense. He lit into Dinkins's "term of indifference" and the "swirling masses of garbage" left by street vendors, promising to criminalize offenses like panhandling, pointing to the Squeegee Men as the kind of dangerous nuisance destroying life in the city.

At every bridge and tunnel and a few major intersections, crews of shifty characters would squirt a filthy potion on your windshield, smear it across with a squeegee, then demand payment for their services, clearing a good $100 a day. Everyone hated Squeegee Men, the public expression of Dinkins's lack of control, lack of interest in day-to-day life in New York. Dinkins responded with one of his unsatisfying truisms: killers and rapists, he said, were the real enemy, not Squeegee Men. But his inability to even admit that Squeegee Men were annoying damaged his campaign more than either the Mollen Commission or the Crown Heights Report. He turned to Kelly, who knew it wasn't so easy or legal to sweep people off the streets. "You want to reduce crime?" Kelly asked. "You give me fifty men and suspend the Constitution. I'll reduce crime." With the help of George Kelling, his staff found pertinent laws on the books, then hit the locations every two hours to either issue summons or make arrests. After a month of pressure, most Squeegee Men were gone. While he'd forever take credit, Rudy Giuliani actually had little to do with getting rid of them. But the fact that no one had considered this extortion worth stopping seemed to prove Moynihan's point. Major Democrats moved to Giuliani; Wagner called Dinkins a decent man but not a leader, and Koch blasted him for "an administration in utter disarray." Latinos pulled away; Bronx president Fernando Ferrer's eventual endorsement was muted.

The mayor couldn't thread the political needle: New Yorkers didn't want to be controlled, but they wanted someone *in* control. They liked the Times Square plan because they wanted edginess and craziness, sex and thrills—but they wanted to choose them. They wanted to trust and be trusted again, put their chairs anywhere in Bryant Park. Lost was the fact that the energy of urban life, the diversity of culture, the food, the glamour were all actually improving. October ended with models striding down the catwalk in DKNY, the first Fashion Week show at Bryant Park, inspired by the huge fashion industry party during the Democratic convention. The tents of "Seventh on Sixth" would become symbols of the next New York. But if Bill Clinton felt your pain, Dinkins seemed to only muster a shrug.

It's a myth that bleeding-heart liberals closed their eyes and pulled the Republican lever. Though some of the White Democratic leadership voted Rudy, the rank and file went for Dinkins in roughly the same proportion as they had four years before; 8 to 1 in Crown Heights and 14 to 1 in St. Albans, but the turnout was below 1989 levels. And with all that, Dinkins still might have won if Governor Cuomo hadn't allowed the ballot to include a referendum on whether Staten Island could secede from New York City. Still sore that the elimination of the Board of Estimate had stripped the borough of some effective power, huge turnout there pushed Giuliani to a 45,000-vote win.

In his farewell address, Dinkins begged the City Council to stay the course of the city's liberal traditions. "Now more than ever," he said, "New Yorkers will look to their Council to protect the most proudly progressive government on God's earth." On December 31, 1993, its last day, the Dinkins administration signed the Memo of Understanding with Disney. Crime was already down 60% on 42nd Street; the streets of Times Square were judged 98.9% clean, and the Boomers were taking control. New York City was about to shed its skin.

III. Reformation

Chapter Eighteen

More Like the Rest of America

Without a coat in the January cold, Rudy Giuliani earnestly announced the coming of Reformation New York from the steps of City Hall while his eight-year-old son, standing at his side, blew kisses. "Dream with me of a city that can be better than the way it is now," intoned the mayor, as stout little Andrew mouthed something to a friendly face. "Believe with me that our problems can be reduced, not magically resolved," he asked while the boy waved, Windsor-style, to the crowd. "Plan with me to make the realistic changes that will actually make people's lives better than they are right now . . ." As the mayor charged to the climax, Junior jutted his chin like a mini-Mussolini, pumping a fist as he chanted along with his father's oddly imperial closing, "It should be so and it will be so!" Inspiring, hopeful, tinged with autocracy, and undercut by some public acting out, Rudy's first day hinted at the eight years to come.

Reformation New York couldn't be simply proclaimed, though. In City Hall, a swaggering cadre of dapper young lawyers called Yesrudys swept out Dinkins's "policy gals"; La Guardia's desk returned and his portrait, too, just in case anyone missed the connection between the two bad-tempered Fusion Republicans. "It always appeared to me," said Giuliani, "that the City of New York traditionally did better . . . when the Mayor was not a complete captive of one political party or the other." Six days a week at 8:00 a.m., he sat at the head of a table with his twenty or so central players, going through the day's business, a meeting he'd started every morning with since 1981, to him "the cornerstone to efficient functioning within any system." But Rudy was able to head straight to the furnace precisely because the last two mayors had made signs and left tools; his promised "reinventing and reengineering" would be variations on their themes, "the common sense approach of Ed Koch," he said, "will echo again." His head of Economic Development John Dyson delivered the breakthrough news that he wanted to bring "an entrepreneurial spirit to government"—virtually the same words he'd used sixteen years before when he did the same job for Hugh Carey. Only now, all of this would be swallowed whole by City Hall, not taken grudgingly as medicine, though ultimately Giuliani would use budget tricks, just like Dinkins, and spend too much when Wall Street took off, just like Koch. Eight years from now, Reformation New York would stand transformed, yet it would also find itself more beholden than ever to Wall Street and in many other ways only more desperate, for reasons not entirely in Giuliani's control.

Control, though, was central to Rudy's plans. "People," he once said, "are wrongly taught there is something wrong with 'authority.'" He planned to make full use of the powers charter reform had handed the mayor's office; the 8:00 a.m. meeting made the trains run on time, but it also centralized power. Reformation New York would be the product of his personal concept of justice. "You found America a paradise," said Don Corleone to Amerigo Bonasera in Giuliani's favorite book, *The Godfather.* "You had a good trade, you made a good living, you thought the world a harmless place where you could take your pleasure as you willed. You never armed yourself with true friends." Now Rudy, son of a Mob enforcer, would be that "true friend."

His City Hall—and soon much of Reformation New York—would be a matter of Us vs. Them, and he quickly made it clear who "Them" were. Since the 1972 incident involving Ben Ward, the NYPD had considered the Nation of Islam mosque a no-go location, but as reports (false, it later turned out) crackled across his radio that officers were being held hostage, Giuliani ordered in the police. Though the scene de-escalated without force, he'd sent his message. And Them wasn't just a matter of race—Giuliani's resolve to make New York "more like the rest of America" was not universally shared; just when chat rooms and bulletin boards were letting the rest of America freely express their identities the way New Yorkers did every day, Giuliani intended to send everyone back to where they'd run away from. Koch had understood chaos as New York's defining quality; he got the madness. Rudy didn't like madness.

Unless it was *his*. While Andrew's mugging at the Inaugural had been sweet and humanizing (sort of), it also had thousands of New York parents picturing how they'd clock their own kid if they did something like that, and that was the sticky thing about making control the price of order—justice got lost. What would happen when it was your kid screwing around? When it was you?

Rekindle Your Love Affair

Rudy immediately took control of the narrative. Every good thing that happened in New York would now be somehow his doing—he demanded, for instance, that the announcement of the deal with Disney be held at City Hall, though, says Rebecca Robertson, "He had nothing to do with 42nd Street. I promise you." But he also displayed the competence and command Dinkins had never fully mustered. In four February speeches, he outlined a stripped down $31.7 billion budget that proposed $750 million in tax cuts over four years with $1 billion in service cuts and $500 million in union concessions. À la *Reinventing Government,* he'd consolidate or eliminate departments and introduce competition, push regulatory reform, make licensing and inspections easier and more efficient for small businesses. He intended to sell two city hospitals, roll the three police departments into one as Koch had tried, though he resisted civilians doing office work at the NYPD because they weren't used to "paramilitary organizations." Parks, already gutted, would be whittled down further; recycling would be picked up every two weeks. The cuts went on. Almost $300 million from the schools. No more AIDS services. Immigrant Affairs merged with Language Services. He did Mayor School proud, talking at length without notes, but the push-back was immediate, loud, and from all directions. Democrats in the City Council quickly passed a law to slow down privatization, the FCB wanted to take over the budget, and the Citizens Budget Commission insisted the cuts weren't enough. Demonstrations began at City Hall. Giuliani's April approval rating was 12% below Dinkins's during the Great Existential Panic of 1990.

And then the Corleone in Rudy emerged. He made Labor an offer it couldn't refuse: In exchange for creating new salary structures, there'd be no layoffs, and those who left voluntarily would get meager buyouts. The unions blinked. "If he didn't like you," said City Council Speaker Peter Vallone, "it might seem he wanted to kill you." To the mayor's credit, he could be swayed; Fran Reiter, for example, convinced him to keep AIDS Services, and the 8:00 a.m. meeting continued to feature a diverse and combustible range of opinions. But as the first year progressed, he increasingly met any criticism or question with cruelty and belligerence, friends and foes summoned to Gracie Mansion for intense meetings just this side of a Star Chamber. Rudy bullied gentle, ineffective Schools Chancellor Ramon Cortines into resigning. And as this climate of fear settled over City government, patronage flowered; cronies replaced midlevel administrators in places like the hospital system. Ultimately he got most of what he wanted in the final 1995 budget, earning him the title "master strategist" from the *Times*. Yet as much as Giuliani craved such compliments, the press was always part of "Them" for him. "He has a very deep distrust and I think dislike of the press," said *The New Yorker*'s City Hall writer Andy Logan, "and so does everybody who works for him." His twenty-nine-year-old spokesperson Cristyne Lategano warned the entire administration not to speak to reporters and insisted that every bit of information released by the City down to the water levels in the reservoirs had to be run by her.

Outside City Hall "a sense of urban emergency and Day-Glo doom still pervades . . . ," read one spring report. A June poll showed that two-thirds of New Yorkers felt crime was as bad or getting worse. Budget cuts had put the HRA into "unprecedented crisis," and with a third of all jobs in Brooklyn and almost half in the Bronx related to health care and social services, they threatened to further depress the city's broad economy. While parks, schools, and jails neared the brink, and with kindergartens almost bursting, local pols went after easy targets like take-out menus and "growling cupshakers."

Sports fans, though, lived in a sort of heaven. For two months, Madison Square Garden shook every night as the Rangers tried to get off a fifty-four-year schneid, and the Knicks finally got past the Michael Jordan–less Bulls to reach the NBA Finals. "This is everything the theater should be and isn't," said Woody Allen, happy to talk about something other than his marriage. The Rangers won the Stanley Cup, but John Starks, tragic hero, hit 2 of 18 in the Knicks' Game Seven loss. Sensing a top, Viacom sold MSG and its teams to Cablevision, which had never run a sports franchise.

There'd be more dramas and diversions during the summer of OJ, when a tourist bureau ad suggested that you "Rekindle your love affair with New York" now, it implied, that someone else was in charge. David Letterman had moved his show to CBS and the Ed Sullivan Theater, where he put a friendly face on Times Square with regular forays to "Meet the Neighbors," making stars out of Mujibur and Sirajul, and Rupert Jee of the Hello Deli. The Wonderbra arrived, along with Kryptonite bike locks, flip phones, and Starbucks. Tom Colicchio's Gramercy Tavern and a crop of new restaurants including Michael's, Mesa Grill, Nobu, and Jean-Georges anchored dining as a performance art. September began rocking away bad memories. "Calm down, it's fall," said *New York*, swooning under the changing leaves. "The metropolis didn't go up in several balls of flame. Civilization continued." And what more proof did you need of that than the premiere of *Friends*, set in a tidy White fantasy of Lifestyle in New York.

The tide began to turn in Rudy's favor when he endorsed Clinton's crime bill and its funds for social programs he'd just gutted. "My city comes first," said the mayor to congressional Republicans. "Political parties come second." His approval rating broke 50%, something Mario Cuomo noticed as he ran for a fourth term, this time against D'Amato's guy George Pataki. Despite giving signals that he'd sit this one out, Giuliani endorsed Cuomo on live television on October 25, a "Dirty Deal" Republicans packaged to represent everything they hated about New York City. Massive Upstate turnout gave Pataki an easy win, but Rudy had made himself look like the Fusion mayor he'd promised to be, transforming perceptions of his Reaganomic takeover into the rough but necessary medicine of Koch's emergency budgets. Right-minded

New Yorkers could now admit out loud that they liked his crazed relish for the job, his support for illegal aliens and gun control, and the fact that he spent New Year's Eve with gay friends. "Our Loser," *New York* called him.

"NEW YORK IS BACK"

And then it happened.

Not to everyone and not all at once, but more and more people throughout all five boroughs had the same odd experience. Out walking late at night, they suddenly realized they weren't thinking about getting mugged. Or they got onto the subway, sat down, read a little of their book, and then got off at their stop without ever squeezing themselves into an unnoticeable ball of humanity. They weren't awakened by gunfire in the small hours. Brave souls took the "No Radio" signs out of their cars. New Yorkers suddenly noticed changes that had been in the works for years—fifteen or sixteen when it came to things like Bryant Park and the "South Bronx Renaissance" that writer Craig Horowitz pointed to as proof of Giuliani's transformational spirit. Calling developments started in the early '80s "vivid evidence that a resurrection is under way," he marveled at how "[w]hole blocks of vandalized, bombed-out apartment buildings have been reclaimed, renovated, and reinhabited by working-class families." By this time, the housing initiative had created some 50,000 new units. "Abandoned, gutted buildings have been rebuilt," wrote the *Times*, now also alert. "Houses have gone up on empty, littered lots." But the 267 townhouse units of Melrose Court, the new shops and malls in the South Bronx, the Pathmark supermarket slated for 174th Street—Giuliani had had nothing to do with them.

Everywhere a sudden light shone down. The all-type cover of *New York*'s Christmas issue harked and heralded the news that "NEW YORK IS BACK." "The death of this city has been declared so often," it read, "that almost no one realizes life here is actually getting better—safer, nicer, tastier, cheaper, snazzier, more sensible and exciting than it's been in years. Who knew?" Inside, the "celebration of the new, improved metropolis" began "Admit it: You've been feeling better, but don't know why," though it certainly hinted by naming Rudy himself one of the thirty-eight "new, improved" things about New York: "Rudy Giuliani's first year as mayor, though far from perfect, has been so eventful, so thrillingly New Paradigmatic that the Dinkins administration seems even less accomplished in memory than it was in fact." Yet out of the thirty-seven other reasons cited, little was new or in any way related to Giuliani. From Times Square, Chelsea Piers, and Bryant Park to better subways, bustling flea markets, and a wave of coffeehouses, this sudden awakening was the result of policies, plans, and battles of prior administrations and the tireless efforts of individuals who'd fought and labored with their fellow New Yorkers for more than a decade.

One of the most defining elements of Reformation New York was buried at #29 on the list. Precise zoning laws had kept superstores in check, but the few so far had significant impact: Tower Records had anchored the Lower Broadway revival, and New Yorkers accustomed to mom and pop hardware stores fell hard for the Bed, Bath and Beyond on Ladies Mile, gawping at the endless shelves of neatly stacked towels and the walls of kitchen gadgets all at low, low prices. Though economists considered them "a kind of economic strip-mining," they also provided jobs and four times the rent as manufacturing, so in February 1995 Giuliani doubled down on one of Dinkins's ideas and proposed raising the as-of-right for superstores from 10,000 square feet to 200,000. Staples and Kmart had already arrived, with Old Navy, Crate & Barrel, and Filene's Basement on their way. While "Kmart," wrote Wendy Wasserstein, "is a reminder that regular people live in Manhattan" and bad businesses didn't deserve protection, New Yorkers soon noticed more beloved stores going under and less of the regular exchange they were used to having with local shopkeepers. "City life," wrote Wasserstein, "is made up of such daily alliances." But they were torn between Jane Jacobs and convenience, and the *Times* called the City Council's ultimate vote against rezoning "touching and sweetly small-townish." Superstores kept coming; you were a "guest" now wherever you went, from T.J.Maxx to the DMV. Voting and shopping veered closer, toward the same goal: to deliver Lifestyle-like information—fast, cheap, and without human connection.

Everything Is Perfect Again

And so with unemployment down to just over 5%, the Bull pawing, and Clinton in the White House, many Democratic Boomers felt confident that their blend of '60s values, '70s realism, and '80s greed would now lead America to a just and prosperous future. The First Lady wrote *It Takes a Village*, and both sides talked about "community values" while Democrats edged away from liberal stalwarts like Ruth Messinger and Public Advocate Mark Green, and Giuliani purged anyone appointed by Dinkins, Koch, and even Beame. Fernando Ferrer conceded that the Right was "doing the most prolific and profound thinking about the city that's been done in a long time," though Labor had blocked many of those ideas when Democrats had floated them. Now Democrats held the door. Rudy's public approval whiplashed. Was he a maverick or just a loose cannon? If Dinkins's sincere distress over budget cuts had been one cause of the paralysis at City Hall, Giuliani couldn't even pretend he lost sleep when cops teargassed student protestors. But you couldn't pigeon-hole him. In the spring, he spoke out on behalf of illegal immigrants and took on an overwhelmed Children's Welfare Administration caught between twenty-six separate computer systems and tens of thousands of files updated with handwritten notes; a kid moving between boroughs may well have moved between continents. Stiff-arming the Transit and Public Housing Police into the NYPD had been on every mayoral agenda since Lindsay and his new Department of Design and Construction for capital projects proved effective. But the Disruptor in Chief always went too far. It was one thing to sell off the UN Plaza Hotel—no one understood why the City owned it in the first place—but Comptroller Alan Hevesi had to block Rudy in court from selling the rights to the City's water supply. Even Ed Koch, whose name he regularly invoked, said, "I think Rudy's become filled with his own sense of importance." The Financial Control Board continued grumbling and S&P downgraded the City's bonds. And yet there was Rudy, getting cheered at the Pride Parade even as he crammed through another drastic budget.

The upbeat mood rolled on. Instead of graffiti, "brand-train" subway cars would now trap citizen consumers in Fruitopia, Donna Karan, and

Levi's commercials for however long they rode, even as Rudy cut $400 million from what the City kicked in to the MTA. Though Salomon Brothers was on death's door after a bidding scandal that forced out John Gutfreund, the People's Market continued its rise, making the classic sixes and sevens that had dropped almost 25% of their value in three years attractive again; rents were up 30% to 40%, with the "most potent pricing factor," admitted *New York*, "our perception of the city." Private schools reported families returning from the suburbs. Doors were unlocked, windows opened, and in the best and genuine ways Whyte and Olmsted had called for, New Yorkers came back together again on streets, in parks, and through public spaces. "People used to understand that gathering in public was good," said Hugh Hardy, "that's what democracy meant." Feeling safer, their presence created even more safety. Outdoor cafés now lined entire blocks. The 79th Street Boat Basin Café attracted Little Leaguers, Rollerbladers, and junior consultants; "Frederick Law Olmsted would be proud," according to *The New Yorker*. "His 1875 plan to bring the polyglot strands of Upper West Side life together in Riverside Park is fully realized . . ." Gael Greene thought the food at Bryant Park Grill was just fine, but she loved the space even more. Greenmarkets and Gourmet Garage became everyday stops, dog runs were a major topic. The dinosaur halls at the Museum of Natural History reopened, their great skeletons now tails-up, nimble, and more aggressive to reflect the new thinking about dinosaurs, and seemingly everything else in Reformation New York. Along the Hudson, skaters, golfers, and bowlers hit Chelsea Piers, "so user-friendly, so open and primary-color-happy," wrote Alex Williams, "it radiates a Sun Belt–style optimism . . ." Such a thing was now considered a compliment.

The streets were cleaner, too, but mostly in those areas with Business Improvement Districts. Thirty of them operated, and for now they proved useful cover for Giuliani by hiding the realities of his budget cuts. Those areas without suffered under piles of garbage. Once again, the point was made that everyone was a customer, and if you wanted more, you were free to pay more. Many found this logic attractive and empowering, but it threatened to erode the very thing Communitarians lectured about. "We're redefining our sense of community in the narrowest possible manner," said former UDC head Richard Kahan.

On May 30, 1995, the revival of *Damn Yankees* playing at the Marquis, nineteen-year-old rookie Derek Jeter stepped in against the Mariners' Tim Belcher. While the Mets and Giants, Knicks and Rangers had all taken their turns in the spotlight, the most New York of New York teams had floundered. No one living around the Stadium cared much about the Yankees, and the feeling was mutual; team executive Richard Kraft referred to the local kids as "monkeys" and after striking a $500 million cable deal in 1988, Steinbrenner warned that he'd take the team to New Jersey if the City didn't subsidize a new ballpark. Rudy, who tried to derail Dinkins's lucrative USTA deal, got to work on plans for a new Yankeeland while Jeter, waving his bat in little circles, delivered another sign that Reformation New York had arrived, slapping his first Major League hit—a single to left. Both Giuliani and the Yankees' manager, fellow Brooklyn native Joe Torre of the hound dog eyes and managerial record 109 games below .500, would build dynasties on rebuilds handed to them. *New York*'s "Shiny and New" Christmas issue expressed the thrill: "Eurotrash, caviar, shiny mega-baubles, and super-glitzy weddings . . . No more of that wearying recession talk. The economy is booming!" Amid the snark, it also said what few wanted to admit. "The Dow is well over 5,000, and income inequality hasn't been greater in living memory . . . Everything is perfect again—this city, plush-banqueted, deferential, first-class, is your Fabergé egg." A gift from a True Friend.

Chapter Nineteen

Larceny in Everyone's Heart

Rudy Giuliani had built his career on the belief that everyone was a sinner somehow—you just had to catch them at it. Cops, he wrote, "are authoritarian figures." Most of the NYPD wanted him to keep Ray Kelly as commissioner, and their meeting had started reasonably well until Kelly mentioned Community Policing and Giuliani showed him the door. The man he really wanted was Bill Bratton, who'd stood next to President Clinton in the Rose Garden to advocate for the Crime Bill and was ready for something bigger than Boston. "I didn't know Giuliani from a hole in a wall," he wrote later, but he found "in close quarters, [he] can be quite charming and ingratiating." Harvey Dent had met Batman, John Wayne had met Jimmy Stewart; over the next two years, as Giuliani and Bratton fought over who was who, New York would learn that crime doesn't have to define city life.

Bratton immediately named Jack Maple Deputy Commissioner for Crime Control Strategies. "Fatso," as he was not so lovingly called by some of his new police brethren, shared Giuliani's belief that "there's a little larceny in everybody's heart," but without the moral encrustation. To Maple, people committed crimes for all sorts of reasons, so until the human soul was sorted out, he'd be outside catching crooks. The rest of the inner circle looked like the cast of a movie. Though known for misplacing his gun and pager, Chief of Personnel Mike Julian had helped settle the riots in Tompkins Square Park; Chief of Department

John Timoney, iron-jawed and Dublin-born, had run Management Planning and Analysis under Kelly; and finally there was John Miller, former WNBC reporter with his own Johnny Deadline shtick. Sneering at Elaine's the way he sneered at Dinkins's tennis, Giuliani had made it off-limits to City employees, but Bratton, Maple, and Miller came anyway, with Rudy's Gal Friday Cristyne Lategano making appearances as Miller's sassy brunette squeeze. As tables were hopped, cheeks bussed, and men with cigars craned to get a better look at what Candace Bushnell, she of the *Observer's* Sex and the City column, was doing with *her* Cohiba, the group slapped backs and brainstormed how they'd end crime in New York.

In his Transit days, Bratton had always suspected that "[t]he big blue wall was a lot of blue smoke and a few mirrors," so he got the Police Foundation to pay John Linder $137,500 for another "cultural diagnostic" somewhere between Mao and AA. Small groups examined their process in painful detail and came to damning conclusions: the NYPD worked 9 to 5, and essentially took weekends off; putting information in silos stymied effectiveness and efficiency. Terrible morale had less to do with David Dinkins than the fact that uniformed cops were, said Bratton, "bored to tears," urged by the force to just stay out of trouble and not screw over other cops. Even the uniforms were ugly.

Armed with all this, and a grudge from his years in Transit, Bratton now requested resignation letters from the fifteen top officials and booted anyone who didn't believe in his goals of a 10% crime drop for 1994, 15% for 1995. Hierarchy would be flattened, responsibility spread; precinct captains and commanders would get more freedom, but they'd be on the hook. Community Policing would be out until order was reestablished. Instead, uniforms would now have the freedom and responsibility to make arrests on any kind of crime; drugs and guns were the targets. All perps would be charged; all suspects would be interrogated, especially when a gun was involved. The open-air drug trade would be driven off the streets. Some 125,000 copies of a pamphlet outlining new crime-fighting strategies developed by Maple were distributed, and here's where the distinctions between Broken Windows and Quality of Life were officially blurred. As they'd done in Transit, and Kelly had with the Squeegee Men, Bratton and Maple established "stepped-up enforcement" of public nuisance laws already on the books to give cops more probable cause for stops. No more tickets for loose joints or playing loud music; you'd be arrested now, get a warrant check, and be interrogated. But Police Strategy Number 5 in the pamphlet setting all this down was called "Reclaiming the Public Spaces of New York," creating a chicken-or-egg question: Would the arrests be made to clean up public space, or was cleaning up public space the pretext for arresting bad guys?

Things didn't start well. On March 23, Edith and Gerald Schaeffer of Maryland and their two daughters were looking at wedding gowns at Vera Wang in the Carlyle Hotel. While they got ready to say yes to the dress, two men burst in, shot the receptionist, and broke Edith's finger pulling off her diamond ring. When Gerald stepped in, the thieves shot both of them in the abdomen. "I hate this city," screamed one of the daughters. The same day in the South Bronx, a nineteen-year-old girl was shot dead, one of ten homicides. "I hate this city" threatened to become Rudy's version of "Dave, Do Something." Then news broke of yet another crooked precinct, this time the "Dirty Thirty" in Harlem. Unlike Dinkins though, Bratton felt more sympathy than disgust. "I could not forgive truly dirty cops," he'd write later, "but I could understand those others who found themselves jammed up for making a momentary mistake"; a reasonable position, but the exact opposite of the one he and the mayor were now taking on Quality of Life "crimes" that would incarcerate thousands of "jammed up" civilians for making their own momentary mistakes. Between the lines, though, was concern about the age, quality, and training of his cops, something Bratton had once tweaked Kelly for. Despite "taking the handcuffs off," the commissioner raised the minimum age for the NYPD to 22 along with higher physical standards and two years of college. He let go of 148 probational cops in 1994, more than the last three years combined, and banned the chokehold.

What ultimately changed the force, though, was data. At that point, crime statistics were still compiled quarterly for the FBI, *annually* for City Hall, and the department's nineteen data systems were intentionally kept separate, rendering them all but useless. The NYPD had its own Control Crisis, so Maple started with demanding the stats on every crime category for every precinct, every week. With precincts now "mini-police departments," captains could use this information to target efforts, but it would also show whether they were doing their jobs. Then Maple began calling in borough commanders and chiefs for weekly 8:00 a.m. briefings in the second-floor pressroom at One Police Plaza. Soon brass from every precinct came to these "Crime Meetings" to go through their numbers in the same excruciating public way of Linder and Nat Leventhal. Soon Compstat, as it was now known, was held twice a week for three hours, starting at 7:00 a.m.—an hour before Giuliani's meeting. Once a month, each commander presented to a room of now 200 officers.

Compstat turned the top brass into a small world connected more directly to precincts. Maple wasn't finished, though. He and his computer whiz John Yohe began to plot each individual crime in New York City, every day. Projected on 8-foot-by-8-foot monitors in the conference room, the maps revealed the hot spots, the bad corners, and larger trends. For example, 60% of all grand larcenies took place in just three precincts, and Manhattan crime was largely the work of visiting Brooklynites. Compstat got more intense; stars were made, chairs thrown, and there were even a few fistfights, but suddenly the renetworked NYPD was thinking with what felt like one mind. Compstat could have been created years earlier—City Planning was cranking out maps like these back in the mid '80s and Sanitation had been plotting its own hot spot maps in 1987—but the NYPD was so far behind that in catching up, it led a new wave of data analytics.

The impact down the chain was swift. Fear of being "in the barrel" put pressure on cops who no longer had the same time for corruption and over time, as the focus stayed on the volume of police action rather than anything that might measure safety and neighborhood satisfaction, the stress of making numbers would lead to systematic abuses. Right now, though, Bratton's changes were exactly the help that communities, and particularly minority ones, had been begging for—Daughtry, Butts, Youngblood, Farrakhan had all marched against crack houses, given the police detailed reports. Early reviews in the African American community were strong. "He's a professional," said Rangel, and Sharpton agreed: "His actions show he wants to reach out." Standing next to Sharpton, Bratton had said, "I know there are some police officers who are disrespectful of the law-abiding, particularly people of color . . . While I'm white and you're black, I'll be your commissioner."

By the fall, and those first intoxicating moments of anxiety-free urban life, nearly a quarter of uniformed patrol cops still hadn't made an arrest and the "zero-tolerance" approach on the streets had added $14 million in overtime—a "quick" booking could still take six hours of a cop's time. A bullish John Miller predicted that the year-end totals would show "the largest year-to-year percentage decrease not just in this department's history but in all history going back to when the earth was still cooling and dinosaurs roamed the plains." The tough but fair, thinking man's top cop (who also happened to be a Democrat) let wary New Yorkers support Rudy-style law and order without supporting Rudy, and without asking questions even as reports began to emerge of overly aggressive police behavior and the random harassment of People of Color. Misdemeanor arrests shot up—from 175,000 to 500,000 in 1994—with the catch, pointed out *The New Yorker*, "that in all likelihood more than a few of those arrested . . . had violated no law." Kelling and Wilson themselves had some caveats about their own theories back in 1982: "None of this," they wrote then, "is easily reconciled with any conception of due process or fair treatment." While everyone wanted a safer city, minorities would disproportionately pay the price.

The Tipping Point

John Miller had been right about the statistics, if not the dinosaurs. Crime in 1994 went down 12.3%, the leading edge of a coast-to-coast crime drop. There'd been 350 fewer murders in 1994 than in 1993; 650 fewer than in 1990. Even Bratton didn't take all the credit: "Nobody can be sure exactly what is going on," he told the *Times* in an article titled "When Crime Recedes: New York Crime Falls, But Just Why Is a Mystery." What the NYPD *could* own was the start of a virtuous cycle. At first, "fear," wrote Fred Siegel, "declined even more rapidly than crime." Subway ridership was up, and more New Yorkers spending more time in public space dampened opportunistic crime. The next year, murders fell to a 25-year low, making the panic over young Black superpredators appear less like science and more like White panic, but theories on both sides were being disproved. Three-quarters of New Yorkers below the poverty line were statistically in "extreme poverty," and by 1998, more than 600,000 people a month relied on emergency meals, more than twice the number as when Giuliani took office, so if hunger made you a criminal, crime should have been shooting up. Nor were the moral measures that a Manhattan Institute type might look for—single-parent homes, for example—getting any better.

So what ended crime as it was known in New York?

Jack Maple said it wasn't about literally fixing broken windows. "Rapists and killers," he wrote, "don't head for another town when they see that graffiti is disappearing from the subway." Incarceration wasn't the deciding factor either, at least in New York; murders took a quick dive once Compstat was in place, but other crimes continued down the same trend line that had started under Dinkins. Something else was happening. The changes in the NYPD had a profound impact, but they were meeting a unique confluence of conditions.

First, drug use had changed. Whatever cachet crack may have had was gone. Hip Hop glorified making money off of crack; it didn't glorify using it. Marijuana, back up from its low point in 1990, was again the recreational drug of choice. Bratton would later dispute this, but hard alcohol was detected more often in suspects than crack; high taxes levied since Koch had driven down its consumption, so less alcohol could have had even more of a long-term impact than less crack. Of course, "drug use" means among People of Color. Back in the '60s and '70s, drugs had been one big bleary subculture but the '80s had "factionalized" drugs in America. The laws of Reagan's War on Drugs went specifically after People of Color, and when middle-class Whites hit bottom, it was a lot easier for them to not only avoid jail but find open arms in the warm world of recovery and codependency. Heroin, ecstasy, and prescription drug abuse, all up among Whites, were ignored.

Second, crack as a business had "matured," according to Professor Andrew Karmen. A "democratic" drug, crack's low overhead encouraged small, independent dealers, so '70s-style gangs hadn't been the problem as much as the chaos of a free market. As the business consolidated, dealers became "more discrete and businesslike," writes Karmen, "and behaved more responsibly and cautiously." Pagers replaced corner sets and drugs went back indoors, taking guns with them. Shooting had been by far the number one method of murder during the crisis, so fewer guns on the streets meant less mayhem. Yet even indoors, and away from the police, violence dropped—fewer fatal robberies, fewer deadly family fights, fewer drug deals gone bad. Smoking had a communal quality unlike the solitary desperation of the crack house.

The murderers were overwhelmingly poor, Black or Latino, young, and 95% male, which also described most of those murdered, pointing to network theory's tenet that who you know has an enormous influence on you. The best indicator of whether someone is a delinquent is the proportion of their friends who are, and between 1980 and 1990, the demographic of young, poor men of color fell by 30%, leading economist Steven Levitt to surmise that the national crime drop was an unintended result of legalized abortion; others linked it convincingly to the abolishment of lead paint. Many of the social programs now being cut had further helped shrink that risk pool. Attending college, for example, dramatically lowered the risk of being shot. Whatever you thought of open admissions to CUNY, its students were literally saving their own lives by stepping onto campus, yet government spending on prisons far outstripped education; in 1990, 2.28 million Black men were jailed in the US while 23,000 earned a college degree. And then there were the gruesome reasons. Overall, there were fewer criminals because they were dying off. Over the last ten years, they'd done a staggering job of killing each other, along with AIDS, which had driven many needle users to crack. Crime is contagious, and as those in criminal networks big and small died, the networks became weaker, leading to even less crime. Prison may have played an early role, but not the way commonly assumed. The city's prison population had peaked in 1991, before Bratton, when crime had first started to decline. As the NYPD began its arrest campaign, the Vera Institute and Brooklyn DA Charles Hynes were already encouraging courts to consider options aside from prison. The State prison population would peak in 1998, and then both the State and City ones would drop into the next millennium almost as dramatically as crime. Without questioning the destructive injustice of America's prison-industrial complex, crime as it was known in New York City did not end because of mass incarceration.

But there were two more hopeful causes and both pointed to the fundamental role communities had in transforming New York. First, immigration. First- and second-generation immigrants are much less likely to commit crimes than the native born, and hundreds of thousands of them had been moving into at-risk neighborhoods, diluting the percentage of criminals. And many were there because of the second reason, the Housing Initiative that replaced urban entropy with homes. "What happened," says Trina Scotland of the East Brooklyn Congregations, "was that as the mind-set changed, and as the police changed, that's when the crime rate started going down." A Melrose Court resident in the fall of 1994 observed, "I think over the summer there wasn't one time here when I heard gunfire during the night. Because of all the new housing, the area has been cleaned up so much it's unbelievable." "What changed the South Bronx," wrote urbanist Tony Proscio, "was not a sudden influx of wealth but a careful restoration of order—in the built environment, in public spaces, and in people's lives." Civic participation by those considered marginal restored social capital and rewrote the set of acceptable behaviors sociologist Robert Sampson calls "collective efficacy." And broken windows, it turns out, might have mattered after all. Correlating blocks with boarded-up windows to a neighborhood's violent crime rate shows parallel drops from the late '80s to 2000: In Mott Haven, blocks with board-ups went from 64.7 to 17.7 as violent crime went from 48.25 to 19.89; in University Heights, 60.6 to 4.3 and 38.79 to 17.73 respectively; Brownsville, 67.4 to 23.3 and 60.14 to 21.37.

Malcolm Gladwell's June 1996 New Yorker article "The Tipping Point" described a city stunned. "There is probably no other place in the country where violent crime has declined so far, so fast." New York by then was 136th in violent crime in the US. In two years homicides in the 75th Precinct had gone from 126 to 44. "There are now ordinary people on the streets at dusk—," he wrote with wonder, "small children riding their bicycles, old people on benches and stoops, people coming out of the subways alone." Though Gladwell saw crime as a virus, criminologist Franklin Zimring leaned toward Giuliani and Maple's belief that a surprising number of people of every race and class are willing to commit a crime if they think they'll get away with it: someone cheating on their taxes or groping a secretary are white-collar versions of a chain snatcher or pickpocket; by 1995, Bernie Madoff was churning on all cylinders. But enough changes in the surrounding circumstances had eliminated enough opportunities, breaking down networks, stopping contagion, and letting neighborhoods reknit. Pervasive crime didn't have to be a fact of urban life, and while pundits of both parties now accepted that liberal policies had failed, Gladwell pointed out that it was also entirely possible that those policies had kept it from getting even worse. In the end, no one policy or person ended crime as it was known in New York. But ending crime was the tipping point that brought Reformation New York fully to life.

Crime Down. New York Better.

While Bratton had been cleaning up the NYPD, Rudy had applied the full power of City Hall against the Mob, baked into the city's business and woven through its government in networks of kickbacks, bid rigging, and bribery. A decade of investigations and RICO suits by the FBI, Manhattan DA Robert Morgenthau, and the US attorneys of the Eastern and Southern Districts had by now put three of the five Bosses in prison and the Mob was teetering. The push started in February 1995, at Fulton Fish Market, where the soldiers of the Genovese family who directed unloading and parking had pulled wholesalers' revenues down to $800,000 from $2 billion just fifteen years before. When Giuliani announced that the City was taking over, someone torched the Old Market Building along with all its records. Chief of Staff Randy Mastro was put under 24-hour police protection and on a tense night in October, 400 fish handlers armed with hooks took up stools at the old Paris Café, police set up a base at the other end of the market, and testy negotiations commenced until Local 359 finally caved. The unloading companies were replaced, resulting in new revenues and lower seafood prices, and in 1997, the same rules were extended to all other wholesale markets. A free-market mayor had solved the problem with a government takeover.

Meanwhile, Robert Morgenthau and the FBI had been working on the trash haulers' cartel, run by the Luccheses and Gambinos, who added an estimated 40% to the price of commercial hauling in New York. Indictments against twenty-three firms allowed companies to negotiate a price with the carter of their choice, which for many businesses was a windfall: the World Trade Center's bill dropped 80%, Columbia Presbyterian Hospital 60%. The mayor called this "the largest tax cut of his administration." There was a downside, though. Mob control had inflated prices, but once big carters squeezed out small carters with lower prices, the big carters began raising them again, begging the question as to whether the city had just traded Mob control for corporate control. At the State-run Javits Center, Governor Pataki cleaned house the same worker-by-worker way the mayor had at the fish market. Local 295 at JFK already had signed a consent decree establishing a monitor, but two more RICO suits were filed in 1995. By the 1997 trial of Vincent "the Chin" Gigante, famous for shambling through Little Italy in his bathrobe feigning mental illness, New York's next generation of mobsters was loitering in suburban malls while the survivors of the last one played themselves in movies.

But as the Italian Mob weakened, the Russian *Mafiya* stepped in. Earlier waves of Soviet Jews who'd settled in Brighton Beach had included many of the mobsters who'd run the Soviet Union's vast black market, and now the 1990 immigration law had inadvertently let in an uncounted number of the ones who'd helped the KGB turn the former Soviet Union into a kleptocracy. "America is getting Russian criminals," said a Russian investigator. "Nobody will have the resources to stop them. You people in the West don't know our *Mafiya* yet. You will, you will!" Yet the NYPD had no Russian-speaking cops or really any contacts in the Russian community other than some dirty officers working security for its mobsters. "They're going to buy power," said a Department of Justice official. In 1996, Giuliani named Semyon Kislin, said by the FBI to have ties to the Russian mob, to his Economic Board of Advisors; Clinton and Gore also had similar friends. Trump had the drop on everyone, though; he'd made his first visit to Moscow back in 1987.

Yet as the Elaine's Gang winged ever closer to the sun, the rivalry between Bratton and Giuliani put their achievements at risk. In his first week, Bratton had shrugged off complaints from City Hall that a *Daily News* interview was not well received, and things only got worse. The commissioner made no secret that his crew of supercops considered Giuliani a glorified hall monitor, but as the adoring press gave him credit for the turnaround, the NYPD found itself waiting for approval of new initiatives until the mayor could orchestrate their peak political and publicity value; City Hall shut down an all-out assault on drugs in Queens after the *Daily News* ran the cover "BRATTON'S JUGGERNAUT." Yet egos continued swelling. Jack Maple gave interviews in his office next to an undimpled heavy bag and his special moustache-trimming mirror while Bratton planned a parade to celebrate the NYPD's 150th anniversary, on what just happened to be his birthday. Giuliani said no. The romance between Miller and Lategano soured, further poisoning relations between One Police Plaza and City Hall, and then *The New Yorker* published a laudatory profile of Bratton claiming "[t]he great majority of the city's thirty-one thousand police officers have nothing but good things to say about him." And that included the commissioner, who said, "I like what I've become." Giuliani didn't. Within days, Lategano announced PR firings across City government, in particular at the NYPD. Bratton's circle discussed resigning en masse, at which point Miller fell on his sword in a weepy televised speech. But Bratton still went to *The New Yorker's* anniversary party, easily the most popular figure in the administration, including Giuliani. His support among minorities, his ability to crisply execute plans that Rudy turned into morality plays had people talking about a run for City Hall. After a 17% drop in crime in 1995, *Time* put Bratton on the cover, and if that wasn't enough to finish him off, he signed a $350,000 book deal. The mayor chose not to renew his contract that March. Bill Bratton left with a 71% approval rating; the force at 73%, more than twice what it had been four years before. He'd administered a powerful and necessary tonic to a city already on the slow mend, but even George Kelling thought it was time to move away from the NYPD's "militarized bureaucracy model." To follow Bratton, Giuliani chose Fire Commissioner Howard Safir, a "lightweight," according to John Timoney. "The idea that Giuliani is some kind of crime fighter is just horseshit." Not surprisingly, Timoney retired.

On October 26, 1996, John Wetteland got Atlanta's Mark Lemke to pop out to Charlie Hayes and the Yankees won their twenty-third World Series. Amid the party, Wade Boggs climbed aboard a police horse in center field and took a victory lap, sending the Stadium into a frenzy. The equation was simple, wrote Michael Tomasky: "Yankees. Rudy. Crime down. New York better."

Chapter Twenty

Cyber City

The end of crime wasn't the only cause of Reformation New York. Until now, technology had been the means to better management, the handmaiden to change, but over the next five years, technology would become the story, altering nearly every aspect of the city's culture and economy, launched by the search for the answer to the same questions Red Burns and the ITP had been asking since the late '70s: For one, What would the Internet *be*? The World Wide Web had made the Internet simply "work" for everyday people the way Apple had for computers; you no longer had to understand it to use it. Out in its infinite reaches, past the playpens of AOL and Prodigy, you could do text-heavy things like explore Meryl Streep's credits on IMDb or read the *Raleigh News & Observer*. Ted Kennedy had a website, as did the Simpsons and NetBoy, or you could enter random words into a "search engine" like Webcrawler and see what popped up. You could watch things happening in real time across the globe, experience new and direct methods of exchange, interpretation, and connection. But how would it work as a business? Would it be doled out like cable or an open network like the telephone? Would people access it through their computers or their televisions? Would they buy content like books, subscribe like magazines, or watch with ads like network TV?

New York sat atop a deep well of underused human capital, a cohort of recent college graduates forced into McJobs along with thousands of writers, artists, graphic designers, and otherwise underemployed creatives who could make anything you might want to actually look at on the Internet. Those with little urge or opportunity to fall into corporate ruts realized they could try to make their own fortunes. In the fall of 1994, the New York New Media Association had hosted its first Cybersuds gathering under the Statue of Liberty crown at El Teddy's in TriBeCa. If unused real estate had created SoHo, all this unused talent would create Silicon Alley.

The debuts of Netscape and Mozilla, the first real browsers, began the shift from text to images; "People don't like to read," said one Tech journalist. The first banner ads appeared in *Wired*'s website, HotWired, announcing that "The (Second Phase of the) Revolution Has Begun," and spring brought Lexington and Concord. The teaser created by Agency.com for the *Sports Illustrated Swimsuit Edition* got so many hits it crashed Time Inc.'s web portal and suddenly "every old-media company realized it needed a Website," said *New York*, "(although it wasn't clear to most of them precisely why)." Corporate America poured into bare lofts equipped with card tables and whiteboards for meetings with graphic designers, semiotics majors, visionaries, and bullshit artists, holders of the secret knowledge for which they would now have to pay dearly. "The Internet was going to be an incredibly sweet revenge," wrote Michael Wolff, "because nobody who had a real job got it." In the following three months, Agency.com alone took on HBO, Time, Hitachi, American Express, and MetLife as clients. "[T]here are two kinds of people:," explained *The New Yorker* (a little later), "those who get it, and those who don't. To get it means that you understand the extent to which the Internet will change work and commerce in the next millennium . . ." There were no rules or precedents, so the result was a creative explosion; while most of what was produced was unimpressive in practical terms even then, "Early True Believers" like Steven Johnson and Stefanie Syman created FEED, one of the first general-interest online magazines, Word.com, a mixed bag of writing, art, and online play edited by Marisa Bowe, and SonicNet, Nicholas Butterworth's music site.

This Pandora's box had cracked open the same summer as Derek Jeter's debut and those cunning new dinosaurs at the Museum of Natural History, the same summer when crime plummeted and the streets filled. Suddenly there was a future again for New York, and it wasn't just because of Giuliani and Bratton. Only a few mouse clicks away loomed the possibility of a city able to get by without dirty factories *and* less reliance on Wall Street; new, clean, high-paying jobs would build an infinite future for everyone. The standard bemused tone about computer geeks had disappeared in the face of some 10,000 New Yorkers in the field, and in November, *New York* declared the city a "HIGH TECH BOOM TOWN." Of course, not everyone welcomed the Geek Rush. Modesty was not valued by most cybergurus, who believed everything everyone in the "Establishment" had ever known about media, content, and the written word had not so much been rendered stupid and irrelevant, but in fact had always been so. "Everything that can be digital will be," was the motto at ad agency Razorfish, founded in an East Village apartment, and there was no room for disagreement; any brakes, any planning were proof of old thinking. "It's incredibly powerful to feel that you are one of the seventeen people who really understand the world," said Rufus Griscom, who used that incredible power to create a website of "Literate Smut" called Nerve.com. Josh Harris at Pseudo came off to many as "glib and glad-handing, arrogant and solicitous," not to say crazy on those days when he showed up at business meetings dressed as his alter-ego, a sad clown named Lovey. Harris parlayed his sickly childhood in front of a TV into an innate understanding of how the Internet would produce cults of personality. His digital research firm made him a millionaire, and at a time when streaming barely existed, his site Pseudo offered channels for every possible taste.

Those who Got It often blurred over the inconvenient fact that popular tastes and market forces don't equal democracy and embraced how the Internet's new forms of social connection overrode human intimacy. Silicon Alley created new society and spaces in real life, too. Along with its arrogance came a diffidence to the aspirations of earlier generations of New Yorkers, whether it be Downtown Cool or Upper East Side respectability. As venture capital rolled in, Geek Chic lived out that sweet revenge Wolff described in bigger and wilder parties and a post-Grunge understanding of cool that left the Bowery and the Lower East Side behind. Punk wasn't dead, but it wasn't dangerous anymore, either. Hackers were now the mysterious scary ones.

Though much of the $1.1 billion spent in 1995 seemed wasted on glorified commercials that took forever to load, cynicism now was like writing off television in 1941 because you thought the CBS *Television Quiz* was lame. With studies claiming that Tech would create up to 120,000 jobs and the World Trade Center 32% vacant, the City and State signed incentives and Wall Street beckoned. Silicon Alley was about to meet the People's Market, as venture capitalists groomed coders for their IPO road shows. "Tech is the heart and soul of the American economy," wrote James Cramer, "the chief driver of its prosperity, the keeper of its newfound world dominance, and the place where its biggest profits are." If you wanted to pay for college and retire in a place that did more than change your bedpan, you had to invest in Tech. Awash in money, mutual fund managers shoved money at Tech, watched it grow, and then plowed their profits into even more Tech. Wall Street had finally Gotten It. The prospect of Java's landing in 1996, for instance, sent Sun's stock price up 157%, which sounded to the unconvinced like proof of tulip mania, but Java would soon bring all those static websites to life with movement and sound, ending Stacy Horn's cyberspace built of words.

You just had to Get It.

A Victorian Lady Who'd Stepped in Dog Poop

The Media Industry tended to process the Internet with nervous, patronizing references to "geek chic" while deciding whether to shift lunch from 44 at the Royalton Hotel to the suddenly hotter Michael's. "[T]o be Infobahn-hip . . . ," advised *USA Today*, "you have to have your electronic mail address on your business card." The *Times* ventured a tentative foray online with AOL in 1994, though, wrote Jon Katz, it "seemed embarrassed and slightly disgusted with itself, like a Victorian lady who'd stepped in dog poop." The supposedly democratic, even anarchic, qualities of the Internet that would allow anyone to put anything out there whenever they wanted, came at a nervous time as Boomers brought their teenaged tastes with them into adulthood, fearlessly wearing Disney apparel while relegating the Fine Arts to a quiet corner with a cup of tea. Even jazz had aged out and Japanese tourists now filled the seats at venerable clubs.

Old book publishing hands would say their business model had always been illogical, but "even though we knew the change was coming," says Joni Evans, " . . we did it the old way." Nicholas Negroponte, the head of MIT's Media Lab, predicted that bound books would become a thing of the past as soon as "electronic paper" hit the market. Novelist Robert Coover hosted an "online writing space," and publishers, editors, and authors sat through a Microsoft presentation at the New York Public Library about the future of multimedia. No one could say yet whether the Internet would be an experiment or a replacement. Email was on the way to becoming a part of daily life. All this added up to a growing fear that literature was becoming a luxury item. Esteemed editors like Jason Epstein and Gordon Lish retired, Dick Snyder was fired, and by the end of the '90s the consolidating urge that created Time Warner reduced a once-thriving ecosystem of nearly a hundred publishers in the late '70s into less than a dozen behemoths: HarperCollins took Morrow; Penguin took Putnam's; S&S bought Macmillan, which included Scribner's and Atheneum. Random House was in the hands of Harry Evans, deft at promotion but overheard the day after the National Book Awards grousing about "That poet" who "went on and on. Jacklyn . . ." A friend corrected him; her name was Gwendolyn. Gwendolyn Brooks.

Oprah came to the rescue. In September 1996, she announced a new monthly Book Club. "I want to get the whole country reading again," she said. Jacquelyn Mitchard's *The Deep End of the Ocean* immediately became a bestseller and going forward, selection became tantamount to winning the lottery for each lucky author. Evans left in 1997 for *US News and World Report*, and a year later German media conglomerate Bertelsmann took Random House off Si's hands. On the retail side, Barnes & Noble chief Len Riggio saw an almost spiritual promise in his superstores—"a chain becomes a network," he said, "so that people who participate in Barnes & Noble activities, which include shopping, feel something in common with people in faraway places who share the same activities." Yet more than half of all books were now sold outside of bookstores. Powell's in Portland sold books online, as since July 1994 had a company claiming to be "The Earth's Biggest Bookstore," Amazon.com, whose founder, former Wall Street quant Jeff Bezos, had, according to *The New Yorker*, "beguiled the press and won the allegiance of trend-setting consumers by portraying his company as hip and innovative while casting Barnes & Noble as a predatory behemoth." Amazon grossed $16 million in 1996; a year later its sales were $148 million, and it went public at $18 a share.

Magazines and newspapers found themselves in a trickier position when it came to the Internet given that their value came from their immediacy; newspapers in particular were kept afloat on classifieds that Craigslist was stealing away. Some immediately surrendered; the *Village Voice* turned itself into a giveaway in hopes of maintaining circulation, while *Newsday* retreated home to Long Island. Those remaining wrestled with the role of their online presence. The Telecommunications Act in February 1996 drastically changed all Media's future. Deregulating communications sounded very much in the spirit of the Internet, but allowing small fry to multiply just meant more protein for the top predators, and the Internet's good-for-me answers would destroy the economics of culture.

Underneath all these tense encounters between old media and new media, the old dinosaurs and the new ones, was now a three-way generational split. On one hand, Clinton's White House represented the ascendance of the Baby Boomers, though they still considered themselves the kids, permanently young at heart and sexy like Mick Jagger. When Microsoft and GE developed the looser, more immediate MSNBC, *Time* editor Richard Stengel compared an appearance to "having your parents finally listen to your opinions at the dinner table." Some Boomers taking over as cultural gatekeepers did confront issues of identity and diversity, but most kept watching David Letterman and listening to Billy Joel, realizing their great expectations by embracing this New Economy and believing they'd never grow old. To which the Gen X era of slackers, *Reality Bites*, and Larry Clark's *Kids* just rolled their eyes. Along with the cohort right after them, the first to be raised entirely with computers, they made no secret that they didn't care about gatekeepers. Elizabeth Wurtzel, poster girl for her memoir of ennui and depression, *Prozac Nation*, canoodled with David Foster Wallace, en route to canonization for his sprawling and specific novel *Infinite Jest*.

Boomers looked suspiciously at this coming generation, but in order to stay on top of things, they needed to join them in cyberspace, a chilling prospect described with genuine poignance in *The New Yorker* by John Seabrook, who intrepidly expanded his contacts in cyberspace until a few months later when he was "flamed . . . a form of speech that is unique to online communication." Worried that his computer may have been infected with "a worm," Seabrook actually breaks down in tears at the idea that another person has acted toward him with such random malice. The cyber city was cleaner. Its streets were safer. New York now had screens and televisions everywhere; the only form of architectural ornament, said critic Karrie Jacobs, "that's truly ours." Exciting new technologies kept coming—DVDs were here! But something dark was being revealed, and though street crime was reduced by eliminating opportunities, the Internet with its vaunted anonymity was creating infinite chances for new kinds of mugging.

The Dinosaurs Are Coming

After watching his portfolio go up 61% in 1995, Jim Cramer predicted Dow 6500 by Labor Day. If Renaissance New York had discovered its wealth by flipping the American Dream upside down, the desperation of the People's Market had become a gold rush, your return on Cisco mined from a newly discovered vein of capitalism. As John Cassidy wrote, "The rise of Silicon Valley and the Internet was something fresh, untarnished by financial scandal or memories of Vietnam. It gave new life to the most potent American myth of all: that the future is boundless." Even as the knowledge gap created more inequality, there was no real need to share. Young Power Democrats like Steve Rattner converged with old-line Dems like Felix Rohatyn to promote a new guilt-free version of Growth that let the Left fill its coffers and still stand on the right side of the Culture Wars. To them, this People's Market now signaled a nation investing in its future. Treasury Secretary Robert Rubin, a former co-chair of Goldman Sachs, kept chipping away at Glass-Steagall, and Michael Osinski created the software that would make it easy to securitize mortgages; now almost anyone could bundle loans into bonds. Derivatives, though barely understood, became a standard financial product. Cramer's prediction was off—the Dow hit 6500 on November 25, once Clinton had beaten Dole, and despite

Alan Greenspan's warning of "irrational exuberance," the president of the Dallas Federal Reserve heralded "an almost perfect economy." "It has become fashionable among many Wall Street types," wrote *The New Yorker*, "to say that the market . . . will rise forever."

The Right got rich on the same stocks. Now that a Democratic White House had delivered the economy Republicans dreamt of, they built a populist cultural strawman out of the coastal elites they nibbled canapés with at Lally Weymouth's birthday party in Southampton. With its first Republican mayor in a generation, New York sheltered the core of the anti-Clinton Right, from Limbaugh to Peggy Noonan, dipped in Reagan fairy dust, who'd joined the *Wall Street Journal*'s tack toward moral imperatives. Rupert Murdoch had given Roger Ailes, "the Dark Prince of right-wing attack politics," $400 million to build Fox News network; Eric Breindel and Judith Regan got their own shows. "He's a sexist," said Regan of Ailes, "but I'm in favor of sexism." New York Media embraced them all, convinced they were playacting. Meanwhile, as New York lost manufacturing jobs six times faster than the rest of the country, Republicans continued cutting the retraining programs necessary to shift jobs in the New Economy, the need for unskilled labor shrunk, and the economic divide spread wider. In between there was Michael Bloomberg, a Democrat known to send checks to Republicans. In his new autobiography, he stated his intention to give away his entire fortune before he died, though he might have had more than just *tikkun olam* in mind. He hired Patricia Harris, former executive director of Koch's Arts Commission, to direct a philanthropic strategy that would also plug him into the city's power networks; underwriting *The Charlie Rose Show* on PBS, for instance, let him meet Charlie's guests, who might then be seen eating fried chicken and coleslaw at one of his casual dinners at the townhouse on 79th Street. The former frat boy now squired the likes of Liv Ullmann, Marisa Berenson, and Diana Ross.

The City and the business community pulled out all the stops for Tech; the Alliance for Downtown New York and the State pushed for tech companies in the Financial District; the old Drexel Burnham offices had become the New York Information Technology Center. The huge mandated signs of Times Square flashed stock quotes over theatergoers.

The number of American stockowners had indeed doubled since the Bull woke back up again in 1991. Day traders bought or sold an average of six million shares a year at a .02 commission, meaning each paid $120,000 directly to brokers, the croupiers of a game that now had no rules. Amid this explosive growth—Intel up from 6½ to 89, peach-fuzz millionaires reading *Red Herring* on the Jitney—it began to dawn on web visionaries that Tech had become just a new way to feed Wall Street. "The three-kids-in-a-loft phase is over," said Jerry Colonna of Flatiron Partners, New York's leading tech venture capital fund. "You can be a guerilla," said Nicholas Butterworth in November 1996, "or you can get paid." The CEO of iVillage warned that "The dinosaurs are coming," and they officially arrived in 1997 when Microsoft opened an office in Worldwide Plaza to fund start-ups. This, according to Douglas Rushkoff, changed "New York development culture from Mac culture to PC culture." On February 20, 1998, DoubleClick became the first Silicon Alley IPO. Priced at $17 a share, it opened at $29 and went up from there. *Everyone* Got It now. Employment in New Media hit 138,258, much of that fluid, freelance work whose new and liberating nature hid the fact that it came with no security and often little cash, and that entry to this economy was all but closed to the poor and unskilled. Silicon Alley pushed into the remaining manufacturing and wholesaling sections of Midtown and Chinatown, squeezing the remnants of the garment, printing, and flower districts while the City tried to seed firms Uptown to relieve the pressure for space.

A bell rung in August 1998, when everything was nearly sucked to the bottom by the bankruptcy of Long-Term Capital Management, one of the 3,500 mysterious "hedge funds," now the "sporty investment vehicle of the late nineties." The capsizing of Russia's first foray into capitalism left them suddenly owing $125 billion, setting off a 6% plunge in the Dow on August 31 that forced a consortium of banks to frantically inject capital into the American financial system. For the first time, some losers drifted into the gutters of Silicon Alley, but this was the summer of Mark McGwire and Sammy Sosa, making America love baseball again with suspect home runs that no one wanted to question. Viagra hit the market, and the FBI named Osama bin Laden America's most wanted fugitive. The Yankees posted 114 wins and swept the Padres for yet another World Series title. Were they the greatest baseball team ever? Was this the greatest dynasty ever? Were these the greatest years ever in the greatest city in the best of all possible worlds? "Almost every social and economic indicator is moving in the right direction," exclaimed *The New Yorker*, stunned by "an unprecedented, almost unimaginable cascade of good news in the past year." The Monica Lewinsky scandal occupied the news because everything else was going so well.

On November 13, 1998, the whale of all Silicon Alley IPOs landed. An early social media site created by two Cornell students, theGlobe.com, opened at $9 a share and ended at $90, a record 606% percent rise beyond even one of Sammy Sosa's moonshots onto Waveland Avenue. When AOL was added to the S&P 500, it was trading at 238 times expected earnings. Amazon didn't even pretend to have earnings.

Two years before, the RPA had issued a report predicting that new global markets and tech growth would be offset by downsizing and greater competition. FIRE would rise, manufacturing would keep sliding, so the City needed to concentrate on equity. Instead, there was the Internet and there was Viagra; infinite wealth, infinite desire. No risk.

Chapter Twenty-one

Whose World Is This?

Most of New York still existed in real life. Raviolis were stamped on Arthur Avenue, Staten Island mowed its lawns, and there was nothing Disneyfied about life in the 50 acres of Long Island City's Queensbridge Houses, the nation's largest public housing complex. In April 1994, baby-faced Nasir Jones, known as Nas, dropped his debut album about growing up in this place where "Every day was one step away from the end." He'd had an uncommon childhood, at least for Queensbridge. His father, jazz trumpeter Olu Dara, traveled while his mother, Ann, raised him and his brother Jabari with a color TV and bookshelves stocked with Ralph Ellison, Sun Tzu, Malcolm X, and Chinese philosophy, musical instruments in every corner. Their parents had exposed them to the world and expected them to rise in it, but Nas had still found himself on the fringes of the Game until his best friend was murdered. Two years later, he now wanted *Illmatic* to bring you "through hell and back." Over samples of everything from Ahmad Jamal, the *Wild Style* soundtrack, and his father's trumpet, Nas opened a new road for Hip Hop, using his rich, complex poetics—"I rap for listeners, bluntheads, fly ladies and prisoners"—to explore mortality and family in a society of teenagers who considered twenty old age. If *The Chronic* was for driving to In and Out Burger, this was headphone music for navigating the projects; Harvard, writes dream hampton, to Dre's state college. Critics compared it to *Kind of Blue*, *What's Goin' On*, *Native*

279

Son, and *The Basketball Diaries*; *The Source* gave the "reality storybook" its first "Five Mic" review. On the cusp of the Internet, Maastricht, and NAFTA, as Thelma Golden examined artistic representations of the Black Male at the Whitney and Tricia Rose's *Black Noise* launched the academic study of Hip Hop, *Illmatic* made an intimate statement about 50 forgotten acres, asserted identity, history, and reality from the street, and yanked the heart of Hip Hop back home.

But *Illmatic* was just one vision of Black life in America, and in New York City. "Never before have so many blacks done as well," wrote Henry Louis Gates that fall. "And never before have so many blacks done so poorly . . . [T]he realities of race no longer affect all blacks in the same way." The same divides of wealth and generation in the city applied in Black communities, too, and were about to split Harlem apart. Pete Rock's gentle question, earnestly asked on *Illmatic*, became a question for everyone across 110th Street, in Queensbridge, Bed-Stuy, and anywhere Black culture had set roots in New York: "Whose world is this?"

Every Man for They Self

With Rick Rubin now producing Johnny Cash and Russell Simmons "the Hugh Hefner of hip-hop," two other rappers were reigniting New York Hip Hop along with Nas. A six-foot-three, 300-pound Lincoln Navigator of a man, Christopher "Biggie" Wallace, aka Notorious B.I.G., released *Ready to Die* with its party classics "Juicy" and "Big Poppa." Son of Jamaican immigrants, he built a rap sheet dealing on the border of Bed-Stuy and Clinton Hill, but he also cut a tape that got to Sean Combs, who signed him in 1992. Slick and intimidating, Biggie flowed like lava, and *Ready to Die* sold 2 million copies its first year, giving him the title of not just "The King of New York" but Hip Hop, period. The other one was Shawn Carter from the Marcy Houses in Brooklyn by the J and the Z trains, though people called him Jay-Z because of his childhood nickname Jazzy. Five years older than Nas but similarly quiet and intense, Carter discovered writing in the sixth grade from Ms. Lowden at IS 318, but when his father left he slipped into trouble, working both sides of music and drugs in Trenton until, according to his old partner, "He messed with the wrong people," got out of drugs, and put it all on his first album *Reasonable Doubt*. Like a dangerous big brother letting you in on secrets, he told "the story of the hustler" with a lived experience that Nas didn't quite have.

New York Hardcore—as it was known—expressed the day-to-day struggle of "the generation of black people," wrote Jay-Z, "who finally got the point: No one's going to help us. So we went for self, for family, for block, for crew." They were in favor of Civil Rights, but rainbows didn't keep you alive on the streets. "Our struggle wasn't organized or even coherent," he continued, yet many who considered "electoral politics, protest movements, and the like as inherently futile" saw Hip Hop as more than just branding; it was their one true voice. "Hiphop," wrote poet Paul Beatty, "is a politically economically amputeed peoples fist." But its outlaw narratives came tinged with misogyny, homophobia, and pointless murder, and when Tupac Shakur accused New York–based rappers, including former friend Biggie, of his 1994 shooting, he touched off the East Coast–West Coast feud that *Vibe* magazine hyped into a cartoon war; its climax, the murders of both Tupac and Biggie, was an absurdly tragic loss of life and talent, the once almost Existential narrative of the Struggle twisted into a performance of young Black men killing each other for the pleasure of White consumers. Just as crack ebbed and violent crime dropped, Hardcore, writes Greg Tate, defined "an era that was already receding into nostalgia." And there were other narratives. Mos Def, born Dante Smith, had gone to see *Wild Style* with his mom back in the day, and now his affirmative, Black nationalist *Black Star* with Talib Kweli and then his first solo album *Black on Both Sides* flowed out of the Zulu Nation with no pretense that there was romance in dealing crack. "[C]rack was not glamorous, it was not sexy," he told an interviewer. "It destroyed many, many lives, and you see people living through that hell, you don't wanna glorify that shit."

Crack had devastated projects like Queensbridge and Marcy. By 1994, some 600,000 New Yorkers lived in public housing; once the nation's biggest and best system, it had offered stability through the '70s, each project networked to produce degrees of social capital, "better maintained and more secure than most market rentals," writes Terry Williams, with gardens, community centers, and day care that many longtime residents believed Dinkins had undermined by letting the homeless jump the waiting list. Families like the Joneses fought to preserve order; some kids joined gangs like the Decepticons, known for their brutal hammer attacks, but many others went on to college. Now the consolidation of police forces put new, young cops into places where unofficial Community Policing had been in effect, encountering kids who spent a lot of their time outside hanging out. All kids, as Terry Williams writes, are "outlaws to some degree . . . with limited rights, uncharted futures, little privacy, no legal places of their own, few possessions, and an attraction to adult behaviors that for them entail violating the law," and now the NYPD's new strategy was essentially criminalizing being a Black kid, trapping tenants between wanting order and wanting justice. Meanwhile, Albany and City Hall both began to defund public housing. "You have Democrats behaving like Republicans," said the director of one advocacy group, "and the poor are the ones who are taking it on the chin." As Mobb Deep rapped, out of Queensbridge, "Every man for they self in this land we be gunning . . ."

Buy Any Jeans Necessary

"Here we go again," said Reverend Butts when Giuliani had ordered the police into the mosque. Though 14 out of the 51 City Council members were Black, no Blacks held citywide office, and Giuliani had eliminated all ethnic offices. Advisors begged him to meet with Black leaders, but Lategano scheduled little other than token school visits. Giuliani "was not comfortable around blacks who in any way disagreed with him," said Captain Eric Adams, cofounder of 100 Blacks in Law Enforcement. One aide compared him to "the stereotype of the Italian middle-class unassimilated suburban homeowner, grilling the sausages." Giuliani, of course, bridled at any suggestion that he or his policies were in any way racist and many New Yorkers welcomed a mayor who admired Jefferson without qualms about Sally Hemings.

Crime was, obviously, the main thrust of the mayor's drive to bring minority New York under control. Money was the other. While classes were being taught in bathrooms, his FY97 budget asked for $100 million to be cut from schools; since Dinkins, $2 billion had been cut from

Education. Health and Hospitals were down $200 million; libraries, down $43 million; CIGs, $24 million. In 1995, emergency kitchens served 2.7 million meals a month; three years later they'd serve 5.2 million. Welfare, though, was his main target. WNYC quoted Giuliani as saying it would be "a good thing" if the poor left the city. "That's not an unspoken part of our strategy," he said. "That is our strategy." New York City had the nation's largest caseload, and since the NYPD was seemingly showing you could eliminate crime without dealing with social causes, instead of welfare, people would now be sent to work. Giuliani "reinvented" the City's system with changes that, after some arm-twisting, the largely minority unions went along with. Getting benefits would now require unpaid work, mostly for City agencies or with groups like America Works, a for-profit, job-training boot camp that got a fee only if its "clients" lasted seven months in their new positions. Income Support Offices became Job Centers that actively dissuaded people from applying for other aid; getting the full range of available public assistance now required visits to different offices in different boroughs. Clinton signed Welfare Reform in August 1996, starting a new cascade of State and City cuts at a moment when 39% of children in the state were on public aid. By 1997, the City had stripped some 300,000 New Yorkers off welfare.

Though they had reservations about being turned into employment counselors, staffers and managers at the Job Centers generally liked the dress codes and professionalization. Despite their growing fear of the police, the quiet reality was that some middle-class African Americans were also open to Giuliani where he overlapped with Clinton's tough-love attitude—Nas offered lessons about life on the street, but his parents had offered an equally powerful lesson about how to raise young Black men with a fierce, loving presence and high expectations. Over the last ten years, Black New Yorkers had been fighting for basic elements of middle-class life: civil, effective policing; good education; and fair space to work within capitalism. They resisted needle exchange programs and legalizing drugs—"People who think that way can go straight to hell," said Rangel. The Nehemiah Project had become a national template for housing that received bipartisan support, and the apolitical approach of the East Brooklyn Congregations found traction

in the age of Reinventing Government. As *Sesame Street*, inspired by
'70s Harlem, underwent redevelopment, its set relit, repainted, wrote
Michael Davis, to include a "dance studio, a home-based day care center, and a playground, and a new array of spaces that seemed less like
Harlem and more like any gentrified up-and-coming neighborhood
in America," in the real-life Harlem, the larger political upheaval was
about to bring the question of Whose World Is This to a head. Networks would be dramatic reorganized, power redistributed, the built
environment permanently changed.

Housing was the first element. Abyssinian Development Corp. had
put Reverend Butts at the leading edge of efforts to bring the middle
class back to Harlem, and it had also let him make some very powerful
friends like Pataki's man, Randy Daniels, Chase chairman Walter Shipley,
and developer Bruce Ratner, as well as the city's most successful African
American businessmen, Ken Chenault and Richard Parsons. He sat on
the boards of the Central Park Conservancy and the United Way, was
head of the NY Council of Churches. "I've wanted to be mayor of New
York since the third grade," Butts told a reporter. "And I'd like to be a US
senator at some point." Landmarking and preservation were low priorities; said one ADC leader, "Community development is preservation."

Giuliani's own plans for Harlem also started with housing. Though
he had a better relationship with the East Brooklyn Congregations than
Dinkins had ever had, he warned that the sluggish economy would
force City Hall to slow down the $4.2 billion he'd committed. Instead
of more building, he wanted to deal with the *in rem* inventory—some
4,000 occupied structures, most in Harlem. His HPD head, thirty-six-
year-old Dallas native Deborah Wright, had been raised in a family of
Baptist ministers, her path through Harvard Business School to First
Boston not exactly what her aunt Marian Wright Edelman had had in
mind for her. Dinkins had named her to the Housing Authority board
in 1992, and she'd accepted the HPD job after some soul-searching
about working for Giuliani. The Neighborhood Entrepreneurs Program,
or "Building Blocks," she put in place would no longer offer rehabs
to nonprofits and CDCs; instead, it transferred foreclosed properties
directly to, ideally, experienced, local, minority-owned private developers. Delinquent landlords would get help or see their tax liens sold.

The mayor also took control of 125th Street, lined with folding tables piled with Chinese-made tat Senegalese vendors passed off as genuine African merchandise. In October 1994, the NYPD forcibly relocated them to a marketplace on 116th where they would pay taxes, get security, sanitation, and, in theory, a regular flow of tourists and locals who appreciated the Afrocentric merchandise. But the real battle over Harlem would be fought over commercial development, long controlled by the Gang of Four, and it would be a quick rout. Back in 1993, Rangel had pushed the idea of Empowerment Zones with Clinton, and in December, Washington awarded one to New York City with agreements in place from Cuomo and Dinkins to match the $100 million development block grant. The HUDC and Rangel had already allocated 60% to the usual youth and social services. But now Republicans were in charge in Albany and City Hall. Pataki, whose eyes went wide when it came to budget slashing, said he would ante up only a tenth of what Cuomo had committed; if Harlem wanted all of that $300 million pot, the Enterprise Zone would have to focus on economic development. Then he reorganized the HUDC under former Dinkins Deputy Mayor Randy Daniels, who put his friend Reverend Butts on the board and killed plans for the International Trade Center. In two strokes, decades of leverage were stripped from the Gang of Four. "This," said Charlie Rangel, "seems like the end of development in Harlem as we have known it." He was right.

To many, this felt very much like a last chance. "Am I unnerved?" asked State Senator David Paterson. "Yes. But the reason I'm anxious to work with them is because I need Pataki to succeed. I need Giuliani to succeed." But many didn't want the outside investment that would bring Harlem into the broader economy, and the rhetoric got hot. United House of Prayer for All People raised the rent on a building across from the Apollo Theater leased by a Sephardic Jew named Fred Harari, a hike that forced Harari to in turn raise the rent on his sublessor, a popular Black-owned record store that not only wouldn't pay but refused a subsidized relocation. A "don't shop where you can't work" campaign twisted into an anti-Semitic campaign about outside ownership and turned Freddy's Fashion Mart into the next Family Red Apple until Roland Smith walked into the store, shot four people, then set the store on fire, killing seven, before he shot himself. Sharpton decided that he should have called Harari an "interloper" instead of a "white interloper." But an "interloper" hadn't started the situation; the owners of the property were Harlem-based, and the very pro-development community board welcomed the EZ. "Although some might speculate that the board members have been co-opted by outside white interests," wrote Derek Hyra, "this is not the circumstance. Many community board members and other homeowners in Harlem want high-priced housing." Just like Jay-Z, they too "went for self, for family, for block, for crew."

Deborah Wright now moved over from HPD to run UMEZ and by August, 188 applications had been received, including a Robert De Niro–Drew Nieporent renovation of the faded Minton's Playhouse and various superstores. Wright seemed surprised at the uproar after she admitted that only 20% or so would "receive serious consideration." "There is a weird combination of arrogance, distrust and fear of gentrification," she said. "People have got to get beyond that attitude." Two months later, the first grants were announced, including a credit union in Washington Heights and a Latino Cultural Center, but most went to big corporations, with the largest to the Harlem USA mall, with its movie theaters, Disney Store, Gap, and skating rink. The developers quickly leveraged their $11.2 million loan into another $50 million from JPMorgan, proof of what social network theorists call the Matthew Effect: those who have will get more.

Local small businesses, on the other hand, found themselves largely shut out. Instead of offering capital and connection, the UMEZ held them to the same standards the big banks had held them to all these years and rejected them the same way. Deborah Wright felt their pain, but only so much. "[O]ne of the basic tenets of capitalism is that you can't control it," she said, while doling out hundreds of millions of dollars in hopes of doing exactly that. "You've been asking for something to happen—it's here, but that means you now have to compete." Of course, they were now competing with national chains with infinite amounts of capital. Wright handed off the UMEZ to thirty-seven-year-old Terry Lane, who made it plain upfront that he was a businessman first and foremost. The young owners "coming home to Harlem" were often like Lane and Wright, people with "a private-sector sensibility."

"[T]he arrival of the black middle class is not clearly advantageous for the 'underclass,'" wrote Hyra. "For many in the black middle class, 'coming home' refers to returning to culturally significant spaces where poor blacks are no longer welcome." They had no patience for political games, at least the old ones. Governor Pataki finished off the HUDC with a report revealing decades of expense and patronage with almost nothing to show for it: $49,000 to maintain six electric typewriters; a data input firm paid $90 an hour for work that cost $12 an hour everywhere else. "I am betrayed by my own people," said one resident, "and I will shout it from the mountaintop." Even Percy Sutton was knocked off his perch; he'd bought the Apollo Theater in 1980 and renovated it for some $20 million, but an audit showed its funds had been profoundly mismanaged and the State took control.

Harlem began to change. McDonald's raised the rent $31,000 on Copeland's Country Kitchen, forcing them to close. Rejected by the UMEZ, Georgie's Bakery and Donut shop also closed after thirty-five years; Krispy Kreme would sell the donuts now. The new Blockbuster was the third-highest grossing store in the chain, but what good did that do Harlem, aside from some minimum-wage jobs straightening boxes? Sales at Isis & Associates bookstore were down 90% over the last two years. Said the owner, "It's no longer for us." In New York, the wisdom now, as Paul Beatty wrote, was to "buy any jeans necessary."

Giuliani Time

Haitian Konpa is summertime music; skipping guitars over a rolling beat and blasts of party horns all producing lots of close dancing with swaying hips, and lots of fights at Club Rendez-vous in Flatbush, the city's prime Haitian nightclub, New York's home for Tonton Macoute in hiding. On Friday night August 9, 1997, patrols from the 70th Precinct responded to a call there, and in seconds a scuffle turned into a battle royale—men and women, cops and clubgoers all throwing punches and wrestling. During the chaos, Officer Justin Volpe, not especially loved in the station house, got into a scrum with security guard Abner Louima, who was arrested. At the precinct, Volpe hauled Louima into a bathroom and went berserk in a way that shocked a city that doesn't shock easily. In the middle of a standard issue police beating, Officer Volpe shoved a broomstick up the prisoner's rectum and then shoved it back into his mouth, shouting, Louima claimed, "Look what you made me do!" and "It's Giuliani Time!" Two days later, Mike McAlary, diagnosed with colon cancer, his reputation dented by a series of columns that had falsely accused a rape victim of lying, got a tip that something strange and awful had happened over the weekend and talked his way into the Coney Island Hospital room where Louima was being held. NY1 and McAlary broke the story.

Even Giuliani knew a line had been crossed; he instructed cops to come forward with information and cleaned out the precinct. But while it turned out that Louima had concocted "It's Giuliani Time," it was the lie that told the truth about Reformation New York. Contented White New Yorkers were forced to question the terms of their contentment, as African Americans who were hardly gangbangers spoke of their daily harassment by police. Nor was Safir much like Bill Bratton. Described as "charmless, insecure, vindictive, abrupt, overbearing and autocratic," he'd trailed behind Rudy for seventeen years as a special agent for the US Customs, the DEA, and then ran the Marshall's Service with action hero bravado; "There is no hunting like the hunting of armed men," he informed *60 Minutes*. Despite his Courtesy, Professionalism and Respect program, the NYPD was doubling down on arrests. Even George Kelling had concerns. "If you simply add seven thousand cops and put them out there," he said, "then the fact that there's more abuse isn't really a surprise." Safir tripled the Street Crime Unit, throwing hundreds of young, mostly White, mostly suburban, cops into the New York night. Meanwhile, over the protests of Sugar Hill, One Police Plaza reassigned beloved patrolman James Gilmore. Mike McAlary won a Pulitzer for his work on the Louima case; he died eight months later, redeemed.

Nineteen ninety-seven was a huge year for Hardcore Rap, but in the face of Giuliani Time there was less fighting the power and more of what *Vibe* publisher Keith Clinkscales called the "aspirational agenda" of Russell Simmons, who'd sold 40% of Def Jam for some $130 million and now bounced between TriBeCa and Beverly Hills. Mase's debut album *Harlem World*, produced by Sean Combs, fell in step with the UMEZ's vision of Harlem. After Puff Daddy's intro about the "big city of dreams / Harlem USA," Mase got straight to the point like an NEP developer sitting down with his Chase banker: "Do you wanna get money with us," he asked, "do you wanna?" *Harlem World* was a lot of fun and sold 4 million copies. *Wu-Tang Forever* moved 600,000 units the first week, with Wu-Wear, a comic book, and video games on the way. Puffy's Bad Boy Entertainment branched out into restaurants, clothes, and media, while Jay-Z, with *In My Lifetime, Vol. 1* out and *Vol. 2 . . . Hard Knock Life* soon to sell 5 million copies, staked out his own brand categories. Creeping up toward $2 billion in sales, Hip Hop was 12.9% of all music bought, and *Source* sold more copies on the newsstand than *Rolling Stone,* so to celebrate its coming of age, Jay-Z and Puffy hit the Hamptons. Combs invited every famous name on the South Fork to a White Linen party on Georgica Pond. They paused—but only briefly. Next summer it was Jay-Z's turn to throw a Fourth of July bash DJed by Mark Ronson, who'd just done the Met Gala. "Hip-hop," wrote Nancy Jo Sales, "music born on the streets of New York, and high society have merged."

In a way, Bling Rap made sense: "If I hear someone jetting around on a private jet," said Jay-Z, "I want to experience that. I've seen someone get his brains blasted out." At that moment, some 70% of Hip Hop sales were to White buyers and crime was dropping; by 1997, the rate of victimization for Black men between eighteen and forty-four had fallen two thirds in the past five years. Juvenile crime was falling, too. White New Yorkers could squirm, but that was the fun—they had nothing to fear from Hardcore rappers chasing the same Bentleys and Cristal. When Jay-Z and Puffy were both arrested for highly publicized assaults, it just felt like they were renewing their licenses. Reverend Butts hated the lyrics, but the narrative was now the same one he was selling: drop your bucket.

So whose world was this? Right now, it looked like Calvin Butts's. "The African American community is going through a major transition in terms of models of leadership," said Wright, "and Reverend Butts is right in the middle of it." Butts sure looked like a candidate for *something,* at least until he was confronted with some of the racial *realpolitik* the Gang of Four had been dealing with all those years. In June 1997, ADC and Bruce Ratner's company Forest City Ratner got the former

Trade Center site on Lenox to build their own "Harlem Center"; Rangel said local community development had become large-scale development by a company that just happened to be located in Harlem. "I'd always been hesitant because it's very political in Harlem," said Bruce Ratner. But when Butts criticized Giuliani from the pulpit for hospital layoffs, the crackdown on taxi drivers, and police brutality, when he wondered if the City was "moving toward a fascist state," his new rich White friends accused him of returning to his old rabble-rousing ways. Butts had once said he believed Giuliani didn't like Black people and now he thought about it again. "I thought long and hard and I said yes." Rudy Washington came out of the sunken place to defend Giuliani while the likes of Sharpton, Dinkins, and Bill Tatum stood back and watched as Rudy demanded an apology and the State trimmed back its plans for Harlem Center. "Prompted by the movement of the Holy Spirit," Butts ultimately embraced Giuliani on the altar of St. Patrick's Cathedral during Sunday Mass. Hug delivered, respect to the Don shown, the State announced it was going ahead and the City Council approved Forest City Ratner's East River Plaza. But Butts had killed his political future.

By the end of the decade, Central Harlem's population had gone up 22%. The percentage of households earning $75,000 had jumped 35% while the poverty rate remained where it had been since 1980. Building Blocks helped minority homeownership in Harlem, but residential developers focused on high-end rehabs to attract the upper middle class, not more affordable housing. "Harlem is now safe enough," said one Black resident, "there are enough basic services, enough beautiful places," and, added a developer, "so many people have so much at stake, it cannot fail." Mortgage loans over these years went from under $10 million to almost $100 million, with a similar rate of growth in Brooklyn; the banks believed that they could make money now in Black New York. Foreign capital was coming in too, along with more tourists.

While the greatest fear among longtime residents was displacement, tenant laws prevented the mass dislocation of Urban Renewal; instead, smaller, richer families owned bigger houses. Columbia professor Lance Freeman found a more subtle kind of damage. What were lost were mobility and the future. Those in place weren't as likely to be pushed out as feared, but it would probably be impossible for their kids to live nearby; the old community was being made temporary. If Harlem was looking Whiter it was mostly because there were fewer Blacks; from '87 to '96 the White population of Central Harlem was still statistically nil and only went up 1.7% in the adjacent Hamilton Heights neighborhood; the 16% drop in the Black population there was largely due to a growing numbers of Dominicans. As Harlem became more diverse, liquor stores took down their heavy Plexiglas windows and openly displayed their wares—good news—and so were the outdoor cafés sprouting along Lenox, but in the name of Quality of Life, police now wrote tickets for drinking a beer on your stoop when enjoying a cold beer on your stoop on a hot day was known to dramatically improve your quality of life. Even Jack Maple said Broken Windows was designed to catch "sharks, not dolphins," and he worried that the force hadn't changed the "common mind-set among cops that the general public is at best a nuisance and at worst the enemy." According to the architects of the crime drop, it was time to reduce the number of cops and begin reintroducing Community Policing. But more cops were exactly what the mayor wanted. "Why back away from it now," he said, and the *Times* agreed: "It makes sense to support a winning streak." "At the end of the day," said Richard Parsons, "blacks are no different from whites. People want results." But what did that have to do with drinking a beer on your own stoop?

Chapter Twenty-two

Heat Is Quality

The money, the Internet, the crime-free streets—it seemed churlish to complain about life in Reformation New York, where visitors to the Bronx Zoo wandered through tents filled with thousands of flitting butterflies and the renovated Grand Central Terminal drew all eyes to its breathtaking blue ceiling of a winter's night sky. Amid a microbrewery, a half-size replica of the Concorde, and waves of FIRE types stuffed into the sort of corporate towers Johnson/Burgee had planned, the New Victory Theater on 42nd transformed, wrote Paul Goldberger, "the city's roughest street into one of its gentlest," all under huge, blinding signs of everything from Cup O'Noodles to the NBC peacock. Disney's Hercules Electric Parade had rolled through like Patton in Sicily, en route to total conquest: *Beauty and the Beast*, the most expensive show in Broadway history, opened with an astounding $6 million in advance sales, *Pocahontas* premiered on the Great Lawn, and "Disneyfication" became code for the corporate "more like the rest of America" changes that everyone loved and hated. Returning after five years away, writer Fernanda Eberstadt was "shocked by the city's new squeaky-cleanness," the unlikely butterflies and mouse ears delivering a first-hit dizziness that left you cheerfully bewildered.

But what was *real* now about New York, and what wasn't? "How do you document real life," asked *Rent*'s adorable scarf-wearing filmmaker Mark, "when real life's getting more like fiction each day?" Everything was available in Reformation New York, whenever you wanted it. Time in some basic ways had come to a stop; as Peter Schjeldahl observed in a review of John Currin's very old-fashioned new paintings, "'old' and 'new' are exhausted categories. The past is present now . . . If the notion startles, it's because we are not accustomed to it yet; but we soon will be." The built environment made this especially clear. Thirty years of landmarking and Jane Jacobs had left a cityscape that, wrote Brendan Gill, let New Yorkers "hold out our hands to that past and feel ourselves warmed by it." Hugh Hardy seemed to be single-handedly creating this timeless New York with a new Dance Theatre of Harlem, the Bryant Park Grill, renovations at BAM and the Rainbow Room, and a complete redo of Windows on the World.

But at the same time, history was nudged aside by others making their own theme park New Yorks. As Sinatra died, DiMaggio died, and the Ramones finally retired, every cycle of nostalgia was churned through. New generations didn't so much resurrect the past as they re-created it as a stage to play on. Elaine's return came with a wink the old guard didn't see. "The torch has been passed," declared James Kaplan. "It's a halogen torch now; the cool symbolic image of a flame rather than the hot thing itself." Even recent history was at risk; covering the Haring retrospective, Kurt Andersen wrote that the late artist "now seems more like a character in *Rent* than an actual person" and with crime down, violence could be fun; director Quentin Tarantino dressed up torture porn with cool kid in-jokes and deep cuts. More branded dining of the sort Hard Rock Café brought in 1984 turned 57th Street's hardworking blocks of art suppliers, piano stores, and modeling agencies into tourist attractions.

The Tech Boom had, on the other hand, turned some unreal things about money and class into hard realities. Back in the '80s, froufrou dresses and all that Glorious Food at the Temple of Dendur had done the work of proving just how exceptional the rich were whereas, explained Michael Shnayerson, "[t]he new money of the '80s is old money now." Either way, there was a vast amount of it. "It's like the country is on a tilt," said Ian Schrager, "and everyone is rolling into New York." Spy Bar invented bottle service when it found itself with too many customers. "It was about creating a barrier to entry," said owner David

Sarner. An estimated 110,000 streamed to the Hamptons for summer sun and society. The first gifted children of '80s wealth were on their way to law school and MBAs, and now it was *their* turn to maximize potential and minimize risk, perform all necessary steps and play all advantages to debut *their* children into this synthetic realm of privilege now assumed to be a birthright. Old or new, money equaled wisdom and this extended to philanthropy, where the savvy no longer just *gave* their money away; they demanded results! "Venture philanthropy" such as the Robin Hood Foundation taught lucky nonprofits how to earn bigger donations with better performance, thus eliminating the need to ask larger uncomfortable questions as to why they had to exist in the first place.

At the same time, Rudy's effort to impose "one standard" on "one city" had failed to create one cultural reality. Technology, activism, global media, and changing demographics continued to "decenter" the culture; new networks of affinity abounded as the city grew: Through the '90s, some 686,000 people would move to New York City, pulling the population over 8 million for the first time, but that was just the net; over those years, almost 1.25 million foreign-born immigrants would live for some time in New York, with Queens taking the most: Flushing was now 38% Asian, Fresh Meadow, 25%, but now there were also Sri Lankans and Liberians in Staten Island, Arabs in Bay Ridge, Syrian Jews in Gravesend, Ghanaians in Concourse Village, Bangladeshis in Kensington, Chinese and Mexicans in Sunset Park, Albanians in Belmont, all adding their customs and culture. The city's Great Conversation had become a grand buffet, but while the food was better and the people were more interesting than ever, it all felt suddenly impossible to digest. More networks appeared with their own narratives, more hubs, and paths in every direction that few were yet making sense of in terms of common humanity. "The market is flooded with content," wrote John Seabrook. "There are too many film festivals, too many books, too many new bands, too many 'new voices' and 'stunning debuts.'" George W. S. Trow went mad. "People fall off the high wire invisibly," he wrote of this suddenly complex world. "There is no net; they crash." After being briefly committed, Trow was found dead in Naples, Italy.

Yet others plunged headfirst. "Everybody has their own independent culture," said Jeff Koons, "and that culture is as valid as any other culture." The plus of this post-Warhol world was that "cool" now meant doing what you did well and with passion. "There are people who go to work every day in a suit and tie who are bohemian," said Penny Arcade in a 1996 performance piece, "and . . . loads of people who graduate from art school and are completely bourgeois." But Create Your Own culture also made facts a matter of opinion. Re-sorting by class, taste, sexuality, faith, and bank account, people produced their own realities and increasingly clumped with only those who shared theirs, a new Us vs. Them at every turn. "The salient question in this new era," wrote Kurt Andersen, "tend[s] to be epistemological: What do you think you know, and why do you think you know it?"

It was hard to say what was "real" in the art world now. Done with the buzzkill multi-culti stuff, 1995's kinder, gentler Biennial demonstrated to critic Mark Stevens that "no commanding style or attitude now rules the art world." When the *Times* asked a panel of artists and scholars "What is art?," they each said there was no answer. "Now the New York art world is so big," said Jeffrey Deitch, "there are a number of sub-art worlds—the figurative group, the political group, the abstract painters, just to name a few—and they function as self-contained units." Coherence came from the Art Industry, the galleries, auction houses, and MFA programs, the museums packaging artists and styles for the media and new global collectors.

In the mid-'90s, SoHo almost a mall, Art created another neighborhood for itself when Matthew Marks bought a garage on 22nd west of Tenth Avenue by the DIA Center and Joseph Beuys's *7000 Oaks* installation; Paula Cooper and Pat Hearn found their own cavernous places nearby, on gritty blocks below the railroad tracks, among truck drivers and hookers, that made a statement of non-Disney reality as much as economics. Others quickly followed. Ugly, hard to get to, lacking in services and restaurants, Chelsea resisted a casual Saturday afternoon wander. "Even the cops are scared to go there," sniffed David Zwirner. "It's *Blade Runner* on the Hudson." Yet after Marks's big shows of Ellsworth Kelly, Brice Marden, and Richard Serra, *New York* dubbed the area "suddenly as groovy as Avenue A in 1985, if not Wooster Street in

1975." Unlike SoHo and the East Village in their days, though, it had no cheap spaces for working artists. Instead of Artists as Gentrifiers, it was simply Art as Gentrifier, and with no displaced residents, making it as guilt-free as the Internet.

To find an actual artist, you'd have better luck in Brooklyn. *New York*'s listings reviewed all of six restaurants there in June 1995, though getting off the L at Bedford no longer required sprinting to safety and some White people were even staying on until Graham. That fall Annie Herron gave seed money to a California transplant named Joe Arnheim to open a gallery at North 9th Street between Driggs and Bedford called Pierogi, its Flat Files full of works on paper priced low so young artists could sell to young locals. More potters, woodworkers, and furniture makers arrived and Brooklyn's "youse guys" tang suddenly felt more "real" than Manhattan; when Kathy Acker, William Burroughs, and Allen Ginsberg all passed away in 1997, it took over from Downtown. Not everyone heard the news—"the creeping dullness of the place just overwhelms me," wrote Philip Dray. But finally even the *Times*'s Roberta Smith noticed the "struggling gallery scene in the Williamsburg section of Brooklyn." Her roundup included recent real estate deals in DUMBO and finished with open-ended musing about the area's potential. "[T]he inclusive spirit," she wrote, "so basic to the Williamsburg art scene easily rubs off on newcomers." When the *Utne Reader* called Williamsburg "the third coolest neighborhood in America and Canada," the green flag was dropped; Jonathan Lethem published *Motherless Brooklyn*, and the Hipsters descended, their facial hair and thirst for PBR a supposed rejection of Manhattan slickness. In 1980, Trow had written, "A fedora hat worn by me without the necessary protective irony would eat through my head and kill me." Brooklyn was full of unironic fedoras now, worn with the conviction they were somehow "real" if worn there. The city now played itself in a movie, and sometimes it stared straight into the lens. *That* was the real Disneyfication of New York.

As Lifestyle changed from an urgent quest for the next thing into a performance, the Style and Media industries helped those citizen consumers frozen in the face of infinite choice and cultural sprawl to find their characters and roles. Everyone and anyone could have one. After five years away, Fernanda Eberstadt found Fashion now the city's "defining industry," but the Garment District was dying off as haute couture went mass market, taking much of the culture with it. Fashion now, wrote Michael Wolff, was "central to the way we think about brands and celebrity and even intellectual property, and how all this gets parlayed and monetized." Branding would signify meaning and provide order in the decentered world. "Street style" was high style now, Hip Hop's changing signifiers perfect for the constant demands of a seasonal business. Celebrity made you an instant brand and, said one club kid–entrepreneur, "You don't have to really be anything to be a celebrity anymore." "[T]he aristocracy of birth was now irrelevant," said Tina Brown. "All that counted now was the aristocracy of exposure." But becoming a celebrity was hard work, so now Media agreed with Warhol that it qualified as an achievement in its own right; the Warhol retrospective at the Whitney came right on time. ("What people don't know," said Brigid Berlin, "is that at the Factory, we were all Republicans.") *Time's* 75th anniversary party threw DiMaggio, Gorbachev, Leni Riefenstahl, Kofi Annan, and Raquel Welch together in a room. Why? Well, why not?

If you couldn't create, you could buy. Culture, like democracy, like identity, was now a form of shopping, directed start to finish by networks of conglomerated Style and Media. With everyone from Prada to Banana Republic opening flagships, a onetime employee of Holly Whyte named Paco Underhill applied Whyte's public space strategies to what he called "retail anthropology," methods for controlling shoppers that, as Malcolm Gladwell pointed out, went against just about everything Whyte stood for. And as Si Newhouse had planned, Condé Nast called an inordinate share of the shots, through three editors. Thin, elegant, Anna Wintour with her Louise Brooks bob had long ago left *New York* with frank ambitions; when Grace Mirabella, then editor of *Vogue*, met her, she'd asked her what job she wanted, to which Wintour had said, "Yours." After cracking the whip for Si Newhouse at British *Vogue*, she'd brought her bob to *H&G*, where Tina Brown found her presence "a bit like suddenly having a sleek-haired race-horse pawing the other side of the fence." She finally got the magazine in 1988 and her first cover that November of Michaela Bercu in jeans and a jeweled Christian Lacroix jeweled jacket had started the move from high fashion to pop culture.

When Condé Nast bought Fairchild Publications, Newhouse gave her *Women's Wear Daily* and *W*, putting her in charge of arguably the three most influential fashion magazines in the world. In the same building, Graydon Carter had finally made *Vanity Fair* his own by bringing its glamorous Smart Set past back to life. "Graydon is a man who has decided to create the world he dreams of," said editor Jim Kelly; in this case a sophisticated, playful fantasy of what New York would be like if *Spy* ran things. Which to some degree it now did.

The third was Tina Brown, who left *The New Yorker* in January 1999. Like Wall Street, the magazine at this point belonged to New York only because of its importance as a global node. Special issues on women and Black Life in America, unimaginable under Shawn, had approached their topics with a difficult candor, though "sophisticated boom boom" may have peaked when she named Roseanne Barr a guest editor. Brown intended her next magazine, *Talk*, to explore celebrity with a kind of point-and-click immediacy. "I believe heat is quality," she told one reporter. Though she tried to walk it back, the words felt true.

"The padrone of New York glitzocracy," Tina's new backer and head of Miramax, was oversized, abrasive Harvey Weinstein who'd once shouted to a reporter, "It's good that I'm the fucking sheriff of this fucking lawless piece of shit town." He was the ultimate cultural expression of Reformation New York. After ten years as a low-level film distributor with his brother Bob, the Weinsteins broke out in 1989 with *Sex, Lies, and Videotape*. Over the next decade, movies like *Pulp Fiction*, *The Crying Game*, *Clerks*, *Good Will Hunting*, and their two Best Pictures, *The English Patient* and *Shakespeare in Love*, all starring young, beautiful leads such as Gwyneth Paltrow, Uma Thurman, Ben Affleck, and Matt Damon, launched a New York–centric film scene, Harvey's bad temper and unshaved porcine face a throwback to Louis Mayer and Harry Cohn. The perks came with peril, though. "Those who have been witness to his outbursts, public and private," reported Ken Auletta, "describe not a lovable rogue but, rather, a man with little self-control, whose tone of voice and whose body language can seem dangerous . . ." He then quoted a studio head as saying that working with Harvey left them feeling "raped—a word often invoked by those who'd dealt with him." "There is one story that needs to be told about this guy," an executive told David Carr. "And you are not going to tell it." Those in his network had nothing but good things to say: "I think that for every bad story you hear . . . ," said willowy Paltrow, dubbed First Lady of Miramax by Harvey himself, "there are three great ones."

And what of those old corners of New York Society that hadn't been repurposed as retro chic? Nouvelle Society had been absorbed into the vast realm of global wealth where it could hide again. "Society doesn't really exist in New York," said *W* editor Patrick McCarthy. "Nobody even knows these people's names anymore. They don't exist." Jackie O had died, so had Jerry Zipkin and the Duchess of Windsor, their estates auctioned off, and Brooke Astor announced she'd be closing out the Vincent Astor Foundation, having given out some $195 million. Glenn Bernbaum, owner of Mortimer's, died of cirrhosis, a secretive, mean, and lonely alcoholic; Nan Kempner eulogized him by saying, "He could be the bitch of all times." But now where would Society find cheap, bland food served in an atmosphere that made outsiders feel uncomfortable? "People don't like to be treated badly," remarked regular Kenneth Lane. "But they like to see others treated badly." No one mourned Old Society's contraction. A new realm of secret signifiers emerged in plain sight, like Doubles downstairs at the Sherry Nether-land, "the last authentic vestige of New York's café society." "There are just as many extravagant evenings," explained Blaine Trump, "but they're done privately." Thankfully, some old Mortimer's hands opened Swifty's in the fall of 1999, named after Bernbaum's pug Swifty who was named after agent Swifty Lazar, who got the nickname from Humphrey Bogart. Some things, like David Rockefeller, lived on.

We're Going to Miss That Secret World

With high drama, the new realities of gay life in New York met the new unrealities of Broadway in December 1995, when a new musical opened at the Nederlander Theatre. *Rent*'s creator Jonathan Larson had died the night before the show's Off-Broadway opening, adding a meta-layer of tragedy to his rock opera riff on *La Bohème* that swapped TB and the Latin Quarter for AIDS and the East Village. In a time when dance critic Arlene Croce panned Bill T. Jones's *Still/Here* as a "messianic traveling medicine show" because it involved AIDS victims, *Rent* stood out as unapologetically diverse, young, and welcoming to People with AIDS and HIV. Critics loved it, tickets could not be found; here was *Hair* for our time, another show along with *Beauty and the Beast* to bring a new generation to ailing Broadway and "La vie Bohème." Except there really wasn't much authentic or *bohème* about *Rent*. Its tantrum of a plot about beautiful, struggling young artists reenacted a scene already long-gone, in a neighborhood *New York* now considered "a foodie paradise ascending," sanding away the lonely horrors of AIDS and heroin, turning squatters into heroes when the few squatters left on the Lower East Side were blocking construction of affordable housing. Most of all, *Rent* helped pasteurize gay life for straight consumption.

"AIDS," wrote Paul Rudnick, "has simply made gay life a fact." And by 1994, Straight New York was accepting that fact. The Gay Games brought as much money and goodwill to the city as the seven World Cup matches did; gays appeared in ads for IKEA and Benetton. Jann Wenner came out. But as gay life in New York became more visible, the search for a cure wandered in a maze, ACT UP dissolved and noncon-frontational AMFAR became the biggest AIDS advocacy group, leaving straight culture to dictate the terms of acceptance. First, gay sex had to stay indoors like drugs and guns; Giuliani enforced old cabaret laws and new health ones to finish the bleaching of liminal spaces started back in the '80s. "It's certainly easier to be gay now," said Larry Kramer, "although it's not easier to have sex now."

Rent expressed the other, deeper levels of the deal: gay visibility at the cost of gay meaning; gay words under straight control—singing "YMCA" at Yankee games and, as President Clinton instructed the military, "Don't ask, don't tell." Broadway had long offered gay men a place to publicly express coded emotions, but it had lost much of its signifying power since AIDS and the British invasion of *Cats* and *Phantom*. Now here was Larson's show, which bore a more than passing resemblance to the plot and characters of a novel called *People in Trouble* by lesbian activist Sarah Schulman. Beyond the possible appropriation, she saw *Rent* as "a shift in public discussion" of AIDS "from expression to product" not unlike the movies *To Wong Foo, Thanks for Everything! Julie Newmar*, and *Philadelphia*, films about gay life made largely from a straight viewpoint. The switch truly flipped on the new Times Square the night the house lights went down at the New Amsterdam, Rafiki sang "Nants Ingonyama Bagithi Baba" out into the darkness, and Julie Taymor's puppet zebras, elephants, and impalas sprung across the stage. Global and captivating, you couldn't hate *The Lion King*, but Disney *had* managed to produce maybe the least gay musical in theater history. HBO's *Sex and the City*, based on Candace Bushnell's bitchy quartet of fashionably insatiable women fucking their way through an airbrushed Manhattan, now took over as the gayest show in town.

And then the Plague suddenly ended. In June 1996, Dr. David Ho announced the success of protease inhibitors and a year later, death rates were down by half, with 30% fewer hospital admissions. After more than a decade of one generation fighting for its life, the next could fight for the right to get married, have kids, and serve in the military. *Christopher Street* and *Native* shut down, and Giuliani absorbed heat from the Right by supporting legislation in favor of same-sex couples. Gay culture went, in the words of Daniel Mendelsohn, "from épatering les bourgeois to aping them." Kramer reunited with the man who'd left him after *Faggots*. "After twenty years," he said, "I am finally getting everything I wanted." Camp felt as passé as communism; no less an expert than John Waters would soon say it was "just a socially acceptable way of saying it's old-school faggy." The effects of the détente went both ways. "[A]s the community 'matures,'" continued Mendelsohn, "both its substance and its style are increasingly hard to differentiate from those of the straight mainstream," while Giuliani sure seemed to enjoy his evenings in pantyhose and sequins performing at the Inner Circle Dinner. "In a sense," Rudnick had written, "even straight people come to New York to be gay." That was debatable: ACT UP and Queer Theory asked whether being gay was about sex, gender, cultural positioning, or all of the above. But if Rudnick's line was the truth for the post-AIDS world, the city had lost something unique. "Someday we will be accepted," said Vito Russo once, "and the world will understand and accept us, and when that day comes, we're going to miss that secret world."

Chapter Twenty-three

Stand Clear of the Closing Doors

Some places, some moments, naturally generate that tingly New York City energy people travel from around the world to feel, and right now Brenda Barnes, waving her fingers after a manicure at Saks, was feeling it as she rode the late afternoon tide west through Rockefeller Center, past skaters gliding under Prometheus and Radio City Music Hall repolished by (of course) Hugh Hardy. A forty-four-year-old law student without much time to waste, she squeezed around one of Safir's "pedestrian separators" and dashed to the other side of Sixth Avenue where a cop grabbed her arm. Barnes sassed him and, on February 13, 1998, six weeks after Giuliani had posed in front of an enormous American flag to swear his second oath of office, she received the first jaywalking ticket in anyone's memory. Within hours, one of OJ's lawyers took her case and New Yorkers had her back the way they'd had Kris Kringle's against Macy's.

Despite the Louima tragedy and rumors of an affair with Cristyne Lategano, swathed in "the odor of something gone bad in the fridge," Giuliani had cruised to reelection over Ruth Messinger in the fall of 1997 and already looked toward Washington, DC. "How far can Rudy go?" asked the cover of *New York* with a drawing of him as George Washington. "Can we trust him with the bomb?" (To which more than one New Yorker interviewed replied, "Just shoot me now.") Most of the first-term brain trust had left, so Giuliani's network tightened and now, certain that statewide voters would demand the city's total subjugation, he made his second term a crusade against New York and everyday New Yorkers like Brenda Barnes.

After a State of the City speech celebrating its "liberation" from "progressive" ideals, bemoaning single-parent families and bilingual education, Giuliani announced a "zero-tolerance" civility campaign inspired by a piece in the winter 1998 *City Journal* advising firm colonial governance for the wild natives of New York: a 30-mile-per-hour speed limit, a probation period for new taxi drivers, and delivery people would need to carry IDs. City workers would get etiquette guidelines. On their own merits, these weren't terrible ideas—all those tidy European cities liberals loved had laws like these, and who hadn't crashed into a clutch of German tourists waiting for a red light to turn green? But even Jack Maple believed "zero tolerance" was for "brown shirts, red armbands and jackboots" and having one of the most venomous mayors in city history lecturing about civility seemed rich, to say the least. "I suppose," Olmsted wrote long before, "the civilization is to be tested as much by civility as anything else."

Eventually Brenda Barnes had her ticket torn up—the officer cited her for the wrong violation—but Giuliani's moralism certainly tested civilization in New York. He invited the Grammy Awards to leave because their president was rude, invoked his "authority" to make sure you didn't jaywalk. He sued *New York* for bus ads that claimed the magazine was "the only good thing in New York Rudy hasn't taken credit for." Intent on purifying the land, he cracked down on fireworks, forced pornographic book and video stores to sell two thirds non-pornography material, and ran strip joints out of town. If drinkers at a bar so much as swayed their hips, his Social Club Task Force could shut the place down, and often did. "The Giuliani tone of 'normalcy' and wholesomeness is something this corroded city needed to an extent. But only to an extent," wrote Michael Tomasky. "There's only so much wholesomeness New York can take."

As the year went on, Giuliani aimed at even smaller, weaker targets: street vendors, CUNY students, cab drivers, and patients at City hospitals—all largely People of Color. CCNY students on welfare were put on workfare projects that forced 62% of them to either quit college or get off aid. "If you can't get a job," said the mayor who'd cracked down on street vendors, "start a small business. Start a little candy store. Start a little newspaper stand. Start a lemonade stand." City government became even Whiter; homeless spending went down as homelessness went up. Twenty Black and Latino Parks workers sued the City and Henry Stern for discrimination.

Amadou Diallo, a slight twenty-two-year-old Guinean Muslim, was one of those vulnerable New Yorkers. He sold hats and socks and bootleg videos on 14th Street twelve hours a day, seven days a week, and he was standing in front of his building on Wheeler Avenue around 12:20 a.m. the night of February 4, 1999, when four plainclothes members of the Street Crime Unit burst out of a car and told Diallo to stop and keep his hands visible. He didn't right away, though, and when he finally pulled out his wallet, the first two cops unloaded their weapons, bullets flying back at them off the brick wall. One of the shooters slipped and fell, and now they all believed they were in a firefight. Nineteen of the 41 bullets hit, pinning Diallo against the door until he finally went down, his wallet and cell phone spilling out onto the bloody ground. Officer Sean Carroll, at thirty-seven the oldest of the crew, realized their mistake and, weeping, held Diallo's hand as he died.

The outcry was immediate, but as the corpse chilled, Giuliani expressed sympathy only for the police, whose first response had been to search the dead man's apartment for something anything incriminating: "We have a right," he said, "to demand more respect from the citizens of the city for the police officers of the City of New York." The commissioner, who'd claimed that Louima's torture "wasn't related to police activity," had personally amped up this elite unit even as the nothing-but-numbers mind-set was compelling cops to haul tens of thousands of People of Color up against the wall. In *City Journal*, Heather Mac Donald called the uproar "manufactured," missing the irony of claiming—in a magazine that railed against business regulations—that they happily accepted the inconvenience of police stops in exchange for safety. As a grand jury pondered, civil rights advocate Charles Barron organized daily protests outside Police Headquarters that Giuliani dismissed as "a publicity stunt." Instead of attending a hearing on the case, Safir zipped off to the waiting Revlon jet that flew him to Tina Brown's

Oscar party. "It was all a lot of fun," he said afterward. The four officers were indicted for second-degree murder.

Safir and Giuliani were taking the NYPD over the edge. "[T]he very meaning of New York's drop in crime has shifted," wrote *The New Yorker*. Polls showed that all people wanted was for him to express grief and remorse for a terrible mistake, but he didn't; his approval rating dropped 21 points. "[I]f there were a way to get rid of Rudy," said political consultant Hank Sheinkopf, "they'd get rid of him today." Even Donna Hanover wouldn't say whether or not she voted for her husband. Craig Horowitz called it "The Fall of the Supermayor." It wasn't enough for Rudy to just push away New Yorkers with his attitude and policies, though; he also did it physically when he erected checkpoints and concrete barricades around City Hall. "Since when do you run a democracy from inside a Forbidden City," asked Paul Goldberger. But even that wasn't enough. Back in the '80s, developer Larry Silverstein had signed a 99-year lease with the Port Authority for 7 World Trade Center, a deal killed when Rudy took down the big tenant-to-be, Mike Milken's Drexel Burnham. Now Giuliani turned the empty 50,000-square-foot trading floor into his emergency command center: "the Bunker." Behind double-paned windows and Kevlar-reinforced walls, the mayor and his new Office of Emergency Management would survive disaster if not in luxury, then in relative comfort, with monogrammed towels and a humidor of cigars to smoke while the drawbridge was hauled up. Meanwhile, as calls to get the police and fire departments on a shared radio frequency were largely ignored, Rudy hosted the first fundraiser for his run for Moynihan's Senate seat. Now that the president had announced his post–White House office in Harlem, Rudy's likely opponent would be the First Lady, Hillary Clinton.

The Last Parties

Outside the Bunker, New York seemed ready to pop. While Gretchen Dykstra prepared for the world's biggest party, coders scrambled to fix the Y2K glitch before planes fell from the sky, *Who Wants to Be a Millionaire?* premiered, and coach Jeff Van Gundy led the Knicks to the NBA finals with all the ugly luck of finding a winning scratch-off on a bodega floor. The Dow broke 10,000 that spring; insiders harvested cash, and even Greenspan compared the stock market to a lottery. In the fall, Clinton happily signed the Financial Services Modernization Act, ending the era of Glass-Steagall. Dragged from behind Rudy's skirts by the prospect of the Clintons in New York politics, big-time Democrats angled for seats in the apartment of songwriter Denise Rich, now bundling for the DNC as a path into New York society.

Real estate was a religion as strong as the Bull, the residential market resetting to levels unseen. "Our common faith," wrote one observer was, "that the value of our handsome little flat in a doorman building can climb ever higher." "There's more money than space," reported *New York*, "so the space is getting more expensive, and the battles for it fast and bloody." Rents were up 50% to 60% over the last five years while owners doubled their money in two; you almost *had* to buy now if you wanted to stay in the city. One sensitive broker worried that "the normal people . . . making a half a million dollars a year—they won't be able to afford to live here and put two kids in private school." Networks of wealth and social capital bound more tightly than ever; co-ops exacted onerous financial requirements—three, five, even ten times the purchase price held in assets and years of maintenance in escrow no longer uncommon. In once-shaggy places like the Upper West Side and the East Village, community boards and block associations fought homeless shelters and zoning changes. Brooklyn was no longer just attractive, it was a necessity; rents had tripled in five years in Williamsburg, established turf like Park Slope was up almost 20%, and *New York* compared Carroll Gardens's "funky bustle" to "the West Village in the '60s."

But New Yorkers weren't the ones driving the land rush. New York real estate was a preferred venue for laundering Russian and Chinese money and thus fertile ground for Donald Trump, who at fifty-one supposedly had a "new conciliatory style." GE was paying him $25 million to transform the G+W Building at Columbus Circle into the Trump International Hotel. "A lot of our Asian customers have asked us to do feng shui," he said. Another surge of money came from publicly traded real estate investment trusts (REITs) that let anyone on the planet participate in the city's real estate boom without having to actually own property. "Shareholder value" drove development decisions now, not planning.

With less than five months left until the year 2000, a febrile mood took hold and the last parties began. In August, lit by the setting sun, 800 or so of the city's tastemakers and power brokers ferried over to Liberty Island to celebrate the launch of Tina Brown's *Talk*. Candidate Giuliani had nixed plans to hold the event at the Brooklyn Navy Yard after Hillary appeared on its debut cover, so Harvey Weinstein had pulled some bigger strings that let party planner of the decade Robert Isabell turn the symbol of America's embracing mission into a private island for Kate Moss and Tom Brokaw, Henry Kissinger and Madonna, Al Sharpton, Joan Didion, Queen Latifah, Salman Rushdie . . . the list went on. "A velvet, sexually charged darkness engulfed the partygoers," wrote Brown later, "illuminating them only by Christmas-tree lights that strung together the colored Japanese lanterns hanging from the trees." Issued their Glorious Food boxed dinner, the guests reclined on Moroccan pillows eating lamb chops while Macy Gray sang and George Plimpton narrated a Grucci fireworks show. The Twin Towers twinkled in the distance. How could it possibly get better than this? It was, wrote David Carr, "the end of an era, a literal fin de siècle."

Could these years of radioactive growth really continue, everything bigger, faster, and shinier? "[W]e are living in a moment of distorted reality," wrote Michael Wolff. The millennium raced toward a poisoned finish as the wealthy chased infinite wealth and the merely well-off believed they were poor in a time when it was criminal to be poor. Since Reagan, the top 1% had gotten 86% of the stock gains. Something *had* to happen. The Yankees won the World Series. Again. Agency.com went public and was now worth $2.2 billion. Josh Harris connected up four floors in two buildings downtown into Quiet, a month-long experiment to explore, he said, "what the internet will look like when it takes over." Apparently it would look a lot like the new Dutch TV show *Big Brother*: "Citizens" chosen for their off-kilter quirks would get a uniform and a sleep capsule equipped with a screen for watching everyone else. Armed with food, water, weapons, and cameras, they'd survive Y2K no matter what, and be filmed doing it, everything shown online in some combination of *1984* and *The Truman Show*. Elsewhere, Prince's "1999" seemed to play on a loop; free-floating anxiety spread. Sixty-two percent of Americans believed something bad would happen on Y2K. Amid ominous noises by Osama bin Laden, gun sales crept up, and *The Worst-Case Scenario Survival Handbook* was a bestseller; while Giuliani dropped by the Bunker with a mystery lady friend for "inspections," DM of Operations Joe Lhota war-gamed emergency response. By the last week of December, fear and fatigue had become general. Usually ebullient New Yorkers planned quiet evenings at home, restaurants closed, and Broadway went dark to avoid the 1 million people expected for Gretchen Dykstra's party in Times Square.

Tensions ebbed a little that afternoon when planes didn't crash over Sydney, but as midnight crept toward the East Coast, specific threats put three hundred crisis managers in the Bunker with Lhota, and the National Guard deployed in Brooklyn in case Manhattan needed to be evacuated. Sharpshooters manned nearby roofs as a petrified Giuliani climbed up to the platform at 45th and Broadway to drop the ball. Once an annual bacchanal, this New Year's Eve was more of a block party, huge puppets floating through the crowds. Times Square still expressed the urban id, but it no longer craved Jane Dickson's dark shadows; it wanted Tibor Kalman's thrill ride of flashing lights and brand names. In Central Park, a midnight run was about to start, and the American Museum of Natural History opened its glowing blue planetarium with a gala dinner. Inside Quiet, tensions had risen under the pressures of constant filming and Harris's machinations as he preyed on Ugly George's lesson that people tended to do whatever they were told if someone was pointing a camera at them. "People want fifteen minutes of fame every day," he said. The night's banquet started with the ragtag Hungry March Band marching naked down the length of the table, and from there things got fairly messy.

In Times Square the ball fell, second by second, and hit zero . . .

Fireworks went off. Confetti flew. Nothing exploded.

The next morning, the police and fire department raided Quiet, thinking it was a cult. Those crawling out into the light found that New York was still there. The rich were still there. The poor were still there. The Yankees, the cops, and the new Magic Johnson Theater on

125th were all still there. Everything was just where they'd left it. And everyone was still waiting for the apocalypse.

The Morning After

Reverend Butts stepped up and gripped the pulpit at Abyssinian Baptist Church, trembling with anger at yet another thing that hadn't changed. "I feel a little like my Lord," he said. "I want to kick over some *tables*." On February 25, a jury in Albany had acquitted the four killers of Amadou Diallo of all charges. Safir had already disbanded the SCU back in November, and State Attorney General Eliot Spitzer was examining Stop and Frisk; though Blacks made up 24.5% of the city's population, they were 62.7% of those stopped. "There is an evil that permeates the place called City Hall," Butts said. A few weeks later Haitian father of two Patrick Dorismond finished his usual 3:00-to-11:00 p.m. shift as a security guard for the 34th Street Partnership and had a few beers with a friend at the Distinguished Wakamba Cocktail Lounge on 37th and Eighth. As he waited outside for a cab, three undercover cops approached, asking if he had some pot to sell. Insulted, Dorismond got into it with them and as he was calling out for police, Detective Anthony Vasquez shot him dead. First, the NYPD claimed he'd tried to rob them, then Safir released Dorismond's sealed juvenile arrest record, illegally. Giuliani didn't care. "I would not want a picture presented of an altar boy," he said, "when in fact maybe it isn't an altar boy." Confronted on live television with the fact that Dorismond had *literally been* an altar boy, Giuliani just squirmed. His 32% approval rating was the lowest of his term, and two thirds now believed the NYPD was doing a poor or only fair job.

That same week, *Barron's* featured a cover image of a mound of cash on fire with the headline "BURNING FAST." Back in January, AOL had swallowed Time Warner to create the world's largest media company. Though its effect was to devalue content, and content was the whole point of Silicon Alley, Nasdaq set a record in March at 5,048 and there were 84 IPOs lined up. And then *Barron's*. The article simply calculated how long Internet companies would last given their cash reserves and current burn rate. Out of the 207 examined, 51 would be out of cash within the next twelve months; in two years' time, 200. Nasdaq dropped 25% that week. The next week was the Dow's worst since Hitler invaded France, off 9.5%, and by the end of the month, even Jim Cramer waved the white flag on "eighteen months of capitalism sans rigor." To visit some of the ruins: Ventrol went from $243 to $21; Internet Capital Group from $193 to $3.25; Infospace from $1,299 to $22. Nasdaq would eventually lose more than half its value. Razorfish and theGlobe.com were down more than 90%. It wasn't exactly the apocalypse, but it was close. The word *schadenfreude* did not appear once in the *New York Times* in all of 1980. In 1995 it showed up seven times, but in the year 2000, the number hit twenty-eight. For many of those watching the dotcom gurus and Early True Believers plunging back to Earth, *schadenfreude* was all they had, along with vindication that it'd been bullshit all along, a point even some digital boosters now hurried to make. "Silicon Alley was built on hype," said Seth Goldstein of Flatiron Partners. "There was no core asset other than the momentum." Part of the great attraction of *Survivor*, premiering that summer on CBS, was the absence of laptops and websites. Spearing fish in the clear waters off Borneo, even if it meant spending time with the Machiavellian nudist Richard Hatch, sounded very good.

Two drivers of Reformation New York—the NYPD and the Internet—had now been punctured, and the third—Rudy Giuliani—was about to see his political future end. Brushing off polls that had him at 28% in the city, he began to publicly squire Judith Nathan, a forty-five-year-old divorced nurse turned pharma saleswoman, to Italian restaurants, Yankee Stadium, and even the Inner Circle dinner. The press stood down until *Post* photographers snapped the two enjoying a leisurely May stroll after brunch on the Upper East Side, and a week later the same man who'd called for zero tolerance and the Ten Commandments in public schools stood in front of cameras in Bryant Park and publicly confessed to breaking Section 255.17 of the State penal code—he was having an affair and getting a divorce. This was news to his wife, who blamed Lategano. Shameful, sloppy, and cruel, the whole thing disgusted most New Yorkers, but less than two weeks later, things took a dramatic turn when Giuliani announced in a speech one councilmember compared to Scrooge the next morning that he had prostate cancer and was dropping out of the Senate race. While Donna Hanover and the two kids remained in Gracie Mansion, he moved into the spare bedroom of gay friends who favored Tiffany lamps and replica Chagalls.

Rudy now claimed to regret his attitude toward the Dorismonds; he met with minority leaders and in the strongest signal yet that he'd actually changed, he replaced Safir with Bernard Kerik. Orphaned when a pimp killed his prostitute mother, Kerik had dropped out of high school, joined the army, and then bounced between security work in Saudi Arabia and policing in New Jersey until he finally came to the NYPD in 1986, where he hit it off with Giuliani as his driver. When Rudy won in 1993, he named Kerik deputy commissioner of Corrections and then gave him the top job in 1998. Though he'd never passed a promotional exam he was liked and, according to Leonard Levitt, "radiated a childlike innocence" that allowed him to execute some of the soft-power follow-up Bratton had always recommended such as requiring cops to tell people why they were being stopped and frisked and apologize if they weren't arrested. By now the NYPD was paying millions every month in overtime, fattening pensions for veterans who now retired in growing numbers, leaving less for high-quality recruits.

Through the summer, Bill Clinton handed over the Democratic mantle to Al Gore while George Bush sent forth his son George W., a contest told by Media as a wonky do-gooder vs. the kind of guy you'd wanna have a beer with. Donald Trump talked about running on the Reform Party ticket; his manifesto *The America We Deserve* outlined plans to offer jobs to Oprah, Spielberg, and Jimmy Hoffa, bomb North Korea, and levy a 14.25% tax on anyone worth over $10 million. Walter Kirn called him a "master of unconscious camp." Jeff Koons's new piece in Rockefeller Center predicted the meme-filled future ahead, distracting New York with a 43-foot flowering *Puppy*, but when the hanging chads were counted—or not—the Supreme Court made George W. Bush the 43rd President of the United States.

Wall Street hit bottom that spring. Nasdaq sank under 2000, now 61.9% off its high less than a year ago. In one year, nearly $4 trillion in paper wealth had disappeared. From 1982 to 2000, the Dow had risen 1,409%, and money had become the central focus of American life. "I'm old enough to remember when you went into a bar during the summer," said Byron Wien of Morgan Stanley, "they were watching a baseball game. Now they're watching CNBC." According to the NY Fed, the city was now six times more dependent on Wall Street than it had been in 1987; from 1992 to 1997, 56% of the increase in paychecks had gone to Wall Street workers. In the ashes, the Internet's dual future as Chaos and Big Brother began taking shape. Napster arrived, redefining *theft* as *sharing*, while Zara used digital data to pump deliveries into its stores every few days, blowing apart the concept of fashion seasons. Up in the Lipstick Building, Bernie Madoff smiled his slight smile beneath dead eyes, his $6 billion fund still delivering monthly returns the way the Yankees kept delivering pennants. Some on the Street were talking, though, and in May 2001, the SEC knocked on his door again. His aide Frank DiPascali whipped up a nearly flawless digital face for the Ponzi scheme, and the SEC took no action.

What's Next?

It was time for valedictories. Giuliani considered his record a triumph; critics called it a disaster. Neither was entirely right. Crime as a kind of viral sickness had ended, but James Traub wondered whether there'd been an "implicit swap of primal energies for prosperity and peace." If so, he didn't seem too upset. As Bill Clinton joined the Y near his new office and Thelma Golden took over the Studio Museum, Reverend Butts said, "I really think that without Giuliani, we would have been overrun." People were excited about the new subway cars with their recordings to "Stand clear of the closing doors, please," and *you* try getting tickets to *The Producers*. Rudy had probed the limits of his post–Charter Reform power by repeatedly suing the City Council and the Comptroller, and though he'd increased mayoral control, what order he'd brought to City government had come more through technology than Reinventing Government strategies. Rather than tackle any long-term civil service reform, he'd outsourced a middling range of services and back-office work while gutting the managerial tier built up since the Fiscal Crisis to provide patronage jobs for loyalists. Yet while the mayor had, according to the *Times*, "guarded basic city data as though they were state secrets and spent millions of public dollars to deny the release of public information," the example of Compstat let him spread data-driven management, break information silos, and produce real-time data. The City developed its first comprehensive information technology strategy and nyc.gov as a single portal to New York City governance. Business hadn't controlled the administration. Instead, what for Koch and Dinkins been a network of support and control had become a transaction: Giuliani provided safe streets, lower taxes, and retention deals, and all he asked for was more growth. Otherwise, said banker Andrew Alper, there was almost "no relationship" between City Hall and major CEOs, though that wasn't all on Rudy; where there were once 140 *Fortune* 500 headquarters in New York there were now 40 or so, whose leaders felt little connection to the city. "Some of these new business leaders," said the NYCP's Kathy Wylde, "are too focused on business."

Inequality had sharpened. Though New York's strong late-'90s economy helped job growth and wages, and the earned income tax credit had brought more into the workforce, the poor got poorer, and there were more of them. By 2001, around 22% of New Yorkers lived in poverty, just about the same percentage as when Koch took office in 1978; in gross numbers, though, that meant a humanitarian crisis. Given the rise in the city's population, there were now 200,000 *more* in poverty, totaling some 1.6 million, more than the entire population of Philadelphia, Phoenix, San Diego, or Dallas. And yet the City's welfare caseload had dropped almost 50%, to around 400,000, because of Giuliani's campaign to push people off public assistance. Latinos had the greatest drop in welfare use—38%—though that may have been caused by illegal immigrants having a harder time getting aid; among Blacks the drop was only 3%. Workfare requirements kept those with HIV/AIDS, non-English speakers, the disabled, and the mentally ill from getting the help they needed to get off of public assistance permanently. Driving Food Stamp participation down sent emergency food aid up. Pataki had cut State subsidies to the MTA, forcing it to rely on fares and tax revenues that Albany then diverted, and Giuliani never restored his own cuts. Out of sight, signals wore out and the subways began to choke even as more riders piled into them.

The most visible result of Giuliani's term was the ordering of public space and who controlled it. New Yorkers were using it more than they had in decades, but in directed ways. By now there were 41 Business Improvement Districts across the city and both Rudy and the City Council had reined them, and Dan Biederman, in. "The trick of managing a BID is being very respectful to government," said Mitchell Moss, "and that's exactly what Biederman doesn't do." While his Bryant Park experiments with "experiential marketing" brought in needed funds, they also began to give the impression that the park was for rent, and after a scandal involving the harassment of homeless in and around Grand Central Terminal, Biederman was forced to resign as the head of the GCP. On a broader scale, it wasn't clear whether BIDs were fixing broken windows or creating Potemkin Villages, but the real issue for Rudy, it seemed, was their independence. As to Parks, that original Olmstedian democracy had been subsumed by the drive for public order, but that said, parks (or at least two of them) were pointing a way toward the post-Rudy future. By now, Elizabeth Barlow had handed the Central Park Conservancy over to Doug Blonsky, who contracted to maintain the park on a day-to-day level and turned away another overture from Christo for his *Gates* project, this time brought in by Michael Bloomberg. Though most city parks remained in tough shape and workfare labor made up the majority of Parks workers, community groups were developing new parks such as the Bronx River Greenway and Brooklyn Bridge Park. The New York Restoration Project won a legal battle against the City to preserve 100 community gardens. Large stretches of the Hudson River were now usable, and the first 1,000 feet opened of the new Hudson River Park between Houston and Bank Street that would, in time, become five miles of green space, restaurants, and commercial use that paid for its maintenance.

The park that most expressed what the city could be after Rudy was one that Rudy fought to the finish. Property owners in Chelsea had won a ruling to tear down the elevated tracks winding from Gansevoort Street up to the Javits Center at 34th, but they couldn't agree on costs with its owners CSX Transportation, so there it stood; City Planning head Joe Rose called the High Line "the Vietnam of old railroad trestles," but anyone who snuck up there illegally saw a hidden garden of Queen

Anne's lace waist high and watercolor blurs of chive and dwarf iris; iron railings gripped by Virginia creeper; milkweed carried on the wind; sumac, poison ivy, even crabapple trees. CSX asked the Regional Plan Association to explore the idea of a park or a light-rail system of the sort once imagined by Peter Obletz back in the '70s, hoping, as *New York* said, to "fob [it] off on a nonprofit group or a group of entrepreneurs." Two Chelsea residents, Josh David and Robert Hammond, had met at a community board discussion. The neighborhood was boiling over now with more than a hundred galleries, Chelsea Market's artisanal food shops, Martha Stewart Living Omnimedia in the Starrett-Lehigh Building, Jeffrey on 14th, and the new Commes des Garçons store on 22nd. So much had been cleared away in the last decade that the High Line's black beams and dark corners carried new meanings not so much about historic or architectural value but about how we once felt about New York City. To gay men like David and Hammond, it had another meaning. "This was the epicenter of sex club land," says David. Connecting the West Village and Chelsea through a thriving art and style district, the High Line, still transgressive, illegal, and cut across the grid, was a statement of post-AIDS memory and an assertion of presence.

The idea became their obsession. With advice from Phil Aarons, a community activist and former Koch aide, they began to create Friends of the High Line and over the next few months made presentations and enlisted the support of Paula Cooper, Matthew Marks, the Municipal Art Society, and most importantly Amanda Burden, who was on the City Planning Commission. "It was the most beautiful thing I'd ever seen," she says. "I saw it right in front of my eyes. I saw a new neighborhood." With Burden now a part of their network, Friends of the High Line began to raise money and angle it into discussions about the future of the West Side Rail Yards. In April, David and Hammond made their case at a City Council hearing. The City and the owners went first, laying out their reasons for why it should come down. A few even said a park would be great for property values, but, said one, "It's a pipe dream." "Since when," replied Burden in her testimony, "is being a dreamer a bad thing?" With permission from CSX, photographer Joel Sternfeld had been clambering up, especially on days with milky skies, to record what he called "a secret landscape," and when *The New Yorker* published them, the High Line became a sudden public enthusiasm. But to the end, Rudy's interest in infrastructure and planning went only as far as figuring out how to lure the Yankees to the West Side. He planned to sign the High Line's demolition papers before he left office.

Ultimately Rudy *had* united the city—everyone was eager to move past him. The likely Democratic candidates for mayor were Fernando Ferrer and frontrunner Mark Green, a Harvard Law grad and contributor to *The Nation*, who offered to continue a kinder version of Reformation New York. On the other side was Michael Bloomberg. Steered by Patricia Harris, he'd donated some $300 million over the last five years and now had seats on twenty boards. Moynihan's former chief of staff, Kevin Sheekey, assembled Bloomberg's own Mayor School featuring many ex-Koch and Moynihan sorts known more for the quality of their ideas than their political slant. Though pro-choice, pro–gun control and anti–death penalty, he switched his registration from Democrat to Republican and began calling himself Mike. Had he ever smoked pot? "You bet I did," he admitted, "and I enjoyed it." It was hard to imagine Rudy saying that, and that was good, but out in the streets he proved a dismal campaigner who looked like he was trying to buy City Hall. The poor? Well, yes. He didn't exhibit the visceral disgust of most Republicans, but it'd been many years and many billions since he'd parked cars to pay for college. And then there was that salty style: While Bloomberg LP had an excellent record promoting women, it also had a frat house culture he cultivated with dirty jokes and comments on the physical attributes of his female employees—he'd once reportedly said, "I would like nothing more in life than to have Sharon Stone sit on my face." On the other hand, he'd never been accused of sexual harassment, and after the escapades of Rudy, Clinton, and Trump, he cleared the bar. Barely. Everyone assumed Green vs. Bloomberg in the fall.

* * *

That new millennium had started without an apocalypse. Although 78% of New Yorkers had voted for Al Gore, the first year of George W. Bush hadn't given them much to protest, and a cold front from the north the evening of September 10 pushed Hurricane Erin off to the east, averting disaster. Instead, a furious thunderstorm scrubbed the sky, temperatures dropped, and New York edged onto the cusp of fall. The opening of Issey Miyake's new TriBeCa boutique went ahead slightly dampened while on Pier 54, Marc Jacobs debuted a flouncy, colorful Spring Collection that put *Vogue* in mind of "a Berkeley student listening to Donovan or the Strawberry Alarm Clock in the late '60s." Afterward, Sarah Jessica Parker, Monica Lewinsky, and Donald Trump all partied together as a fireboat shot happy streams of water over the Hudson. Jay-Z's new album dropped tomorrow.

So ended Reformation New York, and Manhattan's last day as any sort of rebel island.

Many would later report having strange, frightening dreams.

September 11, 2001

The city, for the first time in its long history, is destructible. A single flight of planes no bigger than a wedge of geese can quickly end this island fantasy, burn the towers, crumble the bridges, turn the underground passages into lethal chambers, cremate the millions. The intimation of mortality is part of New York now: in the sound of jets overhead, in the black headlines of the latest edition.

—E. B. White, *Here is New York* (1949)

Matt Lauer led off *The Today Show* with some ominous news for Knicks fans—Michael Jordan was coming out of retirement. Other headlines buzzed; Congressman Gary Condit and the disappearance of an intern and the EEOC's massive discrimination suit against Morgan Stanley. In the second hour, Tracey Ullman would be along to chat with Katie Couric.

My *God*, it was beautiful outside; cloudless blue skies, temperatures in the seventies for the morning rush, so clap your hands and get started on a fall day all new-sneaker bright, sharp-pencil ready. Yesterday the Dow had fought its way out of another morning plunge, so traders hit their desks hoping things had hit bottom and as usual, Joe Lhota had arrived first at City Hall. More parents than usual were dropping off because public schools were polling places for today's primary. Omelets were served at Hugh Hardy's renovated Windows on the World, while

319

pregnant models wolfed bagels and Krispy Kremes before Liz Lange's maternity fashion show in Bryant Park. The mayor finished a working breakfast at the Peninsula on 55th.

Then.

After slicing the morning sky along the Hudson, American Airlines Flight 11 slammed into the upper floors of Tower One, blasting debris and body parts in a five-block radius, shooting jet fuel down the elevator shafts, blowing apart the lobby, shaking the bedrock, and bringing the world as it was known to an end at approximately 8:46 a.m. The *Titanic* took two hours and forty minutes to sink once it hit the iceberg; Tower One would take 102 minutes.

Thousands leapt to action; others froze. Countless disaster movies had wondered what it would look like if a skyscraper exploded, and now here it was: the glorious cloud of confetti swirling hundreds of feet in the air, bigger than any ticker tape parade, bigger than Times Square on New Year's Eve; the details of countless lives and transactions lost now and falling down onto the graveyard of St. Paul's Chapel, thickly drifted on the crooked crosses and headstones, on the spears of the little gate; converging sirens high and low, bleating, honking, frantically keening like a mother who's lost her child; the rain of bodies, sudden fields of gore made of those who'd chosen a final few seconds of flight over fire.

At 8:54 a.m., Matt and Katie cut to a distant live shot of what was called "an accident," Tower One calmly churning like a giant smoke-stack while inside, fire wardens began leading survivors slowly down well-lit stairwells—both the wardens and the lighting put in place after the 1993 attack. Corporations quickly became families, strangers trapped in elevators, bunched together on landings, digging through rubble became networks for survival. Those stranded above the impact weighed their options, went to the roof, looked down from gashes in the facade. Thousands in Tower Two headed for the elevators. But with no general order to leave, some office workers stayed to wait for instructions, making phone calls because the stock market opened at 9:00 a.m., and the business of New York was business. Others who'd gone down went back up.

More than 200 fire trucks arrived, as did police. Off-duty officers threw on clothes and headed in. In the lobby of Tower One, fire chiefs took stock of the piles of shoes, the concrete and glass crashing down, briefcases, body parts. A man with no skin, staggering by, moaning. The NYFD were regular visitors at the World Trade Center—a place this big always had problems—but *this* . . . For a second the mind wandered and then snapped back to what could be done and what couldn't. The chiefs knew this was too big and too high up to stop; from the start it was rescue-only. But the elevators weren't working, so the bad news spread among the firemen that they'd each have to haul some sixty pounds of equipment up a hundred floors. Another jumper hit the ground and after a flinch, they understood this wasn't a plane crash. It was war. And they were going to the front. Duty broke their dark intuition and they went forward, with little coordination or communication, their radios mostly outdated, their signals unreliable. Giuliani had done little to force Police and Fire to deal with each other—he'd created the OEM to avoid that—so they operated on different frequencies figuratively and literally, and each now led their own rescues.

Joe Lhota had dashed over from City Hall and called Giuliani to report that New Yorkers were plummeting to earth around him. Streaking down Seventh Avenue, the mayor and his bodyguards were at Canal Street watching the winds pull the plume of black smoke south and Lhota was with Bernie Kerik when the second plane tore into the midsection of Tower Two around 9:03 a.m., through two stairwells full of evacuees. Another fireball exploded. Lhota dove under a truck just as a girder landed on it and another rain of metal, glass, paper, and debris large and small pummeled the surrounding streets. Pulled out alive, he went to find the mayor.

The Financial District emptied, sending thousands of refugees in the streets north, into boats along the Hudson, streaming east over the Brooklyn Bridge. The Bunker at 7 WTC was evacuated now, too—no one had ever believed this kind of thing could happen, though it had eight years before. After meeting Lhota at the Fire command post, Giuliani and his team set up at 75 Barclay. The general call to evacuate Tower One was announced, but the process was clogging at the bottom. "Don't look. Just keep moving" police said to those walking out into the light, stunned. Though the South Tower had had a head start, progress there was slow, too. Firemen continued up the stairs, counting on three hours of fireproofing before the flames burnt through to the steel, but the gut-shot it took meant more weight pressing down on its few remaining girders and on top of that, the fires here were worse. Outside, the aluminum façade peeled away. Survivors who couldn't get down blocked stairs went toward the roof, clambering at the openings, mad for air, inadvertently pushing others out. Ceilings caved in. From the street you could see smoke and flames coming from a floor about halfway up, and buckling.

At 9:59 a.m., there was a rumble.

An evil blossom of smoke, pulverized debris, and human ashes black and gray burst against a mocking sky all Pantone Process Blue as the top half of Tower Two plowed down. At City Hall, on the streets spoking out of the World Trade Center complex, thousands stumbling away now ran screaming as the wave billowed out in all directions, a wind of unspoken nature roaring around corners, mounting and bearing down, scouring away what New York had been a million years ago when the most important things were the lilac shirts and marigold pants Marc Jacobs had sent down the runway at Pier 54. Everything went black, all the windows of the Winter Garden blown out as the cloud roared through. When the light finally returned, milky and yellow, the entire city south of Canal was coated in a layer of dust.

Everyone had wondered. Now it had happened. The mayor and his crew, trapped briefly at 75 Barclay, came out into the hellscape to make their way north in search of a place to reestablish City government. Inside Tower One, the pace quickened. It was only a matter of time. The firemen were called out but between chaos and bad radios, the message didn't get to them fast enough.

*   *   *

Twenty-seven years before, a French aerialist named Philippe Petit had strung a high wire between the two brand-new towers of the World Trade Center and on a dank morning of white sky, he'd toed his way forward onto the cable and walked in midair, a black dot miraculously flowing back and forth, lying down, defying all the fear rampant in the streets below. In all the years and all the performance art that had

followed in the city, Petit's walk in the clouds was the greatest, a statement of magical courage and audacious skill brought to their absolute
height in a way that could happen only in New York, New York, the
only city crazy and greedy and brilliant enough to have ordered up
two of the world's tallest buildings at the same time. "My destiny no
longer has me conquering the highest towers in the world," he wrote
later about what he was thinking, "but rather the void they protect."
Petit had danced in that void, that frightening, glorious unknown that
defined New York. And now it had disappeared.

*   *   *

At 10:28 a.m., the antenna on Tower One waved, the top floors shud-
dered, and just like Tower Two drove down, sending another wave
of smoke, and dust, and chemicals through Downtown New York.
Crushing more people than anyone wanted to imagine.

*   *   *

Then silence. The terror would continue in different forms over the
next month. But for now there was silence. Joe Lhota threw himself
into assembling the biggest search and rescue in history, and he also
realized that payroll and welfare checks needed to go out the next day
or there'd be more chaos. The Board of Elections and Governor Pataki
called off all the day's elections. The city now knew terrible things
no other city in America had ever known, the kind of arcane, deadly
knowledge Hiroshima had learned when the atomic bomb printed the
shadows of the vaporized on its sidewalks. Those who were in New York
on September 11, 2001, would never forget the silence of those empty,
blasted streets, their memories of it shoved behind a door that never
fully closes. "Waking comes and at first only that," wrote Roger Angell
about September 12, "and then the flood of what can't be undone."
    But New Yorkers had also learned that every stock horror movie
scene of stampeding mobs and cowards desperate to survive wasn't reality. In fact, calm, courage, and loving-kindness had been the norm. They
hadn't run from each other; they'd stood next to each other, they'd talked

to each other. They'd helped each other with a constant selfless dignity, with humanity so profound that any talk of mere "civility" seemed absurd. They'd carried each other, searched, sacrificed, hauled wheelchairs, urged on, pulled to safety, and given freely to total strangers. In the face of horror and death, they'd trusted each other. That fewer than 3,000 died when it could have been in the tens of thousands spoke to what emergency workers but also average New Yorkers had done. They'd learned that if something terrible happened again, they could more than likely rely on the person next to them, and in the years ahead of constant threats of terror, "New Yorkers," writes Rebecca Solnit, "remained among the least terrified." Many would say afterward that this was the day that New York lost its innocence; in fact, it was the day the city regained it, at least for a while.

The next weeks trembled with loss and fear and were spiked with new terrors. Prescriptions for antianxiety pills jumped nearly 25% in New York City as jet fighters patrolled the skies. A new refugee class formed of the 20,000 residents banned from their homes below Canal, now a battlefield, crime scene, and cemetery, every surface coated in toxic dust. Revolting odors settled over the area; "you could smell them in your eyes," wrote one reporter, a smell high and chemical, rounded with burnt flesh. On September 25, Tom Brokaw's assistant opened an envelope filled with anthrax. Similar envelopes arrived at four other media outlets and then, in October, at the offices of two senators. Five people died. The sender was never found. So on top of the fear of loud sounds, planes, and tall buildings now came the constant possibility of chemical terrorism, of something added to the water or sent through the mail that would kill thousands more. Getting a prescription for Cipro became a sick form of prestige as rumors spread of a subway attack planned for Halloween. "The psychic fallout from the World Trade Center disaster is as persistent as the acrid smoke that still rises," wrote *New York*. FEMA and the National Guard were stationed at the Javits Center, and police checkpoints blocked entry south of Canal. Downtown was for large stretches a ghost town. Uptown, traffic barely moved.

Where the World Trade Center had once stood was now Ground Zero, a burning ten-story mound of rubble, the remains of 220 acres of concrete and steel, 2.2 million square feet of aluminum cladding, 3,000 miles of electrical wire, 40,000 doors, 7,000 plumbing fixtures and, it was initially believed, trapped survivors. In a mania of survivor's guilt, police, fire, and construction crews set immediately on it 24 hours a day, using nearby St. Paul's Chapel as a base. After a week of futility, Fire Commissioner Thomas Von Essen had wanted to shift from rescue to cleanup, but the mayor wouldn't allow it even as the fires kept pumping out fine particles of PCBs, pulverized glass, and concrete, hundreds of tons of lead and asbestos and God knows what other toxins coating façades, lining ductwork, covering every surface inside homes, and creeping deeper and deeper with every breath into the lungs of everyone near Ground Zero, especially those of the responders, who began developing the "World Trade Center Cough." Though testing had just started, the White House scrubbed the preliminary findings and EPA head Christine Todd Whitman declared the air safe, avoiding panic and dodging the responsibility for costly cleanup. City Hall shared the good news, and most workers stopped bothering with hazmat abatement. By the end of the year, a quarter of the 6,500 firefighters on the Pile would be diagnosed with respiratory problems. "I didn't see victims," said one later. "They were dust. And I was inhaling them."

Through all this, New Yorkers lived in a state of terrible grace. As Dorothy Day wrote after the San Francisco earthquake, "While the crisis lasted, people loved each other." Solnit calls these moments "Disaster Utopias." After tragedies of such devastation and size, networks of mutual aid spontaneously form and people, she quotes Charles Fritz, "are thus able to perceive, with a clarity never before possible, a set of underlying basic values to which all people subscribe . . . This merging of individual and society needs provides a feeling of belonging and a sense of unity rarely achieved under normal circumstances." The Frozen Zone created its own disaster utopia. "People who live downtown," wrote Jennifer Senior, "are convinced they're living in a different city from that of people who live uptown." Strangers hugged, Bouley and Odeon served rescue workers, and day spas gave free massages on the street. Suddenly Downtown was restored to its old identity as a more genuine world unto itself.

That generous spirit extended to some degree throughout the city. "From that day, for a month it seems like, everybody was present to everybody," Pat Enkyo O'Hara said. "[T]here was a kind of open vulnerability that people felt." People lived off social capital. Flags and Red, White, and Blue were everywhere, volunteering the norm: handing out water at St. Paul's Chapel, collecting cough drops and breathing masks at school; giving blood. "Altruism itself," wrote Solnit, "became an urgent need." Flowers and candles piled up in front of firehouses, and the city settled into the thick arms of those in uniform. Dense networks got a lot denser—children had never been hugged so hard—but for a time, simply to be in New York was to be part of one network. On Saturday night, September 29, Lorne Michaels opened *Saturday Night Live* standing between Mayor Giuliani, Bernie Kerik, Tom Von Essen, and officials from the Port Authority. "Can we be funny?" asked Michaels. To which Rudy said, "Why start now?" While New Yorkers now had official permission to laugh, grief was still openly displayed and understood; the walls papered with the faces of the missing served as shrines, along with the *Times*'s "Portraits of Grief" section, that provided a full obituary for every victim.

And as New York mourned the dead of the World Trade Center, it felt at times as if it were mourning much more than what had happened on 9/11, that a greater catharsis was taking place. So many had died over the last twenty years, so many had been taken, and New York had never really cried, or at least cried together: all the waiters who sang opera at night, who'd died young and alone; the Bronx kid, good at math, who'd slung glass one night on the wrong corner; all the lives wasted and wasted away on gurneys and crack house floors. New Yorkers had moved on in Reformation New York, they'd also moved past all that death. But wrapped in the cowl of 9/11, the full grief of past decades was released. The photo of the Falling Man echoed Wojnarowicz's tumbling buffalo. As David Carr wrote about the new realities: "Everyone who comes after will never understand," he wrote. "The dust will be with us forever." In many ways, 9/11 was the final vindication of people like Holly Whyte, Jane Jacobs, and Gordon Davis who believed that New Yorkers wanted to trust each other and *did*; that they had a natural inclination to live reasonably and civilly with each other. Some did run to the suburbs, or to Brooklyn; "the river makes a world of difference," reported one broker. But most New Yorkers dug in and talked more to their neighbors, to anyone who would listen, extended themselves and their idea of what their community was with permanent effect. Reformation New York had fallen with the World Trade Center, and while Reimagined New York to come was only possible because of the changes and mutations of the two New Yorks before, it would begin with a delicacy, a gentleness, and a unity never seen in the city before, and certainly not during the last eight years. Unfortunately, as it would turn out, civility and kindness don't necessarily equal justice.

Rudy Giuliani led the way through it all, from the moment he grabbed a reporter from NY1 and delivered his first public statement at 10:54 a.m. in the firehouse at Sixth and Houston. Finished with chemo, he seemed to be everywhere, City Hall always in control of the smallest details. Maybe it was Judy Nathan or confronting his own mortality, but Rudy managed to provide a beacon of empathy and comfort to all New Yorkers no matter who they were, how much they made, or the color of their skin. "Tomorrow New York is going to be here," he said, which was exactly what New Yorkers needed to hear. He inspired duty and confidence, made himself the conduit for the city's grief, attending a near-constant cycle of funerals and memorial services as the Pile burned. The "One City, One Standard" that Giuliani had impressed on New York often against its will was now realized briefly through tragedy and kindness, and it remained in the air as long as the smell Downtown. One could only wonder what Reformation New York could've been if *this* man had governed.

But that grace couldn't last forever.

New kinds of networks formed that would direct the next twelve years, and especially the restoration of Lower Manhattan: The survivors of those killed became a protected group, along with the fire department, understandably, but also the police, who'd just a year before been excoriated for their brutality and excesses. Battery Park City, already an enclave, would've cut itself loose from the island if they could. Those who'd been at the World Trade Center that morning would always have the last word. Conflicts began. The traditional rivalry between the police and fire departments played out on the Pile as the rescue mission sank into a dispiriting search for remains. Both sides claimed Ground Zero as a sacred space: the NYPD had lost 23 on 9/11; the FDNY more than

300, the deadliest day in its history. Most of the FDNY specialists who would have directed all this had died, including the hazmat experts, so inexperienced men took mad risks, scaling tons of intricately enmeshed steel, breathing toxic smoke from the Pile still burning a hundred feet down, objects pulled from it still red-hot and glowing as late as mid-October. Work came to a dead stop whenever someone heard what sounded like a knock or cry for help, yet save for rarities like a sweater and the occasional fireman's boot, almost everything had been turned to dust. "There is despair on the faces of the firemen and in their posture," wrote *The New Yorker*, "hunched forward, heads down." As the days passed, the finding of any police or fire remains became a stylized ceremony; civilians, wrote William Langewiesche, got a 'jaded 'bag 'em and tag 'em' approach." Turf battles broke out, building to an all-out fistfight early in November. The futile mission had merely extended grief without processing it. Without bodies, closure is more difficult, but it began to seem that some never wanted to close the open wound that was Ground Zero and saw instead a permanent rationale for maintaining control; Solnit calls it "elite panic." The official story of 9/11 wrapped everything in flags, even as evidence mounted that the shrinking death toll had as much to do with civilian heroics as the first responders, sacrificed to poor communications. The mayor scolded a rescue worker on live radio who had the temerity to ask for Christmas Day off.

"For many New Yorkers," as Nancy Foner points out, "life in the months after September was mainly business as usual" depending on where you lived and worked, but that was true mainly in a physical sense. Meanwhile, they navigated the rising discord between their traditional liberalism and their anger; their helplessness and their taste for war; the calls from on high to go shopping and get back to normal while the world remained anything but. The monolith Yankees turned their inevitable run for the title into an underdog story full of walk-off homers; "Is This It?" by the Strokes played in countless Brooklyn apartments. For many who lived on what Spalding Gray used to call "an island off the coast of America," *The Daily Show* became a nightly vent as New Yorkers were, as John Homans wrote, "forced to stand up not only for our foreign policy but also for our celebrities, our tract houses, our workaholism, Disney . . ."—in short, many of the things they'd come here to avoid, or were at least still trying to get accustomed to. If Giuliani hadn't entirely succeeded in making the city like the rest of America, 9/11 had now made it more American than anywhere else. Which distracted from how rigged the stock market still was and all the other disquiets and doubts that had grown since the market had popped.

And, sadly, even Giuliani hadn't changed that much. As the rescheduled primary approached in late September, behind the scenes he and his staff floated the idea of overturning term limits just for him; the day before the primary he gave this wan endorsement of the democratic process: "People should go out and vote. If they want to." Afterward, with Bloomberg set on the Republican side and Mark Green to face surprise Dem winner Fernando Ferrer in an October runoff, Giuliani met all three candidates to demand a 90-day extension; if he didn't get it, he'd appeal to the public for an extraordinary third term. "I wouldn't vote for him for anything other than a restricted position in New York," said Ed Koch, who considered a few more months of Rudy a not-entirely terrible idea, with a caveat—"He'd be a danger to the country if he were president." Bloomberg gingerly agreed in hopes of an endorsement and so, inexplicably, did Green, Rudy's mortal enemy, thus blowing a hole in his own campaign. Only when Ferrer called Giuliani's bluff did the "Mayor of the World" pull back, left to be satisfied with the adulation of everyone from Kofi Annan to David Letterman, *Talk* magazine gushing that "New York without Giuliani will be like Rome without Caesar, Brooklyn without its bridge, a bagel without the cream cheese."

Along with Giuliani's old egotism, the city's racial fissures showed again, too. Ferrer accepted Sharpton's endorsement, then seemed surprised when White voters stepped firmly if unenthusiastically behind Green, whose admirable public service career was undercut by a sense that no one admired it more than him. "Mark Green is obnoxious," said Koch, "and Freddy is not. That's a fundamental difference." Green squeaked past Ferrer, but attempts to unify the party fell apart and Labor did the minimum. Meanwhile, Bloomberg spent an unprecedented $74 million, using digital data on virtually every voter to direct personalized messaging, an approach that said all you needed to know about how he'd govern. And yet, given all that, Green remained the favorite, the

Democrat in a city ostensibly full of Democrats; Al D'Amato inadvertently referred to him as "Mayor Green" in an interview. Rudy gave Bloomberg a last-minute low-key endorsement, but even then few pundits took him seriously; "Every sign," wrote Elizabeth Kolbert, "points to his being a Pantalone-like figure who is parted from a great deal of money and humiliated in the bargain." Even Bloomberg expected to lose, but he slipped past Green by 35,000 votes, splitting the Jewish and Latino vote, and pulling 29% of Blacks.

On December 15, the final standing piece of the World Trade Center—a four-story section of the façade called "the shroud"—was taken down and a few days later, the fires deep in the Pile were finally struck.

IV. Reimagination

The Pile, the Pit, and the Bullpen

I t barely snowed that winter, so with tourists watching from special platforms, workers swarmed the Pile nonstop. At lunch, the bars and delis nearby filled with the firemen and construction workers sifting through 8 million tons of rubble; at night, banks of lights bore down, cold and benumbed. Stars and politicians handed out water for the cameras. Corporations made sure their logos were visible on whatever they donated while exhausted workers showered at Stuyvesant High across West Street and slept in the pews of St. Paul's. One survivor, Fritz Koenig's sculpture *Sphere at Plaza Fountain*, was moved to Battery Park; other large pieces of debris went to a hangar at JFK. Ground Zero had its own gravity, sucked you in by your grief, stopped time even as the Pile shrank and talk of change began. Few around it were ready for change, though. This gouge in the earth, forever home to vanished husbands, murdered wives, parents of children left behind, a national trauma and national symbol, now meant so much to so many that it was frozen in the density of its purpose.

About seven hundred yards away, the room that once housed the Board of Estimate swarmed, too, with men and women in smart suits and spectator pumps. Mayor Bloomberg had converted it into a bullpen with cubicles for all his deputy mayors and department heads. No need for an 8:00 a.m. meeting anymore because from now on the mayor would be in the middle of everything at all times. A huge TV

screen playing six different channels hung on the back wall. Buzzing
with information and power, this was the new heart of City Hall. The
last three mayors had all started in mid-crisis, but here was the fog and
fear of real war. More than 100,000 jobs had already been lost; 18,000
small businesses closed, tourism halved, $2 billion down in tax revenue;
the New York Fed estimated $21.6 billion in damage, and any further
retreat from New York could be devastating. Happily, Bloomberg's
first days were free of Giuliani's acid. The morning after the election,
the mayor breakfasted with Fernando Ferrer and didn't only shake
hands with Sharpton at the 100 Black Men gala, he'd gotten applause
at the National Action Network. He'd met with union leaders. Since
1982 Bloomberg had been playing three moves ahead, and that's what
most New Yorkers wanted right now—a unified path forward. Deputy
mayors and department heads weren't allowed to fight publicly, or even
privately; his Reimagined New York would use its inside voice, get its
homework done early, and even tackle the extra credit question. "We are
all suddenly nice," complained the not especially nice Michael Wolff.
"We are all cowed."

Giuliani delivered his last speech bathed in the glow of St. Paul's
chandeliers. Connected to every memory of that day, his opinions on
Ground Zero held immense weight, and he believed it shouldn't be
developed. Instead, he said, "We should think about a soaring monument . . ." With the wind tugging faded pictures of the missing off
lampposts and walls, two impulses pulled at New York. Ground Zero
made it impossible to forget the violation and the anger, the terrible
sacrifices, and many felt all that brutality and pain needed to be permanently stamped into Lower Manhattan. But the sad inescapable
fact was that after only a week or so, it was clear that life would go on.
Samuel Beckett suddenly made sense: the world had ended . . . and
yet life continued. "Every now and then," said NYU's Michael Schill,
"you get to a period when you say the face of the city may be changed
forever." Michael Bloomberg's term would bring the most dramatic
era of physical change since Robert Moses, starting this first year as an
expression of the city's dialogue between its urge to never forget and,
as he once said, just get on with it. This third evolution—Reimagined
New York—would finally drag the city out of its industrial past. But

it would also express the dynamic within Bloomberg himself between money and expertise, between profit and public service. The result would be the most effective City Hall in memory—at what it chose to be effective at.

Never Forget

No one and everyone knew what should happen at Ground Zero. No one and everyone was in charge. One thing for certain was that the City would have surprisingly little to say; Giuliani and Pataki had put the Lower Manhattan Development Corporation (LMDC) in State hands to keep it away from Mark Green, expected to win at the time, and the $20 billion in White House aid had to go through Albany. Nineteen public agencies claimed parts of the sixteen-acre site along with craggy seventy-year-old developer Larry Silverstein, who in a stroke of monumentally bad timing had just signed a 99-year lease to take over the World Trade Center; he'd only missed his usual Windows on the World breakfast because he'd gone to the dermatologist. Known to wring the last penny out of a deal, he had only $14 million of his own money at stake so he wasn't going anywhere. "Generally speaking," said one lawyer, "everybody found him impossible and full of shit." The Port Authority, owner of the sixteen acres, had its own agendas. The mall had been immensely profitable, and the PA needed to restore its bottom line, and on top of that, their offices had been in the towers, colleagues had been killed, so rebuilding was personal. The victims' families clustered into organizations that wanted the whole site as a memorial, while those who lived nearby wanted a memorial but, as Bloomberg said, they didn't "want to live in a memorial." They saw a chance to add stores, housing, and parks to their neighborhood. And finally the nation demanded an expression of defiance that should as much as possible resemble an extended middle finger. The person notionally in charge of all this was George Pataki, running for a third term, who decided that the best thing for his campaign was to kick any real choices to the other side of Election Day. So began a twelve-year melee over Ground Zero.

With the cleanup going faster than anyone thought possible, Pataki charged the LMDC's head, bow-tied pragmatist and Yale urban planner

Alexander Garvin, with a to-do list of massive tasks that included selecting a memorial, revitalizing Lower Manhattan, and working with the Port Authority to plan a new WTC complex. New Yorkers were also to be consulted on what they wanted at Ground Zero; a series of gallery shows, community workshops, and the first of two Listening to the City events hosted by the Regional Planning Association all pointed to a preference for balancing commerce and commemoration that the LMDC reflected in its first Request for Proposals in April. And then the confusion began. With two plans already in play—the Port Authority had assumed *it* would be making the master plan while Silverstein had David Childs of Skidmore, Owings & Merrill working on one, too—the LMDC chose Beyer Blinder Belle to develop six "design alternatives" intended as a starting point for what it and the public believed was *the* plan for Ground Zero. Those who went to their unveiling at Federal Hall on July 12 expecting full-blown designs instead saw little more than shapes arranged in various ways around the site to show possibilities; "six ways to slice the pie," according to the *Times's* Herbert Muschamp. A week or so later, 4,000 New Yorkers at the second Listening to the City event aired their disappointment with jury duty conscientiousness. "The moment provided enlightened democratic engagement at the highest level," wrote Robert Ivy in *Architectural Record*. Thrilled to be asked, they said they wanted a skyscraper and a mixed-use area connected to Lower Manhattan, but most of all they wanted boldness; they wanted "catalytic bigness." Garvin announced an "Innovative Design Study," soliciting plans from seven big-name architects that would signal "that the city has been rebuilt in a triumphant way." This wasn't an official competition—Garvin made it clear there'd be no commitment to build the winner and even reserved the right to mix and match. It'll be a mess, he'd said, but it would be like the writing of the Constitution.

Among big hitters like Norman Foster, Richard Maier, Gwathmey Siegel, and Rafael Viñoly was Daniel Libeskind, an academic architect known for unbuildable sketches, abstract theories, and dressing in black from head to cowboy-booted toes. He was also the only one who visited Ground Zero. Standing next to the slurry wall, he remembered sailing into New York Harbor in 1959, a chubby thirteen-year-old Polish accordion prodigy born of two Holocaust survivors; for twenty years his father had worked in a print shop on Stone Street only a few blocks away. Daniel had gone to Bronx Science; he understood the city's deep vein of schmaltz and recalling his first glimpse of the Statue of Liberty made him decide that memory needed to be central. Two months later, Libeskind led off the live televised presentation of the entries with Memory Foundation—five towers spiraling up in an arc, each gradually higher to the summit of the fifth, 1,776 feet high, together echoing the rising profile of the Statue of Liberty, with a Park of Heroes and a Wedge of Light below that would strike the ground every September 11. Norman Foster followed with two sleek towers entwined so that they "split and kiss and touch and become one," while the superteam of Richard Meier, Peter Eisenman, Gwathmey Siegel, and Steven Holl presented a gargantuan structure out of a dystopian comic. The only other real competitor was Rafael Viñoly, whose THINK consortium planned two elegant framework cylinders the size of the Twin Towers.

For the next six weeks, wrote Paul Goldberger, "there seemed to be a public event about Ground Zero every night." The LMDC's website got 6 million hits and some 100,000 went to see the maquettes, the architects pitched their plans at forums and before every camera because it all was, really, a kind of popularity contest that Libeskind, flag pin always on his black lapel, tugging on emotions, excelled at in a way that the other architects began to find a bit *déclassé*. In February, the LMDC named Libeskind and Viñoly the finalists and battle lines were drawn for one last month that took critique into cattiness. At the final presentation, Pataki called the Viñoly towers "skeletons"; Bloomberg compared them to the Elmhurst gas tanks. Libeskind got the nod.

And yet nothing had been truly settled. "I was sure we hadn't picked his design," says Garvin later. "We had simply picked his plan." Silverstein still had Childs working, there was still a memorial to select, and the PA had its transport hub and mall to design. But American Express, Merrill Lynch, and Bank of New York all let it be known that patience was running low, so Pataki stomped on the pedal. He announced that on July 4, 2004, the eve of the GOP Convention that summer in New York, there'd be a groundbreaking. Of something.

Just Get On with It

The real crisis, though, lay beyond the fence around Ground Zero, in the 205,000 acres where the tourist economy had been gutted, an exodus of people and businesses loomed inevitable, and the problems went deeper than 9/11. New York had already been wallowing in its post-dotcom recession when the planes hit, made worse by Giuliani's lack of engagement with business; thousands of back-office jobs had been moved to Jersey City and Hoboken; biotech had passed the city by, and infrastructure had run down. But unlike Ground Zero, Bloomberg could act here. His electrical engineering degree let him understand more about the city's infrastructure than any of his predecessors; creator of a global conglomerate, he knew finance and management; and a plutocrat, he had deep pockets, even if like most plutocrats he was insulated from the suffering and challenges of everyday New Yorkers. Since the self-funded mayor had no debts to repay, he and his transition chief, the peripatetic Nat Leventhal, were free to name a diverse team of deputy mayors that included Democrats and Republicans, a woman, and an African American. The new administration would also include Koch alumni beyond Harris; people like Deputy Mayor Marc Shaw, Cultural Affairs Commissioner Kate Levin, and many who'd served on the Charter Revision Committee. While they didn't always share the same policy goals, these established Democrats operated as a network within City Hall and academics such as Mitchell Moss and Ester Fuchs had meaningful access.

Bloomberg wasn't just the center of the Bullpen, though; he was the hub of the city now, connected in some crucial way to almost every one of its political, economic, social, and cultural networks. *He* was the Crisis Regime for this crisis, and tasseled loafers up on his desk, he took Rockefeller's philosophy that giving creates power to a new level. "Philanthropy," writes Chris McNickle, "was a form of patriotism to Bloomberg" who charged Patricia Harris with reviving the Mayor's Fund to Advance New York City, started by Giuliani to fund initiatives outside the budget process. Over the next twelve years she would raise $1.4 billion in donations from the city's wealthy and its corporations—*noblesse oblige*, if you knew what was good for you. Business elites, finding the strings of their networks tugged by City Hall, "gave back"; *New York* reported sightings of businessmen nostalgic for "an older New York, where all business was local and all relationships—civic, philanthropic, social, political—were believed to be tied together for the common good." The New York City Partnership brought real estate and business leaders together with unions to create "Rebuild NYC" and, with the mayor himself a member, it replaced the Manhattan Institute as a source of research, ideas, and money. The whole administration was, as Julian Brash writes, "undergirded by a sense of collective identity founded upon social and personal connections." Where the three prior administrations had brought in outside consultants, many in Bloomberg's administration (including Bloomberg) brought more experience in management than government, along with a belief that growth demanded what McNickle calls "muscular management of municipal assets, not laissez-faire policies."

The immediate task was the same as Koch's back in 1978: stop the ship from sinking. This time the mayor had to plug an estimated $11 billion deficit over the next two years. There'd be more borrowing and only one huge new tax, on cigarettes, but otherwise cuts across the board: new stadiums for the Yankees and Mets put on hold, no new headquarters for the New York Stock Exchange, no new spending on the MTA, and more cuts to NYCHA, already in trouble; fewer cops. Housing wasn't an issue when the problem ahead seemed to be keeping people. Really saving the city, though, would require more than twisting knobs and changing tax rates. Rudy's New York had become pickled in nostalgia, and nostalgia had no pull on Mayor Mike. "The past is past," he'd later say about 9/11, "but we can do something about the future." Fusing recovery and strategy, he'd scrape away the old industrial legacy, escape the Boom and Bust cycle, and turn New York into Bloomberg: The City, a site for Twenty-first Century global exchange as innovative, strategic, and full of rewards for hard work as Bloomberg: the Company. This sweeping transformation would be planned and executed by two very different people, each of whom spoke to a side of Bloomberg.

One of them was Daniel Doctoroff, a Michigan native, Harvard grad, and Lehman Brothers veteran, mentored by Koch's former

Deputy Mayor Peter Solomon. Like Bloomberg, he'd largely regarded New York as the place he made money until he'd been swept away by the 1994 World Cup semifinal between Italy and Bulgaria and became obsessed with bringing the Olympics to New York City. He'd hired Alexander Garvin, who'd identified seven sites in four boroughs that fell roughly on a north-south axis along a redeveloped East River shoreline and an east-west one stretching from an Olympic Village in Long Island City across to a stadium at the West Side Yards; hence the name Olympic X. Giuliani supported the bid, and the Jets had offered $800 million to make the stadium their home after the Games. As Bloomberg and Leventhal looked at the task ahead, Doctoroff and his ambitions for Olympic X jumped out as the possible framework and catalyst for a Reimagined New York—whether or not the city actually got the Olympics, the sites would be redeveloped with the IOC deadlines helping to blast through the process. If the deadlines weren't enough to make all this happen, Doctoroff's legendary temper would.

Doctoroff took the position of Deputy Mayor for Economic Development and Rebuilding, and though his choice for City Planning was obviously Garvin, Bloomberg insisted on his 79th Street neighbor, Amanda Burden. "I knew zoning backwards and forwards," says Burden. "I knew exactly what I wanted to do." Some in the development world considered her a hobbyist, and that included Doctoroff. "[S]he initially gave off the appearance of being little more than a dilettante," he wrote of a woman who had a master's in urban planning from Columbia, who'd overseen the design of Battery Park City from 1983 to 1990, and been on the City Planning Commission for a decade. More to the point, she'd been "sarcastic and dismissive" of Olympic X when he'd first presented them to the Commission. They weren't an easy couple, Doctoroff with his trading-floor temper and Burden's politesse, but they would be the two sides of the Bloomberg dialectic, what Burden would call, "building like Moses with Jacobs in mind." Doctoroff's big vision for a "virtuous cycle" of development attracting new taxpayers on to existing infrastructure would be balanced by Burden's detailed, design- and community-centered approach. As Chair of the City Planning Commission and Director of City Planning, Burden now rolled much of her wish list into Olympic X and, pointing to the Summer 2005 IOC vote as a deadline, charged ahead into a rezoning process unprecedented in scope and speed. The Olympic Village in LIC would become 5,000 units of affordable housing; the Brooklyn waterfront would get aquatic sports, but also apartment towers; neighborhood after neighborhood would be transformed under the Olympic flag crowned by a stadium over the tracks of the West Side Yards, centerpiece of a 50-million-square-foot mixed-use development Doctoroff christened Hudson Yards intending to add new office space to the city's aging stock.

In February, Bloomberg outlined the business strategy of Reimagined New York to the Association for a Better New York. Instead of executive swaps and retention deals, City Hall would fully synthesize its strategies, management methods, and interlocking networks with the business community, actively preparing the ground for private intervention and investment wherever possible. New York would "think of its job-creating, tax-paying employers, big and small, as valued clients"—not an original thought, that—and create mixed-use central business districts in all five boroughs. The goal was similar to what Koch, Sturz, and Lipper had all had in mind, but not exactly: growth, of course, but the "profits" would go into transformation this time, not reclamation. And hopefully, enough of those people would be Bloomberg's type of people. "[I]f you want New York to remain the place where people come to make money," wrote Michael Lewis, "make sure it is where they receive the loudest applause when they do it." In November, 9/11 still aching, New York beat out San Francisco to become the US Candidate City.

The Theater of Terror

Ray Kelly had been working as head of global security for Bear Stearns when the planes hit the Twin Towers. An unofficial advisor to Bloomberg, postelection rumors had him taking over Schools with Kerik staying at One Police Plaza, but when the call came, Kelly took Kerik's job. "From the distance," said John Timoney, "the NYPD looks like a brand-new, shiny Cadillac. But as you get closer, you see that the shiny new car has a seized engine. So Ray's got to go in and fix the engine." Morale was bad, and minorities didn't trust the police. Kelly wanted to prove that he could get crime down even further, and that he could do it the right way. "I understood that crime fighting wasn't exactly Mike Bloomberg's top priority," wrote Kelly later. "This meant I had relatively free hand in running the police department as I saw fit." Over the next twelve years he would become, according to *Newsday*'s Leonard Levitt, "the most influential police commissioner in the city's history." Sponsoring cricket leagues and playing steel drums at the Labor Day Carnival, he went in search of cooperation and recruits and expanded the fight against crime with new technologies. But the *real* bad guys now, at least the *worst* bad guys, were the terrorists, and the FBI and national intelligence had let the city down both in 1993 and on 9/11. Counterterrorism, he said, "would require a fundamental rethinking of the role of the police in New York City, a thorough reordering of the department's priorities, and some genuine cultural change." Counterterrorism was Kelly's chance to remake the force in his image.

Just a month or so after his swearing in, the NYPD became the first and only American police force to run international spies, operate its own cyberunit, linguistics team, and infectious disease department, paid for off the public budget by the New York Police Foundation. Heavily armed convoys of black Suburbans—"Hercules" teams—randomly descended on sensitive locations to throw off terrorists, much to the distress of unwitting New Yorkers. The police stopped issuing permits for political protest marches in Manhattan. In May 2002, the *Times* reported with admiration and a drop of suspicion that Compstat had "grown into a sweeping data-collection machine that traces hundreds of factors, many of which appear distant from the nuts and bolts of police work," but how it was getting that information raised serious questions. The NYPD settled a racial profiling case, agreeing to issue an explicit nonracial policy on stops and keep data on them, but an April 2003 ruling granted a wider berth on information gathering—the NYPD no longer needed specific information that a crime was being committed to open an investigation. Against FBI practice, a blandly named Demographics Unit infiltrated Muslim communities. FBI chief Robert Mueller raised an eyebrow—then allowed them to continue. A police force that had regained public trust by letting people live without fear was now justifying wider powers and bigger budgets by teaching them to fear new things.

Mike Has No Such Limitations

A year into his term, Michael Tomasky wrote that Bloomberg still "seemed to have no idea what he'd gotten himself into." "He's a rich man," said one unimpressed citizen, "and he don't give a shit about anybody else." His 41% approval rating plunged further when the budget deficit forced him to sign an 18.5% property tax hike along with a new tax on high incomes and a two-year sales tax increase. "I imagine it has been years," said Brooklyn councilman Bill de Blasio, "since he has to had to grapple with what most of us grapple with." "He's got a sense of the city as an amalgam of balance sheets and management reports," continued Tomasky, "but not as the home of 8 million actual people."

To which Bloomberg shrugged. "Most of us are motivated at least in part by other people," Doctoroff would write. "Mike has no such limitations." Nor was he limited by the big checks he wrote to the RNC. "Bloomberg's a Democrat!" wrote Tomasky. "So are most of his top aides, the vast majority of his commissioners, and the lion's share of his proposals and priorities." In June 2002, the City Council had tripled the tax on cigarettes, now $7 a pack, and in December Bloomberg signed the Smoke-Free Air Act banning smoking in all bars and restaurants. Like the Pooper-Scooper panic, all sentient life in New York was predicted to end without a postprandial Marlboro, yet in the first year alone, some 140,000 New Yorkers quit smoking and smoke-free bars and restaurants would actually show higher receipts. In early March 2003, the 311 system came online, providing direct feedback on City services, and Immigrant Affairs became a permanent department. Without much of a fuss, Bloomberg had gotten control of the schools—most involved just hadn't wanted to hand them to Giuliani. Schools-based clinics were started, reproductive health added to the curriculum. In December, as part of the five-borough growth strategy, he announced a $3 billion program to create or preserve 65,000 housing units, the biggest push since Koch; some of the land would come from remediating toxic industrial brownfields. He signed a Living Wage agreement for home health and childcare workers. But the mayor never bothered lining up political support for any of this; he simply announced it. Fires were down 60% over the past 25 years, so he closed three fire stations, saving a meager $8 million at the cost of an enormous outcry that he entirely ignored. Limiting newspaper boxes and fake art-resellers helped the Manhattan Institute crowd discover their love of civil liberties; "With Giuliani's 'zero tolerance' there was a sense that the policy would benefit everyone in the city," said Walter K. Olsen. "With Bloomberg, it's more like nannyism." (Translation: Enforcing Quality of Life laws against minorities benefits everyone, but moving against things White people do is nannyism.)

An alarm went off, though, in January 2003, when Bloomberg referred to the city as a "luxury product." He said it to support his belief that businesses should not only not get retention deals, but they should pay a premium to reap the benefits of being in New York. Stressing culture, education, research, and medicine would buoy the tourist economy and replace lost manufacturing jobs by making the city "even more attractive to the world's most talented people" who were not at all tired, poor, huddled, or wretched; homeless or tempest-tost like New York's original "customers." But Daniel Libeskind's family hadn't come in search of a luxury product. Who and what would be left behind as New York Just Got On with It?

Chapter Twenty-five

Oz Wasn't Built in a Day

A Pax Bloombergus was now declared. When Officer Richard Neri accidentally shot nineteen-year-old Timothy Stansbury, both Bloomberg and Kelly immediately said the shooting was unjustified, and the mayor spoke at the funeral. The confession of Matias Reyes exonerated the Central Park Five, and after the Louima verdicts were overturned, Bloomberg visited a Black church as well as the 70th Precinct. "The greatest thing he's done," said Ed Koch, "is he's changed the climate of the city so that people are no longer frightened of the mayor"; instead, the day's color-coded alert status told you just how frightened to be of terrorists. Jesse Green wrote that gays and lesbians now felt "surer, safer, more integrally American than anyone dreamed possible in 1970." Drag fabulous gave way to the quotidian *Queer Eye for the Straight Guy*; "gay style," commented one writer, ". . . just feels like New York style." Fifty-eight percent of New Yorkers were in favor of same-sex marriage. But there was a generation gap now. "The young had the choice to live quietly because of the bold fury of the old," wrote Sarah Schulman. "When you meet a queer New Yorker over the age of forty, this should be your first thought." Tony Kushner said audiences were now "wistful" about Larry Kramer. In the process of being reimagined, New York was seemingly too busy and still too bruised to hate.

And "New York" was now more than just Manhattan, even if Bloomberg himself remained a consummate Manhattanite: a transplant, a product of hard work and good luck; a social liberal who liked money and assumed that educated people who could hold up their side at a dinner party should make the decisions; someone who believed he deserved what he had. He'd offered his $10.6 billion Vision for Lower Manhattan in a 31-minute speech Paul Goldberger called "the most sophisticated statement on urban design and planning delivered by any mayor of New York since John Lindsay." But even before his five-borough strategy, New York's understanding of itself had expanded so that the old rivalries between Uptown and Downtown, Upper East Side vs. Upper West Side were now really between Manhattan and Brooklyn. Despite the two-year waiting list for a Birkin bag, *The Nanny Diaries* on the bestseller list, and that new Sally Hershberger salon down the block from Jeffrey, Manhattan's brand of Lifestyle was no longer the cutting edge and now the borough was looking at its faded glory the same sad way Liza Minnelli, embodiment of the city's long gone trouper psyche, had watched a rebroadcast of 1972's *Liza with a Z*. "I was sexy," she said wistfully. The temples of High Culture would always be there, but Lincoln Center, for example, omphalos of the performing arts, had fallen under what Alex Ross called "[a] nimbus of corporate blandness." As the fortunate dropped thousands at Per Se, the real proof of a foodie now was their list of Korean joints in Queens; the farm-to-table, offal eating at Craft and Spotted Pig felt like something brought from Brooklyn, not the other way around. Complaints about the passing of what was small, old, and unique in Manhattan came freighted with what Adam Gopnik called "a Tragedy of the Uncommons; weird things make the city worth living in, but though each individual wants them, no one individual wants to pay to keep them going." Little Italy was a prime example. Giuliani had pulled the San Gennaro Festival out of Mob hands in 1995, so Sorrento Cheese had stepped in as sponsor, and few Manhattanites went there even ironically. For all the tears when Patti Smith played the final show at CBGB, the "genuine" punks were in Red Hook. Paradise Garage was now Bungalow 8, a club so exclusive that noncelebrities need not ask for a table. The 10021 zip code on the Upper East Side was now only America's 255th most expensive to live in. Pat Buckley and Kitty Carlisle Hart died, and Brooke Astor lived in the care of the De La Rentas amid ugly controversy as to whether son Anthony had mistreated her. Brooke had never denied being a bad mother—her man always came first—but, as one friend admitted, Anthony was "pretty drippy." Manhattan really *was* in need of a future.

Nine-eleven had something to do with that, but recovery depended on the neighborhood. While traumatized Battery Park City all but turned its back on the city, by the end of 2002, researchers found that "9/11 no longer permeated community consciousness" in TriBeCa. Further east in Chinatown, though, closed subways and the logistics of getting around checkpoints and closed streets along with sinking retail had strangled the garment industry, and government aid hadn't helped much because it was earmarked for businesses south of Canal even though 80% of Chinatown was north of it. In Harlem, on the other hand, the Gateway Building, Gotham Plaza, and Harlem USA all neared completion, and Reverend Butts wanted to turn Smalls Paradise into an IHOP—it was, he said, just another bar. At 125th and Malcolm X, ADC and Forest City Ratner had dug a huge pit for what would be a Marshall's, a CVS, and a bank branch. Outside of Hamilton Heights, Whites were still relatively uncommon, as was homeownership—only 6% here as compared to 30% in the rest of the city. Across Manhattan, the veneer of calm was thin as the White House pushed forward into a war no one felt quite right about and "God Bless America" at Yankee Stadium went from catharsis to nightly *kabuki*. Muzzled by the manufactured need for wartime solidarity, Media, one of the sources of Manhattan's power, felt dented and dislocated. These were, said one reporter, "apocalyptic times" for the Press; a plagiarism scandal and a surprising pro-war stance based on dodgy reportage brought public apologies from the *Times* while the *Wall Street Journal* tried to fend off Rupert Murdoch. Political analysts like Keith Olbermann, Rachel Maddow, and Paul Krugman pushed back against the embargo on dissent as Jon Stewart, who called his show "fake news," jumped from comedian to pundit as it best served. Books? "I mean, books suck," counseled Michael Wolff, now reduced to writing them. "Books may be the true lowest-common-denominator medium." The dream of a respectable life on the midlist capped with a spot on the Line at Elaine's was indeed dead because few writers dreamed it anymore. Now searchable, the Internet figured in daily choices from buying groceries on FreshDirect and finding a date on Match.com to browsing DailyCandy. Gawker aimed at the media overlords for whom its commentators made lunch reservations. "We have tons of tipsters," said editor Jessica Coen, twenty-five. "Is it accurate? Not necessarily, but it is what it is." Though great art was everywhere, the trick was telling quality from price tag. Damien Hirst participated in a syndicate that paid a reported $50 million for a human skull cast with 8,000 diamonds—a work that *he* created. Was it any good? Did it really matter? The iPod had landed and Woody Allen left for London.

As Nobel Prize winner Joseph Stiglitz called attention to the fact that "Since 1990, the number of people living on less than two dollars a day has risen by more than a hundred million," the world's moneymakers were already finding their way back to Bloomberg's Luxury City. Though McKinsey advised the City to rely less on FIRE, both Wall Street and Real Estate became only more technical and obscure, dealing in sums so huge and abstract that they defied connection to the three meals and roof that millions of New Yorkers now aspired to. The Bull returned, unkillable, after the disinfecting prosecutions of Martha Stewart, Sam Waksal, Bernie Ebbers, Dennis Kozlowski, and just about everyone at Enron, and a campaign by Attorney General Eliot Spitzer, considered by *New York* one of the city's sexiest people, against the whole dotcom era he felt had "degenerated into a conspiracy." Anyone with money or sense now worked at, invested in, or ran a hedge fund, each limited to 499 investors with a minimum level of assets. Unregulated by the SEC, they also enjoyed no government protections, which meant leaving the rich to their own devices; historically, a dangerous idea. Pension funds and foundations handed them billions while small investors could buy shares in funds that invested in hedge funds. Some of these feeders steered to Bernie Madoff, whose growing reputation now drew the money of powerful families and Jewish philanthropies. As many comfortable lives rose atop fraudulent wealth, Madoff told himself he was doing good. John Thain, new head of the Stock Exchange, permitted technology that cut the time for executing a trade from 15 seconds to 300 milliseconds. The trading floor was kept for tourists. The rest of the smart money went to real estate, pumped by falling interest rates. REITs exploded, and starchitects arrived in force: Charles Gwathmey, Jean Nouvel, and Norman Foster all had buildings going up and Richard

Meier's Perry Street apartments—"lavish, late and leaky," according to Deborah Schoeneman—led a string of developments down the lower West Side riverfront where Westway would have been. A building's location mattered less to Lifestyle than its fitness center and Wolf stoves; since 30% of the owners were speculators, any cost concerns were that they didn't cost enough. Meanwhile, rent control wound down—around 100,000 out of 1 million apartments had left over the past decade with thousands more to come, and most Mitchell-Lama buildings converted to market-rate co-ops. Affordable housing was quickly becoming a problem.

What Manhattan did best now was visible on Thursday nights on NBC, when Donald Trump hosted a reality television show made by the producer of *Survivor* called *The Apprentice*, each episode ending with him saying "You're fired" to that week's loser. Seeming to realize that playing himself was the one thing he could do better than anyone else, Trump used this platform to remake his battered image; the three-hour Season Two finale was broadcast live from Lincoln Center.

Eyes rolled, but who was the joke really on when Manhattanites couldn't afford the FastPass for their own city? Increasingly they were feeling like the extras now, while the stars were people like lovely Anna Anisimova, model-cum-NYU student and daughter of a Russian aluminum oligarch who'd not only bought her a $10 million apartment in the new Time Warner Center but also shelled out half a million bucks to rent Denise Rich's Hamptons place. Other shiny, young, unsubtle Russians—*zolotaya molodezh* (golden youth)—flooded Fifth Avenue flagships and followed their ranking on Park Avenue Peerage, run by an Indian teenager in Downstate Illinois. The given argument for not simply marching all these rich new arrivals straight to the guillotine was the hefty tax revenue that appeared when they did deign to pay, and that serving them (and the tourists coming back to be in their vicinity) provided an enormous number of jobs. "For most New Yorkers," wrote Daniel Gross, "this is a maddening spectacle: Who are all these people? When will things return to normal?" Never, was the answer. Whether they liked it or not, New Yorkers were made accomplices to global money laundering, commonplace civilization was traded for a job sweeping at Versailles while the jealous soothed their unquiet souls with Shopping Therapy. Home equity loans and cash advances on 0% interest credit cards went to Barneys, Whole Foods, and spring skiing at Alta; for others it went toward rent.

At least Puff Daddy was a New Yorker. Anna Wintour had taken him under wing, guided him through the Paris shows where he kissed Donatella Versace and signed autographs, his recent acquittal for illegal gun possession waved aside. "Fashion was so corporate, so about the money," said Wintour about the sad days before his fall 2001 show at Bryant Park. He'd sold $250 million worth of clothes since then, so maybe the money *was* still part of it, but he indeed sent a new kind of thrill through fashion in his open-collared white shirt, black pin-striped suit, and diamond earring. "Admit it," he once said to a reporter, "I am impeccable."

To further demonstrate the benefits of anonymous hyperwealth, Bloomberg did something unprecedented. By the summer of 2003, despite dismal approval ratings, the City ended FY03 with a surplus; 9/11 hadn't killed New York. In fact, it was doing pretty well. So with the skies clearing, instead of restoring cuts to NYCHA or upping the City's contribution to the MTA, the mayor gave $400 rebates to the 650,000 households who'd absorbed last year's property tax hit. The course was set for Luxury City and the future. Life south of 110th Street was leafier than ever, and polls began to turn north for Mayor Mike. Hosting the coming GOP convention in Summer 2004 was just the world's capital doing business. Wasn't it just easier to go along for the ride? There'd be lots of jobs taking tickets.

West Side Obsessions

The Rockefeller Center at the heart of Bloomberg's Reimagined Manhattan was to be the 40 blocks of Dan Doctoroff's mixed-use, mixed-income Hudson Yards with the boxy, 75,000-seat West Side Stadium demanded by the IOC. Along with plowing over a healthy chunk of gritty, dreary Hell's Kitchen for needed office buildings, enthusiastic estimates had the development producing $500 million a year in tax revenues. By early 2003, the City's OMB had signed off on its complex financing plan, and the business establishment was largely on board, though out of earshot no one really wanted the stadium, even if that meant losing the Games. Since Doctoroff had moved without much involving the State, the big worry was that State Assembly leader Sheldon Silver, already unhappy about all this attention for Midtown while his Downtown district remained frozen in Ground Zero politics, might kill the whole thing out of spite, including the development they *did* want. The RPA supported rezoning but recommended against the stadium and most New Yorkers agreed; 78% were against it if it didn't pay for itself. James Dolan, owner of its potential competitor Madison Square Garden a few blocks east, spent millions waging a public campaign against it.

Few people were more universally disliked than Dolan for driving the Knicks into the ground, but the more Doctoroff, Bloomberg, and the unions insisted the stadium *had* to happen, the more New Yorkers asked why. "When you invite somebody to your house," said Doctoroff, "you tend to clean it up, because you don't want your guests to think you live like a slob." Which was fair enough. But he also had less homey metaphors in mind: "[A] city was like any other product . . . It had customers. It had competitors. It had to be marketed." And there was the rub. Visitors are a fine reason to get your house in order, but it's another thing to convert it into an Airbnb. It might pay the bills, but it stops being yours. Especially when you're not given a choice—Doctoroff's proposed financing structure, creative as it was, strenuously avoided public budgets, approvals, and elected oversight though the IBO estimated it would cost $1.3 billion more to do it that way. Even as Manhattan Borough President C. Virginia Fields came out against the plans, and the *Times* compared them to "a runaway train," Doctoroff was positive he could bull it through since all that was left was an arcane bit of embedded governance: the public authority running it would have to be approved by the three-man State Public Authorities Control Board, consisting of George Pataki, State Senate leader Joseph Bruno, and Sheldon Silver.

Directly south of the stadium, Amanda Burden hooked her own vision of Reimagined New York to Doctoroff's, to both their benefit. After 9/11, Josh David and Robert Hammond came to the conclusion that "The High Line was about New York moving forward," so even though Giuliani had indeed signed the demolition order on his way out,

Burden got Doctoroff to grant a stay so they could run an economic feasibility study. The result turned the tide—$65 million from the City could yield $140 million over twenty years. But tourism wouldn't be enough. Burden's office came up with the answer: in exchange for their air rights over the High Line, owners alongside could build bigger, higher buildings, most likely luxury apartments. "It wasn't her intention," Josh David says later of Jane Jacobs in the West Village, "but what came of it was the creation of the most expensive real estate in New York City." And something very similar was about to happen on the High Line. Meanwhile, it became clear as Doctoroff pushed the stadium and Hudson Yards through the approval process that rubbing some High Line magic on them might help, so Doctoroff became a fan. Community Board 4 and the City Council approved the High Line; in the fall, part of the Meatpacking District was landmarked, and the intricate process of changing title on the High Line went into motion, based on the examples of Central Park and Bryant Park.

At Ground Zero, though, the confusion only got worse. Garvin had been fired from the LMDC, a suspected mole for City Hall, but at least he wouldn't have to deal with The Memorial. Most agreed that the resulting eight finalists weren't bad; they all made you think, but none of them made you feel. The eventual selection in January 2004 of Michael Arad's *Reflecting Absence* and its waterfalls meant the end of Libeskind's exposed slurry wall, the spiritual core of his plan. "I will fight this," he reportedly shouted at an LMDC meeting, "I am the people's architect!" But by the end of the year, Ground Zero would all but swallow Daniel Libeskind. The July unveiling of the Port Authority transit hub made Santiago Calatrava everyone's favorite architect, his vast ribbed building taking flight with the kind of optimism people had been hoping for at the site. And he was just the first architect to outdo Libeskind that year. Though his plan had been officially "chosen," in reality he and David Childs each kept working on separate ones for the Freedom Tower until Silverstein forced them into what Libeskind called "a forced marriage." Six months later he finally signed off on Childs's less fanciful interpretation of his original plan. The *Times* now called him "the incredible shrinking Daniel Libeskind."

Despite the chaos, on July 4, George Pataki got his wish. Deep in the Pit with a PATH train rolling by, the governor had his photo taken alongside Mayor Bloomberg, New Jersey governor James McGreevey, Silverstein, and a twenty-ton block of Adirondack granite—the symbolic cornerstone of the Freedom Tower. Photos taken and hardhats returned, the boulder was settled into a corner of the Pit, never to see light again. "The significance of that site now," said Jane Jacobs of Ground Zero, "is that we don't know what its significance is."

We Got Played

That same day, a long scroll declaring independence from George II was unwound on the steps of Federal Hall by twenty or so protestors dressed in Colonial Glam. Part Burning Man, part Yippie, they called themselves Greene Dragon after the tavern favored by the original revolutionaries. "We're modern-day patriots," said Johnny America, "taking back our government from the corporate monarchy." In late August, they stuck cardboard horse heads on hundreds of bicycles and wove their "horsicles" through rush hour Lexington Avenue led by a blonde woman shouting, "The Republicans are coming! The Republicans are coming!"

Bloomberg had made the case to suspicious New Yorkers that opening the gates to the convention would be a way for Republicans to give back to the city whose suffering they'd waved as a bloody shirt for three years. After Bush had delivered the $20 billion in aid, the administration had gone back to draining money out of New York—in 2002 the city sent Washington $65.9 billion and got back $54.5 billion; the state was 49th in capital funding for the Homeland Security Grant Program—Wyoming got eight times as much per capita. Even emergency health care for first responders was considered just another liberal handout at a time when Mount Sinai found almost three-quarters of those who'd worked on the Pile had new or worsened respiratory problems, that firemen were developing strange lung diseases and cancers. Meanwhile, Rudy was pulling down six-figure payouts for speeches and running down New Yorkers: "In the wake of the attacks on the World Trade Center," he wrote in *Leadership*, "the great majority of New Yorkers—and all Americans—dug deep and pulled together . . ." Bloomberg badly overestimated his adopted party; House Speaker Tom DeLay announced that the GOP would moor a cruise ship in the Hudson so clean-living delegates could remain unsullied. DeLay didn't go through with it, but Bloomberg looked a fool. Republicans still hated New York City.

And the feeling was mutual. The Iraq War had burned away some complaisance, and the brewing protests were as much against Bloomberg's private-jet attitude as the GOP. The City's response indicated that the administration preferred Free Market to Free Speech. First, at the recommendation of Douglas Blonsky and the Conservancy, it denied two left-wing groups permits to meet on the Great Lawn, claiming the crowds would destroy the grass. This wasn't new. New York's history of curbing public gatherings went back to the deadly 1871 Orange Riot, when it became the first American city to require permits for public parades, and as recently as July 1988, Henry Stern had denied the Anti-Defamation League use of the Great Lawn for a concert explicitly because it was political. The two groups would later sue and force the City to keep the Great Lawn open to large events. Another 29 permits had been issued, with the largest for Sunday's march, organized by United for Peace and Justice, a broad collection of 500,000 people of all races, ages, and economic groups, street art, puppetry, and families who walked in 90-degree heat from Chelsea to Midtown and back down to Union Square, with only scattered arrests. "The police are being very laid back and very mellow," said one spokeswoman, despite the NYPD blimps and surveillance cameras. In typical Ray Kelly fashion, Ray Kelly had nice things to say about UPJ, too. And then the niceties ended. The NYPD had been planning for eighteen months, and when the street art and puppets gave way to clashes, Kelly deployed three mobile riot control units with *Soylent Green* efficiency, scooping up entire groups in flexible orange plastic netting and taking them to Pier 57 to be held for as long as Bush was in town, often longer than the 24 hours that the law provides. Some 90% of their cases were dismissed, and the resulting civil suits cost the City more than $30 million. Kelly thought it went extremely well.

Inside the Garden, Bloomberg refused to sit in the President's box while Dick and Lynne Cheney, Giuliani, Pataki, and Arnold

Schwarzenegger invoked "9/11" and "terrorism," the whole show capped off by an eight-minute film about what else but 9/11, written by Peggy Noonan. "You can't beat the mechanics and the work ethic in New York," said the Bush operative who pulled it together. "The city totally saved our ass." Most Manhattanites saw it differently. "The Republicans picked our pockets," wrote Chris Smith. "Or maybe it's more accurate to say we got played perfectly."

Chapter Twenty-six

"B'klyn Cheers, Trembles"

Across the river, wild plants flourished along the Williamsburg shore. Fire spinners had once practiced in this stretch of dead manufacturing, old Poles in lawn chairs ignored skateboarders who'd built their own skate park, but for most it was just a place to smoke a joint in peace or dip a toe in the water as the sun set behind the Manhattan skyline. After Giuliani was blocked from handing this secret space to waste-transfer companies, Hipsters high on whimsy and low on melanin had transformed it into what Daniel Campo calls "an accidental playground" known as the People's Park. Every Sunday afternoon the Hungry March Band who'd stomped naked over the tables at Quiet back on New Year's Eve 1999 practiced their mashup of klezmer, bhangra, roma, and second line in true Williamsburg style—witty, original, and in love with itself. Most New Orleans high school bands were tighter, but the Hungry March Band revived the idea of a community band that appeared unannounced at funerals, protests, and celebrations. In the spirit of Olmsted, skaters, sax players, and fishermen had all exercised their democratic prerogatives here in close proximity, in good cheer, and without permits. During Rudy's Reformation New York, this self-regulating anarchy had begun to feel more like commonplace civilization than the rules of the Central Park Conservancy. In 2000, the State of New York announced plans for a park here, so the invasives were bulldozed, a fence put up, and now the question was whether the Olympics would come first. One way or another this spot, "neither clean nor safe," according to Campo, would be made clean and safe, no matter what the people of Williamsburg wanted.

Brooklyn had always cultivated the romance of its authenticity against the evils of slick Manhattan, and the endless mourning over the Dodgers leaving was really shorthand for losing first its independence in 1898, and then its blue-collar heart when the piers died. But over the last four decades, the brownstoners in Cobble Hill, L train artists, BAM-goers in black, Park Slope lesbians, Fort Greene neo-soul singers, and Ground Zero exiles had all stitched their Lifestyles over the frames of the old neighborhoods they'd moved into and now, declared *New York*, "what was once a reluctant move has become an enthusiastic, don't-look-back migration." Though few who'd gentrified Brooklyn ever considered themselves gentrifiers, they were. Long before 9/11, *The Brooklyn Rail* had pronounced Bushwick "THE NEW SoHo," railing about the death of manufacturing while calling for more of the same live-work zoning that had killed it in SoHo. Money was obviously driving the process when it came to real estate, but the social and cultural gentrification was led by a new generational tide that had been pushing deeper into the borough since the mid-'90s.

Unlike the original East Village exiles, Hipsters had few delusions about a better world, their rush to "authenticity" through craft traditions, Sazeracs, and snout-to-tail eating, their affection for vaudeville and White trash kitsch, rejected Manhattan Boomer optimism and attached an ironic steampunk anchor to the digital world. But the Authentic Lifestyle rarely meant connection with the existing neighborhood networks; it was, writes Sharon Zukin, "a product with cultural buzz" that let them believe they weren't really gentrifiers. Their Authenticity, a way to "claim moral superiority" and "a consciously chosen lifestyle and a performance," had taken over from Art as a force of gentrification. As right-thinking bestsellers by the likes of Jonathan Safran Foer and Dave Eggers proclaimed—sensitively—that plaid flannel had overtaken gray flannel, the *Rail* reported that "droves of young media-oriented professionals" had moved in. Richard Florida's vaunted Creative Class weren't all necessarily Hipsters, but they shared their interest in "organic and indigenous street-level culture." Amid all these new arrivals in their Cyclones caps were the Brooklynites who'd always been there: the Black community, Orthodox Jews, Puerto Ricans, and White ethnics, all largely working class, so reimagining Brooklyn raised a host of tricky questions. Doctoroff and Burden had their own visions, and so did developers like Bruce Ratner, but most of all so did the communities. Yet who exactly spoke for those communities? Who belonged? Who should decide the future of Brooklyn?

The Doctoroff-Burden dialectic of Growth vs. Placemaking was evident from the start. While Hudson Yards and the stadium were the symbolic core of Olympic X, rezoning would be the process that would permanently reimagine the city, ostensibly adding more affordable housing where there was little cheap land left to give away by transforming unused manufacturing areas into mixed use. But rezoning could go two ways. Doctoroff wanted sweeping change. When he looked across the river, he saw a place in desperate need of Manhattan's gospel of Growth, particularly the vast realm of what used to be called South Brooklyn, encompassing Brownstone Brooklyn and Downtown. Though there were already plans in motion for the Navy Yard, MetroTech, BAM, and Brooklyn Bridge Park, he wanted them wrapped into the kind of single overarching development he had going on the West Side. To start things moving he announced a plan in April 2003 to allow unprecedented densities and heights in Downtown Brooklyn in order to encourage more back-office building to compete with New Jersey. Burden, on the other hand, wanted to turn zoning from a crude map of residential, commercial, and manufacturing into a precision tool for creating locally appropriate solutions. In Jamaica, for instance, more housing was needed for the '90s influx of Indians and Bangladeshis—prices for a single-family home here had risen 77% from 1991 to 2004, and no one wanted them torn down for six-story co-ops—so along with the expansion of Jamaica Station, it made sense to rezone manufacturing parcels into mixed use in hopes of finally creating a "downtown" there. Some neighborhoods could be downzoned to preserve their character; others would be upzoned to encourage density. What Burden didn't believe, though, was that it should all be left to the communities, just as it shouldn't be all up to the marketplace. In true Bloomberg fashion,

City experts would have the final word. Early in 2002, City Planning began twenty-five different rezoning processes.

One of the first covered 175 blocks of Williamsburg and Greenpoint. Politically, the area had been depressed and balkanized for decades between Poles, Italians, Puerto Ricans, and more recently Hasidic Jews, with its history of activism and community development similarly tribal. Groups such as St. Nicholas Neighborhood Preservation Corporation on the Northside and the People's Firehouse, formed in 1975 to protest the closure of Firehouse 212, were largely Polish and Italian, while on the Southside there were Los Sures and El Puente, with the waterfront a no-man's land, particularly that stretch along Kent Street that became People's Park. A coalition of transplants and existing community groups had made the golden years of fire spinning and tuba playing possible when they'd blocked waste hauling there, but environmental justice often leaves a beachhead for gentrification so to head it off, the two neighborhoods had started a joint 197a plan that eventually split apart, with Williamsburg's Hasids more concerned with affordable housing and Greenpoint focused on the shore. Now, as City Planning created its draft rezoning plan, it consulted with subcommittees drawn from existing community groups and took the 197as into account, but only so much: People's Park wouldn't become a power plant; there'd be an esplanade and the State would build that new park; there'd be incentives for affordable housing, preservation of manufacturing, and some 170 blocks inland would be zoned block to block. *But* the 1.6 miles of waterfront between the Williamsburg and Pulaski bridges would be zoned for 40-story luxury residential buildings, and the locals were not happy.

The ULURP procedure required Community Board response, then City Planning approval and finally City Council approval, so communities *were* being heard, both in the creation of the plan and in the debate; the question was *who* was speaking for the community? As in Harlem's redevelopment, the pragmatists involved had participated in creating something that protestors and much of the general public didn't like, but if most people didn't participate in the process, what say could they expect to have? As much as Williamsburg's global brand was anti-gentrification, its new residents didn't do much about it; even Richard Florida admitted that the Creative Class were below average on nearly every measure of social capital—they belonged to fewer clubs, for example, and volunteered less. While City Planning met with the community subcommittees every other week, public meetings about the future of the People's Park drew only the skateboarders. There were "individual people who were amazing," says one young activist; Felice Kirby, for example, was one of the leaders of the People's Firehouse, an urban pioneer who'd moved to Williamsburg in 1979 and later bought Teddy's Bar. She'd joined the networks of the neighborhood to protest, party, live, and work, but few of the new faces along Bedford connected that way. "[A]s an individual," said one self-aware Williamsburg resident, "I make no direct change, for better or worse, to the neighborhood of which I am a part." Many passed up those boring community meetings in order to focus on "authentic" things like crack—"I think what was once a stigma," said gallerist Choire Sicha, en route to a new job at Gawker, "has gotten enough ironic distance to be funny or acceptable." The Creative Class believed in "Protest Politics" but they didn't vote. Any focus on affordable housing came from people like activist Monsignor John Powis and corrupt State Assemblyman Vito Lopez. The Creative Class held up compromised pols like Lopez as the reason for their disinterest, but, worried political scientist Robin Rogers-Dillon, "If the most educated and affluent newcomers to Williamsburg adopt a fashionable disgust with the whole system, the community is unlikely to yield much political power."

One organization, the North Brooklyn Parks Alliance, had been building the case for using the 197a plan instead of the City's, but the Creative Class stood largely on the sidelines until Revel Girl got involved. By day, she was Elana Levin, a recent Sarah Lawrence grad, fearless, theatrical, and no-bullshit, who'd hoped to break into film but after a brief stint at *The Apprentice*, she'd joined the Howard Dean campaign where she discovered that fearless, theatrical, and no-bullshit were valuable qualities for political organizing. In the spring of 2004 she'd helped found Greene Dragon, and now she and the Creative Industries Coalition spread the word that Williamsburg would become the next SoHo if the rezoning went through. At the same time, as *Sex and the City* ended its run with Miranda moving to Brooklyn, some members of what *New York* called the "predominantly young, vaguely creative, and, more often than not, contemptuously fashionable set," formed the Williamsburg Warriors. Dressed in costumes culled from *The Warriors*, gone from cautionary tale to cult classic, they threw fundraisers and warned all who would listen that "our favorite coffee shops will become Starbucks, and our cute little North Seventh pharmacy will become Duane Reade."

With pushback also coming from establishment groups like Catholic Charities and Borough President Marty Markowitz over affordable housing, the Community Board voted no, leading to more negotiations in the run-up to the final City Council vote in May. Meanwhile, developers threw up what they could as fast as they could, and the street theater continued. On a rainy Sunday, a young woman galloped down Bedford Avenue on an actual horse this time, shouting "The Developers are coming! The Developers are coming!" Levin urged locals to rally at City Hall for the final Council hearings, but a sense of bittersweet futility had settled over the neighborhood. On May Day, a Sunday, the Hungry March Band led a parade of families tugging kites, folks in costumes, until they reached the waterfront, and the fence. The locks were cut and people broke into the overgrown acres to chop weeds and plant flowers; others made art or just played. Jane Jacobs sent a letter urging the City Council to accept the 197a instead of the DCP plan, but kites and costumes could only achieve so much. In mid-May, after Vito Lopez squeezed a last-minute $1 million for his girlfriend's day care center, the Council approved the plan after adding more inland density, a legal fund for tenants, and money to help retain manufacturing. Some argued that the community had forced the concessions; others, that this was exactly how ULURP was supposed to work. Either way, the locks were replaced at the People's Park, and Williamsburg joined Cobble Hill and Boerum Hill, Bushwick and even Bed-Stuy as another kind of Lifestyle, the latest iteration of what had started back in SoHo and the Upper West Side. With some 130 buildings going up, artist William Powhida stood before a ten-foot tombstone and gave a eulogy for Williamsburg on the damp stage at Supreme Trading on North Eighth. Greene Dragon lived on, if not the way Revel Girl and Johnny America intended. "The Tea Party stole our shit," says Elana Levin. "They just got rid of the sequins."

Where You Park Your Soul

Bruce Ratner believed he made money doing good—the story many New Yorkers had been telling about themselves for a decade. A Model Cities veteran, Koch's former Commissioner of Consumer Affairs, he'd brought his uncles' Cleveland real estate firm out east, renamed it Forest City Ratner and with what the *Times* called "the bookish and unassuming style of an absent-minded professor" got cut into nearly every major development project in New York. Though he was developing the *Times*'s new building with Renzo Piano, he was best known for taking risks in rough places, albeit with the stern kind of look Bill Clinton gave Sistah Souljah; his Atlantic Center, for example, in Brooklyn, had no entrances to nearby Fort Greene in order to confound—his words—the "tough kids." Atlantic Terminal under construction across the street would be a step up, with a Target, Victoria's Secret. and Chuck E. Cheese, and in 2002 Ratner came up with an old-school, Herb Sturz–style Share the Wealth through Growth idea. With the YankeeNets partnership unwinding, he got City Hall's blessing for the third major development of Reimagined New York: he would buy the Nets, and then use the air rights over the LIRR tracks—exactly the same spot Robert Moses had refused to give the Dodgers—to build a new arena amid a $7.7 billion mixed-use hub full of jobs and housing to be called Atlantic Yards.

Unlike Doctoroff on the West Side, Ratner very publicly assembled a network of community support, presenting his plans in October 2003 at Borough Hall alongside Bloomberg, Marty Markowitz, Nets and Knicks great Bernard King, plus a partial investor who'd taken to calling himself "the black Warren Buffett"—Jay-Z, who'd released "Crazy in Love" that summer with Beyoncé. Ratner promised that the Yards would be "almost exclusively privately funded." Of course, there'd have to be some tax deals, the MTA would have to gift him the air rights, and the State would have to invoke eminent domain on a small patch involving only 100 or so residents, but the unions were lined up. Jay-Z was lined up, and there was talk he could lure over LeBron. What more did you want?

Wait. Did you say "Frank Gehry"?

Yes. Frank Gehry of Guggenheim Bilbao fame was on board, and his concept for an arena caressed at the corners by four towers had Muschamp kvelling over "the most important piece of urban design New York has seen since the Battery Park City master plan." Press release claims that Atlantic Yards would "allow Brooklyn to grow while preserving the character of its already developed neighborhoods" could have been written by Burden herself.

But the development was *huge*, and it wasn't the only one on the boards in Brooklyn. After the announcement, a *Brooklyn Paper* headline read "B'klyn cheers, trembles." With new and unnerving details creeping out in the spring about more money and more displacements, a front-page, full-page map showed everything planned for south of the Navy Yard: Whole Foods, Walmart, and a Fairway; an IKEA in Red Hook. ("I happen to be a supporter of it," said the mayor, "but I think if I lived there, I don't know whether I would be.") The piers would be given over to cruise lines, and Gage and Tollner steakhouse was becoming a TGIF's. "[T]here has been almost no public debate . . . ," noted the *Brooklyn Rail*, but "as much as I may have wanted to find one," the reporter could find "no singly organized conspiracy among the downtown elites."

Nor was there any single organized opposition, especially when it came to Atlantic Yards, where the essential questions of Reimagined New York—and maybe even the whole post–Fiscal Crisis era—bubbled to a head now that the city was bouncing back from 9/11. Could you create a future for the city without displacement and superstores? Who were the "real" residents of Brooklyn? On a border area between Fort Greene, Prospect Heights, and Downtown Brooklyn, no one community claimed Atlantic Yards, so the first protests were led by a mixed bag of body shop owners and bar owners, Pakistanis and West Indians, trustafarians and people like Patti Hagan, former *Wall Street Journal* gardening correspondent who lived amid stacks of newspapers in her nineteenth-century Prospect Heights brownstone. Like Felice Kirby, she'd heeded Koch's call and bought her place in 1979; lived and worked with people in the neighborhood; survived the crack and the crime and now, at sixty, wasn't going without a fight. "Your home is a sacred place," she said. "It's where you park your soul." The opposition ultimately cohered around Develop Don't Destroy Brooklyn and its public face, Daniel Goldstein, a laid-off web designer with a healthy stock portfolio who'd held out on principle while neighbors in his Pacific Street condo gladly took seven-figure buyouts. On the other side, Brooklyn United for Innovative Local Development (BUILD) represented itself as the voice of the community's People of Color. "How high this building is isn't important to people who don't have a job and are out there dodging bullets," said its leader Darnell Canada. Meanwhile, the new Target at Atlantic Terminal was the highest grossing store in the entire chain, and the line for Chuck E. Cheese wound around the third floor. You wanted jobs? Target hired 100 more employees in the first week. So was "authentic" found in the local community with its mass-market tastes, or the mandolin-playing protestors? Many who had doubts stayed quiet: "Jay was such an emotional centerpiece for the stadium," said Mos Def later, "that it almost became sacrilegious to criticize it."

Through endless pro forma hearings and closed meetings, the sense of inevitability mounted. Reverend Daughtry joined in negotiations with Ratner for the city's first Community Benefits Agreement, signed in May 2005, and then Gehry unveiled his second pass: sixteen buildings up to sixty stories high, melting and bending in his signature style beneath a cubist behemoth nicknamed "Miss Brooklyn" that made the borough, according to Nicolai Ouroussoff, "a legitimate cultural rival to Manhattan." But then a drip of costly bad news: Tax filings exposed that Ratner was funding BUILD, meaning that he'd essentially signed a CBA with his own Astroturf. The park wasn't going to be public, just another Privately Owned Public Space. Rising costs meant converting commercial space into luxury residential so three-quarters of the office jobs disappeared and community sentiment shifted; the *Times* suggested paring things down. Gehry himself admitted his latest set of plans had been "horrible." But the deal was done. In December 2005, demolition began for Atlantic Yards. From Ground Zero to the West Side Stadium, from Williamsburg to Prospect Heights, New Yorkers were giving voice to what they wanted from the built environment, but it was rarely what the future had in mind.

Chapter Twenty-seven

Too Big to Fail

On a sunny Saturday morning in early February 2005, volunteers tugged at the covers atop some 7,500 gates arching over the paths of Central Park, allowing the bright orange polyester panels of *The Gates: Central Park, New York, 1979–2005* to spill out and flap in the cold breeze. Now sixty-eight years old, Christo still listened to 1010 WINS as he worked, breaking only to munch on cloves of garlic—"raw, like candies," reported his wife and artistic partner Jeanne-Claude—downed with some yogurt or soy milk. Much else had changed, though, since Gordon Davis had turned them down in 1981. The oddball *arrivistes* had become not only what Calvin Tomkins called "creators of extravagant, useless and unexpectedly gorgeous interventions in the natural order" but brand names—the entire $20 million cost would come from sales of works related to it. *The Gates* had changed, too; drilling into the ground would no longer be necessary. "Now the project is very gentle," said Christo.

What had changed the most was City Hall; Bloomberg had visited the artists after they'd wrapped the Reichstag, and in March 2002, Patricia Harris had brought in Parks Commissioner Adrian Benepe, once an Urban Park Ranger, to discuss how to finally make it happen. Christo was the ideal artist for the Luxury City, his largesse and bold gesture forcing wonders on New Yorkers whether they liked it or not. Snow later in the week had a stunning effect—February was chosen because it was the only month without leaves—and it was easy to forget how thousands had recently been denied their right of free speech in the same park. When the City hosted the IOC at the new Jazz at Lincoln Center in Time Warner Center, the climax was Whoopi Goldberg pulling back the curtains to reveal *The Gates*.

Dan Doctoroff could see the finish line. For ten years he'd shook hands on six continents, spent millions of his own money, turned his obsession into a recovery plan for the entire city, and now all that remained was approval from that Public Authority Control Board in May. The City Council had approved the rezoning but it restricted what money could be used for the stadium. New Yorkers may have called for catalytic bigness after 9/11, but after the Republican convention, the Olympics weren't sounding so exciting anymore. Burden had done what she could to make the whole thing more palatable, forcing the Jets to add parks and more street-level engagement to connect up to the High Line, but she had her doubts, too. Meanwhile, the City threw all kinds of incentives at Lower Manhattan to win over Sheldon Silver. But when the May meeting arrived, he simply didn't put the stadium on the agenda. Asked if it was dead, he said, "It was never alive." Scrambling to save his dream, Doctoroff immediately cut deals with the Yankees and Mets for new ballparks, goods deals for the City (if not the fans) that would produce more revenue through luxury suites, but sound fiscal policy isn't an IOC concern, and Iraq had blown away any residual goodwill. In the final voting, New York finished fourth. Doctoroff returned home, devastated.

The 9/11 Crisis was over. The Olympics weren't coming. New York now allowed itself to lean back into Bloomberg's arms. No detail was too insignificant for Anna Wintour when it came to the Costume Institute Gala, her bob swaying as she directed the effort like a tiny Eisenhower on D-Day. At last year's, Donald Trump had proposed to Slovenian model Melania Knauss. This year's obsession was finding 800 perfect chairs, and it came down to the French sort Holly Whyte had insisted on for Bryant Park. How lucky she had friends in the right places! Trucks pulled up at the park and the Met was allowed to borrow what it needed. The synthesis of style, art, money, and politics that Diana Vreeland had aspired to had fully coalesced under Bloomberg. Manhattan was no longer more like the rest of America; it had fulfilled *New York*'s 1980 prophecy and become "Shanghai in 1937; an international settlement and paradise for the wealthy." The mayoral election hadn't been close. The mayor had cruised into November with unemployment at a twenty-year low, the City's bond rating at an all-time high, and more tax rebates on the way. Between hapless George Bush staring down at the New Orleans levees from Air Force One and the humiliating fall of Bernie Kerik, whose vetting for the top job at Homeland Security led to prison rather than to Washington, DC, people realized, said Mitchell Moss, "that Bloomberg had made government work in New York." The Mayor's Fund had spent $53 million on everything from free eye exams to principal training. His powerful Democratic friends pulled over *their* powerful Democratic friends, and the party put up little resistance. Bloomberg beat Ferrer 59% to 40% with 70% of White votes, 50% of Blacks, and even 30% of Puerto Ricans. There was now a clock on Bloomberg's term—literally. The mayor put one up in the Bullpen to remind everyone how much time remained to get his agenda in place, for the good of the city, yes, but also for his own possible run at the White House.

Kurt Andersen called this "a quieter, less exciting time in the city" than the other two "go-go demi-decades." In December, a two-minute video called "Lazy Sunday" aired on *Saturday Night Live*, a pounding Beastie Boys meets *Seinfeld* rap about Andy Samberg and Chris Parnell deciding to stop at Magnolia Bakery for some cupcakes before going to see *Chronicles of Narnia*. Over the next week it was watched some 1.2 million times on a new website that let anyone upload videos, called YouTube. "Lazy Sunday" was the product of a contented, governable city. Mayor Mike had matters in hand; why not sleep late, grab a cupcake, and "get taken to a dream world of magic"? Keith Haring's Pop Shop on Lafayette closed; Susan Sontag, George Plimpton, and Al Hirschfeld all died, though Brooke Astor, God love her, turned a peppy one hundred, still swimming and doing yoga. Howard Stern moved his gonzo radio show to satellite and became known for long, incisive interviews and Harvey Weinstein said he'd found the cause of his horrible behavior: candy bars. He'd have a few when he got hangry, and his spiking glucose level would set him off. Tech had not only returned, but it was driving job growth, as BuzzFeed, Vice, and Etsy became New York's new brand names.

Ten years had passed since crime drained out of its nervous system; those who came now had no conception of a New York where making it through the day unscathed was a victory. Instead, there were Ray Kelly's constant reminders that Terror could happen again at any moment; keeping yourself and your loved ones safe and happy in the Lifestyle you'd worked so hard to achieve made selfishness a virtue, a way of protecting your children. "Is New York Too Safe?" wondered *New York*. In many practical ways, Reimagined New York *was* delivering on its promise of an enlightened Lifestyle. Its residents were living nine months longer than the average American; some of that came from the crime drop—there'd been a gain of 6.2 years since 1990—but in general, everyone's blood pressure had dropped. Smoking was falling twice as fast as the rest of the country, and now the Board of Health required calorie listings in restaurants. Carts selling fresh produce were placed in low-income areas. New Yorkers walked more and walked faster, and there was even evidence that simply living in New York City was healthy, as *New York* reported on the "social and economic density that has life-giving properties." Density creates networks and belonging to networks "correlates with better health and a longer life." The administration collaborated with community groups on more housing and schools. Those who weren't as networked—the homeless, the elderly, single mothers, and unskilled immigrants—slipped increasingly out of sight.

The City now spent more on the Arts than the NEA spent nationwide. A performance piece in Madison Square Park featuring a hot dog cart morphed into Danny Meyer's Shake Shack. Galleries were full of bright colors, big constructions, and even skateboards, at Deitch. On sunny days, Bryant Park was, according to the *Times,* "the most densely used public space on the planet." Thousands, 50/50 male and female, ate lunch there every day, and a land rush took place at 5:00 p.m. on summer movie nights for spaces on the lawn. Work started on the High Line in February 2006, and the Whitney announced that Renzo Piano would design a new museum at Gansevoort. Adam Sternbergh called the High Line "a 1.45-mile, 6.7-square-acre, 30-foot-high symbol of exactly what it means to be living in New York right now," optimistic and creative, conscious of time and nature, directed by people with incredible resources who wanted to spend their money and exercise their talents on an urban experiment.

Bloomberg personally led the way. In 2004 Bloomberg Philanthropies gave more than $140 million to 843 organizations, many of them favorite charities of his Democratic friends, and replaced budget cuts with money out of his own pocket, an act of generosity whose Rockefellerian expansiveness had its own *Godfather* core; the City's collective political will was being replaced by the wisdom and beneficence of one man who could pull support at his whim. "The mayor," wrote Chris Smith, "has replaced the clubhouse tactic of trading jobs and favors with a monetary system of reward and punishment that's plenty 'political.'" An old West Side longshoreman looked back fondly to the days of Mob control: "Now who do we talk to? The city—it's either their way or no way." The attached power networks didn't hide their clout either: Jerry Speyer and his wife, for instance were on the boards of four schools, the NYCP, the Economic Club of NY, the New York Fed, and Alvin Ailey. Names like Weill, Kravis, Bass, Tisch, Lauder, and now increasingly that of balletomane David Koch shone from the walls of museums, schools, and hospitals, demanding gratitude and reminding everyone who they were. The public-private strategies once used to transform specific sites had become the method of governance. Business Improvement Districts once again sprouted up—26 new ones during the Bloomberg years; as many as Dinkins and Giuliani together.

The integration of all these powerful motivations and resources produced some clear benefits, though; Bloomberg had brought in experts and let them work, with only his standard warning—"Don't fuck it up." In terms of the built environment, especially, they were creating functional, beautiful new public spaces that raised real estate values, and had a tangible impact on daily life. The Department of Design and Construction gave preference to small local architects for libraries and firehouses while adding famous firms like Annabelle Selldorf and Snøhetta to the city's landscape. Marshall Berman praised new low-income housing for looking like a "colorful, accessible version of the thousands of vernacular, ordinary apartment houses that served for generations as emblems of New York." Amanda Burden envisioned a micronetwork of Governors Island, the East River Waterfront, and

Brooklyn Bridge Park. "Under Bloomberg" wrote *New York*, "big thinking is happening again."

Throughout City Hall, rising tax revenues allowed business expertise to shift away from crisis mode toward even more innovation. Much of that also had to do with the return of Dan Doctoroff, who'd regrouped after his father's death and the end of his Olympic dream. New York still had a challenge in front of it, but it wasn't survival now; it was success. Instead of losing people, the City now projected 9 million residents by 2030, and they were coming as the threat of climate change became more obvious. So now, as the Olympics had been his catalyst for remaking New York physically, Doctoroff used sustainability as a way to further professionalize City Hall and continue extending its long-term planning. He asked thirteen agencies to assess what 9 million New Yorkers would mean to them, and then used those answers to begin building an approach to climate change, population growth, and infrastructure that would turn turf wars between agencies into coordinated efforts. In June 2006, the mayor's new Office of Long-Term Planning and Sustainability named an Advisory Board of seventeen stakeholders and experts to develop specific initiatives. Then the City announced a similar cross-agency attack on poverty through the Center for Economic Opportunity that examined underlying issues and measures, and applied experimental, data-driven programs that were scaled up if they worked and cut if they didn't. Unlike Giuliani's workfare, the goal was to end poverty, and Bloomberg dragged the private side to the table with a panel drawn from his network of business, nonprofit, and philanthropic connections.

Bloomberg was even able to get things moving at Ground Zero. In April 2005, with a Master Plan finally agreed to, NYPD counterterrorism experts had deemed the latest design of the Freedom Tower too vulnerable, sending Childs back to the drawing board but, wrote Lynne Sagalyn, "Design fatigue had set in." The new security precautions turned the Freedom Tower into something like an enormous drill bit; bland and well-crafted, but hardly magical. ("Whatever is wrong on that site," says Alexander Garvin, "is the result of the Police Department.") Meanwhile, national politics turned Ground Zero from a shared tragedy into a battlefield in the new Culture War. Another excruciating selection process had winnowed the cultural elements at the site down to the Drawing Center and the International Freedom Center; who'd together share a Snøhetta-designed 250,000-square-foot building, which was 150,000 more square feet than the Memorial was getting. "The Families" didn't like that. "There is this fatigue about 9/11 now thanks to these families who continually complain," said the brother of one victim. "Nine-eleven is not just about the families." In June, the *Wall Street Journal* ran an op-ed by the sister of the pilot of Flight 77 that crashed into the Pentagon, accusing the IFC of promoting anti-American values. The *Post* followed with twenty-six editorials against it; congressmen called for probes of an institution that didn't exist. Bloomberg spoke in favor of the center; Giuliani came out against, as did Senator Clinton, until Pataki decreed that it wouldn't be a part of the complex. According to a lawyer close to the governor, Albany by now considered Ground Zero "a fucking mess," his legacy project throttled by politics and complications to no small degree of his own making. New Yorkers' patience was gone, along with any fantasy that anyone listened to their opinions on any big development. But Doctoroff was able to force Silverstein to open his books, which showed that the developer would likely run out of money in three years, leaving the Freedom Tower half built. The mayor brokered a deal that gave Silverstein three towers; Bloomberg took control of the Memorial, and the Port Authority got most everything else. "Except for those who have a personal connection to the tragedy," wrote *New York*, "people have generally moved on." After Katrina, 9/11 was no longer the only Great American Tragedy. In San Diego, Legoland USA built a 28-foot high, 170,000-brick replica of Libeskind's original design.

"Yet just below the numbers," wrote Chris Smith, "where ordinary people actually live, is a growing disquiet." After all, Magnolia cupcakes cost $3 a piece—you could buy a dozen Hostess ones for that, and the fig leaf of philanthropy could only hide so much. Led by a board that compared libraries to FedEx and Netflix, the New York Public Library concocted plans for a $300 million Norman Foster renovation that threatened to turn the landmark building from a working research site into just another tourist destination. While this would eventually be stopped, the NYPL would take $100 million from Stephen A. Schwarzman, cofounder of the massive investment firm Blackstone, in exchange for renaming it the Stephen A. Schwarzman Building. Before the High Line even opened, it exuded fabulousness. "New York," wrote Adam Sternbergh, "has become like a gorgeous antique that someone bought, refurbished, and restored, then offered back to you at a price you couldn't possibly afford." Jane Jacobs called it "Oversuccess." Between just 2003 and 2007, the salary of the average Wall Street worker went up 140%, a two-bedroom co-op in Manhattan, 59%, dinner out, 58%. It didn't get better if you stayed home—a gallon of milk was up 64%. With good reasons, 79% of New Yorkers believed that it was "becoming a city only for the wealthy." Michael Bloomberg was now just one of 45 Luxury City billionaires on the 2006 *Forbes* 400 list, the first to include only billionaires. The richest New Yorker was now David Koch of the Koch brothers, lavish funder of right-wing—and sometimes wingnut—groups along with the arts.

Still, Democrats raised more money on Wall Street than the Republicans for the 2006 midterm, and Upper East Sider Eliot Spitzer, referred to by *New York* as "Someone in the Governor's Mansion Who Understands Us," replaced Pataki as governor. Goldman, Bear Stearns, and Lehman Brothers all reported record earnings as the Dow glided past 12,000 for the first time. A big run of redemptions in 2005 had forced Bernie Madoff to pull in more money from the brokerage accounts to the Ponzi scheme, but the SEC still didn't want to get too close, and over the next two years, his fund took in $12 billion, enough for a yacht and a jet. "We're all Reaganites now," wrote Kurt Andersen, "or at least no longer socialists by instinct." Over thirty years, real wages had at best crept up; the waves on top weren't stirring action below. Homelessness was shooting up. Stop and Frisk came under renewed scrutiny when a tussle after Sean Bell's bachelor party at a Jamaica strip club ended with four cops pumping fifty bullets into him, thinking he was reaching for a gun. He was not. The situation was complicated by the fact that two of the officers were Black and one was Hispanic. All three were eventually found not guilty, but civilian complaints were up significantly and the NYPD was very, *very* reluctant to share data about stops. The subways were bursting, with ridership at its highest level since 1951, but signs of stress appeared in the system, and as the City focused on extending the

#7 to Hudson Yards and Sheldon Silver forced action on the Second Avenue Subway, Albany gave the MTA, the nation's largest train system, 29% below what it requested for maintenance. Said David Gunn, "No politician wants to cut a ribbon on a rebuilt toilet."

But New Yorkers were living increasingly online anyway. Memes, going viral, and texting were everyday life; Kevin Smith had an astounding 50,000 friends on MySpace, and Wikipedia was correct more often than not. After the 2004 election, an ITP professor named Jonah Peretti attended a meeting in California along with Arianna Huffington to develop a liberal alternative to the Drudge Report. The result was an experiment in gaming search engines using her network of contacts called Huffington Post, launched in May 2005 out of an office in SoHo. The Giuliani presidential campaign was also playing with cyberprofiling; "It's frightening to think," said one member of his team, "that one could sway the future of the free world by toying with who gets to the top of search engines."

On Earth Day, April 22, 2007, under the huge blue whale at the American Museum of Natural History, Mayor Bloomberg announced the culmination of Doctoroff's plan for managing Growth through sustainability—PlaNYC2030: an integrated, citywide strategy intended to create homes for 1 million, improve travel times, put every New Yorker within a ten-minute walk of a park, invest in the water supply, roads, subways, and rails, rely on cleaner, more reliable energy, produce the cleanest air of all American cities, clean up brownlands, preserve wetlands, and reduce emissions by 30%. The 127 specific initiatives already had deadlines, action plans, and funding made possible by four straight budget surpluses. "If we don't act now," asked Mayor Mike, "when?" Aside from a congestion pricing proposal shot down by Sheldon Silver, PlaNYC had the support and financial participation of some 150 environmental, labor, and business groups. With a decades-long timeline of action, it was arguably the most enlightened example of urban leadership New York had ever seen.

Back around 9/11 Jane Dickson had been asked by the MTA to propose an art project for the renovated Times Square station. Flung by an illness, by 9/11, into a space in-between, she'd played with trapeze imagery then; flying and falling and always the question as to whether there'd be a net, but after not hearing back, she'd assumed they had chosen someone else. In fact, the whole thing had fallen between the cracks, and when they called her two years later, she'd been caught safely on the other side. She'd survived, and so had Times Square, and New York, it seemed. Celebration felt in order now; party hats and confetti. *The Revelers*—life-size mosaics of New Year's Eve partiers—is Jane Dickson's permanent mark in Times Square.

Even Marshall Berman, the Upper West Side's last Marxist, reveled in Reimagined New York: "It is more saturated with immigrants, more ethnically diverse and multicultural, than it has ever been, more like a microcosm of the whole world . . . [T]oday's younger generation, unable to live in Manhattan, has learned to explore the city as a whole with a zeal and energy and resourcefulness that my generation, obsessed with Manhattan alone, never even dreamed of." Instead of "I Love New York," the city now had "an integrated market development team" with seventeen offices across the globe. As the clock in the Bullpen counted down and aides explored a presidential run, Bloomberg registered as an Independent. *The Sopranos* ended and *Mad Men* began.

When Ivanka Trump and the new owner of the *Observer*, twenty-six-year-old Jared Kushner, sat down for their first all-business, get-to-know-you lunch set up by mutual friends, something stirred and asked which way to Bethlehem.

You Shouldn't Be Worried

On the morning of August 7, 2007, a brief and powerful storm dumped almost two inches of rain in an hour; a small tornado skipped through Sunset Park and Bay Ridge, and the subway system, flooded in many places, came to a halt. It was, in retrospect, a warning. Another storm came eight days later, when Countrywide Financial Corporation begged $11.5 billion in emergency loans. While the smart money had been going to real estate, so had the stupid money, lured by bank "products" such as borrowing 125% of the mortgage price just to get the extra cash. Buyers were induced to overpay and then simply refinance or flip when it was time to pay it back, while the loans taken out, good and bad, were cut up into CMO bonds, inflating the derivative market alongside the housing bubble; $482.4 billion in 2000 hit $2.14 *trillion* three years later. Countrywide, a mortgage bank run by Bronx-born butcher's son Angelo Mozilo was the nation's biggest supplier of mortgages for CDOs, specializing in "multicultural market communities," meaning subprime mortgages. While he'd been providing capital for communities often left out of homeownership, he'd also set a trap for those who didn't fully understand what they were getting into. As the Dow broke records, the Fed had been raising interest rates, and now all across America, adjustable mortgages were adjusting, balloon payments coming due for hundreds of thousands, thus rendering billions in mortgage bonds worthless. New Century Financial, the nation's largest subprime lender, went down in March and Countrywide was next.

From New York, this looked like a line of dark clouds off to the west; Queens was seeing some foreclosures, but the cash-driven luxury market didn't allow for the no-money-down shenanigans putting up McMansions in Vegas. On the Upper West Side, the new luxury condo at 15 CPW was three-quarters sold, with $1.4 billion in contracts to foreign buyers, corporations, and seemingly half of Goldman Sachs. As long as the stock market kept climbing, New Yorkers considered themselves immune. MetLife, once connected to the city through the construction of both the Empire State Building and Rockefeller Center, had gone public in 2000 and in 2006 put up for sale Stuyvesant Town and Peter Cooper Village, Manhattan's last bastion of middle-income housing. Instead of stepping in, City Hall chose to put its efforts toward Long Island City, letting Tishman Speyer's Rob Speyer, also chair of the Mayor's Fund, beat out a tenant offer to pay $6.3 billion—the biggest real estate deal ever. The new RFP for the development of Hudson Yards had been issued, and jaded New Yorkers greeted the final five designs with, said the *Daily News*, "a collective sigh and a shrug." Huge developers had teamed up with huge corporate tenants to produce huge buildings where rich people could live, buy, and work in luxury. Said one architect, "There'll soon be a Ground Zero downtown and a Ground Zero uptown."

In October, the storm pushed east. Through Barack Obama's surprise win in the Iowa primary, through Eliot Spitzer's sexploits and subsequent resignation, and Heath Ledger's overdose, the housing market softened and the Dow began to fall. From 1991 to 2005, Americans had borrowed $530 billion against homes whose values were falling, yet 6 in 10 didn't have enough savings for three months. By February, new home sales down 30% from the year before, the write-downs began on Wall Street, and the subprime disaster landed in the five boroughs. For many whose real earnings hadn't risen all these years, gentrification had let them use dodgy "mortgage products" to take equity out of their rising real estate—sometimes to indulge, but more often to pay bills. People who'd once owned their homes outright now owed hundreds of thousands of dollars they couldn't afford on properties whose values had sunk below their mortgage. The homeownership that had once settled New York now looked to upend it. In March, Bear Stearns went under after eighty-five years in business. Many figured that was the bottom. It wasn't. Credit, once much too easy to get, became next to impossible. The City's new multi-agency homeless campaign was swamped, real estate development froze in place, doing what the people of Brooklyn couldn't—Forest City Ratner had to stop work. But no new development sent housing prices higher. Tishman Speyer, after agreeing to pay the MTA $1 billion over ten years for a 99-year lease, now pulled out of Hudson Yards and unloaded $10 billion in other holdings including 666 Fifth, sold to Jared Kushner. Related Companies stepped in at Hudson Yards.

But how bad could it get, *really?* New Yorkers had now been through two apocalyptic financial crashes—three for those who'd been around for the Fiscal Crisis—and they'd survived each time, even thrived. Get out now and you'll end up having to buy everything back for more. Just batten down the hatches; don't try to time the market. Ride the excitement of the first serious African American candidate for president and the sideshow that was Sarah Palin. New York, complained Madonna, was "not the exciting place it used to be."

The storm was about to hit.

Capitulation

On the evening of September 12, as Hurricane Ike bore down on Galveston, the CEOs of the city's largest banks sat down around a big oval table at the New York Fed, five floors above a vault holding hundreds of billions in gold. Just weeks before, the US Treasury had bailed out Freddie Mac and Fannie Mae for almost as much—$200 billion. Economist Nouriel Roubini called it "socialism for the rich, the well connected, and Wall Street." The central tenet of the free market was that you assumed your own risks, but as the losses mounted into the last days of summer, not only was virtually everyone betting now, but their bets rode on the outcomes of other bets. What if everyone lost at once?

Staring at the prospect of global financial collapse, Treasury Secretary Hank Paulson had no interest in handing out any more money, especially to Lehman Brothers, whose dire straits had forced this meeting. Especially to Dick Fuld, "the Gorilla of Wall Street" who'd led Lehman for the last fourteen years and into the back alley of subprime mortgages. Aggressive, belligerent, Fuld's large teeth and hooded eyes made him look more like a shark than a gorilla, and indeed he was known to eat spare ribs as a morning snack. Tossed from the Air Force for fighting with a superior officer, he'd gone to Lehman, where he'd risen from intern to CEO. He'd leveraged the company at a 30-to-1 ratio—for every dollar it had in the bank, it owed $30—and now the stock was down 42%. Also swirling around the drain was insurance company AIG, down 50% and on the hook for billions it didn't have.

The storms were hitting all at once.

They had forty-eight hours. Unless the men around this table—Lloyd Blankfein of Goldman Sachs, John Thain now at Merrill Lynch, Vikram Pandit from Citibank, Jamie Dimon of JPMorgan Chase—could come up with a plan, Lehman would be out of business on Monday, starting a cascade that promised to scour the world's economy clean, like the asteroid that killed the dinosaurs. Tim Geithner, head of the New York Fed, broke them into working groups to determine the state of Lehman's assets and prepare strategies. The next morning, hundreds of bankers in weekend casual descended on the Fed's headquarters, grabbed a bagel and a cup of coffee from the buffet, then dove into the numbers. Barclays and Bank of America emerged as potential buyers, but the books revealed the actual debt was higher than anyone suspected. Alarm bells rang for the other banks and particularly for John Thain, whose Merrill Lynch had its own huge exposure to subprimes. Sunday was every man for himself. The other banks abandoned Lehman to bankruptcy—the largest in US history—while they scrambled to work out their own deals. In the weeks ahead, Thain and the two Goldman alums he'd brought with him to Merrill would get bonuses in the tens of millions. And 3 million more American homes would go into foreclosure.

But the storm didn't stop. Amid a 504-point drop in the Dow on Monday, a run began on money market funds that threatened to drain the liquidity out of the economy and burn billions in savings. The decades of casino investing, the transition from pensions to 401(k)s, the explosive growth of capital and democratized, unleashed markets had let banks and financial corporations entwine themselves into every corner of Main Street. Punishing the banks' outlandish greed now would mean wiping out millions of Americans whose pennies and nickels had been what made them all too big to fail. Paulson backed the money market funds and on Friday announced the Troubled Asset Relief Program, TARP, to buy up $700 billion in bad debts.

For a few weeks, the market stabilized as the TARP bill wound through the House until September 29, Rosh Hashanah, and the final vote. As it came to the floor, CNBC ran a split screen of the House on one side and the Dow ticker on the other. HR3997 started off well at 1:27 p.m., 90 yeas to 57 nays immediately tallied. It was a fifteen-minute vote, so after the first batch, things slowed down for five minutes and then it tightened: 143–140 at 1:38. Tied at 161 two minutes later. And then, as the wave of nays began, the Dow took a stunning fall—400 points in the remaining five minutes of the vote, 778 points for the day, $1.2 trillion lost by the final bell. Though the bill was passed in October, markets continued to slide, and cardiologists reported a marked increase in chest pains. The Dow dropped 50% in a year. Pundits called it "capitulation."

In the gilded quarters, quiet conversations were had in the headmaster's office as families that once wrote big checks to the annual fund suddenly needed scholarships. The underfunded MTA raised fares by double digits, a brutal tax on low-income New Yorkers. With the dollar 62 cents to a Euro, foreign tourists flooded in to pick through the city's bones while New Yorkers' own Christmas spending dwindled. Maintenance at NYCHA projects had all but ended. In the outer boroughs, foreclosures concentrated in neighborhoods of color; home prices now fell nearly 70% in Bushwick and East New York, and HUD deemed almost 90% of Brownsville and Jamaica, both with more than half their mortgages in foreclosure, as "At Risk or Borderline."

What the hell was happening? Since 1978 New Yorkers had been told to trust the moneymakers. However dangerous the Long-Term Capital collapse had been, for example, Wall Street's Men in Black had tidied it all up. The men who'd crowded around that conference table on September 12 hadn't been '80s buccaneers; they'd been sober and serious, handed the rudder by Clinton and then the wheel by Bush. If people hadn't exactly trusted them, they'd figured they knew what they were doing. But now, even experts admitted that they didn't fully understand derivatives. No longer beset by violent crime, New Yorkers had been victimized by their white-collar neighbors.

The weekend Lehman Brothers disintegrated, Bernie Madoff had scurried home from Cap d'Antibes. He understood what was about to happen. By December he had requests for $1.5 billion in withdrawals and only $300 million in the bank. Writing checks to his friends and family, he tried to disperse what was left and came clean to his sons, who turned him into the FBI. On December 12, the funds that had invested in Madoff began admitting to clients that their money was gone. Pleading guilty, he'd be sentenced to 150 years. Finance has always had schemers and crooks, but in the heart of moneyed New York, the crimes of Bernie Madoff were unspeakably galling. Mort Zuckerman, Kevin Bacon and Kyra Sedgwick, John Malkovich, Fred Wilpon—*Elie Wiesel*, for goodness sake. Anyone on Park Avenue knew that no one got those kinds of returns every quarter, or at least not legally. Late at night, if they'd thought about it at all, they'd smiled because they believed they had an edge. They'd handed over their money of their own free will, borrowed some more, convinced their relatives to do the same. And Bernie Madoff had made fools of them all.

Everyone had been living in a dream world of magic.

Chapter Twenty-eight

Hard Landings

Just a few days before the inauguration of the first African American President, Captain Chesley "Sully" Sullenberger miraculously landed US Airways Flight 1549 in the Hudson River with no injuries; a sign, it seemed, that things could be set right, that the rise of Barack Obama, a community organizer from Chicago's South Side, had ended the era of "good job, Brownie," Abu-Ghraib, and thousand-dollar tasting menus. The United States could still be a beacon to the world; there would finally be justice.

New Yorkers were caught, though. The unity of 9/11 had been squandered on pleasures spun out of Wall Street gold, but now with burgers appearing on the toniest menus and millions facing unemployment or the loss of their homes, they had little sympathy for the Wall Streeters living high on bailout money. AIG, lucky recipient of $85 billion, gave handsome bonuses to 2,000 executives. Laura Blankfein, wife of Goldman Sachs CEO Lloyd Blankfein, cut the line at a charity gala because she felt she shouldn't have to wait with "people who spend less money than me," while CNBC's Rick Santelli threw a live tantrum deploring federal help for "losers" in foreclosure. The *Times* published the resignation letter of AIG executive Jake DeSantis, who'd quit when told to return half of his (taxpayer-funded) $742,000 bonus. Not only were they convinced they deserved it all, they, like Madoff, considered New Yorkers ingrates—hadn't the taxes they *couldn't* evade, the money they'd spent from retention deals and undertaxed condos, made all the good things happen?

Instead of gratitude, though, New Yorkers aired their resentment. "They don't play by the same rules," said Roberta Gratz, "and that offends me. It's an affront to urban democracy." Reality shows like *The Real Housewives of New York City* and *NYC Prep* offered up the cheesy pretensions of nouveau "stars" who seemed to have no clue how absurd they looked. Fashion Week scaled down. What made this all so galling was the fact that even as State Attorney General Andrew Cuomo clawed back TARP bonuses, New Democrats like him were as much to blame as Republicans. Since the birth of Clinton's New Economy, people like DeSantis, a scholarship kid at MIT, and Lloyd Blankfein, born in the Linden Houses in East New York, had stopped noticing that raising all the boats was drowning those who didn't have one, that their philanthropy staved off structural fairness. Back in the '70s and '80s, a neocon was a liberal who'd been mugged; today it was a liberal whose taxes might be raised. Clinton's Treasury Secretary Robert Rubin had filled the Acela with people like Steve Rattner, journalist turned financier now directing the auto bailout, and his wife Maureen White, finance chair of the DNC. Harvey Weinstein was a big Democrat, too, as was the Devil in Prada herself, Anna Wintour, who at least now admitted that the golden years had been "maybe a little unseemly."

The next generation of Democratic aristocrats was already at the plate. A call from Ted Kennedy (and a $2.5 million pledge) had gotten Jared Kushner, son of big-time bundler Charlie, into Harvard, and now the boy had stepped forward as a real estate scion when he'd bought 666 Fifth Avenue. In October he took the velvety hand of Ivanka Trump, presenting herself as someone serious though she still believed the Trump name represented "the highest caliber of luxury and excellence." The Crash was only good news for the Trumps: "So far," she wrote, "the downturn in the economy has worked out just fine for us."

Gigantic real estate deals foundered. With Stuyvesant Town and Peter Cooper worth less than $2 billion now, Tishman Speyer defaulted, while in Brooklyn, Bruce Ratner unloaded 80% of the Nets, 45% of the arena, and an option to buy 20% of Atlantic Yards to the very tall

Russian Mikhail Prokhorov, a swinging bachelor who swung in and out of Putin's orbit. Miss Brooklyn was shrunk down, then eliminated completely until Gehry was fired altogether in Spring 2009. Brooklyn, as one writer put it, was "left with a possible basketball court in a prairie of blight." Related was allowed to put Hudson Yards on ice until the market improved. Gentrification slowed, for now. Sales in Brooklyn were down almost 60%, and after the 2008 rezoning of 125th Street had added more tourists and tall buildings, the move to Harlem had collapsed. Reverend Butts had once said "a community is more than housing, it's more than business. It's culture," but the Abyssinian Development Corporation had blocked landmarking of the Renaissance Ballroom in hopes of replacing it with condos. Now mushrooms grew on the dance floor the Rens had run on, where Ella and Duke had played, and Oscar Micheaux had screened films.

Even Mayor Mike's plans got thrown: Obama's historic presidential bid had quashed his White House run, but the meltdown offered a sudden rationale to ignore the City's term-limits law and run for a third; who better at the helm than the man with the most money? "I think the business community will feel a sense of relief," said the NYCP's Kathy Wylde, whose job it was to make sure the business community felt relieved. Though 89% of New Yorkers wanted a referendum, he insisted that the City Council decide. Speaker Christine Quinn, lining up her own mayoral run in four years, backed him in return for his support, and the mayor called in the chits of all the recipients of his hundreds of millions of dollars in largesse—religious, zoological, biological, literary, and legal—to testify on his behalf. The Council voted 29–22 to allow him to run. Bloomberg knew he was vulnerable; he spent $100 million against Comptroller William Thompson and reminded Democratic donors who exactly buttered their bread—at one point, none of the 160 people who'd maxed their contributions to Thompson's comptroller race had given him a penny. Yet the mayor made no effort to hide where his sympathies lie; as the Dow crept back up over 2009, he blamed the crash on Fannie Mae, Freddie Mac, and those who took out bad loans; he asked unions for cuts and continued baseline contributions to NYCHA while saying that the financiers deserved their juicy bonuses. "Does the richest man in New York," asked Thompson, "get to live by one set of rules, while the rest of us live by another?" Not surprisingly, the answer was yes. New Yorkers were angry, but "[w]e know we're bought and paid for," said *The New Yorker*'s Hendrik Hertzberg. "We know that there is something unseemly, even humiliating, about submitting ourselves to be ruled by the richest man in town. The truth is that Michael Bloomberg has been a very good mayor." He won, 51% to 46%.

Out in the streets, Ray Kelly spent a healthy part of each day driving around in an SUV loaded with computer screens and fax machines, police calls crackling in the background. Now the longest-serving New York police commissioner, he enjoyed approval ratings above 70% for not just keeping the city safe from terrorism, but for driving crime down to levels below the dreams of Bratton and Maple. Murders had fallen below 500 in 2007, and twice in 2009 the city went nearly a week without a murder. The NYPD would ultimately claim that it stopped sixteen terrorist plots under his watch, from blowing up the Brooklyn Bridge to poison gas in the subways; yes, a few bordered on entrapment, but you couldn't be too careful. A majority of the force were now minorities. Yet with the hundreds of security cameras being installed, the license plate scanners and other electronic surveillance methods, a feeling grew that you were being watched at least as much as you were being protected, a feeling that was a basic fact of life for People of Color. The FBI stopped accepting information from the NYPD, fearing anything it had could have been illegally obtained. Kelly renamed the Demographics Unit the Area Assessment Unit, but little else changed. More pressing was Stop and Frisk, or as Kelly daintily called them, "street inquiries," though that often meant guns drawn, hands-up encounters with entirely innocent New Yorkers. In 2006 alone, the NYPD executed 508,540 stops, four times the number in 2002. Only 2,756 out of around 36,000 officers—less than 8% of the force—made more than half of those stops, with 55.2% of them on African Americans who represented around 26% of the city's population and, as Kelly always pointed out, committed 68.5% of its crimes. Despite twice as many complaints to the Civilian Complaint Review Board, Kelly maintained the increase was due to the reporting required on each stop and the number kept rising; after a dip in 2007, stops broke 531,000 in 2008 and topped that in 2009.

One thing that remained consistent was the arrest rate; no matter how many stops police made, the arrest rate remained around 6%. "My take," said one former captain, "is that this has become more like a 'throw a wide net and see what you can find' kind of thing." Indeed, cops had testified that there were quotas, and numbers were sometimes manipulated by the brass. *Floyd et al. vs. the City of New York* was filed in January 2008 by four men claiming that their civil rights had been violated by stops.

And yet 70% of New Yorkers said they still loved Ray Kelly and the police, and when cops defused what would have been a disastrous car bomb in Times Square in May 2010, the counterterrorism campaign got a boost. New York remained at war with an increasingly blurry enemy and most New Yorkers were willing to compromise privacy (well, mostly the privacy of others) to keep Captain Kelly in the cockpit.

The Last Night at Elaine's

All the tables at Elaine's were full the night of May 26, 2011, there was table hopping and backslapping, but the energy was different from the days of Woody and Plimpton, or even when Bratton and Maple had held forth. After all those years of secondhand smoke, Elaine Kaufman had died of emphysema. The book covers still hung on the walls— *Blue Skies, No Candy* by Gael Greene, *Red-Dirt Marijuana* by Terry Southern, Didion, and Halberstam next to police procedurals—but the old crowd had scattered; if anyone still had a yen to watch a writer eat, they were better off trying to cram into Graydon Carter's clubby Waverly Inn on Bank Street, where they sat under the Edward Sorel murals wondering if they could afford the truffle mac and cheese. This was the last night of Elaine's. Said Gay Talese, "This is saying good-bye to one another."

The "golden age of New York media," said Gawker founder Nick Denton, "is largely over." CNN was on the rocks, the *Times* was staying alive with a new paywall on its site, and both Oprah and Martha Stewart were past retirement age. Letterman publicly apologized for having an affair with an employee, and the struggling New York City Opera had to leave Lincoln Center. Apple and five publishing houses defended themselves against an antitrust suit from, laughably enough, Amazon, which claimed that *they* were trying to monopolize the e-book business. Led by Tech's increasing power, the Culture had essentially *become* the Internet, both infinite in size and shape, open to all, full of new depths and niches and discoveries, but also dominated by a powerful few, susceptible to contagion and quick-burning memes that produced more heat than meaning. The curated self, the business of helping you create your identity through your consumption, aesthetic and otherwise, had leapt online to Facebook and Twitter, to Kickstarter, Artsy, and Foursquare, where it could all be fed to you directly now, raw, mixed with whatever facts and realities you chose to believe. New things came, were cool, were consumed, and moved on in ever faster cycles even as things in general stayed the same. *New York*'s weekly tongue-in-cheek (kinda) graph of the "Undulating Curve of Shifting Expectations" tried to measure the zeitgeist in real time, so among the city's cultural highlights now were beekeeping, Lululemon, *The Good Wife*, and Eataly; *The Book of Mormon* on Broadway. Lines for the Alexander McQueen show wound around the Met while Marina Abramovic sat motionless for most of three months in the new MoMA, staring into the eyes of a thousand visitors. Amid global money, art fairs, and websites, no single artist or trend could define the moment; Art was a state of mind, a community available anywhere, anytime with a click.

But the Crash had created a new kind of nostalgia. Patti Smith bottled all that had gone out of fashion and out of business, been torn down or bought out over the last thirty years all into *Just Kids*, her memoir of Downtown's magic years, back when the Greatest Generation had just been old people. Packaged as punk nostalgia, it was really nostalgia for the culturally comprehensible, Manhattan-centric city where thousands were murdered and nothing worked; for a time when you didn't live in New York as much as survived it; for a Lifestyle only possible now with considerable wealth and constant curation. "This city," Smith told an interviewer, "is not supposed to be the biggest, the baddest, the most expensive, the hippest." Except that it *was*. And always had been. "[I]t is the city of changes," said Florent Morellet, owner of the legendary restaurant forced to close after a 700% rent increase that he'd inadvertently brought on himself with his years advocating for the preservation of Gansevoort Market. "People forget this is what they love about New York. They get old, they get grumpy." And most still wanted it to be the biggest, baddest, and hippest. They wanted *their* chance and Jay-Z's anthem "Empire State of Mind" gave them voice, the soaring Alicia Keys solos taking over for Liza and Sinatra.

In 2008, Jay-Z had left Def Jam, married Beyoncé, and with the release of *The Blueprint 3* the next year became the biggest Hip Hop star of all time, the hub of his own network of music, fashion, real estate, sports, and entertainment that rappers young and old, Q-Tip to Kanye West, plugged into. The plush power of "Empire State of Mind" hit New York City with all the Black and White romance of the first five minutes of *Manhattan.* Jay-Z rapped for those who hadn't made it yet, who weren't old and grumpy yet, who were here precisely for what was new. Few immigrants mourned the New York of Patti Smith, and even Liz Smith, in her eighties, wasn't fondly looking backward: "I can't believe I took it all so seriously," she said of the Trump divorce she'd once made front-page news. "Am I still as big of an asshole? Have I learned anything?"

In June, Mayor Bloomberg, a class from PS 11, and a raft of politicians snipped the ribbon under the Standard Hotel to open the first section of the High Line and a nostalgia-free way to use the past to create a future. From plum echinacea, smokebush, and bluestar all growing between the reinstalled tracks to the sumac and cattails of the Bog at 14th Street, a disused piece of industrial New York had been transformed into a work of landscape art akin to Central Park. Piet Oudolf's intricate four-season garden told a story about the partnership between the city and nature; the birds and bees, the steel and brick, the grasses and allium swaying in front of once-hidden graffiti and fire escapes. The first new buildings along the path, by Gehry, Selldorf, and Nouvel, were excellent, the whole enterprise an example of what enlightened government, personal initiative, philanthropy, and public-private cooperation could accomplish.

If the High Line was a discourse on nature and the city, a path between past and present, it also continued the long discussion about what the City could be, and the conflicted feelings many had about Reimagined New York, as Bloomberg, now a registered independent, lined up with the bankers. With maybe a new dusting of Obama White House optimism, City Hall continued pushing at PlaNYC even after Doctoroff left to run Bloomberg's corporation: 500,000 trees planted by 2011, all wastewater treatment plants compliant, new laws enacted to require energy-efficiency upgrades. Greenhouse gas emissions went down as more hybrids were introduced in the City's fleet; the old Fresh Kills dump in Staten Island was becoming a park. Of course, PlaNYC was an initiative from the mayor's office, and there was no requirement that any of his successors carry it forward, but it put New York City at the global forefront of cities confronting climate change. In March 2010, construction began on Via Verde in the South Bronx, a mixed-income development on a remediated brownfields site, and a few months later the RFP went out for the 5,000-unit Hunter's Point South in Long Island City—what would've been the 2012 Olympic Village. Bids were coming in for what would eventually be Cornell Tech and a foothold in high-tech engineering. Big money still leery of the stock market went into deals for the first supertall skyscrapers, made possible by new building technologies and old zoning rules.

Visible and profound changes in public space were being made by Transportation Commissioner Janette Sadik-Khan. Former DOT head under Dinkins, then deputy administrator of the Federal Transit Administration for Clinton, she tried to rebalance the relationship between cars and people with what she called "tactical urban interventions"; clarifying traffic flows let her pull back enough of the street in spots which, with just a few coats of white paint on the asphalt, became new public spaces. "Once you changed a space," she found, "its new configuration became obvious and unassailable." Nearby businesses reported more foot traffic and increased sales; exactly the kind of metrics Bloomberg loved.

Her biggest fight was over bicycles. During his visit to China in 1979, Ed Koch had seen millions in the streets of Beijing and came home with the suggestion, considered absurd then, that New Yorkers bike more; later, in the years before email, bike messengers brought a certain chic to urban riding, followed by the Hipster obsession with fixed-gears. Sadik-Khan wanted something more blandly European, where biking was just an eco-friendly way to get around, so without any public discussion the DOT created 200 miles of bike lanes that ignited a war between oblivious pedestrians, aggressive drivers, and bikers who felt empowered to ride wherever they wanted as fast as they wanted. Citi Bike, the nation's largest bike-sharing service, would be next.

Data remained the philosophical underpinning of Bloomberg's administration. Where past City Halls had used data largely to measure progress, Chief Analytics Officer Michael Flowers, a former prosecutor in the Manhattan DA's office who'd done logistics in Iraq for the DOJ, led an effort to use it proactively now to solve problems, spurred in part by Obama's mandate to make all Federal data available online. Charged with mining the almost limitless amount of data produced by the City of New York, his office created data-driven approaches to everything from housing inspections to cigarette bootleggers. Of course now the push for transparent, nonpartisan performance had the political benefit of providing *so much* data that problems could hide in plain sight; the Open Data portal on nyc.gov made hundreds of City data sets available, but it was up to you to analyze them. Worse, data could be used to sucker people; the new system for the City's payroll somehow ballooned from a $63 million project to a $700 million one because it was in fact a massive fraud. The company paid back some $500 million and the three middle-aged White men at the center got off with twenty years. Said the mayor, "There will always be one or two bad apples."

Bloomberg's City Hall offered opportunities to New Yorkers who engaged with the process, who picked up papers, created networks, and practiced nonbureaucratic, results-oriented "practical urbanism." Out in East New York, East Brooklyn Congregations, in the hands now of Reverend David Brawley, was turning landfill into a mix of low-income rentals and middle-income co-ops called Spring Creek. Community gardens were growing fresh produce. But those who relied on the City for basic things faced poor service from the likes of Deputy Mayor of Operations Stephen Goldsmith, who commuted from Washington, DC, and former Hearst Magazines head Cathie Black whose reign as Schools Chancellor featured jokes about using birth control to keep down enrollment and shouting at the audience in a community meeting. She lasted three months. While privately funded parks thrived, the Parks Department cut its budget and staff.

Occupy

As the recession staggered on and the stock market recovered, the banks were returning their TARP money with interest in order to get out from under rules forbidding bonuses while in the program. According to TARP's administer Neil Barofsky, it hadn't saved home values or prevented foreclosures; it just bailed out Wall Street. But the passage of Dodd-Frank Wall Street Reform and Consumer Protection Act in 2010 convinced Wall Streeters that they were the persecuted class. (Donald Trump, considering a run in 2012, was second in GOP polls; first with Tea Partiers.) Most bankers considered the whole matter over and were frankly surprised the rest of the world still cared. Wasn't Madoff in prison? "Wall Street," said a sadder but wiser Henry Blodget, "is its own world . . . what matters most is your place in that world, not what the rest of the world thinks of you."

To back him up there was more than just Mrs. Blankfein cutting the line; a paper published in *Proceedings of the National Academy of Sciences* showed "a strong correlation between high socio-economic status and interpersonal disregard." As the galas got shiny again, food stamp use in the city shot up, doubling in the years after the Financial Crisis. The percentage of New Yorkers below the poverty line remained around 20%, with another 20% highly vulnerable. There were almost 50,000 people sleeping on the streets any given night. Suckered by the one-two punch of the Prosperity Gospel and greedy banks, Jamaica had the highest number of fraudulent home loans and foreclosures in the city, and one only development out of the 5,176 predicted during its rezoning. Billions in minority capital disappeared while community groups that once helped people buy homes now tried to save them; White capital and the next wave of gentrification stood ready to take advantage. Even the Yankees piled on. If stadiums were cathedrals of baseball, they'd used their deal with the City to build the Vatican, a vaulted palace in the Bronx that charged $2,625 for a seat behind home plate—and didn't let autograph seekers near them during batting practice, even though they were usually empty, even though taking your kid to see Jeter cost as much as a day at Disney World. All but the richest felt powerless somehow, suckered by the Luxury City.

Though some of his programs helped people find jobs and keep their homes, the mayor seemed oblivious to the degree of New Yorkers' pain. "He's a different guy than he was," said a friend to reporter Joyce Purnick. "He breached his own code of ethics . . . and it bothers him." The idea—or more, the emotion—spread that everything good or bad that had happened in New York City since Ed Koch was tainted by decades of tying the city's fortunes to Wall Street, even the urbanism that had once brought New York back together.

Uprisings that spring in Cairo and Madrid, and protests in Madison, Wisconsin, nurtured a spark of hope that maybe popular opposition could rearrange priorities and rebalance the economy, and Reverend Al Sharpton had his own show now on MSNBC. Through the summer, an ad hoc group of activists began plans for what the Writers for the 99% called "the kind of society that they wanted to live in—a society that takes care of all its members' needs for food, clothing, shelter." Most New Yorkers weren't really asking for that, though, so at noon on Monday, September 17, only 400 or so met at the Charging Bull sculpture in Bowling Green Park and left when confronted by police. Planners had scouted locations in Wall Street and by 3:00 p.m. the group, up to a thousand or so now, stopped at Chase Plaza to eat peanut butter sandwiches and listen to a speech by Roseanne Barr before heading to their final destination—Zuccotti Park, a block-long slice of the Financial District kitty-corner from Ground Zero, one of the first privately owned public spaces created by the 1961 zoning since bought by Brookfield Properties in 2001 along with One Liberty Plaza. After 9/11 it was resurfaced in granite, given chess tables, honey locust trees, a 70-foot Mark di Suvero piece and a new name in honor of Brookfield's CEO John Zuccotti, who'd help set New York City on its post–Fiscal Crisis course of Growth and Productivity. And so this grab bag of mostly underemployed, politically independent young people set up camp in a park named after someone they'd consider one of the roots of all evil, intent on creating their own Reimagined New York without benefit of leaders or demands; "a rejection," wrote Heather Gautney in the *Washington Post*, "of the narcissistic, 'I know what's good for you' form of leadership now pervasive in this country."

Bloomberg and Kelly resisted calls from local businesses to sweep the park clean. Microphones weren't allowed, so the campers used "the human mic"—those closest to a speaker would shout what they were saying phrase by phrase, passing it back in waves, haunting, incantatory, to those farther away, immediately turning a crowd into a literal network. A sympathetic pizza joint began taking delivery orders from around the world and by Wednesday Zuccotti Park had "become a sort of makeshift village," wrote Writers for the 99%, creative and communal in ways opposite to the New York Lifestyle. No one beyond earshot of the drumming paid much attention until video of a cop pepper-spraying a woman went viral and suddenly so did Occupy Wall Street. Unions and universities expressed solidarity, as did tens of thousands of New Yorkers who marched to express their own sense of anger and helplessness if not full support of this odd, invigorating pushback against Power, Wealth, and Style. In mid-October, Brookfield tried to ban camping, but the protestors claimed they were making a statement about homelessness that was, therefore, protected speech and stayed.

"If you enter here," said one activist, "know that this space does not abide by the same rules as the rest of society." But it developed the same problems, and Occupy proved just as unable to deal with them, its ultimate reality more a performance than a new version of Olmstedian democracy. Though activists boasted that they didn't need leaders, leaders had created the whole event and worked in the background; they just had no accountability. A divide developed between the college kids and reform-minded sorts stuck to the west side of the park and the hardcore revolutionaries and class war types on the east. Minorities were underrepresented, their POC Working Group almost shut down. Some middle-class protestors had friends living nearby who offered their showers, but "comfort workers" only sent over presentable sorts, meaning the East Side only got gamier and grouchier. By November, the homeless had discovered the free food. Sexual assault became a problem, along with drug use, and an all-night community watch was organized. "Life in the encampments," writes Todd Gitlin, "grew more agitated and dangerous." By the time Bloomberg gave the okay for the

NYPD to clear Zuccotti Park the morning of November 15, there was more relief than anger among most residents. Outside, Occupy had become a brand, a crunchy version of "punk" thrown in front of any and everything to signify protest, though Jay-Z eventually pulled his line of "Occupy All Streets" T-shirts from Rocawear. "I don't know what the fight is about," he'd tell Zadie Smith. "What do we want, do you know?" It didn't help that protestors were as happy to jeer secretaries and janitors as bond traders. Yet even Bloomberg had heard the message. "The public is getting scared," he told a room of executives. "They don't know what to do, and they're going to strike out . . ."

Over the next year Occupy became a global movement and despite organizing some practical actions, it continued to rely on protest more than active participation in democracy. Nothing fundamental about money, power, or politics really changed, so populist discontent with both parties went in search of new leaders; as Frank Rich claimed, in their mutual hatred of "elites" there was "no air between the right and Occupy Wall Street." The stock market posted solid gains through 2012. Across the street from Zuccotti Park, tourists took selfies in front of Arad's memorial pools, stared at the preserved piece of the slurry wall, then hit Century 21. With revenues coming in lower than anticipated so far, the City, on the hook for interest payments on the debt, was already talking about *more* tax breaks to attract tenants to Hudson Yards. At the end of September, Jay-Z opened Barclay's Center with a week of concerts; at this point there was no evidence Atlantic Yards would add up to much more.

October brought the almost biblical wrath of Hurricane Sandy. Bloomberg spent the weekend before at the OEM office in Brooklyn, ordering evacuations for Battery Park City, City Island, the Rockaways, and much of coastal Brooklyn. The subways were stopped Sunday night and Monday was spent in a state of suspended animation with schools closed, Indian Point nuclear power plant shut down, and the water rising in Red Hook and Gowanus. As the eye hit near Atlantic City, the storm barreled up New York Harbor, a 14-foot surge that inundated some 50 square miles of Staten Island, Brooklyn, Queens, and Downtown Manhattan; 90,000 buildings swamped, surreal scenes of cars bobbing in the waves of what were once streets, water pouring into the subways and PATH trains, transformers exploding, leaving millions without power. Almost 200 homes in Breezy Point burned to the ground. Water cascaded into the Pit at Ground Zero; in Chelsea, mud coated millions of dollars of art; hospital generators went out, and a crane fell in Midtown. Forty-three died, mostly elderly unable to escape the surge.

The next morning a rainbow appeared over the Gowanus Canal. It took three days for the MTA, now led by Joe Lhota, to resume partial service; schools were closed for a week. Dusk brought bands of bewildered Downtown refugees dragging suitcases north. This was no "disaster utopia"; fights erupted at gas stations and looting began in spots. FEMA handed out food to hungry lines, as did Occupy Sandy. The cleanup, like everything else in New York, came last to those not in networks: it took three weeks for light and heat to be restored to NYCHA apartments and along the way, hundreds of sick and elderly New Yorkers were discovered stranded in their homes, revealing the even bigger problem that NYCHA had been left to rot. Six billion dollars were needed to catch up on repairs the City hadn't done while it was borrowing money to help build Hudson and Atlantic Yards. You may need Growth to pay for justice, but you also need the will.

Uncle Eddie and Uncle Bernie

Just a few weeks short of thirty-five years since he'd crashed Hugh Carey's "I Love New York" party, Ed Koch entered NewYork Presbyterian / Columbia Hospital. A stroke had slowed him down, and he'd had a pacemaker implanted in 1991, then there'd been a heart attack. More totem now than elder statesman, he delivered his movie and theater reviews on the radio with a tangy, pastrami accent that brought back the '70s, when the battered city had wondered what the hell had happened since Alfred Eisenstaedt took the VJ Day photo of sailor George Mendonsa kissing Greta Friedman in Times Square—very much against her will, as it turned out. Koch had been surprised when Bloomberg renamed the Queensboro Bridge after him: "I never did a fucking thing for Abe Beame," he admitted at his eighty-eighth birthday party. Slipping away, he'd been very interested in the details of his funeral.

Ed Koch didn't die alone on February 1. A bachelor his whole life, he'd lived long enough to see now-Governor Andrew Cuomo, whom he still blamed for "Vote for Cuomo, Not the Homo," lead the way toward same-sex marriage. But he'd never been all that alone. At his funeral, nieces and nephews described their beloved Uncle Eddie as a rich and regular presence who went to soccer games and read report cards, a surprising image for anyone who remembered a bully whose only concern had been "How'm I doin'?" Ed Koch had never been just one thing, though. The same man reviled by gays and African Americans had also seeded a city of homeowners, immigrants, and new starts that had largely come to pass through the efforts and ideas of the people working in his City Hall, many of whom had returned to sit in Bloomberg's Bullpen. "The people who changed New York are in this room," Koch had said at that final birthday party. "They were there when the change started and they are there to make it even better under Mike Bloomberg." As six police officers lifted the casket and carried his body down the aisle of Temple Emanu-El, the organist began to softly play "New York, New York," the crowd on its feet until about halfway through when they began to applaud. Ed Koch exited to a standing ovation, the organist playing louder and faster, taking the song from a dirge to New York's version of a second line.

As they lowered Koch into his grave in Trinity Church Cemetery, among Audubon, Astor, and Clement C. Moore, the reassessment had started on thirty-five years of Renaissance, Reformation, and Reimagining. There was no one single way to think about Ed Koch, and as the reviews came in on Bloomberg, it was clear he would be just as ambiguous a figure; the visionary hard work, the emphasis on sustainability and innovation pocked by blindness on class, race, and policing, what he did for the poor overwhelmed by his visible sympathies for the rich. Bloomberg's last months were among his worst. Though New Yorkers had gone along with his health initiatives and had taken more than a million rides on Citi Bikes within seven weeks of their May 2013 launch, the mayor finally crossed a line with a ban on sugary drinks in containers larger than 16 ounces. Shot down the day before it was about to go into effect, Justice Milton A. Tingling called it "arbitrary and capricious." The well-to-do didn't drink nearly as much soda, so they tended to think it was a fine idea.

The NYPD and Rikers were darker stains. Under the deeply corrupt Norman Seabrook, head of the Corrections Officers' union, the city's jail had devolved into a hell where the guards ran the gangs and prisoners were under constant risk of attack. As to the police, New York City by now was safer than it had ever been. *Ever.* Twice it went entire days without a single reported shooting, stabbing, or slashing. Murder for the year hit yet another low and the city kept sending fewer and fewer inmates to prison now that the Rockefeller sentencing laws had been repealed in 2009 and busts for small amounts of pot were ended. All credit went to the police—in 2013 Kelly and the NYPD were still polling north of 70%—but anger over Stop and Frisk that summer would permanently damage both his and Bloomberg's legacies. For almost two decades, New Yorkers had been told that the price of safety was aggressive policing and the fact that crime now continued to fall without it cast doubt on not just those millions of Bloomberg-era stop and frisks, but everything that had led to them—though *that* wasn't accurate either. The City had helped break the fever of crime with some extreme measures akin to chemotherapy. But chemotherapy stops. And Kelly's NYPD didn't. It made harsh medicine a daily method, inexplicably redividing the city after 9/11, tearing its sense of justice. Since Kelly had come in, the NYPD had stopped more than 4.4 million people and frisked 2.3 million of them, with no other action taken 88% of the time. While he considered every stop a crime prevented, in fact only 0.1% of them had resulted in conviction, and in 2011, Judge Shira Scheindlin ruled that while the police in the *Floyd* case did have reasonable cause for the stops in question, it was not clear that the department had done enough to stop racial profiling, and sent the case to trial. The public remained split: 50% disapproved of Stop and Frisk; 46% were for it, and that split crossed racial lines, with 56% of Whites and 42% of Latinos in favor, along with 27% of Blacks.

Stop and Frisk became, along with Bloomberg's third term, the central topic of the mayoral race. After twenty years, the Democrats were situated to retake City Hall; the question was Who? Aside from Congressman Anthony Weiner who publicly crashed and burned in a tawdry sexting scandal, there was William Thompson again; City Council speaker Christine Quinn, who'd made Bloomberg's unpopular third term possible; and Park Slope's Bill de Blasio, the Public Advocate who polled well among Blacks drawn to his progressive rhetoric and vocal opposition to Stop and Frisk. His marriage to African American Chirlane McCray and a Brooklynite's gimlet eye on all things Manhattan spoke to geographic and generational power shifts; despite his close ties to Andrew Cuomo, he sealed his perception as the anti-establishment candidate with a commercial featuring fifteen-year-old son Dante baldly stating that his father planned to tax the rich. In mid-August, Judge Shira Scheindlin ruled that Stop and Frisk was an unconstitutional "policy of indirect racial profiling" and appointed a monitor to oversee changes, though by then the force had already largely stopped. Vindicated, de Blasio ran away with the primary and easily beat Joe Lhota. "People will lose their lives as a result," said Ray Kelly of the Stop and Frisk decision. They did not. Crime would continue to fall.

The City seemed to be in as good a shape as it had even been fiscally and physically, geared toward a sustainable, technological future, its credit excellent. Down below, work on the Third Water Tunnel continued, a boring symbol of nonpartisan responsibility on the part of all four mayors. Jobs had come roaring back after the 2008 recession, and Bloomberg claimed that poverty had held steady at 21.2% over all three of his terms, the only big city in the country that could say that. New Yorkers liked Sadik-Khan's bike lanes and the plazas; they liked the 800 more acres of parks—though Parks had cut its staff 40% between 2008 and 2012 even as the Central Park Conservancy boasted a $183 million endowment—and three-quarters of a million more trees. A certain texture was gone though, easy to see on the Upper East Side where almost a third of the apartments between 49th and 70th between Fifth and Park were vacant ten months a year, owned by shell companies and LLCs. The neighborhood was a kind of jewelry store now, apartments tended and traded for their speculative value.

Yet the idea of New York City was bigger and broader than it had ever been. By 2010, 37% of New York's residents were immigrants, two-thirds living in Brooklyn and Queens, and as much as globalization had helped gut the city's manufacturing base, they'd been at least as much responsible for hatching its evolutions as anything done at One Police

Plaza or City Hall. While Wall Street had been mining wealth for itself, immigrants from around the world had rebuilt the day-to-day economy; from 1994 to 2004, businesses in neighborhoods like Flushing and Sunset Park grew by as much as 55%. Half of the city's accountants and nurses, 40% of its doctors, real estate brokers, and property managers were immigrants. While technology and wealth had stripped textures from the city, immigrants had been adding new ones.

In 2005, David Shi, an immigrant from China's Shaanxi Province, opened a bubble tea shop in Flushing that also sold handmade spicy noodles that proved much more popular and profitable than the tea, so his next venture was Xi'an Famous Foods in Flushing's Golden Mall. He brought his son Jason, recently graduated from Wash U., into the business to pull noodles and take orders for thirteen hours a day until he stood next to his father, directing the rollout of new shops that blew up when Anthony Bourdain featured Xi'an Famous Foods on his show. Food, writes Sharon Zukin, was "a good chance to accumulate economic and cultural capital," restaurants "incubators of innovation in urban culture." New York now had more Chinese than any city outside of Asia and "Linsanity" in the Winter of 2012, when the NBA's first Chinese American player, point guard Jeremy Lin, led the Knicks to an unlikely playoff run, had been their coming-out party. New York no longer had a Chinatown; it was an Asian city.

Hip Hop had become New York's most globally influential cultural invention, a way to live among *and* against, but also to move forward; the Jay-Z that played Carnegie Hall to benefit his foundation was the same Jay-Z that had moved a great deal of crack in the '90s. "I've said the election of Obama has made the hustler less relevant," he told Zadie Smith. "Maybe had I seen different role models, maybe I'd've turned on to that." If cool meant, as Robert Farris Thompson had written, "to remember the way one ought to be . . . a return to laughter, people, and responsibility," then Jay-Z and Beyoncé were now as cool as anyone ever had been in New York. Did "authenticity" really matter? "I think hip-hop," said Jay-Z, "has moved away from that place of everything has to be authentic." Nitsuh Abebe described him as "dexterously switching personas," a phrase that seemed to apply to New York through these thirty-five years.

Jeff Koons was gearing up for a massive retrospective at the Whitney, its last big show before moving down to the new building in the Meatpacking District. Ingrid Sischy called him "a great American character one might find in a book by Walker Percy or James Thurber or Sinclair Lewis but updated." One of the priorities of his 128 or so assistants was an 11-foot-tall reproduction of a stack of Play-Doh his son Ludwig had plopped together as a toddler. The wise thing was to hate his million-dollar inflatables and balloon dogs, to doubt his sincerity. But there was *Play-Doh*, begging you to touch it, to become small again, and be starting again, to remember that marvelous thrill of popping the top off a new can, getting your first whiff of that chewy smell, and poking your finger in. Koons had packaged up that innocence and joy into tons of metal and, yes, sold it to some incredibly rich people, but it still had the power to transform. "Acceptance of everything" was his koan-ic motto now. Jeff Koons was as consummately New York as any bombed subway car, selfish and sentimental.

Down in Butner Medium Security prison in North Carolina, Bernie Madoff had made as comfortable a transition as could be hoped for. A celebrity there, he signed autographs for guards, gave investment advice, and made friends with Israeli spy Jonathan Pollard. There was sweeping, and yard time, and reading, and commissary. Visits maybe. But this was his life now, and he had all his remaining years to think. The guy who'd helped democratize Wall Street had assumed the trappings of the Establishment then punched a hole through them. Everyone trusted Uncle Bernie. Everyone had made a bundle off him. He'd let limp dicks think they were geniuses and rabbis pretend to save the world, paid for nursing homes, new tits, and ski vacations, New York's dreams and ego built on the pile of bullshit he'd tended in the Lipstick Building. Madoff believed they deserved to get screwed because they'd been in on the con the whole time.

In City Hall, December 31st, the clock ticked down toward zero. At five or so, Bloomberg climbed up on his desk to deliver a final speech, then exited to an applauding crowd lining his way to the subway and one final ride home.

As the evening deepened, a million people found their way to Times Square. The year before, Hunter College had done a retrospective on

The Times Square Show; Ernst & Young had their offices now where Haring and Basquiat had first hung their work, and there was a Red Lobster in the lobby. Sixty-eight-year-old Debbie Harry counted down *New Year's Rockin' Eve* with Miley Cyrus. Tonight the ball would be lit by electricity created by thousands of volunteers pedaling stationary Citi Bikes and Supreme Court Justice Sonia Sotomayor, born in the Bronx, would start it falling to ring out 2013. David Rockefeller was ninety-seven years old.

It was cold, but not freezing. Across the city, in Nehemiah homes and 740 Park, in Brooklyn Heights townhouses, Parkchester projects and the distant reaches of Queens, New Yorkers waited for midnight, drank another drink, and waited for the confetti, the fireworks, and Guy Lombardo playing "Auld Lang Syne" when they would blow horns, kiss sloppy kisses, and randomly cheer the passage of time like no other city in the world. They held hands and counted down; squeezed hands and forgot about everything that had just happened that afternoon and the entire year just gone by. New York looked up toward the ball falling down and wondered, as it always does, "What's next?"

What could possibly be next?

Epilogue

Yes, what could possibly be next? Decamping for Cadogan Square and a knighthood from Queen Elizabeth, Mayor Mike had handed off a flush New York to lanky Brooklynite Bill de Blasio, Red Sox fan and onetime Sandinista supporter, husband to an African American woman who proudly proclaimed her lesbian past. His voters wanted change and the Soak-the-Rich rhetoric of his inauguration seemed to mark, along with the retirements of Derek Jeter and David Letterman, the end of an era.

Though this era had taught that transforming New York requires leadership, de Blasio displayed little interest or ability in leading all of New York City. Instead of uniting the two cities he'd talked about throughout his campaign, he brought a councilman's mind-set to City Hall, identifying problems and demanding action on behalf of his voters, yet with little of the knowledge, imagination, and most of all desire La Guardia had once shown to achieve them in ways that would elevate the city as a whole. After forty years that favored wealth and business, most New Yorkers were ready for a City Hall that took them into account again when making decisions, with the understanding that someone in charge still had to navigate the unpleasant realities of competing goods and the need to create win-win solutions. But de Blasio had political debts to pay after his election and his anti-Establishment distrust of his own office didn't create Power for the People as much as it repoliticized

City government. The City Council, for example, not only leeched powers from the Mayor, but guided them toward individual members, especially on land use. New and encouraging attempts at community-based planning fell under the control of councilmembers in search of their own slice of the new Neighborhood Development Fund; City departments accustomed to directly engaging with communities now had to go through them and the community development organizations who'd supported de Blasio's election were largely shut out.

Business in all forms was not to be trusted in this administration, so instead of deploying better management as a tool to secure equity, Bloomberg's organizational charts went out the window and Special Advisors stalked the halls. Where the prior four mayors, particularly Bloomberg and Koch, had usually given their experts the political cover to get things done, instead politics now guided most decisions, and de Blasio quickly became known for a corrosive blend of ego and micromanagement, his decision-making process too often a sequence of No, No, Yes . . . the latter coming too late to make the desired impact. By the mayor's reckoning, it wasn't enough for the losers to win, the winners had to lose; City Hall had to demonstrate Robin Hood value. When the de Blasios moved from Park Slope to Gracie Mansion, they did so only after expressing their distaste for having to live among all the swells in Manhattan. Meanwhile, he had his security detail drive him every day to and from the Park Slope Y for his workout, blithely enjoying the same kind of privilege he made a show of rejecting. He found it necessary to balance the admirable choice to send more dollars to small community cultural groups with a proudly worn disinterest in the supposedly elitist Arts. Worst was Universal Pre-K, one of the meaningful policies he did deliver on for everyday New Yorkers. Rolled out quickly and effectively, the program could have been a source of pride for the entire city, but when his former HUD boss Governor Andrew Cuomo stepped in with State money to pay for it without having to "tax the rich," de Blasio was disappointed; for him the tax had been as much the point. On the basis of real improvements like Pre-K, paid sick leave, and new union contracts, de Blasio preached to the country at large from the safety of a bully pulpit built on full coffers and Bloomberg-era plans. Even a generally positive *Daily News* review of his first year called him "a preening, pompous and thin-skinned operator," a "hectoring windbag" who used "his family as political props."

Instead of using Growth to create equity, Growth itself was demonized, but the reality didn't match de Blasio's rhetoric. Whatever belief New Yorkers had that this was *their* city only slipped farther away; a year into his first term, 53% said that quality of life was getting worse, and they didn't mean people drinking beers on their stoop. They meant in part their aching helplessness and anger in the face of unchecked development made viscerally clear by the spindly, supertall skyscrapers shooting up south of Central Park. Where the Empire State Building and the World Trade Center had always been shared civic landmarks, buildings like Central Park Tower and One57 along what was now called Billionaires' Row were pure expressions of privilege, built "as of right" by developers exploiting old zoning laws that didn't anticipate new construction technologies. In Brooklyn, a Chinese corporation bought 70% of Atlantic Yards, renamed it Pacific Park, and built four of the fifteen planned towers, while the opening of Hudson Yards in 2019 made hearts sink. As a real estate deal, it was a work of art; an interlacing of trade-offs, contracts, tax incentives, public authorities, and bonds that rivaled the Eiffel Tower in its intricacy and creativity. It added needed office space, jobs, and tax revenue. But its thatch of clashing skyscrapers looming over a Vegas-style luxury mall made Trump Tower look tasteful. Despite The Shed's nifty telescoping roof and earnest leaders who programmed cutting-edge works from a diverse cast of artists, its massive wheels blocked what view remained as you walked north on the High Line, and few felt a crying need for it, especially with all the other existing arts groups out there begging for money. The logo element in the middle of all this, Thomas Heatherwick's sculpture *Vessel*, a 150-foot, $200 million stairway to nowhere, summed up the aspirations of the age that built it. Though one of its residential buildings was 20% affordable, Hudson Yards was promoted as a haven for the wealthy. As a money-spinning development, it was remarkable. As a place in the city, it failed. To the south, the High Line became increasingly a shade garden as towers rose alongside.

Mayor de Blasio seemed to watch all of this with a frustrating passivity, either helpless in the face of the city's most visible form of inequity or playing a limp version of Bloomberg's game as developers who contributed to his campaign fund suddenly found their projects greenlighted. Meanwhile, greedy landlords and online commerce forced retail shops to close throughout the city, creating block after block of empty storefronts. The mayor confronted other problems with a similar shrug; NYCHA, for one, exactly the sort of thing a progressive mayor was expected to solve. Between 2012 and 2014, NYCHA had chosen to do fewer lead paint inspections to lessen the backlog. Then it falsely certified that it had. Then it lied about it to the City Council. When he'd found out about it all, de Blasio had said nothing and taken no actions against those responsible. But when it was discovered eighteen months later that he'd known, he took no responsibility. Finally, after dozens of boilers in NYCHA buildings failed in January 2017, department head Shola Olatoye resigned with nothing but praise from de Blasio as Governor Cuomo toured vermin-infested homes and Attorney General Letitia James put NYCHA atop her list of the city's worst landlords. With $25 billion in needed repairs, the agency settled with the US government, agreeing to accept a Federal monitor and to spend $1 billion on maintenance.

Worse yet was the MTA, which nearly collapsed after the long fight for its resuscitation. Over the preceding two decades, daily ridership had doubled to 5.7 million, while service had eroded and troubles mounted internally: derailments and signal failures caused systemwide delays; overstuffed union contracts had some LIRR and Metro-North employees making more than $200,000 in overtime while the MTA, shockingly analog in a digital age, regularly blurred, misreported, and otherwise fudged data about delays and needed maintenance. Delays tripled between 2012 and 2017, most of which was blamed, falsely, on riders holding doors open.

Throughout its history, the MTA has been routinely abused by mayors and governors who, despite its vital role in the daily functioning of New York City, have underfunded it, taken it for granted, used it as a political football and piggy bank. Though the State does control the entire MTA, its management should be a joint effort that sees transit as a regional issue. Instead, the mayor and the governor, once friends, blamed each other while doing nothing to improve the MTA. De Blasio argued that since the State controlled the MTA, it was entirely the State's problem and refused to increase the City's share. While he once again shrugged and turned his attention to banning horse carriages in Midtown and a pie-in-the-sky Brooklyn-Queens streetcar, the City paid in just a quarter of what it had in 1990. Cuomo, for his part, pushed capital spending on the Second Avenue Subway line and micromanaged the system as if he were getting under the hood of his beloved Corvette. By the summer of 2017, with the LIRR and Metro-North both shutting down lines for maintenance, and the subways running only 58% on time, the governor declared a state of emergency. Once again, de Blasio belied his own stated values, opposing the "congestion pricing" that would help close the MTA's funding gap by charging drivers for entering certain high-volume parts of the city. Finally Cuomo brought in Andy Byford from Toronto to take over the system and in September 2019, with on-time performance back up to 80%, all parties negotiated a $54 billion capital plan that would include upgraded signals, new cars, and extending the Second Avenue line.

Worst of all, de Blasio couldn't land anywhere solid when it came to public safety, human rights, and the NYPD. After riding opposition to Stop and Frisk into City Hall, he chose for his police commissioner Bill Bratton, who promised to show that the policies he'd introduced under Giuliani could also work without oppression. Indeed both police stops and homicides went down and relations with minority communities improved. But on July 17, 2014, in a sick echo of Radio Raheem's murder in *Do the Right Thing*, Officer Daniel Pantaleo was filmed choking Eric Garner to death on Bay Street, Staten Island. As both Bratton and de Blasio expressed their sorrow, a grand jury chose to not indict Pantaleo, and Garner's last words—"I can't breathe"—became a global call to protest that pushed the Black Lives Matter movement forward. Yet between 2014 and 2017, five cops were killed on the job, three of whom were People of Color. Instead of unifying, de Blasio just flipped from one side to the other, pleasing no one. As the police budget mounted and its union pushed for more secrecy for its members, justice became more elusive.

There *were* positive developments in the de Blasio years. *Hamilton* opened at the Public Theater in 2015, and shows like *Dear Evan Hansen* and *Kinky Boots* spoke to a reaffirmed gay presence on Broadway that no longer needed to code its emotions through Mama Rose. The new Whitney Museum breathed life into the concept of American Art as the ideas behind its 1993 Biennial became watercooler conversation; MoMA closed to reconsider and rehang its collection, and at the Domino Factory in Williamsburg, Kara Walker crafted a massive sphinx out of sugar and the legacy of enslavement. Instead of Joan Collins, now Kendrick Lamar graced the cover of *Vanity Fair*. Though unable to meet all of de Blasio's promises, the City had by August 2019 financed more than 135,000 units of affordable housing and had taken a leading role in advocating for national immigration reform. Along with more legal aid, municipal ID cards were an enormous boon for the 62% of New Yorkers who lived in a household with at least one immigrant, legal or otherwise.

And even though public health, one of Bloomberg's unquestionable successes, slipped back painfully and homelessness only got worse, the real possibility of him being a one-term mayor disappeared on November 3, 2016, when Donald Trump's election as president made the mayor's progressive veneer look positively heroic. With hooting Trumpers, pundits, and self-flagellating New Yorkers now calling the nation's most global city "the bubble," decades of plush New Democrat assumptions came to an end. Amid a mounting sense of disgust and distemper, the exposure of Charlie Rose, Attorney General Eric Schneiderman, and Matt Lauer as sexual harassers brought the #MeToo movement forward, but it was the arrest and rape trial of Harvey Weinstein, the fucking sheriff of this fucking town, that signaled (perhaps) the end of toxic masculinity's hold on culture and cultural power. Secrets long held in plain sight were spoken, lists circulated of "shitty men" in various industries. The *New York Times*'s muddled election coverage and its repeat interviews of supposed "real" Americans in the same handful of rural diners undermined its bedrock position in the minds of New York cognoscenti. Beloved chef Anthony Bourdain committed suicide, The Four Seasons closed, and Cardi B reigned supreme. The dream that Tech could somehow wean the city off Wall Street became more of a nightmare as Facebook, Twitter, and Google revealed their data-harvesting, surveilling ways; though they'd still provide new jobs and capital, they were just the new face of The Man. De Blasio somehow took all this to mean that America wanted him in the White House and began his presidential campaign.

Then in late 2019, Andrew Cuomo and Bill de Blasio sat alongside Amazon executives to make the shocking announcement that New York City had won the company's fourteen-month beauty pageant for a new headquarters. With its long global record of tax evasion, notorious anti-union stance, bullying approach to local governments, and the widespread, if not entirely accurate, belief that it caused the death of mom and pop retail in the city, virtually no one in New York had expected or particularly wanted Amazon, but here were the governor and the mayor presenting a secret deal all but signed and sealed. The company would get a chunk of Long Island City and some $3 billion in tax abatements that would ultimately, in theory, return $13.5 billion in revenue to the City, along with up to 40,000 jobs that could pay as much as $150,000, job training relationships with the nearby Queensbridge Houses, CUNY, and NYCHA, a new school, a new park, and an infrastructure fund for the local community. There would also be a helipad. As tone deaf and secretive as the deal was, it had benefits that New Yorkers needed to openly discuss. But the debacle that followed showed everyone involved at their worst.

Andrew Cuomo, for one, who'd finally elbowed his way into the Governor's mansion. It hadn't been a pretty ride. After law school and a year at a firm that dealt with big-time real estate (Donald Trump was a client), he'd scaled up his HELP transitional housing through Dinkins and into Clinton's HUD, where, as its Secretary, he was known for a brutal management style and enforcer rep that cost him a primary race for governor against Carl McCall. After a time-out in the weeds, he returned to win election as State Attorney General, where he weakened the ground under his rival and then Governor Eliot Spitzer, who ultimately did himself in. David Paterson's short reign in Albany set up Cuomo's 2011 victory. Since then he'd squared up to every player in the State, allowing four breakaway Democrats in the State Senate to effectively keep it in Republican hands, or more precisely, in *his* hands as he helped business every way he could while supporting social issues like same-sex marriage and gun control, and building legacy monuments like a new La Guardia Airport, Tappan Zee Bridge, and, he thought, this sprawling campus for Amazon, another big project to be crammed down New Yorkers' throats with only cursory public review.

But New Yorkers weren't having it. Between the parade of terrible big plans they'd survived the last forty years, Trump in the White House, absurd housing prices, the Blue Wave, and the idea of Jeff Bezos landing on his helipad while they waited for their train, late for work, they wanted the deal aired out. Not necessarily shot down but aired out. After all, even Bloomberg thought the incentives Amazon received were too high. The two City Council hearings were testy; Amazon was not accustomed to being questioned. "We want to invest in a community that wants us," sniffed VP Brian Huseman. No one—not Cuomo, not de Blasio, not the City Council members who'd changed their minds, not the newly elected Representative Alexandria Ocasio-Cortez, or Jeff Bezos—could, or wanted to, dispassionately explain the pros and cons and work in good faith toward a deal that everyone could live with. Despite polls that showed most people, especially those in Queens, just wanted a better deal, Amazon walked away.

The fall of 2019 brought the good news that Rikers would be closed by 2026 and replaced by four satellite jails, an idea that went all the way back to Herb Sturz in the '70s, predicated on a smaller prisoner population as crime continued falling, marijuana was decriminalized in New York, and cash bail was outlawed. Forty-five years after CBGB, David Byrne played Broadway for $400 a pop, Felix Rohatyn and Pop Smoke died, and Michael Bloomberg's presidential run put his years in City Hall under the microscope. The world watched a cruise ship full of people sick with a mystery virus try to find an open port. Then Covid-19 hit Wuhan, China, sending it into lockdown. It tore through Italy. And all the while, millions from Europe continued to enter New York unquestioned, untested. On March 1, 2020, the state reported its first case.

Over the next four, almost apocalyptic months of death and violence, de Blasio's No, No, Yes style would be on full display. Slow to respond, full of conflicting messages and ultimately overruled at every step by Cuomo who, after his own early fumbles, took over Giuliani's post-9/11 role, the mayor looked like a midlevel functionary. Assured by his health commissioner that there was no threat, he started the month telling New Yorkers to go to the movies, then spent three weeks going back and forth with Cuomo as to whether the city should shut down and which one of them had the power to do it. By the time the stay-at-home order was declared on March 20, more than 4,000 cases of Covid-19 had been reported in New York City, with 115 confirmed deaths; a week later there were nearly 45,000 cases and more than 900 deaths. In a month, almost a quarter of a million cases in New York City and 11,784 deaths, almost four times the toll on 9/11, predominantly in the Black and Hispanic neighborhoods of the Bronx and Queens. With the streets empty, sirens everywhere at all times, bodies piled in trucks, and hundreds of thousands suddenly unemployed, de Blasio faced a looming $10 billion budget shortfall and a city wondering just how many lives could have been saved if he and Cuomo had acted faster.

And then, as the epidemic eased in New York, four Minneapolis policemen murdered George Floyd. Protests began the next day, May 26, then amid yet another rash of shocking police homicides papered over by complicit city governments they met the fear, boredom, and desperation of springtime quarantine across America and turned violent. In LA, Memphis, St. Louis, Atlanta, and Philadelphia protests morphed into looting and pitched battles between protestors and police often instigated by officers in *RoboCop* riot gear. On the 29th, the chaos hit New York, with two days and nights of street fights in Brooklyn and Lower Manhattan. Once again de Blasio dithered: he supported Black Lives Matter *and* the cops who drove their car into a crowd; the protestors had the right to protest, *and* the baton-swinging cops with their badges taped over were doing a great job. And once again, Cuomo played him into a corner, sounding more supportive of BLM than de Blasio while at the same time calling him out for losing control. With the governor threatening to send in the National Guard and displace him, de Blasio issued an 8:00 p.m. curfew. The violence settled, the curfew was lifted after a week, and peaceful protests continued. In mid-June, New Yorkers took their first legal steps out of lockdown into recovery.

What could possibly be next?

*   *   *

I've stopped asking that question because it seems to tempt fate. New York City will not die. It won't die because the world needs it too much, because New Yorkers want it too much. The density and the constant dance of shared space; the speed and convenience; arts, commerce, and conviviality all tied together: that's always been the ultimate purpose of cities—to facilitate exchange between human beings. And even if there's another run to the suburbs, the mounting pressures of climate change and economics point to an estimated 80% to 90% of the planet's 8 billion people in cities by 2050. New York City *will* survive this pandemic and upheaval; in fact, a few years of flight might flush out some of the suburban attitudes and global wealth that have drained its flavor. Fewer Karens and cheaper rents would be positive things. Throughout history, epidemics haven't killed cities as much as they've revealed their weak points. The question is, What can we take from these four decades of transformation in New York and apply to its next evolution?

First, nothing is permanent about a city, even if it's Cairo, Athens, or Rome. Empires and buildings rise and fall, businesses open and close, tastes change, borders move, people come and go, time passes. Cities are intensely natural places in this way; they're gooey and transient like wetlands, full of life and decay, washed by regular tides that bring rich and fertile new things along with destruction; not just that "creative destruction" you read about in Econ 101 or the bloodless "disruption" bloodless tech types love so much, but the real life, where will I live, what will I eat destruction of human lives who can't make the call, pass the law, hire the lobbyist that would block it. This ebb and flow of change, the back and forth between Order and Disorder, is necessary to produce capital of all kinds; money, yes, but also the social, intellectual, creative, even spiritual capital that cities are known for. The essential value of power big and small in New York is that it lets you direct change—even stop time if you want—so that you can get your hands on some of it. Having the power to start a business, develop a skyscraper, speak with your council member, enroll your kid in a venerable private school all let you profit somehow, even if it's just sleeping securely because you can afford your rent. Those with avaricious landlords, whose local school closed, whose block isn't landmarked, who don't have insurance, who live week to week, are subject to change, not choosing it. The same goes for those who don't bother going to PTA meetings, who shrug instead of voting. They're simply surrendering what power they have.

Until now, the White, moneyed establishment of New York has always—and I mean going back to the Dutch—dictated how the city would change; that was, for example, the whole purpose of the Regional Planning Association. Which isn't to say that everything the establishment did was nefarious; at times they were progressive and benevolent, but ultimately *they* controlled the lives of generations of New Yorkers by controlling what, when, and how change took place. During the era of this book, redirecting change in some specific ways revivified a moribund New York, but almost immediately some parts of the city were all but drowning under money while others starved and the sluice was rarely moved. When it was, it was usually to scour a place clean. Now Covid is forcing a wave of change on New York City; the demand for racial justice is forcing another. There will be more. The next evolution of New York will depend on the nature of those changes, who will control them, and who will benefit. Decisions must be made with the understanding that New York is not a zero-sum game, an algorithm, or a kindergarten class where we all get the same number of cookies. The city must reenergize itself, reward imagination and investment, but with a greater sense of fairness than it's ever mustered.

Who will do all that?

The '70s Fiscal Crisis and all that followed have taught us that it must be everyone, not just another Crisis Regime. But that doesn't mean a return to the old chessboard metaphor of the Game of New York. As we've seen, this city is a vast network of connections that works much like a brain; when people exchanged ideas, actions, and money with each other, the smarter, cleaner, greener, safer, and more creative it became. Yet the last four decades also left the people of New York fragmented, with too many of them farther away from real power than they have ever been; at the same time too many others became passive consumers of urban life. In order to make sure everyone has access to all the different kinds of capital being produced and has agency in how they get them, we need to not only preserve the huge network of

New York but make that network bigger and denser. Density creates connection and energy. If density helped spread Covid, density also helped spread the acceptance of masks and the first push to flatten the curve in New York.

Rebuilding that network of New York starts with individual New Yorkers. Democracy demands more than just shopping, voting, and opining. The machine of government exists to help us govern ourselves; by voting we choose who will run the machine, but then we all still have the responsibility for doing our own work of what Cassim Shepard calls "citymaking." Successful community groups have shown us that we have agency and we have the responsibility to use it. Start by identifying your Real Life networks. Help others find their own and create new ones. Live *in* your community, not *on* top of it. Get to know your neighbors, join organizations, and shop locally. Become a regular. Go to Community Board hearings; volunteer for something beyond the bake sale for your kid's school. If everyone in your networks looks and sounds like you, shops where you shop and went to the sort of schools you went to, you need some new connections. Virus and violence have released distrust and deep resentment, and masks have become a necessity, but don't be afraid of the people around you. The city will need to connect all its citizens, corporations, and institutions as densely and dynamically as possible, and our masks are signs of solidarity, not fear. Be vulnerable, and be generous with what you have, whatever it is. Take responsibility; as Larry Kramer wrote, pick up pieces of paper. Protest is good; involvement is better; doing both is the best.

All these things create community, a cloud of potential exchange, a network of people connected by shared experience who become stronger the more they exchange with each other. Participation creates power. Strong communities aren't affinity clubs, though; they're the product of people solving problems together. Though density also creates conflict, as Richard Sennett writes, we stress sameness too much when we talk about communities when we should be welcoming the tensions that make us confront real problems and create real solutions. If we're to set new standards for how we live with each other based on more than what we buy, the language we speak, or the color of our skin, New Yorkers will have to redefine Quality of Life in terms of disorder as much as order. We'll have to relearn the value of friction, difference, and uncomfortable moments because we're going to have to depend on each other for our survival. We'll have to share time and place, joy and misery, hard work and sacrifice, failure and triumph. New York has always done best when people in City Hall, in boardrooms, and in neighborhoods move beyond politics and together, even when it's tense, try to find what works best. Communities require functioning, dynamic collective power to force and direct the changes they need.

This work ahead will require leaders who put the good of the city above all else. The greatest failures of Dinkins and de Blasio were their failures of leadership, not of policy. They let the city go adrift, but worse, they made everyone who lived in it *feel* adrift. New Yorkers need a sense that someone is in charge of a place that can turn unstable very quickly, someone who can direct the constant flows of change, who can make choices for the common good and suffer the political fallout that comes with them. Leadership, though, isn't just about City Hall and boardrooms. Grassroots leaders must weave a hundred voices and wills into a single, strong thread to wind with others into a cable that can, with more cables, hold up a bridge in partnership with bigger forces. Reverend Johnny Ray Youngblood and Yolanda Garcia, for example, weren't afraid to hold power. They understood that for all the danger it presents, sometimes the righteous must wrap their hands around the live wire in order to achieve the greater good. In short, people have to step up and find the courage to lead, but no one can lead all the time. They must also let themselves be led by others. The difference between citizens being heard and being listened to is the difference between thirty-eight people saying the same thing at an open mic just to hear themselves talk and one clear voice speaking to power. Functional democracy is not a Babel.

City Hall has its own significant responsibilities. Under Koch, it went effectively from arbitrating between the people of New York and its business institutions to doing what it could to help those institutions, even if it meant circumventing the City's own laws and procedures. The subsequent forty or so years of development in return for Growth and tax revenue turned into a latter-day version of the scam that eased Manhattan out of the hands of the Lenape for $24. Post-Covid New

York desperately needs Growth. It needs economic development, jobs, and an active marketplace. But its health going forward must be measured in more than population and tax receipts. This time we must follow through on the promise to deliver the benefits of Growth to all New Yorkers. Even as City Hall creates positive conditions for investment, it will also have to restore the sometimes adversarial dialogue between government and the private sector in order to equitably and effectively direct recovery and change. If we must build—and maybe more buildings with less density will be one path forward—we must do it with awareness of more than just financial output, and not simply open the throttle without a destination in mind. The processes exist to do that—ULURP, for one—but they need to be fully and honestly exercised. Those who will be most affected need more places at the table and to benefit more directly. All sorts of public-private partnerships will be crucial, but the City must exert the constant political will to make them truly cooperative rather than just handing over the keys.

Public administration must be as nonpartisan as possible. Though it's never been a sexy platform for any politician to run on, maintaining infrastructure, budgeting funds, and using them well to keep it updated and in good working order matters more than splashy new capital projects. The failure of basic things like transit, sanitation, and water, streets, fire protection, and parks undermines confidence in the city more than any particular crisis, but rather than guaranteeing reliable, efficient, equitable services, the answer to problems has usually been more "catalytic bigness," meaning more private development and more capital spending to produce more infrastructure that won't be funded down the line. New York will recover if we just make what we have work well again. To do that we'll need the kind of outpouring of talent that we saw during the Fiscal Crisis and after 9/11, and the political support from City Hall to let it perform.

Reforming the police is another fundamental issue for the next New York. We've learned that crime doesn't have to be the defining aspect of urban life, but at the same time, people do bad things, and we need a police department to keep everyone safe. For twenty years, New York largely flailed in the face of crime, until Bratton and his cohort turned the lens back on to the force itself, cleaned house, applied technology, and restructured the NYPD's systems and philosophy. When all this met social and demographic changes, crime dropped, but expectations quickly became unreasonable, and proactive policing became a combination of untrained social work and the regular, sanctioned harassment of People of Color. Public safety, civil rights, and justice are the foundation of urban life; there must be order, but the definition of "order" must be reached with the whole city in mind, not just to preserve privilege. The real point of metrics must always be *why* things are being measured, not the numbers themselves. Basing performance on stops and arrests, on how many were thrown off the subway, may have been useful in a crisis situation, but consistently pushing for more once the fever broke turned the NYPD into an occupying force, destroying at least as many lives with their tactics as they'd once saved with them.

Stop and Frisk wasn't the only mistake. Like other police departments across America, the NYPD used 9/11 as an excuse to militarize, replacing paddy wagons and nightsticks with armored vehicles and high-octane weapons intended to keep the dreaded mujahideen off our shores, though in practice they were only deployed against New Yorkers at times like the GOP convention and the 2020 riots. The police commissioner can dance in all the samba bands he wants, shake hands at as many AME churches as he can get to in one Sunday morning, but decades of commuter cops in riot gear protecting property rather than humans have turned them into security guards and mercenaries. The dangers of the job aren't an excuse to abuse their power just because they're afraid or racist. The roll call in this book is incomplete, but remains devastating: Arthur Miller, Michael Stewart, the Tompkins Square Police Riot, the Mollen Commission, the Anti-Dinkins Police Riot, the abuse of Stop and Frisk, Amadou Diallo, Patrick Dorismond, Eric Garner, and now the indiscriminate countering of violence in our streets with more violence when what was shown to work best was taking a knee. The farthest One Police Plaza ever goes is to blame the bad apples, but as Chris Rock has said, we expect 100% of airplane pilots to be good, so why shouldn't we expect that of our police? New York City must purge its police department of racism, stand up to the police union, and relieve the NYPD from dealing with mental health and social services in the name of Quality of Life.

New York's future will rely on more technology, but again it must be the means, not the end. In the '70s, the city faced a Control Crisis when the volume of information it had to process overwhelmed its ability to deliver services, a problem everywhere then, public and private. City Hall slowly implemented technology and set metrics until Compstat and to some degree the Reinventing Government impulse improved accountability. Bloomberg took data analysis to a higher, even more creative level, but many times along the way the greater purpose melted away, the big picture became pixelated, and the numbers passed for actual results. Data is essential for nonpartisan urban management, but we need to think in both digital and analog to create meaning. Too many Smart City solutions lack connection to human faces and real lives. As we saw with the NYPD, we need to continually update what we measure and set goals that assess impact and change, not just task performance.

The future will also be in our parks and streets, where Olmsted's belief that safe and lively public spaces express the trust and expectations of people in a democracy is more important than ever. New York's transformation began in the city's public spaces, and those spaces will play a crucial role now as it emerges from the dark moment when Covid and civil unrest rendered them once again contested and dangerous. In the post-Covid world where outdoor spaces are generally safer than indoor ones, public space will be re-contested along new lines measured six feet at a time, so as the supertalls continue to shoot up and apartment buildings across the city turn themselves into bunkers, we must resist the temptation to cower behind locked doors as New Yorkers did—by choice—during its darkest days. We must fight to maintain places that offer room for all of us, not just for personal expression but also for reencountering each other. We must keep the streets alive and safe in all ways because, as Holly Whyte taught us, New York thrives on people in public. Though Gordon Davis showed how to use parks to inspire active participation in urban life, City Hall has consistently cut their budget; this is the time to give them our full support. We must have enough quality public space for everyone, distributed and maintained fairly, with respect for the different ways a diverse population uses space, with conscious programming to help us reconnect. What we don't need are more of the pseudo-public plazas and lobby atria required by zoning trade-offs; while some do work as they were planned, they all exist under a cloud of corporate sufferance, manned by private police who can shut down access under the lamest pretext. City parks also remind us that we do still exist in the natural world, even when we're surrounded by buildings. The city is the opposite of the country, but it's not the opposite of nature any more than a beehive is. We need more grass and trees and basketball courts, but we also need more places where people can get their hands dirty. Community gardens, especially in underserved areas, have proven to create networks by connecting people to each other as they connect to the land, and a garden on your roof, your backyard, or your window sill keeps the urban soul in balance.

The Arts are also necessary for the urban soul, and the next New York will need Culture as a uniting force amid a shattering world. Other eras certainly produced their own great artists and artistic communities, but in the '70s the City and the business community recognized the value of the Arts to the city, financial and otherwise, just as new generations of artists were arriving. Over the next forty years, the visual arts in particular became increasingly a part of our daily lives, seen everywhere from the subways to ever-larger museums and the gallery scene of the moment, scenes that consciously or not yielded an industry and rewrote the city map by becoming the leading edge of gentrification. Arts philanthropy veered dangerously close to a form of civic monogramming—it's hard not to look at The Shed and Diller Island and wonder whether it would've been a greater legacy for all the donors involved to spend that $750 million or so underwriting arts education for every student in New York's public schools. Going forward, keeping New York a place where artists can, and want to, live and nurturing the Arts in our communities will matter more to the city's long-term health than feeding the global Art market.

It's unreasonable to believe that New York will ever eliminate all inequality. It's a basic feature of cities, especially ones that draw the poor in hopes of better prospects or just survival, and there's always been space here for luxury; everyone wants a Big Night on the Town; everyone hears "Empire State of Mind" when they look at the skyline, and the same people who spent thirty years wishing for the return of the dingy, cash-strapped New York of the '70s were the first to wail about the dirty, empty streets during Covid. We love and fear New York, and we dream of it loving us back because it demands the best of us. It demands that we take our shot. And while realizing our dreams is not, at heart, a matter of equality, it can be done with the grace of someone like Senator Robert Wagner, a Yorkville bootstrapper who'd said of his success, "That was luck, luck, luck. Think of the others." Over these three evolutions, though, inequality in New York went from an unfortunate byproduct of complex human society to something actively cultivated and promoted by a new culture of wealth and celebrity valued explicitly because it was so visible. Inequality became the point, and that culture of self-aggrandizement ultimately affected how City Hall saw New York; Abe Beame's dented Chrysler became Bloomberg's Luxury City. Saying that tourists and foreign oligarchs defined the city more than the lives of New Yorkers sent the terrible message that we should care more about Hermès bags than each other.

I don't believe that's what Mike Bloomberg meant to say, but that was the impact, and it's not just a matter of hurt feelings. Studies have shown that the appearance of inequality in a place increases actual inequality. A "Luxury City" is more upset when a Chanel store has its windows broken than when police murder a man. It makes itself increasingly vulnerable, needs ever more heavily armed police to protect its purses. Let it be said that philanthropy is good. Centuries of good New Yorkers have given to good causes with good intentions; Bloomberg's philanthropic example and arm-twisting Mayor's Fund accomplished an enormous amount. But we need a New York built on a bedrock of justice, not just *noblesse oblige*. It's time to admit that they (and that includes me) have too often given money in hopes of propping up a world that's served us well rather than in hopes of realizing significant change. Wealthy New Yorkers must focus more on service than naming rights. They must come to terms with the fact that no matter how many checks they write, their Lifestyles and all they do to preserve them are prime causes of inequality.

As I wrote earlier, New York's greatest work of performance art took place the foggy August day when Philippe Petit walked step-by-step between the Twin Towers, carefully maintaining his balance as he seemed to float in midair. New Yorkers take that walk every day, maintaining our balance between Order and Disorder, inside and out, public and private, trees and steel, construction and destruction, rich and poor, we and me, here today, gone tomorrow. Living in New York requires using all your muscles—that's what's so exhausting; the going back and forth. But it's also what makes us so strong and resilient; we are constantly adjusting, constantly in flex.

What's next is in our hands.

Acknowledgments

I n the making of this book about change, two people stand out for their constancy. My agent and dear friend Lisa Bankoff has believed in me since sometime during the second term of Ed Koch, even when I wasn't sure myself, even during the worst shoals of this book. I will always believe in *her*. And second, Eamon Dolan, son of the Bronx and—I can finally say—my editor. It's been worth the wait. Working with Lisa along the way were Dan Kirschen, Berni Barta, and Tamara Kawar; thanks to you all for your help in getting this book to its home. Enormous thanks to the team at S&S: to Tzipora Baitch for her wise guidance; to Patty Bashe for her copyedit; to proofreader and fact-checker Jason Chappell; and to copyediting manager and lifesaver Jessica Chin; to Briana Scharfenberg and Leila Siddiqi for getting the word out; and to Jon Karp for saying yes.

Before the words came the research. Thank you to Amber Tong Gao, Lucy Sun, Stephanie Neel, and Claire Zajdel, and to Lucy Leventhorpe, who deftly and thoughtfully brought it all under control. Most of all though, I'm profoundly grateful to Sam Reisman, whose careful, comprehensive efforts provided the foundation.

This is also a book about connections, so thanks to all the following who helped connect me with people, information, and images: Lisa Anderson, Claire Austin, Janet Bunde, Katie M. Ehrlich, Mya Jones, Emily Klein, Anne Kumer, Maren Lankford, Allison Malecha, Lori

Nelson, Maria Olivero, Josefina Poniente, Nicole Sexton, Peggy Smith, and Susan Swenson, Michelle Press and Daniel Montoya at Getty, Susan Lennon at Alamy, Lori Reese at Redux, Julia Heavey at the *New York Times*, Matthew Lutz at AP, Anita Duquette at the Whitney Museum of American Art, Jennifer Belt at Art Resources, Lexi Campbell at the Matthew Marks Gallery, Jonathan Kuhn and the fabulous Rebekah Burgess at NYC Parks Photo Archive, Teri Slotkin, Gilbert Santana, Bryan Thomas, the generous Mika Väisänen, and finally Larry Fink and Diana Mara Henry—two real heroes behind the lens.

Though I moved to New York in 1980 for college, my real education has been at the feet of other remarkable teachers: Edward Said, Arthur Loeb, Luis Sanjurjo, Genevieve Young, Richard Saul Wurman, Brian Urquhart, Rudy Crew, Anthony Heilbut, Mike Gecan, and Kurt Thometz. In some way or another, they're on every page of this book.

What follows is a list of people who made a significant contribution, whether they know it or not; friends, neighbors, interviewees, people who let me rant, who challenged me or aimed me in a new direction. Charlie Ahearn, John Ahearn, Kurt Andersen, Dr. Holly Anderson, Joe Arnheim, Andrew Arends, Sue Atkins, Fred Bass, Aimee Bell, Sheila Bennett, Marcy Benstock, Barry Bergdoll, Daniel Biederman, Douglas Blonsky, Duncan Bock, Reverend David Brawley, Jim Broner, Robert Brueghman, Jim Buckley, Amanda Burden, Mickey Cartin, Bill Cohan, Paula Cooper, Katie Danziger, Josh David, Gordon Davis, Jane Dickson, Daniel Doctoroff, Cheryl Effron, Michael Eisner, Jessica Elfenbein, Sasha Emerson, Morgan Entrekin, Joni Evans, Susan Fales-Hill, Joan Feeney, Lorraine Ferguson, Ann ffolliott, Tony Fitzpatrick, Robert Feinstein, Susan K. Freedman, Lance Freeman, Deb Futter, Alexander Garvin, Emma Gilbey-Keller, Ann Godoff, Gary Goldsmith, Douglas Gray, Paul Gunther, Michael Hainey, Michael Hirschorn, William Hoffman, Steve Horowitz, Sidney Howard, Andy Humm, Lewis Hyman, Alfonso Izzi, David Kamp, Bill Keller, Fred Kent, Michael Kimmelman, Helen Klebnikov, Leslie Koch, Phillip Koch, Steve Koch, Mark Konkol, Anne Kreamer, Annik LaFarge, Robert Laird, Min Jin Lee, Franz Leichter, Nathan Leventhal, Elana Levin, Kate Levin, Reinhold Levy, Hilary Lewis, Russell Lewis, Joseph Lhota, Kenneth Lipper, Joanne Lipman, Michael Love, Myron Magnet, Richard Oldenburg, Richard

Panek, Andrew Patner, Bruce Phillips, Ruth Pomerance, Richard Ravitch, Rebecca Robertson, Harvey Robins, Elizabeth Barlow Rogers, Jeff Rosen, Barry Rosenfeld, Gene Russianoff, Julie Sandorf, Trina Scotland, Eben Shapiro, Howard Slatkin, Cara Stein, Neil Steinberg, Tim Stephenson, Timothy Stewart-Warner, Elisabeth Sussman, Elizabeth Taylor, Marvin Taylor, Marc Tessier-Lavigne, Matthew Traub, Adriana Trigiani, Jeff Weidell, Adam Weinberg, Carl Weisbrod, Christopher White, LuAnne Williams, Meg Wolitzer, and Joe Zajdel. EJ Camp, thank you for finding my good side, and as always, thank you, Will Balliett and Vijay Balakrishnan, old friends, for the honest reads. And to all my neighbors in my apartment building, thank you for showing me how to make a village in New York City.

To my son and daughter Nick and Kaye, and to all their friends making their lives in the next New York, it's your city now, fragile but still full of possibilities. I can't wait to see what you do.

And finally there's the Native New Yorker I love best, my wife Suzanne. Everyone knows she's the heart and soul of New York City.

Notes

Introduction

xiv *"Hello from the gutters"*: Jimmy Breslin, "Breslin to Son of Sam," *New York Daily News*, June 5, 1977.

xiv *Some 6.8 million*: Edward N. Costikyan, "Gotham's Shrinking," *New York Times*, February 5, 1979.

xiv *"People see it as bad"*: Michael Goodwin and Anna Quindlen, "New York City Park System Stands as a Tattered Remnant of Its Past," *New York Times*, October 13, 1980.

xviii *"[T]he larger the web"*: J. R. McNeill and William H. McNeill, *The Human Web: A Bird's-Eye View of World History* (New York: W. W. Norton, 2003), p. 5.

Chapter One | "I Love New York" Day

3 *Only six weeks*: Peter Kihss, "Snowstorm Shuts Schools and Offices," *New York Times*, February 7, 1978.

3 *history was consumed*: Jill Jonnes, *South Bronx Rising: The Rise, Fall, and Resurrection of an American City* (New York: Fordham University Press, 2002), p. 8.

3 *150 times a day*: Charles Brecher and Raymond D. Horton, eds., *Setting Municipal Priorities, 1982* (New York: Russell Sage Foundation, 1981), p. 273.

5 *"Nobody was willing"*: Robert Wagner Jr. Oral History, Edward I. Koch Administration Oral History Project, Columbia University, pp. 1–8.

5 *the murder rate*: James Traub, *The Devil's Playground: A Century of Pleasure and Profit in Times Square* (New York: Random House, 2004), p. 121.

6 *twice a year*: Brecher and Horton, eds., *Setting Municipal Priorities, 1982*, p. 188.

6 *"The only agenda"*: Gordon Davis interview.

6 *"Punk wasn't about"*: Legs McNeil and Gillian McCain, *Please Kill Me: The Uncensored Oral History of Punk* (London: Abacus, 1996), p. 318.

6 *everyone believed*: Robert W. Bailey, *The Crisis Regime: The MAC, the EFCB, and the Political Impact of the New York City Financial Crisis* (Albany: State University of New York Press, 1984), p. 117.

7 *Cavanaugh had pulled out*: Franz Leichter interview.

7 *"Many things"*: Robert Wagner Jr. Oral History, Edward I. Koch Administration Oral History Project, Columbia University, pp. 1–8.

7 *an economic panel*: Ken Auletta, *The Streets Were Paved with Gold* (New York: Random House, 1979), p. 76.

7 *Impeaching the feckless*: Leichter interview.

7 *"so distraught"*: Ibid.

7 *a "crisis regime"*: Bailey, *The Crisis Regime*.

7 *at much higher rates*: Lynne A. Weikart, *Follow the Money: Who Controls New York City Mayors?* (Albany: State University of New York Press, 2009), pp. 30–31.

8 *"It would mean"*: Felix Rohatyn, *Dealings* (New York: Simon & Schuster, 2010), p. 158.

8 *Albany and Washington*: Julia Vitullo-Martin and Richard P. Nathan, "Intergovernmental Aid," in Charles Brecher and Raymond D. Horton, eds., *Setting Municipal Priorities, 1981* (Allanheld, Osmun: LandMark Studies, 1980), p. 45.

8 *a record 16.7 million*: Miriam Greenberg, *Branding New York: How a City in Crisis Was Sold to the World* (New York: Routledge, 2008), p. 212.

8 *"below minimum standards"*: Mimi Sheraton, "Promise Unfulfilled at Tavern on the Green," *New York Times*, October 8, 1976.

8 *"I just love it here"*: Andy Warhol quoted in Judy Klemesrud, "'Tavern-on-Green Reopens After $2.5 Million in Work," *New York Times*, September 1, 1976.

8 *"It was really a celebration"*: Andy Warhol, *The Andy Warhol Diaries*, Pat Hackett, ed. (New York: Warner Books, 1989), p. 110.

9 *"It's in danger"*: Paul Mazursky quoted in Andy Logan, "Around City Hall," *The New Yorker*, May 1, 1978.

9 *"brashness, pathos"*: In and Out Around Town, *New York*, April 24, 1978.

9 *"I should hope so, Bob"*: Diana Vreeland quoted in Victor Bockris, *Warhol: The Biography*, 2d ed. (Cambridge, MA: Da Capo Press, 2003), p. 420.

10 *"completely democratic society"*: Charles Kaiser, *The Gay Metropolis: 1940–1996* (New York: Houghton Mifflin, 1997), p. 112.

10 *"[A]ll we do is live in"*: Larry Kramer, *Faggots* (New York: Plume, 1978), p. 314.

10 *"affectional preference"*: Maurice Carroll, "Bias Against Homosexuals Banned by Koch in All Mayoral Agencies," *New York Times*, January 24, 1978.

10 *"good because it's awful"*: Susan Sontag, "Notes on 'Camp,'" *Partisan Review*, Fall 1964.

11 *"The city has to be tolerant"*: E. B. White, *Here Is New York* (New York: Harper and Brothers, 1949), p. 43.

11 *"clock theory"*: Grandmaster Flash, with David Ritz, *The Adventures of Grandmaster Flash: My Life, My Beats* (New York: Broadway Books, 2008), p. 79.

11 *"To be contented"*: Diana Vreeland, *D. V.* (New York: Da Capo Press, 1984, 1997 reprint), p. 133.

11 *"I realized"*: "Ed Koch: Hizzoner," *New York*, April 6, 1998.

11 *New Yorkers believed*: Frank Lynn, "Poll Shows Most New Yorkers Think Koch Will Be Good Mayor," *New York Times*, January 2, 1978.

11 *"The world started"*: Allen Schwartz quoted in Ken Auletta, "The Mayor—1," *The New Yorker*, September 10, 1979.

11 *cajoled him*: Michael Riedel, *Razzle Dazzle: The Battle for Broadway* (New York: Simon & Schuster, 2015), p. 186.

12 *dented '74 Chrysler*: Edward Ranzal, "Chrysler Says City Has Refused Offer to Check On and Fix Koch's Newport," *New York Times*, February 24, 1978.

12 *2,300 miles of potholed streets*: Brian Ketcham and Stan Pinkwas, "That's the Way the City Crumbles," *Village Voice*, September 18, 1978.

12 *"To live on"*: Ed Koch quoted in Ken Auletta, "The Mayor—1," *The New Yorker*, September 10, 1979.

12 *"a liberal with sanity"*: Koch quoted in Sam Roberts, "Koch Against Koch," *New York Times Magazine*, June 11, 1989.

12 *Lindsay kids' treehouse*: "Around City Hall: Ring in the New," *The New Yorker*, January 10, 1994.

12 *"I owed nothing"*: Edward I. Koch with Daniel Paisner, *Citizen Koch: An Autobiography* (New York: St. Martin's Press, 1992), p. 150.

13 *"You're not my partners"*: Ed Koch, La Guardia and Wagner Archives, Video Oral History Project, Ed Koch and Nat Leventhal with Richard K. Lieberman and Stephen Weinstein at Borough Hall, November 13, 2012, p. 19.

13 *cut taxes*: Temporary Commission on City Finances, *The City in Transition: Prospects and Policies for New York* (New York: Arno Press, 1978), appendix I.

13 *poverty in the city*: Mark K. Levitan and Susan S. Wieler, "Poverty in New York City, 1969–99: The Influence of Demographic Change, Income Growth, and Income Inequality," FRBNY Economic Policy Review, July 2008.

13 *"[i]f either he or the Mayor"*: "Slow Start Toward Economic Salvation," *New York Times*, February 16, 1978.

13 *"pressure groups"*: Edward I. Koch with William Rauch, *Mayor: An Autobiography* (New York: Simon & Schuster, 1984), p. 111.

14 *embed on-loan executives*: "Phone Company Executive Named New York's Operations Chief," *New York Times*, February 4, 1977.

14 *"the most conspicuous"*: Bill Moyers, "The World of David Rockefeller—Part 1," *Bill Moyers Journal*, WNET, February 7, 1980.

14 *a vast fortune*: David Rockefeller, *Memoirs* (New York: Random House, 2002), pp. 10–12.

14 *"I idolized Nelson"*: Ibid., p. 36.

15 *Going forward*: Daniel Bell, *The Coming of Post-Industrial Society* (New York: Basic Books, 1973).

15 *fifty books explaining*: James R. Beniger, *The Control Revolution: Technological and Economic Origins of the Information Society* (Cambridge, MA: Harvard University Press, 1986), table 1.1.

15 *bungmakers and spats*: Desmond Smith, "Info City," *New York*, February 5, 1981.

15 *largely split apart*: Marc Levinson, "Container Shipping and the Decline of New York, 1955–1975," *Business History Review*, vol. 80, no. 1 (Spring, 2006).

15 *"Capital," he liked to say, "will go"*: Walter B. Wriston, *The Twilight of Sovereignty: How the Information Revolution Is Transforming Our World* (New York: Charles Scribner's Sons, 1992), p. 61.

16 *"maintenance and enhancement"*: Paul E. Peterson, *City Limits* (Chicago: University of Chicago Press, 1981).

16 *"financial supermarket"* and passim: Phillip L. Zweig, *Wriston: Walter Wriston, Citibank, and the Rise and Fall of American Financial Supremacy* (New York: Crown, 1995), pp. 541–549.

17 *musical chairs*: William Zeckendorf with Edward McCreary. *Zeckendorf: The Autobiography of the Man Who Played a Real-Life Game of Monopoly and Won the Largest Real Estate Empire in History* (Chicago: Plaza Press, 2014), p. 264.

17 *"I must say I was annoyed"*: Rockefeller, *Memoirs*, p. 391.

17 *"In the long run"*: Quoted in Robert Fitch, *The Assassination of New York* (London: Verso, 1993), p. 120.

17 *"Expressways are never"*: Jane Jacobs quoted in The Talk of the Town, *The New Yorker*, May 1, 1978.

18 *"[H]e broke into tears"*: Koch with Rauch, *Mayor*, p. 58.

19 *"a working alliance"*: Jimmy Carter, Public Papers of the Presidents of the United States: Jimmy Carter, 1978, p. 578.

19 *a $4.5 billion workable*: Jac Friedgut, "Financing," in Brecher and Horton, eds., *Setting Municipal Priorities, 1982*, p. 181.

Chapter Two I **Something It Hadn't Been**

21 *the Federal government*: "The Zoo Story," *New York*, March 26, 1977.

21 *"Daddy," said Elizabeth*: Elizabeth Davis quoted in Carter Wiseman, "The New Zoo," *New York*, July 18, 1988.

22 *up to $40 billion*: Tom Boast, "Debt and Capital Management," in Brecher and Horton, eds., *Setting Municipal Priorities, 1981*, p. 120.

22 *"bad enough"*: John Lawe in Brian Ketcham and Stan Pinkwas, "That's the Way the City Crumbles," *Village Voice*, September 18, 1978.

22 *"make the city"*: Carl Weisbrod, Remarks at the Association for a Better New York Breakfast, September 8, 2016, NYC Department of City Planning press release.

22 *"Everybody who was any"*: Davis interview.

22 *his attempts* and passim: Charles Brecher and James M. Hartman, "Financial Planning," in Charles Brecher and Raymond D. Horton, eds. *Setting Municipal Priorities, 1983* (New York: Russell Sage Foundation, 1982), pp. 234–241.

23 *nonpartisan managerial:* The City of New York, The Mayor's Management Report, February 20, 1978, pp. 1–2.

23 *"Removal of incompetents":* The Talk of the Town, *The New Yorker,* February 27, 1978.

23 *"a tone that the glass":* Davis interview.

24 *oversaw 24,000 acres:* The Talk of the Town, *The New Yorker,* February 27, 1978.

24 *"A park is a work of art"* and passim: Frederick Law Olmsted, *Writings on Landscape, Culture, and Society,* Charles E. Beveridge, ed. (New York: Library of America, 2015), pp. 439, 478.

24 *"commonplace civilization":* Adam Gopnik, "A Critic at Large: Olmsted's Trip," *The New Yorker,* March 31, 1997.

24 *Clown Prince:* Thomas Hoving, *Artful Tom: A Memoir* (Artnet Worldwide Corporation, 2009).

24 *another way to use:* Vince Cannato, *The Ungovernable City: John Lindsay and His Struggle to Save New York* (New York: Basic Books, 2001), p. 147.

24 *"systematic pattern":* Glenn Fowler, "Levitt's Aides Find Pattern of Loafing by Park Workers," *New York Times,* April 9, 1978.

24 *"honed a superior wit":* Orde Coombs, "The Prince of Central Park," *New York,* November 8, 1981.

25 *"We have cutbacks":* Gordon Davis quoted in Orde Coombs, "The Prince of Central Park," *New York,* November 8, 1981.

26 *"Like the Jews":* Quoted in Michael Brandow, *New York's Poop Scoop Law: Dogs, the Dirt, and Due Process* (West Lafayette, IN: Purdue University Press, 2008), p. 9.

27 *"a shithole"* and passim: Davis interview.

27 *"I can accept graffiti":* Robert Smithson, "Frederick Law Olmsted and the Dialectical Landscape," in *Robert Smithson: The Collected Writings* (Berkeley: University of California Press, 1979), p. 169.

27 *one survey counted 83%:* E. S. Savas, A Study of Central Park, Center for Government Studies, Graduate School of Business, Columbia University, December 1976, pp. 2–31.

28 *"We're going to hang":* Davis interview.

29 *"What a city does best":* William H. Whyte, "The Center Is the Center Is the Center," April 22, 1976, William H. Whyte Papers, Box 1, Folder 2, Rockefeller Archive Center.

29 *"urban pioneers":* Koch quoted in Lee Dembart, "Koch, in Inaugural, Asks That Pioneers 'Come East' to City," *New York Times,* January 2, 1978.

30 *"My strength":* William H. Whyte, *A Time of War: Remembering Guadalcanal, A Battle Without Maps* (New York: Fordham University Press, 2000), p. 105.

30 *"reassert itself as a good":* William H. Whyte, "Are Cities Un-American?," in *The Exploding Metropolis* (Berkeley: University of California Press, 1993), p. 23.

30 *"Little plans":* Ibid., p. 52.

31 *they helped stanch:* Matthew Gordon Lasner in Nicholas Dagen Bloom and Matthew Gordon Lasner, eds., *Affordable Housing in New York* (Princeton: Princeton University Press, 2016), pp. 173–174.

32 *"New ideas must use"*: Jacobs quoted in Max Allen, ed., *Ideas That Matter: The Worlds of Jane Jacobs* (Owen Sound, Ontario: The Ginger Press, 2011), p. 85.

33 *Everett Ortner*: Kay Holmes, "Redoing Brooklyn Brownstones," *New York Times*, June 14, 1979.

33 *"This summer"*: Rum Rejnis, " 'Back to City' Conference Set," *New York Times*, August 25, 1974.

33 *identified with the borough*: Suleiman Osman, *The Invention of Brownstone Brooklyn: Gentrification and the Search for Authenticity in Postwar New York* (New York: Oxford University Press, 2011), p. 19.

34 *a racist hope*: Rosten Woo with Meredith TenHoor and Damon Rich, *Street Value: Shopping, Planning, and Politics at Fulton Mall* (New York: Princeton Architectural Press, 2010), pp. 55–63.

34 *Since at least*: Richard Plunz, *A History of Housing in New York City* (New York: Columbia University Press, 1990), p. 10.

35 *"a souk"*: Calvin Tomkins, "The Art World," *The New Yorker*, May 19, 1980.

35 *"SoHo was not only"*: Margo Hentoff, "Looks," *Village Voice*, June 12, 1978.

36 *"Because our artists' eyes"*: Ingrid Bengis, "A SoHo Pioneer, But Disenchanted," *New York Times*, June 29, 1978.

36 *The City estimated in 1978*: "Loft Horizons," *Village Voice*, July 31, 1978.

36 *"fervently deplore"*: William H. Whyte, *The Essential William H. Whyte*, Albert LaFarge, ed. (New York: Fordham University Press, 2000), p. 228.

36 *"Moveable chairs"*: Fred Kent interview.

37 *"culture of congestion"*: Rem Koolhaas, *Delirious New York* (New York: Monacelli Press, 1994; new edition), p. 293.

37 *"safety in concrete"*: "Buying Real Estate: Safety in Concrete," *New York*, February 26, 1979.

37 *Private sector employment*: The City of New York, The Mayor's Management Report, April 26, 1979, pp. I–19.

37 *"a revival now going on"*: Joyce Purnick, "Good News, Bad News About New York," *New York*, May 14, 1979.

37 *switched from constructing*: Roistacher and Tobier, "Housing Policy," in Brecher and Horton, eds., *Setting Municipal Priorities, 1981*, pp. 157–165.

37 *Early on, the mayor*: Charles J. Orlebeke, *New Life at Ground Zero: New York, Home Ownership, and the Future of American Cities* (Albany: The Rockefeller Institute Press, 1997), p. 59.

37 *10,243 units in 1979*: The City of New York, The Mayor's Management Report, January 30, 1981, p. xxxi.

37 *"providing housing"*: Alan S. Oser, "About Real Estate," *New York Times*, March 15, 1978.

38 *approved conversion plans*: Leonard G. Sahling and Rona B. Stein, "Co-op Fever in New York City," *Federal Reserve Bank of New York Quarterly Review*, Spring 1980.

38 *"I wouldn't think"*: Harry Helmsley quoted in "Leona and Harry: Money and Love," *New York*, October 3, 1988.

39 *sell it back*: Carter B. Horsley, "Commodore Plan Is Key to the City's Tax-Aid Strategy," *New York Times*, March 28, 1976.

39 *Mayor Beame pled*: Tom Shachtman, *Skyscraper Dreams: The Great Real Estate Dynasties of New York* (New York: Little, Brown, 1991), pp. 286–289.

39 *attended Donald's*: Marie Brenner, "After the Gold Rush," *Vanity Fair*, September 1990.

40 *"The situation is bad"*: William H. Whyte, memo to Rockefeller Brothers Fund, November 26, 1979, William H. Whyte Papers, box 1, folder 2, Rockefeller Archive Center.

40 *"I was sold"*: Dan Biederman interview.

41 *"at its most rewarding"*: Samuel R. Delany, *Times Square Red, Times Square Blue* (New York: New York University Press, 1999), p. 121.

41 *"rats chasing popcorn"*: Charlie Ahearn interview.

42 *$20 million worth*: Shachtman, *Skyscraper Dreams*, p. 294.

42 *129 projects had gotten*: James F. Sterba, "City, Citing Economic Upswing to Take Closer Look at Midtown Commerical Buildings' Tax Abatements," *New York Times*, July 26, 1978.

42 *"the highest prices"*: "Trump Pursued a 'Vision' of Tower with Tenacity," *New York Times*, August 26, 1980.

42 *"There was no question"*: Donald J. Trump, *Trump: The Art of the Deal* (New York: Warner Books, 1987), p. 190.

42 *"We were out"*: Louise Sunshine quoted in Michael Gross, *House of Outrageous Fortune* (New York: Atria Books, 2014), pp. 84–85.

Chapter Three | **New York Equalize You**

43 *"stay back!"*: Peggy Jameson quoted in Joe Conason and Ianthe Thomas, "Crown Heights: Who Controls the Streets?" *Village Voice*, July 3, 1978.

43 *"choked to death"* and passim: Joseph B. Treaster, "Excessive Force in Brooklyn Man's Death Is Denied," *New York Times*, June 18, 1978.

43 *"This city"*: "Mayor's Newsletter," July 1978.

44 *"When you reduce"*: Lee Dembart, "Koch Says He's Failed to Justify Fund Cuts to Minorities in City," *New York Times*, January 11, 1979.

44 *"good-government groups"*: Koch quoted in Ken Auletta, *Hard Feelings: Reporting on the Pols, the Press, the People and the City* (New York: Random House, 1980), p. 30.

44 *distrust for the liberal*: Koch with Rauch, *Mayor*, pp. 27–28.

44 *"The blacks Koch"*: Charles Rangel quoted in "Koch's War on the Poor," *Village Voice*, May 29, 1978.

44 *"Blacks don't vote"*: Koch quoted in Scott Yates, "Don't Know Much About History," *Spy*, January 1990.

44 *"If you can't get"*: Charles Rangel, La Guardia and Wagner Archives, La Guardia Community College/CUNY Oral History Project, Ed Koch with Rep. Charlie Rangel with Richard K. Lieberman, September 16, 2011.

44 *"New York City didn't burn"*: Davis interview.

45 *"the poverty programs"*: Jack Newfield, "Amsterdam News Sells Out Harlem," *Village Voice*, April 10, 1978.

45 *As blue-collar employment*: Michael Javen Fortner, *Black Silent Majority: The*

Rockefeller Drug Laws and the Politics of Punishment (Cambridge, MA: Harvard University Press, 2015), p. 46.

45 *"our foot in the door"*: Major Owens quoted in Jim Sleeper, *The Closest of Strangers: Liberalism and the Politics of Race in New York* (New York: W. W. Norton, 1990), p. 108.

45 *"If you are a nobody"*: Jane Jacobs in *Vital Little Plans: The Short Works of Jane Jacobs*, Samuel Zipp and Nathan Storring, eds. (New York: Random House, 2016), p. 71.

45 *"I'm not here"*: "Mayor Koch Stalks Out of Meeting in Queens in Dispute Over Agenda," *New York Times*, February 28, 1978.

45 *"the power to demand"*: Michael Gecan, *Going Public: An Organizer's Guide to Citizen Action* (Boston: Beacon Press, 2002), p. 7.

46 *"a special cold"*: Ed Chambers quoted in Sam Roberts, "Edwards Chambers, Early Leader in Community Organizing, Dies at 85," *New York Times*, May 1, 2015.

46 *the mayor was heckled*: Arthur Browne, Dan Collins, Dan & Michael Goodwin, *I, Koch* (New York: Dodd, Mead & Co., 1985), pp. 207–208.

46 *"a tragic, unforeseeable"*: Andy Logan, "Around City Hall," *The New Yorker*, December 25, 1978.

46 *"a volcano"*: Edward Hightower quoted in "The City Politic: Crown Heights, One Year Later," *New York*, July 2, 1979.

46 *"the Seven-Mile World"*: Jeff Chang, *Can't Stop, Won't Stop: A History of the Hip-Hop Generation* (New York: St. Martin's Press, 2005), p. 109.

46 *"young urban"*: Russell Simmons with Nelson George, *Life and Def: Sex, Drugs, Money + God* (New York: Crown, 2001), p. 4.

47 *"a way station"*: Robert Farris Thompson, *Aesthetic of the Cool: Afro-Atlantic Art and Music* (New York: Periscope, 2011), p. 78.

47 *"warriors for their"*: Afrika Bambaataa quoted in Jim Fricke and Charlie Ahearn, *Yes Yes Y'all: Oral History of Hip-Hop's First Decade* (New York: Da Capo Press, 2002), p. 44.

48 *"a fight with steps"*: Thompson, *Aesthetic of the Cool*, p. 47.

48 *"[H]ip hop wasn't a nice place"*: Charlie Ahearn interview.

48 *"[H]ip hop gatherings"*: Nelson George, "Introduction," in Fricke and Ahearn, *Yes Yes Y'all*.

48 *"peace guards"*: Kool Herc in ibid., p. 26.

48 *"a religion about"*: Simmons with George, *Life and Def*, p. 39.

48 *Five Percenters bridged*: Ibid., p. 40.

48 *"A shift was occurring"*: Nelson George, "Introduction," in Fricke and Ahearn, *Yes Yes Y'all*.

49 *43,000 apartments*: Michael Sterne, "South Bronx Hub: Worry Amid the Bustle," *New York Times*, January 14, 1978.

49 *"white wine"*: Patti Astor quoted in Michael Hixon, "Patti Astor Revives New York's Fun Gallery in Hermosa Beach," *The Beach Reporter*, June 5, 2018.

50 *"started to talk back"*: Thompson, *Aesthetic of the Cool*, p. 45.

50 *"You better clean"*: Rangel quoted in "Chairman of the Money," *New York*, January 15, 2007.

50 *an estimated 80,000*: Emanuel Tobier, "Population," in Brecher and Horton, eds., *Setting Municipal Priorities, 1982*, pp. 38–39.

50 *Local 23–35*: Emanuel Tobier, "Foreign Immigration," in Brecher and Horton, eds., *Setting Municipal Priorities, 1983*, pp. 195–196.

50 *light manufacturing*: Roger Waldinger, *Still the Promised City? African-Americans and New Immigrants in Postindustrial New York* (Cambridge, MA: Harvard University Press, 1996), p. 131.

50 *The Refugee Act of 1980*: Tobier, "Foreign Immigration" in Brecher and Horton, eds., *Setting Municipal Priorities, 1983*, pp. 182–184.

51 *"Soon we be"*: Tamara Kontorov quoted in "A Little Russia Grows in Brooklyn," *New York*, June 5, 1981.

51 *"most of the people"*: Lloyd Williams, interviewed by Aaliyah Barker, "A People's History of Harlem," NYPL Community Oral History Project, July 24, 2017.

51 *60% of its population*: Lance Freeman, *There Goes the 'Hood: Views of Gentrification from the Ground Up* (Philadelphia: Temple University Press, 2006), p. 26.

51 *40% poverty rate*: Ibid., p. 27.

51 *infant mortality rate*: Michael Sterne, "Residents of Harlem Suffer Worst Health in New York," *New York Times*, April 10, 1978.

51 *keeping buildings from going*: Brian D. Goldstein, *The Roots of Urban Renaissance: Gentrification and the Struggle over Harlem* (Cambridge, MA: Harvard University Press, 2017), ch. 4.

51 *HUDC, a UDC subsidiary*: Greg Thomas, "Pataki's Man in Harlem," *Village Voice*, January 28, 2003.

51 *direct jobs*: Derek S. Hyra, *The New Urban Renewal: The Economic Transformation of Harlem and Bronzeville* (Chicago: University of Chicago Press, 2008), pp. 70–72.

52 *cultural leadership*: Philip Kasinitz, *Caribbean New York: Black Immigrants and the Politics of Race* (Ithaca, NY: Cornell University Press, 1992), p. 151.

52 *"They haven't to know"*: Mighty Sparrow, "Mas in Brooklyn," quoted in ibid., p. 150.

52 *"a giant sponge soaking"*: Quoted in Waldinger, *Still the Promised City?*, p. 108.

52 *"when Koch is through"*: "Koch's War on the Poor," *Village Voice*, May 29, 1978.

53 *"medically indigent"*: Bruce Vladeck assisted by Willine Carr, "Health," in Brecher and Horton, eds., *Setting Municipal Priorities, 1982*, p. 324.

53 *"a declaration of war"*: Fred Samuel quoted in "In the News," *Black Enterprise*, December 1979.

53 *"What was happening"*: Charles Rangel, Ed Koch, and Rep. Charlie Rangel, La Guardia Community College Oral History Project, La Guardia and Wagner Archives, September 16, 2011.

53 *"a mistake"*: Koch, ibid.

Chapter Four | Every Night a Different Channel

55 *"newer than new"*: Ann Magnuson in Klaus Nomi's 1978 debut at New Wave Vaudeville, Irving Plaza (NYC), https://www.youtube.com/watch?v=I4sMKzTIuME.

56 *"Doyens of Punk Rock"*: John Rockwell, "Ramones, Doyens of Punk Rock, in the Big Time," *New York Times*, January 6, 1978.

56 *"To be hip"*: Glenn O'Brien, *The Cool School: Writing from America's Hip Underground* (New York: The Library of America, 2013), p. xi.

56 *"[W]hen people told you"*: Carlo McCormick, "A Crack in Time," in Marvin Taylor, ed., *The Downtown Book: The New York Art Scene 1974–1984* (Princeton: Princeton University Press, 2006), p. 69.

56 *"Oh, maybe ten"*: Marcel Duchamp quoted in Suzi Gablik, *Has Modernism Failed?* (New York: Thames & Hudson, 1984), p. 12.

57 *"[U]nderneath each picture"*: Douglas Crimp, "Pictures," in Brian Wallis, ed., *Art After Modernism: Rethinking Representation* (New York: The New Museum of Contemporary Art, 1984), p. 186.

57 *"desire to confront"*: Jane Dickson interview.

57 *like "stone soup"*: Ibid.

57 *"provided a kind"*: Walter Robinson quoted in Shawna Cooper and Karli Wurzelbacher, *"Times Square Show* Revisited," Hunter College Art Galleries, timessquareshowrevisited.com.

58 *"The public has a right"* and passim: Keith Haring, *Journals* (New York: Penguin Books, 1996).

58 *"a different channel"*: Ann Magnuson, "Conversation: Ann Magnuson and Carlo McCormick," cosponsored by Fales Library NYU and Grey Art Gallery, May 27, 2015.

58 *"coolness and being hip"*: Ann Magnuson quoted in John Gruen, *Keith Haring: The Authorized Biography* (New York: Prentice-Hall Press, 1991), p. 47.

58 *"He was the father"*: Kenny Scharf quoted in Bockris, *Warhol: The Biography*, p. 464.

59 *"a Sphinx"*: Truman Capote quoted in Jesse Kornbluth, "The World of Warhol," *New York*, September 9, 1987.

59 *"most colossal creep"*: Frederick Eberstadt quoted in Bockris, *Warhol: The Biography*, p. 140.

59 *"glamorized and satirized"* and passim: Lita Hornick quoted in ibid., p. 433.

59 *"original bohemians"*: Calvin Trillin, "US: Greenwich Village," *The New Yorker*, June 7, 1982.

61 *"a men's club"*: Jules Feiffer quoted in "If You've Been Afraid to Go to Elaine's These Past 20 Years, Here's What You've Missed," *New York*, May 2, 1983.

61 *"a uniquely relaxed"*: The Talk of the Town, *The New Yorker*, December 11, 1978.

62 *"only a certain class"*: Dick Snyder quoted in Thomas Whiteside, *The Blockbuster Complex: Conglomerates, Show Business, and Book Publishing* (Middletown, CT: Wesleyan University Press, 1980), p. 117.

63 *"lie, bribe and risk mental"*: Hilton Kramer, "Tutankhamun Show in New York at Last," *New York Times*, December 20, 1978.

63 *Mayor's Committee*: Report of the Mayor's Committee on Cultural Policy, October 15, 1974, Martin E. Segal, chair.

63 *18,182 graphic designers*: Richard Goldstein, "Artists: A Shadow Community and Its Permanent Government," *Village Voice*, March 20, 1978.

63 *"a social lubricant"*: Robert Kingsley quoted in Herbert I. Schiller, *Culture, Inc.: The Corporate Takeover of Public Expression* (New York: Oxford University Press, 1989), p. 92.
63 *"corporate equivalent"*: Jack Egan, "Mobil the King: How the Oil Giant Beat the Networks," *New York*, February 12, 1979.
63 *"the world's premier"*: Calvin Tomkins, "The Art World," *The New Yorker*, September 15, 1980.
63 *"a convergence"*: Roberta Smith in "Eyes of Richard Avedon," *Art in America* 67 (January–February 1979), p. 133.
64 *"A little bad taste is"*: Vreeland, *D.V.*, p. 2.
64 *"People with something"*: Margo Hentoff, "Looks," *Village Voice*, June 12, 1978.

Chapter Five | **To Lake Ladoga, and Beyond**

65 *"moxie"*: Maurice Carroll, "How's He Doing?" *New York Times*, December 24, 1978.
65 *"Out there around '83"*: Lee Dembart, "Koch Budget Cut Likely to Cover Hospitals, Prisons and Education," *New York Times*, December 12, 1978.
65 *only 2,500 or so cops*: Nicholas Pileggi, "Open City," *New York*, January 19, 1981.
65 *No one analyzed*: Auletta, *Hard Feelings*, p. 38.
66 *volume of data*: Charles R. Morris, *The Cost of Good Intentions: New York City and the Liberal Experiment* (New York: W. W. Norton, 1980), pp. 49–50.
66 *Control Crisis*: Beniger, *The Control Revolution*.
66 *"completely unauditable"*: Alfonso Izzi quoted in "NYC Saves $300 Million with Computerized System," *American City and County*, November 1983.
66 *nearly lost UPS*: Zweig, *Wriston*, p. 274.
66 *"almost total collapse"*: Rockefeller, *Memoirs*, p. 305.
66 *"garbage in"*: Ibid., p. 308.
67 *"We had no idea"*: Peter Solomon quoted in Desmond Smith, "Brave New City Government," *New York*, May 14, 1984.
67 *"There are now three"*: Robert Wagner Jr. quoted in Jonathan Soffer, *Ed Koch and the Rebuilding of New York City* (New York: Columbia University Press, 2010), p. 186.
67 *"I cracked the whip"* and passim: Nathan Levinthal Jr. Oral History, Edward I. Koch Administration Oral History Project, Columbia University, pp. 1–16.
67 *work conditions*: David Bird, "Sanitationmen, Lacking Job Pride, Resign Themselves to Public's Scorn," *New York Times*, April 23, 1979.
67 *Jets tickets*: The City of New York, The Mayor's Management Report, September 17, 1983, p. 87.
67 *productivity and Project Scorecard*: The City of New York, The Mayor's Management Report, January 30, 1981, pp. xi–xvii, 46.
68 *"day-to-day"*: Nathan Levinthal Jr. Oral History, Edward I. Koch Administration Oral History Project, Columbia University, pp. 2–49.
68 *"Special interest groups"*: Edward Schumacher, "Top New York Executives Plan Coalition to Exert More Influence," *New York Times*, December 19, 1979.

438 | Notes

68 *"catalytic bigness"*: David Rockefeller quoted in "The City," *New York Times*, February 28, 1979.

68 *"third sector"*: Peter Dobkin Hall, *Inventing the Nonprofit Sector and Other Essays on Philanthropy, Voluntarism, and Nonprofit Organizations* (Baltimore: Johns Hopkins University Press, 1992), pp. 77–78.

68 *"what is public"*: Bell, *The Coming of Post-Industrial Society*, p. 322.

69 *"equal partner"*: David Rockefeller, "Ingredients for Successful Partnerships: The New York City Case," *Proceedings of the Academy of Political Science*, vol. 36, no. 2, Public-Private Partnerships: Improving Urban Life (1986), p. 122.

69 *"assume greater"*: David Rockefeller, address at Economic Forecast Conference, LIU, March 12, 1969, David Rockefeller Speeches, box 40, folder 612, Rockefeller Archive Center.

69 *a $258 grant in 1975*: "Introduction," in Brecher and Horton, eds., *Setting Municipal Priorities, 1981*, p. 2.

69 *"Everybody seemed way"*: John Ahearn interview.

70 *"the microchip"*: "The Age of Miracle Chips," *Time*, February 20, 1978.

70 *"small-scale community"*: "The Interactive Telecommunications Laboratory: A Proposal," Alternate Media Center, NYU School of the Arts.

70 *"doctors are against"*: Ruth Spear, "Fear of Frying: A Guide to Buying and Cooking Fish," *New York*, April 10, 1978.

70 *"not our city"*: Marvin Feldman and Cynthia Feldman, "Alas, Manhattan Is Spoiled," *New York Times*, February 9, 1980.

70 *crime was rising*: The City of New York, The Mayor's Management Report, January 30, 1981, p. 4.

71 *"produced a bonanza"*: Rita Reif, "Frenzied Market for Major Art," *New York Times*, November 18, 1979; Rita Reif, "At Auctions in 1979: The Stars That Broke the Records," *New York Times*, January 17, 1980.

71 *"Say you were"*: Andy Warhol, *The Philosophy of Andy Warhol* (New York: Harcourt, 1975), pp. 133–134.

71 *"The market"*: Joseph Kossuth quoted in "The New Queen of the Art Scene," *New York*, April 19, 1982.

72 *"New Yorkers seem"*: James Lardner, "Painting the Elephant," *The New Yorker*, July 12, 1984.

72 *30% of doors*: David A. Andelman, "Study Concludes 'Worst' Subway Is West Side IRT," *New York Times*, October 14, 1980.

72 *"Armies of the Night"*: Robin Herman, "Ads Resumed for a Gang Movie After Sporadic Violence at Theaters," *New York Times*, February 23, 1979.

72 *"a city of the very rich"*: Michael W. Brooks, *Subway City: Riding the Trains, Reading New York* (New Brunswick, NJ: Rutgers University Press, 1997), p. 9.

73 *"Muddling Through"*: Edward S. Seely Jr., "Mass Transit," in Brecher and Horton, eds., *Setting Municipal Priorities, 1982*, pp. 406–409.

73 *Everyone told Ravitch*: James Lardner, "Painting the Elephant," *The New Yorker*, July 12, 1984.

73 *"the course of history"* and passim: Ed Koch, La Guardia Community College Oral History Project, La Guardia and Wagner Archives, June 25, 2010.

74 *as a union town*: Soffer, *Ed Koch and the Rebuilding of New York City*, p. 219.

74 *"seltzer instead of orange juice"*: Koch quoted in Martin Gottlieb, "Times Square Development Plan: A Lesson in Politics and Power," *New York Times*, March 9, 1984.

74 *"Glitzy"*: Herb Sturz quoted in Sam Roberts, *A Kind of Genius: Herb Sturz and Society's Toughest Problems* (New York: PublicAffairs, 2009), p. 237.

74 *"an enormous amount"*: Ibid., p. 4.

75 *"national cesspool"*: Holly Whyte quoted in ibid., p. 229.

75 *"a central location"*: John Ahearn interview.

75 *"capital," says Charlie, "of street culture"*: Charlie Ahearn interview.

75 *"raw, raucous, trashy"*: Jeffrey Deitch, "Report from Times Square," *Art in America*, September 1980.

76 *"you've got to make"*: Charlie Ahearn interview.

76 *"to attack," wrote the* East Village Eye, *"the wasteland"*: Leonard Abrams, *East Village Eye*, September–October 1980.

76 *"the soul"*: Diego Cortez quoted in Suzi Gablik, "Report from New York: The Graffiti Question," *Art in America*, October 1982.

76 *"a bouquet"*: Claes Oldenburg quoted in Norman Mailer, with Jon Naar photographs, *The Faith of Graffiti* (New York: HarperCollins, 2009).

76 *"New York City"*: Joseph Rivera, *Vandal Squad: Inside the New York City Transit Police Department, 1984–2004* (New York: powerHouse Books, 2008).

76 *"[T]he landlord couldn't"*: Dickson interview.

77 *"Only five years ago"*: Carter Wiseman, "How Green Was Our Meadow," *New York*, October 20, 1980.

77 *"had a psychological impact"*: Davis interview.

77 *raised $6.5 million*: Carter Wiseman, "Public Parks, Private Cash," *New York*, October 27, 1980.

77 *"as if it were a patient"*: Elizabeth Barlow Rogers, *Rebuilding Central Park: A Management and Restoration Plan* (Cambridge, MA: The MIT Press, 1987), p. 19.

77 *39 projects*: The City of New York, The Mayor's Management Report, January 30, 1981, p. xxix.

77 *"only what's good"*: Andrew Heiskell with Ralph Graves, *Outsider, Insider: An Unlikely Success Story* (New York: Marian-Darien Press, 1998), p. 236.

77 *"A computer or calculator"*: The Talk of the Town, "Pondering," *The New Yorker*, July 14, 1980.

77 *"most sophisticated"*: Browne, Collins, and Goodwin, *I, Koch*, p. 184.

78 *"most significant"*: Anna Quindlen, "About New York," *New York Times*, May 20, 1981.

78 *"a walking city"*: Christo quoted in "Christo and Jeanne-Claude with Praxis," *Brooklyn Rail*, July 1, 2004.

78 *"What am I"*: Michael Goodwin and Anna Quindlen, "New York City Park System Stands as a Tattered Remnant of Its Past," *New York Times*, October 13, 1980.

78 *"fell into place"*: Keith Haring quoted in Gruen, *Keith Haring*, p. 68.

79 *"a curtain wall"*: Ada Louise Huxtable, "Two Triumphant New Hotels for New York," *New York Times*, October 19, 1980.
79 *"It is urbane and elegant"*: Ibid.
79 *"Just junk"*: Donald Trump quoted in "The Ten Most Embarrassing New Yorkers," *Spy*, October 1986.

Chapter Six | The Age of the Individual

81 *"where I am going to give"*: Brooke Astor quoted in Wendy Goodman, "Selling Off the Money Room," *New York*, April 9, 2008.
81 *Brooke had learned*: Marilyn Berger, "Being Brooke Astor," *New York Times*, May 20, 1984.
82 *"horrible renaissance"*: Phillip Norman quoted in Judy Bachrach, *Tina and Harry Come to America: Tina Brown, Harry Evans, and the Uses of Power* (New York: The Free Press, 2001), p. 85.
82 *fantasia of PRC goods*: Phillip H. Wiggins, "China's Trade Show in the City," *New York Times*, December 6, 1980.
82 *"consumption ethic"*: Zino Klapper, "Sino-Santa Gift List," *Mother Jones*, December 1980.
82 *"money and power"*: Vreeland quoted in Debora Silverman, *Selling Culture: Bloomingdale's, Diana Vreeland, and the New Aristocracy of Taste in Reagan's America* (New York: Pantheon, 1986), p. 3.
82 *"wonderful things"*: Ronald Reagan quoted in John Duka, "The Elite Welcome Reagan, Who Offers Toast to the City," *New York Times*, December 10, 1980.
83 *"The old climate"*: Koch quoted in Steven R. Weisman, "Koch's Performance Wins Mixed Reviews," *New York Times*, October 22, 1979.
83 *A think tank called*: "Intellectual Stock Picking," *The New Yorker*, February 7, 1994.
84 *"A millionaire should not"*: Harry Helmsley quoted in Ransdell Pierson, *The Queen of Mean* (New York: Bantam Books, 1989), p. 181.
84 *the top bracket*: Jack Egan, "Reagan's Tax Cuts: The Rich Get Richer . . . ," *New York*, September 14, 1981.
84 *"The point"*: The Talk of the Town, *The New Yorker*, December 17, 1979.
84 *"a certain mood"*: Marie Brenner, "Letter from the Hamptons," *New York*, September 14, 1981.
85 *"In a true democracy"*: Lisa Birnbach, ed., *The Official Preppy Handbook* (New York: Workman, 1980), p 11.
85 *"I don't want to learn"*: Cornelia Guest quoted in Marie Brenner, "The Deb of the Year," *New York*, January 16, 1982.
85 *"Can you imagine"*: *The New Yorker*, June 5, 1978.
85 *Amid a city record 637,451*: Leonard Buder, "New York Police Say Crime Rate Fell 5.1% in '82," *New York Times*, March 11, 1983.
85 *Chlamydia had arrived*: Janice Hopkins Tanne, "The New Bug in Town," *New York*, October 6, 1980.

86 *"a plutocracy"*: Beth Landman and Alex Williams, "The Brothers McNally," *New York*, January 15, 1996.

86 *"riding inside"*: Eric Fischl and Michael Stone, *Bad Boy: My Life On and Off the Canvas* (New York: Crown, 2012), p. 127.

86 *"Given the choice"*: Calvin Tomkins, "The Art World," *The New Yorker*, June 22, 1981.

86 *"It's no longer chic"*: Patrick Brennan quoted in Craig Unger, "Attitude," *New York*, July 26, 1982.

87 *"IT'S TIME TO GO"*: Jean-Michel Basquiat quoted in *Basquiat: The Unknown Notebooks*, Dieter Buchhart and Tricia Laughlin Bloom, eds. (New York: Skira Rizzoli Publications, 2015), p. 92.

87 *"Papa, I have made it"*: Gerard Basquiat quoted in Jeffrey Deitch, *Jean-Michel Basquiat 1981: The Studio of the Street* (Milan: Edizioni Charta, 2007), p. 90.

87 *"minifestivals"*: Walter Robinson and Carlo McCormick, "Slouching Toward Avenue D," *Art in America*, Summer 1984.

88 *"gay life"*: Ingrid Sischy, *Nothing Is Lost: Selected Essays*, Sandra Brant, ed. (New York: Alfred A. Knopf, 2018), p. 201.

88 *"Many Westerners"*: Thompson, *Aesthetic of the Cool*, p. 29.

88 *"It seemed like"* and passim: Charlie Ahearn interview.

88 *"search for wholeness"*: Robert Farris Thompson quoted in Phoebe Hoban, *Basquiat: A Quick Killing in Art* (New York: Viking Penguin, 1998), p. 81.

89 *"He very much wanted"*: Suzanne Mallouk quoted in Deitch, *Jean-Michel Basquiat*, p. 19.

90 *certain GI infections*: David France, *How to Survive a Plague: The Inside Story of How Citizens and Science Tamed AIDS* (New York: Alfred A. Knopf, 2016), p. 19.

90 *the CDC published*: Randy Shilts, *And the Band Played On* (New York: St. Martin's Press, 1987), p. 68.

90 *"Rare Cancer Seen"*: Lawrence K. Altman, "Rare Cancer Seen in 41 Homosexuals," *New York Times*, July 3, 1981.

90 *the Joffrey Ballet*: France, *How to Survive a Plague*, p. 10.

90 *"Larry was anti-movement"*: Andy Humm interview.

90 *"sobering and scary"*: Ibid.

90 *"Gay liberation then"*: William M. Hoffman interview.

90 *"[N]o relationship," said Kramer later, "could"*: Larry Kramer to Sarah Schulman, Act Up Oral History Project, November 15, 2003, p. 6.

91 *So he wrote* Faggots: Alex Witchel, "At Home with: Larry Kramer; When a Roaring Lion Learns to Purr," *New York Times*, January 12, 1995.

91 *Dr. David Sencer advised*: Soffer, *Ed Koch and the Rebuilding of New York*, p. 308.

91 *"Fuck off"*: "Ed Koch: Hizzoner," *New York*, April 6, 1998.

91 *"I always like to tweak"*: Koch quoted in Michael Kramer, "Ed Koch's Blind Spot," *New York*, October 12, 1981.

91 *"Vicious or not"*: Kramer, "Ed Koch's Blind Spot."

92 *back to the '50s*: Brian Sullivan and Jonathan Burke, "Single-Room Occupancy Housing in New York City: The Origins and Dimensions of a Crisis," *City University of New York Law Review*, vol. 17, issue 1, Winter 2013.

92 *127,000 units in 1970*: Peter Marcuse, "Gentrification, Abandonment, and Displacement: Connections, Causes, and Policy Responses in New York City," 28 Wash. U. J. *Urb. & Contemp. L.* 195 (1985).

92 *78,000 patients*: Randy Young, "The Homeless," *New York*, December 21, 1981.

92 *"We are not a shelter"*: Sarah Connell quoted in Robin Herman, "New York City Psychiatric Wards . . . ," *New York Times*, December 8, 1980.

92 *"Wall Street, Madison Avenue"*: Samuel Ehrenhalt quoted in "A Helluva Town—Jobs Are Up, Inflation Down," *New York*, May 10, 1982.

92 *"average middle-class tenant"*: Hillel Levin, "The Rent Battle," *New York*, May 4, 1981.

93 *GM, Union Carbide*: Robert Rickles and Harold Holzer, "The Sputtering Midtown Revival," *New York*, August 3, 1981.

93 *already baked in*: Roger Vaughan and Mark Willis, "Economic Development" in Brecher and Horton, eds., *Setting Municipal Priorities, 1982*, pp. 170–172.

93 *"Piggy, piggy, piggy"*: Koch quoted in "Around City Hall: It Ain't Over," *The New Yorker*, July 24, 1987.

93 *an $854 million deficit*: Jack Egan, "It's Worse Than We Thought," *New York*, March 6, 1982.

93 *"disorder and crime"*: George L. Kelling and James Q. Wilson, "Broken Windows," *The Atlantic*, March 1982.

93 *he'd asked the NYPD*: Soffer, *Ed Koch and the Rebuilding of New York*, p. 327.

93 *"to protect the rights of New Yorkers"*: The City of New York, The Mayor's Management Report, September 17, 1982, p. 37.

94 *"the most popular mayor"*: Rinker Buck, "How Am I Doing?" *New York*, September 9, 1980

94 *"The rebuilding"*: "Introduction," in Brecher and Horton, eds., *Setting Municipal Priorities, 1982*, p. 4.

94 *"regressive politics"*: Koch quoted in "Transcript of Address Delivered By Mayor Koch at Inauguration Ceremony," *New York Times*, January 2, 1982.

94 *By March 1982, 285*: Shilts, *And the Band Played On*, p. 131.

95 *"I'm worried that I could get it"*: Warhol, *Diaries*, p. 442.

95 *"The Gay Plague"*: Michael VerMeulen, "The Gay Plague," *New York*, May 31, 1982.

Chapter Seven | **Be a Card-Carrying Capitalist**

97 *At his desk at 7:30*: Robert A. Bennett, "Man in the News; Spark for a Rally: Henry Kaufman," *New York Times*, August 19, 1982.

97 *GE trading at 1⅛*: Maggie Mahar, *Bull! A History of the Boom, 1982–1999* (New York: HarperBusiness, 2003), p. 46.

98 *finished at 831.24*: Alexander R. Hammer, "Dow Soars By 38.81; Volume Near Peak," *New York Times*, August 18, 1982.

98 Forbes *published*: *Forbes*, September 13, 1982.

98 *traded 137.3 million shares*: Vartanig G. Vartan, "Stock Turnover Soars to Record as Prices Climb," *New York Times*, August 27, 1982.

98 *"nearly all the doubters"*: Jack Egan, "The Party's Not Over," *New York*, March 14, 1983.

99 *choose between*: Louis Hyman, *Borrow: The American Way of Debt* (New York: Vintage, 2012), pp. 180–181.

99 *on a huge scale*: Michael Osinski, "My Manhattan Project," *New York*, March 27, 2009.

100 *almost every major bank*: Connie Bruck, *The Predator's Ball: The Inside Story of Drexel Burnham and the Rise of the Junk Bond Raiders* (New York: Simon & Schuster, 1988), p. 97.

101 *"old George III"*: Michael Bloomberg, with Matthew Winkler, *Bloomberg by Bloomberg* (New York: John Wiley & Sons, 1997), p. 10.

101 *offered the guy*: Joyce Purnick, *Mike Bloomberg* (New York: Public Affairs, 2009), p. 27.

101 *"bright, aggressive"*: John Gutfreund quoted in Purnick, *Mike Bloomberg*, p. 32.

101 *"He thought he knew"*: Morris Offut quoted in Monica Roman, "Why Is Wall Street Afraid of Mike Bloomberg?" Bloomberg.com, April 29, 1991.

101 *"I noticed"*: Bloomberg, with Winkler, *Bloomberg by Bloomberg*, p. 55.

101 *the punching bag stand*: Steve Fishman, "The Madoff Tapes," *New York*, February 25, 2011.

102 *"screen-based trading"*: Bernie Madoff quoted in Steve Fishman, "The Monster Mensch," *New York*, February 20, 2009.

102 *"You make more"*: Steve Forbes quoted in Mahar, *Bull*, p. 109.

102 *Information Capital*: "Info City," *New York*, February 9, 1981.

102 *Planning could now*: The City of New York, The Mayor's Management Report, January 30, 1984, pp. 228–229.

102 *Satellite dishes*: Desmond Smith, "The City's Coming White-Collar Crisis," *New York*, September 27, 1982.

102 *"If nothing is done"*: "Info City," *New York*, February 9, 1981.

102 *"No city had ever"*: Vreeland in Philippe Jullian, *La Belle Époque* (New York: The Metropolitan Museum of Art, 1982), p. 3.

102 *Costume Institute's 1982 gala*: John Duka, "La Belle Europe Reigns Again at Met Museum," *New York Times*, December 7, 1982.

103 *"Don't forget that"*: Vreeland quoted in ibid.

103 *"People with money"*: Brooke Astor quoted in John Fairchild, *Chic Savages* (New York: Pocket Books, 1989), p. 94.

103 *"oratorical skills"*: Marie Brenner, "Brief Lives: Ivan Boesky Takes a Position," *New York*, May 21, 1984.

103 *"I'll own the world"*: Saul Steinberg quoted in Suzanna Andrews, "Vanished Opulence," *Vanity Fair*, January 2001.

103 *"an untouchable"*: Anonymous quoted in ibid.

104 *a deli in Detroit*: Marie Brenner, "Brief Lives: Ivan Boesky Takes a Position," *New York*, May 21, 1984.

104 *"elaborate stage set"*: John Taylor, *Circus of Ambition: The Culture of Wealth and Power in the Eighties* (New York: Warner Books, 1989), p. 104.

104 *"the Working Rich"*: Jesse Kornbluth, "The Working Rich," *New York*, November 24, 1986.

104 *"the new Republican"*: Warhol, *Diaries*, p. 355.

104 *"more self-righteous"*: Jerome Karabel quoted in Bell, *The Coming of Post-Industrial Society*, p. 428.

105 *"Sometimes," wrote Fairchild, "no, often"*: Fairchild, *Chic Savages*, p. 88.

105 *supports the pillars*: Francie Ostrower, *Why the Wealthy Give: The Culture of Elite Philanthropy* (Princeton: Princeton University Press, 1995), p. 6.

105 *"when they go"*: Marilyn Berger, "Being Brooke Astor," *New York Times*, May 20, 1984.

106 *"She has done"*: Bernice Kanner, "Life with Leona," *New York*, March 12, 1984.

106 *"We don't pay taxes"*: Leona Helmsley quoted in Robert W. Wood, "10 Notorious Tax Cheats," *Forbes*, April 17, 2005.

106 *"a model Trump"*: Jonathan Greenberg, "Trump Lied to Me About His Wealth to Get onto the Forbes 400. Here Are the Tapes," *Washington Post*, April 20, 2018.

106 *"In fifty years"*: Ivana Trump quoted in Marie Brenner, "After the Gold Rush," *Vanity Fair*, September 1990.

106 *"operetta uniforms"*: Natacha Stewart, "Atrium," *The New Yorker*, October 2, 1983.

106 *"New York was conquered"* and passim: Constantine Kondylis quoted in Gross, *House of Outrageous Fortune*, p. 91.

107 *New York City was playing*: Matthew Drennan, "Local Economy and Local Revenues" in Charles Brecher and Raymond Horton, eds., *Setting Municipal Priorities, 1988* (New York: New York University Press, 1988), pp. 24–27.

107 *"commercially driven gentrification"*: Phil Patton, "The Flatiron Is Hot," *New York*, January 28, 1985.

107 *"It was ugly"*: Charlie Ahearn interview.

107 *half the legitimate*: Lynne B. Sagalyn, *Times Square Roulette: Remaking the City Icon* (Cambridge, MA: The MIT Press, 2001), p. 283.

108 *"giving Times Square"*: John Burgee quoted in Carter Wiseman, "Brave New Times Square," *New York*, April 2, 1984.

108 *"undue despair"*: Whyte quoted in Martin Gottlieb, "Keen City Watcher Inspires Times Sq. Debate," *New York Times*, April 26, 1984.

108 *"Bowl of Light"*: Sagalyn, *Times Square Roulette*, p. 245.

108 *"Card-Carrying Capitalist"*: *New York*, May 23, 1983, pp. 48–49.

109 *LBOs and other*: Mahar, *Bull*, p. 51.

109 *"sickness of the town"*: Lewis Lapham quoted in Tina Brown, *The Vanity Fair Diaries, 1983–1992* (New York: Henry Holt & Co., 2017), p. 104.

109 *One-third of Yale's*: Ellen Hopkins, "The Young and the Sleepless," *New York*, June 9, 1986.

109 *"the sign of a top"*: Jim Rogers quoted in "Baby-Boom Bust?" *Manhattan, Inc.*, September 1986.

109 *"Greed is all right"*: Ivan Boesky quoted in Peter Gant, "Ivan Boesky and the End of the '80s Wall Street Boom," *New York Daily News*, August 14, 2017.

Chapter Eight | **They Begin to Blossom**

111 *"the baby boom generation"*: Fran Schumer, "Downward Mobility," *New York*, August 16, 1982.

111 *"When I said I didn't care"*: William Hamilton quoted in ibid.

112 *In July 1982*: Desmond Smith, "The City's Coming White-Collar Crisis," *New York*, September 27, 1982.

112 *"growing breed"*: Ibid.

112 *"status society"*: Bell, *The Coming of Post-Industrial Society*, p. ixxv.

112 *"essentially unfair"*: Charles Kadushin, *Understanding Social Networks: Theories, Concepts, and Findings* (New York: Oxford University Press, 2012), p. 168.

113 *"It was very hippie"*: Bil Rock quoted in Henry Chalfant and Sacha Jenkins, *Training Days: The Subway Artists Then and Now* (New York: Thames & Hudson, 2014), p. 27.

113 *"curated fashion store"*: Ingrid Sischy, "The Rise and Fall of Charivari, the Cult Boutique of Fashion," *Vanity Fair*, September 2016.

113 *"filthy and full of junk"*: Betsy Iger quoted in "The Apartment," *New York*, January 21, 1985.

113 *"one more tool"*: Sally Goodgold quoted in Peter Hellman, "New York's New Left Bank," *New York*, August 30, 1982.

114 *"What a joy"*: Gael Greene, "A Breakthrough on the Western Front," *New York*, October 3, 1983.

114 *"[a]ffluence begat gourmets"*: Karen Cook, "Chow, Manhattan," *Manhattan, Inc.*, March 1986.

114 *"a necessary social ritual"*: Patricia Morrisroe, "Restaurant Madness," *New York*, November 26, 1984.

114 *Le Bernardin*: Gael Greene, "Le Bernardin Beguiles Our Crocodile," *New York*, February 24, 1986.

114 *"cute little devils"*: Peter G. Davis, "A Disc Is Still a Disc," *New York*, December 3, 1984.

114 *"Not since the advent"*: Patricia Morrisroe, "Living with the Computer," *New York*, January 9, 1984.

115 *"I'm gonna tell everyone"*: Warhol quoted in Phoebe Hoban, "Looks Great, Manny, But Will It Sell?" *New York*, August 5, 1985.

115 *Computer banking*: Phoebe Hoban, "Dialing Your Dollars," *New York*, February 25, 1985.

115 *Louis Rukeyser's*: Dan Dorfman, "Wall Street Weak in Review," *New York*, January 14, 1985.

115 *Money had gone*: Fran Schumer, "Is Sex Dead?" *New York*, December 6, 1982.

115 *personal ads thrived*: Patricia Morrisroe, "Strictly Personals," *New York*, March 19, 1984.

115 *"yuppies and AIDS"*: Alexander Liberman quoted in Brown, *The Vanity Fair Diaries*, p. 222.

115 *"Intense Families"*: Richard Sennett, *The Uses of Disorder: Personal Identity and City Life* (New York: Alfred A. Knopf), 1970.

115 *devoted an entire*: New York, October 4, 1982.

115 *"formal 'play dates'"*: Michael Stone, "Trying to Raise Children in the City," *New York*, February 2, 1987.

116 *"special talents"*: Camille Hopkins, "The Smart Set," *New York*, October 29, 1984.

116 *"an upper tier"*: Katherine Davis Fishman, "Middle-Class Guide to the Public Schools," *New York*, January 13, 1986.

116 *"a brand-name college"*: Michael Stone, "Pressure Points," *New York*, March 10, 1986.

116 *"Our father is a lawyer"*: New York, June 10, 1985.

116 *effective property tax*: "Twenty-Five Years After S7000A: How Property Tax Burdens Have Shifted in New York City," Independent Budget Office, December 5, 2006.

116 *"without doubt"*: Peter Hellman, "New York's New Left Bank," *New York*, August 30, 1982.

117 *"a real schism"*: Linda Reiner quoted in Patricia Morrisroe, "The New Class," *New York*, May 13, 1985.

117 *"Fuck you, Jack"*: "How to Win Friends and Influence People, Part III," *Spy*, April 1988.

117 *61% of its residents*: Chelsea's Housing and Vacancy Report: New York City 1987, NYC Department of Housing Preservation and Development, 1987, p. 153.

118 *"not a penal sentence"*: Louis Winnick quoted in Carter Wiseman, "The Housing Squeeze—It's Worse Than You Think," *New York*, October 10, 1983.

118 *"The whole notion"*: Fritz Ertl quoted in Patricia Morrisroe, "Exodus," *New York*, November 25, 1985.

118 *37% of owners had higher*: Housing and Vacancy Report: New York City 1987, NYC Department of Housing Preservation and Development, 1987, pp. 186–188.

118 *"Holly lifted a scrim"*: Amanda Burden interview.

118 *"extension of the city"*: Amanda Burden quoted in Carter B. Horsley, "Young Firm Shaping Future of Two Areas," *New York Times*, June 28, 1981.

118 *"largest and most expensive"*: Albert Scardino, "Big Battery Park Dreams," *New York Times*, December 1, 1986.

119 *"a treadmill"*: Ellen Hopkins, "The Young and the Sleepless," *New York*, June 9, 1986.

119 *number of psychologists*: Terri Minsky, "Prisoners of Psychotherapy," *New York*, August 31, 1987.

119 *Wellbutrin*: Allison Robbins, "New Ups for Old Downs," *New York*, May 25, 1981.

119 *"new class of poor"*: New York, February 17, 1986.

119 *"The most dramatic"*: Felix Rohatyn quoted in Sam Roberts, "'75 Bankruptcy Scare Alters City Plans Into 21st Century," *New York Times*, July 8, 1985.

119 *trash incineration*: Jane Goldman, "What's Bugging You," *New York*, May 27, 1985.

119 *Manufacturing continued*: The City of New York, The Mayor's Management Report, September 17, 1983, p. xxxix.

120 *"begin to blossom"*: Wallace Shawn, *Aunt Dan and Lemon* (New York: Grove Press, 1985), pp. 95–97.

121 *"Any homosexual"*: Michael Daly, "AIDS Anxiety," *New York*, June 6, 1983.

121 *The City Council shot down*: Andy Logan, "Around City Hall: Been Down So Long It Looks Like Up," *The New Yorker*, April 11, 1983.

121 *"active surveillance"*: The City of New York, The Mayor's Management Report, January 13, 1983, p. 209.

121 *the Salvation Army*: France, *How to Survive a Plague*, p. 122.

121 *Sencer said the worst*: Ibid., p. 340.

121 *"a vast empty space"*: Andrew Holleran, *Ground Zero* (New York: New American Library, 1988), p. 189.

121 *"[S]topping promiscuity"*: Ibid., p. 119.

122 *Douglas Crimp argued*: Dangerous Bedfellows, ed., *Policing Public Sex: Queer Politics and the Future of AIDS Activism* (Boston: South End Press, 1996), p. 76.

122 *Intravenous drug users*: Shilts, *And the Band Played On*, p. 457.

122 *One-third of the beds*: "St. Vincent's Remembered," out.com, August 17, 2010.

122 *"I considered myself"*: Hoffman interview.

122 *"a comprehensive expansion"*: Koch quoted in Shilts, *And the Band Played On*, p. 556.

122 *57% of Americans*: https://news.gallup.com/poll/1651/gay-lesbian-rights.aspx.

122 *"AIDS rewrote"*: Marvin Taylor interview.

122 *50% of Manhattan's gay*: Kaiser, *The Gay Metropolis, 1940–1996*, p. 283.

123 *sex clubs and parties*: Dangerous Bedfellows, ed., *Policing Public Sex*, p. 76.

123 *the deaths of longtime*: Sarah Schulman, *The Gentrification of the Mind: Witness to a Lost Imagination* (Berkeley: University of California Press, 2012), pp. 23–35.

123 *Singles inhabited 53%*: Housing and Vacancy Report: New York City 1987, NYC Department of Housing Preservation and Development, 1987, p. 7.

123 *"Why didn't you come"*: Harvey Robins interview.

124 *"Art is not democratic"*: Richard Serra quoted in "Man of Steel," *The Guardian* (UK), October 5, 2008.

124 *"Art for the people"*: Charles Osgood, *CBS News Sunday Morning*, October 20, 1982.

124 *"all but unthinkable"*: The Talk of the Town, *The New Yorker*, March 28, 1983.

124 *"taken the rich"*: Robin Leach quoted in Ron Rosenbaum, "The Frantic Screaming Voice of the Rich and Famous," *Manhattan, Inc.*, January 1986.

125 *"New York was the big time"*: Brown, *The Vanity Fair Diaries*, p. 21.

125 *"sophisticated boom boom"*: Ibid., p. 108.

125 *"We give intellectuals"*: Ibid., p. 176.

125 *"gift of instinctive collusion"*: Ibid., p. 131.

126 *"an honorable man"*: George W. S. Trow quoted in Craig Unger, "Murmurings at *The New Yorker*," *New York*, November 28, 1983.

126 *hardcover sales*: Edward Tivnan, "Doubleday Rocks and Rolls," *New York*, February 7, 1983.

126 *"It was suddenly"*: Joni Evans interview.

126 *"Money is the Opposite"* and passim: Haring, *Journals*, p. 114.
126 *"apotheosis"*: Charlie Ahearn interview.
127 *"back to his roots"*: Patti Astor quoted in Hoban, *Basquiat*, p. 137.
127 *"just one of those kids"*: Warhol, *Diaries*, p. 462.
127 *"the downtown cultural elite"*: Haring quoted in Gruen, *Keith Haring*, p. 91.
128 *"[t]he party was over"*: Kenny Scharf in *The Nomi Song*, 2004.
128 *"You give them a group"*: Rick Prol quoted in Cynthia Carr, *Fire in the Belly: The Life and Times of David Wojnarowicz* (New York: Bloomsbury, 2012), p. 253.
128 *"a kind of Junior Achievement"*: Craig Owens, *Beyond Recognition: Representation, Power, and Culture* (Berkeley: University of California Press, 1992).
128 *"Art that is bright"* and passim: Calvin Tomkins, "The Art World," *The New Yorker*, April 14, 1986.
128 *"the Warhol Economy"*: Elizabeth Currid, *The Warhol Economy: How Fashion, Art & Music Drive New York City* (Princeton: Princeton University Press, 2007).
128 *"The MTA thought"*: Lee Quiñones quoted in The Talk of the Town, "Buffed Out," *The New Yorker*, February 26, 1990.
129 *"Hip Hop as a culture"*: Charlie Ahearn interview.
129 *"forced out"*: Tom Pollak quoted in "The Lower East Side," *New York*, May 28, 1984.
129 *"continue to exist"*: Carlo McCormack quoted in Tiernan Morgan, "The East Village Eye: Where Art, Hip Hop, and Punk Collided," hyperallergic.com, November 12, 2014.
129 *"Warhol TKO"*: Vivien Raynor, "Art: Basquiat, Warhol," *New York Times*, September 20, 1985.
129 *"Oh God"*: Warhol, *Diaries*, p. 680.
129 *"endless celebrities"*: Haring quoted in Gruen, *Keith Haring*, p. 142.
129 *"[B]y 1985 and 1986"*: Scharf quoted in ibid., p. 140.
129 *"speedy regress"*: Tad Friend, "Downhill from Here," *Spy*, October 1986.
129 *"To be cool"*: Thompson, *Aesthetic of the Cool*, p. 26.
130 *"very effective"*: Haring, *Journals*, p. 134.
130 *"overinstitutionalized"*: Gablik, *Has Modernism Failed?*, p. 13.
130 *"artists and collectors"*: Paula Cooper interview.
130 *"become much more"*: Eric Fischl interview with a.m. Homes in Betsy Sussler, Suzan Sherman, Ronalde Shavers, eds., *Speak Art!: The Best of Bomb Magazine's Interviews with Artists* (New York: G+B Arts International, 1997), p. 67.

Chapter Nine | The Devil and Ed Koch

133 *"walks a dog"*: Bess Myerson quoted in Browne, Collins, and Goodwin, *I, Koch*, p. 129.
133 *"Berlin cabaret"*: David W. Dunlap, "Singing a Song of City Hall," *New York Times*, May 12, 1985.
134 *"at the height"*: Warren Leight, book, and Charles Strouse, music and lyrics, *Mayor* (New York: Samuel French, Inc., 1987), p. 9.
134 *"[I]t has been a long time"*: Ed Koch, The City of New York, The Mayor's Management Report, September 18, 1985, p. viii.

134 *shifted City Hall*: Raymond Horton, "Human Resources," in Brecher and Horton, eds., *Setting Municipal Priorities, 1988*, pp. 187–191.

134 *Arts for Transit*: Sandra Bloodworth and William Ayres, *Along the Way: MTA Arts for Transit* (New York: Monacelli Press, 2006), p, 162.

134 *"Once a train"*: George L. Kelling and Catherine M. Coles, *Fixing Broken Windows: Restoring Order and Reducing Crime in Our Communities* (New York: Simon & Schuster, 1996), p. 116.

135 *conservative option*: Jack Newfield and Wayne Barrett, *City for Sale: Ed Koch and the Betrayal of New York* (New York: Harper & Row, 1988), p. 168.

135 *"economic success"*: "Introduction," in Charles Brecher and Raymond Horton, eds., *Setting Municipal Priorities, 1986* (New York: New York University Press, 1985), p. 5.

135 *Accidentally on purpose*: Newfield and Barrett, *City for Sale*.

136 *"I was born in this building"*: Koch quoted in Susan Heller Anderson and Maurice Carroll, "New York Day By Day," *New York Times*, February 2, 1984.

136 *neighborhood preservation*: Bloom and Lasner, eds., *Affordable Housing in New York*, p. 245.

136 *Washington Heights*: Robert W. Snyder, *Crossing Broadway: Washington Heights and the Promise of New York City* (Ithaca, NY: Cornell University Press, 2015).

136 *65% of Harlem*: Goldstein, *The Roots of Urban Renaissance*, p. 157.

136 *"pragmatic and sensible"*: Ed Logue quoted in Michael Goodwin, "New Plan, Dependent on US Aid, Is Offered to Rebuild South Bronx," *New York Times*, July 20, 1980.

137 *choose their own siding*: Philip Shenon, "Taste of Suburbia Arrives in the South Bronx," *New York Times*, March 19, 1983.

137 *restocked with fish*: William E. Geist, "Residents Give a Bronx Cheer to Decal Plan," *New York Times*, November 12, 1983.

137 *"who have bought them"*: Koch quoted in Jonnes, *South Bronx Rising*, p, 376.

138 *"a renewed sense"*: Samuel G. Freedman, *Upon This Rock: The Miracles of a Black Church* (New York: HarperCollins, 1993), p. 334.

138 *Mugavero sold him*: Ibid., pp. 337–338.

138 *"fragile roots"*: Reverend Johnny Ray Youngblood quoted in ibid., p. 339.

138 *140,000 units*: The City of New York, The Mayor's Management Report, February 14, 1985, p. vii.

138 *"give the project a soul"*: Sandy Frucher quoted in David L. A. Gordon, *Battery Park City: Politics and Planning on the New York Waterfront* (Amsterdam: Gordon and Breach, 1997), p. 90.

138 *Soviet officials*: Fitch, *The Assassination of New York*, p. 138.

138 *to their communities*: Ibid., p. 91.

138 *"[C]lassic Robin Hood"*: William B. Eimicke quoted in Jeffrey Schmalz, "Albany Accord Reached on Apartments for City," *New York Times*, March 19, 1986.

138 *"I got so mad"*: Ed Koch, La Guardia and Wagner Archives, Video Oral History Project, Ed Koch and Nat Leventhal with Richard K. Liegerman and Stephen Weinstein at Borough Hall, November 13, 2012, p. 8.

138 *75,000 low- and middle-income*: Joyce Purnick, "Cuomo and Koch Agree on Housing . . . ," *New York Times*, May 24, 1985.
138 *throw everything*: The City of New York, The Mayor's Management Report, September 18, 1985, pp. 253–263.
139 *"a manhood question"*: Sturz quoted in Roberts, *A Kind of Genius*, p. 236.
139 *"a person's biceps"*: The Talk of the Town, "Notes and Comments," *The New Yorker*, July 30, 1984.
139 *"purpose of Westway"*: Marcy Benstock quoted in The Talk of the Town, "Campaign," *The New Yorker*, July 19, 1982.
140 *"dreamy English major"*: Marcy Benstock interview.
140 *"13,400 and 124,600"*: James P. Sterba, "Westway Expected to Invigorate Area," *New York Times*, December 10, 1978.
140 *"significant adverse impact"*: Arnold H. Lubasch, "Biologist Revises Statement on Westway's Bass Impact," *New York Times*, July 4, 1985.
141 *"Westway," Dovel firmly testified, "like other"*: William Dovel quoted in Arnold H. Lubasch, "Biologist Says Westway Poses No Threat to Bass," *New York Times*, June 30, 1985.
141 *voted against emergency funding*: The City of New York, The Mayor's Management Report, January 30, 1986, p. 111.
141 *"the last frontier"*: Edith Fisher quoted in Joseph Giovannini, "New York Harbor Being Redesigned," *New York Times*, November 11, 1986.
141 *"If you had asked me"*: Ruth Messinger quoted in Jim Sleeper, ed., *In Search of New York* (New Brunswick, NJ: Transaction Publishers, 1989), p. 67.
142 *Small business*: Vaughan and Willis, "Economic Development," in Brecher and Horton, eds., *Setting Municipal Priorities, 1982*, p. 166.
142 *pro-development appointees*: Carter Wiseman, "Donald Trump's Fantasy Island," *New York*, January 20, 1986.
142 *the price of doing business*: John Taylor, "Pushing the Outer Limits," *New York*, April 10, 1989.
142 *"largely abdicated"*: Carter Wiseman, "Brave New Times Square," *New York*, April 2, 1984.
142 *"the job of urban"*: Messinger quoted in Albert Scardino, "They'll Take Manhattan," *New York Times*, December 7, 1986.
142 *"function as referee"*: Ibid.
142 *lot on Greenwich Street*: Howard Blum, "Shearson Picks Manhattan Site for New Center," *New York Times*, January 16, 1984.
142 *development rights to the Coliseum*: Kenneth Lipper interview.
142 *"Overall benefit to the city"*: Jonathan Greenberg, "Clash of the Titans," *Manhattan, Inc.*, January 1986.
143 *The price tag*: Ibid.
143 *"Critics of the Coliseum sale"*: Robert Kiley quoted in John Taylor, "The Shadow," *New York*, October 5, 1987.
143 *restaurant to be built*: Deirdre Carmody, "Vast Rebuilding of Bryant Park Planned," *New York Times*, December 1, 1983.

143 *"single most democratic"*: Orde Coombs, "The Cherry Orchard," *New York*, July 5, 1982.
143 *"[A] tree-loving pixie"*: Elisabeth Bumiller, "Guarding the Turf, Stepping on Toes . . . ," *New York Times*, July 23, 1995.
144 *fifteen times the capital funds*: The City of New York, The Mayor's Management Report, September 18, 1985, p. vi.
144 *"encourage residential"*: Ibid., p. 264.
144 *"not a yuppie park"*: Norman Cohen quoted in Susan Heller Anderson, "Plans Aims to Double Union Square," *New York Times*, July 16, 1987.
144 *"Reluctantly," wrote Brendan Gill*: Brendan Gill, "The Skyline," *The New Yorker*, November 9, 1987.
145 *"bright, festive, gaudy"*: Tony Hiss, "Reflections: Experiencing Places—II," *The New Yorker*, June 29, 1987.
145 *Power is little pieces*: Larry Kramer, *Reports from the Holocaust: The Making of an AIDS Activist* (New York: St. Martin's Press, 1989), p. 135.
146 *hit a rough patch*: Jeanie Kasindorf, "The Mayor Takes His Full Cut," *New York*, September 9, 1985.
146 *"[T]he line between a bribe"*: Franz Leichter quoted in Charles Brecher, Raymond D. Horton, with Robert A. Cropf and Dean Michael Mead, *Power Failure: New York City Politics & Policy Since 1960* (New York: Oxford University Press, 1993), p. 126.
146 *"Since you lost"*: Carol Bellamy quoted in Michael Kramer, "It's Me. The Mayor," *New York*, September 9, 1985.
146 *"Being Mayor," he'd later write, "forces you"*: Edward I. Koch, "How'd I Do?" *New York Times*, December 31, 1989.

Chapter Ten | **From Queens Come Kings!**

147 *"Welcome, Massa"*: "Around City Hall: Been Down So Long It Feels Like Up," *The New Yorker*, April 11, 1983.
147 *"Anyone else who would"*: Rangel quoted in Michael Kramer, "Blacks and Jews," *New York*, February 4, 1985.
147 *"[O]h you should have"*: Warhol, *Diaries*, p. 515.
147 *Koch refused to stand*: Sam Roberts, "Hearing on Police Cut Off in Harlem," *New York Times*, July 19, 1983.
147 *Real incomes rose*: Emanuel Tobier with Walter Stafford, "People and Income" in Brecher and Horton, eds., *Setting Municipal Priorities, 1986*, p. 59.
148 *Only 14% of New Yorkers*: Ibid., pp. 68–71.
148 *Blacks actually lost 11,000 jobs*: Thomas Bailey, "Black Employment Opportunities" in Charles Brecher and Raymond D. Horton, eds., *Setting Municipal Priorities, 1990* (New York: New York University Press, 1989), p. 99.
148 *"all of the industries"*: Roger Waldinger, "Race and Ethnicity" in ibid., p. 64.
148 *population considered "Other"*: Housing and Vacancy Report: New York City 1987, NYC Department of Housing Preservation and Development, 1987, p. 3, xvi.
148 *Whites leaving*: Louis Winnick, *New People in Old Neighborhoods* (New York: Russell Sage Foundation, 1990), pp. 137–138.

452 | Notes

149 *2,733 African Americans*: Carol Camp Yeakey and Clifford T. Bennett, "Race, Schooling, and Class in American Society," *Journal of Negro Education*," vol. 59, no. 1 (Winter 1990).
149 *the new generation*: Chang, *Can't Stop Won't Stop*, p. 223.
149 *"dirty religion"*: Louis Farrakhan quoted in E.R. Shipp, "Tape Contradicts Disavowal of 'Gutter Religion' Attack," *New York Times*, June 29, 1984.
149 *Black political establishment*: Sleeper, *The Closest of Strangers*, p. 205.
149 *"nosy and newsy"*: Wayne Dawkins, *City Son: Andrew W. Cooper's Impact on Modern-Day Brooklyn* (Jackson: University Press of Mississippi, 2012), p. 91.
149 *exodus of the Black*: William Julius Wilson, *The Truly Disadvantaged: The Inner City, the Underclass, and Public Policy* (Chicago: University of Chicago Press, 1987).
150 *HUDC joined in*: Greg Thomas, "Pataki's Man in Harlem," *Village Voice*, January 28, 2003.
150 *145 vacant brownstones*: Alan S. Oser, "Perspectives; Harlem Rehabilitation Struggle Leaves Casualties," *New York Times*, December 4, 1994.
150 *a significant role*: Greg Thomas, "Pataki's Man in Harlem," *Village Voice*, January 28, 2003.
150 *Building Harlem*: Goldstein, *The Roots of Urban Renaissance*, p. 216.
150 *"from Strong Island"*: Greg Tate, *Flyboy in the Buttermilk: Essays on Contemporary America* (New York: Fireside, 1992), p. 138.
151 *at once prosperous*: Peter Blauner, "'Fat Cat' and the Crack Wars," *New York*, September 7, 1987.
151 *"Hip hop was not just"*: Bill Stephney quoted in Chang, *Can't Stop Won't Stop*, p. 212.
151 *"anger, style, aggression"*: Frank Owen quoted in ibid., p. 231.
151 *"They made costumes"*: Russell Simmons quoted in Alex Ogg with David Upshal, *The Hip Hop Years: A History of Rap* (New York: Fromm International, 2001), p. 78.
151 *"a bit of a suburbanite"*: Simmons with George, *Life and Def*, p. 69.
151 *had paid Def Jam's*: Lynn Hirschberg, "The Music Man," *New York Times*, September 2, 2007.
151 *"young male fantasies"*: Simmons with George, *Life and Def*, p. 70.
151 *"Hip Hop crazy"*: Chuck D with Yusuf Jah, *Fight the Power: Rap, Race, and Reality* (New York: Delacorte Press, 1997), p. 59.
152 *"bring a higher level"*: Stephney quoted in ibid., p. 78.
152 *"Crack is a businessman's"*: Haring quoted in David Sheff, "Keith Haring: Just Say Know," *Rolling Stone*, August 10, 1989.
153 *$50,000 a kilo in 1980*: Nelson George, *Hip Hop America* (New York: Viking Penguin, 1998), p. 40.
153 *"[W]hen it landed in your hood"*: Jay-Z, *Decoded* (New York: Spiegel & Grau, 2010), p. 12.
153 *"CRACK, SUPER DRUG"*: Quoted in Goldstein, *The Roots of Urban Renaissance*, p. 205.

153 *"multigenerational chaos"*: George, *Hip Hop America*, p. 41.

153 *Rates of child abuse*: The City of New York, The Mayor's Management Report, February 10, 1988, pp. 375–395.

153 *150,000 New Yorkers*: Terry Williams, *Crackhouse: Notes from the End of the Line* (New York: Penguin, 1992), p. 10.

153 *In East New York*: Freedman, *Upon This Rock*, p. 50.

153 *Coogan's Restaurant*: Snyder, *Crossing Broadway*, pp. 176–177.

154 *murder had fallen to*: Andrew Karmen, *New York Murder Mystery: The True Story Behind the Crime Crash of the 1990s* (New York: New York University Press, 2000), p. 4.

154 *"out to get me"*: Bernard Goetz quoted in Myra Friedman with Michael Daly, "My Neighbor Bernie Goetz," *New York*, February 18, 1985.

154 *1.7 million felonies*: Ester Fuchs and John Palmer Smith, "Criminal Justice" in Brecher and Horton, eds., *Setting Municipal Priorities, 1986*, pp. 364–367.

154 *"keep the junkies moving"*: Ray Kelly, *Vigilance: My Life Serving America and Protecting Its Empire City* (New York: Hachette Books, 2015), p. 49.

154 *"Nobody seems to know"*: Robert McGuire quoted in Karmen, *New York Murder Mystery*, p. 84.

154 *"stranger policing"*: George Kelling quoted in William Bratton with Peter Knobler, *Turnaround: How America's Top Cop Reversed the Crime Epidemic* (New York: Random House, 1998), p. 82.

154 *"No precinct commander"*: Leonard Levitt, *NYPD Confidential: Power and Corruption in the Country's Greatest Police Force* (New York: St. Martin's Press, 2009), p. 32.

155 *pulled officers out*: Sam Roberts, "'73 Police Report Says Ward Didn't Release 16 at Mosque," *New York Times*, November 20, 1983.

155 *pushed hard for Ward*: Roberts, *A Kind of Genius*, p. 201.

155 *Operation Pressure Point*: The City of New York, The Mayor's Management Report, September 17, 1984, p. 12.

155 *focused on Quality of Life*: The City of New York, The Mayor's Management Report, February 14, 1985, p. 3.

155 *Off on a bender*: Levitt, *NYPD Confidential*, p. 17.

155 *"abuse of authority"*: The City of New York, The Mayor's Management Report, September 17, 1984, p. xviii.

155 *"something brave"*: LL Cool J quoted in Samuel G. Freedman, "To Some, Davis Is 'Hero' Amid Attacks on Blacks," *New York Times*, January 2, 1987.

156 *"This incident," said Ed Koch, now a year into his third term*: Koch quoted in Robert D. McFadden, "Black Man Dies After Beating by Whites in Queens," *New York Times*, December 21, 1986.

156 *"The Civil Rights movement"*: Al Sharpton and Anthony Walton, *Go and Tell Pharaoh: The Autobiography of the Reverend Al Sharpton* (New York: Doubleday, 1996), p. 53.

156 *"I learned before I got out"*: Al Sharpton quoted in Catherine S. Manegold, "The Reformation of a Street Preacher," *New York Times Magazine*, January 24, 1993.

156 *"You're going to be like Garvey"*: Sharpton and Walton, *Go and Tell Pharaoh*, p. 35.

157 *"You ain't nothing but"*: Ibid., p. 105.

157 *began to shift away*: Kasinitz, *Caribbean New York*, pp. 247–248.

157 *"a coon show"*: Sharpton quoted in Ronald Smothers, "23 Black Leaders and Koch Attack Pervasive Racism," *New York Times*, January 1, 1987.

157 *"a third of New Yorkers"*: Richard J. Meislin, "Racial Divisions Seen in Poll on Howard Beach Attack," *New York Times*, January 8, 1987.

158 *Goldman Sachs*: Ellen Hopkins, "Blacks at the Top," *New York*, January 19, 1987.

Chapter Eleven | **Building the Bonfire**

159 *"We're in a time"*: Arthur Schlesinger Jr. quoted in Bernice Kanner, "What Price Ethics?" *New York*, July 14, 1986.

159 *TB, VD, AIDS, child abuse, and homelessness*: The City of New York, The Mayor's Management Report, January 30, 1986, pp. 281–286, 353.

159 *"Money," wrote Michael Bloomberg, "was emerging"*: Bloomberg, with Winkler, *Bloomberg by Bloomberg*, p. 80.

159 *"Smart, fun, funny, and fearless"*: Spy, October 1987.

160 *"short-fingered vulgarian"*: "April Is Cruel, But We're Nice," *Spy*, April 1988.

160 *"In order to get"*: Rohatyn quoted in Ron Rosenbaum, "Meet Felix and Liz Rohatyn: Society Dissidents," *Manhattan Inc.*, April 1986.

160 *"They want to be seen"*: Annettee Reed quoted in Kathleen Teltsch, "Rohatyns Set Off Debate by Faulting Gala Events," *New York Times*, May 11, 1986.

160 *"This is what I appreciate"*: Brown, *The Vanity Fair Diaries*, p. 179.

160 *Three out of the four*: Newfield and Barrett, *City for Sale*, p. 340.

161 *"John Gotti broke"*: Jack Newfield, "Little Big Man," *New York*, June 24, 2002.

161 *American air freight*: James B. Jacobs with Coleen Friel and Robert Radick, *Gotham Unbound: How New York City Was Liberated from the Grip of Organized Crime* (New York: New York University Press, 1999), p. 62.

161 *A trade show at Javits*: Ibid., p. 71.

161 *Concrete cost up to 70%*: Ibid., p. 109.

161 *"the monetary costs"*: Ray Rowan, "The Mafia's Bite of the Big Apple," *Fortune*, June 6, 1988.

161 *"a kind of folk hero"*: Andy Logan, "Around City Hall: Knowing the Right People," *The New Yorker*, October 26, 1987.

162 *"You should be guilty"*: Rudolph Giuliani quoted in Nancy Collins, "Gotcha!," *New York*, May 25, 1987.

162 *"Jesuitical view"*: James Stewart, *Den of Thieves* (New York: Simon & Schuster, 1991), p. 289.

162 *"He told me he wanted"*: Kathy Livermore quoted in David Saltonstall, "Giuliani Candidacy Sparks Pride Among Italian-Americans," *New York Daily News*, October 8, 2007.

162 *press coverage*: Stewart, *Den of Thieves*, p. 288.

162 *"expressed dismay"*: Nathaniel C. Nash, "An Insider Scheme Is Put in Millions," *New York Times*, May 13, 1986.

163 *"I'm probably considerably"*: Giuliani quoted in Nancy Collins, "Gotcha!" *New York*, May 25, 1987.

163 *by the end of 1986*: Timothy Curry and Lynn Shibut, "The Cost of the Savings and Loan Crisis: Truth and Consequences," *FDIC Banking Review*, vol. 13, no. 2, 2000.

163 *old structure of one bank*: Robert G. Eccles and Dwight B. Crane, *Doing Deals: Investment Banks at Work* (Boston: Harvard Business School Press, 1988).

163 *"Hit and run"*: Michael Lewis, *Liar's Poker* (New York: W. W. Norton, 1989), p. 128.

163 *"eerie popular feeling"*: Ibid., p. 204.

163 *"Well, you've got the name"*: Gutfreund quoted in Taylor, *Circus of Ambition*, p. 128.

163 *in 1987, $1 billion*: Chris Smith, "Take Me Out to the Card Game," *New York*, June 20, 1988.

163 *"a vast crisis"*: Robert Heilbroner, "Reflections: Hard Times," *The New Yorker*, September 14, 1987.

164 *"Oh I'm not going to make it"*: Warhol quoted in Jesse Kornbluth, "The World of Warhol," *New York*, September 9, 1987.

165 *"I wish someone great"*: Andy Warhol, *America* (New York: Harper & Row, 1985), p. 11.

165 *"people with bad teeth"*: Warhol, *Diaries*, p. 703.

165 *"If there's this many"*: Ibid., p. 777.

165 *More than 2,000 mourners*: Grace Glueck, "Warhol Is Remembered by 2,000 at St. Patrick's," *New York Times*, April 1, 1987.

165 *"How will anybody"*: Haring, *Journals*, p. 156.

166 *"along with Roy Cohn"*: Brown, *The Vanity Fair Diaries*, p. 234.

166 *"The End of the Beginning"*: "AIDS: The End of the Beginning," *New York Times*, December 29, 1987.

166 *"soft whisper of sadness"*: Sischy, *Nothing Is Lost*, p. 204.

166 *"the Statue of Liberty"*: Bob Hope quoted in "Hope's Joke," *Los Angeles Times*, July 30, 1986.

166 *doctors openly complained*: Lilli Scott, "Fear in the Foxholes," *New York*, January 4, 1988.

Chapter Twelve | **The Age of Atonement**

171 *"a big one out there"*: H. Ross Perot quoted in Alison Leigh Cowan, "In the Aftermath of Market Plunge, Much Uneasiness," *New York Times*, October 19, 1987.

171 *Bill Gates was #29*: Associated Press, "Forbes Releases List of 49 Billionaires," October 12, 1987.

171 *"statistical arbitrage"*: Scott Patterson, *The Quants: How a New Breed of Math Whizzes Conquered Wall Street and Nearly Destroyed It* (New York: Crown Business, 2010), p. 41.

171 *"The entire universe"*: Migene González-Wippler, *Santera: The Religion* (New York: Harmony, 1989), p. 97.

172 *a large institution*: Mark Carlson, "A Brief History of the 1987 Stock Market Crash with a Discussion of the Federal Reserve Response," Finance and Economics

Discussion Series, Divisions of Research & Statistics and Monetary Affairs, Federal Reserve Board, Washington, DC, November 2006.

172 Titanic-*like oblivion*: Richard Dewey, "The Crash of '87, From the Wall Street Players Who Lived It," *Bloomberg Markets*, October 16, 2017.

172 *"complete fear"*: Paul Tudor Jones quoted in ibid.

172 *watched their fortunes*: Donald Bernhardt and Marshall Eckblad, "Stock Market Crash of 1987," *Federal Reserve History*, November 22, 2013.

172 *"the first global crisis"*: Jim Chanos interview, Bloomberg, October 16, 2017.

172 *Dow fell 3.5 points a minute*: Taylor, *Circus of Ambition*, p. 217.

172 *"The Plunge"*: William Glaberson, "The Plunge: A Stunning Blow to a Gilded, Impudent Age," *New York Times*, December 12, 1987.

172 *"expansiveness and the money"*: John Taylor, "Nervous About the Nineties," *New York*, June 20, 1988.

173 *"status theorist"*: Tom Wolfe quoted in "The Book on Tom Wolfe," *New York*, March 21, 1988.

173 *What action there was*: Bryan Burroughs and John Helyar, *Barbarians at the Gate: The Fall of RJR Nabisco* (New York: Harper & Row, 1990) p. 108.

173 *121 of the S&P*: Mahar, *Bull*, p. 51.

173 *Amid warnings*: The City of New York, The Mayor's Management Report, September 17, 1987, Introduction.

173 *fifty money-saving*: James A. Krauskopf, "Federal Aid" in Brecher and Horton, eds., *Setting Municipal Priorities, 1990*, pp. 131–132.

174 *office space in Pittsburgh*: Shachtman, *Skyscraper Dreams*, p. 321.

174 *17 million tourists helped*: Tony Hiss, "Reflections: Experiencing Places—II," *The New Yorker*, June 29, 1987.

174 *"PROTECT ME"*: Jenny Holzer, "Protect Me from What I Want" (art piece).

174 *"If there's one thing"*: Ivan Karp quoted in Talk of the Town, "Welcome Back," *The New Yorker*, June 22, 1987.

174 *"certifiably chic"*: Edward Zuckerman, "Confessions of an Outer Borough Exile, Part I," *Spy*, April 1988.

176 *"immoral"*: Kelling quoted in Michael Tomasky, "Quality of Life," *New York*, December 23–30, 1996.

176 *"The Subway"*: *New York*, September 25, 1989.

176 *"New York's changed"*: Vincent Gallo quoted in Hoban, *Basquiat*, p. 305.

176 *"not a surprise"*: Haring quoted in David Sheff, "Keith Haring: Just Say Know," *Rolling Stone*, August 10, 1989.

177 *tipped the box*: Ann Magnuson, "Conversation," May 27, 2015.

177 *"fat and rich"*: Diane von Furstenberg, "Voice of New York," *New York*, April 11, 1988.

177 *World Financial Center*: Julie Baumgold, "The Bubble Bursts," *New York*, April 19, 1993.

177 *"Behind every great fortune"*: Honoré de Balzac, *Le Père Goriot*.

177 *"It is refreshing"*: Liz Smith, "Donald Trump," *New York*, April 25, 1988.

177 *borrowed $407.5 million*: Jonathan O'Connell, David A. Fahrenthold, and Jack

Gillum, "As the 'King of Debt,' Trump Borrowed to Build His Empire. Then He Began Spending Hundreds of Millions in Cash," *Washington Post*, May 5, 2018.

177 *"perhaps the greatest"*: *New York*, September 12, 1988.

177 *"running for president"*: Donald Trump quoted in "The Spy 100," *Spy*, October 1988.

177 *"We have dined out"*: Brown, *The Vanity Fair Diaries*, p. 265.

177 *"is divided into people"* and passim: Liz Smith quoted in "The Voice of New York," *New York*, April 11, 1988.

178 *"cleared by the* SEC*"*: Georgia Dullea, "Candlelight Wedding Joins 2 Billionaire Families," *New York Times*, April 19, 1988.

178 *"We tried very much"*: Gayfryd Steinberg quoted in ibid.

178 *"embittered and vengeful"*: Adam Gopnik, "The Art World: Originals," *The New Yorker*, May 23, 1988.

178 *"best party in Manhattan"*: Brown, *The Vanity Fair Diaries*, p. 278.

179 *beaten by police*: Robert D. McFadden et al., *Outrage: The Story Behind the Tawana Brawley Hoax* (New York: Bantam Books, 1990), p. 81.

179 *an unfavorable opinion*: Frank Lynn, "Metro Matters," *New York Times*, September 5, 1988.

179 *"Fire, Liar and Wire"*: Reverend Lawrence Lucas quoted in Dawkins, *City Son*, p. 190.

179 *1,867 homicides*: Eric Pooley, "Fighting Back Against Crack," *New York*, January 23, 1989.

179 *89,331 involved*: The City of New York, The Mayor's Management Report, September 17, 1989, p. 550.

179 *26% of kids*: Brenda G. McGowan and Elaine M. Walsh, "Services to Children," in Brecher and Horton, eds., *Setting Municipal Priorities, 1990*, p. 268.

180 *63% of welfare families*: Housing and Vacancy Report: New York City 1987, NYC Department of Housing Preservation and Development, 1987, p. 92.

Chapter Thirteen | **A Psychic Turning Point**

181 *"sinking like a rock"*: Lou Reed, "Romeo Had Juliette," *New York*, 1989, Lou Reed (BMI), SongID2152041.

181 *"The Toughest Weenie"*: Philip Weiss, "The Toughest Weenie in America," *Spy*, November 1988.

181 *made an enemy*: Fred Siegel, *The Prince of the City: Giuliani, New York and the Genius of American Life* (San Francisco: Encounter Books, 2005), p. 27.

182 *Koch's own polling*: Chris McNickle, *The Power of the Mayor: David Dinkins, 1990–1993* (New Brunswick, NJ: Transaction Publishers, 2013), p. 29.

182 *"I was too proud"*: Koch quoted in ibid., p. 29.

182 *"The city is war-weary"*: Quoted in Joe Klein, "Been Down So Long It Looks Like Up to Me," *New York*, February 20, 1989.

183 *support the Times Square*: Sleeper, *The Closest of Strangers*, p. 277.

183 *"a lousy candidate"*: Quoted in Joe Klein, "Mr. Softy," *New York*, January 16, 1989.

183 *the right to run*: "City Room," *New York Times*, November 15, 2007.

183 *"Wolf pack teen"*: *New York Daily News*, April 24, 1989.

183 *"only one goal"*: Pete Hamill, "A Savage Disease," *New York Post*, April 23, 1989.

183 *"become permissible"* and passim: Joe Klein, "Race," *New York*, May 29, 1989.

184 *"waves of vagrants"*: Andrew Kirtzman, *Rudy Giuliani: Emperor of the City* (New York: Perennial, 2001), p. 23.

184 *"to cede greater"*: Christopher Byron, "Sweatshirt Justice," *New York*, October 2, 1989.

184 *"the unwillingness"*: Joe Klein, "Brotherhood Week," *New York*, September 11, 1989.

185 *"cultural mulatto[es]"*: Trey Ellis, "The New Black Aesthetic," *Callaloo*, no. 38 (Winter 1989).

185 *"art-school dilettante"* and passim: Joe Klein, "Spiked," *New York*, June 26, 1989.

185 *"Every time you take a veil off"*: Ed Koch quoted in "Around City Hall: It Ain't Over," *The New Yorker*, July 24, 1989.

185 *"sort of like Babar"*: Joe Klein, "War of the Sound Bites," *New York*, August 14, 1989.

185 *took Ailes's advice*: Rudolph W. Giuliani with Ken Kurson, *Leadership* (New York: Hyperion, 2002), p. 191.

186 *"I'm tired of hearing 'sorry'"*: Moses Stewart quoted in "Around City Hall: Fighting the Power," *The New Yorker*, September 11, 1989.

186 *"They are blowing"*: Gabe Sargomento quoted in Nick Ravo, "250 Whites Jeer Marchers in Brooklyn Youth's Death," *New York Times*, August 28, 1989.

186 *"a fancy schvartze"*: Jackie Mason quoted in Kirtzman, *Rudy Giuliani*, p. 25.

186 *"silly and irrelevant"*: Giuliani quoted in David Dinkins, with Peter Knobler, *A Mayor's Life: Governing New York's Gorgeous Mosaic* (New York: Public Affairs, 2013), p. 163.

186 *"snarling, unfocused"*: Kirtzman, *Rudy Giuliani*, p. 24.

186 *Milken's indictment*: Stephen Labaton, " 'Junk Bond' Leader Is Indicted by US in Criminal Action," *New York Times*, March 30, 1989.

187 *"be sent overseas"*: Sheryl McCarthy quoted in "Around City Hall: Rudy's People," *The New Yorker*, May 2, 1994.

187 *his first marriage*: "Around City Hall: Inexakte," *The New Yorker*, November 6, 1989.

187 *New York's voters*: John H. Mollenkopf, *New York City in the 1980s: A Social, Economic, and Political Atlas* (New York: Simon & Schuster, 1993), p. 61.

187 *"Seizing the soul"*: Daniel Patrick Moynihan quoted in Browne, Collins, and Goodwin, *I, Koch*, p. 185.

187 *"Make the best"*: "Mr. Peeper's Nights: Almost Too Chic to Die," *New York*, November 20, 1989.

187 *"I leave with joy"*: Koch quoted in Richard Levine, "Koch Takes His Leave from City Hall," *New York Times*, December 30, 1989.

188 *"Everybody was fat"*: James Lynch quoted in Weikart, *Follow the Money*, p. 60.

189 *"last nine years"*: Larry Kramer quoted in Sara Rimer, "New Gadgets and Vistas Welcome Citizen Koch," *New York Times*, January 4, 1990.

189 *"You were a terrible mayor!"*: Koch quoted in Maer Roshan, "Ed Koch vs. Al D'Amato: I'm Right, You're Wrong," *New York*, May 14, 2001.

Chapter Fourteen | Dave, Do Something!

191 *make cuts*: McNickle, *The Power of the Mayor*, pp. 69–73.
191 *"I don't hate just Jews"*: Sonny Carson quoted in James Barron, "At P.S. 262, 2 Principals Now Occupy One Post," *New York Times*, November 10, 1989.
192 *lose $12.3 million*: The City of New York, The Mayor's Management Report, February 15, 1990, p. iii.
193 *"the best sex"*: Marla Maples, *New York Post*, February 16, 1990.
193 *"didn't even know"*: "Around City Hall: Starting Out," *The New Yorker*, March 12, 1990.
193 *New York would lose*: McNickle, *The Power of the Mayor*, p. 62.
193 *"in much better shape"*: Norman Steisel quoted in Peter Blauner, "The Big Squeeze," *New York*, April 2, 1990.
193 *"didn't understand"*: Davis interview.
193 *"I wish I could say"*: Dinkins with Knobler, *A Mayor's Life*, p. 129.
193 *"heard as a man"*: Ibid., p. 139.
194 *The reporters present*: Joe Klein, "The Panic of 1990," *New York*, October 1, 1990.
194 *"I'm a follower"*: David Dinkins quoted in "Around City Hall: New Look," *The New Yorker*, February 12, 1990.
194 *"no sense of strategy"*: Ray Horton quoted in Joe Klein, "Fantasy in Blue," *New York*, October 15, 1990.
194 *"gets to be a function"*: Dinkins quoted in Dean Baquet, "Slaying Sets Off Anxiety by Tourists," *New York Times*, September 5, 1990.
194 *"has been observed"*: Dinkins quoted in "Dinkins Says He'll Show Anger at Violent Crimes," *New York Times*, September 6, 1990.
194 *"DAVE, DO SOMETHING!"*: *New York Post*, September 7, 1990.
194 *"In the past"*: Wagner Jr. quoted in Joe Klein, "The Real Deficit: Leadership," *New York*, July 22, 1991.
195 *"The city has careened"*: Joe Klein, "The Panic of 1990," *New York*, October 1, 1990.
195 *Lew Rudin convened*: Josh Barbanel, "Using 1975 Tool, Business and Labor Leaders Form Fiscal Council," *New York Times*, October 25, 1980.
195 *Cops hesitated*: Constance L. Hays, "Dinkins Issues Call to Citizens to Fight Crime," *New York Times*, September 10, 1990.
195 *a one-bedroom*: Housing and Vacancy Report: New York City 1991, NYC Department of Housing Preservation and Development, 1991, p. 134.
195 *"a great deal of sullenness"*: Irwyn Greif quoted in John Taylor, "Nervous about the Nineties," *New York*, June 20, 1988.
195 *"Most everything's been done"*: Melvyn Masters quoted in ibid.
196 *"camp lite"*: Paul Rudnick and Kurt Andersen, "The Irony Epidemic," *Spy*, March 1989.

196 *"public order"*: Fred Siegel quoted in Joe Klein, "The Panic of 1990," *New York*, October 1, 1990.

197 *consultant John Linder*: Chris Smith, "The NYPD Guru," *New York*, April 2, 1996.

197 *20% of New Yorkers*: Bratton with Knobler, *Turnaround*, p. 177.

197 *"the most demoralized"*: Ibid., p. 144.

197 *Bratton prioritized*: Ibid., p. 143.

197 *"Taking Back the Subway"*: "City Journal Interview: Victory in the Subways," *City Journal*, Summer 1992.

197 *Monthly ejections*: Ibid.

198 *"even the powerful people"*: Jack Maple quoted in "The Crime Buster," *The New Yorker*, February 24, 1997.

198 *secret life*: Michael Daly, "The Cop Who Loved the Oak Bar," *New York*, April 11, 1983.

198 *set up undercover*: Michael Daly, "Hunting the Wolf Packs," *New York*, June 3, 1985.

198 *just a lieutenant*: Jack Maple with Chris Mitchell, *The Crime Fighter* (New York: Broadway Books, 1999), p. 19.

198 *"many of the people"*: Bratton with Knobler, *Turnaround*, p. 154.

199 *"the catalyst"*: Ibid., p. 173.

199 *"the Marine Corps"*: Ibid.

199 *Many in the force*: Peter Blauner, "The Rap Sheet on Lee Brown," *New York*, January 22, 1990.

200 *"Lee Brown's definition"*: William Bratton quoted in "City Journal Interview: Victory in the Subways."

200 *Jheri Kurl Gang*: Playthell Benjamin, "Sugar Hill Blues," *New York*, May 12, 1997.

200 *"a remarkable request"*: Kelly, *Vigilance*, p. 75.

200 *"breezed right past"*: Ibid., pp. 60–61.

200 *Department of Substance*: McNickle, *The Power of the Mayor*, p. 218.

201 *from 834 in 1973* and passim: Judith A. Greene and Vincent Schiraldi, "Better by Half: The New York City Story of Winning Large-Scale Decarceration While Increasing Public Safety," *Federal Sentencing Reporter*, vol. 29, no. 1, October 2016.

201 *"I've never seen"*: Thomas P. Walsh quoted in John Tierney, "As Crime Drops in Midtown, Even Criminals Credit Police," *New York Times*, April 24, 1991.

201 *"petty and unsophisticated"*: Joe Klein, "New York to Dave: Get Real!," *New York*, May 27, 1991.

201 *"electronically enhanced"*: Red Burns, "From the Chair," *Interactions: The Interactive Telecommunications Program Newsmagazine*, May 1989.

202 *"community of personalities"*: Stacy Horn quoted in Thomas A. Stewart, "Boom Time on the New Frontier," *Fortune*, September 27, 1993.

202 *"Like salons"*: Stewart, "Boom Time on the New Frontier."

202 *post, flame*: Trish Hall, "Lifestyle: Coming to the East Coast: An Electronic Salon," *New York Times*, January 29, 1990.

202 *"It is a revealing"*: Stacy Horn, *Cyberville: Clicks, Culture, and the Creation of an Online Town* (New York: Warner Books, 1998), p. 6.

202 *widely prescribed*: Fran Schumer, "Bye-bye, Blues," *New York*, December 18, 1989.

202 *"You feel that"*: Ibid.

202 *"modern technological society"*: Peter Kramer, *Listening to Prozac* (New York: Viking Penguin, 1993), p. 172.

203 *Fox and cable channels*: Michael Stone, "Hard Times," *New York*, November 19, 1990.

203 *"To viewers"*: Edwin Diamond, "War Watch," *New York*, February 4, 1991.

203 *talking nonstop*: Marie Brenner, "After the Gold Rush," *Vanity Fair*, September 1990.

203 *pick through the garbage*: Christopher Byron, "Trump Is Us," *New York*, June 18, 1990.

203 *borrowed $30 million*: Timothy L. O'Brien, *TrumpNation: The Art of Being the Donald* (New York: Grand Central Publishing, 2005), p. 143.

203 *No one wanted*: Christopher Byron, "1990 Winners and Sinners: Business," *New York*, December 24–31, 1990.

203 *"Oh, he'll be back"*: "The Spy 100," *Spy*, October 1990.

204 *Since 1987*: Crown Heights' Housing and Vacancy Report: New York City 1991, NYC Department of Housing Preservation and Development, 1991, p. 289.

205 *"David Dinkins has failed"*: Mike McAlary, "Dave Lets City's Wounds Fester," *New York Post*, August 23, 1991.

205 *Dinkins's approval rating*: "Around City Hall: Low Hopes," *The New Yorker*, August 26, 1991.

205 *"They're not people"*: "Around City Hall: The Unpeaceable Kingdom," *The New Yorker*, January 27, 1992.

Chapter Fifteen | **Mayor School**

207 *"looks quite healthy"* and passim: Peter D. Salins, "Is New York Going Down the Tubes?" *City Journal*, Fall 1990.

207 *"the left-liberal side"*: Jim Sleeper quoted in James Traub, "Intellectual Stock Picking," *The New Yorker*, February 7, 1994.

207 *"city government is tired"*: Joe Klein, "Going Private," *New York*, March 5, 1990.

208 *"bureaucratic institutions"*: David Osborne and Ted Gaebler, *Reinventing Government: How the Entrepreneurial Spirit Is Transforming the Public Sector* (Reading, MA: Addison-Wesley, 1992), p. 23.

209 *"in the back all alone"*: Mike Gecan interview.

209 *"government accomplishing"*: Abraham Biderman quoted in Alan Finder, "New York Pledge to House Poor Works a Rare, Quiet Revolution," *New York Times*, April 30, 1995.

209 *"a breach of faith"*: Frucher quoted in Eric Lipton, "Battery Park City Is Success, Except for Pledge to the Poor," *New York Times*, January 2, 2001.

210 *"Fuck you"*: Myron Magnet interview.

210 *"What happened"*: William Stern quoted in "Liberalism and the City," *City Journal*, Autumn 1991.
210 *amazing coincidence*: Charles Murray, *Losing Ground: American Social Policy, 1950–1980* (New York: Basic Books, 1984), pp. 30–31.
210 *As Magnet explained*: Myron Magnet, *The Dream and the Nightmare: The Sixties Legacy to the Underclass* (New York: William Morrow & Co, 1993), pp. 197–200.
210 *"the decentralized flexible"*: Joe Klein quoted in "Liberalism and the City," *City Journal*, Autumn 1991.
210 *"the moral foundations"*: Jonathan Rieder quoted in ibid.
211 *"All New Yorkers"*: Robert F. Wagner Jr., *New York Ascendant: The Report of the Commission on the Year 2000* (New York: Harper & Row, 1988), p. 176.
211 *"They say it's because"*: Jim Little quoted in Richard Lyn Cook and Stephen Pleasants, "Victims," *New York*, April 9, 1990.
211 *Lemann questioned*: Joe Klein, "Life Without Father," *New York*, April 29, 1991.
211 *"triumph of individualism"* and passim: Alan Ehrenhalt quoted in "Liberalism and the City," *City Journal*, Autumn 1991.
212 *"I came from the Left"*: Reverend Calvin O. Butts quoted in Joel Dreyfuss, "Harlem's Ardent Voice," *New York Times*, January 20, 1991.
212 *who "charmed" him*: Butts quoted in David M. Halbfinger, "With Attack on Giuliani, Pastor Returns to Fiery Past," *New York Times*, May 22, 1998.
212 *some 6,000 units*: Emily M. Bernstein, "A New Bradhurst; Harlem Trades Symbols of Decay for Symbols of Renewal," *New York Times*, January 6, 1994.
212 *"The idea that prosperity"* and passim: Yolanda Garcia quoted in Peter Stand, Yolanda Garcia, and Eddie Bautista, "Melrose Commons, A Case Study for Sustainable Community Development," Barbara Olshansky, ed., Planners Network, 1996.
212 *he couldn't find one*: "Around City Hall: Two Cities," *The New Yorker*, June 8, 1992.
213 *nearly one million*: US Census data, 1980, 1990.
213 *"Migrant knowledge"*: Richard Sennett, *Building and Dwelling: Ethics for the City* (New York: Farrar, Straus and Giroux), 2018.
213 *first Korean grocer*: Pyong Gap Min, *Ethnic Solidarity for Economic Survival: Korean Greengrocers in New York City* (New York: Russell Sage Foundation, 2008), p. 13.
213 *"a welcome twist"*: Peter Hellman, "What's Better Now," *New York*, May 22, 1989.
213 *some 175,000 Koreans*: Min, *Ethnic Solidarity for Economic Survival*, p. 50.
213 *rise more than 40%*: NYC Department of City Planning, "The Newest New Yorkers, 2013 edition," ch. 2.
214 *"almost entirely ignored"*: James Traub, "Intellectual Stock Picking," *The New Yorker*, February 7, 1994.
214 *"innovations like privatization"*: Giuliani quoted in "How to Save New York," *New York*, November 26, 1990.
214 *"out there pitching"*: Biederman interview.
214 *"The Quality of Urban Life"*: *City Journal*, Spring 1992.

214 *"I don't know"*: Giuliani quoted in Myron Magnet, "What City Journal Wrought," *City Journal*, Autumn 2015.

214 *"Imagine having a politician"*: Ibid.

215 *summer would bring*: Eleanor Dwight, "Field of Dreams," *New York*, April 20, 1992.

215 *"All the hiding places"*: Andrew Heiskell quoted in Bruce Weber, "After Years Under Wraps, a Midtown Park Is Back," *New York Times*, April 22, 1992.

215 *"Will they be able"*: Ron Wood quoted in ibid.

215 *"another city altogether"*: Paul Goldberger, "Architecture View; Bryant Park, An Out-of-Town Experience," *New York Times*, May 3, 1992.

215 *"phenomenal" drop*: George James, "Midtown Crime Reported Down Sharply," *New York Times*, June 2, 1992.

215 *"to ratify the future"*: The Talk of the Town, "Light the Lights," *The New Yorker*, April 1, 1991.

215 *"jogging paths"*: Karen Cook, "A Fine Line," *Manhattan, Inc.*, April 1987.

215 *"hit his stride"*: Donald Zucker quoted in Eric Pooley, "Air Dinkins," *New York*, May 25, 1992.

216 *"bullshit"* and passim: Giuliani quoted in Kirtzman, *Rudy Giuliani*, p. 41.

216 *Fully one-third of the NYPD*: James C. McKinley Jr., "Officers Rally and Dinkins Is Their Target," *New York Times*, September 17, 1992.

Chapter Sixteen | The End of the One-Tribe Nation

217 *"THOUGHT POLICE"* and passim: Jerry Adler et al., "Thought Police," *Newsweek*, December 24, 1990.

217 *"Multiculturalism is a lie"*: Maggie Gallagher, "The Myth of Multiculture," *City Journal*, Spring 1991.

218 *"Money was no object"*: Evans interview.

218 *"I don't sit around"*: Judith Regan quoted in Rebecca Mead, "Pop Vulture," *New York*, October 25, 1993.

218 *2 million books*: Jeanie Kasindorf, "Living with Martha," *New York*, January 28, 1991.

218 *"ratlike cunning"*: Harry Evans quoted in Michael Gross, "Tina's Turn," *New York*, July 20, 1992.

218 *"the money culture"*: Tina Brown quoted in Bachrach, *Tina and Harry Come to America*, p. 212.

218 *"cultural vandalism"*: Michael Gross, "Tina's Turn," *New York*, July 20, 1992.

218 *"I am distraught"*: Brown quoted in Margalit Fox, "George Trow, 63, a Critic of American Culture, Dies," *New York Times*, December 1, 2006.

219 *"calmly embittered spirit"*: Adam Gopnik quoted in Kay Larson, "Pop Goes the Easel," *New York*, October 15, 1990.

219 *"fat cannibal"*: David Wojnarowicz, "Postcards from America: X-rays from Hell," *Close to the Knives: A Memoir of Disintegration* (New York: Vintage, 1991), p. 114.

219 *the social highlight*: Paul Taylor, "AIDS Guerillas," *New York*, November 12, 1990.

219 *"shake the boundaries"*: David Wojnarowicz, "Do Not Doubt the Dangerousness of the 12-inch Politician," *Close to the Knives*, p. 153.

220 *"three of four years"*: Larry Kramer, "Larry Kramer: Queer Conscience," *New York*, April 6, 1998.

220 Untitled (One Day This Kid . . .): David Wojnarowicz, 1989. Estate of David Wojnarowicz and P.P.O.W. Gallery.

221 *"Black people were the first"*: Chuck D with Jah, *Fight the Power*, pp. 179–180.

221 *"sold so many pieces of himself"*: Sharpton quoted in Michael Klein, *The Man Behind the Sound Bite: The Real Story of the Reverend Al Sharpton* (New York: Castillo International, 1991), p. 243.

221 *"my night journey"*: Sharpton and Walton, *Go and Tell Pharoah*, p. 182.

221 *"throw my hair"*: Sharpton quoted in Jim Sleeper, "Moving the Black Middle Class," *The New Yorker*, January 25, 1993.

222 *"bebop predecessor"* and passim: Adilifu Nama, "It Was Signified" in Michael Eric Dyson and Sohail Daulatzai, eds., *Born to Use Mics: Reading Nas's Illmatic* (New York: Civitas Books, 2010), p. 19.

222 *"the hardest-working intern ever"*: Andre Harrell quoted in Andrew Cable, *A Family Affair: The Unauthorized Sean "Puffy" Combs Story* (New York: Ballantine Books, 1998), p. 29.

222 *"the coldest year"*: Simmons with George, *Life and Def*, p. 179.

222 *"the official bling-bling"* and passim: Simmons quoted in O'Brien, *TrumpNation*, p. 198.

222 *"the Def Jam brand seem"* and passim: Simmons with George, *Life and Def*, p. 113.

223 *"do not equate"*: Adilifu Nama, "It Was Signified" in Dyson and Daulatzai, eds., *Born to Use Mics*, p. 21.

223 *"neighborhood work"* and passim: John Ahearn interview.

223 *"more as guardians"*: Jane Kramer, *Whose Art Is It?* (Durham, NC: Duke University Press, 1994), p. 37.

223 *"not of the community"*: Arthur Symes quoted in ibid., p. 94.

224 *predominantly Hispanic*: Tom Finkelpearl, *Dialogues in Public Art* (Cambridge, MA: The MIT Press, 2001), p. 85.

224 *"a disquiet to the day"*: John Ahearn quoted in ibid., p. 91.

225 *"low-key, inclusive"*: David Brody, *Brooklyn DIY: A Story of Williamsburg Art Scene 1987–2007*, directed by Martin Ramocki," artcrical.com, March 1, 2009.

225 *"electro-mechanical bricolage"*: Ibid.

225 *"human parts are recycled"*: Jonathan Fineberg, "A long time ago in a galaxy far, far away . . ." in Jonathan Fineberg, ed., *Out of Town: The Williamsburg Paradigm* (Urbana-Champaign: Krannert Art Museum, University of Illinois, 1993).

225 *"global metaculture"* and passim: Kit Blake, "Metaculture" in Fineberg, ed., *Out of Town*.

225 *"It is here"*: Annie Herron quoted in Brad Gooch, "The New Bohemia," *New York*, June 22, 1992.

226 *"a street fair, New Music performance"*: James Kalm, "Brooklyn Dispatches," *Brooklyn Rail*, April 6, 2009.

226 *"We feel protected"*: Jeff Gompertz quoted in Brad Gooch, "The New Bohemia," *New York*, June 22, 1992.

226 *"Bacchanalia"*: James Kalm, "Brooklyn Dispatches," *Brooklyn Rail*, June 2008.

226 *"Everything's changing"*: Charles Garbacki quoted in Lynette Holloway, "Neighborhood Report," *New York Times*, September 19, 1993.

226 *"a direct rebuke"*: Michael Gross, "All the Pretty Young Things," *New York*, March 15, 1993.

227 *"territory of controversy"*: Elisabeth Sussman interview.

227 *"I hate the show"*: Michael Kimmelman, "Art View," *New York Times*, April 25, 1993.

227 *"a pious, often arid show"*: Roberta Smith, "At the Whitney, A Biennial with a Social Conscience," *New York Times*, March 5, 1993.

227 *"Mope art"*: John Taylor, "Mope Art," *New York*, March 22, 1993.

227 *"the moment in which today's"*: Jerry Saltz, "Jerry Saltz on '93 in Art," *New York*, February 1, 2013.

227 *"[I]dentities declare communities"*: Elisabeth Sussman, "Coming Together in Parts: Positive Power in the Art of the Nineties," in Elisabeth Sussman with Thelma Golden, *1993 Biennial Exhibition* (New York: Whitney Museum of American Art, 1993), p. 12.

227 *"embracing of the margins"*: Thelma Golden, "What's White . . . ?", in ibid., p. 35.

227 *"art you got"*: Sussman interview.

227 *"socially marginalized"*: Lisa Phillips, "No Man's Land: Art at the Threshold of a Millennium" in Sussman with Golden, *1993 Biennial Exhibition*, p. 54.

227 *"symbolic violence"*: Coco Fusco, "Passionate Irreverence: The Cultural Politics of Identity," in ibid., p. 78.

228 *"identity, difference, otherness"* and passim: Roberta Smith, "At the Whitney, A Biennial with a Social Conscience."

228 *"culture of victimization"*: John Taylor, "Don't Blame Me!," *New York*, June 3, 1991.

228 *"rolling tide of undocumented"*: Christopher Byron, "Where Have You Gone, Roger Maris?," *New York*, June 10, 1991.

228 *"a loosely confederated"*: Thomas A. Stewart, "Boom Time on the New Frontier," *Fortune*, September 27, 1993.

228 *"a revolution of random"*: Craig Bromberg, "Here Come the Gizmos," *New York*, August 17, 1992.

229 *"I think what will happen"*: Jaron Lanier quoted in The Talk of the Town, "Jaron Lanier Is Virtually Sure," *The New Yorker*, December 27, 1993.

Chapter Seventeen | **You Were on Your Own**

231 *Rollerbladed*: Rebecca Mead, "Money Machine," *New York*, November 22, 1993.

231 *Goldman Sachs had advised*: Mahar, *Bull*, p. 85.

231 *crafty benefits counselor*: John Cassidy, "Striking It Rich," *The New Yorker*, January 14, 2002.

232 *6% of households*: "US Household Ownership of Mutual Funds in 2001," *Fundamentals: Investment Company Institute Research in Brief*, vol. 10, no. 4, September 2001.

232 *"There might be better"*: Michael Bloomberg quoted in R. L. Stern, "A New Guy Can Do It Better," *Forbes*, November 25, 1991.

232 *"nice and complicated"*: Donald Trump quoted in Mark Singer, "The World of Mar-A-Lago," *The New Yorker*, May 19, 1997.

233 *"now his currency"*: Julie Baumgold, "Fighting Back," *New York*, November 9, 1992.

233 *"an interior life"*: Mark Singer, "The World of Mar-A-Lago."

233 *"When Trump is back"*: Donald Trump quoted in Baumgold, "Fighting Back."

233 *real median household*: Housing and Vacancy Report: New York City 1993, NYC Department of Housing Preservation and Development, 1993, p. 74.

233 *"I hit the street"*: Luc Sante, "Commerce," in Marshal Berman and Brian Berger, eds., *New York Calling: From Blackout to Bloomberg* (London: Reaktion Books, 2007), p. 104.

233 *Mechanic David Peter*: Catherine S. Manegold, "Explosion at the Twin Towers . . . ," *New York Times*, February 27, 1993.

233 *Joseph Cacciatore*: Charles J. Shields, *The 1993 World Trade Center Bombing* (Philadelphia: Chelsea House, 2002), p. 43.

233 *food was cooked*: Jim Dwyer et al., *Two Seconds Under the World* (New York: Crown, 1994), p. 19.

233 *some 200,000 people*: Ibid., p. 17.

233 *"Point of View"*: *New York*, November 12, 1990.

234 *a cavern 200 feet by 150 feet*: Dwyer et al., *Two Seconds Under the World*, p. 53.

234 *The TV stations*: James Bennet, "Explosion at the Twin Towers: The Towers, Flaws in Emergency Systems Exposed," *New York Times*, February 28, 1993.

234 *"on your own"*: Karen Eggleston quoted in Martin Gottlieb, "Explosion at the Twin Towers: The Response; Size of Blast 'Destroyed' Rescue Plan," *New York Times*, February 28, 1993.

234 *theme from Barney*: Shields, *The 1993 World Trade Center Bombing*, p. 45.

234 *the last people*: Ibid., p. 52.

234 *Six had died*: Kelly, *Vigilance*, pp. 90–91.

235 *"The emperor"*: Ada Louise Huxtable, "Times Square Renewal (Act II), a Farce," *New York Times*, October 14, 1989.

235 *"The ground was covered"*: Dickson interview.

236 *"opportunity to go"* and passim: Rebecca Robertson interview.

236 *"positive chaos"*: Robertson quoted in Pranay Gupta, "Her 'To Die For' Projects Include Times Square and the Seventh Regiment Armory," *New York Sun*, March 9, 2006.

236 *"things that would change"* and passim: Robertson interview.

236 *"should be a zoo"*: Tibor Kalman quoted in Sagalyn, *Times Square Roulette*, p. 300.

236 *"cure the street"*: Kalman quoted in Liz Farrelly, *Tibor Kalman: Design and Undesign* (New York: Watson-Guptil Publications, 1998), p. 44.

237 *"You had to trust"*: Kalman quoted in ibid., p. 47.

237 *never graduated*: Heiskell with Graves, *Outsider Insider*, pp. 163–164.

237 *"Impeccably stylish"*: David W. Dunlap, "1935: A Family Battle for Succession," *New York Times*, November 5, 2015.

238 *"obsessed"*: Michael Eisner interview.

238 *"We owed a lot to Lester Eisner"*: Jacobs quoted in *Villager*, May 12–18, 2004.

239 *"best Broadway musical score"*: Frank Rich, "The Year in the Arts: Theater/1991," *New York Times*, December 29, 1991.

240 *"A few porn shops"*: Gretchen Dykstra quoted in Traub, *The Devil's Playground*, p. 195.

241 *"In the great wave of moral"*: Daniel Patrick Moynihan, "Defining Deviancy Down," *The American Scholar*, vol. 62, no. 1 (Winter 1993), p. 21.

241 *other sorts of deviance*: Andrew Karmen, "'Defining Deviancy Down': How Senator Moynihan's Misleading Phrase About Criminal Justice Is Rapidly Being Incorporated into Popular Culture," *Journal of Criminal Justice and Popular Culture*, vol. 2, no. 5, 1994.

241 *"a post-ideological"*: John Taylor, "Dark Shadows," *New York*, October 25, 1993.

241 *"This is a stronger, safer"*: Dinkins quoted in John Taylor, "Rudy's Shot," *New York*, October 11, 1993.

241 *fully a third of Blacks*: "Around City Hall: Change Partners," *The New Yorker*, June 14, 1993.

242 *only 11% Black and 14% Hispanic*: Eric Pooley, "Bulldog," *New York*, February 22, 1993.

242 *"the most prudent"*: Ray Kelly quoted in McNickle, *The Power of the Mayor*, p. 294.

242 *"What you've got to do"*: John Timoney quoted in Bratton with Knobler, *Turnaround*, p. 205.

242 *"a very, very good way"*: David Garth quoted in Alison Mitchell, "Political Memo: Police Hearings Effects Defy the Usual Wisdom," *New York Times*, October 3, 1993.

242 *discounting the drop*: Craig Horowitz, "How Bad Is It?," *New York*, October 18, 1993.

242 *"During the years"*: Pete Hamill, "How to Save the Homeless and Ourselves," *New York*, September 20,1993.

243 *"term of indifference"*: Giuliani quoted in Catherine S. Manegold, "Fight Vowed by Giuliani on Narcotics," *New York Times*, September 10, 1993.

243 *"You want to reduce crime?"*: Ray Kelly quoted in Bratton with Knobler, *Turnaround*, p. 202.

244 *"utter disarray"*: Koch quoted in Catherine S. Manegold, "Assailing Dinkins, Koch Backs Giuliani," *New York Times*, October 15, 1993.

244 *"Seventh on Sixth"*: Jeanette Walls, "Intelligencer," *New York*, October 4, 1993.

244 *huge turnout*: James Dao, "The 1993 Elections: New York City Roundup; Secession in Jeopardy?," *New York Times*, November 4, 1993.

does not apply.

244 *"Now more than ever"*: Dinkins quoted in Alan Finder, "Dinkins Encourages Council to Retain His Key Programs," *New York Times*, December 22, 1993.

Chapter Eighteen | More Like the Rest of America

247 *"Dream with me"* and passim: Giuliani quoted in "'The New Mayor: Transcript of Inaugural Speech: Giuliani Urges Change and Unity," *New York Times*, January 3, 1994.
247 *Yesrudys swept*: Kirtzman, *Rudy Giuliani*, p. 66.
247 *"It always appeared to me"*: Giuliani quoted in Siegel, *The Prince of the City*, p. x.
248 *"the cornerstone"*: Giuliani with Kurson, *Leadership*, p. 29.
248 *"common sense approach"*: Giuliani quoted in "'The New Mayor; Transcript of Inaugural Speech: Giuliani Urges Change and Unity."
248 *"entrepreneurial spirit"*: Alison Mitchell, "Former Head of Power Authority Is Chosen to Be a Deputy Mayor," *New York Times*, December 18, 1993.
248 *"wrongly taught"*: Giuliani quoted in Siegel, *The Prince of the City*, p. 142.
248 *"You found America"*: Mario Puzo, *The Godfather* (New York: Signet, 1978), p. 21.
249 *"the rest of America"*: Giuliani quoted in Siegel, *The Prince of the City*, p. xv.
249 *"He had nothing"*: Robertson interview.
249 *$31.7 billion*: Steve Lee Myers, "Looking Toward Budget, Giuliani Places His Bets," *New York Times*, February 6, 1994.
249 *slow down*: E. S. Savas, *Privatization in the City: Successes, Failures, Lessons* (Washington, DC: CQ Press, 2005), pp. 120–121.
250 *"If he didn't like you"*: Peter F. Vallone, *Learning to Govern: My Life in New York Politics from Hell Gate to City Hall* (New York: Chaucer Press, 2005), p. 210.
250 *summoned to Gracie Mansion*: Bratton with Knobler, *Turnaround*, p. 279.
250 *climate of fear*: Kirtzman, *Rudy Giuliani*, p. 98.
250 *"master strategist"*: "Budget Showdown at City Hall," *New York Times*, June 23, 1994.
250 *"very deep distrust"*: Andy Logan quoted in William Glaberson, "Giuliani and Reporters: Disparate Views of Mayor's Image," *New York Times*, July 4, 1994.
250 *"a sense of urban emergency"*: Laura Jacobs, "So Deep," *New York*, April 25, 1994.
250 *A June poll showed*: Clifford Krauss, "New York City Crime Falls But Just Why Is a Mystery," *New York Times*, January 1, 1995.
250 *"unprecedented crisis"*: Marva Hammons quoted in Alison Mitchell, "HRA Chief Tells Council of Deep Cuts," *New York Times*, September 27, 1994.
250 *"growling cupshakers"*: Alex Williams, "Stop That Bike!" *New York*, July 18, 1994.
251 *"This is everything"*: Woody Allen quoted in The Talk of the Town, "Everything You Ever Wanted to Know About Knicks," *The New Yorker*, June 6, 1994.
251 *never run a sports franchise*: Murray Chass, "ITT-Cablevision Deal Reported to Buy Madison Square Garden," *New York Times*, August 28, 1994.
251 *"Calm down, it's fall"*: "Fall Preview," *New York*, September 14, 1994.

251 *"My city comes first"*: Giuliani quoted in Siegel, *The Prince of the City*, p. 131.

252 *"Our Loser"*: Eric Pooley, "Our Loser," *New York*, November 21, 1994.

252 *"vivid evidence"*: Craig Horowitz, "A South Bronx Renaissance," *New York*, November 21, 1994.

252 *"Abandoned, gutted"*: Alan Finder, "New York Pledge to House Poor Works a Rare, Quiet Revolution," *New York Times*, April 30, 1995.

252 *"NEW YORK IS BACK"* and passim: Bob Ickes, "The New, Improved New York," *New York*, December 19, 1994.

253 *"economic strip-mining"*: Bert Flickinger III quoted in Sarah Ferguson, "The Invasion of the Superstores," *New York*, March 13, 1995.

253 *proposed raising*: Steven Lee Myers, "Giuliani Proposes Changes in Zoning to Aid Superstores," *New York Times*, February 19, 1995.

253 *"regular people"* and passim: Wendy Wasserstein, "When Superstores Were Truly Super," *New York Times*, October 27, 1996.

253 *"City life"*: Ibid.

253 *"touching and sweetly"*: Kirk Johnson, "Bargain, Yes. But Not in Our Backyards," *New York Times*, December 15, 1996.

254 *Giuliani purged anyone*: Eric Pooley, "Inside Rudy's Brain," *New York*, February 27, 1995.

254 *"most prolific and profound"*: Fernando Ferrer quoted in "New York's Liberals Have Fallen and They Can't Get Up," *New York*, July 10, 1995.

254 *cops teargassed*: Eric Pooley, "Rudy's Problem Children," *New York*, April 10, 1995.

254 *moving between boroughs*: "A Reporter at Large: The Protector," *The New Yorker*, April 21, 1997.

254 *"I think Rudy's become"*: Koch quoted in Joyce Purnick, "Metro Matters: A Vocal Ally of Giuliani Is Now His Toughest Critic," *New York Times*, June 26, 1995.

254 *"brand-train"*: Alex Williams, "Sub Text," *New York*, March 20, 1995.

255 *dropped almost 25%*: Peter Hellman, "The Return of the $100,000 Closet," *New York*, April 24, 1995.

255 *"most potent pricing"*: Peter Hellman, "Rents Run Amok," *New York*, June 27, 1996.

255 *Private schools reported*: "Gotham," *New York*, January 23, 1995.

255 *"People used to understand"*: Hugh Hardy quoted in Julie V. Iovine, "Tenacity in the Service of Public Culture," *New York Times*, December 12, 1995.

255 *"Frederick Law Olmsted"*: "Tables for Two," *The New Yorker*, July 26, 1999.

255 *Gael Greene thought*: Gael Greene, "Forget Paris," *New York*, June 5, 1995.

255 *"so user-friendly, so open"*: Alex Williams, "Chelsea Piers," *New York*, April 22, 1996.

255 *"We're redefining"*: Richard Kahan quoted in Eric Pooley, "Biederman's Little Acre," *New York*, May 1, 1995.

256 *local kids as "monkeys"*: Richard Kraft quoted in Matt Bai, "Yankee Imperialism," *New York*, July 25, 1994.

256 *"Eurotrash, caviar"*: Alexandra Lange, "Now That's Swanky," *New York*, December 28, 1995.

Chapter Nineteen | Larceny in Everyone's Heart

257 *"authoritarian figures"*: Giuliani with Kurson, *Leadership*, p. 178.
257 *Community Policing*: Levitt, *NYPD Confidential*, pp. 41–42.
257 *he really wanted*: Bratton with Knobler, *Turnaround*, p. 191.
257 *"I didn't know Giuliani"*: Ibid., p. 190.
257 *"there's a little larceny"*: Maple with Mitchell, *The Crime Fighter*, p. 45.
257 *known for misplacing*: Julia Marsh, "Failed NYPD Reform Chief Once Sued the City Over Small Desks," *New York Post*, February 21, 2015.
258 *Sneering at Elaine's*: John Miller quoted in James Kaplan, "Forever Elaine's," *New York*, July 8, 1996.
258 *"[t]he big blue wall"*: Bratton with Knobler, *Turnaround*, p. 209.
258 *Mao and AA*: Chris Smith, "The NYPD Guru," *New York*, April 2, 1996.
258 *"bored to tears"*: Bratton quoted in George James, "Bratton Puts Focus on Beat for Shake-up," *New York Times*, January 24, 1994.
258 *requested resignation*: Dennis Hevesi, "Bratton Asks Police Aides for Resignation Letters," *New York Times*, January 9, 1994.
259 *"I hate this city"*: James Barron, "Gunman Wounds Two in Robbery at an East Side Bridal Shop," *New York Times*, March 24, 1994.
259 *"I could not forgive"*: Bratton with Knobler, *Turnaround*, p. 205.
259 *148 probational cops*: "The C.E.O. Cop," *The New Yorker*, February 6, 1995.
259 *banned the chokehold*: Bratton with Knobler, *Turnaround*, pp. 245–247.
260 *Manhattan crime*: Maple with Mitchell, *The Crime Fighter*, p. 114.
260 *chairs thrown*: Levitt, *NYPD Confidential*, p. 69.
260 *"He's a professional"*: Rangel quoted in Clifford Krauss, "Roles and Goals for an Energetic Bratton," *New York Times*, January 22, 1994.
260 *"His actions show"*: Sharpton quoted in ibid.
261 *"I know there are some"*: Bratton quoted in ibid.
261 *nearly a quarter*: Karmen, *New York Murder Mystery*, p. 88.
261 *"quick" booking*: Eric Pooley, "Officer Lucifero's Escape from Booking Hell," *New York*, August 22, 1994.
261 *"year-to-year"*: Miller quoted in James Kunen, "Comment: Quality and Equality," *The New Yorker*, November 28, 1994.
261 *"in all likelihood"*: Ibid.
261 *"None of this," he wrote then, "is easily"*: George L. Kelling and James Q. Wilson, "Broken Windows," *The Atlantic*, March 1982.
261 *Crime in 1994 went down 12.3%*: Siegel, *The Prince of the City*, p. 149.
261 *"Nobody can be sure"*: Bratton quoted in Clifford Krauss, "New York City Crime Falls But Just Why Is a Mystery," *New York Times*, January 1, 1995.
261 *"rapidly than crime"*: Siegel, *The Prince of the City*, p. 149.
262 *more than 600,000 people*: "Who Feeds the Hungry? Mapping New York City's Emergency Food Providers," *Food for Survival*, 2000, pp. 8–9.
262 *"Rapists and killers"*: Maple with Mitchell, *The Crime Fighter*, p. 154.
262 *Marijuana was back*: Andrew Golub, ed., *The Cultural/Subcultural Contexts of*

Marijuana Use at the Turn of the Twenty-First Century (New York: The Haworth Press, 2005), p. 11.

262 *less alcohol*: Karmen, *New York Murder Mystery*, pp. 185–187.

262 *"factionalized"*: George Kalogerakis, "Stoned Again," *New York*, May 1, 1995.

262 *Heroin, ecstasy*: Ibid.

262 *"matured"* and passim: Karmen, *New York Murder Mystery*, pp. 172–173.

263 *communal quality*: Golub, ed., *The Cultural/Subcultural Contexts of Marijuana Use*, p. 28.

263 *Black or Latino, young, and 95% male*: Karmen, *New York Murder Mystery*, p. 64.

263 *unintended result*: John J. Donohue III and Steven D. Levitt, "The Impact of Legalized Abortion on Crime," *Quarterly Journal of Economics*, vol. CXVI, issue 2, May 2001.

263 *abolishment of lead paint*: Jessica Wolpaw Reyes, "Lead Exposure and Behavior: Effects on Antisocial and Risky Behavior among Children and Adolescents," *Economic Inquiry*, vol. 53, no. 3 (August 2014).

263 *students were literally saving*: Karmen, *New York Murder Mystery*, pp. 209–215.

263 *yet government spending*: Michael Eric Dyson, "'One Love,' Two Brothers, Three Verses," in Dyson and Daulatzai, eds., *Born to Use Mics*, p. 130.

263 *2.28 million Black men*: Thelma Golden, *Black Male. Representations of Masculinity in Contemporary American Art* (New York: Whitney Museum of American Art, 1994), p. 13.

263 *needle users to crack*: Karmen, *New York Murder Mystery*, pp. 238–240.

264 *because of mass incarceration*: Franklin E. Zimring, *The City That Became Safe: New York's Lessons for Urban Crime and Its Control* (New York: Oxford University Press, 2012), pp. 207–209; Judith Greene and Vincent Schiraldi, "Better by Half: The New York City Story of Winning Large-Scale Decarceration While Increasing Public Safety," *Federal Sentencing Reporter*, vol. 29, no. 1 (October 28, 216), pp. 22.

264 *First- and second-generation*: Robert J. Sampson, *Great American City: Chicago and the Enduring Neighborhood Effect* (Chicago: University of Chicago Press, 2012), pp. 256–257.

264 *"What happened"*: Trina Scotland interview.

264 *"I think over the summer"*: Sara Morales quoted in Craig Horowitz, "A South Bronx Renaissance," *New York*, November 21, 1994.

264 *"What changed the South Bronx"*: Tony Proscio quoted in Siegel, *The Prince of the City*, p. 290.

264 *"collective efficacy"*: Sampson, *Great American City*, p. 27.

264 *"There is probably no other place"* and passim: Malcolm Gladwell, "Dept. of Disputation: The Tipping Point," *The New Yorker*, June 3, 1996.

265 *wholesalers' revenues down*: Selwyn Raab, "Fish Market's Problems Revert to New York City," *New York Times*, March 27, 1994.

265 *tense night in October*: Dan Barry, "At the Fulton Fish Market, Tradition Gives Way to Tension," *New York Times*, October 18, 1995.

266 *against twenty-three firms*: James B. Jacobs, with Coleen Friel and Robert Radick,

Gotham Unbound: How New York City was Liberated from the Grip of Organized Crime (New York: New York University Press, 1999), p. 196.

266 *"the largest tax cut of"*: Ibid., p. 203.

266 *"America is getting Russian criminals"* and passim: Boris Urov quoted in Robert I. Friedman, *Red Mafiya: How the Russian Mob Has Invaded America* (New York: Warner Books, 2000), p. v.

267 *a* Daily News *interview*: Kirtzman, *Rudy Giuliani,* p. 95.

267 *"BRATTON'S JUGGERNAUT"*: Levitt, *NYPD Confidential,* p. 103.

267 *undimpled heavy bag*: Ibid., pp. 44–45.

267 *"[t]he great majority of the city's"* and passim: "The C.E.O. Cop," *The New Yorker,* February 6, 1995.

267 *"militarized bureaucracy model"*: Kelling quoted in Michael Tomasky, "Quality of Life," *New York,* December 25, 1996.

268 *"lightweight"*: Timoney quoted in "Gotham," *New York,* May 27, 1996.

268 *"The idea that"*: Timoney quoted in Robert Sabbag, "Rudy's Cop," *New York,* June 3, 1996.

268 *"Yankees. Rudy."*: Michael Tomasky, "Can Anything Beat Rudy?," *New York,* November 11, 1996.

Chapter Twenty | Cyber City

270 *"People don't like to read"*: Jason Calacanis quoted in Casey Kait and Stephen Weiss, *Digital Hustlers: Living Large and Falling Hard in Silicon Alley* (New York: HarperCollins, 2001), p. 20.

270 *"The (Second Phase of the)"*: Gary Wolfe, *Wired,* October 1, 1994.

270 *"every old-media company"*: Michael Krantz, "The Great Manhattan Geek Rush of 1995," *New York,* November 13, 1995.

270 *"The Internet was going to be"*: Michael Wolff, *Burn Rate: How I Survived the Gold Rush Years on the Internet* (New York: Simon & Schuster, 1998), p. 26.

270 *following three months*: Kait and Weiss, *Digital Hustlers,* p. 33.

270 *"two kinds of people"*: Erik Larson, "The World of Business: Free Money," *The New Yorker,* October 11, 1999.

270 *"Early True Believers"*: Vanessa Grigoriadis, "Silicon Alley 10003," *New York,* March 6, 2000.

271 *"HIGH TECH BOOM TOWN"*: *New York,* November 13, 1995.

271 *"incredibly powerful"*: Rufus Griscom quoted in Vanessa Grigoriadis, "Silicon Alley 10003," *New York,* March 6, 2000.

271 *"glib and glad-handing"*: Michael Krantz, "The Great Manhattan Geek Rush of 1995," *New York,* November 13, 1995.

272 *much of the $1.1 billion*: David S. Bennahum, "Too Hot Java," *New York,* January 7, 1996.

272 *create up to 120,000 jobs*: Kait and Weiss, *Digital Hustlers,* p. 59.

272 *World Trade Center 32%*: Michael Indergaard, *Silicon Alley: The Rise and Fall of a New Media District* (New York: Routledge, 2004), p. 43.

272 *"Tech is the heart and soul"*: James J. Cramer, "Playing the Futures Market," *New York*, November 13, 1995.

272 *"[T]o be Infobahn-hip"*: *USA Today* quoted in Larry Doyle, "Geek Chic," *New York*, June 13, 1994.

272 *"seemed embarrassed"*: Jon Katz, "The Times Enters the Nineties; Doesn't Like It Much," *New York*, June 27, 1994.

273 *"even though we knew"*: Evans interview.

273 *Novelist Robert Coover*: The Talk of the Town, "The Pleasures of the Hypertext," *The New Yorker*, June 27, 1994.

273 *New York Public Library*: Peter Landesman, "And the Word Was ROM," *New York*, June 28–July 3, 1995.

273 *Dick Snyder was fired*: "Intelligencer," *New York*, June 27–July 4, 1994.

273 *name was Gwendolyn*: Evans quoted in Linda Hall, "Whithering Hype," *New York*, November 28, 1994.

273 *"the whole country"*: Oprah Winfrey quoted in David Streitfeld, "On Oprah: People Who Read," *Washington Post*, September 26, 1996.

273 *"a chain becomes"*: Len Riggio quoted in David Kirkpatrick, "Barnes & Noble's Jekyll and Hyde," *New York*, July 19, 1999.

274 *"beguiled the press"*: Ibid.

274 *Amazon grossed $16 million*: "Remember When Amazon Only Sold Books?," *Los Angeles Times*, June 18, 2017.

274 *"having your parents"*: Richard Stengel quoted in David Ellis, "Not Necessarily the News," *New York*, March 24, 1997.

274 *canoodled*: Elizabeth Wurtzel, "Beyond the Trouble, More Trouble," *New York*, January 31, 2008.

275 *"a form of speech"*: John Seabrook, "Brave New World Dept.: My First Flame," *The New Yorker*, June 6, 1994.

275 *"that's truly ours"*: Karrie Jacobs, "Video Killed the Gargoyle," *New York*, February 17, 1997.

275 *Jim Cramer predicted*: James J. Cramer, "Fortune Telling," *New York*, January 15, 1996.

275 *"The rise of Silicon Valley"*: John Cassidy, "The World of Business: Striking It Rich," *The New Yorker*, January 14, 2002.

276 *"almost perfect economy"*: Robert McTeer quoted in John Liscio, "Apocalypse Later," *New York*, January 20, 1997.

276 *"It has become fashionable"*: The Talk of the Town, "Grant's Tomb," *The New Yorker*, January 13, 1997.

276 *"the Dark Prince"* and passim: David Brock, "Roger Ailes Is Mad as Hell," *New York*, November 17, 1997.

276 *"He's a sexist"*: Regan quoted in ibid.

276 *New York lost manufacturing*: Michael Tomasky, "Port in a Storm," *New York*, July 29, 1996.

276 *fried chicken and coleslaw*: Chris Smith, "The Mayor and His Money," *New York*, October 3, 2005.

276 *the old Drexel Burnham*: Indergaard, *Silicon Alley*, p. 4.

277 *each paid $120,000*: John Cassidy, "Striking It Rich," *The New Yorker*, January 14, 2002.

277 *Intel up from 6½*: John Cassidy, "Dept. of Disputation: Bear Headed," *The New Yorker*, July 28, 1997.

277 *"The three-kids-in-a-loft"*: Jerry Colonna quoted in Matthew McCann Fenton, "Silicon Allies," *New York*, April 7, 1997.

277 *"be a guerilla"*: Nicholas Butterworth quoted in Indergaard, *Silicon Alley*, p. 1.

277 *"The dinosaurs are coming"*: Candice Carpenter quoted in Jason Chervokas and Tom Watson, "Silicon Alley Trades Attitude for Maturity," *New York Times*, September 23, 1996.

277 *"New York development culture"*: Douglas Rushkoff quoted in Kait and Weiss, *Digital Hustlers*, p. 41.

277 *"sporty investment"*: Peggy Edersheim Kalb, "Funds & Games," *New York*, January 19, 1998.

278 *"Almost every social and economic"*: Joe Klein, "Comment: Giving Clinton the Silent Treatment," *The New Yorker*, January 10, 1999.

Chapter Twenty-one | Whose World Is This?

279 *nation's largest public housing*: Bloom and Lasner, eds., *Affordable Housing in New York*, p. 100.

279 *"Every day was one step away"* and passim: Nas in *Nas: Time Is Illmatic*.

279 *"I rap for listeners, bluntheads"*: Nas, "Memory Lane (Sittin' in Da Park)," *Illmatic*, Columbia, 1994.

279 *Harvard, writes dream hampton*: dream hampton, "Born Alone, Die Alone" in Dyson and Daulatzai, eds., *Born to Use Mics*, p. 242.

280 *"reality storybook"* and passim: Minya Oh, "Five Mic Review," *Source*, 1994.

280 *"Never before have so many blacks"*: Henry Lewis Gates Jr., "Comment: The Black Leadership Myth," *The New Yorker*, October 24, 1994.

280 *"Whose world is this?"*: Nas, "The World Is Yours," *Illmatic*, 1994.

280 *"Hugh Hefner of hip-hop"*: The Talk of the Town, "A Run for the Money," *The New Yorker*, October 14, 1996.

281 *"He messed with the wrong people"*: Zack O'Malley Greenburg, *Empire State of Mind: How Jay-Z Went from Street Corner to Corner Office* (New York: Portfolio/Penguin, 2011), p. 29.

281 *"the story of the hustler"*: Jay-Z, *Decoded*, p. 10.

281 *"the generation of black people"*: Ibid., p. 86.

281 *"electoral politics"*: James Braxton Peterson, "It's Yours," in Dyson and Daulatzai, eds., *Born to Use Mics*, p. 84.

281 *"politically economically"*: Paul Beatty, "No Tags Back," *Joker, Joker, Deuce* (New York: Penguin Books, 1994), p. 33.

281 *"already receding"*: Gregory Tate, "An Elegy for *Illmatic*" in Dyson and Daulatzai, eds., *Born to Use Mics*, p. 239.

281 *"[C]rack was not glamorous"*: Mos Def quoted in Charles Aaron, "The *Spin* Interview: Mos Def," *Spin*, August 1, 2009.

281 *offered stability*: Terry Williams and William Kornblum, *Uptown Kids: Struggle and Hope in the Projects* (New York: G. P. Putnam's Sons, 1994), pp. 21–23.

281 *"better maintained"*: Ibid., p. 23.

282 *"outlaws to some degree"*: Ibid., p. 93.

282 *"You have Democrats behaving"*: Arthur Levin quoted in "The Political Scene: Dollface," *The New Yorker*, January 15, 1996.

282 *"Every man for they self"*: Mobb Deep, "Shook Ones Pt. II," 1994.

282 *"Here we go again"*: Butts quoted in Eric Pooley, "Rudy and Race," *New York* February 7, 1994.

282 *Lategano scheduled*: Kirtzman, *Rudy Giuliani*, pp. 154–155.

282 *"was not comfortable"*: Eric Adams quoted in Deborah Hart Strober, *Rudolph S. Giuliani: Flawed or Flawless?* (New York: John Wiley & Sons, 2007), p. 146.

282 *"Italian middle-class"*: Quoted in Kirtzman, *Rudy Giuliani*, p. 186.

282 *admired Jefferson*: Giuliani with Kurson, *Leadership*, p. 38n.

283 *2.7 million meals a month*: "Who Feeds the Hungry? Mapping New York City's Emergency Food Providers," *Food for Survival*, 2000, pp. 7–8.

283 *"That's not an unspoken part"*: Karmen, *New York Murder Mystery*, p. 226.

281 *largest caseload*: Demetra Smith Nightengale et al., "Work and Welfare Reform in New York City During the Giuliani Administration: A Study of Program Implementation," *Urban Institute*, July 31, 2002, p. iii.

283 *eliminate crime*: Snyder, *Crossing Broadway*, p. 194.

283 *Income Support Offices*: New York City Bar, "Welfare Reform in New York City: The Measure of Success," July 1, 2002.

283 *300,000 New Yorkers*: Giuliani with Kurson, *Leadership*, p. 162.

283 *African Americans were also open*: Sharon Zukin, *Naked City: The Death and Life of Authentic Urban Places* (New York: Oxford University Press, 2010), p. 79.

283 *"People who think"*: Rangel quoted in Craig Horowitz, "The No-Win War," *New York*, February 5, 1996.

284 *"dance studio"*: Michael Davis, *Street Gang: The Complete History of* Sesame Street (New York: Viking, 2008), p. 320.

284 *"I've wanted"*: Butts quoted in Craig Horowitz, "The Anti-Sharpton," *New York*, January 26, 1998.

284 *"Community development"*: Karen Phillips quoted in Goldstein, *The Roots of Urban Renaissance*, p. 235.

284 *slow down the $4.2 billion*: Alan Finder, "Success of Housing Program Rests on Economy," *New York Times*, May 2, 1995.

284 *some 4,000 occupied structures*: Alan S. Oser, "Perspectives; Speeding the Recycling of City-Owned Buildings," *New York Times*, March 27, 1994.

284 *no longer offer rehabs*: Ibid.

284 *experienced, local*: Shawn G. Kennedy, "Mayor Cutting City's Roster of Building," *New York Times*, September 15, 1994.

284 *tax liens*: Shawn G. Kennedy, "New York Outlines a New Policy on Seizure of Buildings for Taxes," *New York Times*, October 31, 1995.

285 *Senegalese vendors*: Paul Stoller, *Money Has No Smell: The Africanization of New York City* (Chicago: University of Chicago Press, 2002), p. 18.

285 *"the end of development"*: Rangel quoted in Brett Pulley, "End of Urban Agency Draws Fears of Neglect," *New York Times*, March 30, 1995.

285 *"Am I unnerved?"*: David A. Paterson quoted in Robin Pogrebin, "New Yorkers & Co.: The Political Dance of Calvin Butts," *New York Times*, December 3, 1995.

285 *a Sephardic Jew*: Dan Barry, "Death on 128th Street: The Dispute," *New York Times*, December 9, 1995.

285 *"don't shop where you can't"*: Jim Sleeper, "From the Ashes of the Harlem Tragedy," *Washington Post*, January 21, 1996.

285 *shot four people*: Joe Sexton, "Death on 128th Street: The Victims," *New York Times*, December 9, 1995.

286 *an "interloper" instead*: "Al Sharpton Goes Home," *New York Post*, January 3, 1999.

286 *"some might speculate"*: Hyra, *The New Urban Renewal*, p. 137.

286 *"serious consideration"* and passim: Thomas J. Lueck, "A Jazz Club, A Lingerie Shop and the Gap Vie For Harlem Aid," *New York Times*, August 20, 1996.

286 *"basic tenets of capitalism"*: Deborah Wright quoted in ibid.

286 *made it plain*: Robert Kolker, "In the Zone," *New York*, January 31, 2000.

286 *"a private-sector sensibility"*: Craig Horowitz, "The Battle for the Soul of Harlem," *New York*, January 27, 1997.

287 *"black middle class"*: Hyra, *The New Urban Renewal*, p. 132.

287 *"I am betrayed"*: Ann Jackson quoted in Jim Dwyer, "Financial Fiasco in Harlem Urban Corp. Built Apt. Money Pit, Squandered Millions, Report Sez," *New York Daily News*, February 16, 1997.

287 *some $20 million*: Horowitz, "The Battle for the Soul of Harlem."

287 *Georgie's Bakery*: Dorothy Pitman Hughes, *Wake Up and Smell the Dollars!* (Los Angeles: Amber Books, 2000), p. 51.

287 *"It's no longer for us"*: Isis quoted in Kirk Johnson, "Uneasy Renaissance on Harlem's Street of Dreams," *New York Times*, March 1, 1998.

287 *"buy any jeans necessary"*: Paul Beatty, "No Tags Back," *Joker, Joker, Deuce*, p. 29.

288 *"Look what you"* and passim: Justin Volpe quoted in Marie Brenner, "Incident in the 70th Precinct," *Vanity Fair*, December 1997.

288 *"charmless, insecure"*: Robert Sabbag, "Rudy's Cop," *New York*, June 3, 1996.

288 *"There is no hunting"*: Howard Safir quoted in Levitt, *NYPD Confidential*, p. 130.

288 *"If you simply add"*: Kelling quoted in Michael Tomasky, "The Brutal Truth," *New York*, September 8, 1997.

288 *One Police Plaza*: Playthell Benjamin, "Sugar Hill Blues," *New York*, May 19, 1997.

288 *"aspirational agenda"*: Keith Clinkscales quoted in Nancy Jo Sales, "The Mix Master," *New York*, May 10, 1999.

288 *for some $130 million*: Simmons with George, *Life and Def*, p. 193.

288 *"big city of dreams"* and passim: MA$E, "Puff's Intro," *Harlemworld*, 1997.

289 *with Wu-Wear*: The RZA, with Chris Norris, *The Wu-Tang Manual* (New York: Riverhead Freestyle, 2005), p. 71.

289 *Creeping up toward*: Kelefa Sanneh, "The Music Industry: Gettin' Paid," *The New Yorker*, August 20 and 27, 2001.

289 Source *sold more copies*: James Surowiecki, "Hip-Hopped Up," *New York*, April 5, 1999.

289 *"music born"*: Nancy Jo Sales, "The Mix Master," *New York*, May 10, 1999.

289 *"If I hear someone"*: Jay-Z quoted in Nancy Jo Sales, "Hip Hop Go the Hamptons," *New York*, August 9, 1999.

289 *At that moment, some 70%*: Kelefa Sanneh, "The Music Industry: Gettin' Paid," *The New Yorker*, August 20 and 27, 2001.

289 *the rate of victimization*: Karmen, *New York Murder Mystery*, p. 55.

289 *"The African American"*: Wright quoted in Craig Horowitz, "The Anti-Sharpton," *New York*, January 26, 1998.

290 *"I'd always been hesitant"*: Bruce Ratner quoted in David W. Dunlap, "The Changing Look of the New Harlem," *New York Times*, February 10, 2002.

290 *"a fascist state"*: Butts quoted in Dan Barry, "Butts, Harlem's Prominent Pastor, Calls Giuliani a Racist," *New York Times*, May 21, 1998.

290 *State trimmed back*: Amy Waldman, "Feud with Mayor Cited in Project Cutback," *New York Times*, February 2, 1999.

290 *"the Holy Spirit"*: Butts quoted in Jonathan P. Hicks, "Pastor's Embrace of Giuliani Sparks a Debate," *New York Times*, May 3, 1999.

290 *Central Harlem's population*: Chris Smith, "Real Estate 2000: Uptown Boomtown," *New York*, April 10, 2000.

290 *focused on high-end rehabs*: Hyra, *The New Urban Renewal*, p. 48.

290 *"now safe enough"*: Philmore Anderson quoted in Smith, "Real Estate 2000: Uptown Boomtown."

290 *"so many people"*: Eytam Benjamin quoted in ibid.

290 *more subtle kind of damage*: Freeman, *There Goes the 'Hood*, p. 30.

291 *it would probably be*: Ibid., p. 163.

291 *from '87 to '96 the White Population*: Housing and Vacancy Reports, New York City 1987 and 1996.

291 *Plexiglas windows*: Freeman, *There Goes the 'Hood*, p. 34.

291 *"common mind-set among cops"*: Maple with Mitchell, *The Crime Fighter*, p. 211.

291 *"Why back away from it now"*: Giuliani quoted in Karmen, *New York Murder Mystery*, p. 101.

291 *"At the end of the day"*: Richard Parsons quoted in Craig Horowitz, "The Anti-Sharpton."

Chapter Twenty-two | **Heat Is Quality**

293 *"roughest street"*: Paul Goldberger, "An Old Jewel of 42nd Street Reopens, Seeking to Dazzle Families," *New York Times*, December 11, 1995.

293 *astounding $6 million*: Michael Goldstein, "Broadway's New Beast," *New York*, March 14, 1994.

293 *"squeaky-cleanness"*: Fernanda Eberstadt, "Bland Ambition," *The New Yorker*, November 4, 1996.

293 *"document real life"*: Jonathan Larson, "Rent," *Rent*, 1993.

294 *"'old' and 'new'"*: Peter Schjeldahl, "The Art World: The Elegant Scavenger," *The New Yorker*, February 22 and 31, 1999.

294 *"hold out our hands"*: Brendan Gill, "Comment: Looking Backward," *The New Yorker*, January 5, 1998.

294 *"The torch"*: James Kaplan, "Forever Elaine's," *New York*, July 8, 1996.

294 *"a character in* Rent*"*: The Talk of the Town, "The Culture Industry," *The New Yorker*, July 7, 1997.

294 *"new money of the '80s"*: Michael Shnayerson, "The Champagne City," *Vanity Fair*, December 1997.

294 *"on a tilt"*: Ian Schrager quoted in ibid.

295 *"a barrier to entry"*: David Sarner quoted in Rebecca Milzoff, "Taking the Fifth," *New York*, October 23, 2006.

295 *An estimated 110,000*: Ethan Smith, "Where Goes the Neighborhood," *New York*, June 25–30, 1997.

295 *"flooded with content"*: John Seabrook, "The Big Sellout," *The New Yorker*, October 20, 1997.

295 *"off the high wire"*: George W. S. Trow, *My Pilgrim's Progress: Media Studies, 1950–1998* (New York: Vintage Books, 1999).

296 *"independent culture"*: Jeff Koons, *Conversations with Norman Rosenthal* (London: Thames & Hudson, 2014), p. 283.

296 *"people who go to work"*: Penny Arcade quoted in Schulman, *The Gentrification of the Mind*, p. 29.

296 *"salient question"*: Kurt Andersen, "The Culture Industry: The Age of Unreason," *The New Yorker*, February 3, 1997.

296 *"What is art?"*: Quoted in Louis Menand, "A Critic at Large: What Is 'Art'?," *The New Yorker*, February 9, 1998.

296 *"Now the New York"*: Jeffrey Deitch quoted in Edith Newhall, "Art for Argument's Sake," *New York*, March 24, 1997.

296 *"Even the cops"*: David Zwirner quoted in ibid.

296 *"suddenly as groovy"*: Alex Williams, "Go West, Young Dude," *New York*, January 1, 1996.

297 *"the creeping dullness"*: Philip Dray, "I Am a Renter," in Berman and Berger, eds., *New York Calling*, p. 228.

297 *"struggling gallery"* and passim: Roberta Smith, "Art Review; Brooklyn Haven for Art Heats Up," *New York Times*, November 6, 1998.

297 *"the third coolest"*: Jay Walljasper and Daniel Kraker, "The 15 Hippest Places to Live," *Utne Reader*, Nov–Dec 1997.

297 *"A fedora hat"*: George W. S. Trow, *Within the Context of No Context* (New York: Atlantic Monthly Press, 1997), p. 4.

298 *"defining industry"*: Fernanda Eberstadt, "Bland Ambition, *The New Yorker*, November 4, 1996.

298 *"central to the way"*: Michael Wolff, "Runway Runaway," *New York*, October 9, 2000.

298 *"You don't have to really"*: Mark Ronson quoted in Nancy Jo Sales, "Caution: These Kids Are About to Blow Up," *New York*, July 13, 1998.

298 *"[T]he aristocracy of birth"*: Tina Brown, *The Diana Chronicles* (New York: Doubleday, 2007), p. 17.

298 *"What people don't know"*: Brigid Berlin quoted in Paul Alexander, "Tsuris in a Soup Can," *New York*, December 22, 1997.

298 *"retail anthropology"*: Malcolm Gladwell, "The Science of Shopping," *The New Yorker*, October 27, 1996.

298 *"a sleek-haired race-horse"*: Brown, *The Vanity Fair Diaries*, p. 256.

299 *"Graydon is a man"*: Jim Kelly quoted in Jennifer Senior, "Graydon Rides the Wave," *New York*, December 11, 2000.

299 *"heat is quality"*: Brown quoted in Michael Wolff, "All Talk," *New York*, January 25, 1999.

299 *"The padrone"*: David Carr, "The Emperor Miramaximus," *New York*, December 3, 2001.

299 *"the fucking sheriff"*: Harvey Weinstein quoted in ibid.

299 *"have been witness"*: Ken Auletta, "Annals of Communications: Beauty and the Beast," *The New Yorker*, December 16, 2002.

299 *"raped—a word"*: Ibid.

299 *"There is one story"*: Quoted in Carr, "The Emperor Miramaximus."

300 *"I think that for every"*: Gwyneth Paltrow quoted in ibid.

300 *"Society doesn't really"*: Patrick McCarthy quoted in Michael Gross, "Scenesters," *New York*, December 22, 1997.

300 *Astor Foundation*: Brendan Gill, "Our Local Correspondents: A Party for Brooke," *The New Yorker*, April 21, 1997.

300 *"bitch of all times"*: Nan Kempner quoted in Meryl Gordon, "No More Mr. Nice Guy," *New York*, October 5, 1998.

300 *"treated badly"*: Kenneth Lane quoted in ibid.

300 *"last authentic vestige"*: Melinda Blau, "The Doubles Standard," *New York*, April 7, 1997.

300 *"extravagant evenings"*: Blaine Trump quoted in Michael Gross, "Social Life in a Blender," *New York*, February 2, 1998.

301 *"traveling medicine show"*: Arlene Croce, "A Critic at Bay: Discussing the Undiscussable," *The New Yorker*, December 24, 1994.

301 *"a foodie paradise"*: Peter Kaminsky, "Tompkins Square Riot," *New York*, March 23, 1996.

301 *Lower East Side*: Chris Smith, "Live Free or Die," *New York*, July 8, 1996.

301 *"AIDS," wrote Paul Rudnick, "has simply"*: Paul Rudnick, "Gaytown, USA," *New York*, June 20, 1994.

301 *"certainly easier"*: Larry Kramer, "Larry Kramer: Queer Conscience," *New York*, April 6, 1998.

301 *"public discussion"*: Sarah Schulman, *Stagestruck: Theater, AIDS, and the Marketing of Gay America* (Durham, NC: Duke University Press, 1998), p. 44.

302 *death rates*: David France, "The Best Hospitals: AIDS," *New York*, June 9, 1997.

302 Christopher Street: John Istel, "HIV-Negative," *New York*, February 10, 1997.

302 *"épatering"*: Daniel Mendelsohn, "We're Here. We're Queer! Let's Get Coffee!," *New York*, September 30, 1996.

302 *"After twenty years"*: Kramer quoted in Alex Witchel, "At Home With: Larry Kramer; When a Roaring Lion Learns to Purr," *New York Times*, January 12, 1995.

302 *"just a socially acceptable"*: John Waters quoted in Susan Dominus, "Hairspray It On," *New York*, July 22, 2002.

302 *"community 'matures'"*: Mendelsohn, "We're Here. We're Queer! Let's Get Coffee!"

302 *"even straight people"*: Rudnick, "Gaytown, USA," *New York*, June 20, 1994.

302 *"Someday we will be accepted"*: Vito Russo quoted in Mendelssohn, "We're Here! We're Queer! Let's Get Coffee!"

Chapter Twenty-three | Stand Clear of the Closing Doors

303 *"pedestrian separators"*: Safir quoted in Jeffrey Goldberg, "Sore Winner," *New York Times Magazine*, August 16, 1998.

303 *dashed to the other*: David Rohde, "Officer Apprehends a Perpetrator. The Charge Is Jaywalking," *New York Times*, February 14, 1998.

303 *Cristyne Lategano*: Jennet Conant, "The Ghost and Mr. Giuliani," *Vanity Fair*, September 1997.

303 *"the odor of something"*: Michael Tomasky, "No (Real) Apologies," *New York*, October 27, 1997.

303 *"Can we trust him with the bomb?"*: Mark Jacobson, "Rudy's Oval Office Dream," *New York*, November 10, 1997.

303 *"Just shoot me now"*: Quoted in ibid.

303 *first-term brain trust*: Michael Tomasky, "Solo Act," *New York*, March 10, 1997.

304 *"liberation"*: Siegel, *The Prince of the City*, p. 217.

304 *"zero-tolerance"*: Maple with Mitchell, *The Crime Fighter*, p. 213.

304 *"I suppose," Olmsted wrote long before, "the civilization"*: Frederick Law Olmsted, "The Real China," in Olmsted, ed., *Writings on Landscape, Culture, and Society, Beveridge*, p. 21.

304 *Social Club Task Force*: Ethan Brown, "Bar Codes," *New York*, May 1, 2000.

304 *"The Giuliani tone"*: Michael Tomasky, "Dirty Joke," *New York*, August 24, 1998.

305 *"If you can't get a job"*: Giuliani quoted in Jason DeParle, "What Welfare-to-Work Really Means," *New York Times Magazine*, December 20, 1998.

305 *Amadou Diallo*: Michael Cooper, "Officers in Bronx Fire 41 Shots, and an Unarmed Man Is Killed," *New York Times*, February 5, 1999.

305 *Officer Sean Carroll*: Heather MacDonald, "Diallo Truth, Diallo Falsehood," *City Journal*, Summer 1999.

305 *first response*: Jim Dwyer, "Truth Missing After Apt Search," *New York Daily News*, March 21, 1999.

305 *"a right," he said, "to demand"*: Giuliani quoted in David M. Herszenhorn, "The Diallo Shooting: The Mayor," *New York Times*, April 1, 1999.

305 *"police activity"*: Safir quoted in Goldberg, "Sore Winner."

305 *"manufactured"*: Heather MacDonald, "Diallo Truth, Diallo Falsehood," *City Journal*, Summer 1999.

305 *"a publicity stunt"*: Giuliani quoted in Kirtzman, *Rudy Giuliani*, p. 243.

306 *"a lot of fun"*: Safir quoted in Kevin Flynn, "Safir Faces Criticism After Oscar Trip," *New York Times*, March 23, 1999.

306 *"[T]he very meaning"*: Elizabeth Kolbert, "The Perils of Safety," *The New Yorker*, March 22, 1999.

306 *"[I]f there were a way"*: Hank Sheinkopf quoted in Craig Horowitz, "The Fall of Supermayor," *New York*, April 19, 1999.

306 *"Supermayor"*: Craig Horowitz, "The Fall of Supermayor," *New York*, April 19, 1999.

306 *"Forbidden City"*: The Talk of the Town, "Comment," *The New Yorker*, November 9, 1998.

306 shared radio frequency: Jim Dwyer and Kevin Flynn, *102 Minutes: The Untold Story of the Fight to Survive Inside the Twin Towers* (New York: Times Books, 2005), pp. 57–60.

307 Greenspan compared: James Surowiecki, "Bubble Wrap," *New York*, February 15, 1999.

307 Denise Rich: Lisa DePaulo, "Nouveau Rich," *New York*, January 25, 1999.

307 *"Our common faith"*: Alex Williams, "Peak Experience," *New York*, April 12, 1999.

307 *"more money than space"*: Carl Swanson, "Real Estate 2000: Bubble Jeopardy," *New York*, April 10, 2000.

307 *"the normal people"*: Alexa Lambert quoted in ibid.

307 years of maintenance: Tracie Rozhon, "TURF: When Money Isn't an Asset," *New York Times*, April 13, 2000.

307 block associations: Bruce Lambert, "MAKING IT WORK: The Community Counselor," *New York Times*, September 25, 1994.

307 *"new conciliatory style"*: Karrie Jacobs, "Acquired Taste," *New York*, December 8, 1997.

307 *"Asian customers"*: Donald Trump quoted in Karrie Jacobs, "Small World, After All," *New York*, January 27, 1997.

308 Hillary appeared: Dan Barry, "In Losing Its Party Location, a Magazine Gains the Buzz," *New York Times*, June 23, 1999.

308 *"sexually charged"*: Tina Brown, "Farewell to the King of Parties," thedailybeast .com, July 12, 2009.

308 while Macy Gray sang: Alex Kuczynski, "For Talk Magazine, Eclectic Party and a 'Hip' List," *New York Times*, August 3, 1999.

308 *"the end of an era"*: David Carr, "David Carr 10 Years Ago, an Omen No One Saw," *New York Times*, August 2, 2009.

308 *"distorted reality"*: Michael Wolff, "The E Decade," *New York*, December 6, 1999.

308 the top 1% had gotten 86%: Alex Williams, "To Have and Have More," *New York*, June 14, 1999.

308 *"what the internet"*: Josh Harris quoted in *We Live in Public*, Ondi Timoner, director, 2009.

309 *Sixty-two percent of Americans*: Massimo Calabresi, "The Terror Countdown," *Time*, December 27, 1999.

309 *Giuliani dropped by*: Michael R. Blood, "Mayor's Bunker Dazzles—Almost," *New York Daily News*, June 8, 1999.

309 *"fifteen minutes"*: Harris quoted in Andrew Smith, "We're in the Business of Programming People's Lives," *Wired*, March 15, 2019.

310 *"a little like my Lord"*: Butts quoted in Eric Lipton, "The Diallo Case: The Overview; From Pulpits to Politics, Angry Voices on Diallo," *New York Times*, February 28, 2000.

310 *Blacks made up 24.5%*: Dan Barry, "The Diallo Case: The Police; One Legacy of a 41-Bullet Barrage is a Hard Look at Aggressive Tactics on the Street," *New York Times*, February 27, 2000.

310 *"There is an evil"*: Butts quoted in Angela Mosconi, "Butts Rips Rudy Over Racial Divide; Says Mayor's Failed to Unite Cops, Community," *New York Post*, February 28, 2000.

310 *Anthony Vasquez*: William K. Rashbaum, "Undercover Police in Manhattan Kill an Unarmed Man in a Scuffle," *New York Times*, March 17, 2000.

310 *"I would not want a picture"*: Giuliani quoted in Jim Dwyer, "Rudyspeak 101: Turn It Around," *New York Daily News*, April 9, 2000.

310 *two thirds now believed*: Adam Nagourney with Marjorie Connelly, "Giuliani's Ratings Drop Over Actions in Dorismond Case," *New York Times*, April 7, 2000.

310 *devalue content*: Indergaard, *Silicon Alley*, p. 134.

311 *51 would be out of cash*: Jack Willoughby, "Burning Up," *Barron's*, March 20, 2000.

311 *worst since Hitler*: Floyd Norris, "The Markets: Market Place; Today's Opening Bell Could Be A Test Case for the Lessons of 1987," *New York Times*, April 17, 2000.

311 *"capitalism sans rigor"*: James J. Cramer, "Bubble Trouble," *New York*, May 1, 2000.

311 *Ventrol went from*: Ibid., and Saul Hansell, "'Buy!' Was Cry, as Stock Bubble Burst," *New York Times*, March 4, 2001.

311 *Razorfish and theGlobe.com*: Kait and Weiss, *Digital Hustlers*, p. 297.

311 *In 1995 it showed up*: Philip B. Corbett, "The Age of Schadenfreude," *New York Times*, January 13, 2009.

311 *"built on hype"*: Seth Goldstein quoted in Kait and Weiss, *Digital Hustlers*, p. 299.

311 *had him at 28%*: John Zogby, "Outrage Goes Only So Far," *New York Times*, March 30, 2000.

311 *divorced nurse*: Sarah Kershaw, "One Woman's Year in the Spotlight's Heat; Friends Call Judith Nathan Stunned by the Media Circus of New York," *New York Times*, June 16, 2001.

311 *Inner Circle*: Joyce Purnick, "Metro Matters; 'Good Friend,' a Marriage, and Voters," *New York Times*, May 8, 2000.

311 *blamed Lategano*: Kirtzman, *Rudy Giuliani*, p. 281.

311 *Scrooge the next morning*: Ibid., p. 287.

312 *the spare bedroom*: Frank Rich, "Journal; 1 Mayor, 2 Guys, 1 Shih Tzu," *New York Times*, August 4, 2001.

312 *claimed to regret*: Elisabeth Bumiller, "Mayor Tried to See Family of Dorismond," *New York Times*, June 8, 2000.

312 *prostitute mother*: Craig Horowitz, "Tears of a Cop," *New York*, April 4, 2005.

312 *"childlike innocence"*: Levitt, *NYPD Confidential*, p. 189.

312 *"unconscious camp"*: Walter Kirn, "In Trump We Trust," *New York*, January 17, 2000.

312 *61.9% off its high*: Jonathan Fuerbringer, "The Markets: Stocks and Bonds; Markets Plunge in Wide Sell-Off; Nasdaq Falls 6%," *New York Times*, March 13, 2001.

312 *"I'm old enough"*: Byron Wien quoted in Floyd Norris, "With Bull Market Under Siege, Some Worry About Its Legacy," *New York Times*, March 18, 2001.

313 *the city was now six*: David Kirkpatrick, "Street Addict," *New York*, May 1, 2000.

313 *56% of the increase*: Ibid.

313 *blowing apart*: James Surowiecki, "The Financial Page: The Most Devastating Retailer in the World," *The New Yorker*, September 18, 2000.

313 *"implicit swap"*: James Traub, "Giuliani Internalized," *New York Times*, February 11, 2001.

313 *"we would have been overrun"*: Butts quoted in ibid.

313 *repeatedly suing*: Norman Vanamee, "Gotham," *New York*, November 17, 1997.

313 *outsourced a middling*: Savas, *Privatization in the City*, pp. 135–136.

313 *"guarded basic city data"*: Dan Barry, "The Giuliani Years: The Overview," *New York Times*, December 31, 2001.

314 *first comprehensive*: The City of New York, Reengineering Municipal Services 1994–2001, The Mayor's Management Report, Fiscal Supplement 2001, pp. 271–273.

314 *nyc.gov*: Thomas J. Lueck, "Mayor and Biggest Rivals Come Together, Virtually," *New York Times*, June 24, 2000.

314 *"no relationship"*: Julian Brash, *Bloomberg's New York: Class and Governance in the Luxury City* (Athens: University of Georgia Press, 2011), p. 31.

314 *"Some of these new"*: Kathy Wylde quoted in Robert Kolker, "The Power of Partnership," *New York*, November 26, 2001.

314 *earned income tax credit*: Howard Chernick and Cordelia W. Reimers, "Welfare Reform and New York City's Low-Income Population," *Economic Policy Review*, vol. 7, no. 2, September 2001.

315 *"The trick of managing"*: Mitchell Moss quoted in Hugo Lindgren, "BID for Power," *New York*, August 17, 1998.

315 *"experiential marketing"*: Biederman interview.

315 *harassment of homeless*: Bruce Lambert, "Ex-Outreach Workers Say They Assaulted Homeless," *New York Times*, April 14, 1995.

315 *Biederman was forced*: Charles V. Bagli, "Business Group Fails to Mollify Giuliani," *New York Times*, September 24, 1998.

315 *workfare labor*: Ted Smalley Bowen and Adam Stepan, "Public-Private Partnerships for Green Space in NYC," School of International and Public Affairs, Case Consortium@Columbia, May 2014.

315 *community gardens*: Jennifer Steinhauer, "Ending a Long Battle, New York Lets Housing and Gardens Grow," *New York Times*, September 18, 2002.
315 *now usable*: The Talk of the Town, "Everybody In Dept.," *The New Yorker*, September 9, 2002.
315 *couldn't agree on costs*: David Halle and Elisabeth Tiso, *New York's New Edge: Contemporary Art, the High Line, and Urban Megaprojects on the Far West Side* (Chicago: University of Chicago Press, 2014), p. 160.
315 *"Vietnam of old railroad"*: Joseph Rose quoted in Thomas J. Lueck, "Up, but Not Running on the West Side," *New York Times*, July 25, 1999.
316 *"fob [it] off"*: Alex Williams, "Lower West Side Story," *New York*, October 4, 1999.
316 *"This was the epicenter"*: Josh David interview.
316 *"most beautiful thing"*: Burden interview.
316 *"It's a pipe dream"* and passim: Quoted in Joshua David and Robert Hammond, *High Line: The Inside Story of New York City's Park in the Sky* (New York: Farrar, Straus and Giroux, 2011), p. 32.
316 *"a secret landscape"*: Joel Sternfeld quoted in Annik LaFarge, *On the High Line* (New York: Thames & Hudson, 2014), p. 67.
317 *more for the quality*: Brash, *Bloomberg's New York*, p. 81.
317 *"You bet I did"*: Bloomberg quoted in Meryl Gordon, "Citizen Mike," *New York*, April 16, 2001.
317 *"Sharon Stone"*: "Profiles: The Mogul Mayor," *The New Yorker*, April 29, 2002.
318 *"a Berkeley student"*: "Spring 2002 Ready to Wear: Marc Jacobs," Vogue.com.

September 11, 2001

319 *"The city, for the first time"*: White, *Here Is New York*, pp. 50–51.
320 *shaking the bedrock*: Dwyer and Flynn, *102 Minutes*, p. 20.
321 *signals unreliable*: Ibid., pp. 57–59.
323 *"My destiny"*: Philippe Petit, *To Reach the Clouds: My High Wire Walk Between the Twin Towers* (New York: North Point Press, 2002), p. 179.
323 *"Waking comes"*: Roger Angell, Talk of the Town, "Tuesday, and After," *The New Yorker*, September 24, 2001.
324 *"the least terrified"*: Rebecca Solnit, *A Paradise Built in Hell: The Extraordinary Communities That Arise in Disaster* (New York: Penguin Books, 2009), p. 224.
324 *Prescriptions for antianxiety*: Ariel Levy, "Pill Culture Pops," *New York*, June 9, 2003.
324 *"you could smell them"*: Jennifer Senior, "Fallout," *New York*, September 20, 2004.
324 *rumors spread*: John Homans, "Psych Ops," *New York*, November 12, 2001.
324 *"The psychic fallout"*: Sarah Bernard, "The Crash After the Crash," *New York*, October 15, 2001.
324 *220 acres of concrete*: Charles B. Strozier, *Until the Fires Stopped Burning: 9/11 and New York City in the Words and Experiences of Survivors and Witnesses* (New York: Columbia University Press, 2011), p. 3.
325 *most workers stopped*: Solnit, *A Paradise Built in Hell*, pp. 214–215.

325 *6,500 firefighters*: Tina Kelley, "At Least a Quarter of Ground Zero Firefighters Ill," *New York Times*, December 20, 2001.

325 *"I didn't see victims"*: Adrienne Walsh quoted in Chris Smith, "FDNY," *New York*, September 11, 2011.

325 *"While the crisis lasted"*: Dorothy Day quoted in ibid.

325 *"Disaster Utopias"*: Solnit, *A Paradise Built in Hell*, p. 21.

325 *"are thus able to perceive"*: Charles E. Fritz quoted in ibid.

326 *"People who live downtown"*: Jennifer Senior, "The Circles of Loss," *New York*, October 1, 2001.

325 *Strangers hugged*: Steve Fishman, "Down by the Frozen Zone," *New York*, October 1, 2001.

325 *"From that day"*: Pat Enkyo O'Hara quoted in Solnit, *A Paradise Built in Hell*, p. 209.

326 *"Altruism"*: Ibid., p. 197.

326 *"Can we be funny?"*: *Saturday Night Live*, September 29, 2001.

326 *"Everyone who comes after"*: David Carr, "18 Truths About the New New York," *New York*, October 8, 2001

326 *"the river makes a world"*: Melinda Magnett, "To Buy or Not to Buy," *New York*, October 22, 2001.

327 *"Tomorrow New York"*: Giuliani quoted in "Person of the Year," *Time*, December 31, 2001.

328 *"despair on the faces"*: Ben Younger, "Damage Report," *The New Yorker*, October 15, 2001.

328 *"bag 'em and tag 'em"*: William Langewiesche, *American Ground: Unbuilding the World Trade Center* (New York: North Point Press, 2002), p. 70.

328 *"elite panic"*: Solnit, *A Paradise Built in Hell*, p. 37.

328 *had the temerity*: Michael Tomasky, "2001: A Race Odyssey," *New York*, December 24, 2001.

328 *"For many New Yorkers"*: Nancy Foner, ed., *Wounded City: The Social Impact of 9/11* (New York: Russell Sage Foundation, 2005), p. 5.

328 *"an island off the coast"*: Spalding Gray, *Swimming to Cambodia* (New York: Theater Communications Group, 1985), p. 27.

328 *"forced to stand up"*: John Homans, "Psych Ops," *New York*, November 12, 2001.

329 *"People should go out"*: Giuliani quoted in Craig Horowitz, "Crashing Green's Party," *New York*, October 8, 2001.

329 *"I wouldn't vote"*: Koch quoted in "Ed Koch vs. Al D'Amato," *New York*, October 8, 2001.

329 *"without Giuliani"*: Quoted in Williams Cole, "Against the Giuliani Legacy, Part Four," *Brooklyn Rail*, January 1, 2002.

329 *"Mark Green is obnoxious"*: Koch quoted in Elizabeth Kolbert, "The Long Campaign," *The New Yorker*, October 22, 2001.

330 *"Mayor Green"*: Al D'Amato quoted in "Ed Koch vs. Al D'Amato," *New York*, October 8, 2001.

330 *"a Pantalone-like figure"*: Elizabeth Kolbert, "One More Week," *The New Yorker*, November 5, 2001.

330 *splitting the Jewish*: Chris McNickle, *Bloomberg: A Billionaire's Ambition* (New York: Skyhorse Publishing, 2017), pp. 43–44.

Chapter Twenty-four | The Pile, the Pit, and the Bullpen

333 *8 million tons of rubble*: "9/11 by the Numbers," *New York*, September 6, 2002.
334 *More than 100,000 jobs*: Lynne Sagalyn, *Power at Ground Zero: Politics, Money, and the Remaking of Lower Manhattan* (New York: Oxford University Press, 2016), pp. 7–9.
334 *"suddenly nice"*: Michael Wolff, "Saint George," *New York*, December 10, 2001.
334 *"We should think"*: Giuliani quoted in Josh Barbanel, "World Trade Center Project Needs to Be More Than Real Estate Deal," *New York Daily News*, June 5, 2008.
334 *"Every now and then"*: Michael Schill quoted in Josh Barbanel, "Remaking, or Preserving, the City's Face," *New York Times*, January 18, 2004.
335 *only $14 million*: Robert Kolker, "Who Wants to Move to Ground Zero?," *New York*, April 18, 2005.
335 *"Generally speaking"*: Quoted in ibid.
335 *"live in a memorial"*: Bloomberg quoted in Jennifer Senior, "The Memorial Warriors," *New York*, September 11, 2002.
336 *"slice the pie"*: Herbert Muschamp, "Visions of Ground Zero: An Appraisal; An Agency's Ideology Is Unsuited to Its Task," *New York Times*, July 17, 2002.
336 *"The moment provided"*: Robert Ivy, "Editorial," *Architectural Record*, August 2002.
336 *they wanted a skyscraper*: Paul Goldberger, *Up from Zero: Politics, Architecture, and the Rebuilding of New York* (New York: Random House, 2004), pp. 67–68.
336 *"rebuilt in a triumphant way"*: "Larger Visions for Downtown," *New York Times*, October 12, 2002.
337 *"split and kiss"*: Daniel Libeskind, *Breaking Ground: Adventures in Life and Architecture* (New York: Riverhead Books, 2004), p. 45.
337 *"a public event"*: Goldberger, *Up from Zero*, p. 142.
337 *"skeletons"*: Edward Wyatt, "Ground Zero: The Site," *New York Times*, September 13, 2003.
337 *"we hadn't picked"*: Alexander Garvin interview.
338 *"Philanthropy," writes Chris McNickle, "was a form of patriotism"*: McNickle, *Bloomberg*, p. 202.
339 *noblesse oblige, if you knew*: Kate Taylor, "Bloomberg Lured Donors for New York Programs," *New York Times*, November 20, 2013.
339 *"an older New York"*: Robert Kolker, "The Power of Partnership," *New York*, November 26, 2001.
339 *replaced the Manhattan Institute*: Robert Kolker, "Home for the Holidays," *New York*, January 6, 2003.
339 *"collective identity"*: Brash, *Bloomberg's New York*, p. 94.
339 *"muscular management"*: McNickle, *Bloomberg*, p. 133.
339 *"The past is past"*: Bloomberg quoted in Chris Smith, "Bloomberg, Michael," *New York*, August 26, 2011.
340 *"I knew zoning backwards and forwards"*: Burden interview.

340 *"gave off the appearance"* and passim: Daniel L. Doctoroff, *Greater Than Ever: New York's Big Comeback* (New York: Public Affairs, 2017), p. 37.

340 *"building like Moses"*: Burden quoted in Scott Larson, *"Building Like Moses with Jacobs in Mind": Contemporary Planning in New York City* (Philadelphia: Temple University Press, 2013), p. 3.

340 *"virtuous cycle"*: Doctoroff, *Greater Than Ever*, p. 70.

341 *"job-creating"*: Bloomberg quoted in ibid., p. 48.

341 *"[I]f you want New York"*: Michael Lewis, "Manifestoes for the Next New York, . . . ," *New York Times*, November 11, 2002.

341 *"From the distance"* and passim: Timoney quoted in Craig Horowitz, "The Twice-Top Cop," *New York*, January 14, 2002.

342 *"I understood that crime fighting"*: Kelly, *Vigilance*, p. 181.

342 *"the most influential police"*: Levitt, *NYPD Confidential*, p. 235.

342 *"fundamental rethinking"*: Kelly, *Vigilance*, p. 166.

342 *off the public budget*: Matt Apuzzo and Adam Goldman, *Enemies Within: Inside the NYPD's Secret Spying Unit and bin Laden's Final Plot Against America* (New York: Touchstone, 2013), p. 82.

342 *"sweeping data-collection"*: William K. Rashbaum, "Crime-Fighting by Computer: Scope Widens," *New York Times*, March 24, 2002.

343 *"seemed to have no idea"*: Michael Tomasky, "Rudy Who?," *New York*, January 14, 2002.

343 *"He's a rich man"*: quoted in Elizabeth Kolbert, "The Un-Communicator," *The New Yorker*, February 22, 2004.

343 *"I imagine it has been years"*: Bill de Blasio quoted in Jennifer Steinhauer, "City Hall Memo; Bloomberg, With Year Inside, Shows What Outsiders Can Do," *New York Times*, December 21, 2002.

343 *"He's got a sense"*: Michael Tomasky, "Put on a Happy Face," *New York*, November 4, 2002.

343 *"Most of us are motivated"*: Doctoroff, *Greater Than Ever*, p. 242.

343 *"Bloomberg's a Democrat!"*: Michael Tomasky, "Polls Vaulting," *New York*, July 28, 2003.

343 *the land would come*: Jennifer Steinhauer, "Mayor Calls for Thousands of New Homes," *New York Times*, December 11, 2002.

344 *"With Giuliani's 'zero tolerance'"*: Walter K. Olson quoted in Ethan Brown, "Ticket Master," *New York*, May 23, 2003.

344 *"luxury product"*: Bloomberg quoted in Diane Cardwell, "Mayor Says New York Is Worth the Cost," *New York Times*, January 8, 2003.

344 *"even more attractive"*: Bloomberg quoted in Brash, *Bloomberg's New York*, p. 121.

Chapter Twenty-five | **Oz Wasn't Built in a Day**

345 *"The greatest thing"*: Koch quoted in Elizabeth Kolbert, "The Mogul Mayor," *The New Yorker*, April 14, 2002.

345 *"surer, safer"*: Jesse Green, "The New Gay Moment," *New York*, March 5, 2001.

345 *"gay style"*: Simon Dumenco, "The Buysexual Agenda," *New York*, August 8, 2003.

345 *"had the choice"*: Schulman, *The Gentrification of the Mind*, p. 6.

345 *"wistful"*: Tony Kushner quoted in Michael Specter, "Nowhere," *The New Yorker*, November 22, 2004.

346 *"most sophisticated statement"*: Goldberger, *Up from Zero*, p. 135.

346 *"I was sexy"*: Liza Minnelli quoted in Liesl Schillinger, "Suddenly Liza," *New York*, March 6, 2006.

346 *"[a] nimbus of corporate blandness"*: Alex Ross, "Musical Events: Coming Apart," *The New Yorker*, April 1, 2002.

346 *"Tragedy of the Uncommons"*: Adam Gopnik, "The Critics: Times Regained," *The New Yorker*, March 22, 2004.

346 *Sorrento Cheese*: Bill Tonelli, "Arrivederci, Little Italy," *New York*, September 27, 2004.

346 *only America's 255th most expensive zip code*: Forbes.com, 2006.

347 *"pretty drippy"*: Quoted in Meryl Gordon, "The Family Astor," *New York*, August 4, 2006.

347 *"no longer permeated"*: Foner, ed., *Wounded City*, p. 12.

347 *government aid*: Ibid., p. 184.

347 *homeownership—only 6%*: Randy Daniels quoted in Craig Horowitz, "How Harlem Got Its Groove Back," *New York*, July 15, 2002.

347 *"apocalyptic times"*: Franklin Foer, "The Journal at Sea," *New York*, September 12, 2005.

347 *"Books may be"*: Michael Wolff, "Book Review," *New York*, January 31, 2003.

348 *"tons of tipsters"*: Jessica Coen quoted in Sonia Zjawinski, "Meet the Bloggers," *New York*, February 10, 2006.

348 *a reported $50 million*: Alan Riding, "Alas, Poor Art Market: A Multimillion-Dollar Head Case," *New York Times*, June 13, 2007.

348 *"Since 1990, the number"*: "Books: Master of Disaster," *The New Yorker*, July 15, 2002.

348 *"degenerated into a conspiracy"*: John Cassidy, "Annals of Finance: The Investigation," *The New Yorker*, March 30, 2003.

348 *Madoff told himself*: Steve Fishman, "The Madoff Tapes," *New York*, February 25, 2011.

348 *executing a trade*: Noam Scheiber, "The Brain in Thain," *New York*, December 21, 2006.

349 *"lavish, late and leaky"*: Deborah Schoeneman, "Will Calvin Klein Sue?," *New York*, September 17, 2004.

349 *fitness center and Wolf stoves*: S. Jhoanna Robledo, "The Height of Fashion," *New York*, November 7, 2005.

349 *thousands more to come*: David W. Chen, "Bit by Bit, Government Eases Its Grip on Rents in New York," *New York Times*, November 19, 2003.

349 *half a million bucks*: Phoebe Easton, "How Much Is That in Rubles?," *New York*, July 26, 2004.

349 zolotaya molodezh: Amy Larocca, "The Russian-American Princess," *New York*, May 16, 2008.

349 *an Indian teenager*: Isaiah Wilner, "The Number-One Girl," *New York*, May 14, 2007.

349 *"For most New Yorkers"*: Ibid.

350 *"Fashion was so corporate"*: Anna Wintour quoted in Guy Trebay, "Fashion Statement: Hip-Hop on Runway," *New York Times*, February 9, 2002.

350 *"Admit it"*: P. Diddy quoted in Michael Specter, "I Am Fashion," *The New Yorker*, September 9, 2002.

350 *out of earshot*: Charles V. Bagli, "In Business and Civic Circles, Unease Over Stadium Plan," *New York Times*, February 9, 2004.

351 *RPA supported*: Charles V. Bagli, "Report Suggests Forgetting About Stadium on West Side," *New York Times*, July 20, 2004.

351 *78% were against*: Ibid.

351 *"When you invite somebody"*: Dan Doctoroff quoted in Robert Kolker, "Olympic City, N.Y.," *New York*, October 28, 2002.

351 *"[A] city was like any other product"*: Doctoroff, *Greater Than Ever*, p. 68.

351 *"a runaway train"*: "Stop the Stadium in Its Tracks," *New York Times*, December 4, 2004.

351 *"moving forward"*: David and Hammond, *High Line*, p. 39.

352 *"It wasn't her intention"*: David interview.

352 *"I will fight this"*: Daniel Libeskind quoted in Joe Hagan, "The Breaking of Michael Arad," *New York*, May 12, 2006.

352 *"a forced marriage"*: Libeskind, *Breaking Ground*, p. 243.

352 *"the incredible shrinking"*: Robin Pogrebin, "The Incredible Shrinking Daniel Libeskind," *New York Times*, June 20, 2004.

353 *"The significance"*: Jacobs quoted in The Talk of the Town, "Urban Studies," *The New Yorker*, May 17, 2004.

353 *"modern-day patriots"*: Johnny America quoted in "Political Protest as Street Theater," *Hartford Courant*, August 30, 2004.

353 *"The Republicans are coming!"*: Quoted in "Greene Dragon Group Stages Anti-Republican Bike Ride," nyc.indymedia.org/es/2004/08/40953.html.

353 *the city sent Washington*: Ryan Lizza, "Bush to New York: Here's Your $20 Billion—Now Drop Dead," *New York*, June 14, 2004.

353 *Rudy was pulling*: Chris Smith, "Shrinking Mike," *New York*, May 24, 2004.

353 *"In the wake"*: Giuliani with Kurson, *Leadership*, p. 278.

354 *permits for public parades*: Lisa Keller, *Triumph of Order: Democracy & Public Space in New York and London* (New York: Columbia University Press, 2009), p. 167.

354 *Another 29 permits*: Diane Cardwell, "Preparing for the Convention: Demonstrations; For the Convention, Demonstrations Start Early, as Do Arrests," *New York Times*, August 26, 2004.

354 *"The police are being"*: Leslie Cagan quoted in "The Republicans: The Convention in New York," *New York Times*, August 30, 2004.

354 *planning for eighteen months*: Kelly, *Vigilance*, p. 186.

354 *went extremely well*: Robert Kolker, "Law Pre-Enforcement," *New York*, September 20, 2004.

355 *"You can't beat"*: Stuart Stevens quoted in Chris Smith, "The Republicans Picked Our Pockets," *New York*, December 9, 2004.

355 *"The Republicans picked"*: Ibid.

Chapter Twenty-six | "B'klyn Cheers, Trembles"

357 *"an accidental playground"*: Daniel Campo, *The Accidental Playground: Brooklyn Waterfront Narratives of the Undesigned and Unplanned* (New York: Fordham University Press, 2013).

358 *"neither clean nor safe"*: Ibid., p. 5.

358 *"what was once a reluctant move"*: Wendy Goodman, "BROOKLYNism," *New York*, May 1, 2006.

358 *"THE NEW SoHo"*: Lori Ortiz, "Bushwick Is THE NEW SoHo," *Brooklyn Rail*, December 1, 2000.

358 *"a product with cultural buzz"* and passim: Zukin, *Naked City*, p. 43.

358 *"droves of young"*: Theodore Hamm and Williams Cole, "Inequality in Brooklyn," *Brooklyn Rail*, August 1, 2002.

358 *"organic and indigenous"*: Richard Florida, *The Rise of the Creative Class, Revisited* (New York: Basic Books, 2012), p. 148.

359 *risen 77% from 1991 to 2004*: Brad Lander, Testimony to the City Planning Commission on the Jamaica Plan, Pratt Center for Community Development, May 23, 2007.

360 *a power plant*: Thomas J. Lueck, "City Opposes Power Plant on Waterfront," *New York Times*, May 13, 2003.

360 *170 blocks inland*: Tara Bahrampour, "City Seeking to Rezone Brooklyn Waterfront," *New York Times*, June 19, 2003.

361 *"individual people"*: Elana Levin interview.

361 *"no direct change"*: Theresa Kimm, "Confessions of a New Kid on the Block," *Brooklyn Rail*, November 1, 2004.

361 *"once a stigma"*: Choire Sicha quoted in Carl Swanson, "Crack Is . . . Back?," *New York*, November 18, 2002.

361 *State Assemblyman Vito Lopez*: Paul Vitello, "Vito J. Lopez, Ex-New York Assemblyman Tainted by Scandal, Dies at 74," *New York Times*, November 10, 2015.

361 *"educated and affluent"*: Robin Rogers-Dillon, "Zoning Out: The Politics of North Brooklyn," *Brooklyn Rail*, October 1, 2001.

361 *"predominantly young, vaguely creative"*: Zev Borow, "Will the Last Hipster Please Turn Out the Lights," *New York*, November 19, 2004.

362 *"our favorite coffee shops"*: Jennifer Bleyer, "To the Ramparts, Hipsters, and Hold the Latte," *New York Times*, March 6, 2005.

362 *developers threw up*: Diane Cardwell, "City Sees Way to Get Mix of Homes on Brooklyn Waterfront," *New York Times*, December 27, 2004.

362 *the DCP plan*: Diane Cardwell, "City Is Backing Makeover for Decaying Brooklyn Waterfront," *New York Times*, May 3, 2005.

362 *how ULURP*: Tom Angotti, "Zoning Instead of Planning in Williamsburg and Greenpoint," *Gotham Gazette*, May 17, 2005.

363 *artist William Powhida*: James Kalm, "Brooklyn Dispatches," *Brooklyn Rail*, March 7, 2007.

362 *"The Tea Party stole our shit"*: Levin interview.

363 *"the bookish and unassuming"*: Charles V. Bagli and Joseph Berger, "Nets Helped Clear Path for Builder in Brooklyn," *New York Times*, September 26, 2012.

363 *"tough kids"*: Ratner quoted in Diane Cardwell, "Different by Design Soon to Be Less So; Rethinking Atlantic Center with the Customer in Mind, *New York Times*, May 26, 2004.

363 *"the black Warren Buffett"*: Jay-Z, "Threat," *The Black Album*, 2003.

363 *"almost exclusively"*: Ratner quoted in Diane Cardwell, "A Grand Plan in Brooklyn for the Nets' Arena Complex," *New York Times*, December 11, 2003.

364 *"the most important"*: Herbert Muschamp, "Courtside Seats to an Urban Garden," *New York Times*, December 11, 2003.

364 *"preserving the character"*: Brooklyn Atlantic Yards press release, December 2003.

364 *"B'klyn cheers"*: *Brooklyn Paper*, January 24, 2004.

364 *"I happen to be"*: Bloomberg quoted in "For Ikea, Next Stop Bloomberg . . . ," *Brooklyn Paper*, October 16, 2004.

364 *"almost no public"*: David Vine, "Billions for Brooklyn—No Questions Asked," *Brooklyn Rail*, December 1, 2003.

364 *"a sacred place"*: Patti Hagan quoted in Lynda Richardson, "Public Lives; One Eye on the Wrecking Ball, Feet Firmly Planted," *New York Times*, February 5, 2004.

365 *"How high this building"*: Darnell Canada quoted in "Packed House," *Brooklyn Paper*, February 21, 2004.

365 *highest grossing store*: "Ratner's 'Terminal' Opens to Huge Crowd," *Brooklyn Paper*, July 31, 2004.

365 *"emotional centerpiece"*: Yasiin Bey quoted in Amos Barshad, "Yasiin Bey, the Former Mos Def, Poetry-Slams the Barclays Center, Hopes for Jay-Z Summit," *Vulture*, February 7, 2013.

365 *city's first Community*: "Daughtry Breaks with 'God Squad,' " *Brooklyn Paper*, October 9, 2004.

365 *"cultural rival"*: Nicolai Ouroussoff, "An Appraisal; Seeking First to Reinvent the Sports Arena, and Then Brooklyn," *New York Times*, July 5, 2005.

365 *just another Privately Owned*: "No Arena Park . . . ," *Brooklyn Paper*, October 1–8, 2005.

365 *office jobs disappeared*: Nicholas Confessore, "Routine Changes, or 'Bait and Switch'?" *New York Times*, November 6, 2005.

365 *Gehry himself admitted*: "Gehry: My Design Was 'Horrible,' " *Brooklyn Paper*, November 26, 2005.

Chapter Twenty-seven | Too Big to Fail

367 *"raw, like candies"*: Jeanne-Claude Christo quoted in Adam Sternbergh, "The Passion of the Christos," *New York*, January 14, 2005.

367 *"creators of extravagant, useless"*: Calvin Tompkins, "Onward and Upward with the Arts: *The Gates* to the City," *The New Yorker*, March 29, 2004.

367 *the entire $20 million cost*: Ibid.

367 *"Now the project is very gentle"*: Christo quoted in "Christo and Jeanne-Claude with Praxis," *Brooklyn Rail*, July 1, 2004.

367 *February was chosen*: Ibid.

368 *Whoopi Goldberg*: "Around City Hall: Bloomberg's Game," *The New Yorker*, April 4, 2005.

368 *she had her doubts*: Robin Pogrebin, "An Aesthetic Watchdog in the City Planning Office," *New York Times*, December 29, 2004.

368 *"It was never alive"*: Sheldon Silver quoted in Purnick, *Mike Bloomberg*, p. 148.

368 *produce more revenue*: Committee on New York City Affairs, "Report on the Financing of the Hudson Yards Infrastructure Project," New York City Bar, May 16, 2007.

368 *Donald Trump had proposed*: Deborah Schoeneman, "Trump Canard: Wedding Bling," *New York*, May 24, 2004.

368 *the Met was allowed to borrow*: Amy Larocca, "The Charity Ball Game," *New York*, April 29, 2005.

369 *"Bloomberg had made"*: Moss quoted in "His American Dream," *New York*, December 1, 2006.

369 *Mayor's Fund had spent*: Chris Smith, "The Mayor and His Money," *New York*, October 3, 2005.

369 *a quieter, less exciting time"*: Kurt Andersen, "Delirious New York," *New York*, November 28, 2005.

369 *"get taken to a dream world of magic"*: The Lonely Island, "Lazy Sunday," *Saturday Night Live*, December 17, 2005.

370 *"Is New York Too Safe?"*: Mark Stevens, "Is New York Too Safe?," *New York*, October 17, 2005.

370 *there'd been a gain of 6.2 years*: Clive Thompson, "Why New Yorkers Last Longer," *New York*, August 10, 2007.

370 *Smoking was falling*: Tom Farley, MD, *Saving Gotham: A Billionaire Mayor, Activist Doctors, and the Fight for Eight Million Lives* (New York: W. W. Norton, 2015), p. 64.

370 *Carts selling fresh produce*: Ibid., pp. 85–88.

370 *"social and economic density"*: Clive Thompson, "Why New Yorkers Last Longer."

370 *"the most densely used"*: Alan Feuer, "A Park Cleans Up Its Act," *New York Times*, October 20, 2006.

370 *a 1.45-mile, 6.7-square-acre"*: Adam Sternbergh, "The High Line: It Brings Good Things to Life," *New York*, April 27, 2007.

371 *Bloomberg Philanthropies*: Chris Smith, "The Mayor and His Money," *New York*, September 23, 2005.

371 *"The mayor," wrote Chris Smith, "has replaced"*: Ibid.

371 *"Now who do we talk to?"*: Billy Cox quoted in Geoffrey Gray, "No Safe Harbor," *New York*, January 5, 2007.

371 *"colorful, accessible version"*: Marshall Berman, "Introduction," in Berman and Berger, eds., *New York Calling*, p. 34.

372 *"Under Bloomberg"*: Alexandra Lange, "Building the (New) New York," *New York*, May 26, 2006.

372 *"Design fatigue had set in"*: Sagalyn, *Power at Ground Zero*, p. 292.

372 *"Whatever is wrong on that site"*: Garvin interview.

373 *who'd together share a Snøhetta-designed*: Robert Kolker, "The Grief Police," *New York*, November 29, 2005.

373 *"There is this fatigue"*: Chris Burke quoted in ibid.

373 *"a fucking mess"*: Ed Hayes quoted in Kurt Andersen, "Ground Zero to Sixty," *New York*, May 13, 2005.

373 *"Except for those who"*: Stephen Rodrick, "Rudy Tuesday," *New York*, February 23, 2007.

373 *170,000-brick*: Eric Wolff, "Libeskind Alive! (At Least in SoCal)," *New York*, September 10, 2007.

373 *"Yet just below the numbers"*: Chris Smith, "Mike's Managerial Missteps," *New York*, March 23, 2007.

373 *investment firm Blackstone*: Robin Pogrebin, "A $100 Million Donation to the NY Public Library," *New York Times*, March 11, 2008.

374 *"a gorgeous antique"*: Adam Sternbergh, "The High Line: It Brings Good Things to Life," *New York*, April 27, 2007.

374 *"Oversuccess"*: Anthony Flint, *Wrestling with Moses: How Jane Jacobs Took On New York's Master Builder and Transformed the American City* (New York: Random House, 2009), p. 190.

374 *a gallon of milk was up 64%*: Lionel Beehner, "Rich Get 140% Richer," *New York*, September 21, 2007.

374 *Democrats raised more money*: Greg Sargent, "Wall Street Shorts the GOP," *New York*, May 8, 2006.

374 *"Someone in the Governor's"*: Chris Smith, "Because at Long Last, There's Someone in the Governor's Mansion Who Understands Us," *New York*, December 14, 2006.

374 *Goldman, Bear Stearns*: Daniel Gross, "The Streak," *New York*, April 30, 2006.

374 *"We're all Reaganites now"*: Kurt Andersen, "American Roulette," *New York*, December 22, 2006.

375 *"No politician"*: David Gunn quoted in Chris Smith, "Who Failed the C Train?," *New York*, January 28, 2005.

375 *Kevin Smith had an astounding*: Ben Wasserstein, "The Man with 50,000 Friends," *New York*, July 14, 2006.

375 *an experiment in gaming*: Michael Shapiro, "Six Degrees of Aggregation," Columbia Journalism Review, May–June 2012.

375 *"It's frightening to think"*: Gillian Muessig quoted in Geoffrey Gray, "Internet Dating with the Prez Candidates," *New York*, May 10, 2007.

375 *"If we don't act now"*: Bloomberg quoted in Thomas J. Lueck, "Bloomberg Draws a Blueprint for a Greener City," *New York Times*, April 23, 2007.

375 *PlaNYC had the support*: C. J. Hughes, "A Critical Look at Pliancy, Four Years After Its Launch," *Architectural Record*, September 29, 2011.

376 *"It is more saturated"*: Berman, "Introduction," in Berman and Berger, eds., *New York Calling*, p. 32.

376 *"integrated market"*: NYC&CO press release, June 8, 2006.

376 *Countrywide Financial Corporation*: Vikas Bajaj, "Mortgage Lender Moves to Shore Up Cash," *New York Times*, August 16, 2007.

376 *$482.4 billion in 2000*: Daniel Gross, "Bottom's Up," *New York*, July 2, 2004.

377 *"multicultural market"*: Connie Bruck, "Angelo's Ashes," *The New Yorker*, June 29, 2009.

377 *$1.4 billion in contracts*: Gross, *House of Outrageous Fortune*, p. 272.

377 *$6.3 billion*: Charles V. Bagli, *Other People's Money* (New York: Dutton, 2013), p. xxvi.

377 *"a collective sigh and a shrug"*: Ethan Rouen "Public responds to proposals to rebuild Hudson Yards area," *New York Daily News*, November 19, 2007.

377 *"There'll soon be a Ground Zero"*: Dan Sclare quoted in ibid.

378 *yet 6 in 10*: Duff McDonald, "The Catastrophist View," *New York*, November 5, 2007.

378 *new home sales down*: US Census Bureau Press Release, March 26, 2008.

378 *including 666 Fifth*: Steve Cuozzo, "The Scandalous History Behind Kushner's Ritzy Midtown Building," *New York Post*, April 18, 2017.

378 *"not the exciting place"*: Madonna quoted in Rich Cohen, "Madonnarama!," *Vanity Fair*, May 2008.

379 *"socialism for the rich"*: Nouriel Roubini, "Public Losses for Private Gain," *The Guardian* (UK), September 18, 2008.

379 *eat spare ribs*: Steve Fishman, "Burning Down His House," *New York*, November 27, 2008.

379 *but the books revealed*: James B. Stewart, "Eight Days," *The New Yorker*, September 14, 2009.

380 *cardiologists reported*: Beth Landman, "Hedge Funds and Heartache," *New York*, January 31, 2008.

380 *70% in Bushwick*: "An Opportunity to Stabilize New York City's Neighborhoods: A Fact Sheet on the Neighborhood Stabilization Program," Furman Center for Real Estate and Urban Policy, New York University, July 2009.

Chapter Twenty-eight | **Hard Landings**

383 *2,000 executives*: Michael Shnayerson, "Wall Street's $18.4 Billion Bonus," *Vanity Fair*, March 2009.

383 *"people who spend"*: Jessica Pressler, "Wall Street Wives Doing Their Part to Stimulate the Economy," *New York*, August 5, 2009.

384 *"They don't play"*: Roberta Gratz quoted in Gross, *House of Outrageous Fortune*, p. 309.

384 *"a little unseemly"*: Wintour quoted in Amy Larocca, "68 Minutes with Anna Wintour," *New York*, September 4, 2009.

384 *Ted Kennedy (and a $2.5 million pledge)*: Shawn Boburg, "For Trump Son-in-Law and Confidant Jared Kushner, a Long History of Fierce Loyalty," *Washington Post*, November 27, 2016.

384 *"the highest caliber"* and passim: Ivanka Trump, *The Trump Card: Playing to Win in Work and Life* (New York: Simon & Schuster, 2009), p. 178.

385 *"left with a possible"*: Justin Davidson, "Basket Case," *New York*, February 6, 2009.

385 *down almost 60%*: Andrew Rice, "The Opportunist's Guide to Real Estate," *New York*, April 24, 2009.

385 *"a community is more than housing"*: Butts quoted in Robin Pogrebin, "Neighborhood Report: Harlem; Helping the Renaissance Ballroom Live Up to Its Name," *New York Times*, June 18, 1995.

385 *"I think the business community"*: Kathy Wylde quoted in Frank Lombardi and Kathleen Lucadamo, "Michael Bloomberg to Run for Third Term as New York City Mayor, Despite Term Limit Laws," *New York Daily News*, September 30, 2008.

385 *Though 89% of New Yorkers*: "New Yorkers Split on Bloomberg Third Term as Mayor," Reuters, October 21, 2008.

385 *spent $100 million*: Max Fisher, "How Bloomberg Got Away with Buying New York," *The Atlantic*, November 3, 2009.

385 *"Does the richest man in New York"*: William Thompson quoted in McNickle, *Bloomberg*, p. 266.

386 *"bought and paid for"*: Hendrick Hertzberg quoted in Max Fisher, "How Bloomberg Got Away with Buying New York."

386 *Murders had fallen*: Christine Hauser, "Fewer Killings in 2007, But Still Felt in City's Streets," *New York Times*, January 1, 2008.

386 *the city went nearly a week*: Al Baker, "New York on Track for Fewest Homicides on Record," *New York Times*, December 28, 2009.

386 *illegally obtained*: Apuzzo and Goldman, *Enemies Within*, p. 149.

386 *"street inquiries"*: Kelly, *Vigilance*, p. 184.

386 *55.2% of them on African Americans*: Emily Vasquez, "Numbers Show How Police Work Varies by Precinct," *New York Times*, February 5, 2007.

386 *twice as many complaints*: Al Baker and Emily Vasquez, "Number of People Stopped by New York Police Soars," *New York Times*, February 3, 2007.

386 *stops broke 531,000 in 2008*: Christine Hauser, "Police on Pace to Make Record Number of Stops in '09," *New York Times*, May 12, 2009.

387 *"My take," said one former captain*: John A. Eterno quoted in Al Baker, "New York Minorities More Likely to Be Frisked," *New York Times*, May 12, 2010.

387 *70% of New Yorkers*: Al Baker, "Police Stops Hit Record in 2009," *New York Times*, February 18, 2010.

387 *died of emphysema*: Enid Nemy, "Elaine Kaufman, Who Fed and Fussed Over the Famous, Dies at 81," *New York Times*, December 2, 2010.

387 *"This is saying good-bye"*: Gay Talese quoted in Manny Fernandez, "Too Much Fun to Feel Sad at the Farewell to Elaine's," *New York Times*, May 26, 2011.

387 *"golden age"*: Nick Denton quoted in Michael Idov, "The Demon Blogger of Fleet Street," *New York*, September 22, 2010.

388 *"This city"*: Patti Smith quoted in Vanessa Grigoriadis, "Remembrances of the Punk Prose Poetess," *New York*, January 7, 2010.

388 *"[I]t is the city of changes"* and passim: Florent Morellet quoted in David Amsden, "The 25th Hour of Florent Morellet," *New York*, May 23, 2008.

389 *"I can't believe I took"*: Liz Smith quoted in Jonathan Van Meter, "The Original Gossip Girl," *New York*, September 22, 2008.

390 *PlaNYC was an initiative*: Tom Angotti, "PlaNYC at Three: Time to Include the Neighborhoods," *Gotham Gazette*, April 12, 2010.

390 *"tactical urban interventions"*: Janette Sadik-Khan with Seth Solomonow, *Streetfight: Handbook for an Urban Revolution* (New York: Penguin Books, 2016), p. 20.

390 *"Once you changed a space"*: Ibid., p. 84.

391 *providing* so much *data*: Alan Feuer, "The Mayor's Geek Squad," *New York Times*, March 23, 2013.

391 *$500 million*: Benjamin Weiser, "3 Found Guilty in CityTime Corruption Trial," *New York Times*, November 22, 2013.

391 *"practical urbanism"*: Cassim Shepard, *Citymakers: The Culture and Craft of Practical Urbanism* (New York: Monacelli Press), 2017.

392 *returning their TARP*: Dealbook, "10 Large Banks Allowed to Exit US Aid Program," *New York Times*, June 9, 2009.

392 *Donald Trump*: "Trump's Appeal Divides Tea Party Loyalties in Crucial States," Reuters, March 15, 2016.

392 *"Wall Street," said a sadder but wiser Henry Blodget, "is its own world"*: Henry Blodget quoted in John Heilemann, "The Wall Street Mind: Triumphant . . . ," *New York*, April 8, 2011.

392 *"a strong correlation"*: Lisa Miller, "The Money-Empathy Gap," *New York*, June 29, 2012.

392 *doubling in the years*: McNickle, *Bloomberg*, p. 228.

392 *remained around 20%*: Ibid., pp. 303–304.

393 *"He's a different guy"*: Purnick, *Mike Bloomberg*, p. 176.

393 *"the kind of society"*: Writers for the 99%, *Occupying Wall Street: The Inside Story of an Action That Changed America* (Chicago: Haymarket Books, 2011), p. 8.

393 *speech by Roseanne Barr*: Ibid., p. 16.

393 *"a rejection"*: Heather Gautney, "What Is Occupy Wall Street?," *Washington Post*, October 10, 2011.

394 *"makeshift village"*: Writers for the 99%, *Occupying Wall Street*, p. 21.

394 *"If you enter here"*: Gan Golan, "The Office of the People" in Ron Shiffman et al., eds., *Beyond Zuccotti Park* (Oakland, CA: New Village Press, 2012), p. 71.

394 *"Life in the encampments"*: Todd Gitlin, *Occupy Nation: The Roots, the Spirit, and the Promise of Occupy Wall Street* (New York: itbooks, 2012), p. 43.

395 *"what the fight is about"*: Jay-Z quoted in Zadie Smith, "The House That Hova Built," *T, The New York Times Style Magazine*, September 6, 2012.

395 *"The public is getting scared"*: Bloomberg quoted in Michael Goodwin, "Mike's a Bit Pro-Occupied," *New York Post*, November 20, 2011.

395 *"no air between"*: Frank Rich, "The Class War Has Begun," *New York*, October 21, 2011.

396 *NYCHA had been left to rot*: Eric Lipton and Michael Moss, "Housing Agency's Flaws Revealed by Storm," *New York Times*, December 9, 2012.

396 *"I never did a fucking thing"*: Koch quoted in John Cassidy, "Postscript: Ed Koch, 1924–2013," *The New Yorker*, February 1, 2013.

397 *"The people who changed New York"*: Koch quoted in "Mayor Edward I. Koch Speaks at His 88th Birthday Celebration at Gracie Mansion," https://www.youtube.com/watch?v=xOoAhDVomFs.

397 *"arbitrary and capricious"*: Justice Milton A. Tingling quoted in Michael M. Grynbaum, "Judge Blocks New York City's Limits on Big Sugary Drinks," *New York Times*, March 11, 2013.

398 *Twice it went entire*: Rocco Parascandola, "City Goes Entire 24 Hours Without a Shooting, Stabbing or Slashing for the Second Time in Year," *New York Daily News*, November 9, 2013.

398 *fewer and fewer inmates*: McNickle, *Bloomberg*, pp. 277–278.

398 *Kelly and the NYPD*: Wendy Ruderman, "Keep Kelly Atop Police Department, New Yorkers Say in Poll," *New York Times*, January 17, 2013.

398 *only 0.1% of them had resulted*: McNickle, *Bloomberg*, p. 88.

398 *50% disapproved*: Ruderman, "Keep Kelly Atop Police Department, New Yorkers Say in Poll."

399 *"People will lose their lives"*: Kelly, *Vigilance*, p. 294.

399 *poverty had held steady*: Robert Doar, "Fighting Poverty the Bloomberg Way," AEI.org, March 26, 2014.

399 *cut its staff*: Bowen and Stepan, "Public-Private Partnerships for Green Space in NYC," p. 1.

399 *almost a third*: Andrew Rice, "Stash Pad," *New York*, June 27, 2014.

399 *37% of New York's residents*: Nancy Foner, ed., *One Out of Three: Immigrant New York in the Twenty-First Century* (New York: Columbia University Press, 2013), pp. 1, 41.

400 *"a good chance to accumulate"*: Sharon Zukin, *The Culture of Cities* (Malden, MA: Blackwell, 1995), p. 160.

400 *"I've said the election"* and passim: Jay-Z quoted in Smith, "The House That Hova Built."

400 *"dexterously switching personas"*: Nitsuh Abebe, "Carnegie, Rockefeller, Carter? Jay-Z's American Dream," vulture.com, February 8, 2012.

401 *"a great American character"*: Sischy, *Nothing Is Lost*, p. 265.

401 *Play-Doh*: Jeff Koons quoted in " 'Capturing a Feeling of Creation': Jeff Koons on Play-Doh," Christies.com, May 16, 2018.

401 *"Acceptance of everything"*: Koons quoted in Sarah Thornton, *33 Artists in 3 Acts* (New York: W. W. Norton, 2014), p. 108.

Epilogue

404 *"a preening, pompous"* and passim: Harry Siegel, "De Blasio's Pretty Nice New York," *New York Daily News*, December 16, 2015.

406 *"NYCHA had chosen"*: Greg B. Smith, "NYCHA Lied About Inspecting Thousands of Homes for Toxic Lead Paint, Federal Probe Finds," *New York Daily News*, July 27, 2017.

406 *city's worst landlords*: Ameena Walker, "NYCHA Claims Top Spot on Annual List of NYC's Worst Landlords," *Curbed New York*, December 19, 2018.

406 *daily ridership*: Brian M. Rosenthal, Emma G. Fitzsimmons, and Michael LaForgia, "How Politics and Bad Decisions Starved New York's Subways," *New York Times*, November 18, 2017.

406 *overstuffed union contracts*: Asher Stockler,"MTA Drowning in Overtime Pay; One Worker Earned More Than New York Mayor and Governor Combined," *Newsweek*, May 18, 2019.

406 *fudged data*: "The Crisis Below: An Investigation of the Reliability and Transparency of the MTA's Subway Performance Reporting," New York City Comptroller's Office, February 8, 2019.

410 *even Bloomberg*: J. David Goodman, "Amazon Pulls Out of Planned New York City Headquarters," *New York Times*, February 14, 2019.

410 *"invest in a community"*: Brian Huseman quoted in Joseph Pisani, "Gone in a New York Minute: How the Amazon Deal Fell Apart," AP News, February 16, 2019.

420 *"luck, luck, luck"*: Senator Robert Wagner quoted in Andy Logan, "Around City Hall: Ring in the New," *The New Yorker*, January 10, 1994.

420 *Studies have shown*: Alana Semuels, "The Dangers of Visible Inequality," *The Atlantic*, September 9, 2015.

Index

510 | Index

Jackson, Jesse, 149, 157, 181, 182, 187, 221
Jackson, Mahalia, 156
Jackson, Reggie, 19
Jacob Riis Park, 27
Jacobs, Jane, xix, 17, 30–32, 35, 36, 45,
    51, 117, 119, 211, 214, 238, 239, 253,
    294, 326, 352, 353, 362, 374
Jacobs, Karrie, 275
Jamaica, Queens, 359, 392
James, Letitia, 406
Janis, Sidney, 128
Janklow, Mort, 62, 126
Japan, 93
Javits Center, 161, 266, 324, 266
jaywalking, 303, 304
Jay-Z, 153, 280–81, 286, 289, 318, 363,
    365, 389, 395, 400
Jeter, Derek, 256, 270, 393, 403
Jews, 149, 213, 266
    Hasidim, 46, 204–5, 360
JFK Airport, 161, 266, 333
jobs, see employment
Jobs, Steve, 115
Johnson, Philip, 85, 108, 145, 235, 236
Johnson, Steven, 270
Jones, Bill T., 300–301
Jones, J. Raymond, 44
Jones, Paul Tudor, 172
Jones, Russell Tyrone, 240
Jones, Shavod, 155
Jordan, Michael, 319
JPMorgan, 286
Judd, Donald, 34
Julian, Mike, 257
junk bonds, 99–100, 162, 186, 187, 203
Just Kids (Smith), 388

Kadushin, Charles, 112–13
Kahan, Richard, 118, 255
Kaiser, Charles, 10
Kalm, James, 226
Kalman, Tibor, 175, 236, 237, 239, 240, 309
Kanner, Bernice, 106
Kaplan, James, 294

Karabel, Jerome, 104–5
Karmen, Andrew, 262–63
Karp, Ivan, 174
Katz, Jon, 272
Kaufman, Elaine, 60–61, 387
Kaufman, Henry, 97, 111
Kelling, George, 134, 135, 154, 176, 196,
    198, 214, 243, 261, 267, 288
Kelly, Jim, 299
Kelly, Ray, 200, 205, 216, 234, 242,
    243, 257–59, 341–42, 345, 354, 370,
    386–87, 394, 398, 399
Kempner, Nan, 84, 300
Kennedy, Ted, 384
Kent, Fred, 36, 118
Kerik, Bernard, 312, 321, 326, 341, 369
Khashoggi, Adnan, 42
Khomeini, Ayatollah, 180
Kiley, Robert, 134, 143, 176, 197
Kimmelman, Michael, 227
Kirtzman, Andrew, 184, 186
King, Bernard, 363
King, Larry, 60
King, Martin Luther, Jr., 212, 221
King, Rodney, 201, 227, 228
Kirby, Felice, 361, 364
Kirn, Walter, 312
Kislin, Semyon, 266
Kissinger, Henry, 308
Klein, Calvin, 59
Klein, Joe, 183–85, 195, 207, 210
Kluge, John, 125
Koch, David, 371, 374
Koch, Ed, xiv, xix, 3, 10–14, 17–20,
    22, 23, 25, 29, 37, 42, 43–46, 49,
    50, 52–53, 65–69, 76, 79, 82, 83,
    93–94, 107–8, 123, 124, 133–42, 146,
    147–50, 154–57, 160, 173, 176, 180,
    182, 185–89, 192–93, 195, 199, 208,
    232, 243–44, 248, 249, 251, 254,
    262, 314, 329, 339, 341, 345, 363,
    364, 390, 393, 396–97, 404, 415
    AIDS epidemic and, 91, 94, 120, 122,
    123, 209